Praise for

ROBERT MORRIS

"Rappleye argues that Morris, a merchant who procured supplies for the Revolution and became its chief treasurer, has been unduly neglected in favor of more philosophical Founding Fathers, and this book provides an illuminating account of the Revolution's improvised and even dodgy finances."

—*The New Yorker*

"Pages to savor, packed with new research and an overall new look at our founding history that is long overdue. What Mr. Rappleye reveals to us is a historical truth that is as important today as it was during our perilous struggle for independence. That lesson is: You cannot have a stable society or a functioning government that fosters liberty unless you have a sound financial foundation supporting them."

—James Srodes, *The Washington Times*

"*Robert Morris: Financier of the Revolution* brings to life one of our least appreciated Founding Fathers. The world needs to know more about Morris, and this highly readable book will surely foster more research and writing."

—*Concord Monitor* (New Hampshire)

"Passionate biography of a Founding Father. . . . In fluid prose, Rappleye ably resurrects an underrated contributor to the early American republic. Provides thorough coverage of a deserving subject."

—*Kirkus Reviews*

"This book deserves to be in the historic reading section of high school and university libraries."

—*Pennsylvania Magazine*

"The first full-length modern biography of an extraordinary, forgotten founder of the American republic, Rappleye's book, the best ever about its subject, is an effective work of rehabilitation. . . . Rappleye (*Sons of Providence*) brings Morris and his world brightly alive. Nothing of the financier's full life (his privateering for the war effort; his pioneering trade with China; the "overconfidence" that brought his downfall) escapes Rappleye, and his judgments are balanced and astute. . . . [Gains] Morris the standing he so much deserves among the great figures of the founding era."

—*Publishers Weekly*

"Charles Rappleye's biography of [Robert Morris is] a welcome addition to the recent spate of books on the remarkable men who created this country. For it was Morris who, over and over again at critical moments, found ways to ensure that the rebels had the money and matériel they needed. Mr. Rappleye's *Robert Morris* is a great story, told with narrative skill and scholarly authority. . . . Rappleye has done a marvelous job of explaining why this mostly forgotten Founder deserves our gratitude."

—*The Wall Street Journal*

"Important in the American Revolution but obscure in popular history, Robert Morris is here introduced to a general readership and also defended from aspersions from preceding academic biographers. The author's first intent is well met in a fluid narrative of Morris' mercantile acumen. . . . within a well-structured, readable account of Morris' eventful life, Rappleye ably brings forth the financial substrate of the American Revolution.

—*Booklist*

ALSO BY CHARLES RAPPLEYE

Sons of Providence: The Brown Brothers, the Slave Trade,
and the American Revolution

All American Mafioso: The Johnny Rosselli Story (with Ed Becker)

ROBERT

*Financier of the
American Revolution*

MORRIS

Charles Rappleye

Simon & Schuster Paperbacks

NEW YORK · LONDON · TORONTO · SYDNEY · NEW DELHI

Simon & Schuster Paperbacks
A Division of Simon & Schuster, Inc.
1230 Avenue of the Americas
New York, NY 10020

First Simon & Schuster trade paperback edition November 2011

SIMON & SCHUSTER PAPERBACKS and colophon are
registered trademarks of Simon & Schuster, Inc.

For information about special discounts for bulk purchases,
please contact Simon & Schuster Special Sales at
1-866-506-1949 or business@simonandschuster.com.

The Simon & Schuster Speakers Bureau can bring authors
to your live event. For more information or to book an event,
contact the Simon & Schuster Speakers Bureau at
1-866-248-3049 or visit our website at www.simonspeakers.com.

Designed by Paul Dippolito

Manufactured in the United States of America

1   3   5   7   9   10   8   6   4   2

The Library of Congress has cataloged the hardcover edition as follows:

Rappleye, Charles.
Robert Morris : financier of the American Revolution / Charles Rappleye.
p.   cm.
Includes bibliographical references.
1. Morris, Robert, 1734–1806.   2. United States—History—Revolution,
1775–1783—Biography.   3. United States—Politics and government—1775–1783—
Biography.   4. Governors—Pennsylvania—Biography.   I. Title.
E302.6.M8R37   2010
973.3092—dc22
[B]   2010020461

ISBN 978-1-4165-7091-2
ISBN 978-1-4165-7092-9 (pbk)
ISBN 978-1-4165-7286-2 (ebook)

To my wife Tulsa Kinney:
mind, body, soul.

CONTENTS

PART III · THE NEW REPUBLIC

ROBERT MORRIS

INTRODUCTION

I first came across Robert Morris in the research for my last book, *Sons of Providence*, a story from the time of the American Revolution. John Brown, a prominent Rhode Island merchant, was spearheading opposition to the prospect of new, federal taxes, which he considered just as oppressive as the taxes imposed by Parliament. Morris was the leading advocate for the new funding plan; I was struck by his compelling arguments in support of the national government, and at his audacity in dispatching Thomas Paine to Providence to lobby for the cause.

The source material for this remarkable episode was contained in *The Papers of Robert Morris*, a nine-volume collection issued under the stewardship of historian E. James Ferguson over the course of twenty-five years, with the last volume published in 1999. The scope of Morris's endeavors, the depth of his frustration, and the lucidity of his prose stuck with me in the months it took to finish my manuscript.

Once that book was published I returned to Morris. I was surprised to find that despite the publication of the Morris papers, no modern-day biographer had taken advantage of Ferguson's labors to produce a full treatment of this central figure in America's founding saga. Indeed, Morris had been all but forgotten in the recent surge of interest in the nation's founding era.

This was more than just a disservice to a remarkable career. Morris's absence from the story leaves a gaping hole in our understanding of the social and political struggles that bedeviled the revolutionary war effort, led to the writing of the Constitution, and helped launch America as a financial powerhouse. The more I learned of Morris, the easier became the choice of what my next project should be.

The most recent books on Morris, prior to this biography, are major works from 1954 and 1961 covering his four-year tenure as superintendent of finance in the revolutionary government. In this position Morris acted in the capacity of treasury secretary at a time when finances were the most urgent and vexing problem confronting the new nation. More than that, Morris was the chief civil officer in the government, with full authority to hire and fire any employee of Congress or the armed forces. In a very real sense he was, as one of his critics complained, a "pecuniary dictator."

His ascendance may not have been a great moment for American democracy—though his appointment was made by a unanimous vote in Congress—but it was very good for the progress of the Revolution. Faced with an empty treasury, a worthless currency, and an economy in disarray, Morris leaned heavily on his own personal fortune to provide crucial aid to General George Washington and salvage the credit of the rebel government with key allies in Europe, and he projected in detail the scheme for federal revenues that came to be known as Alexander Hamilton's funding program.

At the same time, Morris laid the foundation for a financial system that would establish America as the world's economic leader. He introduced the concepts of banking and commercial finance on a national basis, and persuaded a skeptical public to endorse his vision and set it in motion. He conceived, and in the years to come would implement, measures to restore the nation's credit and encourage capital formation that speak directly to the financial crisis that confronts the world today.

This was the period of Morris's greatest influence, a time of prominence and prodigious exertion acknowledged—albeit in passing—by most of our more sagacious historians. But as I delved further, I found that Morris was deeply engaged in the war effort and the affairs of Congress from the very onset of America's split with England. He was active in the early opposition to the Stamp Act, was instrumental in the clandestine and today little-known effort to arm the rebel colonies, and worked closely with Benjamin Franklin in forging ties to France, a critical source of support throughout the Revolution. For three critical months in the winter of 1777, when Congress fled Philadelphia for the relative safety of Baltimore, Morris ran the operations of the American government virtually single-handed.

Just as interesting was Morris's political odyssey. By nature open, warm, and gregarious, just as comfortable in a grog shop as in the parlors of Philadelphia's mercantile elite, Morris was in the beginning of the war a reluctant but consensus candidate for a series of important state and national offices. Over time, as the old social order was shaken by the new political forces of democracy and liberty, Morris came to be identified as a spokesman for wealth and stability, and was excoriated by early radicals like Samuel Adams as a corrupting influence on the "Republican virtue" they hoped the Revolution would foster.

But Morris was no ideologue. Pragmatic, creative, "addicted to hard work," as one student of his career put it, Morris shrugged off his critics and focused his exceptional energies on problems that crashed in waves against the rickety bulwark of the nascent national government. His perseverance and his steadfast integrity won him the allegiance of his fellow founders—Franklin, Hamilton, James Madison, John Adams (though never his cousin Sam), and especially Washington—and he became the leader of the faction that, four years after the peace with Britain, wrote the new Constitution.

Among this collection of imposing and often brilliant men, Morris was a principal character, a leader and an icon who dominated the councils of the Revolution. Yet he was also enormously controversial. He was rich in an era when popular ideology celebrated austerity. He was skeptical of the virtues of democracy and an unabashed global capitalist—a man ahead of his time. During the Constitutional Convention and in the first sessions of the novel United States Senate, he often let surrogates handle the floor debates because he knew that the simple fact of his endorsement could kill the measures he supported.

This infamy has persisted to the present day, taken up by historians still grinding axes that were fashioned at the time. The consequence is a curiously warped version of our national story, one that prizes the rhetoric and ideology of the founding epoch and fails to credit the essential pragmatism that distinguishes the American Revolution from so many other subsequent social upheavals. To paint Morris out of the picture ignores the fundamental ways in which his instincts and insights helped shape the nation that America became.

Another source of fascination was Morris's commercial career. His critics then and later held that Morris made his fortune by graft and corruption, siphoning off precious funds from the public efforts to finance the war. But a close study of his business activities demonstrates that his deep engagement in government procurement usually cost him dearly, losses he sustained by his unparalleled mastery of trade and international markets. Foreign merchants and even the courts of Europe sought him out, granting him exceptional and exclusive franchises simply because he was the best-connected and most capable entrepreneur in America.

All this made more poignant and more arresting the final chapter of Morris's life and career. His deals and his endeavors expanded steadily in scope, reaching heights that can only be termed phenomenal—sole management of tobacco trade with France, land deals that encompassed literally millions of acres. In the end, perhaps inevitably, Morris overreached, convinced that his salvation would arrive with one more sale, the emergence of one more critical trading partner. That reprieve never arrived, and in 1797, at sixty-three years of age, Morris surrendered to the sheriff of Philadelphia and was confined to debtor's prison.

This somber denouement comes as little surprise to anyone familiar with the rollicking, boom-and-bust cycles of early American capitalism. But for Morris it helped becloud a remarkable career of private and public enterprise, of risk and painful dilemma in the context of the unprecedented break between Britain and her former colonies. As a consequence, and in a twist of historiographical irony, Morris's memory today is preserved best by his critics and his enemies. Take, for example, the recent book *Taming Democracy*, a broad-brush polemic which holds that the true story of the Revolution is one of the popular will being usurped by a small, self-interested elite. Here, leftist historian Terry Bouton finds Morris to be "the most powerful man in America—aside, perhaps, from George Washington. Indeed, the degree of authority he possessed over the economy was probably never matched in the subsequent history of the United States." Bouton presents Morris in caricature, and ignores the hard lessons of experience that pushed him to the fore. But his grand appraisal of Morris's stature, and his high estimate of Morris's power, are beyond dispute.

What follows, then, is the full story of Robert Morris, his ascent, his political evolution, his tenure as the chief executive of the revolutionary government, and his seminal contribution to the formation of the republic. Among the most powerful and influential of America's founding fathers, his career wends its way through the central events of his time, providing new light on the key controversies of the Revolution and its aftermath. There is much in the way of policy and legislation, but there is also a very human tale of struggle and triumph, of ambition and tragedy. I tried to steer carefully through the shoals of controversy, the political debates that bedeviled the founders and resonate to the current day. I sought to deal fairly with the many charges leveled against Morris in the course of his career, and with his vigorous and generally successful rebuttals. But most of all, I strove to illuminate the character and vision of a self-made man who shaped the destiny of a new nation, helping to make America what it is today.

PART I

REVOLUTIONS

— *Chapter 1* —

"A Character I Am Proud of"

I n the angry, dark days of the Revolution, and in the epochal political struggles that followed, the foes of Robert Morris denounced him as the leader of the "aristocratical" party, seeking to restore the social order that the American patriots had done so much to overturn. But to those who knew his story, this was one accusation that made no sense. In a time when fate was often determined by rank of birth, Morris hailed from obscurity.

Robert Morris was born in the booming British port of Liverpool on the last day January 1734. His grandfather was a sea captain; his father, who shared his name, was a broker, or factor, in the employ of a shipping firm. His mother was recorded as an Elizabeth Murphet, but there is no record of her marriage to Morris. It appears the child was born out of wedlock. According to family lore, Murphet was soon out of the picture, and young Robert was raised by his maternal grandmother. Morris later professed no recollection of his mother.

When his namesake was still a toddler the senior Robert Morris shipped out to the New World, dispatched by his employers to Oxford, a small trading port at the mouth of the Tred Avon River on Maryland's Eastern Shore. He soon established a reputation as a shrewd and savvy businessman, "a mercantile genius thought to have no equal in the land." His base in trade was in tobacco, the primary export of the Chesapeake region, raised on slave plantations carved out of lush primeval forest. Morris bought leaf from growers and stored it in a company warehouse on the Oxford wharf, but soon branched out. He formed partnerships with factors at other ports, won contracts to provide uniforms for Maryland troops during King George's War, and invested in at least one slaving voyage from Africa.

He was an innovator, a pioneer who helped modernize the early tobacco trade. According to one contemporary account, he was "the first who introduced the mode of keeping accounts in money, instead of so many pounds of tobacco . . . as was formerly the case." And he persuaded his fellow tobacco factors to appoint independent inspectors to assay the quality of the crop offered at different warehouses. This practice gave rise to an inspection law that Morris pushed through a reluctant legislature. "If he had any public political point to carry," one associate recalled, "he defeated all opposition."

Well liked among his friends, Morris was remembered for his "cheerful wit and sound judgment"; "as a companion and bon vivant, he was incomparable." He could also be haughty and sometimes overbearing, severe with servants and slaves. Over the course of a decade, he came to dominate commercial life in Oxford, and helped raise the port to a prominent position on the Chesapeake.

When his son reached thirteen years of age, Morris sent for him to join him in America. Young Robert arrived sometime in 1747 and lived briefly at Oxford. He stayed in the handsome wood-frame house his father maintained on the town's main street, and studied under an Anglican clergyman. Robert was tutored in mathematics—the universal language of business— and gained a smattering of Latin.

As the years went by, Robert demonstrated many of the qualities that marked his father—the gregarious nature, the business acumen, the spirit of innovation—but these traits had to be inherited, not instilled. Just two years after his arrival, the father decided his son needed more than the hamlet of Oxford could provide. He sent Robert off to Philadelphia in charge of a friend named Robert Greenway, a merchant who doubled as a librarian at the Library Company, one of the civic projects fostered by Ben Franklin.

Situated on a tongue of land between the Schuylkill and Delaware rivers, home at that time to roughly twenty thousand people, Philadelphia rivaled Boston as the largest settlement in British North America. Designed by founder William Penn to embody a stolid practicality, the houses were tidy, compact, and built of pale red brick; the streets broad and straight, with right-angle corners, flagstone sidewalks, and beginning around 1750, lit by whale-oil lamps, the first on the continent. The main street in town was High, or Market, which featured an arched arcade of market stalls down the middle—brick, of course—and which was thronged three days a week with country vendors and city shoppers.

It was a cosmopolitan city, the original Quakers living at close quarters with recently arrived Germans, Scotch-Irish Presbyterians, a handful of Catholics, a small set of British Anglicans, and roughly a thousand African slaves, many of them domestic servants. There were capacious stone churches, grassy commons, and several libraries. People prided themselves on their civic works; the Quakers operated a hospital, and the Anglicans staffed America's first college of liberal arts. Ben Franklin had helped organize both, a testament to his political dexterity and his broad influence in his adoptive home.

The pride of the town was the new State House, two stories tall, with a handsome bell tower and flanked by two blocky office buildings, all spare, straight, and brick with trim painted white. Behind, to the south, lay a spacious public yard enclosed by a wall seven feet high where legislators liked to stroll between sessions. But Philadelphia was also urban, and subject to blight. Many side streets were unpaved. Dung, dirt, and trash collected waist high on the roadsides and a boggy, sometimes fetid swamp snaked from the Delaware almost to the center of town. In the summer, when flies, gnats, and mosquitoes descended in clouds, the heat could be overbearing. The only respite was to find a seat under the awnings that tented city stoops.

For young Robert Morris, tall and sandy-haired, with a Celtic complexion and pale blue eyes, the crush of people in the streets and the din of wagons and livestock clattering over the cobblestones probably felt a bit like home. Bustling Philadelphia bore more resemblance to Liverpool than the tiny hamlet of Oxford. And there were plenty of distractions for a teenage boy—taverns and coffeehouses of every description, and on the north edge of town, in a district known as Helltown, cockfights and bull baits drew raucous crowds.

Robert lived with his sponsor Greenway, but the long-limbed youth showed little interest in books. He was soon placed as an apprentice in a shipping firm, contracted to spend the next seven years learning the modes and the skills of the commercial life, or as papers confirming another apprenticeship of the time described it, "the Art, Trade, or Mystery of Merchandize."

The firm that took him on was headed by a British-born merchant named Charles Willing. Quartered at the southern end of the Philadelphia waterfront, Willing operated a countinghouse, warehouse, a retail store, and below those, a wharf, berth to his several square-rigged frigates. To the north, sixty more piers stretched two full miles along the west bank of the Delaware. This was the seat of the Pennsylvania shipping trade, the industrial heart of the city and the busiest port in the colonies. It was a scene of constant hubbub: smiths and sailmakers toiling in their shops, captains and mates hollering after jack-tar seamen, stevedores and draymen wrestling the great wooden barrels called hogsheads used to ship the staples of trade—flour or sugar, wine or rum. It was the perfect setting for Robert to start in the path followed by his father.

As a teenage trainee, Robert began at the bottom, sweeping floors and helping to sort the various imported goods that arrived on the firm's several ships. Before long he was brought into the countinghouse as a clerk, churning out the voluminous, painstaking correspondence that was the lifeblood of the shipping trade. In the days before Xerox, before telegraph or typewriters, it was all done longhand—sailing orders for captains, detailed cargo lists, and letters to foreign factors, especially Thomas Willing, Charles's brother and financial broker in Bristol, England—all with copies drawn up for the home office. These early papers Morris signed with his initials, and the subscription "for my masters."

In his youth Morris longed to return to his home in England, but he never had the chance. Instead, the young apprentice impressed Charles Willing with his jovial nature, his energy, and his diligence. The Willing trading house, overlooking the river craft, the coastal schooners, and the tall masts of the seagoing ships that rode the easy current of the Delaware, became his home.

In July 1750, when he was thirty-nine years old, the senior Robert Morris was awakened by a troubling dream. One of his vessels had just arrived from England, and the ship's captain was to host a party to celebrate a safe voyage. In his dream, Morris envisioned the party ending in tragedy: on his way back to shore, a salute fired from the ship would somehow deal him a fatal blow. Upon awakening, Morris considered begging off the afternoon engagement, but that would be a breach of protocol. Instead, when he arrived on board ship, he confided to the captain his premonition, and asked him to forgo the customary salute. The captain agreed, but he apparently neglected to inform the crew. When the festivities wound down, Morris and his party climbed into a longboat for transport back to the Oxford wharf. As they pulled away, the ship's cannon roared out a broadside salute. The guns weren't loaded but the charges were live, and the cotton wadding from one of the guns caught Morris above the elbow, breaking his arm. The wound became infected, and within three days Morris was dead.

Robert Morris learned of his father's decease in a letter. The senior Morris had always been distant from his son, and now he was gone. All that was left was a will, which provided that the father's assets be liquidated and placed in the hands of his teenage boy, an estate appraised at two thousand five hundred pounds sterling. Also named in the will were the father's two sisters, who remained in England. There was no mention of Elizabeth Murphet, but there was a bequest for Sarah Wise, a Maryland resident, who was to receive two hundred fifty pounds in local currency "for the good will and affection I have for her," as well as one hundred pounds for her daughter, and one hundred more for "the child of which Sarah Wise is now with child." This infant appears to have been another illegitimate son, a half-brother to young Robert, who recorded later that, "no sooner had I fixed myself in the world than I took charge of this brother." Thus did Robert Morris find himself, at sixteen years of age, an orphan in the New World, an apprentice possessed of a modest fortune, living with Robert Greenway and looking after the affairs of a baby half-brother.

The estate left by his father was substantial for the time, but it was probably superfluous; the Willing firm was fast assuming a leading position in colonial trade, and Robert grew with the company. Before long he was shipping out as cargo master on trading ventures, sailing the Caribbean to select the most promising markets and driving dockside bargains to obtain the best cargo for the return trip. He landed at Kingston, Havana, and Port-au-Prince on Hispaniola, learning the ways of ships and sailors on seas that were sometimes hostile.

In 1761, during one of the recurrent European wars, his vessel was captured and Morris was briefly confined to a French jail. As the story goes, he was released at the behest of an itinerant preacher and turned out on a barren shore in Cuba. He was penniless, but he encountered a Frenchman and won his favor by repairing his broken watch. With the assistance of his new friend Morris made his way to a port, and from there back to Philadelphia. The adventure was considered a mark of his ingenuity; it also afforded Morris insight into the perilous life of the mariners who helmed the ships of the great trading houses.

But it was in the Willing home office in Philadelphia that Morris made his mark. Here he spent long hours keeping ledgers and accounts, and tracking valuations in the bewildering array of currencies that crossed his desk—British pounds, French livres, Dutch florins, Spanish reales, and of course the currencies of the several colonies, each of which fluctuated against each other and against the trade standard, the British pound sterling. More arcane still were the primary medium of international trade, bills of exchange, promissory notes drawn by a merchant or factor against a distant creditor, usually on the other side of the Atlantic. These paper obligations provided a critical channel for commercial capital, and were marketed in their own right.

Besides his aptitude for numbers, Morris demonstrated a natural feel for markets and the nerve to put his instinct into action. The story is told of one early occasion, when Charles Willing was away on business, Robert learned from an arriving ship captain that the price of flour had jumped in the foreign market. Robert promptly purchased all the flour then available in Philadelphia, leaving competing merchants to pay advanced prices while Willing & Co. shipped the available supply to Europe. This was an astonishing display of bravura for a boy still in his teens, an early example of the adroit maneuvers that would carry Morris to the heights of power and influence in the world of American commerce.

Morris seemed impervious to the looming threat that shadowed the life of the colonial trader—constant, gnawing risk. A successful trading venture could yield a fortune, especially in wartime, but such voyages were plagued by shipwreck, spoilage, shifting markets, and privateers—freelance pirates licensed by one belligerent state or other to raid rival shipping. Loans had to be supported when they came due, and impatient creditors assuaged. The constant prospect of failure was enough to drive some to distraction; George Clymer, a prominent Philadelphia merchant, longed to leave the trade due to "its peculiar precariousness." Robert Morris, on the other hand, seemed energized by the high-stakes game of international shipping. One of his earliest surviving letters, written in November 1759, captures his saucy audacity. He writes to celebrate a recent infusion of cash: a debtor "has paid us a good deal of money which reprieves us from gaol one month more," Morris wrote. But the respite would only be temporary. "Our damned creditors are hungry as the Devil and we tumble hogsheads of sugar and bills of exchange and paper money down their throats every day but all won't do unless a fresh supply comes soon."

Morris's counterpart in the Willing firm, a colleague who soon became his friend, was Thomas Willing, his father's eldest son and his partner in the trading house. Two years older than Robert, Thomas Willing had the social polish and family connections that an outsider like Robert lacked. Through his mother, Mary Shippen, Thomas was related to one of Philadelphia's most prominent families, pillars of the Anglican church and influential in the politics of the colony. And by his father, Thomas was born into a mercantile concern with one foot in Philadelphia and the other in England, where

his uncle and namesake ran a trading house of his own. Following the opposite path to Robert's, Willing was sent to England in his early teens, to live
with his paternal grandmother and enroll in a private academy; the last six
months of his stay he studied law at London's famed Inner Temple.

Thomas returned to America in 1750 and joined his father in business.
He was formally admitted as a partner the next year, and the trading house
renamed Charles Willing & Son. Their practice followed the contours of
the British imperial economy: the firm exported Pennsylvania produce,
primarily wheat, to Europe, and imported wine, manufactured goods, and
immigrants—usually indentured servants from the continent, but also
slaves from Africa and from British plantations in the Caribbean. Within the
house, it appears that Morris managed shipping activities, while the Willings focused on building their credit in Europe and extending the firm's
reach in western Pennsylvania through trade with the Indians. Charles
Willing also embraced the high profile that attended mercantile success: he
was a justice of the peace and served twice as mayor of Philadelphia.

Morris's position with the firm, and his bond with Thomas Willing, were
altered dramatically with the death of Charles Willing in 1754. There was
an element of irony in the circumstances of his demise: the thousands of
indentured servants arriving in Philadelphia, many of them on Willing's
ships, had introduced "jail or ship fever" to the local population, the "sick-
ness spreading in the town . . . owing to the unhealthiness of the vessels
and the Palatine passengers." Obliged as mayor to make rounds of the "pest
house," Charles Willing contracted the fever and died on November 29.

This left Thomas, twenty-three years old, in charge of the family business and the male head of a household that included his mother and eight
younger siblings. The weight of these obligations only reinforced his dutiful and instinctively conformist nature; before long, even his friends referred to him as "Old Square Toes."

Thomas quickly assumed his father's public functions as well. He took
a seat on the City Council in 1755, and held a variety of offices for the
next twenty years, including stints in the Assembly, two terms as mayor
of Philadelphia, and ten years as an associate justice on the colony's Supreme Court. As his responsibilities multiplied, Willing came to rely more
and more upon Robert Morris. When Morris turned twenty-one, his seven-
year apprenticeship was complete, and he became a full-fledged employee,
a virtual partner with Thomas. In the spring of 1757, Willing decided to
make it official, dissolving the old firm and creating Willing Morris & Com-

pany. It marked an extraordinary leap for Morris: his rapid transition from apprentice clerk to vested partner was an unprecedented ascent for an outsider at a time when family connections were largely determinative, especially in staid Philadelphia.

Announcing his decision, Willing credited Morris as a "sober honest lad," and declared that the two of them would team up "to more advantage than either could do singly." That Morris brought a rare degree of acumen and vigor to the partnership is evident; his sobriety, however, appears to be a bit of an embellishment. Letters Morris received from friends around this time suggest that he was a young man who enjoyed a drink and a night on the town. One such correspondent, a friend and trading partner in Jamaica, boasted to Morris that, "drunk I shall be today, having a half dozen friends and a batch of true London claret. This town is turned devilishly debauched." There's no record of Morris's answer to his friend, but in the years to come he gained a reputation for grand parties and a bountiful wine cellar. At a time when business was routinely conducted by "a numerous body of twelve o'clock punch drinkers," when Philadelphia boasted more than one hundred taverns, and a hundred more houses licensed to sell rum by the quart, Robert Morris was a first-class carouser.

On at least one occasion, Morris's revelries led to more than just a hangover. That is to say, sometime around 1763, Morris sired a baby girl. She was born out of wedlock, like Morris himself, and little is known about the mother. The child was named Mary, and known to her family and friends as Polly; she did not live with Morris, but he appears to have provided for her room and board, and she apparently obtained a good education in Philadelphia. Polly was married in 1781, around age eighteen, and remained in touch with Morris during her adult life. Robert was also managing the affairs of his half-brother, Thomas; he enrolled him in school and, around the time the boy turned sixteen, took him on as a clerk in the countinghouse.

Morris's family life, then, was a bit chaotic, but his focus was on business. He lived close by the docks on Front Street, just a short stroll from the Willing business complex. His day entailed drudgery at his writing desk in the countinghouse, attending arrivals and supervising the lading of outgoing vessels, and meeting with vendors and other merchants at the City Tavern, at the India Queen, or at any of a dozen other dens where merchants did their business. Working days were long, varied, and convivial, and perhaps best captured in this observation by a foreign traveler of the life of the American merchant:

They breakfasted at eight or half-past; and by nine were in their counting houses, laying out the business of the day; at ten they were on their wharves, with their aprons around their waists, rolling hogsheads of rum and molasses; at twelve, at market, flying about as dirty and diligent as porters; at two back again to the rolling, heaving, hallooing, and scribbling. At four they went home to dress for dinner; at seven, to the play; at eleven, to supper, with a crew of lusty Bacchanals who would smoke cigars, gulp down brandy, and sing, roar, and shout in the thickening clouds they created like so many merry devils, till three in the morning.

The next morning, of course, it started all over again.

In pursuing the day-to-day business of the trading house, Robert Morris was performing the same duties as most of the other traders on the Philadelphia waterfront. What set the firm of Willing & Morris apart, what helped elevate them above their competitors, was their spirit of creativity.

Underwriting insurance was one typical innovation; with rates in England high and sometimes prohibitive, Willing in 1756 pooled eighty thousand pounds with five other Philadelphia merchants to insure their own vessels and offer policies to other traders. The firm's advance position in the Indian trade gave rise to another fiscal experiment. This substantial line of business was regulated by the colony to prevent abuses and the frontier violence that resulted; Willing was named to a nine-member Indian Affairs board that was empowered to finance the trade by borrowing private capital at 6 percent interest. This opened a whole new practice of underwriting government projects through bonds and other promissory notes, and Willing took a direct hand in most of the early negotiations.

It's hard to say what role Morris played in designing these novel arrangements; most of the paperwork that survives is subscribed by Willing. But Morris was working closely with his partner, gaining hands-on insights into the process of credit and capital formation at a time when most entrepreneurs engaged only in those operations they could finance from their own funds. Even as a passive observer, he may have recognized the same creative spirit at work that his father had introduced to the Maryland tobacco trade. In retrospect, these early projects look seminal: Morris later put the same principles to work on a grand scale, endeavoring to restore the finances of a beleaguered national government. It was a mercantile world, but Morris and his partner were practicing capitalism.

Borrowing and pooling private funds became especially attractive at the close of the French and Indian War, when the British government levied a series of new tariffs and trade regulations. These included the Currency Act, which barred colonial governments from issuing paper money. Colonial currencies were commonly issued as loans against real property and recalled through taxes, but they suffered destabilizing inflation during the course of the war, and so were abolished. The resulting squeeze on commerce, combined with a surge in the exchange rates for British pounds, stripped the colony of capital; said one Pennsylvania trader, "Cash is monstrous scarce—I believe we must learn to barter."

Rather than curtail their operations, Willing and Morris sought to raise funds. In 1766 they combined with seven other leading merchants to issue "joint and several promissory notes," available to the public, payable in sterling after nine months, and bearing 5 percent interest. This was a daring new approach to the problem of capital scarcity, the functional equivalent of a bond market operating with paper that could serve as an alternate medium of exchange. So daring, in fact, that it sparked a panic of sorts among competing traders who feared the authors of the new notes might corner the export market for flour. That December, nearly two hundred merchants and retailers announced in the *Pennsylvania Gazette* they would refuse to accept the promissory notes for "any payment whatsoever." Two weeks later, "a great Number of Inhabitants" broadened the critique in a petition to the Assembly. The opposition denounced the plan as the "partial schemes of private men," and suggested "many other Companies, actuated by Motives of private Gain," would issue their own notes, leading the entire mass of new paper to depreciate. They asserted as well that "the power and right" to issue currency "is, and ought to be, lodged in the Legislature of the Province alone."

No record survives of an answer to the petition, but Morris offered the obvious counterarguments in similar controversies years later—that private financing would allow the merchants to assemble ventures, and that such ventures would benefit the community as a whole; enhancing, literally, the commonwealth. As to issuing currency, that was a gray area. It was true that the commercial paper was intended to pass for money. But using the bonds would always be a private decision, a transaction between consenting individuals. Commercial houses did business through letters of credit all the time; this would just make interest-bearing debt more widely available. Whether private issues would hold their value was hard to predict, but if the notes were redeemed on schedule, depreciation would appear unlikely.

The critics of the plan lodged their complaint with the king's attorney general for Pennsylvania. Surprisingly, the ruling was amenable. Banks were expressly forbidden in the colonies under the mercantile code of the empire. But the official opinion held that transactions in the merchants' paper represented a private association, and as such were probably legal. The fears of the public carried more weight with the Assembly, however, which found that the notes carried "a manifest tendency to injure the trade and commerce of this Province." In a place and time when routine banking operations were still a foreign practice, the idea of a trading market in private securities was simply ahead of its time.

The promissory notes were a financial response to the British revenue acts; Willing and Morris took an active role in formulating a political response as well, and here they moved in concert with popular sentiment. Willing was already a politician, but for Morris the controversy marked his first appearance on the public stage. Tellingly, it was brought on by the initial rupture between Britain and her colonies in America.

The spark was a new revenue measure called the Stamp Act, a schedule of fees that would apply to virtually any transaction involving paper—official stamps were to be required for all court papers, deeds, bonds, and leases, as well as newsprint, advertisements, almanacs, even playing cards. Parliament passed the act in March 1765, to take effect November 1. Legislatures throughout North America reacted sharply, and patriot merchants and artisans organized chapters of the shadowy Sons of Liberty to lead the opposition in the colonial ports.

The response in Pennsylvania was muted, however, the consequence of local factions that had dominated the politics of the colony for a generation. Power was divided between the Quakers, who dominated the Assembly, and the Penn family, the founders of the colony who shared the governorship as a hereditary right. William Penn's sons had long since left the Quaker church, and feuded with the legislature over taxation, political appointments, Indian policy—any pretext for a fight. Ben Franklin, no Quaker but very much a politician, shared the opposition's antipathy for the proprietors, and served as a leader of the Quaker party in the Assembly. So deep was the party divide that in 1764 the Assembly sent Franklin on a lobbying mission to England. He spent the next ten years pressing the king's ministers to revoke the original colonial charter and replace the Penns with a governor appointed by the crown.

With both the Penns and the opposition Quakers busy courting royal favor, the government was all but immobilized in the face of the Stamp Act crisis. Even Franklin was nearly caught on the wrong side of the nascent rebellion; once the act was announced, early in 1765, he collaborated with officials in London to name John Hughes, one of his Assembly allies, as the local commissioner administering the new tax. In the months that followed, indignation swept the colonies. Riots broke out in Boston, New York, and Newport, Rhode Island; in September, Hughes wrote to Franklin, "The spirit or flame of rebellion is got to a high pitch amongst the North Americans, and it seems to me that a sort of frenzy or madness has got such hold of the people of all ranks, that I fancy some lives will be lost before this fire is put out."

By now, the popular movement fully outpaced Pennsylvania's elected government, and when the actual stamps arrived, on the morning of Saturday, October 5, leaders of the resistance gathered at the London Coffee House to lay their plans. A committee was selected to treat with Hughes and demand that he resign his commission: they included James Tilghman, a prominent attorney; Charles Thomson, an ironmonger and leader of the local Sons of Liberty; William Bradford, owner of the coffeehouse and publisher of the *Pennsylvania Journal*; and several merchants, among them Robert Morris.

At the direction of this committee, boys were sent out with muffled drums to beat a tattoo through the broad avenues of the city, and the bells in the church steeples and the State House were tolled with muffled clappers. The low, insistent tones spread across Philadelphia like a whispered rumor, and by afternoon more than a thousand people had gathered on the lawn behind the State House. They were ill-tempered and boisterous; Hughes had been hanged in effigy the night before. The committee offered a series of rousing speeches, then headed off as a group to confront Hughes at his home. There they found that another crowd had assembled—this a body of several hundred, led by the White Oaks, an association of shipwrights allied with Franklin and the Quakers, who vowed to protect Hughes, stamps or no.

From inside the house, Hughes sent word that he was ill and confined to bed, but the committee insisted, and with the grudging consent of the Oaks, a conference was held at bedside. Speaking for the committee, Tilghman and Morris demanded that Hughes resign. Hughes was intransigent; if the committee wanted him to resign, they would have to indemnify friends in England who had put up bond against his performance. Still, there was a mob nearby ready to tear the house down—as had already happened to stamp collectors in several other colonies—and another mob stood ready to battle them. Morris and Tilghman presented a compromise: Hughes could simply promise not to enforce the act unless Maryland and Delaware did so first. Hughes asked for time, and the committee gave him two days to deliberate. The group then returned to the State House yard to report their progress.

This was a primitive form of shuttle diplomacy, the committee navigating between two angry mobs and one recalcitrant collector. Shouts were raised that the patriots should march on Hughes's house after all, but Morris and Tilghman pleaded patience, citing Hughes's infirmity, and promising resolution the next Monday. The grumbling assembly settled for a stalemate, and as darkness fell over the city, the angry crowd dispersed into the cool evening. As the threat faded, the White Oaks headed home as well.

The episode marked a turning point for Pennsylvania, and for Robert Morris. No longer would the critical decisions facing the colony be confined to the Assembly, where Quakers wrangled for control with the Penns and their adherents. Now the fundamental questions of war and peace, of loyalty to or separation from Britain, would be debated out-of-doors, subject to the surging and unruly passions of tavern caucuses and mobs in the street. For Morris, it was a ticklish first foray into the realm of popular democracy. Accustomed to the more finite responsibilities of shipmaster and business executive, he now found himself attempting to steer a political movement. Already he was learning that while a leader might point the way with argument and reason, what course the crowd would follow was hard to predict.

Morris and the committee visited Hughes the following Monday and obtained a signed statement suspending his powers. The immediate crisis had been neutralized, but the Stamp Act itself remained in effect. In Pennsylvania as in the other colonies, the movement shifted ground: Parliament and the British ministry had ignored pleadings and petitions; now they had to be pushed.

The means settled upon was economic boycott. First in Boston and New York, then in Philadelphia, the leading merchants agreed to stop all imports of British goods, thus depriving England of the crucial colonial market. There was a distinct element of self-interest in the boycott, as many merchants were already burdened by a backlog of imports, but the movement was couched in terms of colonial rights, and the slogan "No taxation without representation" became a rallying cry in town squares from New England to South Carolina.

In Philadelphia, Morris's partner Thomas Willing now assumed the lead position. He was the most prominent on a committee of eleven merchants that met in early November to draw up formal resolutions vowing to end all imports from Britain until the Stamp Act and the revenue laws were repealed. Copies were drawn up and circulated throughout the city, and within weeks, more than four hundred merchants and shopkeepers, Robert Morris included, signed on to the boycott. The effects were immediate, and pronounced. In Philadelphia, the merchants' committee inspected all incoming ships to ensure that no contraband was unloaded; in Britain, trading houses and manufacturers sustained a sharp decline in trade. This pressure combined with factional divisions in Parliament to force a stunning retreat in British policy: in March 1766, Parliament repealed the Stamp Act.

News of the repeal touched off a season of celebration throughout the colonies. In Philadelphia, Morris joined the mayor and scores of other leading citizens in a festive banquet at the State House. The evening closed with twenty-one toasts, each marked by a seven-gun salute from cannon arrayed on the yard. In the surrounding streets fireworks and bonfires lit the night, while on the waterfront, the White Oaks led a parade—now everyone was a patriot—and revelers were treated to drafts from huge bowls of punch set outside the doors of the London Coffee House. But events were soon to show that the protests against the Stamp Act were to be the beginning, not the end, of the quarrel with England.

The logic of the British ministry was simple: Britain had run up an enormous debt in her war with France. The people of England were already heavily taxed, and the king and Parliament thought it only reasonable that the colonies should contribute to the defense of the empire. The colonists had an equally simple response, famously articulated by John Dickinson, a wealthy, London-trained attorney aligned with the Penn family in the colonial legislature, in his "Letters from a Pennsylvania Farmer." For more than a century, Dickinson argued, American settlers had faced all the dangers and hardships of the new world on their own. They owed England their allegiance, but that was all.

The dispute festered for most of the next decade, with Charles Townsend, King George's chancellor of the exchequer, imposing one revenue measure after another, and the colonists increasingly defiant. Boston was the most confrontational, but in all the major ports, committees were formed to institute boycotts, to write petitions, and to organize resistance to the Townsend Acts.

Robert Morris sat on a number of these committees, but it would be a stretch to call him an activist. He was a committeeman, garrulous and sociable, and when the merchants were called to associate, he usually went along. But more than that, Morris was a merchant, twenty years along in a career that had brought him from obscurity to wealth and prominence. War with England was a distant prospect, the worst of several possible outcomes, and still just a distraction. In the mid-eighteenth century, life in Philadelphia had much to offer a rising member of its civic elite.

With a population of roughly thirty thousand in 1774, Philadelphia had grown by half since Morris had arrived, and it was growing still. There was a new hospital, a new jail—four stories high, with a cupola for a crown—a new poorhouse, and the ornate new Carpenters' Hall. City Tavern was built by subscription in 1773 and immediately supplanted the London Coffee House as the most elegant suppertime destination. Business was conducted behind drawn curtains in paneled booths; larger assemblies convened in the fabled Long Room.

Social life was constrained by the dour modes of the Quakers, but there were a few well-loved diversions: the Jockey Club sponsored races in the springtime, balls were held at the State House, and a Dancing Assembly met every Thursday evening, enlivened with a punch that called for two hundred limes and five gallons of rum. Despite occasional straitlaced protests, plays were performed at the Southwark Theatre, built of brick— "a real playhouse," one memorialist recalled, "albeit a poor, shabby little structure."

The city nurtured a lively intellectual scene, anchored by Franklin's American Philosophical Society. There were more than twenty print shops, more than thirty bookstores, and, in 1776, seven newspapers, each catering to its own slice of the social and political spectrum. But Morris found little attraction in the charms of a literary salon; he was drawn more to the clubs—associations, societies, and fraternal orders that cited a variety of civic causes as reasons to congregate, usually over a bountiful meal. Morris was a great joiner, and famous for his appetite. Even when he didn't qualify, he was invited—the members of the Hibernian Club, which met at Griffith's Tavern to celebrate their Irish ancestry, made Morris an honorary member, along with governor John Penn and other luminaries. In 1772, Morris helped found a club of his own, the Society of the Sons of St. George. Their vocation was to assist and support British immigrants; in one case, they put up bond to release three of their countrymen from debtor's prison. They met at Byrne's Tavern, "under the Sign of the Clock," just a block from Morris's dockside home. The president of the society was the rector at the Anglican church, but the vice president, and master of ceremonies, was Morris.

During the summers, when the plains by the Delaware stifled in sultry humidity, the town's gentry would retreat several miles up the Schuylkill, to where that quiet stream slipped over an abutment and dropped 150 yards in a frothing cascade. There was an old "aristocratic" tavern there, which served as the weekend headquarters of the Mount Regale Fishing Company. Formed in rivalry to the Quakers' own exclusive club, Mount Regale hosted the city's affluent Anglicans—the Penns, George Clymer, Thomas Willing, and, by the middle 1760s, Robert Morris. Women were admitted only on special occasions. These "fishing societies" were only nominally devoted to trolling the river; their primary function was feasting. A typical Mount Regale menu included beef, fowl, ham, tongue, lamb, salad, peas, pies, cream cheese, lemons, wine, and, of course, rum.

The one mark of status that Morris tended to eschew was government office. At a time when commercial success was often reflected in an appointed or electoral post, Morris was content to let Thomas Willing serve as the public face of the firm. The sole exception was job-related; in 1766, Morris was among seven men appointed as port wardens for Philadelphia, responsible for licensing river pilots and inspecting arriving cargoes. He held the post for ten years, solidifying his position as a leader on the busiest waterfront in North America.

Morris confirmed his membership in Philadelphia's civic elite with his marriage in the spring of 1769 to Mary White. She was the daughter of Thomas White, a lawyer who had assembled an estate of seven thousand acres near Annapolis, then moved to Philadelphia. White was as close to an aristocrat as colonial society would admit, a leader in the city's small but influential Anglican enclave. As members of Britain's official religion, the Anglicans rivaled the Quakers in enterprise, and aligned against them in politics by supporting the proprietors. White had two children by his second marriage; Mary's older brother, William, was in training for Anglican priesthood.

The wedding was performed in March under the tallest spire in the city, at Christ Church just above Market Street; Robert was thirty-five years old, and his bride was nineteen. The couple promptly set about raising a family in Morris's home on Front Street. Mary took up the duties of a Philadelphia matron, supervising servants and managing a social calendar; Robert obtained a family pew at Christ Church, their tenancy reserved by a small brass plaque engraved with their names. The highborn Anglican congregation included the Willings, Ben Franklin, several judges, and Philadelphia mayor Samuel Powel.

In December, Mary bore the couple's first child, a boy named after his father. He was the first of seven children they would raise together. Morris's family circle also included his half-brother, Thomas. Around the time the boy turned sixteen, Morris brought him into his firm, "to instruct him in the profession from which he was to draw his future support." Thomas thrived there, but in his off-hours fell into a hard-drinking crowd, "worthless companions," in Robert's eyes, who "soon carried him into the practice of their follies and vices." To break this pattern, Morris sent his brother to Spain, to work for a trading company and learn Spanish and French. Around the time of his marriage, Morris recalled his brother to Philadelphia, where Robert and Thomas Willing agreed to take him on as a junior partner at Willing & Morris.

The following year Morris moved to join the select set of gentry that maintained second homes outside the city. He purchased a farm on a low bluff overlooking the Schuylkill a couple of miles northwest of Philadelphia, and soon set about erecting his country seat. Morris dubbed his new estate The Hills, and built a two-story mansion with a complex of smaller structures, including a coach house, several greenhouses, and quarters for a full-time gardener. The grounds were cultivated in the British style, with meandering walks and ornamental ponds among groves of trees. From the raised piazza flanking the house, Mary and Robert Morris could gaze over the spires of the churches in town and the topmasts of the ships docked along the Delaware, all to the serenade of rustling leaves and the sonorous hum of cicadas.

The Hills served as a weekend retreat for Robert and Mary; it also served as a forum for Robert to cultivate his commercial connections. Guests would make the trip out from town to wander through the gardens, enjoy a banquet at the Morris table, and drink from a cellar stocked with the finest wine and spirits that Europe could produce. A large man, his six-foot frame already filled out with two decades of Philadelphia cuisine, Morris was a warm and generous host, and he loved nothing better than to sit late after dinner trading stories over a glass of wine. "I dine at The Hills every Sunday," he wrote to a friend a few years later. "Thus you see I continue my old practice of mixing business and pleasure and have ever found them useful to each other."

It was not recorded if Mary brought a dowry to the marriage, but Morris was likely able to finance his new acquisition himself. In the early 1770s, as the crisis with Britain deepened, the pace of business at Willing & Morris only accelerated. They expanded their commercial fleet to nine ships owned outright, with shares held in several more. Their operations were generally secret, as was customary for a competitive firm. Yet they were so extensive that, even before word of its trading patterns leaked out, rivals could track them by the shifting price of commodities.

The scope of the firm's commerce was reflected in the correspondence of a competitor named William Pollard, who wrote in bafflement to a Liverpool correspondent that, despite a drop-off in trade to the British plantations in the Caribbean, the price of flour, bread, and wheat in Philadelphia remained "the highest ever known." What Pollard didn't realize was that, beginning in 1769, a series of severe hurricanes had forced the Spanish government to suspend its strict embargo on trade with foreigners and enlist a small circle of Philadelphia traders to stave off impending famine. Old Square Toes and his audacious partner were the first to seize on this new opportunity, sending cargoes of flour to Spanish posts in New Orleans and Puerto Rico; still other ventures, in conformance with Spanish trade regulations, went all the way to Cádiz before being transshipped back to Havana.

So dominant was the position of Willing & Morris in this new trade that in 1772, the Spanish monopolists charged with provisioning the Caribbean posts complained to royal authorities that the Philadelphia firm was supplanting their operations. The king's ministers rejected the petition; the monopoly had proved to be "an embarrassment to itself and to the Spanish nation," the ministers declared, and the private trade would continue. That same year, with local supplies exhausted, Willing & Morris sent half a dozen ships as far as Quebec in search of flour to satisfy Spanish demand.

All this trade rested on a framework of international contacts, agents in overseas ports who would see to distribution in local markets, negotiate with sovereign authorities, and arrange financing for return shipments. Key to these deals was credit: in the days before commercial banks or other means of international exchange, merchants had to rely on loans extended from distant trading houses, collectible against third parties who in turn maintained accounts for the original borrower. Notes were paid over time—thirty, sixty, even ninety days from the date they were presented for collection—which meant that, given the months involved in crossing the Atlantic, accounts could take a year or more to settle. Morris became a master of exploiting these time intervals to satisfy lenders, extend his purchasing power, and maximize the carrying capacity of the Willing & Morris commercial fleet.

Morris ran this trading operation from his desk on the Philadelphia waterfront, writing detailed sailing orders, juggling bills of exchange, relaying reports on commodity prices, and building trust and confidence with foreign factors he would never meet. His tools were rudimentary—a quill pen and leaves of parchment—but he was a globalist, practicing international finance at its most sophisticated.

Morris was just a junior partner at his firm, but his rapid advance and his social skills marked him as a leader in Philadelphia's commercial fraternity. His growing stature was showcased in 1773, when John Penn was dispatched from England to replace his brother Richard as governor of Pennsylvania. The merchants of Philadelphia held a dinner in their honor to mark the occasion, but as the richest and most powerful men of the colony gathered for the fete, the hosts recognized an awkward predicament: the Penn brothers detested each other. The solution was devised through the seating chart: "Mr. Bob Morris, the head man at the merchants' feast, placed Governor Penn on his right hand, and his brother, the late governor, on his left," one attendee recorded. The evening closed with a series of toasts, and the event was recorded a success, but not without deft management by Morris: through the length of the festivities, neither Penn brother spoke a word to the other.

Morris's place of honor at the head table underscores his principal accomplishment in his life thus far: not fortune per se, but to have earned the designation and reputation of "merchant." At a remove of two centuries this may appear somewhat prosaic, but in colonial America, where most people made a living by toil, the station of the merchant was something quite rarefied. They lived by their wits, but more than that, they lived by their character: partners and investors had to rely on a merchant's word as his bond; financial arrangements rested on individual credit, established through a past record for fair dealing. It was presumed that these assets flowed from a scrupulous sense of personal integrity, attributes Morris cultivated and took pride in. To him, the title of merchant implied moral as well as financial standing. "I declare that the character of a real merchant, a generous, open and honest merchant, is a character I am proud of," Morris said later, setting out his personal credo in a public statement. "It is the profession to which I have been bred from my earliest youth, the station in which it has pleased God to place me."

For all his social and financial success, Morris was not especially grandiose. At a time when many members of Anglican gentry wore wigs, or powdered their hair, Morris wore his plain and swept back. One foreign visitor described him as "very simple in his manners," and "without ostentation." Another acquaintance, comparing Morris to another opulent merchant, found the latter's abode to be "more gaudy, but less comfortable" than Morris's. According to a list composed by an eccentric Swiss immigrant in 1774, Morris was among the select group of eighty-four Philadelphians to own a horse-drawn conveyance, but where the rich rode in ornate coaches drawn by teams of four or six horses, Morris made due with a "chariot," a more modest carriage with a pair or perhaps a single horse.

That year, Morris's household consisted of his wife, three young children, and several servants, including at least one slave, a domestic servant named Hero. At that time, the taxable estate of Morris's partner, Thomas Willing, was assessed at more than five hundred pounds; by contrast, Morris's was assessed at £115, about the same as a prosperous blacksmith. Though his new estate at The Hills was probably not included in the tax estimate, Morris was, on the eve of the Revolution, a man on the rise, but not quite arrived.

Still, his prospects were bright, his circumstances comfortable, and his position in Philadelphia society secure. The only cloud on his horizon was the one drifting in from the east: the conflict between the colony where he resided and the land of his birth. In the four years following repeal of the Townsend Acts, even through another round of committee activity in response to a tax on tea, Morris managed to stay clear of the controversy. But the violent Boston tea protests augured a new stage in the dispute, and when British authorities retaliated with the Intolerable Acts, closing the Port of Boston and placing the city under martial law, Morris was already looking wistfully to the bygone days of harmony in the empire. "Poor Bostonians," Morris wrote in June. "*Poor America*. This is the beginning of troubles, but its better to die bravely than be starved by pickpockets. God send our children and grandchildren may see as happy days as we have done."

Chapter 2

SUING FOR PEACE, ARMING FOR WAR

N ews of the punitive measures against Boston rekindled the flame of resistance in Philadelphia. A circular letter, addressed to their fellow colonists by the Massachusetts radicals in May 1774 to call for a new and comprehensive boycott of British trade, arrived in the most urgent fashion, carried into town by Paul Revere after a hard ride of six days. With the Assembly in recess, the Boston letter was debated in a series of stormy meetings, at City Tavern, at the London Coffee House, and at the Bunch of Grapes Inn. There were no rules at these sessions, and little decorum. Speakers were shouted down, oaths exchanged; as one participant recounted, "The tumult and disorder were past description." During one speech the militant patriot Charles Thomson, rail-thin but a fiery orator, got so worked up that he fainted in mid-sentence and collapsed to the floor.

Robert Morris and his fellow traders regarded these scenes with some trepidation. They were reluctant to engage in another boycott, as commercial relations within the empire were already strained. And they were leery of the firebrands in Boston. Those defiant patriots had brought the wrath of the king upon their own heads; Pennsylvania remained at peace, her trade flourishing, her patriotic ardor dampened by the peaceful mores of the Quakers.

Morris, moreover, took no part in the elaborate disquisitions on colonial rights that preoccupied so many of his contemporaries. In all the time he would spend in the high councils of the Revolution, in all the debates over form and policy, Morris rarely ventured into the realm of theory. He was a pragmatist who moved easily within the mainstream of political action.

Still, Morris understood that a breach had opened between America and her parent state, and there was no question in his mind over where he stood. "For my part I am a native of England but from Principle am American in this dispute," he wrote to James Duff, a British factor who looked after Willing & Morris interests in Spain. As to tactics, he endorsed the moderate approach espoused by John Dickinson, who had emerged as an uncertain leader of the colonial resistance. Long after the first shots were fired, Morris believed that a peaceable reunion with England was possible. "I recommend constantly a steady, manly, but decent and peaceable opposition as most likely to ensure success," he told Duff. In this instance, success meant reconciliation. "I pray God both for the sake of that country and this that such may be the issue."

Morris maintained this sensibility throughout the summer of 1774, as the people of Philadelphia sought to craft an answer to the Boston letter. Dickinson and Charles Thomson took the lead, seeking to unite the fractious Pennsylvania movement in a broad coalition. The core idea was to convene a Congress of all the colonies—the details could be sorted out there.

To that end, the patrician Dickinson assembled a meeting of sixty civic leaders at Carpenters' Hall, who selected a committee to administer what was fast becoming a mass movement. The roster totaled forty-three members and spanned every political, religious, and economic faction in the city. Morris and his partner were both included. The Committee of 43 met the public a week later, on June 18, before a crowd of several thousand at the State House yard. Dickinson shared the podium with Thomas Willing, and together they introduced the new committee, and floated the idea of a Provincial Convention. Both proposals won enthusiastic endorsement, and the Convention was set for July.

Faced with the prospect of a popular uprising, Governor Penn called the Assembly back into session. It met four days before the Provincial Convention, and for the next week, Philadelphians were treated to the spectacle of two representative bodies in session at the same time; the Assembly in the State House, and the Convention two blocks down Chestnut Street at Carpenters' Hall. On July 21, the members of the Convention presented the Assembly with their resolves, committing Pennsylvania to the boycott and proposing Dickinson, Willing, and a young attorney named James Wilson as delegates to Congress. Crowded into the galleries at the State House, the members of the Convention waited expectantly, but the burgesses, most of them Quakers, said nothing. According to one wry account, the members of the Assembly sat "with their hats on, [wearing] great coarse cloth coats, leather breeches and woolen stockings in the month of July. There was not a speech made the whole time, whether their silence proceeded from their modesty or from their inability to speak I know not."

Abashed and deflated, the Convention returned to Carpenters' Hall, authorized the Committee of 43 to continue in force as a "Committee of Correspondence," and adjourned. The next day, after meeting all morning in closed session, the Assembly endorsed the idea of a colonial Congress and named a slate of conservative delegates; none of the three nominated by the Convention was included. The delegates were to seek "the best Prospect of obtaining a Redress of American Grievances," according to specific instructions issued by the Assembly. But they were to go no further: "You are strictly charged to avoid every Thing indecent or disrespectful to the Mother State."

John Penn and the Assembly had delivered a blunt, procedural blow to the popular movement against Parliament and the crown; the Convention had been dismissed without a word and all its recommendations ignored. Still, for all the blank stares they gave Willing and his associates that afternoon at the State House, they must have sensed the ground shifting beneath them. They embodied the formal, elected government of the colony, but the popular movement was swirling past them, carrying the Committee of 43, and the Provincial Convention, along with it.

The same phenomenon was unfolding throughout the colonies. In New York, the Boston circular letter was ignored by the Assembly and answered by a Committee of 51. In Maryland and Delaware, and to the south in Virginia, and North and South Carolina, standing governments were bypassed by provincial conventions that endorsed the boycott. In resisting the authority of Britain, the people of America were defying constituted authority at home as well.

Over the spring and summer of 1774 this amorphous movement began to acquire distinct and substantial features. Goaded by escalating parliamentary measures designed to punish the people of Boston, ad hoc committees of correspondence and town meetings in every colony endorsed the still-conjectural Congress. On June 17, the Massachusetts House of Representatives sharpened the focus, proposing that the new body convene in Philadelphia on the first day of September. In the weeks that followed, legislatures or provisional conventions in every colony but Georgia named slates of delegates.

Just how Robert Morris regarded this momentous shift in American political culture is hard to say. He was no political adventurer, and in the years to come often found himself at odds with the passions of popular politics.

Yet in the turbulent period after the Stamp Act, Morris sat on several of the committees that rose up to fill the vacuum left by the paralysis of the official government. He respected the prerogatives of formal authority, but did not hesitate to move when that authority was compromised. Above all, Morris was a patriot—it was a maxim with him that "The individual who declines the service of his country because its councils are not conformable to his ideas makes but a bad subject; a good one will follow if he cannot lead." The only question was, with the lines of sovereignty blurred, where did patriotic duty lie?

Once the problem of allegiance was settled, Morris was free to act. As much as he was a member of the establishment, he had little investment in the status quo. In an era when institutions lasted for generations, his life had been marked by constant change: the departure from his homeland, the loss of his father, the rapid rise from apprentice to partner. The future might be uncharted, but Morris would face it with equanimity, always on his own terms.

The members of the First Continental Congress began arriving in Philadelphia in early August. Some, like Sam Adams and his cousin John, were already famous; others were making first impressions, like George Washington, the reserved and sometimes awkward colonel from Virginia. For Pennsylvanians, the wrangling over factions and provincial councils ceased, and all eyes focused on the new, continental body. Recorded Joseph Reed, a lawyer active in the Provincial Convention, "We are so taken up with the Congress that we hardly think or talk of anything else."

As their first act, the arriving delegates were treated to Philadelphia's extravagant brand of hospitality; "mighty feasts," one termed it; "sinful feasts," said another. Morris presided at many of the festivities, and appears to have formed an especially collegial connection with Washington, inviting him to dinner and hosting him for a weekend retreat at The Hills. He also found affinity with the New York delegation, comprised chiefly of moderates who, like him, had entered politics only reluctantly as the conflict with Britain escalated. John Jay, decorous and somber—"plain as a Quaker," in the estimation of Abigail Adams—but also inexorable in legal and political pursuits, became close friends with Morris and a reliable political ally.

But there was business to attend to, and through all the merriment, the delegates and their hosts warily appraised each other. Some of the delegates, especially those of Virginia, rallied to the radicals from Massachusetts, while others regarded them with suspicion, calling them "the violent party." The Pennsylvania delegates soon emerged, along with those of New York, as their moderate counterpart.

The Congress turned its formal attention to the contest with England on the last week of September. On Tuesday the 27th, it voted unanimously to cease all imports from the British Empire, the boycott to begin December 1. The obvious corollary to the ban on imports was a ban on exports to Britain, but this would have more immediate and dire effects for the Americans. The southern colonies, with economies built exclusively on export commodities like tobacco and rice, were especially vulnerable. Even the Virginia delegates, for all their brave rhetoric, pleaded that an export ban be postponed for at least two years. That led to a compromise: nonimport would begin December 1; if that brought no relief from Britain, nonexport would commence in September 1775. This compact, an agreement among the colonies to engage in economic warfare against England, was drafted in early October and termed the Continental Association.

For the first time, the colonies had joined in formal opposition to their mother country. But the Congress could only advise; it had no formal authority, no way to enforce its policies. To that end, the Congress called for committees to be elected "in every county, city, and town" in America that would monitor commercial activity and publicize any violations of the Association, "that all such foes of the rights of British-America might be publicly known, and universally condemned as the enemies of American liberty." Entrusting the boycott to local, elected committees was a brilliant solution, at once removing the Association from the jurisdiction of the colonial legislatures, several of them still loyal to the crown, and at the same time energizing the popular movement for American liberty. With the groundwork laid for concerted action in support of the rebels at Boston, the Congress adjourned until the following May. The delegates enjoyed another round of banquets, followed by a ball, and then departed for home.

The action now returned to the individual colonies. In Philadelphia, a radical faction led by the city's mechanics, as artisans and craftsmen were called at the time, took the initiative, nominating a slate of sixty men to the Committee of Inspection and Observation that would enforce the new boycott. Their ticket included John Dickinson, Charles Thomson, and a dozen other members of the Committee of 43, but it dropped the more conservative elements of that body, including many of its Quakers. The city's moderates answered with a rival slate; it included a third of those named on the mechanics' ticket, including Dickinson, but it replaced radicals like Thomson with the city's more prosperous, conservative merchants, and a number of the Quakers rejected by the mechanics.

Robert Morris was named on both tickets. This was in part simply pragmatic. As a port warden, Morris was well situated to monitor shipping activity, and four of the seven wardens found themselves nominated—though only Morris was chosen by both sides. It was also a measure of his reputation: Morris was known to be capable, fair, and honest, just the sort of person to iron out trading disputes. And it reflected Morris's status as a political outsider who carried no baggage from the colony's factional wars. It was telling that his partner Thomas Willing, co-chair of the Provincial Convention, was named on the moderate ticket, but not the mechanics'.

Ballots were cast November 12, and left little doubt where popular sentiment lay. The mechanics' ticket received 499 votes; the moderates just eighteen. Turnout fell well below the standard for Assembly elections, but that was due to the nature of the contest. Quakers, loyalists, and the disaffected stayed away; this was a vote to see who would lead the resistance.

For the next several months the new committee occupied itself in directing the boycott—inspecting cargoes, hearing appeals from merchants seeking exemptions, and sequestering the banned imports that arrived in port. Such merchandise might be sold, but any proceeds were to be sent to aid the citizens of Boston. At the same time, the committee served as a political forum, calling for a second Provincial Convention and proposing that the colony raise and arm a militia. The Convention met in Philadelphia in January, but more moderate voices held sway, and the plan to arm the province was shelved.

Robert Morris was active in enforcing the rules of trade but he took no part in the Convention. Politics held no charm for him, and besides, he had very little time. The conflict with England had led some European houses to tighten credit terms for American merchants, forcing Willing & Morris to scramble for foreign exchange. All trade with the British Empire was scheduled to end that fall; Morris was determined in the interval to make one last, great effort to shore up his capital accounts across the Atlantic.

In the winter of 1774, Morris sent out a veritable flotilla to Europe, on his own and with an array of partners. He summarized this activity in a letter to one of his factors at Cádiz, Spain. "I have pushed freely and boldly this season having loaded from 50 to 60 sail of stout ships since the 1st of November," Morris wrote in February. "Some are gone up the Mediterranean some to Lisbon but mostly for England." Morris may have exaggerated the number of vessels he'd sent out—he was probably seeking to impress his Spanish correspondent. Still, even half that amount represented a staggering figure, more shipments of flour and wheat than his firm usually dispatched in a year.

Morris included elaborate instructions on how he expected his factor to handle the funds earned through sale of the flour. Some were to go to outstanding debts on the continent; for the balance he requested "bills at long sight" from firms at London and Rotterdam. By collecting long-term obligations from Europe, Morris was laying away funds against hard times ahead. "Our exchange must inevitable come down very low and it will then be a great advantage to have money coming in as it will furnish us with supplies for which we can remit our own drafts on different people that employ us" Morris wrote. "Hence we shall propose to repeat this measure." He deplored the prospect of "civil war," as he termed it, but should it come he would be ready.

As if to confirm the firm's aggressive posture that winter, Willing & Morris in January launched two new ships: the *Pomona* and the *Black Prince*. Each was registered at two hundred tons, the largest of the thirty vessels registered that month in Philadelphia; the celebrated mariner John Barry called the *Black Prince* "the finest ship in America." She was put to work at once, sailing under Barry for Bristol, England, on December 28; she returned April 23, and was sent out again May 1, this time for London.

Morris was so consumed with getting his ships out that he had little time for public affairs. "The very extensive concerns in business which fall under my management oblige me to decline any active part, otherwise I should probably have had a large share in the public transactions," he explained to his Spanish agent.

Had the conflict with England receded, Morris would likely have maintained that course, attending to the affairs of the countinghouse while his partner navigated the byways of Philadelphia politics. But the friction at Boston continued to escalate. With the patriot movement rising around him, British commander Thomas Gage occupied the city of Boston, fortified his position there, and built his force to 3,500 men. Pressed by his superiors to take more decisive action, on April 18 Gage ordered an expedition of more than five hundred soldiers to seize military supplies the rebels had sequestered at Concord. The troops set out about midnight. An advance force reached Lexington around dawn, only to find a body of Minutemen, as the militia were termed in New England, drawn up on the village green to meet them. Shouts rang out, then volleys, and the first battle of the American Revolution was under way.

Word of the fighting outside Boston reached Philadelphia four days later. As it happened, the date was April 23, the traditional day for celebrating England's patron saint. Accordingly, that afternoon found Robert Morris in the Long Room at City Tavern, presiding over more than a hundred prideful Britons at the annual feast of the Society of St. George. As the story goes, an express rider galloped up to the tavern door, burst in on the proceedings, and announced the news from Boston. The assembly immediately broke up in alarm, the many loyalists in the room knocking over tables and chairs in their rush for the exit. Legend holds that the exodus left Morris at the head table, glass raised in mid-toast, facing an empty room. After years of talk, petition, and boycott, the worst had come to pass: America and England were at war.

The Congress returned to Philadelphia in May 1775 to find the city transformed. "The martial spirit throughout this province is astonishing," John Adams wrote in a letter home. "It arose all of a sudden, since the news of the battle of Lexington." Gone was the wary skepticism that had greeted the zealots from Massachusetts the previous autumn. Hundreds of horsemen rode out to greet their arrival; every bell in the city chimed in unison. Militia companies drilled on the commons every day of the week, including even Quakers. "Uniforms and regimentals are thick as bees," Adams reported.

This new, more rebellious spirit infused the Pennsylvania Assembly as well. Reversing its position from the year before, the Assembly dropped the more conservative voices from its congressional delegation, and added the three men recommended by the Provincial Convention: John Dickinson, James Wilson, and Thomas Willing. Another addition was Benjamin Franklin, returned at long last from ten years in London. At seventy years of age, he was beloved of both the Quakers and the patriot activists. Always a cagy politician, Franklin's stance on the conflict with England was largely unknown, but his fame added luster to the Pennsylvania delegation, and to Congress itself.

As much as the Assembly tried to keep up, events moved faster still. In mid-June, Congress appointed George Washington to take command of the impromptu rebel army massing outside Boston; he departed days later, taking along as aides-de-camp the patriot lawyer Joseph Reed and Thomas Mifflin, a Quaker merchant so enamored of the cause that he was willing to forsake the teachings of his pacifist church. The next week Congress called on Pennsylvania to raise eight companies of "expert riflemen"—more than six hundred men. And at the end of June, word arrived of the pitched battle at Bunker Hill.

The fighting was taking place in a province far removed from the peaceful plains of Pennsylvania, but the conflict was escalating rapidly. Moreover, with the rebel Congress directing the war from Philadelphia, there was every reason to expect that the Quaker city would soon become a target. Finally, on the last day of June, the Pennsylvania Assembly moved to place the colony on a war footing. It endorsed the militias that had been parading in the streets, issued orders for the purchase of firearms and equipment, and, most important, established a twenty-five-man Committee of Safety to supervise the defense effort. The committee roster comprised the most prominent political figures in the colony, including Ben Franklin and John Dickinson, as well as its leading merchants, among them Robert Morris. Franklin and Morris formed a strong friendship, and came to rely on each other in the political squalls that lay ahead.

Now Morris was on two committees, one for enforcing the Continental Association, one for defense of the city. But where service on the Committee of Inspection and Observation was practically nominal—no budget, no mission but literally to observe—the Committee of Safety was charged with arming 4,500 men, launching a provincial navy, building forts on the Delaware, and obtaining munitions. For the Assembly, the Committee of Safety served as a foil to insulate itself from a warlike duty it never really wanted; for Morris it marked the opening of a career of active public engagement that would continue for the next twenty-five years.

The Committee of Safety commenced operations the following Monday in the white-paneled Assembly Room at the State House. As their every act would constitute treason against the crown, their proceedings took place in secret, with minutes to be divulged only upon order of the committee itself. They agreed to meet six days a week, and because Congress occupied the hall during the day, sessions began at six o'clock in the morning. Fewer than half of the twenty-five members showed up to the first meeting, establishing the mode for the next year: many held title on the committee, but most of the work fell to a core group. As their first act, the committee named Ben Franklin as president, but at his age, and with his obligations in Congress, he could be little more than a figurehead. The committee soon recognized Morris's strengths as an administrator, and when Franklin was absent, Morris took the chair.

• • •

Morris's primary assignment from the committee was to obtain gunpowder. As the most prominent merchant among the committee's active members, he was the natural choice for the job. But it was no simple task: Parliament had banned the sale of arms or ammunition to the colonies months before, and the dearth of powder was a national concern. Most of the gunpowder to be found in North America had been seized in daring patriot raids on British garrisons, but that supply was squandered by the amateur soldiers at Boston. Arriving there to assume his new command, Washington found his forces "exceedingly destitute" of powder. The shortage was so critical that Washington deceived his own troops, filling powder barrels with sawdust to conceal the deficit.

The only solution was to purchase contraband explosives abroad and smuggle them in. Morris promptly set about staging these ventures on his own, with a variety of partners, and through other merchants under contract to the committee. This was risky business, a combination of espionage and arms smuggling under the nose of British consuls in foreign ports and warships cruising the high seas. Morris employed every form of subterfuge he could devise to ensure a cargo would get through: false papers for ships, false sailing orders, false cargo registers.

Many ships were captured, but many more got through. By early August, Morris and a second merchant on the committee requested compensation for twenty-five thousand pounds advanced from their own funds to underwrite trading ventures. That was a large fortune, enough to outfit half a dozen outgoing voyages, tackle, cargo, and all. The returns began coming in almost immediately; one shipment of powder, totaling more than three thousand pounds, was received August 21. A week later, Morris deposited another two tons of powder in the committee's new magazine.

Congress was seeking gunpowder at the same time Pennsylvania was sometimes turning to the same contractors Morris used for the committee. In September, the Congress called on Morris himself, and advanced him a total of eighty thousand pounds to obtain powder in Europe. It was by far the largest munitions contract Congress had yet made. It also sparked the first dispute over procurement within the new national government.

Morris had agreed to send a ship to Europe bearing thirty thousand pounds in hard currency; the gunpowder purchased there was to be shipped back to America at a rate of £14 per barrel. The venture would yield a profit estimated at twelve thousand pounds, depending on the cost of powder. Following the practice established in its first powder contracts, Congress agreed to provide the capital, along with insurance. Here the point was confused—whether the insurance was to cover just the first cost of the gunpowder, or the full venture, profits included.

The uncertainty over coverages sparked a heated policy debate. The deal had been executed between Morris and Ben Franklin, who signed for the Congress, but neither was on hand to explain the discrepancy when questions arose. Fortunately for Morris, Thomas Willing was in attendance that day, and he was able to intercede with the other members. Morris was "a man of reason and generosity," Willing told his colleagues, and while the terms appeared a bit cloudy, Congress could revise the contract as it saw fit. Other delegates pointed out that the price of gunpowder had already risen to £19 per barrel, making the deal something of a bargain for the government. If gunpowder was to be obtained—and that was essential—the merchants involved would have to be compensated.

But for some delegates, like Eliphalet Dyer, a stern-minded military veteran from Connecticut, the sheer size of the deal, and the numbers involved, was too much to stomach. "There are not ten men in the colony I come from who are worth so much as will be made clear by this contract," Dyer declared. This drew a snort from George Ross, an attorney, a Pennsylvania delegate from Lancaster, and a colleague of Morris's on the Committee of Safety. "What does this matter to the present debate, whether Connecticut men are worth much or no?" Ross scoffed. "It proves that there are no men there whose capital or credit are equal to such contracts. That is all."

To some degree, Ross was engaging in a bit of sectional boasting—as the entrepôt for the fecund hinterlands of the Delaware and the Susquehanna, commercial operations in Philadelphia dwarfed those of the other colonial ports. But the effort to supply the army would bedevil the Congress for the duration of the war. To some of the more puritanical members of Congress, the very idea of trade was anathema—as Richard Henry Lee of Virginia declared at the time, "The spirit of commerce is a spirit of avarice." Yet with no navy and no formal foreign alliances, matériel would have to be obtained through the enterprise of private merchants like Morris. They would have to find some profit in the business; how much they would make, and how they should be compensated for losses, was the subject of constant, sometimes contentious negotiation.

That Congress resolved its doubts about Morris is apparent from its proceedings two days later, when his firm was awarded a separate contract to obtain powder, cannon, and small arms. And in the end, the wrangling over profits and insurance came to naught; the captain of the ship *Lion*, dispatched under the initial gunpowder contract, returned from Europe bearing cash but not armament, the captain having found that the kingdoms of Europe were leery of offending England, and "watchful to prevent the exportations."

The second contract proved even more disappointing. Seeking to move quickly, Morris had purchased a ship and sent it to Hamburg under direction of William Duncan, a "worthy active young gentleman" from Philadelphia. Morris had the ship sail "in ballast," carrying just enough cargo to keep her upright on the sea. Rather than burden the voyage with a trading mission, he'd sent with Duncan bills drawn against Willing & Morris accounts in Europe, credits that would finance the munitions for the return voyage. After the launch, Morris waited patiently, his high hopes turning to concern, and finally resignation. "It unfortunately happened" that the ship and captain were never heard from again, Morris recorded three years later. "Mr. Duncan must have perished in her."

Despite such setbacks, the efforts of Morris and the Committee of Safety soon yielded a steady stream of gunpowder. Throughout the month of August, the committee dispatched wagonloads of the critical stuff to answer calls from New York and New Jersey, to supply a Canadian expedition being staged by General Philip Schuyler at Albany, and to Washington's army at Cambridge. During this same period, official committees and private merchants in most of the other colonies also were scrambling to obtain gunpowder. They met with varying degrees of success, but all of them together secured less than half the powder and saltpeter obtained by Pennsylvania and its Committee of Safety. Thus in the autumn of 1775, well before the colonies declared independence and even as he was negotiating his first contracts with the Continental Congress, Robert Morris was already the principal actor in supplying powder to the American war effort.

While Morris waged his campaign to obtain gunpowder in secret, he and the Committee of Safety led a very public effort to prepare the city for battle. On the marshy flats fronting the Delaware south of the city, teams of workmen built a small fleet of ships for a new Pennsylvania Navy. Most were specifically designed for river defense; swift, narrow vessels propelled by sweep oars and mounting a single heavy-gauge cannon in the bow. An elaborate system of spiked-timber obstructions was sunk in the river channel, the locations secret to all but committee members and a cadre of trusted pilots. And the committee moved to organize the scores of volunteer militias that had sprung up around the city, issuing standardized pay scales, purchasing equipment, and selecting officers.

For all the patriotic enthusiasm, fissures soon appeared that threatened to undermine the popular consensus. The rebel militias flat-out rejected the regulations issued by the committee. In part, the split was rooted in simmering religious rivalry; Quakers had been exempted from service, which offended the Scotch-Irish Presbyterians who dominated the militias. Pay scales were denounced as too low, and the militias insisted on electing their own officers. Some radical elements went further, denying the authority of any free-standing committee. Sovereignty, they said, derived only from the people, as expressed through popular convention or the Assembly itself. Similarly, the captains named to helm the row-galleys challenged the committee's choice of the fleet's commanding officer. It was fast becoming apparent that the new ethic of liberty clashed with the top-down imperatives of military command.

Morris's seat on the committees embroiled him in the city's more vengeful displays of patriotic spirit. By late summer, the zealots in the movement had lost patience with the city's loyalists, and moved to silence two of the most vocal. One, an attorney named Isaac Hunt, had the temerity to defend a merchant charged with violating the Continental Association by selling imported linen. Hunt spoke for his client at both the Committee of Inspection and Observation and the Committee of Safety. On a Wednesday morning in early September, about thirty militiamen marched to Hunt's house, called him out, loaded him in a horse-drawn cart, and paraded him through the streets of the city to the beat of a drum. A growing crowd of "jolly tars, market people and others" trailed along, throwing rocks and shouting threats.

The crowd now proceeded to the house of a second infamous Tory, a physician named John Kearsley. When some raucous demonstrators banged on his window, he appeared in his doorway brandishing a gun. The mob set upon him, thrust him in the cart with Hunt, and proceeded to the London Coffee House. In the street before the entrance, the throng surged around the cart, both dissidents disheveled and smeared with blood, Kearsley bellowing in rage and his captors roaring back. The pair was finally released upon the intervention of Mayor Samuel Rhoads, but when Kearsley was escorted home, his house was pelted with stones and all its windows shattered.

Isaac Hunt left Philadelphia the next day, sailing before dawn for Barbados, but Kearsley remained. Incensed at his rough treatment, he sat down with two collaborators, drew up a detailed scheme for an invasion of Pennsylvania, committed it to paper, and sent it off to London. His letters were intercepted, and Kearsley was brought up for trial before the Committee of Safety.

This put Morris in a difficult position; Kearsley was a vocal loyalist, but also a respected physician, a member of the American Philosophical Society, an Anglican, and a fellow officer at Morris's club, the Society of St. George. Morris sat as chairman when the committee heard the case. The trial took up most of a Saturday afternoon, before a packed audience in the city's Masonic Lodge, around the corner from City Tavern. The telltale letters made the verdict inescapable, and after Morris signed the order committing his friend to jail, Kearsley was escorted to prison by a contingent of militia marching to the sound of the fife and drum. Guilty he might be, but Kearsley's case had to be sobering for Morris: the ugly riot before the Coffee House was well known around town. Instead of bringing them together, the conflict with Britain was driving Philadelphians into angry, hostile camps.

In the past, with the tenor of politics turning harsh, Morris might have retreated from the fray, but now he became more engaged. In August, an election was held to select a new, expanded Committee of Inspection. Three slates of candidates were offered; Morris was named on two—the radical, or mechanics ticket, and a moderate ticket dominated by Philadelphia's mercantile interests. Thomas Willing's name appeared on the third, more conservative ticket; Morris's did not. Though they were partners in the same firm, and despite his role as co-chair at the first Provincial Convention and his seat in the Congress, Willing was identified with the civic establishment, while Morris personified a new mode of leadership. In citywide balloting on August 16, the radical ticket prevailed.

It should be noted that all these committee tickets were broad-based—Franklin, John Dickinson, Thomas Mifflin, and Joseph Reed were each named on all three—and did not serve as strict guides to the attitudes of the nominees. That is to say, Morris was an active patriot, but he was no zealot, and continued to make clear his hope that the colonies would reconcile with Great Britain. His inclusion on the radical slate was more a reflection of his competence as an administrator and his central role on the Committee of Safety. Still, though politics were growing ever more partisan, Morris enjoyed the confidence of most of his fellow citizens—artisans and merchants; Presbyterians, Anglicans, and even Quakers.

In September, Morris capitalized on this broad base by running for a seat in the Assembly. He'd never before run for public office, but these were extraordinary times, and we can surmise his reasons for stepping out of character. First, of course, was the growing prospect of a split with England. Morris would not stand mute while others made decisions that would shape America's future. More immediately, the stalemate with the militias had made clear that the key dilemmas confronting the Committee of Safety would have to be decided by the Assembly. If Morris took those matters seriously—and it appears that he did—he would have to join the Assembly to see them through. Finally, any assessment of Morris's thinking has to account for his financial interest. Congress' policy of nonexport went into effect September 9, idling most of Philadelphia's commercial fleet. Affairs at the countinghouse wound down to the point that Morris sent his half-brother, Thomas, now a partner in the firm, back to Europe. As the election approached, Morris may have believed a post in the Assembly would allow him to drum up more business.

Morris wasn't the only bystander drawn to the political arena that year. With an array of new and more radical elements challenging the colony's traditional elite, the election of October 2 was, as one recent historian observed, "the most hotly contested in Philadelphia since the Quaker-Proprietary battles of 1764 and 1765."

Considering the martial displays in the streets and the militant tracts appearing in the press, the results of the balloting were relatively tame. Charles Thomson, by then known as "the Sam Adams of Philadelphia," was passed over, as was Anthony Wayne, a dashing militia colonel and member of the Committee of Safety. Rather, it was the more centrist of the patriot activists, Robert Morris included, who won the contested seats. Of the ten candidates running from Philadelphia, John Dickinson tallied the largest total vote.

The new Assembly got down to business toward the end of the month. In deference to Congress, which held sessions at the same time, the Assembly moved its meetings to a smaller room on the second floor of the State House. These were close quarters, but a physical acknowledgment of the fact that Philadelphia was now a national as well as a provincial capital.

Morris was immediately paired with Dickinson on several key committees, including one assigned to settle the charged question of militia service. The program crafted by this Assembly committee sought to answer the primary militia complaints: Quakers and others who refused service would be fined, and those who signed on would be paid through the issue of eighty thousand pounds in new paper currency. It was a watershed decision, marking the first time in Pennsylvania history that Quakers would be penalized for their pacifist beliefs. But it remained a compromise, leaving both sides of the controversy dissatisfied. The increasingly radicalized militia soldiers maintained their demand that all Pennsylvanians share equally in the defense of the colony, and many denounced the pay scales as insufficient—which they were. The Assembly's earnest attempt at a solution served as a stopgap, but the underlying tensions continued to build.

The Assembly sought middle ground as well in selecting a new delegation to Congress. The two most radical delegates, Thomas Mifflin and George Ross, were dropped; in their place were named Andrew Allen, scion of a family long identified with the colonial establishment and closely aligned with the Penns; and Robert Morris. This appointment completed in the space of a few short weeks Morris's remarkable migration from political outsider to active membership on the highest public bodies in America. He was now a member of the Committee of Safety, which served as the executive agency of the provincial government; the Committee of Inspection, which enforced the edicts of Congress; the Pennsylvania Assembly; and the Continental Congress. He was no longer a private man. From here forward, all the trials and controversies that would arise to confront the people of America would be his own.

The leader of the Pennsylvania delegation, and its strongest voice in Congress, was John Dickinson. Elegant, articulate, possessed of a vast estate, Dickinson had earned renown throughout America for his early, ardent defense of colonial rights. But in the opening weeks of the Second Congress, Dickinson emerged as the voice of the moderate delegates from the central colonies—New York, Pennsylvania, Maryland—who held reconciliation with Britain as the primary object of the American resistance. This stance placed Dickinson in opposition to what came to be known as the "Eastern faction," so called because it was led by the Adamses of Massachusetts. With their colony occupied by British forces and a rebel army already in the field, they pressed for a policy of armed confrontation. This faction was based in New England but closely tied to the Lee brothers and their allies in Virginia; together they comprised the Lee-Adams bloc in Congress, or to borrow another phrase from the time, the Lee-Adams "junto." This faction regarded Dickinson and the moderates as "fearful, timid, skittish," in the words of John Adams; the "timid members," as Thomas Jefferson called them.

It was true that they were fearful. To the end, Dickinson and his allies felt that war should be avoided if at all possible. Britain possessed the world's most powerful military machine; moreover, without England as their sponsor, the colonies would be left vulnerable to the other European powers and their surrogates in North America—the French in Canada, and the Spanish in the Floridas and to the west. But there was an ideological as well as a tactical split, a fundamental difference in attitude and worldview that ran through the heart of the Congress.

The Eastern faction, with their Virginia allies, hungered for a final division with Britain, with the colonies incarnated as independent states founded on the supposed "Republican" virtues of self-determination and self-reliance—Sam Adams dreamed of a "Christian Sparta." The moderates recoiled at the idea, seeking instead to preserve the ties with England while staking out new political rights within the imperial system. In this, they spoke for the vast majority of Americans. Ben Franklin, who came very late to the radical position, commented in 1775 that he had "traveled almost from one end of the continent to the other, and kept a variety of company, eating, drinking, and conversing with them freely, and never had heard in any conversation from any person, drunk or sober, the least expression of a wish for separation" from England.

Confident of broad public support and of his own stature as a patriot, Dickinson and the moderates held sway in the Congress through most of 1775. In July, Dickinson won endorsement of his Olive Branch Petition, a final appeal to the king to intervene with his ministers in favor of his loyal subjects in America. And when individual colonies asked for advice, Congress directed them to arm the populace, but to restrict their militias to defensive measures.

John Adams found this caution exasperating, but he was careful to stifle his rhetoric. "We have been obliged to act with great delicacy and caution," Adams wrote in his diary, "to keep ourselves out of sight, and to feel pulses, and to sound depths; to insinuate our sentiments, designs, and desires by means of other persons, sometimes of one province, sometimes of another." Closed sessions, and the deference to authority that was customary at the time, kept congressional factions largely hidden from the public. But within the Assembly chamber at the State House the lines were sharp and distinctly felt. By midsummer, Dickinson and John Adams were no longer on speaking terms.

In November, word arrived from England that King George had refused even to read the Olive Branch Petition. But Dickinson was intransigent, and in the Assembly he composed a new set of instructions to hold the Pennsylvania delegates to his moderate line. The delegates were directed to "exert your utmost endeavors . . . to obtaining redress of American grievances." But Dickinson set firm limits. "We strictly enjoin you" to "dissent from, and utterly reject, any propositions . . . that may cause, or lead to, a separation from our Mother Country, or a change in the form of this government."

This position may appear inherently equivocal—to prepare for war while suing for peace—but Robert Morris embraced it. Writing to a British correspondent soon after he was named to Congress, Morris said, "I am unhappy to tell you that as yet nothing is done towards peace & reconciliation but on the contrary every thing breathes War & Bloodshed." To Morris this left America no choice but to take up arms. "On this side it seems absolutely necessary to provide for a vigorous defense . . . seeing that every account we receive from England threatens nothing but destruction." Here he expressed confidence in the strength of the colonies. "These threats will prove vain while Americans continue united."

Still, Morris insisted, "It is just doing bare justice to assert that nobody wish for independence on Great Britain; the People all call out for reconciliation on Constitutional terms, and they do not act against Great Britain until drove to it." His tone was heartfelt. "We love the people of England. We wanted no other friends, no other allies."

Lest his reader mistake fealty for frailty, Morris emphasized the point. "Alas, if [the British] cannot be content to consider us brothers entitled to the same freedom, the same privileges they enjoy, they cannot expect a people descended from their own flesh & blood . . . to sit down tamely & see themselves stripped of all they hold dear." Here Morris neatly described the painful personal dilemma posed by the rebellion, and its resolution. "For my part I abhor the name & idea of a rebel, I neither want or wish a change of King or Constitution, & do not conceive myself to act against either when I join America in defense of Constitutional Liberty." He had marked out for himself a careful path between the adventurist rebels of America and an overreaching British Parliament.

Morris was not a revolutionary, but he was a nationalist, and he was asserting this position as an actor in a new, national arena. His sole objective was the national interest, and at this point Morris continued to believe the best choice for America was to retain its ties to the empire. "I am now a member of the Continental Congress & if I have any influence or should hereafter gain any it shall be exerted in favor of every measure that has a tendency to procure Accommodation on terms consistent with our just claims."

At the time Morris made his first appearance in the Congress, on Friday, November 3, the ideological feud within that body had receded before the pressing issues of logistics. War had yet to be formally declared, but there were armies in the field—besides Washington at Boston, two armed expeditions were marching to Canada—and defenses to erect. With no executive office and little staff, the Congress managed its affairs through subcommittees composed of the delegates themselves. It was a poor vehicle for administration, and a capable executive like Morris soon found his services in demand.

Morris received a crucial assignment in December, when he was named to a committee charged with obtaining arms and ammunition. Here he was performing the same delicate, urgent business for the Congress that he handled at the Committee of Safety, but the scope of his responsibilities was greatly expanded. Again, all the work performed by the committee was patently treasonous, and all its transactions were covert. It was titled the Secret Committee of Trade, or, more simply, the Secret Committee.

Morris was new to the committee but he was already well acquainted with its operations. In fact, he was already doing business with it under the powder contracts Congress debated in September. The committee was formed days before that deal was inked, and Thomas Willing was one of its original members; his resignation, on grounds that the committee's night meetings were inconvenient, prompted Morris's nomination. Ben Franklin was also a member, and he and Morris would collaborate here as they did on the Committee of Safety. Aside from Franklin and Samuel Ward, chairman of the committee and a former governor of Rhode Island, the members shared a mercantile background and were generally aligned with Dickinson's moderate politics.

The committee handled its contracts in a clubby, often incestuous manner. The Willing & Morris contract was just one example; Philip Livingston, John Alsop, and Francis Lewis, all of New York, were other members who obtained contracts with the committee, as did John Langdon of New

Hampshire, and Silas Deane of Connecticut. The chairman, Samuel Ward, was more a politician than a merchant, but he made sure several of the early contracts went to his friends in Newport and Providence.

This mode of business would appear designed for corruption, and the committee eventually faced accusations of self-dealing. But the in-house deals were dictated at least in part by the nature of the committee's operation. First, as its activities were secret, there would be no advertising of contracts, no competitive bids; transactions were necessarily limited to insiders. Second, the committee operated well within the parameters of colonial commerce, where personal contacts were the primary and often the sole consideration in routine business deals. Proximity was a factor as well; since the committee was situated in Philadelphia, it would be difficult, especially in wartime, to hammer out terms with third parties in distant ports. In one case, Deane advised a Connecticut associate to make the trip to Philadelphia himself in order to secure a contract. And there was a limited pool of merchants who were capable of mounting the international trading ventures that the committee authorized. Of that small circle, Willing & Morris stood at the center.

Despite the opportunities for graft, it is beyond dispute that the committee performed an important duty for the Congress, establishing clandestine supply lines that were essential to mounting an armed response to Britain. That the Congress turned to its own members to do so may have been its only viable option.

Further, not all the contracts went to committee members or even their friends. Especially in Philadelphia, there were many cases where the committee did reach outside its circle in awarding contracts. Last, and perhaps most important to keep in mind, the committee ventures were dangerous and highly speculative. Contractors generally gained only on commissions charged for assembling and selling cargoes. Advances from the committee paid for outgoing cargoes, but the returns went directly to the government; insurance covered risk of capture but not sea risk and not the ships themselves. Experience would show that, for all the advances made by the committee, few of the merchants involved profited from them.

Still, the Secret Committee contracts entitled merchants to engage in foreign ventures at a time when most such trade was barred by the continental embargo. Contractors obtained a decided advantage simply by keeping their ships and wharves in operation. They were serving their government and themselves at the same time. It was just the sort of high-risk, multifaceted operation that Robert Morris relished.

At the outset, the Secret Committee acted at the orders of the Congress, which issued specific requisitions as different needs arose. Gunpowder was first, of course, and weapons. Soon after came new orders for sailcloth, which American mills were too primitive to produce; medicines, hardware, lead for bullets, and more powder. Each order was funded to a rough estimate of the quantity of stores needed, and the contracts then executed by the committee. It was a demanding business, requiring interminable hours drawing up contracts and sailing orders.

The contractors received their advances in paper money, new Continental dollars that the Congress was having printed by the million. Even this basic chore required direct intervention: among the first tasks assigned Morris by the Congress was to "call on the several persons appointed to sign the Continental bills and desire them, with all possible expedition, to finish numbering and signing said bills, as the money is much wanted." Just how "said bills" were to be supported was a problem the Congress left to a later day.

In December, Morris took on still another responsibility when he was appointed to the Marine Committee. The Congress had begun in September to raise a navy; its first step was to purchase the *Black Prince* from Willing & Morris and refit her as a warship. By December it had converted three other merchantmen, but now it grew more ambitious, voting to build thirteen new naval vessels at ports from New Hampshire to South Carolina. The project was daunting; one delegate derided it as "the maddest idea in the world." But others, led by John Adams and including Morris, felt that some answer to British naval superiority was indispensable.

By the fall and winter of 1775, Morris had his hands full. His days began at dawn, with meetings of the Pennsylvania Committee of Safety. From there he went to the Pennsylvania Assembly, which continued in session until November 25, or to the Congress—conveniently for Morris, all these bodies met at the State House. In the afternoons he might have slipped out for a few hours at the countinghouse; in the evenings, he sat with the Secret Committee, usually at one of the town taverns, often late into the night. At home, Morris and his wife now had four children between one and eight years of age. Fortunately for Mary, she had servants to help with the young ones; during this hectic period, she likely saw little of her husband.

— *Chapter 3* —

INDEPENDENCE

Early in December 1775 two Frenchmen arrived at Providence, Rhode Island, aboard a sloop bearing gunpowder from the West Indies. The pair were learned, ambitious, and cloaked in mystery. Pierre Penet and Emmanuel de Pliarne said they were engaged in trade, and the sloop's captain confirmed they had helped at Cape François, a French port on the island of Hispaniola, to secure the powder he had brought to Providence. Beyond that, the two adventurers said they were on a mission, the nature of which could be divulged only to George Washington.

The Rhode Island patriots were much impressed, and Governor Nicholas Cooke provided a letter of introduction to the general. Penet and Pliarne traveled overland to Cambridge and laid out their scheme to Washington at his headquarters. They were connected with the French ministry, they said, and could obtain large quantities of powder and arms for the rebels. Washington found the plan "very eligible," but wisely deferred to Congress. The general confirmed his endorsement by writing a letter of introduction to John Hancock, the Massachusetts merchant prince then sitting as president of Congress, and by underwriting the cost of their trip to Philadelphia.

Penet and Pliarne appeared before Congress December 30 and were referred to the Secret Committee. The two Frenchmen were freelance ambassadors without portfolio; they had no papers, no commission from the French court. Penet said he was a merchant of some standing in Nantes, and Pliarne had apparently spent time as an armorer with the French fleet. But their bearing, and the letters from Washington and from Rhode Island, were persuasive. In a meeting on Friday, January 1, an agreement was reached, and Robert Morris named agent for their account. Morris was to dispatch eight trading cargoes to France; in return, Penet and Pliarne would ship fifteen thousand stands of small arms and a variety of other munitions, with more to follow.

48

The deal with Penet and Pliarne represented a watershed in the continuing effort to arm the colonies. It seemed to confirm what many had begun to hope: that of all the powers in Europe, France, England's inveterate enemy, was the most likely source of aid to the breakaway colonists. Just as important, it suggested a new mode in the arms trade. To this point, supplies were obtained by individual American traders roaming Europe and the West Indies to find entrepreneurs willing and able to assemble return cargoes of contraband munitions. Now, those very entrepreneurs were reaching out to the Americans.

The negotiation was just as significant for Robert Morris. While the full Congress had weighed the approach of the Frenchmen and referred them to the committee, the terms of the deal with Penet and Pliarne were the exclusive domain of the committee. As the wise head on the Secret Committee with long experience in Europe, it would have been Franklin who led the deliberations. But the execution of the contracts was left to Morris. His business expertise, his knowledge of international trade and shipping, were making him indispensable.

Morris was fast assuming the same stature on the Marine Committee. Since early December, the Willing & Morris facility at the south end of Front Street had been utilized as a staging area for the converted merchant ships that were to comprise the first squadron of the new Continental Navy. The firm's warehouse and wharf were piled high with rigging, armament, and hogsheads stuffed with rum, meat, and hardtack bread. Uniformed troops from Pennsylvania's Continental contingent—the Pennsylvania Line—stood guard around the clock to keep scavengers away.

On the morning of Monday, January 4, handbills were posted at taverns along the waterfront calling officers and seamen to muster immediately at the Willing & Morris wharf. By afternoon, close to seven hundred men were milling on the pier, toting their duffels and sea chests and clambering onto skiffs that would ferry them out to four converted merchant ships moored in the river.

Robert Morris elbowed his way through the hubbub, shouting orders and keeping a sharp eye on the confusion in his dual capacity as proprietor of the premises and member of the Marine Committee. In the coming year, when Commodore Esek Hopkins proved ineffective, Morris would emerge as the navy's de facto commander. He patronized the career of great fighting sailors like John Barry and John Paul Jones, supervised construction and supply of new vessels, and directed the movements of the Continental warships, issuing detailed sailing orders in the firm, precise diction of a seasoned naval captain. It was his insight to recognize that America's "infant fleet" could never challenge the British navy directly; instead he directed attacks against "defenceless places" far from the main theater of fighting, in the Caribbean and as far away as the English Channel, forcing the enemy to divide her sea forces.

On January 30, Morris added another leaf to his congressional portfolio when he joined yet another committee, this the Committee of Secret Correspondence. This panel, which included Franklin, Dickinson, and John Jay, was charged with the delicate business of establishing alliances with foreign powers, ties essential to surviving the confrontation with Britain. The committee was the State Department of the nascent national government. Primarily charged with diplomatic relations, its functions overlapped with the Secret Committee, as foreign allies would serve an increasing—and crucial—role in obtaining supplies. Like the Secret Committee, the Committee for Secret Correspondence was largely autonomous, and as the name implies, its activities were strictly covert.

Here again, Morris was brought in as the Congress' can-do, all-purpose administrator. His initial role was to supply the diplomats with swift-sailing packet boats that might slip the British cruisers and deliver urgent correspondence to Europe. But the appointment afforded Morris a unique vantage point at the center of the government's most critical functions. He and Franklin were the only delegates assigned to both secret committees, and thus were the sole members privy to all confidential contacts with foreign agents and governments. At the same time, through the Secret Committee and the Marine Committee, Morris took part in all the efforts to supply the armed forces.

Nor was his engagement limited to policy and supervision. His firm, his ships, and his personal contacts were all deeply engaged in carrying out government assignments. This function was expanded again between January and March, when the Secret Committee issued a final round of contracts to answer the growing demands of the army. These were the largest requisitions yet, totaling more than three hundred thousand dollars for arms and gunpowder, and cloth for tents, sails, and uniforms. The funds were divided among eight different contractors, but the lion's share, more than half the total, went to Robert Morris. Still another contract, a single advance of two hundred thousand dollars to buy gifts to secure the allegiance of Indian tribes on the frontier, went to a consortium of New York merchants, all of them members of the Secret Committee, but Morris had a hand here as well, serving as the initial receiver of the funds. He would broker the entire operation.

At first glance, these contracts would suggest that Morris had a stranglehold on the committee system and used his political clout to siphon into his own coffers an inordinate, even scandalous share of the largest expenditures yet to be issued by the Congress. In each of these transactions, Morris was essentially making deals with himself. But this interpretation fails to take into account the circumstances at the time, and the thinking of the men involved. Remember, at this point the Congress was little more than a loose alliance of colonies, a debating society with no administrative apparatus and no formal authority outside its own chamber. Everything that was to be done had to be done in-house.

Recall, too, that the Second Continental Congress had begun its operations in July 1775. By early 1776, the delegates had gained a fair amount of experience, and that experience led them to rely increasingly on Robert Morris. The specific operations of the Secret Committee were largely unknown to the Congress as a whole, but within the committee itself there was never the slightest hint, in the minutes or in the letters of the individual delegates, of dissent or controversy over the large and growing share of assignments that went to Morris. Nor was the committee stacked with Morris's friends or political allies. The first Committee chairman, Samuel Ward, was a mainstay of the Eastern faction, as was the Virginia plantation owner Richard Henry Lee, who joined the Committee in March. Morris's strongest personal tie on the committee was to Franklin, his collaborator on the Pennsylvania Committee of Safety.

Rather than a measure of political muscle, Morris's accumulation of contracts was a reflection of his growing stature in the eyes of his colleagues. Energetic, resourceful, with an enormous capacity for work, Morris took on one task after another as his fellow delegates flagged under the burden of endless meetings and mounting perplexities. By early February, Morris complained that his eyes were failing him, a condition he attributed to being "harassed the whole time by much public business, of which . . . more than one man's share falls to my lot."

Morris was still a minor figure in the politics of the Congress, which remained the province of better-known and more experienced politicians like John Adams and John Dickinson. But Morris was generally acknowledged as the body's consummate capitalist, the member who, more than any other, understood how to put money to work. The delegates relied on his commercial instincts primarily in the arena of foreign affairs, as when Morris was named with Franklin, Dickinson, and Adams to draft the policies the new United States would adopt in its dealings with other nations of the world. The result was the Plan of 1776, which proposed that any foreign treaty should emphasize free trade and free shipping. These principles ran in direct contradiction to the British Rules of Trade, and reflected instead commercial priorities grounded in the real-world experience of Robert Morris.

When it came to domestic issues, Morris followed the same agenda. He gave full voice to his laissez-faire principles early in the war when Congress was considering steps it might take to revive American commerce. "For heaven's sake what is meant by a Chamber of Commerce?" Morris wondered in a letter to a fellow delegate. "Do they mean to combine the jarring interests of these states into commercial systems that will adapt the minds of their respective traders? It is impossible. Do they mean to lay restrictions and form regulations? They are pernicious."

To Morris, the primary role government should take in affairs of commerce was to get out of the way. "I assert boldly that commerce ought to be free as the air, to place it in the most advantageous state to mankind in general." The imperatives of the market were more than sufficient to stimulate the energies of the American merchants. "Our traders are remarkable for their spirit and daily forming those enterprises you wish for," Morris wrote his friend. "Their own interest and the public good go hand in hand and they need no other prompter or tutor."

John Adams, who opposed Morris on the critical question of independence and generally kept him at arm's length, nevertheless appreciated his contribution to the national council. "You ask what you are to think of Robert Morris?" Adams wrote to a friend in the army in April. "I'll tell you what I think of him. I think he has a masterly understanding, an open temper and an honest heart: and if he does not always vote for what you and I think proper, it is because he thinks that a large body of people remains, who are not yet of his mind. He has vast designs in the mercantile way. And no doubt pursues mercantile ends, which are always gain; but he is an excellent member of our body."

In March 1776, Samuel Ward contracted smallpox. When he died three weeks later, Robert Morris was named to replace him as chairman of the Secret Committee. There was no question and no dissent. It was an obvious choice, the perfect fit for his abilities and the natural culmination of his rise within the revolutionary government.

None of this should be taken to suggest that Morris enjoyed immediate or unbroken success in the arms ventures commissioned by Congress. In fact, by the time the final round of contracts was issued, in February and March 1776, few of the early ventures to Europe had been completed. They were still in progress, the ships either in transit or their captains abroad, hustling to assemble return cargoes. Delays were to be expected at a time when Atlantic crossings took a month or more; wartime ventures to acquire munitions took even longer.

The exploits of Thomas Mason, a Philadelphia ship captain who helmed one of the earliest arms ventures, serve as an example. This was a private voyage, divided in thirds among Mason, Robert Morris, and another investor. Mason provided the ship and crew while Morris and the third partner supplied financial backing and a cargo of flour. Mason set out in early August 1775, "loaded as deep as prudence would admit."

Mason arrived in Spain after thirty days at sea and contacted a Willing & Morris factor in the port city of Ferrol. There was no demand for flour at the time, but with American ports closing, the factor agreed to advance five hundred pounds to Mason and keep the hogsheads stored on Morris's account until prices improved. His ship's hold now empty, Mason sailed to Bordeaux and began to cast about for armaments. The results were mixed. Gunpowder was available, but under French law only for shipment to Africa, where it was always in demand for the slave trade. And saltpeter could be had, but only if destined for Holland; neither could be shipped under an American flag.

Mason deliberated for two days. Either choice would require him to deceive the French authorities, and his contract with Morris called explicitly for gunpowder. Mason decided on the saltpeter as the simpler subterfuge, but he then learned the bills of exchange he carried for funds might not be honored, as Britain had moved to block all American credit. Undeterred, Mason presented himself at the offices of Berard Bros., a banking firm recommended by Morris. The bankers informed Mason it would take about three weeks to forward the bills to London to find out if they might be negotiated. All right, Mason said, and in the meantime he would load his ship on their account; if the bills came back without funds, he would remain in France "as hostage" until hard payment arrived from Philadelphia.

Berard Bros. agreed to these terms and Mason set about preparing his ship. Now arrived Nicholas Biddle, another Philadelphia captain, at the helm of the aptly named brigantine *Chance*. Biddle was also seeking an arms deal, this on account of Congress, and carried cash to secure the deal. Biddle agreed to guarantee Mason's payment, freeing Mason to ship out. On September 20, a new twist arrived in the mail. It turned out that most of Morris's notes had been honored after all, but the same post brought news that the French government had been alerted to the false shipping papers, and issued orders to seize Mason and his cargo. Here the two captains settled on a new scheme: Biddle would head for America in Mason's ship, and Mason would remain behind, using the balance of their funds to gather another cargo for the *Chance*.

Mason contacted the port authorities and promised to meet with them the following day. That night, Biddle made his departure in Mason's vessel. Mason was arrested the next morning, but with no ship in hand, he was soon released. The intrepid captain then purchased a load of gunpowder and two thousand muskets, and chartered a Dutch freighter, ostensibly to take the contraband to Amsterdam. In late December, Mason made a rendezvous with the Dutch vessel at sea, transferred the cargo to the *Chance*, and sailed for the open ocean. He arrived at Philadelphia early in February and was invited by Morris to recount his exploits before the Secret Committee. As Mason recorded, "I received the general thanks of Congress for the integrity of my transactions."

Not all ventures were so complicated, but nor were they so successful. Answering the contract with Penet and Pliarne, Morris arranged for eight ships to be loaded with tobacco and other cargoes and sent out to France. Each was dispatched by different subcontractors, some from Philadelphia but others from Virginia and South Carolina. Half the ships were captured, and of the other four, one was penned up on the York River in Virginia by enemy cruisers; another was diverted from its intended destination when it encountered a British ship off the coast of France.

The Royal Navy posed a daunting threat, but American privateers were a menace as well. The captain and crew of the privateers were entitled to keep the ships and cargoes they seized, "prizes" that could make them rich from a single voyage. The swashbuckling captains of these sea raiders often failed to distinguish between friend and foe; two of the four ships Morris lost in the Penet venture were to American privateers. The captured vessels were eventually released, but the delays stalled payments to the French partners for years, hindering future shipments of arms.

It didn't help that the British were alerted early on to the clandestine efforts of the Secret Committee. This damaging exposure arose from the voyage of the *Dickinson*, sent out by Bayard, Jackson & Co., a Philadelphia contractor to the committee. The *Dickinson* departed in March in convoy with several Willing & Morris vessels. Upon approaching the coast of France, the crew mutinied and steered the ship into Bristol, England. The leader of the uprising, first mate John Sands, was apparently a British spy; he had taken careful notes on the cargo and destination of the other ships in the convoy. Sands provided the port authorities at Bristol his notes from the ship's papers, which included instructions to a French factor detailing an arms deal the *Dickinson* was to finance. Sands's account was published in the press, leading to official British protests against French assistance to the rebels. At least one Willing & Morris ship was captured as a direct result of Sands's betrayal, while the formal protest forced French authorities to denounce trade with the rebels—still another obstacle facing the arms traders of the Secret Committee.

The constant delays, the changes in venue, and the long gaps in communication meant that the specific contracts tended to blend together. If one venture stalled, whatever funds remained were rolled over to finance another. Instead of discrete missions, the contracts issued to Morris by the Secret Committee and by the Pennsylvania Committee of Safety, as well as the third-party contracts that he supervised for both entities, evolved into one ongoing enterprise, with Morris acting as strategist, chief agent, underwriter, and, on occasion, a contractor himself.

As the weeks stretched into months, with new contracts issued on top of the old, Morris developed a new, more general system of handling the business. Individual contractors were gradually replaced by a network of agents empowered to handle funds and cargoes, and to manage contacts with foreign suppliers. Some of these agents were based in America; others were sent to foreign ports. All of them reported to Morris.

The first agent selected for a foreign post gives an idea of the ad hoc nature of the business, and of Morris's general mode of operation. The agent was Stephen Ceronio, a young Italian from Genoa. An idealist drawn to America by the dream of fighting for liberty, Ceronio arrived in Philadelphia with a letter of introduction to Willing & Morris. He worked for a time in the firm's countinghouse, and forged a close bond with Morris; he later referred to Morris as his "capital friend . . . in America, the Adopted Father." Morris later sponsored a sojourn to America by Ceronio's brother

Ange. As to Stephen, Morris found him to be "capable and faithful to the last degree."

In February 1776, after Ceronio had worked with Willing & Morris for less than a year, Morris tabbed him for assignment to the Caribbean. It was characteristic of Morris to settle large responsibilities on the shoulders of young, sometimes untried men, much as Thomas Willing had done for him early in his career. In most cases, it worked to his advantage; Morris had an eye for mercantile talent, and his appointees repaid him in trust and unswerving loyalty.

Stephen Ceronio was based at Cape Francois in order to handle transshipment of munitions from Europe through the neutral ports in the Caribbean. He worked from there and made side trips to St. Eustatius, St. Thomas, and St. Croix, always clearing his activities with the local authorities. His first task was to receive shipments from the Pennsylvania Committee of Safety, and use the proceeds to buy gunpowder. Soon thereafter, he was performing the same business for Congress.

In all the ports of call he visited, Ceronio posed as an agent for Willing & Morris, a cover story that allowed him to conduct shipping operations for the Secret Committee without raising suspicion. It was also true, in part, as he often managed private transactions for the Morris firm while attending to official, secret business. This dual role offered other practical advantages: it helped to pay for his presence in the Caribbean, as commissions on the sporadic government contracts were too meager to support him. And it allowed Ceronio to mix private and public cargoes on the same vessel. This provided further cover, and avoided the need to hold scarce munitions while awaiting a full cargo. It also, of course, extended the reach of Morris's private operations.

Ceronio was named at Morris's sole initiative; the next agency to be assigned was more complicated and more crucial, a joint project of the Secret Committee and the Committee of Secret Correspondence. This was an extension of the collaboration between Morris and Franklin, the only delegates to share membership on both committees, and answered the designs of both men. The agent would be posted in Paris, with the twofold mission of securing arms in Europe, and sounding out potential allies in the struggle against Britain. Spain, Holland, Germany, even Russia, were all rivals with England and might befriend the rebel colonies, but France, still chafing at her defeat in the French and Indian War, was a more likely source of help.

This candidate for this critical mission would have to possess the manner and bearing of a diplomat, experience in business, and strong political support in Congress. Morris and Franklin discussed the project in the weeks after Christmas of 1775, and in January, they settled on Silas Deane, a delegate to the First Continental Congress from Connecticut.

The son of a blacksmith, Deane was a Yale graduate who had married high on the social ladder and entered the West Indies mercantile trade in partnership with his brothers Simeon and Barnabas. In Congress he sat as an original member of the Secret Committee and obtained several of its early contracts. When fighting broke out at Lexington, Deane demonstrated a sense of daring initiative when he helped organize and personally finance Benedict Arnold's expedition against the British fort at Ticonderoga. There Arnold joined forces with Ethan Allen to effect a stunning victory, which also netted the Continental Army its first artillery. Short and stout, his wife the daughter of a former governor, Deane was plainspoken with a practical but expansive mind that tended to conceive grand schemes. Among his colleagues in Congress he was "reckoned a good man, and much esteemed."

Deane sometimes lacked tact, however, especially in dealing with his fellow delegates from Connecticut, and late in 1775 the provincial Assembly declined to return him to Congress. But Deane was too immersed in the war effort to stay home. He was already pursuing financial opportunity in the munitions trade, and was committed to maintaining a role in the American cause. Just as important, he'd formed strong friendships with Morris and Franklin during his time in Philadelphia. Relieved of his duties in Congress, he was the ideal candidate to carry out the foreign mission.

Deane received his official commission in early March. He was to pose as a merchant from Bermuda while secretly pursuing arms and clothing for 25,000 men, the purchases to be made on the credit of the Continental Congress. At the same time, he was to approach the French court and propose a formal alliance. He was essentially a one-man embassy, with open-ended powers to solicit aid of any sort, material, financial, or political, that he might discover on the continent.

Morris arranged for Deane's passage and provided him with the sort of detailed sailing instructions that were his custom with factors and sea captains. The first leg of the journey would take Deane to Bermuda, then under loose British control. He was to present himself to the Customs House, report his ship's register as lost, and procure new, Bermudian papers. If that failed, he might contact a local captain who had sailed under Morris, and have him register the ship under his name, with the same result—

Bermudian registry, which would shield him from British seizure. To further abet the cover story, the papers "ought to be dated 1 January 1776, but the farther back the better," Morris advised. That accomplished, Deane should hire a new crew, mate, and master, telling them he was bound for London. Only upon approaching the English Channel should he reveal his true destination as Bordeaux. Morris knew Deane was an experienced merchant, but he was leaving nothing to chance.

There were delays as usual—bad weather, enemy cruisers off the coast—but Deane finally reached Bermuda in late April. It took ten days to settle arrangements for the next leg of the journey, and Deane used the interval to exercise his strategic inclinations. He conducted a detailed survey of British forces on the main island, and proposed seizing the port there and using it as a base for privateers to harass shipping from the British Caribbean. Morris commended Deane's "useful hints" and referred the plan to Congress, but it died under the press of other business.

Before his departure, in a mark of trust that would be repeated by many an adventurer, Deane deposited with Morris funds to support his family. He then sat down to pen a final letter to his wife, displaying a penchant for melodrama well suited to the travails that lay ahead. "I am about to enter on the great stage of Europe," he wrote, "and the consideration of the importance of quitting myself well, weighs me down." Deane could scarcely conceal his eagerness for the mission, offering an apology for his absence that would have provided cold comfort to his distant partner. "I wish as much as any man for the enjoyments of domestic ease, peace, and society, but am forbid expecting them soon; indeed, must be criminal in my own eyes, did I balance them one moment in opposition to the Public Good and the Calls of my Country."

It was a strange period, this time of unrelenting activity in preparation for a war that many still hoped to avoid. Nobody felt the contradiction more directly than Morris: he was the most active player in the procurement campaign, and yet remained an ardent advocate of reconciliation. The arms trade at least provided a sense of movement, the impression that things were being accomplished. The political situation, in Congress and throughout the colonies, remained frozen between the poles of continued negotiation and outright independence. Resolution came only haltingly, with Americans moving through stages to break heartfelt allegiances and establish themselves as independent states.

England provided plenty of incentive. Frustration with the upstart colonists turned to outright indignation when the Continental Army took the field, giving rise to punishing raids that brought fire and death to the ports of Falmouth, Maine, in October 1775, and Norfolk, Virginia, on New Year's Day of 1776. These outrages convinced the radicals that independence would come soon, "since our enemies themselves are hastening it." But it took the publication of Thomas Paine's seminal work *Common Sense* to bring the idea of outright separation from Britain into the political mainstream.

Only recently emigrated from England, Paine brought a foreigner's clear-eyed view to bear on the tangled emotions so many Americans felt for their "parent" state. Writing in plain and trenchant prose, Paine was the first to argue that independence from England was not just a possible outcome of the quarrel with Parliament, but a desirable one. He ridiculed the proposition that England should dominate her vast dominion in America: "There is something absurd," he said, "in supposing a continent to be perpetually governed by an island." More shocking, Paine invoked reason and scripture to denounce the very idea of monarchy. The bedrock for the whole system of British sovereignty was "an unwise, unjust, unnatural compact." William the Conqueror was a "French bastard," and King George nothing more than a "royal brute."

The logic of his argument, and the way Paine flouted the respectful modes of conventional address, seemed to crystallize American resentment against the crown. First issued in Philadelphia in mid-January 1776, Paine's tract became an overnight sensation, with tens of thousands of copies in print, and extracts published in newspapers throughout the colonies. Before the month was out, George Washington had written from far-off Boston to acclaim Paine's "sound doctrine and unanswerable reasoning"; two months later, he reported, "I find that 'Common Sense' is working a powerful change in the minds of many men."

Yet while *Common Sense* effected a sea change in public opinion, the Congress took longer to come around. This was due in part to a degree of institutional inertia: most delegates, like those from Pennsylvania, were restrained by explicit provincial instructions, and in the spring of 1776, none had been authorized to endorse independence. Moreover, within the body, the very fervor of the New England faction had begun to work against them—the constant pressure had galvanized Dickinson and his allies into entrenched opposition.

The next great shove toward the precipice came, ironically, via Robert Morris. On a cold and drizzly Tuesday afternoon in the last week of February 1776, Morris received an anonymous packet of papers delivered by one of his merchant ships. The vessel had been carefully searched upon her departure from Bristol, England, but the papers, stowed at the bottom of a barrel of bread, had escaped detection.

Morris perused the documents in the chilly gloom of the countinghouse: among them was a printed copy of the Prohibitory Act, a new law passed by Parliament just before Christmas in retaliation for the warlike posture of the colonies. It repealed the punitive measures taken against Boston, and in their place declared all the thirteen colonies represented at the Congress to be renegades, their decision to raise armies placing them outside the protection of the king. All American shipping was now subject to seizure, as were any foreign vessels engaged in trade with America. Also in the packet was an unsigned letter transmitting the printed act. It was even more foreboding: 26,000 troops had been raised for an invasion, with plans to attack Boston, New York, Virginia, and North Carolina.

On its face, the Prohibitory Act was the final step in a series of measures from Parliament making untenable Morris's hopes for reconciliation. Yet the act contained a curious caveat: the prime minister, Lord North, would appoint a peace commission empowered to grant pardons to individuals, and to treat with any colony or town that might seek terms of accommodation with the crown. A second letter advised that a vocal minority in Parliament under the Marquis of Rockingham stood with the Americans, but only so long as they avoided outright independence. These mixed messages were typical of both sides in the conflict—with the ministry and with the Congress, every murmur of peace drowned out by the clamorous call to arms.

Morris headed out that night, probably to the City Tavern, where he shared the news with the members of Congress he found there; the next day he delivered the startling sheaf of papers to the State House. The business of the Congress was suspended and the delegates sat with rapt attention while the letters and the text of the Prohibitory Act were read. Richard Smith of New Jersey observed dourly, "The bill is very long & cruel." Within weeks, British warships took up station off the Delaware to enforce the new prohibition on trade.

News of the Prohibitory Act had an immediate impact on Congress. John Adams termed it an "Act of Independency, for King, Lords and Commons have united in sundering this country and that I think forever. It is a compleat dismemberment of the British Empire." More concretely, faced with an outright embargo on trade, the Congress now passed a bill authorizing American sea captains to raid British shipping on the high seas. These privateers posed a greater strategic threat to the British than all the American land forces, and represented a substantial escalation in the conflict. Even John Jay, a leader with Dickinson of the peace faction in Congress, embraced the prospect of war on the ocean.

Remarkably, though his coalition was eroding, Morris still clung to the idea of a negotiated settlement with Britain. He was confident, as he told a number of his friends, that America had the resources to prevail in a test of arms. But he was just as sure that outright war would be ruinous to both countries. Moreover, despite the gaudy appeal of uniformed militias and patriotic parades, Morris feared that the majority of Americans were still not ready to put life and treasure on the line in a war for liberation from England.

Still, Morris recognized that time was running out. His only hope was the slim opening proffered in the Prohibitory Act—the peace commission. In the weeks after the copy of the act arrived, reports filtered in that negotiators had been appointed, that they were headed toward America. "Where the plague are the commissioners?" Morris wondered in April. "It is time we should be on a certainty and know positively whether the liberties of America can be established and secured by reconciliation, or whether we must totally renounce connection with Great Britain & fight our way to a total independence."

While Morris was waiting for a reprieve from across the sea, a new core of political militants was working in Philadelphia to break the stalemate at home. The immediate object of this clique—"friends of America," they called themselves—was the annual election of the Committee of Inspection and Observation, scheduled for February 16. Tramping through the snow to after-hours caucuses at taverns and at Carpenters' Hall, the radicals drew up a "mechanics" ticket that would reflect the new schism. As in previous committee elections, the shift in character of this new ticket was incremental. The ticket returned about two thirds of the committee's hundred incumbents, but the deletions included some of the city's leading moderate voices. Robert Morris was left off, as were several of his colleagues on the Committee of Safety.

The committee election stirred little controversy and the mechanics ticket won without opposition. But two weeks later the committee called for a new Provincial Convention, serving notice that it would challenge the Assembly and the Committee of Safety for political direction of the province. The convention was to address two issues central to the war effort: better pay for the militia, and rescinding the instructions that barred the Pennsylvania delegates in Congress from endorsing independence.

Suddenly, the lines that defined several political entities operating in Philadelphia began to blur. The radicals of Massachusetts and Virginia, until recently regarded with suspicion by the people of Pennsylvania, now found common ground with the local patriots. In Congress, in the Assembly, and in the committees, support for independence, an idea that was anathema just months before, was becoming the litmus test for anyone holding public office. For Morris, his removal from the committee marked a subtle but critical transition. Just a year before, a wave of dissent had borne him from outside the political establishment to membership in every important public body in the province. Now, in what must have felt like a dizzying turn of fortune, his brief tenure in office marked him as a member of the establishment who was an obstacle to the popular movement.

As the architect of Pennsylvania's resistance, John Dickinson recognized the threat the Provincial Convention posed to his radical-moderate coalition. And as a member of both the Committee of Inspection and the Assembly, he was in perfect position to effect a compromise. Meeting with members of both bodies on March 8, he achieved just that; the committee dropped its call for a convention, and the Assembly agreed to enlarge its membership by seventeen seats—four in Philadelphia and thirteen from the western countries. This answered a long-standing complaint against the proprietors and the Assembly—that the Quakers maintained their sway in the colony by limiting representation in the western provinces. More important, it offered the radicals an opportunity to formally test their strength. The election for the new Assembly seats, slated for May 1, would serve as a popular referendum on the question of independence.

For the next two months, all of Pennsylvania was in a state of ferment. Patriot activists—the Independents—and their moderate counterparts huddled in nightly meetings, developing strategies and candidate slates. Thomas Paine was active here, along with Benjamin Rush, a young physician who had still to make his mark in Philadelphia. Members of Congress, frustrated with their own stalemated deliberations, paid close attention, with John and Sam Adams consulting with the radicals on a daily basis. Pennsylvania had become the great stumbling block in the road to independence; the overthrow of the moderates there might finally clear the way.

The central question in the election was separation from England, but the political dispute soon took on a broader and more fundamental character. Paine and the Independents were seeking a new social order, within the province as well as without, more democratic and more open, stripped of the privileges that rank and wealth had long assumed. On this both sides agreed, the moderates warning that a vote for independence would threaten Pennsylvania's charter government and the Assembly itself, bringing to a close a century of social peace, religious tolerance, and political liberty.

These arguments were made at great length in tavern hall speeches, from pulpits around town, and in the press. Scribes writing as "Civis," "Plain Truth," and "Cato" rose up to rebuke *Common Sense*, deriding Paine as "a crack-brained zealot for democracy." Paine, always ready for a fight, answered in kind, now signing himself "The Forrester"; he was soon joined by "Cassandra" and "Dialogus." What began as a "terrible wordy war on the subject of independence" soon evolved into a free-wheeling cultural and political debate. The militant patriots were derided as "violent men" who would lead the province into "the dark and untrodden way of Independence and Republicanism." The Independents attacked the economic interests represented by the moderates, introducing the prospect of class conflict for the first time.

Writing in the *Evening Post*, "A Tradesman" declared that the merchants feared independence because it would threaten their monopoly position in the provincial economy. "They get all the profit and will soon reduce and control the people as the East India Company controls Bengal." In the same vein, "Cassandra" warned of "an aristocratical junto" that was "straining every nerve to frustrate our virtuous endeavors and to make the common and middle class of people their beasts of burden." Rising prices, a natural result of depressed trade, were cited as evidence of conspiracies at work. "Several persons," the Committee of Inspection announced, "have formed a cruel design to add to the distresses of their suffering fellow-citizens and country by collecting great quantities and exacting exorbitant prices" for staples like rum, sugar, and salt.

Since he was already a member of the Assembly, Robert Morris was not a principal in election for new representatives. Still, he had to count himself among the "great and over-grown rich men" targeted by the Independents, especially when, days before the election, Thomas Willing was named a candidate on the moderate ticket. By the eve of the voting, Morris and most of the Philadelphia electorate recognized how much was at stake. A vote for the moderates would endorse the status quo embodied in "their ancient happy Constitution"; a vote for the Independents would hasten the break with England and deal a blow to those at home who had "grown rich from nothing at all and engross every thing" to themselves.

The balloting on May 1 was tense and closely watched; when the sheriff moved to close the polls at six that evening, the Independents mounted a vigorous protest, and the voting continued until after midnight. The tallies were close but the result came as a shock; Pennsylvania voters had repudiated the radical agenda and elected the moderates in a near sweep. In the city, moderates took three of the four open seats; Willing was the only one to fall short, and even the sole radical elected, George Clymer, was a prosperous merchant. In the frontier counties the margins were more decisive, meaning that for all the strife in the streets and in the press, the Assembly would remain a bulwark of social order and a barrier to the independence movement. For the Philadelphia militants and their allies in Congress, the message was clear: any real change would have to come from outside Pennsylvania's established government.

During the week after the election, the war of words became a tangible, audible reality. On May 7, the British warships stationed off the coast began moving up the river, refilling water casks and, as one contemporary supposed, "making themselves acquainted with the channel for no good purpose." The next day, under a balmy spring sky, the galleys of Pennsylvania's provincial navy rowed out to confront the forty-four-gun frigate *Roebuck*, the twenty-gun *Liverpool*, and several support ships, and the sound of cannon fire rumbled across the Delaware.

Thoroughly outgunned, the galley captains retreated to the shallows and lobbed shot from more than a mile distant. Still, they fought with persistence, and nightfall found the *Roebuck* stranded on a sandbar well below the city. In the meantime, with the attention of the British commanders occupied by the row-galleys, the armed Continental schooner *Wasp* slipped in to score a clean capture, taking one of the *Roebuck*'s tenders, a transport brig called the *Betsey*.

The next morning, the *Roebuck* floated free and sailed back with her squadron to Philadelphia, where more than twenty vessels sallied out to meet them. The fight lasted all day, drawing thousands of spectators to the riverbank, where they cheered their plucky little fleet and sipped refreshments in the hazy afternoon. In town, all was confusion. Drummers beat the militias to arms and families began loading possessions on wagons to retreat to safer ground. From the State House, Robert Morris and the Committee of Safety did what they could to direct the fighting. They met before dawn and sat into the evening, issuing orders to the captains, assigning men from the Continental frigates to the row-galleys, and sending out stores of powder, shot, and beer. As the chairman of the Committee of Safety and member of the Marine Committee of Congress, Morris served as the fulcrum, coordinator of the Continental and provincial forces.

The cannonades ended at sundown with the British cruisers in retreat. Morris and his colleagues must have felt some sense of accomplishment, as the provincial defense force had stood its first test under fire. And it afforded Morris another opportunity to exercise his keen appreciation for raw talent—days after the fighting, on his authority as a member of the Marine Committee, he elevated Joshua Barney, first mate of the *Wasp*, to the rank of lieutenant in the Continental Navy. Barney was then just seventeen years old, but he was to prove, in the estimation of one naval historian, "an exceptional leader . . . perhaps the country's finest fighting sailor."

It was a small victory, the first tangible contact with a war that until then had hovered on the Pennsylvania horizon like a mirage. But coming as it did just days after a critical election, at a time of elemental shifts in attitude and allegiance, the skirmish on the river took on outsized implications. It soon became apparent that the close approach of British ships, and the sight and sound of their big guns, served to undermine the moderates' tenuous grip on the reins of power in Pennsylvania.

Within Congress, John Adams exploited the shock of the river battle to press his campaign for independence. For more than a year, Adams had determined that the key to achieving separation from England lay in breaking up the existing colonial governments. "To contrive some method for the colonies to glide insensibly, from under the old government, into peaceable and contented submission to new ones," Adams confided in his diary, was "the most difficult and dangerous part of the business." And of all the colonies that stood in his way, Pennsylvania, with the largest economy and the largest city in America, was crucial.

On May 10, with gunsmoke from the river battle still hanging in air, Adams moved a resolution calling upon American patriots to establish new governments "where no government sufficient to the exigencies of their affairs have been hitherto established." The language was a little obtuse, but a preamble added days later made it clear. "Any government under the crown of Great Britain . . . should be totally suppressed." There was little question within the State House that the first such government would be that of Pennsylvania.

The sharp language of the preamble brought a long-overdue showdown between the radical and the moderate factions in Congress. Argument ran for two full days, with the moderates on the defensive. James Duane of New York, whose provincial legislature had refused even to endorse the Continental Association, rose to point out that Congress lacked the authority to meddle in the internal affairs of the member colonies. "You have no right to pass the resolution," Duane declared, "any more than Parliament has." But that was the marvel of the times: when the people raised arms against the king, then no formal authority remained, nor any formal limits on authority. The only arbiter was "the people," however that voice might manifest itself. Here, Adams was calling on the people to overthrow the provincial governments.

Duane was concerned with more than the limits of congressional powers. He was still hoping to avoid a final break with England. Buttonholing Adams during a recess in the floor debate, Duane called the preamble "a machine for the fabrication of independence." Adams, no longer coy about his ultimate objective, smiled back. "It is independence itself," he said, and promised that a formal resolution for independence would soon follow. To Duane, it was all still premature. He reminded his colleagues that the Parliament had dispatched a peace commission, and they could be en route that very day. "Why all this haste," Duane asked. "Why this urging? Why this driving?"

The question was especially pertinent to Pennsylvania, whose Assembly was the immediate target of Adams's thrust. John Dickinson was absent, so the argument fell to James Wilson, a brilliant young lawyer who had opened his practices in Dickinson's law office. Wilson saluted the premise that "all power originates from the people," but insisted that the sitting Assembly remained a legitimate popular institution. "In this province, if that preamble passes, there will be an immediate dissolution of every kind of authority; the people will instantly be in a state of nature." But that was just what Adams was aiming for. Only when existing institutions were swept away could the popular movement for independence find full expression in Congress.

On May 15, debate over the preamble came down to a vote, and after all the long months of compromise and delay, the radicals of the Eastern faction finally prevailed. Still, the victory was close and contentious; the call to erect new governments passed by six states to four, with Georgia absent and two states abstaining. The Maryland delegates were so upset with the result that they walked out of the session, announcing they could proceed no further until they received instructions from their constituents at home.

For Adams, however, the vote was cause for celebration. "This day the Congress has passed the most important resolution that was ever taken in America," he wrote, one that comprised "a complete separation" from Britain, "a total independence, not only of Parliament but of her crown." Later, Adams termed the vote on new governments "an Epocha, a decisive event."

That afternoon, the directive to replace any governments resting on royal authority was made public for the first time, announced outside the London Coffee House. Only one man cheered; the rest of the crowd appeared stunned. "We stared at each other," recorded James Allen, a moderate recently elected to the Assembly. "My feelings of indignation were strong, but it was necessary to be mute. This step of Congress, just at the time commissioners are expected to arrive, was purposely contrived to prevent overtures of peace." Allen vowed then to oppose the radicals within the Assembly, "for if they prevail there, all may bid adieu to our old happy Constitution & peace."

Reverberation from the river battle took a bit longer to work its way through the local political scene, but with similar effects. In the days after the action, gossip on the waterfront and in the taverns accused the captains of the row-galleys of cowardice in failing to capture the stranded *Roebuck*. Stung by the criticism, the captains lashed out against their civilian overseers. The *Roebuck* had escaped, the captains said, because Morris and his colleagues had failed to supply enough gunpowder to maintain the offensive against the frigates. Soon the city's militia leaders, who had long been at odds with committee policies, embraced the captains' cause. The allegations were layered with ugly insinuations. "Several of the Committee of Safety are suspected Tories," one of the critics wrote in the *Pennsylvania Gazette*, "and are highly improper to be at the head of military secrets and affairs."

The dispute dragged on for more than a month. A committee of the Assembly was appointed to investigate the affair, but their finding in favor of the Committee of Safety only served to undermine the stature of the Assembly itself. In June, the row-galley captains announced they would no longer answer the orders of the committee or the commodore it appointed. Morris and the Committee of Safety answered with an "Address to the Public" that sounded much like a resignation. The committee members, said the address, "are not so blinded by Self Love, or so lost in their own importance, as not to perceive lately that both Confidence and Authority are considerably shaken and impaired; not resting on a foundation altogether popular, their existence has been beheld with Jealousy, & by an opposition formed on mistaken or unworthy principles, their Conduct in almost every branch of the public service has been traduced and vilified."

This was not simply an idle defense of the members' honor. At stake, said the committee, was the principle of military command, which was being eroded by the idea of elected officers and voluntary service. "Military Authority is not of a nature to be participated, and when attempted, the greatest mischiefs commonly flow from it," the committee warned. "Should this unfortunately prove so in our case, the Committee are not responsible." This was a joint statement, but it clearly summarized Morris's thinking on democratic practice in wartime. Considering that it arose from the first flare-up in what might prove to be a long contest, the dispute did not bode well for the defense of the city.

For all the political and tactical fallout it generated, the river battle had still another result, one of enormous interest to Robert Morris. With the British gunships sidelined to repair damage from the fighting, Morris pushed out a fleet of merchant ships, some of them carrying freight destined for France. At the same time, several inbound ships, held up at the capes of the Delaware by British patrols, made their dash into port. Morris reported these developments in early June in an optimistic letter to Deane. "We have some trade revived and consequently a better prospect of making remittances to you than at the time you sailed." Remittances were the key—agents and munitions deals were critical, of course, but without return shipments of tobacco, flour, or some other valuable cargo, trade with the powers of Europe would soon run dry.

And if government cargoes could get through, there was no reason why commercial cargoes couldn't also make it. Writing in an expansive mood, Morris now outlined to Deane, apparently for the first time, a scheme of private trade that he believed might profit both men. "The Scarcity of Goods all over this Continent affords a fine opportunity to private adventurers," he wrote. Here Morris was exercising his merchant's instinct for opportunity. With trade at a standstill, even the most basic articles would bring windfall prices to anyone nimble enough to supply them. Nothing fancy, just "Woolens & Linens, Pins, needles etc. etc. suited for the consumption of this country" would suffice handsomely. Morris encouraged Deane to seek out European partners "of good reputation & Capital" to engage by halves or thirds, splitting the ventures between Morris and himself, and to ship in French vessels via the Caribbean. "You may depend the goods if once introduced here will sell for immense profits and at the same time be most useful to America." A win-win proposition.

Morris was less sanguine, but just as clear-eyed, in a companion letter he wrote to Deane assaying the political situation in the colonies. He decried the "great division amongst ourselves" over the question of independence, but suggested that the hard line taken by king and Parliament "has put an effectual stop to those divisions . . . As His Majesty has totally destroyed all hopes of reconciliation." Surprisingly, in light of his strong beliefs on the question, Morris expressed no frustration on the point, no animus for his political opponents. This may derive from his self-identity as a merchant and not a politician, but whatever the cause, Morris would demonstrate time and again a certain distance, a sense of equanimity, in the heat of political contest.

Morris then offered Deane a prescient forecast of events then unfolding. "Every body see it in the same light and it will bring us all to one way of thinking, so that you may soon expect to hear of new governments in every colony and in conclusion a declaration of Independency by Congress. I see this step is inevitable and you may depend it will soon take place." As much as some moderates blamed the radicals for the drift to war, Morris placed the blame squarely on the enemy. "Great Britain may thank herself for this event, for whatever might have been the original designs of some men in promoting the present contest I am sure that America in general never set out with any view or desire of establishing an Independent Empire. They have been drove to it step by step. . . . The Dogs of War are now loosed upon us. We are not dismayed but expect to give a good account."

Over the next several weeks the dramatic events Morris anticipated transpired, with the slow-motion slide from respectful dissent to outright rebellion gathering an inexorable momentum. On May 20, spurred by the call from Congress for new governments, the Philadelphia radicals gathered more than four thousand impatient patriots in the State House yard. Standing for two hours under a driving rain, the crowd roared its approval as a series of speakers denounced the moderate government. "The rage of the people burst out in protest against their present Assembly, who had instructed the delegates not to vote for independence," recorded one out-of-town visitor who happened to be in attendance.

All pretense to amicable debate was abandoned. Speakers who defended the Assembly were insulted or threatened. "The people behaved in such a tyrannical manner that the least opposition was dangerous," the same visitor reported. Consequently, the resolutions of the rain-soaked rally were unanimous: the Assembly instructions to its delegates in Congress were "dangerous," the Assembly itself lacked legitimate authority, and the people of the colony should assemble in a Constitutional Convention to found a new popular government.

The new Assembly, the body elected the week before the river battle, held its first session on May 20, the same day as the rally on the State House yard. Once again, Pennsylvania had two popular bodies meeting simultaneously, this time a stone's throw apart. But the Assembly now found itself hamstrung from within; house rules required a quorum of two thirds of the members, and the radicals, though a minority, had enough strength to shut down the proceedings simply by walking out.

For the next three weeks, Morris and John Dickinson sought to maneuver through increasingly narrow options. On most days, the Assembly met only to adjourn for lack of a quorum. Still the pressure mounted; on June 7, Richard Henry Lee of Virginia introduced in Congress a resolution asserting that "these United Colonies are, and of right ought to be, free and independent States." Lee spoke with erudition and melodious voice—"the Cicero of America," some called him—and his moral conviction left the opposition cowed.

The Pennsylvania moderates scrambled to keep pace. On June 5, the Assembly assigned Dickinson, Morris, and five others to draw up new instructions for the delegates. In Congress, Dickinson, Morris, and James Wilson pleaded for time. They voted against Lee's resolution, arguing that public support for independence was "fast ripening," but "if a declaration should now be agreed to, these delegates must retire and possibly their colonies might secede from the union." This was an unlikely gambit, but it won a delay of three weeks for a final vote. Back at the Assembly, jammed into their temporary quarters on the second floor of the State House, Dickinson and Morris reported on June 15 that "the situation in public affairs is so greatly altered, that we now think ourselves justifiable in removing the restrictions" against independence. In the meantime, the moderates gathered six thousand signatures denouncing the popular convention and endorsing the authority of the Assembly.

It all came too late. The tactics of debate, petition, and ballot were inadequate to a time of surging popular passions. The vote endorsing new instructions for the delegates was the last one taken by the "antient" Pennsylvania Assembly; the body never again mustered a quorum under its original charter. On June 18, a conference of ninety-seven delegates from across Pennsylvania met at Carpenters' Hall to draw up rules for a convention "for the express purpose of forming a new government in this province, on the authority of the People only." The revolution at home had toppled the standing government.

On July 1, a wet and gloomy day, Congress resumed its debate on independence. With the Assembly in suspension, Morris and the Pennsylvania delegates were on their own. After nine hours of heated argument, the vote was put, and to their dismay, the radicals found the body still divided. Maryland had finally come around, but Delaware's two delegates were split. New York abstained, and South Carolina and Pennsylvania voted against independence.

This was a genuine setback, as even the most ardent advocates for breaking ties with England believed that all the colonies must concur for the rebellion to succeed. Still, they had reason for optimism: after the vote was taken, Edward Rutledge of South Carolina averred that, despite its stance against independence, his delegation would join the others if the decision was unanimous. Delaware would come around as well with the arrival of a third delegate, Caesar Rodney, who was then hurrying to Philadelphia. That left Pennsylvania, which had divided narrowly against. John Dickinson, the principled moderate, had voted no, along with Morris, his partner Thomas Willing, and a pacifist Quaker, Charles Humphreys. But James Wilson had deserted his mentor Dickinson to vote in favor, along with John Morton, the speaker of the defunct Assembly, and Benjamin Franklin. The close vote gave the radicals some cause for hope.

Caesar Rodney arrived the next day after riding eighty miles through thunder and rain, and Congress resumed the debate. With Delaware now in line, all eyes turned to Pennsylvania. Morris and Dickinson held out to the last, but finally decided they should not, on their own, frustrate any longer the majority in Congress. With the fateful question hanging in the balance, the pair quietly stepped out of the Assembly room. In their absence, Pennsylvania voted in favor of independence by a margin of three to two.

Some accounts hold that it was the venerable Franklin who met Morris and Dickinson in conference and persuaded them to stand aside. But whatever impelled them, the two moderates had surrendered their ardent convictions in deference to the popular will. So it was that "the greatest question was decided, that was ever debated in America." The British colonies of North America were now independent states.

There is little source material on the question, but it is worth considering why Morris held out to the end against a final break with England. He already believed independence was "inevitable"; certainly it was when he decided, with Dickinson, to retreat from the State House at the critical moment on July 2. And it was apparent to all that, when the question was called, failure to vote for independence would be roundly unpopular. Even the Pennsylvania Assembly, an institution that had endured for nearly a century, had fallen sacrifice to the public enthusiasm for independence.

What was Morris's motive? Loyalty may have been a factor, to Dickinson, and to the moderate faction that had argued so long for a negotiated settlement. The letters that survive reveal no ties of endearment between Morris and Dickinson, but Dickinson had always maintained a posture of conscientious sincerity, first as a critic of Britain, and then as a political moderate. He may well have earned Morris's respect, even his fealty.

Morris also may have simply voted his conscience. His only statement on the question came in a letter to Joseph Reed, then serving on Washington's command staff. "I have uniformly voted against and opposed the Declaration of Independence," Morris wrote, "because in my poor opinion it was an improper time and will neither promote the interest nor redound to the honor of America, for it has caused division where we wanted Union." This was the standard moderate position, but in light of the dissension in Pennsylvania, also a reasonable one.

Either way, whether rooted in loyalty or in conviction or both, Morris held his ground to the last. It's hard not to conclude that, while he was a pragmatist and a man of commerce, when it came to questions of public policy, Morris was also a man of principle.

— Chapter 4 —

WAR AND POLITICS

The Declaration of Independence was presented to the public for the first time on July 8, 1776, a sunny Monday afternoon. "A great concourse of people" assembled in the State House yard to hear John Nixon, the sheriff of Philadelphia, read the text line by line. The throng answered with lusty huzzahs, and then broke into smaller groups for the satisfying work of tearing the king's arms down from above the door of the State House, and at the courthouse nearby. It was at that moment, for all the weighty deliberation that graceful building would host before and after, that the State House earned the appellation Independence Hall, though the term would not come into use for another fifty years.

That evening, under clear skies and bright stars, crowds gathered to torch the royal insignia in bonfires and toast the birth of a new republic. But despite the communal cheer in Philadelphia and throughout the colonies, the polity in Pennsylvania remained deeply divided, with the old order dismantled and the new one yet to be formed. The moderates were disaffected, outright Tories met regularly, and even the core radicals began to squabble over control of the movement. In the interim, with the Assembly defunct, the Convention called to write a new state constitution also ran the affairs of state, raising militia corps and making official appointments.

The Convention met almost daily for the next three months, shuttling between the State House and the committee room at Philosophical Hall nearby. Benjamin Franklin was elected president and gave his imprimatur to proceedings, but old as he was, infirm with gout and occupied with so many other responsibilities in Congress, he left the drafting of the new constitution to others—upstart radicals Timothy Matlack and James Cannon, principally, as well as Benjamin Rush, none of them much experienced in politics. The Convention was rent by internal divisions until, by the time it issued the new constitution in late September, Rush and other prominent militants were already denouncing it.

One area of early consensus within the Convention, however, was the need for a new delegation to Congress that would reflect the militant ethic prevailing in the province. In balloting July 20, the conference retained Franklin, Wilson, and Morton, and voted to drop those delegates who had opposed independence. They were replaced with Benjamin Rush, George Clymer, and several other radicals, all political unknowns.

The sole exception in this purge was Robert Morris. The decision to keep him in Congress generated no comment or discussion in the press or the letters of the time, but was extraordinary nonetheless. True, Morris had distinguished himself on the Committee of Safety, but he had also alienated commanders in the militia and the provincial navy, and had been a mainstay in the last meetings of the old, discredited Assembly. Moreover, much of the best work he'd done in Congress—his management of the arms trade—remained a secret to all but a tiny core of insiders. That he was retained in the delegation can only be taken as a mark that he had established the reputation to which he had long aspired, for integrity, for sagacity, and for sheer competence. Change was afoot, but in a time of genuine crisis, even the most ardent ideologues recognized Morris as indispensable.

Morris himself expressed what must have been a genuine sense of astonishment at his reappointment, along with some degree of dismay. "I did expect my conduct in this great question [the vote on independence] would have procured my dismission from the great Council, but find myself disappointed, for the Convention has thought proper to return me in the new delegation," he confided to Joseph Reed. "Although my interest and inclination prompt me to decline the service, yet I cannot depart from one point which first induced me to enter the public line: I mean an opinion that it is the duty of every individual to act his part in whatever station his country may call him to in times of difficulty, danger and distress. While I think this a duty, I must submit, although the councils of America have taken a different course from my judgment and wishes."

True to his word, Morris returned to Congress. And when the Declaration of Independence was finally drawn up for signature, on August 2, Morris set aside his qualms and appended his signature. There is no question that, of all the signers, Morris was the most reluctant. Yet the ensuing years would show that, having done so, none of his colleagues did more to bring it into fruition.

. . .

Even as he was wrestling with the dilemma of independence, Morris was continuing to build the trading network that would supply the arms of the Revolution. The West Indies were a crucial nexus, both a neutral market where American cargoes might be traded for arms and supplies, and a base for transshipping munitions from Europe. Stephen Ceronio was in place early in the contest, but among the hundreds of islands in the Caribbean there were scores of ports and enough business to keep several agents busy.

In several instances Morris relied on the existing Willing & Morris agents to handle the government's business—John Dupuy at Môle, St. Nicholas, a French port on Hispaniola, and Cornelius Stephenson and Henricus Godet on the Dutch island of St. Eustatius. Factors for other Secret Committee merchants were folded in, including Samuel Curson at Eustatius and Isaac Gouverneur at Curaçao. Each of these agents received shipments from America on both private and public account, and made purchases for the government, often out of their own funds. But the key figure in the Caribbean, the most active trader and the one in closest communication with Robert Morris, was William Bingham.

Just twenty-four years of age, Bingham was the son of a prominent Philadelphia merchant, had a master's degree from the College of Philadelphia, and already owned several ships of his own. He spent the first part of 1776 employed as a secretary to the Committee of Secret Correspondence, and in June, Morris and Franklin sent him to St. Pierre on Martinique, a French island at the eastern edge of the Caribbean. As in the case of Silas Deane, this was a joint appointment of both secret committees; like Deane, Bingham was to pose as a private merchant while pursuing arms deals and establishing a diplomatic connection with the French authorities. Morris described Bingham to Deane as "a young gent of good education, family & fortune; his correspondence has yet a good deal of the fanciful young man in it, but experience will cure him of this."

Bingham's first venture demonstrates the multiple assignments common to the Continental agents. He was to obtain ten thousand muskets for the Secret Committee. He was to negotiate preferential treatment for American privateers by the authorities on the French islands. He was to receive and send on to America a shipment of gunpowder commissioned by Willing & Morris under contract to the colony of Virginia. And he was to ship linens and other goods to Morris on private account, with Bingham taking a half-share. Above all, Morris admonished, he was to "keep doing something constantly." Risks were great, but so was demand; prices were so high that "one arrival will pay for 2 or 3 or 4 losses."

With these orders in hand, Bingham departed Philadelphia aboard the Continental sloop of war *Reprisal*, armed with eighteen six-pound guns and helmed by the enterprising Captain Lambert Wickes. True to the nature of the sea lanes at the time, Wickes and the *Reprisal* took three enemy vessels as prizes, and upon her arrival at St. Pierre, had to fight off a British warship before making harbor. There Bingham learned that two ships sent with cargoes intended to fund his operations had both been captured. Still, Bingham received a warm reception from the Count D'Argout, the French *intendant* on the island, and he was soon sending a steady stream of ships to the American coast.

Another key post was at New Orleans. As the gateway to the Mississippi, New Orleans was the source of munitions and supplies for western outposts ranging from Natchez all the way up to Pittsburgh. It was a vast region yet to be settled under European dominion, but where emissaries from Britain, France, and Spain all maintained loose alliances with the native Indian tribes. One great fear of the American rebels was that the British would incite the western Indians to rise against the former colonies in a reprise of the French and Indian War; the answer was to fortify western outposts with arms shipped up the Mississippi. New Orleans would also serve as a transfer point for clandestine arms arriving from Spain.

Fortunately for Congress, Morris already had a contact in place in New Orleans, an Irish mariner and trader named Oliver Pollock. Morris had sailed the Caribbean with Pollock during his apprenticeship under Charles Willing; Pollock later settled in New Orleans, became a confidant of the Spanish governor, and among various enterprises sold flour shipped to him by Willing & Morris.

Pollock's first wartime service to Congress was to intercede with the local authorities when a visiting British sloop of war seized the *Lady Catherine*, a ship sent by Morris on a munitions venture in 1776. Pollock managed to obtain her release and returned her to Philadelphia in November with a letter offering to assume official duties for the Secret Committee. Morris folded Pollock into his network in June.

In France, the focal point for all of Morris's international operations, Silas Deane's early progress was even more promising. Deane reached Paris in July and was immediately contacted by Pierre Penet. Pursuant to his contract with Congress, Penet had assembled a substantial shipment of arms, but his credit had been stretched to the limit and he had yet to see any remittances. Deane avoided making promises, but assured him that Congress would honor its commitments. That was enough for Penet, and he agreed to ship the matériel with no further delay.

Days later, Deane procured an audience with the French foreign minister Comte de Vergennes, a career diplomat renowned for a serene demeanor, a subtle mind, and a steely will. The meeting was held at Versailles, the opulent palace of the French king, Deane following a courtier through a maze of mirrored halls and gilt doorways until he reached Vergennes's small corner office. Vergennes spoke no English but was attended by his first deputy, Conrad Gerard, who served as interpreter. During a session that ran more than two hours Vergennes proved to be more welcoming than Deane had dared hope: he applauded Deane's pose as a Bermuda merchant, assured him he could rely on his personal protection anywhere in Paris, and, most important, said he had no objection to any kind of exports from France. Of course, relations with Britain would preclude an open arms trade with the rebel colonies, but that was just for appearances. Deane could buy all the arms and powder he wished; if he ran into any problems with local police or customs authorities, Vergennes promised to intervene.

Deane left the meeting stunned at his good fortune, but there was more to come. Vergennes was too discreet to do so in person, but after the meeting, Gerard wrote Deane to suggest that he partner in the arms trade with Caron de Beaumarchais. This was a most unlikely connection. Beaumarchais was a famous figure in Paris, a bon vivant, a hanger-on at the royal court, and a playwright, author of the recent hit *The Barber of Seville*—the one thing he was not was a merchant. But Beaumarchais was an ardent admirer of the American rebels, and he had formed a plan worthy of a dramatist: he would set up a false front, a fictional merchant house that he dubbed Roderigue Hortalez & Co., which would ferry arms across the Atlantic. Gerard assured Deane that Beaumarchais would have no trouble fulfilling any contracts Deane might have in mind.

Deane took Gerard at his word and met with Beaumarchais soon thereafter. The pair took an immediate liking to each other—Deane was charmed by Beaumarchais's flamboyant self-confidence, and Beaumarchais with Deane's idealistic enthusiasm. The two forged a close partnership, and within weeks were traveling together to armories and powder mills across France, and arranging for ships and insurance. All purchases were made on Beaumarchais's seemingly inexhaustible credit.

If it all seemed too easy, that was because Deane did not know the remarkable events that preceded his arrival. As early as September 1775, Beaumarchais had been urging King Louis XVI and his ministers to find some way to aid the American rebels. This was an easy point to carry; Vergennes, even more than his sovereign, had been aching to avenge France's disgrace in the Seven Years War. France's armed forces were decrepit; she was in no position to challenge England overtly. But an uprising in North America would cleave Britain's empire, leaving her wounded and vulnerable.

Beaumarchais proposed the Hortalez scheme in February. By May, Vergennes and Beaumarchais together had persuaded the king to secretly contribute one million livres—about two hundred thousand pounds sterling—to the American cause, and Vergennes made quiet overtures to Spain for an equal contribution. Spain, also hostile to Britain, agreed to pitch in, and in June, Beaumarchais received his first allotment of cash. More than that, the king in April ordered a complete retrofit of the French sea and land forces. This would prepare France to wage war against Britain, and rendered the existing arsenals surplus. These weapons—tens of thousands of muskets, and hundreds of cannon—would provide Beaumarchais an immediate source of supply.

All this was in place before Silas Deane reached Paris. In the months that followed, Deane pursued his mission diligently, seeking financing, making purchases on the Indian contract, arranging shipments for Hortalez, and, when time allowed, pursuing the private deals suggested by Robert Morris. But his primary goal of locating arms to send to America was already assured.

Deane was the lead man for American operations in Europe, but he was not alone. Arthur Lee, brother of Richard Henry Lee, was in London studying law at the time, and in December was requested by Congress to provide intelligence on European politics. His assignment was something of a sop to the Eastern faction in Congress, which had been largely passed over in the Secret Committee and foreign appointments. His brother was certainly a partisan, in the factional disputes dividing the American patriots, but Arthur Lee took things to extremes. As soon as he learned of his appointment, he wrote home to challenge the membership of the Committee of Secret Correspondence. Jay and Franklin, in particular, were "men whom I cannot trust. If I am to commit myself to an unreserved correspondence, they must be left out, and the Ls [Lees] or As [Adamses] put in their places." The committee ignored this show of pique, but the contentious spirit of the Lee brothers would roil politics in America for years.

Arthur Lee had discussions with Beaumarchais in London in May, but was supplanted when Deane arrived in Paris, a snub that did nothing to improve his sour humor. Another Lee brother, William, moved to London with Arthur in 1768, made a living as a merchant, and was so well established by 1773 that he was elected one of two sheriffs of London. Two years later, indicating just how divided the British were over policy toward the colonies, Lee was elected a city alderman. Together, the Lee brothers served as a sort of adjunct embassy for the Eastern faction of Congress, monitoring and often criticizing the activities of the other American agents.

Morris also placed his own personal representatives in this crucial arena. One was John Ross, a successful, fiercely independent and sometimes caustic Scottish merchant who had moved to Philadelphia in 1768. Ross was a partner with Morris in one of the larger Continental contracts and sailed to Spain in May to look after their joint concerns. He wound up in Hamburg, purchasing gunpowder and dodging the German authorities, who took their official policy of neutrality more literally than did France and Spain.

Morris's other man on the spot was his half-brother Thomas. Robert had sent him to Europe when the export trade was stilled by the embargo in 1775; now he directed him to catch up with Deane in Paris, and Thomas was waiting there when Deane arrived. Writing to Deane in August, Robert described Thomas as a "Master of the [French] language, tractable, capable, & quick of apprehension." But Deane would have to keep an eye on Thomas, Robert confided. "He has been a wild youth heretofore but if he is now sensible of former follies he may be the more valuable man for it."

Morris realized this was a bit of a gamble, but he was optimistic by nature, and had seen some indication of Thomas's reform. Several letters from Thomas, and from correspondents in Spain and Marseilles, "induced me to believe he had discarded all his follies," Morris wrote later, "& I determined to win him to the pursuit of his own good, by placing an intire confidence in him."

Robert's confidence may also have been colored by his desire to have a partner looking after his interests. In any case, he expressed high hopes for his lone sibling, and for the prospects of a joint enterprise with Deane. "I wish him to become a good historian, to understand the politics of most countries in Europe as they regard one another as well as the particular police of each kingdom or state; in short it is my advice that instead of passing his time in pleasurable pursuits he should make use of his present opportunity and advantage & lay the foundation of a Character that may become respectable and conspicuous in the world." Morris closed by invoking once again his mantra of combining self- and public interest, this time through the offices of his brother. "It seems to me the present opportunity of improving our fortunes ought not to be lost especially as the very means of doing it will contribute to the service of our country at the same time."

By the summer of 1776, Morris's network of international agents and factors exceeded in scale any commercial operation ever staged from North America. This was a direct consequence of the war, of course: securing supplies for the Continental Army and the Continental Navy was a truly national project requiring, for the first time, the concerted effort of all thirteen colonies.

Similarly, Morris and his agents were transcending, for the first time, the mercantile restrictions imposed by the British Board of Trade. The Morris network sought business in all the countries of Europe and in all their dominions in the Caribbean. And they drew on an unprecedented pool of capital—the funds advanced by Congress combined with the resources of the European traders who, like Beaumarchais, assembled shipments on their own credit against future remittances from America.

While this network was, strictly speaking, a creature of the Secret Committee, it all revolved around Morris. He wrote the orders, he distributed the funds, and in many cases his own firm served as cover to conceal the operations of the government. Often the agents cut private deals with Morris as well, shipping separately or in the same conveyances. Some of the ships were consigned privately, some cargoes went on naval vessels, some private ships sailed in convoy under navy protection.

For the next two years Morris did what he could to coordinate these far-flung operations, but most of the time he was working in the dark. Deane strove to keep Morris informed, writing long letters, often in elaborate secret code or in invisible ink, but communications were slow and frequently failed to get through. The British had an extensive network of spies that routinely pilfered the mails; Deane's closest confidant in Paris, an American expatriate named Edward Bancroft, turned out to be a double agent in pay of the British. And messages were often lost on the high seas. Shipboard couriers kept dispatches in a bag weighted with shot; upon the approach of a hostile sail, the papers were thrown overboard. The long stretches of silence left both Deane and Morris exasperated.

In the meantime, closer to home, Morris was consumed with the business of financing the clandestine arms trade by getting remittances from America to Europe. The optimism he felt in June when he got the trading fleet out from Philadelphia had been shaken by a series of reversals. Several ships had been captured at sea, and several others, vessels loaded with flour at New York to fund the Indian contract, never left port, their cargoes commandeered to feed Washington's troops. "I am much concerned that we have been so unfortunate in our remittances to you," Morris wrote to Deane in August. "You will think yourself unlucky in these untoward Circumstances and you have really been so, but this must not dispirit us, for you may depend on it, I will persevere in making you the necessary remittance with all possible expedition."

The project of getting cargoes to Europe—and receiving those that came in—quickly grew into a domestic network just as elaborate as the foreign operation, with Continental agents posted in each of the thirteen colonies. Many of these agents were officially appointed by the Marine Committee to supervise construction of the new frigates and dispose at auction prizes captured by the navy or by privateers; most took on Secret Committee duties as a sideline, and also engaged in private business with Morris.

The tricky nature of these dual, public-private relationships, and the potential for conflicts of interest, is illustrated by a letter Morris wrote to John Bradford, the Continental agent at Boston. Morris did not know Bradford personally; he was appointed on the recommendation of John Hancock. In this letter, Morris was showing Bradford the ropes. He first commended Bradford for securing a public cargo of remittances to send to Europe; Bradford's efforts "gave me pleasure because it convinced me you had the Public Interest at heart." Morris then went on to propose a private scheme, asking Bradford to keep an eye out to buy any goods selling for steep discounts at public auctions, then holding them for resale during the lean winter months. These might be purchased on private or public account; the private goods charged to Morris "& my friends," with Bradford participating as a one-half or one-third partner, depending on his contribution to the purchase.

Just whose account the purchases went to might be sorted out later; "I will procure you either Public or private orders for them," Morris wrote, "and in the mean time you may avail yourself of the means pointed out by the Secret Committee to make any of those payments until Funds are provided." Bradford would receive a standard 2.5 percent commission for his services, plus his share of the profits on the private ventures.

To Morris, any questions of propriety would be answered so long as everyone involved came out ahead. "I have much in my power or under my influence both Public and private," Morris told Bradford. "My desire is to serve justly and faithfully every interest I am connected with."

• • •

Each region under Morris's jurisdiction in America presented distinct problems, some of them political and some logistical; all eventually found their way to Morris, who tackled them with his customary energy, exhorting his agents with calls to duty and prospects for profit.

The strategic situation was dictated in large part by the disposition of the enemy. The British had evacuated Boston in March; by June they had shifted to New York, and their fleet effectively sealed off the middle states. The seas off New England were largely open, but the region produced little of value for European markets. The South had useful exports but lacked boats and sailors; one of Morris's continuing projects with Bradford was obtaining ships from New England—on Continental account and his own— sending them to the Carolinas for cargoes, and thence to Morris's agents in the West Indies. Many, however, were captured en route.

The most important article in the export trade, the one with the strongest market in the Caribbean as well as in France, was tobacco. Here Morris worked through Benjamin Harrison and Carter Braxton, both members of Congress from Virginia, to buy as much leaf as possible. This dragged Morris into a thorny political feud, as Harrison and Braxton were aligned against the Lee brothers in a long-standing provincial rivalry. In addition, because sellers charged more when the buyer was the government, Morris had his agents make all their buys on the Willing & Morris account. This subterfuge served the public interest but engendered more personal animosity toward Morris; Virginia planters feared that Philadelphia capitalists would only take the place formerly occupied by British trading houses, leaving the planters facing the same debt burden as before the war.

By the end of 1776, Morris had largely cornered the market in tobacco, but getting it to Europe proved even more difficult. The green leaf made for a heavy and bulky cargo, requiring large, sluggish vessels to return a profit, and these ships fared poorly against the British cruisers. Through 1776 and into the following year, more than half the tobacco ventures put out by the Secret Committee were taken, and many more were delayed for months waiting for a chance to get to sea.

Morris had more success, though on a more modest scale, trading out of ports in the Carolinas, where the British presence was thin and the Outer Banks provided excellent cover for crafty sailors. The key agents here were Joseph Hewes, a delegate to Congress from North Carolina, and John Dorsius, the Willing & Morris factor at Charleston; as ever, they dealt on public account for the Secret Committee, and on private account with Morris, often shipping dual ventures on the same vessel. These agents sent small, fast boats laden with rice and indigo to the Caribbean, where they helped finance the operations of William Bingham and Stephen Ceronio. Bingham in particular established a profitable private trade to the southern ports, but the volume of cargoes on public account could not keep pace with the need for capital, and the debts incurred by Morris's foreign agents mounted steadily.

Morris handled all these arrangements, foreign and domestic, virtually on his own. In August he confessed to Deane, "I have been so exceedingly harassed with public business of various kinds that it has not been in my power to be so good a correspondent as I always intended." The Secret Committee was happy to let him carry most of the workload, and by September attendance at the Committee of Secret Correspondence had dwindled until just Morris and Franklin were conducting the business. John Jay marked his absence blithely in a friendly letter to Morris: "As long as your whimsical constituents shall permit the gentleman to whom I am writing to remain among those honest and able patriots in Congress in whose hands I think the interest of America very safe, the Congress will possess too great a stock of abilities to perceive the absence of my little mite." For Morris, borne down with responsibilities that only seemed to multiply, this endorsement may have rung a bit hollow.

It was not until September that Morris learned from two correspondents— neither of them Deane—that the French had agreed to send major shipments of arms on credit through the fictitious house of Hortalez. This new development changed the entire outlook of the rebellion. The Congress had made a dangerous gamble when it decided to challenge the forces of Britain; by securing aid from one of the powers of Europe, the Americans now might at least confront force with force.

But at this point the agreement with France was strictly covert, one that would require what Franklin termed "impenetrable secrecy" to preserve their new ally from Britain's wrath. Consequently, on October 1, Morris and Franklin requested that Congress confirm their diplomatic standing. The answer came in a statement signed by John Hancock giving Morris and Franklin exclusive authority "to direct all matters in their department on behalf of the United States." That same day, Morris and Franklin together crafted a singular document recording just how they planned to exercise that authority. Having received the momentous news from France, the two had determined that "It is our indispensable duty to keep it a secret, even from Congress," because "We find, by fatal experience, the Congress consists of too many members to keep secrets." Besides, the pair continued, "It is unnecessary to inform the Congress of this intelligence at present, because Mr. Morris belongs to all the committees that can be properly be employed in receiving and importing the expected supplies."

This was not the end of the matter; the prospect of a French alliance was too important to keep bottled up, and by the middle of October, Congress had adopted a new and more ambitious strategy: they would send two more commissioners to join Deane in Europe and seek a formal treaty with France. Those selected were regarded as two of the wisest heads in Congress—Franklin and Thomas Jefferson—but when Jefferson declined, citing his wife's ill health, he was replaced by Arthur Lee.

At the same time, the Secret Committee authorized a separate addition to the Paris embassy: the appointment of Thomas Morris to act with Deane as commercial agent for the rebel colonies. This appears in part an act of political balancing—Richard Henry Lee's brother was joining the delegation, so Robert's brother would as well. But there was also a tactical imperative at work: by now, Morris recognized that his remittances were not getting through, and he directed his brother to help augment Deane's credit by tapping the Willing & Morris reserves in England. Further, Thomas would be posted at the port of Nantes and would receive all Secret Committee shipments to Europe, with orders to forward the proceeds to Deane in Paris. As before, Morris implored Deane to "be attentive to his conduct and if need there be, to spur him [Thomas] up to a diligent, honest & faithful discharge of his Duty."

Morris confided to Franklin that he would have liked to join the embassy himself, but there was little chance Congress would let him go. Franklin sailed October 26 on the *Reprisal*, recently returned from Martinique. His departure deprived Morris of his closest ally in Congress, but having one more trusted friend in France turned out to be valuable in the end.

The fateful decision to make a total break with England brought a period of calm in the politics of the Congress. Having finally won the ultimate point, the Lee-Adams faction seemed to mellow in its dealings with the moderates; Richard Henry Lee proved especially useful to Morris by monitoring and endorsing the activities of the Secret Committee. And Morris found common ground with John Adams, working with him to draw up a Plan of Treaties that emphasized free trade and discouraged formal alliances that might entangle the emerging nation in third-party conflicts. Shaped by

Morris's globalist outlook, the plan became the template for American foreign policy for generations.

In Pennsylvania, however, the Declaration seemed to have the opposite
effect. Rather than close a period of political turmoil, it marked the beginning of a decade-long contest for control of the former colony. If political
authority truly resided in the people, just what form should it take? How
would a new republic address the old questions of class, rank, and sovereignty, of wealth and equality? More than any other colony, Pennsylvania
became the testing ground for the radical notions of liberty and popular authority that formed the core tenets of Whig ideology.

To some degree, this was a consequence of John Dickinson's long effort
to bind together the various elements of the resistance movement against
Britain in one broad coalition. In every other colony, factions of the home-
grown elite had divided, with the more radical activists assuming leadership in the drive for independence. In Pennsylvania, these factions hung
together under the banner of reconciliation and made the Assembly the
instrument of their power and influence. This worked for a time, but insulated the elite from the popular movement, and when the reckoning came,
the whole edifice of local authority collapsed.

What ensued was a democratic uprising. The old Quaker and Anglican
elites were replaced by more recent immigrants, most of them Scottish
and Irish Presbyterians, who had been largely excluded under the original
charter government. Poorer, more rural, and less educated, these relative
newcomers tended to be jealous of the wealth of the urban elites, and felt
bitterly their long exclusion from power.

These resentments were brought to bear in the Pennsylvania constitutional convention that met in Philadelphia from early July through September of 1777. Delegates were selected by local committees dominated by the
militias, ensuring Presbyterian control. Moreover, representation was apportioned geographically, meaning a preponderance of delegates from the
rural parts of the state, "honest well-meaning country men," according to
one typical assessment, but "intirely unacquainted with such high matters."

The primary object of these outsiders was to ensure the displacement
of the old elites. "We are determined," wrote one of the radicals at the
convention, "not to pay the least regard to the former Constitution of this
Province, but to reject every thing therein that may be proposed, merely
because it was part of the former Constitution. We are resolved to clear
every part of the old rubbish out of the way and begin upon a clean foundation." The very idea that government was an art, and might be perfected in

its design, was rejected out of hand. "You learned fellows who have warped your understanding by poring over musty old books, will perhaps laugh at us, but, know ye, we despise you."

Some of the rhetoric espoused by the radical leadership shared early signs of the social revolutions of a later era—a rudimentary class analysis, the leadership's avowed allegiance to the "common people." This reached its highest expression in a proposed clause which held "That, an enormous Proportion of Property vested in a few individuals is dangerous to the Rights, and destructive of the Common Happiness, of mankind; and therefore every free State hath a Right by its Laws to discourage the possession of such Property." But this egalitarian measure went beyond the more modest aims of the convention, and was rejected in the final document. This was not so much a class movement as a contest for political power.

Instead of pushing a social agenda, the delegates focused on establishing a frame of government that would allow the purest expression of popular democracy, embodied in a unicameral representative legislature. The other familiar elements of government apparatus, the executive and the judiciary, were correspondingly weakened. There would be no governor, but rather a Supreme Executive Council composed of twelve members and which, despite its imposing title, had no veto, little institutional authority, and a built-in rotation of officers explicitly designed to prevent what was termed in the constitution itself "the danger of establishing an inconvenient Aristocracy." Likewise, judges would be appointed by the legislature and limited to seven-year terms, instead of the life terms that formerly insulated them from political influence.

The authority of this new government was to be guaranteed by an oath, administered to officeholders and all prospective voters, swearing allegiance to the constitution. Loyalty oaths were commonplace at the time, but this one represented a divisive innovation in Pennsylvania, effectively denying suffrage to Quakers and other conscientious objectors. The only way to amend the new constitution was via an elected Council of Censors, a novelty from Roman times, which would convene once every seven years.

The convention closed its business on September 26 by scheduling elections for a new Assembly, with voting slated for November 5. There was no plebiscite on the constitution itself, no means of ratification, and the new framework immediately came under attack from all sides. Several of the early radicals, like the physician Benjamin Rush and merchant George Clymer, joined with the Philadelphia moderates to decry the loyalty oaths and the unicameral legislature. Newspaper pundits invoked Montesquieu on the theory of mixed government: "When the Legislative and Executive powers are united in the same person, or in the same body of magistrates, there can be no liberty." Even John Adams, who had done so much to unseat the old Assembly, bridled at the "absurd democratical notions" the constitution embodied.

The radical sponsors of the constitution denounced their critics as Tories and "wealthy men" seeking to preserve long-standing privileges. The moderates answered with a careful and detailed public letter. "We think it our duty to declare to you, that we wish for no alterations to be made in the Constitution, which shall affect the great and fundamental principles of a free government." Their opposition was not to democracy, but to the frame of the new government. "We esteem the sacred power of the people to be above all other power. . . . By our preference of a mixed and tempered legislature to that established by the Convention, we declare that we wish for a government that shall not suffer the poor and the rich alternately to be the prey of each other."

Robert Morris had more than enough on his hands dealing with the logistical concerns of the war effort, but he could not long ignore the political dispute now rending the province. In mid-October he joined several hundred moderates in the State House yard for a two-day counter-convention to coordinate opposition to the new constitution. Morris had to feel a strange sense of déjà vu, returning to the scene of the Stamp Act demonstrations and the first Provincial Convention, this time to challenge not the old order, but the new one. Still in its early stages, the revolution in Pennsylvania had already completed one full turn, Morris making the transit from critic of the established authorities to member of the revolutionary establishment—the Committee of Inspection, the Committee of Safety—and now back to the opposition.

The State House rally marked Philadelphia as the seat of resistance to the state's new frame of government, and Morris as a leader of the dissidents. In the days before the Assembly election, Morris joined John Dickinson on a slate of candidates promising to revise the constitution, and on November 5 both were elected to the new body. The city voters so abhorred the radical frame of government that they refused even to cast ballots for the Executive Council, and those critical seats went unfilled.

At this point Dickinson cut something of a tragic figure, casting about for a role to fill. After his defeat in opposition to independence, he had quit the Congress to command a battalion of the Pennsylvania militia that saw action in July and August. But when he was passed over for higher command, he resigned his commission and stepped back from public life. Now ensconced in the minority faction of the new Assembly, Dickinson joined Morris in adopting the same tactics the Assembly radicals had employed in the spring—they threatened to boycott the proceedings, depriving the new body of a quorum.

Faced with deadlock, the Assembly's radical, "country" leadership agreed to a deal: if the moderates would attend the sessions of the legislature, the radicals would agree to call a convention in January to revise the new constitution. This was approved by a vote of the Assembly in late November, but was rescinded the following day. Thoroughly frustrated, Dickinson once again retreated from the political fray, but Morris lingered on, attempting to coordinate military affairs between an increasingly dysfunctional Assembly and the Congress. This was urgent business, for the war, so long a distant menace, was now drawing close.

George Washington had scored a quick and easy victory in his first confrontation with the enemy forces at Boston. With the British garrisoned inside the city, Washington had placed the cannon captured at Ticonderoga on a high hill overlooking the town. The general was bluffing—he had no powder to fire the guns—but the deception worked, and the British mounted a hasty seaborne evacuation to Halifax.

But when the fighting started in earnest, Washington and the Continental Army suffered a string of ominous reversals. The action commenced in New York in June after the British amassed the largest overseas expedition ever mounted by the empire—land forces of thirty thousand troops supported by thirty warships, many more tenders, and ten thousand seamen. Washington was also at peak strength, with nineteen thousand troops, though he had little artillery and no cavalry. Their superior numbers and training gave the British a distinct advantage. Over the next six weeks the Americans were driven from fortified positions first on Long Island and then on Manhattan, losing thousands of soldiers to capture and retreating just in time to salvage the main body of the army.

These early battles exposed command weaknesses on both sides. The British forces were deployed under direction of two brothers, General William Howe and Admiral Richard Howe. Together they waged a hesitant and faltering campaign, letting weeks slip by at a time when more aggressive action might have destroyed their oft outgunned foe. Some observers credit the sluggish pace to ineptitude, but another factor was the Howe brothers' personal view of the war. Both Howes, in fact, opposed the idea of coercion as the means to rein in the colonists, and both were members of the minority peace faction in Parliament. Consequently, when the brothers were named joint commanders of the British forces in North America, they insisted that they also be empowered to negotiate with the rebels.

These were the "peace commissioners" so longed for by Morris and the other American moderates, but the mixed nature of their mission defeated any chance for a settlement. Soon after Richard Howe arrived in America in June, he asked Washington for a truce and a parley; in September he held talks with John Adams and Franklin. In both cases the American patriots refused to believe the British commanders were in earnest, and the negotiations came to naught. But so long as there remained a prospect of meaningful dialogue, both Howe brothers were leery of bringing the full weight of their forces to bear on the rebels, and their efforts lagged as a consequence.

As for Washington, he had plenty of excuses for his failures in the field—supply problems, green troops—but he also demonstrated a tendency to vacillate, leaving key judgments to councils of war that rendered split and tentative decisions. Nor did Washington have much help—his second-in-command, Charles Lee, a former colonel in the British army and no relation to the Lee brothers of Virginia, proved remarkably incompetent and, more than that, fiercely jealous of his chief. Lee compounded his dishonor when, late in the year, he left his troops to spend the evening at a tavern and there was captured by a mounted British detachment.

If both armies were listless in the field, there was no question which had gained the upper hand. November found Washington slogging across New Jersey, a harsh winter closing in, his army depleted by desertion and harried by German and English troops under Charles Cornwallis. In the wake of the British advance, Richard Howe tested the mettle of the American civilians, promising full pardons to any who came forward to seek protection of the crown. To the chagrin of the New Jersey patriots, thousands did.

By early December Washington had abandoned New Jersey altogether, crossing the Delaware into Pennsylvania and arranging what remained of his army. His troops were exhausted and ragged—"many of 'em entirely naked," in Washington's memorable lament—and they were hungry. The commissariat had been capably run by Joseph Trumbull, son of the Connecticut governor, but as the fighting moved south, his lines of supply dried up. New Jersey had been "swept clean," and in Pennsylvania, farmers were now refusing to accept Continental currency, which had fallen into a steady decline in value. Moreover, purchasing was complicated there by the corrupt administration of Carpenter Wharton, the head of the provincial commissary.

The sudden arrival of Washington in Pennsylvania, with the British close on his heels, sent shock waves through Philadelphia. Word filtered in that Howe was headed for the city; by December 2, "the shops were shut, and all business except preparing to disappoint our enemies [was] laid aside." Bands of militia roamed the streets, accosting suspected Tories, breaking into their homes and banishing hundreds to the countryside. Before long a sense of panic set in, with "people of all ranks" packing household goods onto carts and fleeing the city. General Israel Putnam, a veteran of the fighting at Bunker Hill, placed the city under martial law, ordering that any vendor refusing Continental money would find his goods confiscated. Robert Morris relayed the sense of dismay in a letter to Deane. "Our affairs are amazingly altered for the worse within a few weeks," he reported. "We have been much alarmed for the safety of this city."

Amid the confusion, Washington called for reinforcements, but weeks went by with no response from the militia. Samuel Adams blamed the Quakers, the Tories, and John Dickinson, who Adams said had "poisoned the minds of the people" with his appeals to reconciliation, "the effect of which is a total stagnation of the power of resentment." Morris remarked on the same phenomenon, but he blamed Congress itself, and the "winter cabals" that had brought down the old Assembly in early 1776. "Our [new state] Constitution is disliked, the People divided, unhappy, and consequently weak," Morris told John Jay. If not for the internal strife, Morris believed, Pennsylvania's "strength might have been drawn into proper exertion & her capital would never have been made to tremble."

On December 14, with Howe's troops ranged along the Jersey side of the Delaware from Pennington to Bordentown, waiting only for hard ice to cross into Pennsylvania, Putnam advised the Congress to abandon Philadelphia. Many delegates opposed this as an unseemly display in time of emergency, but more saw wisdom in preserving the national leadership, and the decision was taken to remove to Baltimore, a hundred miles to the south. Over the next several days, the delegates joined the pell-mell exodus from the city.

Robert Morris elected not to go with them. He had too much business engaged, too many ships due into port, to leave them unattended. But he believed the threat real enough that he sent his wife off with their four children and the domestic slave Hero to stay with her stepsister in Bush

Town, a small village just north of Baltimore. He prepared to follow them at a moment's notice, sending his vital papers off for safekeeping, packing his belongings in a wagon and ordering the livestock he kept at The Hills to be slaughtered.

Mary set out on a frosty December morning, her coach crammed with household belongings, the road itself crowded with wagons and travelers. The journey south was filled with anguish and foreboding. Her son Thomas, not yet five years old, was afflicted with a painful boil on his leg; her daughter Hetty was still just a toddler. Like her husband Mary had never embraced the idea of rebellion against Britain; now the war was upon them, and all her worst presentiments were at hand. "Indeed, my spirits were very unable to the task after that greatest conflict flying from home," Mary wrote to Robert soon after her departure. "The sufferings of our poor little Tom distressed us all."

Even as Mary was writing that letter, Robert Morris paused from his official duties to survey the abandoned city. Many of the Quaker families had stayed on, believing they had no quarrel with the British, but otherwise the frozen streets were deserted, save for sick and injured soldiers straggling in from the front. "It looks dismal and melancholy," Morris wrote.

For the next three months, Morris set aside all his personal commercial affairs, his time fully consumed in attending the business formerly transacted by the Congress and its many committees. At the outset he routinely exceeded his authority, directing the operations of the Continental fleet, distributing what stores came in to port, answering incessant pleas for funds, and supervising every other government function. On December 21 his endeavors received official sanction when Morris was appointed with George Clymer and George Walton of Georgia, the only other delegates remaining in Philadelphia, to "execute Continental business." All three were active, but they often lost touch with each other, and most of the critical decisions fell to Morris. At this crucial juncture, he was essentially serving as chief executive of a beleaguered government facing its most severe trial.

Morris thrived under the hectic pace and took pride in what he was able to achieve. "I believe we dispatch about 7/8ths of that damned trash that used to take up 3/4ths of the debates in Congress," he wrote at one point, a rare boast from a man who usually accepted the shortcomings of others without complaint. Still, it was a taxing, desperate interval. "The business of this committee engrosses my whole time & increases daily," Morris wrote to Jay. "I am now the veriest slave you ever saw."

•　•　•

Thomas Paine, traveling with Washington's army in the dispiriting retreat across New Jersey, sought to rally the flagging morale of the soldiers and the citizenry. Writing on a drumhead by the light of a campfire, Paine composed the first in a series of essays titled *The American Crisis*. "These are the times that try men's souls," Paine intoned in one of his more enduring passages. "Lay your shoulders to the wheel," he exhorted. "Let it be told to the future world, that in the depth of winter, when nothing but hope and virtue could survive, that the city and the country, alarmed at one common danger, came forth to meet and repulse it."

Brave words, but hope was dwindling, and the difficulties mounting. Enlistments in the Continental Army were coming due, some on December 1, many more at the turn of the year, and most of Washington's demoralized troops had decided to head for home. Writing to his brother on December 18, the American commander confided, "If every nerve is not strained to recruit the new Army with all possible expedition, I think the game is pretty nearly up."

In Philadelphia, Morris was thinking the same way. "The unfortunate case of American Affairs at this period leaves [no] room for joy in the mind of a true friend to this country," he wrote in a letter to Deane. "Our people knew not the hardships & calamities of war when they so boldly dared Britain to arms," Morris mused. "Every man then was a bold patriot, felt himself equal to the contest and seemed to wish for an opportunity of evincing his prowess, but now when we are fairly engaged, when Death & Ruin stare us in the face and when nothing but the most intrepid courage can rescue us from contempt & disgrace, sorry I am to say it, many of those who were foremost in noise, shrink coward-like from the danger. . . . Dejection of spirits is an epidemical disease, and unless some fortunate event or other gives a turn to the disorder, in time it may prevail."

For all their misgivings, Morris and Washington pressed on, Washington at his camp on the banks of the Delaware, and Morris from the deserted city twenty miles away. In fact, in this moment of crisis, the two men found each other. In certain respects, they could not have been a more unlikely pair. Where Morris was warm and open, Washington was cool and distant; where Morris was of uncertain lineage, Washington was the epitome of landed gentry, literally born to the manor. But what they shared was more essential, more important in the crucible of the Revolution. Both were wealthy and essentially comfortable with colonial society, and neither was inclined to rebellion, but once the contest was under way, both accepted early, central roles. And both were leery of the simple maxims of ideology;

they were fundamentally pragmatic problem solvers, clear thinkers who confronted obstacles with dogged persistence.

In time, these two key figures came to recognize a certain kinship, though it's hard to say exactly when. Morris had first met Washington at the Philadelphia Jockey Club in 1773 and appears to have formed a personal bond with Washington during his early attendance at Congress; Robert and Mary had hosted Martha Washington at The Hills in July. But here in the crisis, the two men became collaborators, Washington calling on Morris for assistance only he could provide. In late December, Morris provided essential service by wresting from the confusion on the docks crucial, just arrived cargoes of blankets and stockings, as well as muskets, pistols, gunpowder, and lead. He secured wagon teams for transport and forwarded the critical provisions to the Delaware camp. These supplies allowed Washington to stage his daring Christmas Eve expedition across the Delaware.

By nightfall on Christmas Day, Washington had achieved his first great victory, a stunning conquest of the Hessian troops at Trenton that revived public faith in the army, and the soldiers' confidence in themselves. But the rebel forces remained in genuine danger, surrounded by the enemy and threatened with dissolution. Over the next few days Washington stayed in close correspondence with Morris, making urgent requests that Morris hastened to answer. Washington sent an express rider December 30 asking Morris to press Carpenter Wharton for provisions from the city—a large body of troops remained on the west bank of the Delaware, unable to move for want of food. Morris promptly intervened, upbraiding Wharton and giving him a draft on Congress for forty thousand dollars; the wagons started moving that afternoon. At the same time, Washington pleaded for funds he needed to pay his spies—"Silver would be most convenient," was the general's gingerly phrase. This was no small request, as Morris had consigned all his own hard money to Congress. But that same night he raised from several sources a motley mound of coin: Spanish milled dollars, English crowns and shillings, a French half-crown.

Another request arrived the next day, this one larger and more urgent. Washington was confronted with "the great and radical evil which pervades our whole system . . . like an axe at the tree of our safety, interest and liberty"—the short-term enlistments of his soldiers. Washington had a simple scheme for this new crisis: he would plead with them to stay on patriotic grounds, but he would also entice them with a bounty of ten dollars. That sum was barely nominal—unskilled laborers were getting two dollars a day at the time—but it was more money than many of the soldiers had seen for weeks. It was also more than the general could lay hands on. "If it be possible, sir, to give us assistance do it," Washington pleaded. "Every man of interest and every lover of his country must strain his credit upon such an occasion."

Once again, Morris responded with alacrity. How he found funds, at a time when every source had been exhausted, has now been reduced to legend. One early biographer poses a conversation between Morris and a rich Quaker in the city; David Hackett Fischer, writing in 2004, quoted "a lady of old family in Philadelphia" to advise that Morris himself dug up a chest of coin buried in that rich Quaker's garden. Whatever the means, Morris found the money, and sent it out to Washington the next day. At dawn on New Year's Day, Morris was in his office, writing a quick note to accompany the funds. "I am up very early this morning to dispatch a supply of fifty thousand dollars to your excellency. You will receive that sum with this letter but it will not be got away so early as I could wish for, none concerned in this movement except myself are up. I shall rouse them immediately."

Morris took the opportunity to close his message on a personal note. "The year 1776 is over. I am heartily glad of it & hope you nor America will never be plagued with such another. Let us accept the success at Trenton as a presage of future fortunate events."

— *Chapter 5* —

MASTER OF THE
SECRET NETWORK

A great stillness settled over the rebel colonies of North America in the cold, early months of 1777, as if the first clashes as of the opposing armies had left both sides stunned.

In northern New York, from a guard post at Fort Ticonderoga overlooking Lake Champlain, a Pennsylvania volunteer wrote Morris to share his melancholy mood. "It's now as cold as I ever felt in my life," the shivering soldier reported. "Three men froze to death last night in their tents." To the east, the British commander Henry Clinton sailed with six thousand men to the deep-water harbor of Newport, Rhode Island, and took up quarters virtually unopposed. Situated at the mouth of Narragansett Bay, his position bottled up the little American navy that Morris had worked so hard to launch a year before. After a season of ineffectual cruising, Commodore Esek Hopkins had put in for repairs at Providence; now he would remain there, effectively neutralized.

To the south, William Howe gave off his pursuit of Washington and crowded his forces into New York, while his brother Richard doubled the number of ships assigned to the blockade, sealing off what was left of American trade. Washington withdrew as well, collecting his troops on the heights at Morristown, New Jersey, and establishing his headquarters in a tavern on the village green. Further south, at Baltimore, Congress operated at a sluggish pace, the delegates removed from the seat of action and chafing at their self-imposed purgatory. Baltimore was a poor replacement for Philadelphia, its streets unpaved and deep in mud, its taverns coarse and inadequate. "The Damndest Hole in the World," Benjamin Harrison groused to Morris, an "infernal sink."

With the Congress and his family out of town, Morris was stuck in a limbo of his own. Philadelphia was quiet, its streets blanketed in snow, the broad Delaware choked with ice. Trade was already off due to the blockade and the weather; the declining state of the Continental currency depressed it even more. Morris stayed busy enough in the daytime, shuttling between committee offices, the countinghouse, and the waterfront, where he harangued teams of seamen and stevedores—"I have scolded the officers like a gutter-whore," he said of one laggard crew.

Whatever doubts Morris harbored about the extent of the powers he exercised were allayed by the mail he received from Baltimore. William Hooper, a delegate from North Carolina, told Morris that, "Congress seems unanimously sensible of the obligations which they owe you, and you may boast of being the only man whom they all agree to *speak* & I really believe *think* well of." John Hancock wrote in the same vein: "Without the least appearance of Flattery I can assure you your whole conduct since our Flight is highly approved, & happy I am that you remained . . . indeed all depends on you."

On Sundays Morris continued making his way out to The Hills, hosting there a circle of friends that included George Clymer and George Walton, the only other delegates to Congress still in town; Franklin's son-in-law Richard Bache, who ran the post office in Franklin's absence; and James Mease, a merchant recently named clothier to the Continental Army. But most evenings he spent largely on his own, reading correspondence from his dispersed connections and scratching out letters by lamplight.

For all the carousing he did in his youth, Morris was by now an established family man, and he missed his wife and brood. "The absence of my family sits grievously hard on me as I never parted with them before," he confided to a friend. From her temporary quarters in Maryland, Mary did what she could to keep in touch. Her letters suggest a certain degree of formality—"Dear Mr. Morris," they began—but that might be expected of a couple where the husband was twice the age of his wife. Still, she had already borne him four children, and there was a bond of genuine affection. In one letter, after the formal salutation, she addressed him as "My dearest husband."

Along with news of their children, Mary shared with Robert her concerns about the war, and growing interest in his affairs. "I wish you would inform me a little more of the Mercantile world," she wrote not long after their separation, "whether any of the many vessels you expected in this fall, are arrived, and what their success." Mary would never assume the stature of a partner in Morris's many enterprises, but their relationship was a close one, and grew stronger as the years went by.

More disturbing to Morris was the family news he received from Europe. Despite the admonitions Robert had made to Silas Deane and to Franklin to keep an eye on the affairs of his brother, Thomas Morris had reverted to the ways of his youth. Soon after being placed in charge of all congressional business in Europe, he'd moved from Paris to London and then all but disappeared, ignoring his business contacts and leaving urgent letters unanswered. Rumors soon began to circulate that Thomas was spending most of his time drinking.

Morris first learned of Thomas's dissipation from James Duff, the factor in Cádiz, who said Thomas had stopped answering his letters and had quickly run through a thousand pound line of credit. Nor had any of the Willing & Morris contacts in London seen or heard from him. Robert feared the worst, and wrote immediately to Deane. "This letter from Mr. Duff alarms me most exceedingly, as it will make me most unhappy if the Public business should have suffered by his Appointment. . . . I give you notice of my alarm the moment I have received it, that either his neglect or abuse of the trust reposed in him, if any there be, may be remedied the soonest that is possible."

Morris wrote the same day regarding Thomas to his friend John Ross, asking him to "examine into his conduct to the very bottom." If the rumors were true, Robert planned to "get him back here and let him go into our army." The news from Cádiz, he wrote, came as "a very heavy disappointment."

Along with the note to Ross, Robert sent a second letter addressed to Thomas directly, which Ross was to deliver if he could confirm Thomas's misconduct. In this second missive, Robert said the rumors "give me the most horrid presages of what I am to expect." The elder sibling chided his half-brother sternly. "Your follies as a boy I always forgave, expecting one day you would despise them and reap the fruits of your abilities, but if you have introduced them into the European World in the character of a man and a merchant, I fear it will all be over & that your future prospects must be gloomy indeed."

Robert held on to the hope that Ross would find no cause to deliver that letter, but he could not suppress the nagging fear that he had pushed Thomas too quickly, or at least that he had gambled rashly in trusting him with such high responsibilities, both for the government and for Willing & Morris. On other occasions Morris's tendency to trust his feel for the hidden capacities of his subordinates turned out brilliantly, but here he had allowed his wishes to guide him. The letter from Duff came as a sobering awakening, and Morris felt his error deeply. He was, he told Thomas, "Unhappy to the last degree in having to write you in this style and can hardly find strength to add that I look on you with pitying eyes for I was once your affectionate friend."

In fact, the commissioners in Paris were already well aware of the problem. Two months before, Deane sent a letter to Morris breaking the news with as much tact as he could muster. "I am entering now on a most delicate affair, which is affecting your brother," Deane wrote. "You may have given him in your [letter] of August 11 a just character; but, my dear friend, I am afraid from good advice from London, that pleasure has got too strong hold of him." Within days of his arrival, Thomas had slipped into a life "so dissolute and expensive that it very essentially injured the reputation of your house, of which he was considered as being a member."

By January 17, after Franklin had joined Lee in Paris, matters had come to a head. On that date, the three commissioners formally requested that Thomas be replaced. "We are sorry to say that irregularities of Mr. Thomas Morris render it absolutely necessary that some other person should be immediately appointed in his place."

The timing of the report from Cádiz could not have been worse. Not only was Robert heavily invested, personally and financially, in Thomas's performance, but he knew that Thomas would soon have still another monitor on the scene. This came on the initiative of Richard Henry Lee, who in Robert's absence was steering the Committee of Secret Correspondence in Baltimore. Lee moved carefully, informing Morris that he planned to place a second commercial agent in France, but not mentioning his name. Morris readily agreed to the measure, even after learning that the new agent would be Lee's brother William, the alderman from London.

There were other parallels between Richard Henry Lee and Robert Morris. Lee had accounts in England, as did Morris, and with Lee's tobacco shipments blocked by the British embargo, he was concerned to find his credit steadily eroding. In addition, besides his two brothers, Richard Henry had two sons living in England. Lee hoped to place the eldest— named, ironically, Thomas—as a secretary to William. "My earnest wish," he advised Arthur Lee in April, "is to put them both in a situation to be of service to their country, and beneficial to themselves." Quietly, steadily, Lee was moving to expand the family presence in Europe, and to wrest control of the trade mission from Morris.

For the time being, Thomas retained his commission, turning up at his post in the port of Nantes in January and resuming his commercial activities. There he worked largely through Pierre Penet and his firm, Pliarnet & Penet, who were happy to exploit his connection with the leading commercial house in America. Thomas's most important contribution was to strike a contract with the Farmers General, an aristocratic combine that controlled most foreign imports to the kingdom, for supply of tobacco. But he was obviously discontent, and made plans in February to leave Europe altogether. This was a curious flight of fancy that conflicted with all his assigned duties, and it came to naught; Thomas remained in Nantes, and resumed his correspondence with his brother. For his part, Robert remained uncertain, for him an unusual and uncomfortable condition. As late as June, he wrote to Bingham that "I am Embarrassed between a desire to serve [Thomas] and my doubts if he will serve himself and do honor to my recommendations of him. A little more time will convince me one way or another."

By that time, Thomas was again completely abandoned to his appetites. One associate reported bluntly, "He is drunk at least 22 hours out of every 24 and never without one or two whores in company."

Robert Morris wouldn't know the full story until late in the year, as communications between Congress and its agents abroad had almost wholly broken down. This was maddening to Deane, whose tenure in France was becoming more and more anxious. "Eight months with but two letters, when so much depended on the most exact and constant correspondence, has been the most trying scene of my life," Deane complained in a December letter to Morris.

In fact, after the first exhilarating meetings with Beaumarchais and Vergennes, Deane had encountered a series of setbacks. The biggest problem was Viscount Stormont, the British ambassador at Paris. Aggressive and tempestuous, his actions informed by a network of spies, Stormont learned early on of the Hortalez scheme, and protested loudly to Vergennes against any violations of French neutrality. To save face, and despite his promises to Deane, Vergennes issued a string of conflicting orders to the local authorities at ports across France, first to seize contraband bound for America, then to release it. Ships were loaded in secret, then unloaded under police orders, then loaded again. Deane and Beaumarchais responded to these maneuvers with frantic appeals to Vergennes and lavish bribes to the local authorities, driving up the cost of their operation.

In the meantime, Morris continued his effort to push out remittance shipments. From their separate stations in Philadelphia and Baltimore, Morris and Richard Henry Lee schemed constantly to deploy the few armed vessels of the Continental Navy to open sea lanes and escort cargo ships, but to little effect. Morris vented his frustration in a steady stream of invective. "These damn Men of War plague us exceedingly," he told John Jay; "The enemies ships gall us confoundedly," he complained to Bingham in February. In June he told Deane, "We are so cursedly hampered with the Numerous Cruizers along our coast, that remittances are precarious & very difficult to be got out."

The dangers of the sea war sometimes hit close to home. In April one of Morris's own vessels, returning from France with a cargo of arms and powder, was heading up the Delaware when she was spotted by a British patrol. A chase ensued, and with three British warships closing fast, their guns blazing, Captain James Anderson headed for shore. He beached his vessel, got his crew into longboats, and prepared to dynamite the ship rather than let her fall to the enemy. Unfortunately, Anderson himself perished in the blast. "She blew up with a most terrible explosion," the British commander recorded, "forming a column of liquid fire to a great height . . . showering down burnt pieces of wood etc. which covered a space round about for near one half a mile in the water." Recounting the episode to her mother, Mary Morris lamented, "Mr. Morris has met with a great loss, as well as the continent."

With few shipments arriving from America, Deane cast about for other means of credit. Pierre Penet and other merchants had plenty of cargoes ready to sail, but without remittances they could not sustain the ventures. Separately from Thomas Morris, Deane developed his own deal with the Farmers General, securing a million-livre advance to underwrite munitions ventures against return shipments of tobacco. On his private account, Deane arranged shipments through his brother Simeon, a tobacco trader who joined him in Europe to speculate in private trade. And Silas managed to persuade Le Ray de Chaumont, a major French merchant, to underwrite a joint venture with Robert Morris as a partner. These amounted to a fraction of the European trade Morris had envisioned, but it was a start.

Perhaps Deane's greatest financial coup was to secure from Vergennes in January a loan of two million pounds. The Congress had requested ten times that amount, hoping France would underwrite the entire war effort, but Vergennes deemed that sum "impossible." Still, the smaller sum would cover the expenses of the American mission in Paris, and leave open the prospect of additional loans in the future.

At last, in winter and early spring, Deane's endeavors with Beaumarchais began to bear fruit. The first shipment from Hortalez, aboard the frigate *Amphitrite*, put out to sea on December 14. True to the tangled nature of the entire project, the *Amphitrite* returned to port after disputes arose among her passengers, and her departure was delayed another two months. But in January, two more vessels got under way.

The departure of these critical shipments from France was the culmination of months of dogged work by Deane and Beaumarchais, but it may have been the arrival in December of Ben Franklin as head of the American embassy that finally broke the ice. Franklin was already renowned for his achievements in science; his new status as a revolutionary leader made him hugely popular in France and raised the American struggle to the status of a cause célèbre. By January, Franklin, Deane, and Arthur Lee had opened a new round of talks with Vergennes. They wanted funds, they wanted warships to convoy trading vessels, but, most of all, they sought an outright declaration of war against Britain.

Vergennes stalled. He had already ventured heavily; this was the time to let events take their course, and the first great plot was now unfolding. On March 17, the first Hortalez vessel, the *Mercure*, arrived at Portsmouth, New Hampshire, bearing more than three hundred tons of matériel, including cloth for tents and uniforms, and a large supply of gunpowder. John Langdon, former member of Congress and the Continental agent in New Hampshire, took command of the cargo, dispatching part of it to Washington at Morristown, and the rest to the garrison at Ticonderoga.

A second Hortalez ship, the *Seine*, sent to New England but blown well off course, arrived at Martinique on March 18. There William Bingham took charge, breaking down the cargo for shipment by smaller, faster vessels to the mainland. He left fourteen cannon on board the *Seine*, mixed in a variety of local produce, and sent her off to Boston. She was captured by the British en route, the only one of Beaumarchais's ships lost to the enemy. This was unfortunate, but most of the cargo had been shifted to other transports.

Morris's network was now in full swing, with agents in Europe dispatching cargoes to receivers placed from Martinique to New Hampshire.

By June, a total of eight ships had set out, carrying more than two thousand tons of supplies for the Continental Army. Deane had been driven to distraction, and Beaumarchais had exhausted all the funds advanced by France and Spain and had plunged deep into debt. But the illicit pipeline from France was open at last and Washington would enter the campaign of 1777 with a full complement of cannon, small arms, tents, and uniforms.

This was the primary goal of the American mission, but even as it was being realized, Congress was looking for more. As early as October, the new members of the Committee of Secret Correspondence, under the sway of Richard Henry Lee, had decided to send emissaries to Vienna, Tuscany, Holland, and Prussia. This was a distinct overreach, rooted in the almost naive confidence in American arms and ideals that had distinguished the Eastern faction in Congress from the beginning. Franklin opposed the scheme even before he embarked for Paris, offering a typically wry admonishment: "A virgin state should preserve the virgin character, and not go about suitoring for alliances, but wait with dignity for the application of others."

In the months ahead, Tuscany, Vienna, and Prussia all spurned the American suitors, but Spain was a different case. Closely allied with France through Bourbon family ties and a shared enmity for Britain, the Spanish king had already demonstrated his interest in supporting the American rebels. In late January, the three commissioners in Paris sought to capitalize on that opening by sending Arthur Lee to Madrid. The selection of Lee was partly by process of elimination—Deane had too many engagements in Paris to leave, and Franklin was too old. But personality played a role as well; Lee's severe and suspicious nature quickly alienated his fellow commissioners and, more importantly, Vergennes. All three were relieved to see Lee depart.

Lee never made it to Madrid. So fearful was the Spanish court of British surveillance that they sent an emissary to intercept Lee at Burgos, a provincial town in the northern highlands. The meeting took place March 4. Lee was typically blunt, pressing for an audience in the capital and an open declaration of war against England, but the Spanish agent curtly fended him off: "You have considered your situation," he told Lee, "but not ours." Still, the effort was not in vain. As Deane had in Paris, Lee found a plan for secret aid already in motion. Ammunition and clothing were being collected for the Americans at the Spanish ports of Havana and New Orleans, awaiting only a means of transport to the rebels. In addition, James Gardoqui, a prominent merchant of the northern port of Bilbao, would serve as the Spanish counterpart to Beaumarchais, secretly shipping arms direct from Spain at Lee's direction. Gardoqui sat in on the Burgos meeting as an interpreter, and held private talks with Lee afterward to iron out the details.

Partisan that he was, Lee was careful to consign the Spanish cargoes not to Morris, but to Elbridge Gerry, a merchant from Salem, a member of Congress from Massachusetts, and a confirmed adherent of the Eastern faction. The connection wasn't purely political, as Gerry was already engaged in private trade with Gardoqui. For the next three years, Gerry mixed the subsidized cargoes with his own private shipments, and Lee maintained his own backchannel conduit for foreign aid.

In Philadelphia, as the panic of December began to fade, life returned to a semblance of normalcy. Some of the city's conservatives, including Joseph Galloway, a longtime political ally of Franklin's, had seized on Howe's offer of clemency and defected to the British, but many of the families that had fled made their way back. "Matters are returning to the old channel," James Allen recorded in his diary.

The Assembly had resumed its sessions in January. Morris did not attend; he said he was "too busy," though his disdain for the Pennsylvania militants and their constitution was another likely factor. In his absence, on February 5, the body named a new delegation to Congress. The slate was a distinctly radical one, with the exception, once again, of Morris. This would end his conflicted tenure in the Assembly, as the new constitution barred members from holding more than one public office at a time. Still, Morris accepted the appointment grudgingly, writing a stiff letter that referred to himself in the third person: "Although his private business suffers exceedingly by giving up his time and attention to the public, yet . . . he means to serve his country to the extent of his abilities in the present struggle for liberty."

The central complaint here, that his mounting government obligations forced Morris to neglect his private interests, was by now a recurring theme. As early as October Morris told John Bradford that "My time is so engrossed by Public business that I have but little left to employ in speculation." Three months later, he wrote to John Langdon that his congressional duty "engrosses so much time I cannot attend my own business." This was especially exasperating to a man of Morris's competitive instincts. Writing later in reference to his firm, Morris vented his frustration: "Their whole time and attention as well as that of all their clerks & people was engaged in this [government] business by which they got a commission that hardly paid the rent of their stores & charges of clerks & etc. Their neighbors at the same time making rapid fortunes by private business which they had no time to attend."

But if Morris's trading enterprises suffered during this time of trial, his fortunes did not. The most dynamic theater of combat in the war against England was on the open sea, and here Morris deployed his capital to great advantage. With the Continental fleet pent up by the British blockade or still on shipyard stocks, most of the fighting was carried out by privateers, usually converted merchant ships carrying a few cannon and a swarm of cutthroat sailors armed with swords, pikes, and pistols. They couldn't match the firepower of the British warships, but enemy freighters made easy targets—in one celebrated case from 1775, the Boston-based schooner *Lee*, sporting four guns and manned by a crew of fifty, captured a British transport four times her size without firing a shot, landing tons of gunpowder, two thousand muskets, and a three-thousand-pound mortar to augment Washington's armament. Sale of prizes—the ships and cargoes seized by the privateers—made fortunes for the crews, captains, and owners, and opened a seaborne bonanza that lasted for the duration of the war.

The result was a seesaw battle all along the Atlantic seaboard, with raiders chasing cargo ships and the Royal Navy exacting retribution. Each side wreaked havoc on each other; by the end of 1776, British merchants had lost 350 sail, while the rebels, by April 1777, had seized 120 ships in the West Indies alone. The riches reaped by the privateers caused real problems on land, as fighting sailors routinely deserted the ships of the Continental Navy—and sometimes even their regiments in the army—to join the gold rush at sea. Still, as chairman of the Secret Committee, Morris recognized the strategic importance of privateering. He authorized William Bingham to commission as many sea raiders as he could muster, and soon after granted the same authority to Deane, though on a more limited scale. Along with Ben Franklin, Morris savored the idea of carrying the war to England's home waters, but such operations caused problems for the friendly, neutral states of Europe.

Morris refrained at first from personal investment in the free-for-all. His partner Thomas Willing refused any engagement in privateering, and for a time Morris agreed; in view of his "extensive connections and dealings with many worthy men in England," he "could not consent to take any part of their property." By December, Morris changed his stance. "Having had several vessels taken from me & otherways lost a great deal of property in this war," he told Bingham, "I conceive myself perfectly justifiable in the Eyes of God & Man to seek what I have lost from those that have plundered me." Still, his first step was tentative—an agreement with Bingham to invest as a silent partner with him and Captain George Ord, a daring sailor who won fame in a powder raid on Bermuda in 1775 and helmed the *Lady Catherine* on her eventful voyage to New Orleans. Morris advised Bingham to obtain and fit out a "stout" ship for Ord, and that he christen it the *Retaliation*.

Ord performed brilliantly, capturing thirteen prizes in his first cruise, and then headed out for more. Encouraged by these results, Morris announced to Bingham in April that "My scruples about Privateering are all done away. I have seen so much rapine, plunder & Destruction . . . that I join you in thinking it a duty to oppose and distress so merciless an enemy." With that, Morris and Bingham underwrote a new venture under a French-Canadian seafarer named Coctiny de Prejent. Sailing from Philadelphia, Prejent scored a string of captures, but he turned out to be more of a pirate than his sponsors bargained for; instead of paying off their shares, Prejent invested his winnings in raising a small fleet of privateers under his command. Prejent became a genuine menace to the British, but a total loss for Morris and Bingham.

There were other complications. Continental Navy ships on duty in the Caribbean were directed to Bingham in Martinique when they needed repairs, and Bingham often had to pay for the work out of his own and his partner's winnings from privateering. Still, Morris was fortunate to have Bingham on his side when their raiders dragged prizes into port. Bingham's close ties with the French authorities in Martinique—he paid a one percent tithe to the *intendant* for all prizes sold—made the port of St. Pierre the premier venue for selling off captured ships and cargoes. On one afternoon in 1777, a British spy counted eighty-two ships in the harbor awaiting auction.

Bingham appears to have been Morris's primary partner in the privateering game, but there were many others. By 1780 his privateering ventures reached the breadth of his Secret Committee network; he sent out ships with Deane and John Ross in Europe, and with Oliver Pollock in New Orleans. There is no tally of the profits Morris and Bingham realized by their privateering ventures. But Morris's good fortune became notorious in Philadelphia; during a wartime visit to the Quaker city, the French diarist François Jean de Chastellux recorded that Morris "is, in fact, so accustomed to the success of his privateers, that when he is observed on a Sunday to be more serious than usual, the conclusion is, that no prize has arrived in the preceding week."

By early February, Morris had gained enough confidence in the military situation that he wrote Congress to urge its return to Philadelphia. As with almost any question to come before the body, this set off another sectional dispute between the moderates and the Eastern faction. For the time being, Sam Adams and Richard Henry Lee were content to stay put, and their inclinations set the tone. "I wish Congress may remove back with all my heart," Benjamin Harrison said in a letter to Morris. "However I am told the Yankees are against it. If so we go not; they Rule as absolutely as the Grand Turk in his dominions."

But if he was distant from the scene of debate, Morris remained the fulcrum for the operations of the government, and he pressed his fellow delegates to address glaring flaws in administration that threatened to undermine the entire project of the Revolution. One such weakness was the committee system: lacking a chief executive or a civil bureaucracy, the business of government was handled exclusively by committees of the Congress, which sputtered for lack of consistent membership and direction. Morris addressed the point directly in a letter to his colleagues on the Committee of Secret Correspondence. "If the Congress means to succeed in this Contest they must pay good Executive Men to do their business as it ought to be & not lavish millions away by their own mismanagement. I say mismanagement because no Men living can attend the daily deliberations of Congress & do executive parts of business at the same time."

Morris reiterated the point in a letter to Deane, this time adding a sour note on politics. "You may depend on this. So long as that respectable body [Congress] persist in the attempt to execute as well as to deliberate on their business it never will be done as it ought & this has been urged many & many a time by myself & others but some of them don't Like to part with power or to pay others for doing what they cannot do themselves." The question was still new to the young government, but executive autonomy would become a key battleground within the Congress. For the ideologues of the Lee-Adams faction, the committee system, however cumbersome, was the democratic answer to the patronage and corruption of royal administration. Granting authority to individual managers, even in the military, represented a retreat from revolutionary principles, and the radicals would resist it doggedly.

The second critical concern Morris grappled with at this time was the declining value of the paper money issued to finance the war. He described the problem in stark terms in his lengthy letter to Deane. "I must add to this Gloomy Picture one circumstance more distressing than all the rest because it threatens instant & total Ruin to the American cause unless some radical cure is applied & that speedily. I mean the Depreciation of the Continental Currency, the Enormous Pay of our army, the immense expense at which they are supplied . . . and in short the extravagance that has prevailed in most departments of the public service have called forth prodigious emissions of Paper money, both Continental and Colonial. . . . All this amounts to real depreciation of the money."

Morris was not alone in his concern over Continental funds. Beginning with the first run of $2 million in June 1775, the emissions had become routine, periodic, and massive—climbing first to $3 million, then to $5 million every three months. By the end of 1776, notes for $25 million were in circulation. The individual states were also printing their own money at the time, leaving merchants and vendors to choose between a variety of increasingly unstable currencies. The money passed handily at first, the only exceptions being Quakers and other religious dissidents who sought to avoid any participation in the war. But by December, when Washington's troops were shivering and hungry in their camps on the Delaware, farmers and wagon drovers in Pennsylvania were uniformly refusing the government's scrip.

The first response to the failure of the currency was to blame enemies of the Revolution for seeking to sabotage the war effort. As early as April 1776, the Committee of Privates, a militia group in Philadelphia, was denouncing "certain monopolizers whose prosperity arises from the miseries of mankind." Similar accusations against "forestallers" and monopolizers would reverberate for the duration of the war.

By autumn, the continued decline of the revolutionary currency elicited a more penetrating critique from Pelatiah Webster. Born in Connecticut and graduated from Yale, Webster was a public intellectual who served as a sort of American counterpart to Adam Smith. Webster moved to Philadelphia before the Revolution and made his fortune in trade, but his primary avocation was a continuing study of the workings of money and credit. In the first of what became an occasional series of newspaper essays on public finance, Webster in September 1776 called for extensive taxation to support the revolutionary government. "The Continental money is to be considered as a debt fastened on the person and estate of every member of the United States," Webster argued. The debt "is already a heavy one . . . it is still increasing fast, and without a speedy tax, and a very sufficient one, it will grow upon us beyond any possibility of payment."

Taxation was the means by which the government might control the total supply of money, Webster reasoned, and the supply of money determined its ultimate worth. "I conceive the value of the currency of any state has a limit, a *ne plus ultra*, beyond which it cannot go; and if the nominal sum is extended beyond that limit, the value will not follow."

But taxation required a political response, and in a war being fought expressly to defy the taxing authority of Parliament, the idea of the revolutionary governments imposing heavy domestic taxes was anathema. Besides, Congress had no power to tax; it could print money, but had no means for funding it.

As fall turned to winter, prices were rising throughout the colonies. Some of the increase was due to wartime shortages, but the underlying weakness of the Continental currency was becoming apparent to all. In late December, New England legislators convened in Rhode Island to devise measures "to support the Credit of our Currencies to prevent the oppressing the Soldiers and Inhabitants of Extravagant Prices." Over the course of a week's debate the delegates followed Webster's lead, calling for "no further Emissions of currency" and "such taxes upon the Inhabitants as their abilities will bear." Then they went further, denouncing the "unbounded avarice of many Persons" and decided that "Rates and Prices . . . be affixed and settled."

The resolves of the New England convention were taken up by the Congress at Baltimore in February. The question of taxes got little attention, but the call for price controls generated an extended debate. Some of the major figures in Congress, including Samuel Adams and Richard Henry Lee, saluted the idea as "wise and salutary." But there was sharp opposition, largely from the Pennsylvania delegates but from among the radicals as well as the moderates. Benjamin Rush summarily dismissed the claims of market manipulation: "The extortion we complain of arises only from the excessive quantity of our money." Price controls, he said, would do little to change the picture. They amounted to "Nothing but an opiate. It may compose the continent for a night, but She will soon awaken again to a fresh sense of her pain and misery." John Witherspoon, head of the college at Princeton, mentor to James Madison and a delegate from New Jersey, agreed. "Remember," he argued, "laws are not almighty. It is beyond the power of despotic princes to regulate the price of goods."

Robert Morris would tackle the issues of taxation and price controls in due time, but these were essentially political questions that went beyond the scope of the established powers of the government. At this point in his career the pragmatic Morris limited his concerns to more practical steps to support the sinking dollar. His letter to Deane was one such response; he pressed for an increased loan from France or possibly Holland, as well as warships to open shipping lanes to America, by which France would gain access to friendly commerce, reaping in America "the Luxuriant produces of the finest Soil in the World."

On the domestic front, Morris advocated government borrowing to reduce the amount of bills in circulation. This would at least ground the national finances in loans, rather than simply passing scrip on the credit of Congress, which was rapidly sinking. In Morris's view, all parties would benefit; investors would find a safe harbor against inflation, while the loans would draw down the "immense sum" then outstanding. The first step toward loan financing was taken in October 1776, when Congress established a Continental Loan Office that would offer for public sale five million dollars in certificates bearing 4 percent interest. Response to the loan program flagged, however, as several state treasuries were also seeking to raise funds by offering notes bearing the same rate of interest. In February, Morris pushed Congress to raise the rate on the Loan Office Certificates to 6 percent.

This occasioned a new division among the delegates at Baltimore. Rush and several others supported the higher rate, but the southern states feared that paying more would only increase the cost of the war without yielding additional funds. When he learned the motion had died on a split vote, Morris wrote Rush to press the matter. "If the Congress do not embrace this measure at once they are undone. Every department of Public business is in want of money, they cannot make it fast enough & if they will not borrow on the terms other people do, what must follow?" The message apparently got through, as Congress raised the rate after a second debate on February 26. This was the first of several steps taken to encourage loans, and did help to slow, but not to reverse, the decline of the currency.

As with the problem of organization, the question of finances became a recurrent theme, though here the Congress deferred to Morris's expertise. In May he was named, along with Witherspoon and William Duer of New York, to a committee "to devise ways and means for defraying the expenses of the coming year." The committee reported back in June after receiving word of the French loan of 2 million livres. The commissioners—Franklin and Deane—proposed devoting those funds to paying interest on the Loan

Office Certificates, thereby extending further the government's credit. This plan was endorsed by Morris and his committee, and debated all through the summer.

The risks of going deeply in debt to France struck fear into Henry Laurens, a merchant and plantation owner from South Carolina. "What folly, what madness," Laurens fumed to a friend. "Easy access to the Treasury of France will only hasten our ruin." He compared accumulating loans to "A young man borrowing money from a designing Sharper upon the credit of an expected Heirship." John Adams also recoiled at the prospect of debt financing. "Taxation," he said, "Taxation and Economy are our only effectual Resources."

All that might be true, but with financial demands pressing and immediate, Congress really had little choice. The committee report was finally put to a vote in September, and passed ten states to two, with just five delegates voting against. The war would be fought on credit, and France would serve as the lender of last resort.

Aside from his committee work, Morris did what he could locally to push the loan program through fiscal legerdemain. One such instance he described in detail; encountering two entrepreneurs heading for Boston "with a large sum of money," Morris prevailed on them to invest their funds in Loan Office Certificates, and to auction them for any capital they might need in New England. They agreed, but only upon Morris's guarantee that the Continental agent in Boston would cash out the certificates if the public sale stalled. This was typical of Morris; in finance as in trade, he never hesitated to throw the weight of his personal influence into pursuing the duties of his office.

In late February, Morris was chafing at the absence of Congress, and at the continued alarms that arrived by express rider from the army's headquarters in New Jersey. There was still fresh snow on the ground, and the British remained in their winter redoubts, hampered by the scarcity of wagons and lack of forage for their horses. Why, then, should Washington continue to press Morris, as he did repeatedly, to prepare for invasion by removing all excess supplies of food and military equipment from the city?

Morris's frustration prompted a remarkably candid exchange between the two leaders who had quickly emerged as central figures in the Revolution. Writing to Washington on February 27, Morris confessed that, "I have been backward about removing the public stores" from Philadelphia, "well knowing that a panic is sooner caused than retrieved." He reminded the general that "the expense & loss or Waste arising by such removal amounts to almost the same thing as a total destruction of them."

This was more than a tactical question. Morris was asking Washington to consider the larger question of leadership, and the impact of his orders on the public mind. "I do not like to be too sanguine & yet it is very necessary in a Contest like this we are engaged in to view the best side of the picture. . . . Remember good Sir, that few men ever keep their feelings to themselves, & that it is necessary for example sake that all leaders should feel & think bold in order to inspirit those that look up to them."

Having opened on the subject of Washington's gravitas, a trait already familiar to both friends and foes of the commander from Virginia, Morris plunged ahead. "Heaven (no doubt for the noblest purposes) has blessed you with a firmness of mind, Steadiness of Countenance and patience in sufferings that give you infinite advantages over other men. This being the case you are not to depend on other people's exertions being equal to your own. One mind feeds and thrives on misfortunes by finding resources to get the better of them, another sinks under their own weight, thinking it impossible to resist, and as the latter description probably includes the majority of mankind we must be cautious of alarming them." Here Morris pressed his point. "I hate deception and cannot wish anything like it would ever escape you, but I really think if the bright side of our affairs were sometimes to be painted by your pen or sanctified by your name, it would draw forth the exertions of some good men sooner than distress does from others."

Look at the bright side! Coming at a time when Washington was contemplating a summer campaign against an adversary of twice his strength, this singular bit of advice may have brought a smile to the general's face. But this was Morris's nature: "I am one of those people who think the best part of the Community will ultimately swim at the top, notwithstanding others get the uppermost during the general jumble," Morris told the general. "I can see the way to liberty and happiness through the Cloud or mist before us."

Washington's answer to Morris was prompt but politic. "The freedom with which you have communicated . . . is highly pleasing to me," the general wrote March 2. "For be assured, Sir, that nothing would add more to my satisfaction, than an unreserved Correspondence with a Gentleman of whose Abilities and attachment to the Cause we are contending for, I entertain so high an opinion of as I do of yours." But Washington could not endorse Morris's buoyant outlook. He acknowledged the problems confronting William Howe, but held that those very problems would serve as "an inducement, if no other, to shift Quarters"—from the Jerseys and New York to Philadelphia.

On the question of managing public perceptions, Washington said he was indeed keeping his own dark presentiments private. "My Opinions on these several [military] matters, are known only to those who have a right to be informed. . . . I have endeavored to conceal them from every one else." That was why the general wanted supplies for the army evacuated now. "By these means the business may be done imperceptibly as it were, and the people not distracted by Fears that may prove groundless."

The discussion over strategy was not a critical one. Morris had no interest in disputing Washington's authority, and had already, as he informed the general, "given orders to every department to remove all stores not immediately wanted, as fast as they can." More important was the sense of mutual trust that this exchange helped to foster. Morris made sure to confirm his high regard in a closing note to the general. "The good opinion you are pleased to entertain of me makes me very happy because there is no man's opinion I reverence more."

Congress came back to Philadelphia in March, with Mary and the Morris children trailing not far behind. Both arrivals were a source of genuine relief for Morris. His three months of service as the de facto chief executive left him exhausted, with his eyes bleary and painful from the grind of paperwork. Mary declared herself "Very happy to find myself at home after so long an absence, with the terrible apprehensions we fled with of never seeing it again," and Robert stole the opportunity to take a brief leave from the government.

It was a good time to step back from the pressures and intrigues of Congress. The extended hiatus in backwater Baltimore was more than the delegates had bargained for, and many of Morris's friends and allies decided to head home—John Jay, Robert and William Livingston, James Duane all returned to New York, while Benjamin Harrison, Joseph Hewes, William Hooper, and Edward Rutledge dispersed to the south. Even his venerable Philadelphia collaborator Ben Franklin was in faraway Paris. "What is to become of America and its cause," Morris worried in his exchange with Washington, "if a constant fluctuation is to take place amongst its Counselors & every change we find reason to view with regret?"

At least there was Hancock, the slim, handsome, sometimes peevish president of the Congress. He was rich, generous, and loved fine wine, and in Philadelphia, Hancock had discovered a genuine affinity for the self-made Morris. "I have really had my hands, Head & Heart full of business since I saw you last but thank God my spirits never failed," Morris wrote to Hancock in February. "I hope soon to take you by the hand and pass that social hour that gives an honest soul more real joy, than all the follies & Vanitys in the World."

But the Boston radicals—the Adamses and Elbridge Gerry—had always looked down on their hometown merchant prince, with his taste for lavender suits and liveried servants. Hancock was growing tired of their machinations, and of his long absence from home, and he too began talking about leaving the government.

This prospect prompted speculation over a successor, and within the remnants of the moderate faction Robert Morris was touted as a viable, even the likeliest, candidate. Morris would have none of it and he squelched the rumor wherever he encountered it. It was enough, however, to impress Mary with her husband's growing stature. She related this bit of political intrigue in a letter to her mother. Morris was to have been "complimented . . . with the Presidentship," Mary enthused. "Don't you feel quite important? I assure you I do, and begin to be reconciled to Independence."

Even aside from his yen to return to business, Morris was probably wise in resisting the lure of higher office, for the flow of politics in Congress was running against him. With the departure of so many political moderates with wide experience in administration and commerce, the militant Lee-Adams faction took a firmer grip on the reins of the government. Convinced that the problems of the Revolution lay in a simple lack of "virtue," they launched a series of ill-advised reforms.

One immediate target was the commissary department, where they believed personal corruption, not the weak currency or unwieldy logistics, had led to privation in the army. In short order, and following their anti-authoritarian ethic, the Puritans of the Eastern faction moved to decentralize the agency by splitting it in two, and then stripped department chiefs of the power to name their own subordinates. Purchasing agents were put on salary instead of commission and required to pay in prices set by Congress. Joseph Trumbull, the respected head of the department, fought the changes and then quit in disgust, followed by most of his top aides. By August, this critical agency was in shambles. "The whole Race of Commissaries look like cats in a strange garret staring at each other," one deputy quartermaster complained. "Not one of them knows what he is about."

Another focus of the Eastern faction was management of foreign affairs. All but closed out of the diplomatic appointments in the early stage of the war, "Richard Henry Lee seized the opportunity" to refashion the internal apparatus for handling America's critical alliances in Europe. With Robert Morris on the sidelines, Congress renamed the Committee of Secret Correspondence as the Committee for Foreign Affairs, appointed Thomas Paine as the committee secretary, and named James Lovell as chairman. A former schoolmaster from Massachusetts, Lovell was shrewd and dedicated, a Latin instructor at a school whose graduates included both Hancock and Sam Adams, and who was briefly jailed by the British as a patriot activist. Lovell was also stern and censorious, a natural addition to the Lee-Adams clique. Lovell had little regard for Silas Deane, and was soon working to undermine Deane in favor of Arthur Lee.

Nor was Deane much endearing himself to the rest of the Congress. At the outset of the conflict with Britain, the patriot leaders, fearful of their own lack of military experience, had asked their agents to solicit experienced foreign officers to enlist in the cause. Now the foreigners were arriving in droves, some of them French idealists eager to fight in the cause of liberty, but others sheer mercenaries seeking military honors and commensurate salaries. Worse, many arrived bearing commissions for command issued by William Bingham, Arthur Lee, Ben Franklin, and especially Deane.

Inevitably, these ambitious soldiers of fortune found their way to Philadelphia, and called, at all hours, on the members of Congress. "I must also request to spare me all you can in the introduction of French Officers to me," Morris wrote to Bingham in February. "Really they are flocking over in such numbers from every port by every ship that I don't know what to do with them."

This was more than a trivial annoyance. Pressed by uniformed Frenchmen with commissions in hand, Congress made numerous appointments that caused deep resentment in the army. Much of this resentment recoiled back on Congress, and then back on Deane; in July, Lovell made it the basis of a formal motion for Deane's recall. It failed then, but became a new source of acrimony between the delegates.

Some of the foreigners proved more valuable than others. Among the last to arrive, with a crew of fourteen other volunteers in tow, was Gilbert du Motier, the Marquis de Lafayette. Making his way overland after an Atlantic passage that ended in South Carolina, Lafayette tracked down Hancock and presented him with a letter of recommendation from Deane. Hancock fobbed him off on Robert Morris, who said he would meet them the next morning. Morris arrived, well after the appointed hour, and presented the bedraggled travelers to James Lovell, delegate from Massachusetts. "This gentleman speaks French very well," Morris advised. "Deal with him from now on." With that, he turned on his heel and went back to work.

Morris was not always so curt; in fact, he became a confidant of Lafayette's and his private banker. Lafayette placed his funds with Morris and drew an "allowance" for his personal expenses. When he exceeded his allotment, as he often did, Morris advanced him loans from his own account.

Muddled as was the state of Congress in early 1777, the affairs of Pennsylvania were approaching the point of total breakdown. After months of political stalemate, the new government had finally seated its Supreme Executive Council, but even here the radicals failed to muster a clear mandate. The new president of the council, a Quaker merchant named Thomas Wharton, Jr., could offer only lukewarm support for the government he was to lead. "There are many faults, which I hope one day to see removed," he mused to a friend. "If a better frame of government should be adopted, such a one as would please a much greater majority than the present one, I should be very happy."

As it was, most of the citizens of Philadelphia, and many throughout Pennsylvania, had by now settled into firm opposition to the new Assembly. Militia call-ups went unanswered, taxes went unpaid; judges, constables, and sheriffs, elected to office, refused to serve. James Allen, several of whose family members had left the city to join the British but who himself joined the militia, recorded a blunt assessment in his diary. "The government of this province, or state as they term it, is truly ridiculous; not one of the laws of the Assembly are regarded; no courts open, no justice administered."

The primary source for resentment against the government was the test oath, which was viewed as a cudgel wielded by the militants against their enemies. Also troubling was the sense that, like the ruling clique they unseated, the members of the new Assembly were engaging in the time-honored practice of patronage. "The clamors of the red-hot patriots have subsided into easy places and offices of profit; the posts of mere *trust* go a-beggin," one critic wrote. The sheer hypocrisy of the new regime left this commentator fuming. "When I reflect on the times I am seized with the blue devils."

With popular support for the Assembly waning, a dwindling core of militants moved to revive enthusiasm for the new constitution. They organized, in early March, as the Whig Society, named after the liberal political faction in England that opposed the monarchy and whose views, transplanted to America, formed the theoretical framework for the independence movement. The Philadelphia Whigs were a loose-knit circle of intellectuals with but little connection to the Scotch-Irish frontiersmen whose resentment of the cosmopolitan elite had given impetus to the new government. Some, like the astronomer and mathematician David Rittenhouse, and Thomas Young, a physician and former protégé of Sam Adams in Boston, had been active in the early drive to unseat the old Assembly; others, including the painter Charles Willson Peale, had little political experience, but were attracted by the ideas of democracy and the "New Man," freed of the corruption and social forms of the old world, that the Revolution promised to raise up.

Peale became the president of the Whig Society almost on a whim. He attended a meeting of the group "out of curiosity more than for any other reason"; when candidates were called for the top office, nobody answered, and the idealistic artist consented to be drafted. That none of the firebrands of 1776 were ready to stand for leadership says much about the curious inconstancy of this most utopian strain of the revolutionary movement. United in their opposition to the provincial elite, the militants had little to bind their ruling coalition, and only a vague idea of their own objectives.

Toward the end of March, the Peale and Whig Society published a manifesto of sorts, a defense of the state constitution just as lukewarm as that pronounced by President Wharton. "We have not that fond notion of our own political wisdom, as to imagine ourselves . . . infallible in such arduous undertakings as the formation of constitutions," they conceded in an address published in the *Pennsylvania Gazette*. But now was not the time to argue. "A noisy and ill-natured wrangling, about the designs of the framers or opposers of the constitution, can answer no other purpose than to injure or disgrace us."

Thomas Paine was at camp with Washington and not present in Philadelphia for the convention that wrote the constitution, but he became an icon for the militants and embraced their cause as his own. Back the capital in March, Paine joined the Whig Society and weighed in on the public debate. "That the present constitution has errors and defects is not to be doubted," he wrote, but that was to be expected. The new government was an experiment in newfound liberty: "We *must* begin somewhere," Paine wrote. He dismissed the outcry against the constitution as mere factional squabbling. "I have ever been of the opinion, and still am, that the whole matter is more personal than political." As to the issues in dispute, Paine considered them overblown. "There is nothing immediately dangerous" in the new government; the danger lay in disputing it. This is where the critics of the Assembly disagreed. The breakdown of authority in wartime, they said, threatened the province with "anarchy and ruin."

The approach of the enemy army brought the quarrel over the constitution to a head. Beginning in March, the British army mustered from its winter slumber in Manhattan to begin a series of maneuvers in New Jersey. William Howe failed then to launch a serious campaign, but his feint presented enough of a threat that Washington ordered all military stores removed from the capital. The Congress, alarmed again just weeks after returning from Baltimore, called on the state to throw up fortifications and assemble three thousand troops for defense of the city. But they were dismayed to find that, at that point, there was no state to answer—the Assembly had adjourned, the Supreme Executive Council was in recess, and the operations of the government were in disarray. Chortled one newspaper writer, "Was lost, a *new invented* Government."

William Duer, recently returned from New York, moved that Congress step into the vacuum, and on April 15, a council of war was held. Robert Morris was on hand with the rest of the Pennsylvania delegation; they sat down with Wharton; the state Board of War, dominated by moderates like Richard Bache; and, for the Congress, Duer, Sam Adams, and Richard Henry Lee.

The upshot was sensible enough: a resolution finding the existing state government "incapable of any exertion," and conferring emergency powers on Wharton and the Board of War. But the Pennsylvania militants cried foul, denouncing the conference as a plot to discredit the Assembly. Duer dismissed their protests out of hand. "If Congress had not interposed, this state would have fallen an easy prey to a very small body of the enemy's army. It is to be hoped . . . that a little Quackery will save a powerful State, which must have fallen a sacrifice to a speculative system of politics."

This was the end of the intervention by Congress, but the Philadelphia moderates would not let matters rest there. When the Assembly finally reconvened in May, it was confronted by an ultimatum from a new coalition of moderates led by the Pennsylvania delegates in Congress—Robert Morris, James Wilson, Benjamin Rush, and George Clymer. Deprecating the "weakness and languor" of the government, these leaders of Philadelphia's elite promised to cease their opposition if the Assembly would agree to call a new convention that would weigh amendments to the constitution.

This was a revival of the same bargain the Assembly had agreed to, and then reneged on, in December. But the forty-two signers of the petition comprised a new and more imposing opposition than the militants had faced before. Rush and Clymer, after all, had been early advocates of the new government. And many of the signers had distinguished themselves in the early stages of the war. Jonathan Maxwell Nesbitt was a Presbyterian merchant who ran privateers and rode with the Philadelphia Cavalry; John Cadwalader was a general in the state militia and had fought with Washington in New Jersey. Just as important, the petition roster carried the weight of high office in the national government. Aside from the Pennsylvania delegates it included Richard Peters, secretary to the congressional Board of War, and Charles Thomson, the radical activist from the early days of the resistance, now secretary of Congress. These critics of the constitution could hardly be dismissed as Tories.

The renewed call for a convention sparked another round of salvos in the Philadelphia press, but after a month of wrangling, the Assembly came halfway, voting to hold a referendum on the question of calling a convention. This partial victory for the moderates only inflamed the militants in the Assembly. They stepped up their campaign against those who refused to swear allegiance to the new regime, and in September, with the collaboration of the Congress, they rounded up twenty of the city's leading Quakers and banished them to the Virginia frontier. Conditions there were harsh, and at least two of the Quakers died in exile, martyrs to the cause of nonviolence.

Everyone in Philadelphia believed the British would make an attempt against the city in the summer of 1777, but nobody could say when it might happen. The Howe brothers seemed just as uncertain. Huddled in New York, they meditated on two primary strategies. The first was to drive north up the valley of the Hudson, seeking a rendezvous with a strong force of eight thousand troops heading south from Quebec under command of "Gentleman Johnny" Burgoyne, a flamboyant major general and a rival of William Howe for the favor of the British ministry. The other option was to head south and take possession of the rebel capital.

Burgoyne set out in June, quickly recaptured Fort Ticonderoga, and then drove south into the wilds of upstate New York. Howe vacillated a month longer. Finally in late July he got word of Burgoyne's rapid progress and, eager for laurels of his own, settled on Philadelphia. Remarkably, he decided to move by sea, rather than hazard a march through the Jerseys. On July 23 he crammed thirteen thousand troops aboard his brother's fleet and sailed out from Staten Island.

With Howe dithering, Robert Morris took steps to ensure that this time, come what may, he would keep his family together. In April he purchased at Manheim, sixty miles west of Philadelphia, the estate of Baron Henry William Stiegel, an eccentric German immigrant who had erected an iron furnace and glassworks, and then went bankrupt. The Castle, as Stiegel called his palatial mansion, was draped in tapestries and included, among its many rooms, a chapel.

By early May, the Morrises had packed up their house in town and removed to The Hills, from which they might make a quick escape to the countryside. "We intend sending off our best furniture to Lancaster, with all the linen we can spare," Mary explained in a letter to her mother, "that our flight may be attended with as few encumbrances as possible." She was seven months pregnant with her fifth child, and Mary was already feeling wistful about departure from "dear Philadelphia." The family would remain in their country house "if possible, in the enjoyment of all that's beautiful to the eye and grateful to the taste; for, as if to add to our mortification, are we obliged to leave it; nature never appeared so lovely, nor promised such a profusion of her gifts."

The Howe brothers finally made their appearance July 29, their fleet moving majestically up the Delaware, but then suddenly reversed course and were gone. What prompted this detour has been a matter of conjecture ever since, but for three weeks Washington's army was "compelled to wander about the country like Arabs" under a sweltering summer sun, hoping to anticipate the British landing force. The Howes finally reappeared in the northern reaches of the Chesapeake, landing August 22 at the small Maryland port Head of Elk.

Washington hastened to meet them, marching his forces south and passing directly through Philadelphia. Here, for the first time, Congress and the citizens of the capital got a chance to see the Continental Army on parade. Washington did what he could to put on a show, arranging his regiments in ranks twelve deep, marching to the sound of fife and drum. The men dressed as well as their tattered state would allow, those without hats sporting a sprig of green in their hair, "to indicate hope."

The army took two hours to pass through the city, their progress cheered by throngs on either side. The troops created a distinctly rustic impression compared to the more precise maneuvers of their British counterparts, but they inspired confidence nonetheless. "We now have an army, well appointed between us and Mr. Howe," John Adams wrote to his wife Abigail, "so that I feel as secure here, as if I was at Braintree," his home ground in Massachusetts.

But disposition of forces did not ensure the outcome, and over the next two weeks the fortunes of war turned against Washington. He blocked the British advance on September 11 at Brandywine Creek, twenty miles southwest of Philadelphia, but in fighting that commenced at dawn and continued until nightfall, suffered a series of reverses that ended in a rout. Thereafter Washington was forced into his now too familiar mode of anxious retreat, his troops tired and hungry, his commanders disappointed.

A week after the debacle at Brandywine, Washington dispatched his youthful aide Alexander Hamilton with a small troop of cavalry to torch flour mills on the banks of the Schuykill River and keep them out of enemy hands. When his party was surprised by a squad of British dragoons, Hamilton made a narrow escape, and then sent an urgent message to John Hancock: "If Congress have not left Philadelphia, they ought do it immediately without fail." The capital was to be abandoned to the enemy.

Hancock received Hamilton's express after midnight, and the alarm was instantly cried in the streets. "It was a beautiful, still, moonlit morning," Thomas Paine wrote of the exodus, "and the streets were as full of men, women, and children as on a market day."

There was no need for panic; Howe, progressing at his usual leisurely pace, did not reach Philadelphia for another week. From his redoubt at The Hills, Morris had the time to load Mary, their four youngsters, the infant baby, Charles, several servants and slaves, all their belongings, and Robert's papers and account books onto a "caravan of covered wagons." Heading out onto the crowded, rutted highway, they made their way to Manheim.

Morris's choice of sanctuary was fortunate, as the Congress retired first to Lancaster, and then across the Susquehanna to York, both towns within a day's ride of The Castle. York was little more than a hamlet, a village of fewer than two thousand residents with inadequate lodgings and poor food—even the water tasted bitter. Some members of the Eastern faction found lodging with Daniel Roberdeau, a wealthy merchant and leader of the Pennsylvania radicals who maintained a mansion in York, but most had to scrounge for cramped quarters.

While Morris enjoyed far better accommodations than his fellow delegates, he shared with them a sense of gloom: theirs was a government in exile, their army ineffectual, their cause in doubt. With the days growing short and the nights growing cold, they had to acknowledge the fact that prospects for a quick end to the conflict had vanished.

— *Chapter 6* —

CONGRESS IN EXILE

I n September, even before the British army began its march on Philadelphia, Robert Morris began making plans to leave the government.
He had been engaged constantly in state and Continental business
for more than three years, and was convinced that only a separation would
allow him the time to put his financial house in order. Besides, the crucial affairs under his direction had settled into a stultifying, disagreeable
routine. Supplies continued to flow in, many of them shipped by Beaumarchais, but it was nearly impossible to make remittances. The network of
agents Morris had placed in foreign ports was now operating almost exclusively on their own credit, the individual agents sinking steadily into debt.

Then there was the matter of Robert's half-brother, Thomas. The January letter from the commissioners at Paris asking that Thomas be replaced
had finally arrived in June and was presented to the full Congress. This was
hugely distressing to Morris, "exposing me to feelings the most Poignant
I ever knew," as he put it in an angry letter to Silas Deane. It was not just
the move against Thomas, but that Franklin and Deane had lodged official
charges and forced Robert to make a public defense of his brother, that
Morris found so distressing.

In his view, Robert had asked his two friends in Paris to look out for
his brother, and they had betrayed him. Morris took it personally, and addressed Deane petulantly. "Perhaps I have flattered myself with the expectation of more Friendship from the Doctor [Franklin] and you than I had a
right to, and shall therefore Correct the Error in the future."

Worse for Robert, Thomas had prevailed upon some of his merchant
associates on the Nantes waterfront to dispute the accounts from Paris, reviving in Morris the hope that his brother might be the victim of mercantile rivalry, and not his own foibles. "These same Gentlemen from Nantes
inform me that [Thomas's] employment is sought for by others whom

121

the commissioners wish to gratify at his expense," Morris wrote Deane. In particular, Morris suspected the motives of Jonathan Williams, Franklin's nephew, who served his uncle as personal secretary, and whom the commissioners had assigned to handle the sale of prizes because Thomas was so often unavailable. Robert shared the letters from Thomas with the Congress, and managed to preserve Thomas's appointment as commercial agent.

This was a critical error in judgment on Morris's part, one he compounded by writing Thomas to recount the charges made by the commissioners, and affirm his personal support for him. Robert continued to entertain doubts about Thomas—he expressed them freely to William Bingham, among others—but now the defense of his brother had become a point of pride.

The facts of the matter were worse than Robert could have imagined. His emissary on the scene, John Ross, had made several contacts with Thomas, each one more disappointing. In July he found him "being without intermission abandoned to the most disgraceful pursuits of debauchery . . . engaged, as I am informed, he is with the lowest Reptiles of human society." Ross reported his findings to Deane. "Poor unfortunate and inconsiderate mortal! He is entirely lost, & be assured, too far gone to retrieve."

Ross determined then to remove Thomas from his post, but Thomas was intransigent; he would not step aside until he heard direct for his brother. When Robert's endorsement arrived in September, Thomas made a great display of his vindication. He nailed a copy of the letter to a post in his office on the Nantes waterfront, then traveled to Paris to confront his accusers. Thomas bragged of the support he'd received in Congress, and announced, as Deane recorded, that "he should hereafter despise us, and treat us with the greatest contempt."

The whole imbroglio was disastrous for the American embassy in France. As the receiver of what remittance shipments did get through, and as the manager of prizes brought in by privateers, Thomas Morris controlled the funds the commissioners needed to maintain their credit and finance their operations. In addition, the breakdown of the finances fulfilled all the dark visions of Arthur and William Lee, who eagerly sought grounds to attack Deane and Franklin. Suspicion and blame were family traits with the Lees, attitudes they polished in letters to each other. Soon after their first meeting, William Lee had concluded the worst of Deane, ascribing to him "the faithless principles, the low, dirty intrigue, the selfish views & the wicked arts of a certain race of Men."

When William Lee met with Thomas Morris at Nantes in August, he remarked on his "strange and unhappy conduct," and immediately began lobbying his brothers in Congress to be appointed in his place. To Deane and Franklin, however, William and Arthur Lee joined with Morris in demanding that Williams be replaced, leaving Thomas Morris and William Lee to run the commercial agency in tandem. The Paris commission was now sharply divided, with Deane and Franklin on one side, the Lees on the other, and Thomas Morris a foil the Lees adroitly manipulated.

All this would come clear to Morris months later, when letters from Deane, John Ross, and other principals finally caught up with him. Until then he was left to live with his fears about his brother's conduct, the doubts clouding all his engagements in the covert munitions trade. In the meantime, the secret committees had been reformed—the Secret Committee as the Committee of Commerce and the Committee of Secret Correspondence as the Committee for Foreign Affairs—and their business largely taken up by new members. It seemed like an opportune time to make a clean break.

But such a separation would require a thorough statement of the accounts of the Secret Committee, a "Herculean labor," as Morris termed it in September. In fact, he had been requested by Congress in January, and again in June, to provide accounts for all the secret transactions made under his auspices, but by the fall he had made little progress. Part of the problem was due to the nature of Secret Committee trade: because shipments of munitions violated neutrality agreements, virtually every Secret Committee cargo was loaded in haste and literally in the dark, and often without invoices. Surprise inspections by port authorities meant that cargoes were transferred from one ship to another, the contents left in jumbled confusion for the receivers in America to sort out. Private goods mixed with public cargoes added to the muddle. And financing was scrambled as well, with funds for failed contracts transferred to answer others, and proceeds from remittances applied to whatever ventures the different agents might be pursuing at the time.

Committee subcontractors did little to help matters. These shippers were required to provide invoices and vouchers to document their expenditures, but they encountered the same delays as the committee members themselves; accounts were usually tardy and often never rendered at all.

As a result, the committee's affairs were in turmoil. Many contracts were simply recorded in the minutes of committee meetings, compiled along with the orders issued to individual contractors. The progress of the war only compounded the disorder. Beginning with the departure of Congress to Baltimore, the papers of the committee were often in transit. With the move to Lancaster, they were on the road again, stalling any effort to sort out the accounts.

The removal to Manheim threw Morris's personal financial affairs into confusion as well. Thomas Willing had elected to stay in Philadelphia and test the limits of General Howe's benevolence; within a week of Morris's departure, Willing learned that bills they had drafted against trading partners in London totaling more than £36,000 had been rejected, leaving the firm unable to finance ventures or pay off creditors. "To have such a demand come upon me unprepared as I am to satisfy it, is terrible indeed," Willing wrote to Morris in dismay. He had always been the more cautious partner; this sudden setback sent him into a panic. "Ruin & a Jail, stare me in the face," he continued. "If the news is true, I fear I shall sink under it—you alone can calm my fears if it is false, or put me in a way to extricate myself if you believe it is true."

Two weeks later, Willing wrote again. It turned out the first reports he'd received had been exaggerated. Some transactions had been stalled when mail to England was blocked in New York, and several sizable payments were due to arrive soon in Philadelphia. Still, the firm was in arrears, due in large part to the shenanigans of Thomas Morris. "My good friend," Willing wrote carefully, "the accounts . . . of Tom's behavior in London lead me to believe he has injured Us with our friends there; his Dissipation, extravagance, and total neglect of them, & of all business, was a poor return for the Confidence & Credit given him—I fear he is not so well reclaimed from his folly's as you seem to think. . . . God grant he may now attend to bringing all our affairs to a conclusion; if he does not, or squanders the Substance in his hands, we shall be disgraced."

Remarkably, Willing never blamed Robert for his brother's antics, never chided him for placing Thomas in such a critical position. Instead he appealed to him as the one person with the sagacity to manage the various demands on their commercial house. "I beg of you to let me know what steps I shall take," Willing wrote, "tell me what you know of the matter, what funds we can use at present, & what prospect you have of providing against the whole extent of this unexpected demand."

Beyond the pressure of the immediate crisis, Willing missed the personal contact, the intimate collaboration that had marked their partnership for more than twenty years. "I lament from my soul this cruel separation from the Man that I love, & when I think of your banishment from that stage on which you have trod with such unrivalled reputation, I feel an Anguish not to be expressed." This was a rare display of emotion for a man renowned as a pillar of sober industry. "We cannot, must not part forever," Willing wrote. "This is your proper scene, & here we must one day meet again."

As it happened, their separation would last nine months, through a long winter of exile for the Congress, for Morris, and for the Continental Army. This interregnum, with the capital occupied and the rebel government dispersed, was a time of transition, retrenchment, and recrimination among revolutionary leaders state and national. None of the early zealots had anticipated such a protracted and difficult contest; with frustration building, the leaders began to lash out.

The state government set the tone. Upon removing from the capital to Lancaster, the Assembly canceled any plans for a political convention to revise the constitution, and then closed its sessions altogether. Power devolved to the Council of Safety, which ruled the state by decree and administered what one historian later called "a reign of terror." Bands of militia roamed the countryside, confiscating livestock, firewood, and other supplies from the "disaffected"—those citizens who declined to take the oath of allegiance to the state constitution. "The prevailing idea now," James Allen wrote in his diary, "is that no man has any property in what the public has use for. The militia . . . plunder without ceremony."

There was little recourse to the radical government. Some of the moderates wanted to continue fighting for the oft delayed plebiscite on the constitution, but Morris felt the moment had passed. As he explained to James Wilson, "I think it is dangerous to the state to give opposition whilst it is invaded. Let us settle the Grand Contest in favor of America, & then amend & alter the Constitution to the liking of the majority and the happiness of the whole." For the time being, opponents of the hard-line government would just have to lie low.

The new tenor in Congress was ushered in by the departure of John Hancock. As president Hancock had been diligent and evenhanded, but he never made much of an impact on the general administration; nor did he overcome the animosity of the radicals, especially those from his home state.

Upon announcing his decision to leave, Hancock gave a magnanimous speech thanking the delegates for their support, and praying that "every thing which may tend to distract or divide your councils be forever banished." That hope was dashed that very afternoon, when it was moved that the Congress return thanks to Hancock for his two years of service. The motion raised the hackles of the Eastern faction, who protested that "it is improper to thank any president for the discharge of the duties of that office." This stern pronouncement displayed both the particular disdain the radicals reserved for Hancock, and the moralistic frame of their worldview. The debate dragged through two roll-call votes until Hancock finally received his plaudits, with all four of his fellow delegates from Massachusetts voting against. Morris was not present for the vote, but Hancock made sure to remember him; before leaving York, he sent Morris funds to pay for a case of wine he had borrowed, and a gold knob for his walking stick, "a small token of his real regard & friendship."

With Hancock's departure the radicals sought to place Francis Lightfoot Lee, another of the Lee brothers, as president. But the full Congress was not ready to confer that sort of power on the Eastern faction; they settled instead on Henry Laurens of South Carolina, a wealthy plantation owner who had made his fortune in the slave trade. A sometime rival to the Charleston firebrand Christopher Gadsden, Laurens occupied middle ground between the radical and moderate delegates in Congress. He was not so politically adept as the Lees and the Adamses, but he shared their belief in American "virtue," and harbored the same mistrust of the moderates of Pennsylvania and New York. He called them "the property men," and determined early on that their self-interest could undermine the entire project of the Revolution.

"Our greatest enemies are within ourselves and not among those men who oppose us by arms or honestly and openly profess themselves averse from our measures and politics," Laurens wrote in August, soon after joining the Congress at Philadelphia. The true "enemies" were those who had balked at making the final break with England. It had been more than a year since the debates over independence, but to Laurens that remained the litmus test. "Almost every man of them were the most vigorous in opposing the measures of the British Ministry until they perceived that opposition proceeding to a serious War," Laurens observed, "then fear of the loss of life & estate shocked their faith. They wished to remain neuter [neutral], they still acknowledged that America had been greatly aggrieved but withdrew from the Councils and Society of their former colleagues under pretenses, some that Independence had been declared too soon, others that it had never been their design to be Independent."

This description seems tailored to John Dickinson, but would also easily encompass the rest of the moderates—Duer, John Jay, and certainly Robert Morris. From the outset, Laurens would regard their every act with suspicion. "They are cunning men," Laurens wrote, "and their cunning is exceedingly baneful to a cause which in their hearts they wish well. If we lose that Cause it will be the direct effect of their timidity & their pernicious examples."

If Laurens brought a critical eye to the national council, he was especially skeptical of Morris. Even before leaving South Carolina for Philadelphia, he heard mutterings among the traders on the docks at Charleston that members of the Secret Committee were shipping private goods on government vessels. Upon arriving at Congress, several delegates shared with him the same concern. The practice of mixing private and public cargoes in the committee ventures was raising eyebrows, and Morris was the center of suspicion.

Soon after Laurens was named president of Congress, Samuel and John Adams left York, Sam for Massachusetts and John as still another diplomat in Europe. But the Eastern faction remained the driving force in the government, under the adroit direction of James Lovell and Richard Henry Lee; Laurens would sometimes buffer them, and sometimes join them.

Through a most convoluted circumstance, Robert Morris found himself uncomfortably exposed early in November before the zealots of both the state and national governments. The unwitting instigator was John Brown, a former clerk in the Willing & Morris countinghouse, who was sent by Thomas Willing to deliver a secret message that originated with the British high command.

After a year of fighting, William Howe was still hoping to end the war via his peace commission rather than his artillery. On the morning of November 2 he sent a note from his quarters in Philadelphia to Willing, asking for a conference. When Willing obliged, Howe posed a series of questions: Was his partner, Robert Morris, still in Congress? Was it true Morris was still open to reconciliation? And were there any terms under which Congress might yet rescind the Declaration of Independence? To the first two queries, Willing answered with a qualified yes—he couldn't say for sure. As to the Declaration, Willing said he had never subscribed to the document, and rescinding it might yet be possible. But Willing was baffled by the thrust of Howe's inquiry; his understanding, as he put it to the general, was that "conquest and confiscation was his sole object."

Howe professed to be aghast. "How can that be?" he asked. This was not the rapacious commander of patriot propaganda. Howe was genial and earnest, as Willing recorded in a memoir of the meeting. "The consequence of the campaign must be ruin & destruction of the country," Willing quoted the general as saying. "I wish to avoid it with all my heart. . . . I had rather settle the matter in an amicable way than gain 10 victories."

Howe then laid out terms for a cease-fire: the rights of the colonists would be restored to the status of 1763—self-rule, no taxes, a general amnesty. The rebels might even retain their arms. Just return to the imperial fold, and "I should be glad to withdraw troops tomorrow and go home." These terms were all that the rebels had ever asked for, the sort of deal that might have averted the war in the first place. Much had passed since then, of course, but Willing thought the Congress might yet entertain the appeal. He sent for Brown, described to him Howe's offer, and dispatched him to deliver it to Morris. Willing then added his own endorsement. "I told him to tell Morris this was the proper time for America to make her bargain. . . . No blame can be imputed on us for being instruments, however unworthy, of conveying terms of peace to our bleeding country."

This last was a serious miscalculation. Brown set out the next morning, spent a night on the road, and, arriving at Manheim, waited three days for Morris to return from Congress. When Morris got there, late on a rainy Saturday night, Brown related the whole improbable tale. Morris then summoned William Duer, who was apparently staying at Manheim, and after a second interview with Brown, the two delegates returned to York to share the intelligence with Congress, where it was "freely spoken of."

Agreeable as the offer from Howe may have appeared to those still hoping for reconciliation, the majority in Congress regarded it as tantamount to treason, and a warrant was issued for John Brown's arrest on "suspicion that he is employed by the enemy for purposes inimical to these states." He was located in Lancaster and jailed by the Council of Safety, the charge now expanded to encompass "forming combinations with the enemy for betraying the United States into their hands."

This was not what Morris had in mind when he presented Howe's offer. He and Duer hustled Brown back to Lancaster to post bail, promising to turn him over to Congress. Back the trio went to York, their carriage lurching over the rutted rural roads, but the delegates refused to meet with Brown, and remanded him back into custody. Now the incident seemed to mushroom. Henry Laurens relayed news of Howe's overture to George Washington, who had never accepted his counterpart's avowed ambition for peace. "It has been the unvaried custom of the enemy from the commencement of the present contest to try every artifice and device to delude the people," Washington wrote Congress from his camp outside Philadelphia. "The message through John Brown was calculated for this end."

But if Washington dismissed Howe's entreaty out of hand, he was more flexible in assessing blame. "I am surprised Mr. Willing should suffer himself to be imposed on by such flimsy measures," he wrote. Fortunately for Brown, he and Willing had been active in getting supplies to American troops held by the British in the capital, and Washington pronounced him a "worthy, well-disposed man."

Still, Brown remained in jail, confined by a Council of Safety that found, after an inquiry, that "John Brown is employed to tell a ridiculous tale of peace . . . to gull us into a sham treaty." It was left to Morris to intervene. He could not spare the time for another visit to York, but he penned an ardent appeal to Thomas Wharton, who was sitting as president of the Council of Safety. Since Brown was "innocent in his intentions," Morris wrote, "I cannot feel myself easy whilst he is confined in jail."

Morris was aware, of course, that association with Brown could only undermine his stature at a time when passions against "collaborators" ran high throughout occupied Pennsylvania. But he made no effort to distance himself from Brown. He cited Washington's "unsolicited testimony" in Brown's behalf, then added his own. "My connections in business with Mr. Brown are well known; he was many years a faithful servant in my employ and is justly entitled to my Friendship." Morris pleaded that Brown be handed over to his custody; "I am certain his conduct and conversation will be such as cannot produce any evil consequences to the public."

Brown was finally released in January, his ordeal marking the close of William Howe's last bid for a negotiated peace. It was probably true, as Washington said, that Willing's part in the affair was ill-conceived, and that Morris was rash in conveying Brown's message to the full Congress. But if Morris was impetuous he was also fearless, and fiercely loyal. To his credit, though sometimes to his detriment, Morris was always ready to speak his mind.

It was not just the moderates and suspected Tories that came under scrutiny of the ideologues in this season of suspicion. In October and November, as the days grew short and the first flurries of snow blew east from the heights of the Allegheny Mountains, the leaders of the Revolution turned their skeptical eyes on their commander in chief.

George Washington had made one last effort to dislodge Howe in Octo-

ber, leading a three-pronged dawn assault on enemy positions at Germantown, five miles east of Philadelphia. But after an initial surge the American
forces were thrown back, leaving Howe in sole possession of the city. In
the weeks that followed, Washington was reduced to standing guard on the
outskirts of town as the enemy settled into the warm, sturdy town houses
of the rebel capital.

Two weeks after the defeat at Germantown, word arrived of a distinctly
different engagement on the west bank of the Hudson River at Saratoga,
two hundred miles north of Manhattan. After two days of battle, the northern division of the Continental Army, under Major General Horatio Gates,
forced the surrender of John Burgoyne and his entire army of five thousand
men. Gates himself never got close to the fighting, preferring to direct his
forces from a redoubt well to the rear; the hero of the day was Benedict Arnold, who was seriously wounded pressing flanking attacks from horseback
in defiance of direct orders that he retire. The other heroes of Saratoga,
unsung until long after, were Beaumarchais and Silas Deane, for it was the
arms delivered at Portsmouth that the American forces carried into battle.

Saratoga was a huge development, proving for the first time that the
American rebels could defeat British regulars in a pitched battle. And despite the passive role he played, the laurels for the victory went to Gates,
a former major in the English army who had moved to Virginia in 1772.
Preening, unctuous, and ambitious, Gates had fought alongside Washington in the French and Indian War, and when the Revolution came, Washington appointed him to high command. Now flush with victory, Gates
nurtured hopes of displacing Washington as chief of the rebel forces.

For Washington the victory at Saratoga came as a mixed blessing. It dramatically altered the landscape of the war, eliminating a serious threat from
the north and heartening devotees of the Revolution at home and abroad.
Yet it also threw into harsh light Washington's own performance, which,
aside from the bold thrust at Trenton, was marked by disappointment, defeat, and retreat.

It remains a testament to Washington's bearing and personal charisma
that, after two difficult years in command, he was still considered by Morris
and many others as indispensable to the cause. But this very stature made
the ideologues of the Eastern faction in Congress uneasy. They were leery
of the whole idea of centralized command, preferring instead the romantic notion of citizen soldiers directed by civilian committees. John Adams
grumbled early on about the "superstitious veneration" surrounding Washington; beginning in October, in their councils at York, Benjamin Rush,

James Lovell, and Richard Henry Lee—and in correspondence from Boston, Sam Adams—all raised their voices to question Washington's competence, his character, and his tenure.

Robert Morris took no part in the early stages of this debate. His goal remained a complete separation from the affairs of government, and in early November, he obtained from the Supreme Executive Council a formal six-month leave from his duties in Congress. Morris was overjoyed. He planned one last visit with the delegates at York; after that, "I expect to have more command of more time than has fallen to my lot for some years." But that final visit generated a new assignment—Morris was dispatched, with two other delegates, to visit Washington and "consider the best and most practicable means for carrying on a winter's campaign with vigor and success, an object which Congress have much at heart."

The obvious intent of sending this delegation was to spur Washington to action, as if the news from Saratoga wasn't incentive enough. But when Morris arrived at Whitemarsh, the camp Washington had established outside the city, the reality of the situation put such an offensive out of the question. The British forces were well entrenched, rendering any assault foolhardy. On the American side, the breakdown of the quartermaster and commissary departments, and the decline of the Continental currency, were taking a heavy toll. Officers were grumbling about inadequate pay, discipline was breaking down, and both officers and men lacked clothing for the winter. Weeks before the delegates arrived at camp, with the ground already frozen, Washington had offered a ten-dollar bounty for the best plan for fashioning shoes from raw hides. Little came of this scheme; by December, close to half his troops were barefoot.

As if to highlight Washington's predicament, William Howe marched his entire force out of Philadelphia to test the American position. For three days, the two armies feinted and skirmished, but the rebels held high ground and Howe decided against a major action. Watching the redcoats retreat to their fortifications, Morris and the other delegates from Congress shared Washington's sense of frustration. In conference the following day, the delegation agreed: there would be no winter campaign; Washington and his army would find shelter someplace suited for defense but close enough to Philadelphia to keep the British in check.

Then Morris and the committee went further. In resolutions penned by Morris, the committee proposed "That a reform may take place in the army, and a proper discipline be introduced, we wish to see the Military placed on such a footing as to make a Commission a desirable object to the Officer, and his Rank preserved from degradation and contempt." With that preamble, the committee recommended that officers be promised a pension of half-pay for life, commencing at the end of the war.

The plan had the virtue of being deferred compensation—Congress would not need to produce the funds until the fighting was over. But it stood in direct contradiction to the ideology of the Revolution. In New England especially, patriots feared that pensioned soldiers would corrupt the virtuous social order they were fighting to establish. As James Lovell put it to Sam Adams, pensions represented a "mode of introducing into Society a set of haughty idle imperious Scandalizers of industrious Citizens and Farmers." Most of the Eastern faction in Congress agreed, and the proposal was tabled.

Washington broke camp at Whitemarsh the night of December 10. The delegates from Congress made their way east to York; the army followed more slowly, delayed along the way by a clash with a mounted force under Cornwallis. The British raiders repulsed an American vanguard and made off with two thousand sheep and cattle; the rebel army trudged on, short of food, many shoeless, until they reached a frozen notch in the hills called Valley Forge.

Morris arrived back at Manheim to find that the impending scandal over the conduct of his brother had finally burst. He was dismayed to find two letters from John Ross, written in August and September but only arriving December 17. Now it was confirmed, in the most vivid terms, that Thomas was incapacitated by drink, defiant of intervention, and a tool in the hands of his merchant associates in Nantes.

Morris reacted swiftly, his pace quickened by chagrin. The day he received the news from Ross he drew up three letters, the first to the Committee of Commerce at York, the second to the firm Pliarne & Penet, and the third a draft of a formal communication from the committee to his brother. To the committee he explained that he'd been misled by Thomas and his partners until "alas the scene is changed and this day I had the Mortification to receive a letter from my confidential friend [Ross] assuring me that my Brother's Conduct is exceedingly blamable." To Pierre Penet he ordered that all accounts be promptly settled and closed. And to Thomas, Morris wrote, "We have received Authentic information through your Brother [this in Robert's hand], that you have unhappily preferred dissipation to business and are so bent on the pursuit of pleasures as to be an improper Agent. . . . You are therefore, hereby dismissed."

This was just the first round in a virtual parade of contrition that lasted through the end of the year. On Christmas Eve, Morris wrote to John Brown, the secretary of the Marine Committee (and no relation to the Willing & Morris clerk), "I am sorely hurt by his [Thomas's] conduct and mortified to the very Soul. . . . I have now done with him forever." Days later he wrote Franklin to apologize for doubting him and Deane: "I blame myself much for having written that unfortunate letter of the 29th June to Mr. Deane, and more so for having given way to Suspicions that I am now perfectly convinced were injurious to you and him. . . . It is said that repenting sinners are entitled to forgiveness and in that case I am sure Mr. Deane and you must receive me back."

But his most elaborate confession and appeal was to Henry Laurens. Just months into his presidency, Laurens had established himself as an independent force in Congress, exercising the powers of his office with more vigor than Hancock ever did. He was also officious, censorious, and a stickler for detail, much to the dismay of the overburdened secretary of Congress, Charles Thomson.

Morris sought to salvage his reputation before this imperious southern solon with a lengthy discourse drafted the day after Christmas. He detailed the entire story of his dealings with his brother, from their shared paternity to Thomas's early performance in the countinghouse, from his travels in Europe to his congressional appointment. Robert glossed over the doubts about Thomas that he'd shared with friends along the way. "No part of his conduct had ever given me the least cause to suspect any want of integrity," Morris asserted. "Could I have had the least idea of what has happened, I would sooner have perished than he should have been trusted."

At this point Robert was protesting too much. There had been plenty of warnings that Thomas was spinning out of control, warnings Morris had ignored. But his flaw had been more pride than avarice, and his anguish in the end appeared genuine enough. "My distress is more than I can describe," he wrote Laurens. "To think that in the midst of the most ardent exertions I was capable of making to promote the interest & welfare of my country I should be the means of introducing a worthless wretch to disgrace and discredit it, is too much to bear."

Laurens judged this performance "very affecting," and among the moderates in Congress Morris's reputation for integrity and competence remained largely intact. In the eighteenth century nepotism was taken as a matter of course, as was, apparently, the possibility of human foibles. It may have been that the cohesive nature of family ties in that era tempered the impulse to righteous indignation—everyone had a crazy uncle or a wastrel son in their immediate circle. But for whatever reason, despite the caustic language that characterized political debate, it was rare to find family association invoked against an adversary. Ben Franklin's only son, for example, was the Tory governor of New Jersey, but while that was a source of deep resentment for Franklin, it was rarely mentioned by even his most severe critics.

The letters from Europe, and Morris's abrupt turn against his brother, came too late to arrest the harm done to the American mission in France. Thomas had created serious problems, both for the government and for the Willing & Morris firm, by mishandling cargoes and accounts, but that malfeasance might have been repaired. More lasting damage arose from the rift between the Lees and their fellow commissioners—Deane and Franklin.

The ostensible cause of the division was William Lee's resentment at the employment of Franklin's nephew Jonathan Williams. Lee recognized, as he wrote to Richard Henry Lee in September, that Thomas Morris was "actually in a continual state of madness from inebriety and intemperance." But Lee also knew that his own appointment as commercial agent rested on the same authority as Thomas Morris's had; his only recourse was to push Williams aside and form a makeshift partnership with Morris. But Deane and Franklin remained steadfast in support of Williams. Their own effort to get Thomas recalled had been rebuffed early in the year by Congress and by Robert Morris, and they found Williams perfectly capable as Thomas's stand-in.

Around this time, William Lee received a new appointment; he was paired with Ralph Izard, a South Carolina merchant then staying in Paris, as diplomatic emissaries—Lee to Prussia and Vienna, Izard to Tuscany. This was part of the new, more aggressive strategy of "militia diplomacy" adopted in Congress under the influence of Richard Henry Lee and James Lovell. But those European courts had no interest in the American rebels, and Lee and Izard remained in Paris. They were joined there in December by Arthur Lee after his own mission to Berlin ended in embarrassment, his papers purloined by spies and his petition spurned by the king.

Frustrated and idle, living on government expense, the Lee brothers and Izard spent the weeks that followed fulminating against Franklin and Deane. The appointment of Williams over Thomas Morris, they decided, was a scheme to disguise "public plunder," and they made it their job to unmask the evildoers.

To Arthur Lee, the Jonathan Williams agency was just a sideshow in a larger, more nefarious plot. The key was Hortalez & Co., the false front created by Beaumarchais. Lee had learned of this subterfuge when it was first conceived; as he now recalled his early talks with the playwright-diplomat, the munitions were to be supplied free to America. The whole project of getting remittances back was a ploy designed by Deane and Beaumarchais to enrich themselves!

This version of the Hortalez project was either diabolical—a fabrication by Lee designed to discredit Deane—or delusional; one historian termed it "evidently a failure of memory." The fact was that even in his preliminary discussions with Lee, back in 1776, Beaumarchais had made it clear that remittances were critical to his operation. Lee acknowledged the terms in writing at the time, and those letters remained in Beaumarchais's hands. Now, in the fall of 1777, Lee asserted the opposite: the arms were a gift from France to America, no return shipments were required, and any remittances were "gratuitous."

Lee made these charges officially, to the Committee on Foreign Affairs, and privately, to his brother and to Sam Adams; he suggested the only remedy was to recall Deane and Franklin. At the same time, in Paris, both William and Arthur Lee disputed every decision requiring joint consent of the commissioners and complained constantly over perceived slights to their dignity. Protesting to Deane the appointment of Jonathan Williams, William Lee complained in December that "you have as good a right to order your servant to take the coat off my back and put it on his own." Lee continued with the vow, "I pass over in silence, with Christian forbearance, the personal injustice and injury that has been done to me." The letter itself, of course, rendered that statement absurd.

Annoying as William Lee could be, Arthur was even worse, prompting Deane and Franklin to close ranks against his wheedling demands. In Arthur's presence they maintained a frosty cordiality, but between themselves, only half in jest, Deane and Franklin diagnosed his disposition as mental illness; to his friend Bancroft, Deane wrote in January, "Arthur Lee must be shaved and bled, or he will be actually mad for life."

Franklin had longer personal experience with Lee, and understood that Lee would exact a price for being ignored. He wrote to James Lovell in December to preempt Lee with a defense of Deane's conduct. Deane was, Franklin wrote, "an able, faithful, active, and extremely useful servant of the public, a testimony I think it my duty to take this occasion of giving to his merit unasked, as . . . I perceive he has enemies." Franklin also assured

Lovell and Congress that Deane had done all he could to avoid encumbering the army with French volunteers. "I, who am upon the spot . . . know of the infinite difficulty of resisting the powerful solicitations of great men who, if disobliged, might have it in their power to obstruct the supplies [Deane] was then obtaining."

But Franklin's intervention, like Robert Morris's with his brother, came too late. In November, on the motion of Richard Henry Lee, Congress stripped Deane of his commission and recalled him from Paris. "He died at the last very easie," recorded William Williams, a delegate from of Connecticut, "though there had been at sundry times before, the most violent and convulsive throes and exertions on the same question." How Deane's constituency evaporated is unclear, but Robert Morris's pique over Deane's failure to chaperone Thomas was one likely factor.

For his part, Richard Henry Lee said he moved for recall simply because anger in Congress against the French officers had made Deane's position untenable. "I find myself obliged to think that he has pursued his best judgment for the good of his Country," Lee wrote soothingly to Samuel Adams. Of course, Lee was aware that Deane's departure would make more room for his brothers in Europe, but he was too circumspect to share this prospect with Adams. Instead, he confided obliquely, "This is a matter of great delicacy."

Word of Deane's recall did not reach the commissioners until the spring. News of the victory at Saratoga traveled much faster, and in the interim, helped to break the stalemate with Vergennes. Convinced now that the Revolution might actually be viable—and concerned that the British might now seek a settlement with the rebels—Vergennes got word to Deane he was willing to enter into a formal, public alliance with Congress.

This was the prize that Deane and Franklin had been striving for. A treaty would mean continued French aid, and possibly a war between France and England, forcing King George to contend with multiple foes. The details were hammered out in a series of meetings, and the treaty signed on February 6. Arthur Lee proved contentious to the end, arguing that he should sign the treaty twice, in deference to his dual appointment to the courts of France and Spain. Vergennes's deputy, Conrad Gerard, finally had to step in to mediate, and signatures were affixed—one per diplomat.

Despite this signal achievement, there was little mirth in the American mission at Paris. The feud with the Lees had cast a pall over all their endeavors, and now tragedy began to haunt their affairs. Deane, already weighed down by work and bickering, learned in October from a newspaper that his wife had died in Connecticut. In late January, Penet's partner, Emmanuel de Pliarne, one of the arms dealers who set the whole munitions trade in motion, drowned while attempting to cross the Potomac. That same day, poisoned with alcohol and despair, Thomas Morris died in his room at a Nantes lodging house.

Even in death, Thomas Morris served as a pawn in a game played by stronger, willful men. His decease set off an unseemly scramble among the contending parties in the American mission, their objective being the locked chest where Thomas kept his commercial papers. The chest was held by the local police, who would release it only on authority of the commissioners in Paris. John Ross appealed to Franklin and Deane that they order the papers released to him in his capacity as private agent for Robert Morris, but, wary of offending the Lees, the commissioners deferred to William Lee. Thus it was Lee who first secured the trunk, and spent four days combing it, seeking evidence of malfeasance. Apparently he found none, as none of the many accusations he made later derived from the Thomas Morris trove.

At this point Ross arrived at Nantes and demanded that Lee turn over any private papers pertaining to Robert Morris. Lee, of course, refused, setting off a dispute that dragged on for weeks. Lee finally consented to turn the papers over to Ross under the supervision of Deane and Franklin, and carted the chest to Paris for the handoff. But Deane found better things to do on the appointed day, and Franklin flat declined to serve as arbiter in this messy dispute. Lee finally left the trunk, locked, in Franklin's custody, where it remained for more than a year. This closed the quarrel over the papers, but opened a festering feud between the Lee brothers and Ross, and, by extension, Robert Morris. Hereafter, the Lees included Morris in their suspicion that private interest had polluted the public project at Paris.

In the meantime, Thomas Morris was buried. To those who knew Thomas in his waning days, the funeral he received must have evoked the uneasy discomfort of a black farce. His trading partner at Nantes, Pierre Penet, arranged for services "conducted in the most genteel and decent manner a Popish country will allow the Protestant religion"—a nighttime procession of forty-eight servants, each carrying a lighted torch, attended by several thousand spectators. John Paul Jones, the celebrated seafarer who considered Robert Morris his patron, happened to be in port fitting out a privateer, and contributed a thirteen-gun salute.

Penet described this pageant in a detailed letter to Robert, but if he was hoping to exploit the sentiment of a bereaved sibling, his efforts were wasted. When he learned of Thomas's demise, Robert expressed only stern resentment. "He has paid the last tribute to his follies and vices by a premature death which I consider the best thing that could have befallen him," Robert wrote in May. "I lament only his loss of virtue, not the loss of the man whom I had determined to renounce."

The fractious arguments dividing the American mission in France were matched, even exceeded, by the growing discontent in Congress and in the army. The chaos in the commissary and quartermaster departments left the soldiers at Valley Forge to suffer the blasts of December without tents, with few blankets, and, for days at a stretch, with no food. Delegates demanded answers there and at the hospital department, where thousands of sick and dying soldiers were warehoused with insufficient staff, medicine, or bedclothes. "In short," James Lovell summarized in a report to Sam Adams, "every great Plumb pudding that Congress has ever made has produced quarreling & envy, more or less, on this and the other side of the water."

Lovell was himself deeply engaged in the one dispute that actually threatened to destroy the rebel government—the drive to unseat George Washington. Frustration with the general crested during the two weeks Morris spent at the camp at Whitemarsh. Lovell and Richard Henry Lee took the lead, along with Benjamin Rush, in a sub-rosa bid to replace Washington with Horatio Gates. They collaborated with disgruntled members of the army itself, principally Thomas Mifflin and, not surprisingly, Gates himself.

Mifflin was especially audacious. A personal aide to Washington in the early stages of the war, Mifflin spent most of 1777 as quartermaster general, and his poor performance contributed to the desperate shortages that plagued the army in Pennsylvania. Mifflin resigned this critical post in October and began agitating in earnest against his former commander, huddling at his estate in Reading with disgruntled officers and anti-Washington delegates. In November, Mifflin was handed a platform when he was named to a newly constituted Board of War that would revise the administration of the army. Mifflin pressed Richard Henry Lee to add Gates to this body, and Lee agreed.

Washington learned of the resentments rising against him in an explicit letter from Lafayette, who was briefly visiting York. "There are open dissentions in Congress," Lafayette confided to his mentor, "parties who hate one another as much as the common enemy; men who, without knowing anything about war, undertake to judge you and to make ridiculous comparisons. They are infatuated with Gates."

All these maneuvers were undertaken with great caution, as Washington remained the most prominent—and most popular—public figure in the Revolution. But Mifflin spoke candidly in a letter he sent Gates urging him to hasten south from New York. "The list of our disgusted patriots is long and formidable—their resentments keen against the reigning cabal"—this a reference to Washington and his commanders. "This army will be totally lost unless you come down here & collect the virtuous Band who wish to fight under your banner."

Gates did indeed come to York, and was named president of the new Board of War in late November. Among its first acts, as if to confirm its status as a rival center of command, the board named Thomas Conway, a French officer and a committed critic of Washington, as inspector general of the army. This was more than Washington could swallow. "I have been a slave to the service," Washington wrote to Lee, "but it will be impossible for me to be of any further service if such insuperable obstacles are placed in my way."

Conway got his appointment, but Washington's threat to resign froze any new advances against his authority. Washington was fortunate, too, in the allegiance of Henry Laurens, whose son John was a member of Washington's inner circle, an aide-de-camp who served along with Alexander Hamilton and Tench Tilghman. As president, Laurens was able to track the covert maneuvers of Washington's enemies, a clique historians later dubbed the "Conway Cabal." Subtle and always fearful of public exposure, this group was described by Laurens as "prompters and actors, accommodators, Candle snuffers, Shifters of scenes, and mutes."

Word of the schemes against Washington traveled slowly, even within the high councils of the government, but by January the general's allies were rising to his defense. Robert Morris learned of the intrigues from Richard Peters, who had retained his position on the Board of War despite his loyalty to Washington. Peters reported to Morris that he himself had been accused of plotting against the general, and asked Morris to denounce any such rumors. Soon after, Morris heard from Tench Tilghman as well. "You must have seen and heard some thing of a party forming against him," Tilghman wrote from Valley Forge. "I have never seen any stroke of ill fortune affect the General in the manner that this dirty underhanded dealing has done. It hurts him the more because he cannot take notice of it without publishing to the World that the spirit of faction begins to work among us."

This last point seems almost naive today, but was considered critical at the time. In leading what was still a novel Revolution, the Congress was striving to project a public face of unanimity and purity of purpose. The wrangling and backbiting might be a routine by-product of democratic politics, but for appearances' sake, it all had to be concealed from public view.

In his reply to Peters, Morris made clear where his loyalties lay: "I really think it a horrid thing that mankind should ever combine to support each other in unworthy attacks on Worthy Characters." Morris had personal ties to both Mifflin and Gates, but he immediately recognized the larger implications of the threat to Washington. "The General will not suffer alone in any loss of character, his Country and his Country's Cause will inevitably suffer more or less with him. . . . Let us therefore withstand these attempts against the first Man in this World & unite our endeavors to procure him such Force as will enable him to shine with that Splendor he Merits."

Morris had by this time embarked on the leave of absence he had obtained, but then delayed, back in November. His retreat was interrupted by several trips to consult with Congress at York, but he spent most of the time at Manheim, enjoying his family and entertaining with his customary, munificent hospitality. Congress might have been driven from the capital, but Morris lived out this interregnum like a baron on his fief, with servants, stables, and a courtyard where the clatter of hooves and coaches echoing off cobblestones announced the arrival of powerful friends from government, business, and the army.

Officials attending Congress at York frequently stopped by for a respite at Manheim. General Horatio Gates made the trip, as did Baron von Steuben, the Prussian soldier of fortune who would introduce martial discipline to the ragged troops at Valley Forge. Delegates from Congress visited as well, especially Morris's legislative ally William Duer, a wealthy lawyer, merchant, and landowner who shared his host's devotion to fine wine. Another frequent guest was Mary's brother William White; he had recently been ordained an Episcopal priest, and had accepted appointment as chaplain to Congress. William was close to his sister and very fond of Robert.

The Castle at Manheim was capacious, but life never returned to the comfortable routine of the city. The Morris household was shaken during this time by the flight of Hero, one of several domestic slaves, who made his way back to occupied Philadelphia. Morris asked Thomas Willing to seek out Hero and send him back, but the elderly servant would not be moved. Willing located Hero living in a hovel in one of the city's cramped side alleys. "I tried every way to get him to come to me," he wrote Morris. "I saw and talked with him but all in vain. He said you were a good Master, but he don't like the country & cannot consent to go out." Willing let the matter rest there.

Morris was insulated at Manheim from the constant interruptions of office, but his days were full of work. With the principals separated by armies in the field, he had decided to dissolve the house of Willing & Morris, a partnership that had prospered for more than twenty years. At the same time, he set about rendering the accounts of the Secret Committee. The books had been delayed at York until late December; now he could undertake the task in earnest.

Morris set to it with a sense of urgency, as the wheel of recrimination in Congress was now turning against him. Morris heard the first rumblings in early February, when Duer and another delegate alerted him that, as Morris put it later, "some matters to my prejudice had been insinuated by a Member in Congress respecting these books." Morris was being delicate here; the source of the "insinuations" was Henry Laurens, who complained loudly of "the great expenditures of Money by the Secret Committee . . . and the unsettled state of their accounts." Until now, Congress had been content to let Morris direct the affairs of the munitions trade on his own. Now the president, in league with the Eastern faction, was questioning Morris's integrity.

Morris responded with a combination of energy and indignation that would become increasingly familiar to his adversaries in the government. He produced a series of reports detailing his tobacco ventures, public and private; his statement of the "mysterious Commerce" with Hortalez; and his orders rerouting outgoing cargoes from Thomas Morris to John Ross. These he submitted along with an offer to return the books to the committee immediately. They were welcome to sort out the mess themselves.

This produced what amounted to an apology from Congress, along with a hint at the source of the criticism. The Committee of Commerce, by then depleted to just two members, had no problem with Morris's performance; in fact they were glad for him to retain their books, and would continue to consult him "whenever we find ourselves embarrassed."

What had riled the committee, and provoked resentment in Congress at large, was a decision Morris had taken in November in one of his last acts as a committee member. He had commissioned, without consulting Congress, an armed venture sending Thomas Willing's brother James down the Mississippi to collect gunpowder from James Pollock, the Continental agent in New Orleans. Along the way, Willing was to capture or destroy any British settlements he encountered on the river, and consult with Pollock about further ventures against enemy posts east of New Orleans. James Willing had lived for several years at Natchez, and had traveled to Philadelphia in the fall to propose the venture.

Considering the wide range of missions previously authorized by the committee, this expedition was fairly unexceptional. But as Morris well knew, it was a politically volatile assignment. The Board of War in July had proposed a more ambitious military expedition to the south, which won enthusiastic support from Morris, Duer, Benjamin Harrison, and others. But the plan was scotched after two days of debate, due chiefly to the opposition of Henry Laurens. By staging the Willing expedition, Morris had quietly circumvented Laurens.

In the event, James Willing proved to be something of a counterpart to Thomas Morris—fond of drink and hard to manage. His expedition did indeed flush the enemy from their settlements on the Mississippi, but it also prompted the British to fortify their defenses at Pensacola and other key posts. And once he arrived in New Orleans, Willing tarried for months, taxing Pollock's resources and straining relations with the Spanish governor. When Willing finally departed, it was by sea; his vessel was captured and Willing spent a year in British custody in New York.

This was all in the future; in question in February was how the mission got started in the first place. It was during a hearing before the Committee of Commerce that word of the Willing expedition leaked out to the full Congress. That prompted the controversy over the committee books, but as one member reported to Morris, it was the expedition that caused the resentment: "Some of the members were dissatisfied with that undertaking."

From this point forward, Laurens seemed to mark Morris as an outright adversary. His misgivings appeared confirmed in April, when a report reached him that John Swanwick, a clerk in Morris's employ, was accused of traitorous correspondence with the enemy. Laurens called on Morris to make "the immediately most diligent and effectual inquiry"; it was the John Brown affair all over again.

The facts of the case were a bit more innocuous. Swanwick's father was indeed a Tory, a former British excise officer who gained notoriety as a zealous wagon master during the enemy occupation of Philadelphia. The crime of his son John, then just fifteen years of age, was of trading letters with his father.

Morris handled the matter carefully, promising a "strict examination," which he conducted with a lieutenant colonel from the army standing in as witness. He reported back a week later, assuring Laurens of Swanwick's "perfect innocence."

The rift between Morris and Laurens assumed more historic dimensions in the debate over half-pay pensions. This provision, first raised by Morris in December, was revived after a second committee was sent to camp in January. Shortages of food and clothing were the obvious, pressing challenges confronting the troops at Valley Forge, but Washington was also beset with constant requests from officers seeking leave or outright dismissal. Substantial pensions, Washington was convinced, were the only means to maintain the officer corps. "I do most religiously believe," he said in April, "that the salvation of the cause depends on it."

Unfortunately for the general and for his supporters in Congress, Henry Laurens opposed the measure just as strongly. "It would lay the foundation of a standing army, of an Aristocracy," Laurens wrote. Every American made sacrifices; soldiers should fight for patriotism, not compensation. The president had joined his son John to defend Washington against his disgruntled commanders, but now he cleaved to the New England stalwarts. So firm were his convictions, the senior Laurens declared, that "had I heard of the Loss of half my Estate, the amount would not have involved my mind in such fixed concern as I feel from the introducing of this untoward project."

But faced with the prospect of actual dissolution of the army, the Eastern faction itself was divided. Torn between their republican ideology and their home state general, the revolutionary leaders from Virginia—especially the Lee brothers, Francis Lightfoot and Richard Henry—defected to the moderates. With the familiar party lines breaking down, debate over half-pay dragged out for more than a month. Leading the opposition to Laurens were William Duer and Gouverneur Morris, a new delegate from New York and key member of the committee conferring with Washington. Laurens fought the moderates to a standstill in endless argument—"We murder time," cursed Charles Carroll of Maryland; "chat it away in idle impertinent talk."

Another issue that was killing congressional time was the question of union. Even before the prospect of war with England arose, Ben Franklin,

John Dickinson, and other champions of American liberty had been calling for the separate colonies to band together. But now they were in command of their own affairs, the delegates at York found that union raised thorny issues of sovereignty that would bedevil them until years after the war.

How would the new states of America be represented in the national forum—by population, or as equal entities? How should taxes be assessed—by land values or by some other measure—and should the new national government levy them at all? And who would resolve the question of competing claims to frontier lands, claims that had roiled relations between the colonies for years?

Congress resolved in April to tackle these issues in earnest, setting aside two days of every week to hammer out a pact they called the Articles of Confederation. The first step was easy enough; all agreed that the states would remain sovereign, combining as a league to address matters of national scope. But that raised the question of what powers the central government might exercise, and talks began to drag, through September and on into November. The final result was what might expect from a council of wary new states—a "league of friendship" under which "Each State retains its sovereignty." Questions of war and peace were the province of the national Congress, and Congress could borrow and spend to mount armed forces, but was barred from levying taxes; all other affairs civil and fiscal were reserved to the states. The Articles were wordy and convoluted—"a little deformed," one delegate wrote to an absent colleague, "you will think it a Monster." But it was "the best that could be adapted to the circumstances," and on November 15 the Articles were forwarded to the states for ratification.

As he was on leave from Congress Robert Morris was secluded at Manheim for much of the wrangling on these important questions, but he rejoined the delegates in the spring and played a role in both. On March 5, 1778, after the Articles were endorsed by the state Assembly, Morris singed the document in the name of Pennsylvania. Other states held out, however, and the Articles would not take force for another three years.

The question of half-pay did not come to a head until May, when its opponents proposed referring the measure to the states for decision—a backhanded way to kill it. With the two Pennsylvania delegates in attendance divided, Duer and Gouverneur Morris sent an urgent appeal asking Robert to attend for the vote. "Massachusetts is against us," Gouverneur urged. "Think one moment and come here the next."

Morris did as he was bade, arriving in time to swing the Pennsylvania delegation into opposition, and the measure was defeated six states to five. Days later Laurens reluctantly agreed to a compromise: officers would receive half-pay for seven years, but not for life; and soldiers and noncommissioned officers who stayed through the end of the war would receive a bonus of eighty dollars. The new terms won the endorsement of every state, with just two hard-line delegates from New England—Lovell of Massachusetts and Oliver Wolcott of Connecticut—voting in opposition.

As with the Articles, this was not the end of the struggle over half-pay. It raised defining questions of the Revolution—the status of the army, the powers of the national government, the contest between "virtue" and "Mammon," as Laurens termed it—and Congress would revisit the issue repeatedly in the coming years. But the vote was a stinging setback for Laurens, and surely confirmed his worst impressions of Robert Morris.

As well, the episode signaled the arrival of Gouverneur Morris as a figure on the national scene. Just twenty-five years old, Gouverneur was descended from one of the great families that dominated politics in New York and was raised on a landed estate overlooking the East River in what is now the Bronx. A lawyer known for his brilliant mind and a rapier wit, Morris was full of contradiction—thoughtful but sometimes whimsical, a tireless worker but also a famous hedonist, a born aristocrat who lobbied for reconciliation but who helped author the revolutionary constitution in New York.

He was no relation to Robert Morris, but the two shared a devotion to fine wine, hard work, and General Washington—in 1776, Gouverneur had been Washington's liaison to the New York provincial Congress, and formed a deep attachment to the Virginian. Robert Morris clearly enjoyed the time he spent with the audacious young delegate, and came to refer to him playfully as "my namesake." Their collaboration in promoting half-pay inaugurated a lasting friendship and a core political alliance.

While Congress wrestled with its internal divisions, two ships bearing contending diplomatic missions were making their way across the Atlantic. The *Andromeda*, dispatched from England, carried a new, five-member peace commission that would present new terms of conciliation authorized by the prime minister, Lord North. The second was the *Sensible*, a warship that put out from Brest bearing Silas Deane's brother Simeon, who carried copies of the new treaty with France.

It appeared, for a time, as if the outcome of the American rebellion hung on the race between these two vessels; that the British terms so fully answered the colonial grievances that, absent the surety of a foreign alliance, the Congress would actually accept accommodation. At least the British commissioners hoped so. And while the *Sensible* arrived first, her captain had to steer north to avoid the Royal Navy, depositing Simeon Deane at Casco Bay on April 13. The *Andromeda* reached New York a day later, and the terms of appeasement were immediately published in the loyalist press.

It soon became apparent, however, that three years of fighting had pushed American resentment beyond any terms of reunion. George Washington set the tone, writing Congress on April 17 to denounce "this insidious proceeding," and exhort the delegates to "expose in the most striking manner the injustice, delusion, and fraud it contains."

This reaction came as little surprise; the members of the peace commission were aware that similar entreaties from Howe had been summarily dismissed. One of the commissioners decided on his own not to await the event, but to stage a private campaign to obtain a more charitable hearing. George Johnstone was a former royal governor of West Florida and a vocal defender of the colonists in Parliament; he had several longtime friends now sitting in Congress, and made personal appeals to them sweetened with the promise of a substantial reward for a successful intervention.

Robert Morris was one of those friends, and was the first to receive one of Johnstone's letters. But even for Morris, the days of holding out for a reprieve from the king were over. Whether chastened by the experience of John Brown, or hardened, like the rest of the Congress, by the ordeals of the war, Morris immediately notified Henry Laurens of this backchannel entreaty, and forwarded Johnstone's letter to him. The missive "unfolded to me what I suspected from the first," Morris wrote; "the government of Great Britain are alarmed at our forming Foreign alliances and from that apprehension have sprung Lord North's Conciliatory Measures." The Johnstone letter was read before the full Congress on April 27.

A week later, after a grueling passage overland from Maine, Simeon Deane arrived at York. Now all doubts were wiped away. The upstart colonists had won the open endorsement of one of the great powers of Europe. Spain would follow suit a year later, though only by half—she would ally secretly with France against England, but never entered an alliance with the Americans. Still, the nature of the game had been altered dramatically. On May 4, Congress ratified the treaty with France and issued a fresh call to the patriots of America. "Arise then! To your tents, and gird you for the battle!"

That same day, the benighted members of the peace commission arrived in Philadelphia. Untenable as their effort already appeared, they were stunned to find Delaware Bay crowded with hundreds of ships brought in to evacuate loyalist families from the American capital. Unbeknownst to the peace commissioners, the Howe brothers had been recalled and replaced by one of their sharpest critics, General Henry Clinton, with orders to consolidate the British forces at New York.

William Howe had lost his command, but he tarried in Philadelphia another six weeks. He and his army had enjoyed a comfortable winter in the city, and Howe consented when his officers proposed a lavish fete in his honor, a twelve-hour costume pageant that its organizers dubbed the "Mischianza." While Howe's men prepared for this most inapt extravaganza, the peace commission did what it could to revive its project, making several direct appeals to Congress, but each was ignored. On June 16, the commission's last day in Philadelphia, Johnstone again took matters in his own hands. He wrote new letters to Morris and to Joseph Reed, both reputed holdouts for reconciliation.

It was a slim chance, made even less likely when Johnstone included in each appeal an overt promise of a bribe; to Morris he suggested "that honors and emoluments should naturally follow the fortune of those who have steered the vessel in the storm and brought her safely into port." Morris turned his letter over to Laurens and it was later published in the Philadelphia press.

On June 17 the peace commissioners sailed from Philadelphia to New York. They continued issuing proposals from the loyalist stronghold there, but their entreaties produced only ridicule. This brought to ignominious conclusion the ill-starred effort to solve through negotiation the dispute between England and her colonies. It was fitting that their last-ditch appeal was to Morris, the man who cried out, two years before, "Where the plague are the commissioners!" He had been England's most sympathetic ally in the rebel government; now he, too, had turned his back on his former countrymen.

When Johnstone wrote this final appeal, Morris was at Valley Forge for another conference with Washington. He found the army in far better shape than at Whitemarsh in December. The ranks were reinforced with new recruits, an esprit de corps had been introduced by Baron von Steuben, and the new head of the commissary, Jeremiah Wadsworth, was acting with vigor, securing flour from New York and cattle from Connecticut. The privation and sufferings of the long hard winter were over.

The British army departed Philadelphia on June 18, sending their heavy equipment by water and marching north with Henry Clinton. Washington convened a council of war where it was decided not to confront Clinton, but to await an opportunity to strike at his columns in their progress through New Jersey. For the time being, Washington assigned Benedict Arnold, still hobbled by the leg wound he sustained at Saratoga, to enter the capital and maintain order.

Morris knew he'd be returning to Manheim to collect his family, but he could not resist the temptation to see firsthand the state of his longtime hometown. Traveling with an advance guard a day ahead of Arnold's column, he entered Philadelphia on June 18, three hours after the last of the redcoats had departed.

Chapter 7

THE RETURN OF
SILAS DEANE

Approaching Philadelphia from the north, Morris surveyed a landscape transformed by war. The fine country estates on the outskirts of town—The Hills included—had been gutted or leveled outright, fences torn up and trees cut down. "Nothing but wanton desolation," one early visitor recorded. Entering the city itself, Morris and his friends found many of the buildings abandoned and the air fouled by stench, filth, and clouds of flies. "The Town exceedingly Dirty & disagreeable, stinks Intolerably," Jonathan Maxwell Nesbitt, one of Morris's companions, wrote to a friend. The floor of the State House had been opened for use as a latrine. Close by, British soldiers had dug a great, open pit where they dumped the bodies of dead prisoners and starved horses.

The physical state of the shattered capital was startling to a longtime resident like Morris, who told a friend that "my mind was much engaged in contemplating the ravages of a cruel and merciless enemy." What most struck Morris was the "thin visages and meager carcasses" of those who had endured the occupation. The loyalists had spent the winter enjoying balls and feasts with their British patrons, but most of them had departed; those who remained had survived the winter on short rations, their privation reflected in their "lank bodies."

Morris spent a week in town. He was on hand the morning of June 19 when thousands of spectators cheered the arrival of Benedict Arnold. And he probably enjoyed a reunion with Thomas Willing, who had remained during the occupation with his wife and ten children. Willing had walked a fine line, refusing to take loyalty oaths either to the crown or to Pennsylvania; finally in May, under threat of forfeiture of his estate, he swore fealty to the state, but his delay was long remembered by the patriot activists.

The week in town also afforded Morris a firsthand view of General Arnold's new and brazenly corrupt civic administration. Whether due to the wound he received at Saratoga, or the plaudits awarded to Horatio Gates, Arnold had become embittered, and apparently decided to obtain some measure of compensation. Within days of his arrival, Arnold issued an order closing the city's shops and ordering all merchants to report their holdings to the army, in order that commissaries might purchase whatever they deemed necessary at a cost price. At the same time, Arnold secretly arranged with clothier general James Mease to divert some of those cut-rate purchases to their own account for resale. The scheme came to haunt both Arnold and Mease.

As the military government settled into city quarters—Arnold took residence in a slate-roof mansion vacated by the British general Henry Clinton—Morris got back on the road to Manheim. He returned to Philadelphia with his wife and family in time to attend an Independence Day feast at the City Tavern, where eighty diners were entertained by a full orchestra and raised thirteen toasts, each followed by the crash of cannon fire. Outdoors the streets were crowded with revelers, buoyed by reports that Washington had prevailed in a pitched battle with the British army at Monmouth, New Jersey. The night ended with fireworks as Philadelphians celebrated the liberation of their capital.

The Congress resumed sessions on July 7. With the State House in shambles, temporary quarters were established at Pennsylvania College. The delegates had just resumed their old haunts in the battered city when they were called upon to host their first state visit.

Three weeks after the last British sail disappeared below the Delaware capes, a new fleet appeared in the river. This was a French battle squadron featuring twelve ships of the line, each mounting more than fifty guns, and five frigates. Here was the first physical evidence of the new alliance with France. Here, as well, were two of the diplomats who had made the expedition possible: Conrad Alexander Gerard, former assistant to Vergennes and now the first French ambassador to America; and Silas Deane, recalled to his homeland after three years abroad.

It took a week for the squadron to make its way to Chester, ten miles below Philadelphia. Disembarking July 12, Gerard and Deane were greeted by a delegation from Congress led by John Hancock, recently returned from Massachusetts. Gerard was then escorted to Philadelphia, arriving inside Hancock's canary-yellow carriage to a salvo from the provincial artillery and salutes from soldiers drawn up along Market Street. Deane followed several days later, joining Gerard in residence as a guest of General Arnold.

So far, so good. The grand entrance up the Delaware, in company of an admiral, an envoy, and a dozen warships, had all been scripted in advance. Caron de Beaumarchais had been Deane's closest collaborator in Paris, and he saw an attack on his friend as a challenge to his own honor. He hoped an extravagant bit of theater would cast Deane's return in the best possible light.

Deane had been stunned when word of his recall arrived early in March. He was given no reason, only requested in three cordial lines to report back to Congress in person on "the state of affairs in Europe." Deane's first reaction had been despondence. After all the animosity, all the frustrations, and despite all he had achieved, his rivals had reached across the water to oust him. He decided then he would remain in Paris. "This worthy American . . . is dejected," Beaumarchais wrote soon after. "He has lost his head."

It was Beaumarchais who changed Deane's mind. Spirited, dynamic, always game for intrigue, the playwright convinced Deane that the recall might be turned to advantage. He should challenge his accusers based on the record of his accomplishments and the goodwill of the French court. And Beaumarchais would supply Deane with the 1776 letter from Arthur Lee acknowledging that payments were due for the Hortalez supplies. Lee's allegation that Deane used the remittances to line his pockets would be discredited by Lee's own hand.

As Beaumarchais described his meeting with Deane, the two friends traded ideas: Beaumarchais volunteered to write a detailed memorial of Deane's endeavors. Deane warmed to the scheme, and it was he who proposed that the king send a fleet to demonstrate his commitment to his new allies, and that Deane would sail with them. Yes, Beaumarchais agreed, and the king would send along "some special favor," a mark of personal esteem.

When Beaumarchais pitched the whole package to Vergennes, the foreign minister embraced it. All preparations were made in secret; Vergennes specifically directed that Arthur Lee not be told, as he mistrusted Lee's contacts with England. Deane and Gerard set sail a month later, carrying the memorial and other documents from his friend, a separate endorsement from Vergennes, and a portrait of the king in a jeweled frame. All these he waited to present to Congress . . . and waited. For two weeks he heard nothing; on July 28 he wrote a brief note to Laurens. Still nothing.

As the weeks wore by, the optimism of the plans laid with Beaumarchais wore off. Nothing was said about the sole complaint raised against Deane in Congress—the annoying applications by French officers for posts in the military—and there was certainly no pressing interest in learning his views on Europe. The deepening silence was ominous.

Deane had some idea of what he was up against. He knew he had incurred the enmity of Arthur and William Lee, and he was aware that two other Lee brothers, Richard Henry and Francis Lightfoot, were influential members of Congress. But he could not have realized the pitch of acrimony that had seized the leadership of the Revolution during the schemes against Washington and the wrangle over half-pay. Those disputes had rekindled the long-standing mistrust in Congress between radical and moderate factions, and Deane's status became the new flashpoint. As early as June, according to Henry Laurens, the delegates had "absolutely taken sides."

Deane did not know, either, the huge blow-up his quiet exit from France had set off among the commissioners at Paris. When Arthur Lee and Ralph Izard learned they had been kept in the dark, they worked themselves into high dudgeon over the insult they had sustained, and each turned on Franklin. Izard could be ignored, but Lee had more standing, and his accusations were grave. Franklin had done "violence to the authority which constituted us together," Lee fumed. More specifically, Lee accused Franklin of concealing the accounts of public transactions, which "you and Mr. Deane have constantly taken to yourselves." Lee demanded an answer: "Why do you act so inconsistently with your duty to the public, and injuriously to me?"

Franklin answered sharply. "It is to the public that I am accountable," Franklin wrote Lee, "and not to you. I have been a servant to many publics, through a long life . . . there is not a single instance of my ever being accused before of acting contrary to their interest or my duty. I shall account to the Congress when called upon, for my terrible offense of being silent to you about Mr. Deane's and Mr. Gerard's departure."

As to Lee's insinuations about keeping secret the public accounts, Franklin sagely observed that the accusation was designed more for the Congress than for him. "What can they understand by it but that you are the only careful, honest man of the three [commissioners], and that we have some knavish reasons for keeping accounts in the dark and you from seeing the vouchers?" In truth, Franklin wrote, the accounts were readily available for Lee's inspection. "The infinity of business we have had here is the true and only reason I know of why they have not been settled."

Franklin then accosted Lee for his demeanor through all the time they'd spent in Paris. "It is true that I have omitted answering some of your letters, particularly your angry ones, in which you, with very magisterial airs, schooled and documented me, as if I had been one of your domestics. . . . I saw your jealous, suspicious, malignant and quarrelsome temper, which was almost daily manifesting itself against Mr. Deane and almost every other person you had any concern with. I therefore passed your affronts in silence, did not answer, but burnt your angry letters, and received you when I next saw you with the same civility as if you had never written them." Franklin's retort, of course, only incensed Lee further, and in the months that followed, Lee shared his invective with Izard, with his brothers, and with Congress.

The commissioners tried to keep these disputes private, but Vergennes, who made it his business to know all the secrets in Paris, soon caught on. He had done what he could to support Deane, but would not jeopardize his prospects by taking sides any further. In his first dispatch to Gerard in America, Vergennes remarked on "the storm against Deane," and advised that his deputy "not become involved in this affair."

It is worth a pause, at this juncture, to delve a little more deeply into the remarkable fraternal combine that orchestrated Deane's recall. Who were the Lee brothers, and how did they exert such a powerful influence over the Continental Congress?

To a large degree, the four Lees who were active in the Revolution—Richard Henry, Francis Lightfoot, William, and Arthur—were typical of the landed gentry that dominated life in the Tidewater region in Virginia. Bracketed by the Potomac and the James Rivers, this was a land of verdant tobacco plantations where slaves worked the fields under the shadow of imposing mansions. Isolated on their vast estates, the planters prized self-sufficiency as a mark of moral rectitude, and twined the patience and rigor of agricultural life with the outward trappings of the landed aristocrat—lavish furnishings, lacquered carriages, and the latest fashions from England.

It was a life of opulence but also of profound insecurity, as the land barons struggled to preserve the income that their pretensions required. The result was a sort of wary pride, alert to any threat that might pierce the facade of their genteel independence. "The public or political character of the Virginians corresponds with their private one," a British visitor observed years before the Revolution. "They are haughty and jealous of their liberties, impatient of restraint, and can scarcely bear to be controlled by any superior power."

It was an attitude that became increasingly hard to sustain. Beginning around 1760, the combination of expensive lifestyle, overplanting, and a weak market for tobacco drove the planter class into mounting debt. On the eve of the Revolution, the planters of Virginia accounted for as much debt to Britain as did the other twelve colonies combined. The constant fear of their creditors, one royal functionary observed, "renders them uneasy, peevish, and ready to murmur at every occurrence."

The Lee brothers were members of this fretful class, but their anxieties ran even deeper. They were raised among nine siblings in a great, brooding brick mansion called Stratford. Their father, Thomas Lee, was a third-generation planter, the family's "empire builder," who assembled an estate of thirty thousand acres in the Northern Neck, a district lying between the upper tidal reaches of the Potomac and the Rappahannock Rivers. Upon the patriarch's demise in 1750, when Richard Henry was eighteen years old and Arthur ten, Stratford and most of the land went to the eldest son, Philip Ludwell Lee. A smaller share went to his second son, Thomas Ludwell Lee, and smaller pieces still were assigned to Richard Henry and Francis Lightfoot. William and Arthur were enjoined to pursue a "profession or trade."

Thus when William and Arthur went to England for their education, they stayed to seek their fortune—there was little in Virginia to hold them. Francis Lightfoot settled on a remote tract of land well to the west of the Tidewater, while Richard Henry spent the next five years at school in the English countryside. He returned to live under Philip's roof, reading classics and wrangling over the title to his inheritance. It took eight years for Richard Henry to obtain title to a fine estate overlooking the Potomac, and raise a mansion that he named Chantilly.

Widely scattered but united in their straitened circumstances, the four younger brothers maintained a powerful bond through a steady and intimate correspondence. Not to say they were informal; their address was crafted, their musings thoughtful and thorough. There were discourses on politics—Thomas Lee held office though most of his life, as did all four brothers—and during the war, on matters of state and the military situation. But this correspondence also served as a forum for moral declaration and denunciation, a sort of internal dialogue that opens a window on a fierce social outlook. Even in an age of elaborate diatribe, the language of the Lees stood out, by turns secretive, scornful, paranoid, sometimes outright pathological.

Their adversaries inhabited a dark domain. They were "wicked," "evil," "designing," often in combination; Richard Henry warned of "the art, cunning, and industry of wicked, vicious and avaricious Men." Some of these evildoers were particularly nefarious: Ben Franklin was "the meanest of all men, the most corrupt of all men," an "old, corrupt Serpent." We have already heard William's portrait of Deane as a practitioner of "low, dirty intrigue"; Richard Henry was just as eloquent: Deane and his ilk "will shoot up in any soil, and the foulness about them thicken for a time the purest streams." Nor was the Lees' invective reserved to individuals. Scots in general were "an uncivil, unsociable people, and utterly strangers to politeness." John Ross was either "an insignificant Scotch peddler," or "the dirty Scotch peddler." Wartime profiteers were "Rascally Tory Jew engrossers."

Faced with such a treacherous world, the Lees sometimes felt overwhelmed. Deane and his followers "have done everything in their power to traduce me," Arthur Lee complained at the height of his campaign against Deane. "These are dangerous men." When the calumnies closed in, the Lees could only rely on their own sense of merit—a quality they always claimed for themselves—to carry them through. "Virtue must . . . drive vice and folly off the ground," Richard Henry counseled. William Lee agreed: "We must wrap ourselves in virtue and be contented."

Arthur may have been the most disturbed by the temperament that was his legacy. Even John Adams, a political ally, conceded to James Lovell that while he considered Arthur "an honest man, faithful and zealous," there was also "an acrimony in his temper, there is a jealousy, there is an obstinacy . . . and an affectation of secrecy, the fruit of jealousy, which renders him disagreeable often to his friends, makes him enemies, and gives them infinite advantages over him."

Of all the family patriots—the elder brothers were never enthusiastic in the rebel cause—Richard Henry Lee was the fulcrum. Tall and rail-thin, his appearance was as severe as his diction, with sharp features, a long, aquiline nose, and just one functional hand, the other having been maimed in a shooting accident. He was a fine speaker and a subtle politician, feared by his adversaries for "his smooth discourse, and art of cabal."

Richard Henry Lee began his career in public office at age twenty-six with a seat in the Virginia legislature, the House of Burgesses, which met at Williamsburg. Here he adopted the role of skeptical outsider, as if compensating for his limited means by holding tighter to the ideals of industry, thrift, sacrifice, and all-encompassing "virtue." He challenged the prerogatives of the entrenched landowners and alienated his neighbors with an early speech against slavery, though he felt compelled by circumstance to persist owning and trading in African bondsmen. By time of the Revolution, Lee had consciously rejected the mores of his Virginia peers in favor of the Puritan ethic of New England. He venerated Sam and John Adams, and once confided to John, "The hasty, unpreserving, aristocratic genius of the south suits not my disposition."

This remarkable transfer of allegiance helped extend the reach of the Eastern faction in Congress. It was not just the Lees—Henry Laurens and a handful of other southerners also found allure in the Puritans' stern moral outlook—but the Lees provided the most lasting and durable strand in this intersectional bond. At a time when Americans were divided by culture and custom, the Lee brothers united with the Adams cousins around the theme of "Republican virtue."

Two seminal episodes from his early career shed light on Richard Henry Lee's political character. The first was a crusade Lee waged against John Robinson, the colonial treasurer, speaker of the House of Burgesses, and a dominant figure in the life of the colony. Virginia's paper money was depreciating, and the British Board of Trade threatened to outlaw the currency unless the decline was arrested. Suspicion grew that the problem lay with Robinson; he was responsible for destroying outdated notes as they came in through taxes, but gossip held that he was actually putting the money back in circulation via "loans" to his friends.

For four years, Richard Henry Lee led the "hot, young, and giddy" members of the House in a campaign to have Robinson audited. The treasurer died in 1766, and an examination of his accounts proved all the rumors true: Robinson had doled out more than one hundred thousand pounds to some of the wealthiest planters in the colony. They were named publicly and called to account, and Lee was vindicated as a fearless, and fearsome, politician. More important to Lee, he was confirmed in his view that the world was rife with evil, checked only by the cleansing scourge of virtue.

The second incident came around the same time, when news of the Stamp Act reached the colonies. Richard Henry's first reaction was to ask a friend in London to secure for him the lucrative post of stamp distributor. But when he was passed over for the appointment, Lee took a leading role in opposition to the act, including personal attacks on George Mercer, the man named to administer the stamps in Virginia.

Richard Henry's protest culminated in September 1765, when he led a bizarre procession from Chantilly to a nearby courthouse, where they conducted a mock trial of Mercer. The actors in this charade were Lee's family slaves, some costumed and others entirely naked, with Richard Henry playing the role of priest, on hand to take Mercer's "confession." A cart carried stuffed dummies identified as Mercer and the author of the Stamp Act, Prime Minister Grenville, which were tried, hung, and then burned. The strangest part of this display was that the effigy of Mercer looked more like Lee himself than it did Mercer, and the "dying words" Lee proclaimed sounded like a statement of his own contrition. "It was the inordinate love of gold that led me astray from honor, virtue and patriotism," Lee intoned, and then he added, in Latin, "To what do you not drive a man's heart, O accursed lust for gold?"

Mercer's allies made the most of this peculiar performance when they publicized Richard Henry's own failed bid for the stamp distributor post in the *Virginia Gazette* under the title "An Enemy to Hypocrisy." Reviewing the episode in a 1980 essay, the historian Pauline Maier observed, "It is tempting to conclude that all the accusations of corruption hurled out by the Lees over a quarter century in politics were built upon their own guilt."

Driven by pride, insecurity, and their own internal demons, the Lee brothers by 1778 had established themselves as an independent force within the councils of the Revolution, with two brothers in Congress, and two more holding government appointments in France. They first fixed on Silas Deane as an impediment to their sway in Europe, but soon came to see the battle as a much larger struggle. To the Lees, Deane and his cohorts, especially Robert Morris, were "avaricious and ambitious men" who threatened the very core of the revolutionary project.

Deane finally got his hearing before Congress on Saturday, August 15. Gouverneur Morris marked the event the day before in a letter to John Jay. "Your friend Deane, who hath rendered the most essential services, stands as one accused. The Storm increases and I think some one of the tall trees, must be shorn up by the roots."

After all the buildup, the inquiry got off to an inauspicious start. Deane presented testimonials from Franklin and Beaumarchais, and then began a narration of his endeavors in Paris, but here he was interrupted. A motion was made that he present his statement in writing, and he was asked to leave the hall. After a long debate and two roll-call votes he was ushered back in and asked to return the following Monday.

Deane appeared as requested and began again, but was again interrupted and asked to return again two days later. Wednesday came, but the hearing was postponed to Friday. That afternoon, Deane finally had his audience. He completed his statement, and was granted "leave to withdraw."

There was no answer, no challenge, no rebuttal. Deane's enemies, it appeared, were stalling.

Deane could well be excused for feeling exasperated. It was odd enough that he was recalled just as the primary objects of his mission had been realized; it was extraordinary to find that the charges he was called home to face had yet to be formulated.

Robert Morris was on hand for the Deane hearings, and was probably relieved to find them so thoroughly inconclusive. He was well aware that, as the sponsor of Deane's mission, he was himself on trial. And by this time, Morris's long dominance over the secret munitions trade was becoming a genuine liability.

The critical view of Morris at this time was summarized by Theveneau de Francey, an agent sent by Beaumarchais to America in early 1778 to press Congress for the laggard shipments of remittances. Morris had supported the policy of payment, but wanted the cargoes to be handled by American agents in France, not sent directly to Beaumarchais. Francey contested this intermediary role for the agents and won a partial victory; he conferred several times with Morris and found him charming "on every occasion," but resented his support for the Continental agents.

Writing to Beaumarchais in July, Francey vented his frustration with Morris. "As he is the only merchant in Congress who has ever conducted large commercial operations, his opinion is law." This was the view held by the enemy as well; Paul Wentworth, chief of the British Secret Service, described Morris in a 1778 memo as "Active, zealous, a great and the most useful partisan on the continent, bold and enterprising, of great mercantile knowledge, fertile in expedients and an able financier."

But while Francey shared that high opinion of Morris's sagacity, he did not trust him. "He has a very great influence and a very great credit, and as, in the beginning of the Revolution especially, no one could render greater service to America than he, through his connections in the four quarters of the globe, he has done whatever he pleased." And that, Francey said, was to enhance his own standing. "He works for himself in working for the republic."

To this point, Morris would not disagree. It was his maxim, the foundation of his agency system, to harness the pursuit of private profit to the exigencies of the government. But Francey then went further, alleging that Morris defrauded the government when it served his aims. It was Morris's agents who assembled the remittance cargoes, Francey said, and Morris's vessels that shipped them. "He always takes care to insure the tenth or twelfth part of the cargo belonging to him, and the vessel is thus sent by his agent from Virginia, consigned to his agent in France, and as this Virginia agent is not required to render any account of his shipment, they have ample time to ascertain whether the vessel has arrived or been taken. In the first case it belongs to Mr. Morris; in the second, it belongs to Congress."

This conception of Morris's self-dealing was held by a number of delegates—certainly Henry Laurens subscribed to it—but according to Francey, "not a member of Congress has had the courage to call him to account." For the time being, Deane would have to suffice as a substitute target.

Francey's explicit charge against Morris would soon become the subject of public inquiry. But the idea that Morris was making a killing in Secret Committee trade is belied by his continuing effort to put the entire project behind him. True, the secret ventures had produced some real moments of triumph. The Hortalez scheme had yielded enough timely arrivals of supplies to equip the army for the 1777 campaign, and John Ross, venturing as a partner with Morris, had also dispatched several shiploads of gunpowder and arms from neutral ports in northern Europe. But the failure of remittances to Europe had brought the entire network to a near-standstill. Beaumarchais, Penet, and Chaumont had all exhausted their capital and were clamoring for payment.

The secret agents in the Caribbean were in the same fix, leaving Morris to plead their case before Congress. Both Ceronio and Bingham "have suffered exceedingly by making advances for the Public," Morris wrote to the Marine Committee. "If Mr. Ceronio does not receive remittances it is probable he may be Imprisoned; he has been threatened with that fate by his Creditors & he has served us with zeal and fidelity that merits much better things." In his desperation, Ceronio seized at Cape François a shipment of furs sent out by Oliver Pollock at New Orleans to cover his own mounting debts. The Continental agents were now preying upon each other.

Nor had his private business proved as lucrative as Morris had hoped. His collaboration with Deane had produced just three ventures; of these, one vessel was captured, one arrived to some success, and one, a privateer meant to cruise off the coast of France, never sailed. Morris appears to have gained by joint trading ventures staged by Bingham out of Martinique, but here as well, profits never matched expectations.

After his return to Philadelphia, Morris devoted all his energy to severing his ties to the government. He asked Congress to appoint a new committee to settle the Secret Committee books; when that measure stalled, Morris hired a private accountant to work on the committee books. He finally turned them over, updated but still unsettled, toward the end of July.

While Morris was closing out his government operations, he was establishing connections that would serve as a foundation for renewed private enterprises. The key was America's new status, thanks to the alliance with France, as a player in the international arena. Where at the outset the Congress sent agents abroad to solicit trade and alliances, now the European powers were sending accredited agents to America. They made their way to Philadelphia, and there soon encountered Morris.

Among the more exotic of these foreign visitors was Juan de Miralles, a Spanish trader out of Havana. Given to colorful silk suits, extravagant entertainments, and munificent displays of generosity, Miralles relished his role as a man of mystery. He had royal commission to seek supplies of flour and sound out prospects for a formal alliance, but like Silas Deane, Miralles traveled under cover as a private merchant. He landed in South Carolina in early 1778 and made his way through Virginia, stopping there to meet with Governor Patrick Henry. When he reached Philadelphia in early July he set about cultivating contacts in the government, including Henry Laurens.

With Morris, however, Miralles needed no introduction. The two had been trading partners before the Revolution, when Morris had helped secure critical supplies of grain for the Spanish islands. Now Morris became Miralles's "sponsor and chief promoter" in the rebel capital; they partnered in ships and several other enterprises, and became warm personal friends. Morris was, once again, finding success by mixing business and pleasure.

Morris also struck up a commercial relationship with the French mission at Philadelphia. Here the connection ran through John Holker, another foreigner traveling with a secret commission from his home government. Holker's father was a British expatriate who moved to Paris, went into trade, and became one of the key suppliers to Beaumarchais. In late 1777, Vergennes asked the younger Holker to travel to America and report back on the political situation and the prospects for trade. Holker made contacts in Maryland and Virginia, and presented himself to Congress at York in June.

Morris met Holker at the July 4 dinner in Philadelphia. The entrepreneur-envoy with the high-level contacts pressed Morris to serve as his agent in America, helping him to manage "large Concerns and important Business . . . committed by his friends in France to his care." Morris demurred at first, citing his endeavor to settle his tangled government accounts, but Holker was persistent. Gerard arrived soon after and appointed Holker both consul to Philadelphia and agent for the French marine. These endorsements may have convinced Morris of Holker's consequence; in any case, Morris agreed to take up the business and was soon heavily engaged with Holker in trading ventures, and in rounding up supplies for the French fleet.

With his business interests again multiplying, Morris was now attending Congress only sporadically. He was on hand for Deane's initial appearances, and spoke with him privately on occasion to lay plans for future business ventures, but Morris seemed little concerned with the accusations against him. "I think our friend D has much public merit," Morris wrote Jay in early September. Deane "has been ill used, but will rise superior to his enemies."

Here Morris was being a bit too sanguine, as Richard Henry Lee at last presented his case against Deane a week later. Lee had in hand several letters from Arthur Lee leveling vague charges of misconduct, but he set these aside in favor of allegations by William Carmichael, a wealthy Maryland native who served briefly as a volunteer secretary to Deane and Franklin in Paris. Carmichael had recently returned to Philadelphia, and would testify, Lee said, to show that "Deane had misapplied the public money." Moreover, Deane had conspired to exclude Arthur Lee from the negotiations with the French ministry, leading to "an open rupture" in the Paris commission. Asked by the Congress to reduce his charges to writing, Lee asserted, "Mr. Carmichael condemned Mr. Deane's conduct toward Mr. [Arthur] Lee and was pointedly severe in reprobating the system and measures that he had pursued in his public character, which he said he would fully unfold when he came to America."

Carmichael was a curious choice for star witness. It was true that he had cast aspersions against Deane, but he bore even more animus toward the Lees, and the feeling was mutual. William Lee had written in January to warn Richard Henry "in the strongest manner against the wiles and intrigues of Mr. Carmichael . . . weigh with caution, but trust not any thing that comes from him." Richard Henry shared these misgivings, and conveyed them to Arthur in a coded letter just days before presenting his case to Congress. "You were not mistaken in the union you supposed would be formed here between Carmichael and Deane; they go hand in hand & are closely allied in forming faction." Still, Carmichael was the only witness Lee could produce. "I wish we had all the evidence on your side, but . . . we must call for his evidence."

In typical Lee fashion, Richard Henry saw Deane's effort to defend himself as a plot against his brothers. "I assure you that envy, selfishness, and Deane's arts have created a strange spirit among many, and will require on your parts great wisdom and much caution in all your conduct and correspondence."

Carmichael was called to testify on the last day of September, and the hearings extended a week. His statement proved thoroughly inconclusive, introducing into the annals of Congress the lexicon of the reluctant witness: "I did not pay sufficient attention to answer with precision," "I do not recollect," and this unique construction, "I cannot at present absolutely charge my recollection with what I had reason to believe at that time."

The substance of Carmichael's testimony proved equally disappointing to the Lee faction. The worst charge he could make—and this without clear evidence—was that Deane had supplied public funds to help Beaumarchais complete work on a privateer he was fitting out to cruise against enemy shipping. This was an ambiguous claim at best, as the mission was well within Deane's purview, and as Deane and Beaumarchais were constantly forced to juggle funds to cover deficiencies in payments owed by Congress.

The inquiry might have ended there, but Deane's critics were in no mood to let the matter drop. More accusatory letters had arrived, from Arthur Lee and Ralph Izard, and new hearings were scheduled. In the meantime, Congress decided to end the bickering in France by appointing Franklin "minister plenipotentiary," giving him sole control over the embassy at Paris. Richard Henry Lee could only cringe. "The Doctor is old and must soon be called to account for his misdeeds," he confided to Arthur Lee; "therefore bear with him, if possible."

The sputtering examination of Silas Deane seemed to confirm Robert Morris in his decision to leave Congress. The floor debates had descended into unremitting enmity, and Morris's primary contributions to the war effort appeared to be over. But as much as he longed to leave politics altogether, developments in Philadelphia now conspired to draw him back into the public arena.

In the first few weeks after liberation from the British occupation the city's radical and moderate factions had observed an uneasy cease-fire. All had shared the tribulations of exile, and all felt uneasy, upon their return to the city, to find that many who remained had adopted the style and manners of the British. Worse, the loyalists seemed unabashed. "The avowed Tories are I think more inveterately so than ever," Morris wrote to a friend.

Resentment against these presumed collaborators prompted the city's political leadership to form a Patriotic Society, which would ferret out and punish "sundry persons, notoriously disaffected to the American cause." The roster of the society included radicals like Thomas Paine and *Pennsylvania Journal* publisher William Bradford, but also moderates like Morris, James Wilson, and Thomas Mifflin; Joseph Reed, recently retired from duty as adjutant to George Washington, cultivated ties to both sides.

The group was conceived as a means to demonstrate civic solidarity, but its operation soon began to look more like a witch-hunt. Spurred by the Patriotic Society activists, the Supreme Executive Council published the names of 139 suspected collaborators. Over the next two months, those accusations were reduced to forty-five cases of treason submitted to a grand jury. Of these, twenty-three were taken to trial, most of them argued by Joseph Reed, serving the state as a special prosecutor. Here the Patriotic Society came to a divide; the lead defense attorney was James Wilson, the moderate who had only reluctantly joined Ben Franklin to vote for the Declaration of Independence.

Wilson's presence at the bar meant the cases would be hard-fought. Trained under John Dickinson, Wilson had the appearance of a schoolboy, with thick round glasses and a small, pursed mouth, but he was a stubborn litigator with a keen legal mind. Besides, the cases appear to have been substantially overcharged—most of the true loyalists had departed with the British. In the end, juries acquitted all but four of the accused traitors. Two of those convicted, Abraham Carlyle and John Roberts, both of them Quakers, were sentenced to death.

The fate of these two unfortunates soon became a cause célèbre. The jurors in both cases pleaded for clemency, as did the justices of the state Supreme Court, and thousands more signed petitions submitted to the Supreme Executive Council pleading for mercy. The president of the council, Thomas Wharton, had died suddenly in May; his successor, George Bryan, one of the authors of the radical constitution, joined Reed in taking a hard line: some example had to be set to keep the Tories in check. The executions were carried out November 4, and memorialized by the Quaker diarist Elizabeth Drinker: "They have actually put to death, Hanged on ye Commons, John Roberts and Abraham Carlyle. An awful day it has been."

The passions raised in the effort to save Roberts and Carlyle now spilled over into the annual elections to the state Assembly. Wilson and Benjamin Rush worked frantically to organize the critics of the sitting government, Wilson calling on moderates to help determine "whether the state of Pennsylvania shall be happy under a good Constitution, or oppressed by one of the most detestable that ever was formed."

Robert Morris left no record of his engagement in this contest, but he stood for Assembly on the November ballot. He was elected, along with George Clymer and Thomas Mifflin, as part of an opposition slate from Philadelphia. This hard-fought race marked the close of Morris's three-year tenure in Congress. The loss of his energy was widely felt—in particular, the Committee of Commerce, successor to the Secret Committee, never recovered the initiative that Morris had brought. His absence was also felt on the waterfront, where repairs to the Continental fleet soon came to a standstill. "Mr. Morris has left the Marine [Board]," one sea captain observed, "and everything is going to the devil as fast as can."

The state Assembly divided along party lines on the first day of the new session, when Morris and the other moderates insisted on amending their oath of office to allow them to press for revisions to the constitution. Startled to find that fully a third of the house had opted for the modified oath, the Assembly leaders agreed to schedule for April the plebiscite on the state constitution that had been derailed by the British invasion a year before. The Assembly then voted to ease the penalties levied against those who refused to swear loyalty to the state, and agreed unanimously to seat Joseph Reed, who derived support from both parties, as president of the Executive Council.

Robert Morris was instrumental here; with Gouverneur Morris acting as intermediary, Robert sat down with Reed and promised to support his presidency if Reed would consent to the plebiscite. To seal the deal, Morris and Thomas Mifflin underwrote the cost of a huge banquet at City Tavern to celebrate Reed's presidency. Morris sat at the head table along with Conrad Gerard and Don Miralles. It appeared, however briefly, that some degree of compromise had been achieved.

Outside the sphere of politics, the months after the British withdrawal saw dramatic changes to daily life in Philadelphia. The return of the government brought a surge in purchasing—the commissary and quartermaster departments combined to spend $39 million in 1778, a fourfold increase over the year before. At the same time, and partly as a consequence of the rise in spending, the Continental dollar lost value at an accelerating rate. Prices of flour, beef, and molasses doubled in July alone, and doubled again in December. The result was dramatic economic dislocation, with some traders and government functionaries making fortunes, and large numbers of working people slipping into distress. "If I was to mention to you the price of the common necessaries of life, it would astonish you," Franklin's daughter Sarah wrote to her father. "It takes a fortune to feed a family in a very plain way."

The success of the few—with Robert Morris among the most conspicuous—was celebrated in a season of profligate merriment. General Benedict Arnold, Conrad Gerard, and Juan de Miralles all competed to put on the most lavish dinner parties, Arnold spurred not just by ego but also by his passionate romance of Peggy Shippen, the celebrated belle of a family known for Tory leanings. "I know of no news unless to tell you we are very gay," Mary Morris wrote her mother in November. "We have a great many balls and entertainments."

Mary could not help but comment on Arnold's amorous pursuits, which were then the talk of the town. "Even our military gentlemen here are too liberal to make any distinctions between Whig and Tory ladies—if they make any, its in favor of the latter . . . it originates at Headquarters, and that I may make some apology for such strange conduct, I must tell you that Cupid has given our little General a more mortal wound than all the host of Britons could."

As frivolous as the affairs of Philadelphia society appeared, the doings of Congress looked even worse. Unable to devise an answer to the sinking currency, the delegates whiled away weeks in courts-martial, in wrangling over jurisdiction with the Pennsylvania state government, and in protracted feuding over Silas Deane. They refused Deane permission to return to France, but also refused to grant him a hearing on Lee's charges. For some delegates this aimless dance was infuriating. "We are plagued to death with quarrels and recriminations relative to our commissioners abroad," Cyrus Griffin of Virginia wrote in October. "It is absolutely necessary that Deane should be sent over to Europe . . . but some gentlemen are determined to ruin an innocent Character." Griffin said he was so disgusted he was ready to quit Congress altogether.

All of this took place behind closed doors; it was Deane who finally took the dispute public. Frustrated with four months of impasse, he wrote an angry tract striking back at the Lees and published it December 5 in the *Pennsylvania Packet*. Addressed "To the Free and Virtuous Citizens of

America," the statement was self-serving to the point of maudlin, but it was also incendiary. "I was content," Deane wrote, "even while sacrificed to the aggrandizement of others; but I will not see an individual, or family, raised upon the ruins of the general weal." This was an oblique reference to the Lees; Deane then made it explicit. Arthur Lee had bungled his diplomatic assignments, and William Lee—the London alderman—had bulled his way into the commercial agency; both, Deane wrote, "gave universal disgust to the nation whose assistance we solicited."

This was just an introduction. Deane went on to charge that the Lee brothers were secretly scheming with British spies. One, a regular associate of Arthur Lee's, had recently arrived in America and had conferred with Richard Henry Lee. Far from being the patriots they posed to be, the Lees were conspiring to derail the alliance with France. Deane would have shared this crucial intelligence with Congress, he said, but "their ears have been shut against me."

Despite its dramatic flourishes, Deane's attack on the Lees was misguided, even foolhardy. He was playing a game at which the Lees themselves were far more adept: guilt by accusation, guilt by association. In a time when party lines were fluid in Britain as in America, the charge of conferring with suspected enemies was a hard one to make stick. All the Lees had to do—which they did—was claim ignorance, and the case against them collapsed. Richard Henry Lee had been, with Sam and John Adams, the earliest advocate of independence in the Congress; few were now ready to doubt his patriotism.

Yet Deane's decision to go public with his defense was a transformational event for the Continental Congress. There was plenty of vitriol in the public prints in those days, aspersions cast by innuendo, association, satire, and jest. But a certain decorum was observed—names of the subject were dropped in initials, or identified by reputation. And the author was generally pseudonymous: "A Farmer," "Agricola," "Watchman." Here, Deane had published his tract over his own name. He called the Lees by name, and made explicit, and errant, accusations. He did so as a former member of Congress, disputing a standing member of Congress, for all the world to see. Until now, even the most mortal struggles of the body—the debate over independence, the challenge to Washington, the hand-wringing over the commissaries—had been effectively concealed from public view. The minutes were published on occasion, but they were skeletal, and the proceedings themselves were always secret. The Congress had nurtured a facade of unanimity, one many of them believed should spring naturally from the soil of a liberated republic.

Now the national council stood exposed, not by the substance of Deane's charges, but presenting them publicly. There was no longer any question that Congress was riven by factions, warring among themselves, fighting for power. The veneer of strong and serene leadership at the helm of the American insurgency had been stripped away. John Adams, the new commissioner in Paris, feared all this and more when he learned of Deane's publication. "It appeared terrible to me indeed," he wrote in his diary. "It would wholly lose us the confidence of the French court," and could "endanger a civil war in America." There could only be two results, Adams decided. "There appeared to me no alternative but the ruin of Mr. Deane or the ruin of his country."

With the veil of their decorum pierced, the warring delegates abandoned all restraint in the flaming discord that ensued. Deane was actually scheduled to appear in Congress on Monday, days after his grievances hit the streets of the city. When the session convened, Henry Laurens demanded that Congress rescind the invitation and repudiate Deane. His colleagues did as they often did—they stalled, tabling the president's motion and delaying Deane's hearing. Laurens was furious. He stewed for the next thirty-six hours, and on Wednesday, at the opening of business, stood to deliver a blistering attack on Deane.

He felt wounded, Laurens said, not for himself, but "for the honor and dignity of this House, the great Representative of an infant Empire, upon whose conduct the Eyes of Europe are fixed." But Congress had failed to act. After a long and stern oration, Laurens announced, "as I cannot consistently with my own honor, nor with utility to my country, considering the manner in which the Business is transacted here, remain any longer in this chair, I now resign it."

The president of Congress had quit. This act of pique appeared rash, especially when John Jay, just arrived from New York and a friend to Deane, was chosen as his replacement. Edward Langworthy of Georgia laughed at Laurens's "Phantasticability and absurdity." But if the president's dramatic gesture drew snickers in the House, it sent tremors of dismay through the patriot leadership.

To George Washington, visiting Philadelphia from his camp at White Plains, New York, it all appeared of a piece—the high life of the capital, the harsh animus in Congress, the affairs of the nation "on the brink of ruin." Writing to his friend Benjamin Harrison, Washington offered "A picture of the times, and of Men; from what I have seen, heard, and in part know I should in one word say that idleness, dissipation and extravagance seem to have laid fast hold of most of them. That Speculation, peculation, and an insatiable thirst for riches seems to have got the better of every other consideration." This severe assessment may have derived in part from the censorious influence of Henry Laurens, who hosted Washington on this foray into the capital. It reflected, as well, sheer enthusiasm, as the city sought to honor the general. Nathanael Greene, in town at the same time, found himself exhausted by the tribute. "Our great Fabius Maximus was the glory and admiration of the city," Greene recorded. "Every exertion was made to show him respect," with balls and dances that routinely ran till after midnight, "but the exhibition was such a scene of luxury and profusion they gave him more pain than pleasure."

Just as vexing to Washington was the distraction of Congress with the fallout of the Deane affair. "Party disputes and personal quarrels are the great business of the day," Washington wrote, "whilst the momentous concerns of an empire, a great and accumulated debt; ruined finances, depreciated money and want of credit are but secondary considerations and postponed from day to day, week to week, as if our affairs wore the most promising aspect."

The weeks that followed only confirmed Washington's fears, as the shock waves from Deane's bombshell spread ever wider. The Lee brothers, first Francis Lightfoot and then Richard Henry, published angry denunciations, countered by several anonymous essays defending Deane. But it was Thomas Paine who opened a broader, deeper debate. The Revolution's most accomplished pamphleteer had been silent for much of the year, holding his pen in check during his term as secretary to the Committee on Foreign Affairs. There he perused all of Arthur Lee's reports disparaging Deane, and forged strong ties to Richard Henry Lee, James Lovell, and President Laurens. Now he became their spokesman.

In a series of articles beginning in mid-December and continuing almost daily into January, Paine dismissed the charges against the Lees and turned the harsh light of inquiry back on Deane himself. Over his famous signature "Common Sense," Paine denounced Deane for his "barbarous, unmanly and unsupported attack" on the Lees, and then went on the attack himself. He cited his review of secret state papers—the Arthur Lee letters—to assert that the supplies from Beaumarchais were "a present," requiring no payment in return. He questioned Deane's statement of his accounts, suggesting "concealment of papers that looks like an embezzlement." And he called on every state to investigate any "mercantile connections" between their representatives in Congress and Deane—as a precedent, "Pennsylvania should begin."

To this point Paine seems to have been circling closer and closer to Robert Morris; now he turned to the charge of mishandling public funds, and referred to Morris by name. "Hitherto our whole anxiety has been absorbed in the means for supporting our independence, and we have paid but little attention to the expenditure of money, yet we see it daily depreciating; and how should it be otherwise when so few public accounts are settled?" Expanding on the point to "awaken the attention of the public," he cited the specific case of Robert Morris and the books of the Secret Committee. He had taken them into his possession, held them for close to a year, and returned them unsettled, failing to answer for two million in public funds.

No misconduct was alleged here per se, but the implications were obvious. Until now Morris had, by inclination and by the nature of his charge from Congress, kept secret all his activities in connection with the government and its agents. This afforded him an air of mystery, but also an aura of delinquency. Paine had given those suspicions the added weight of published revelation. Morris had little choice but to answer.

Morris made his reluctance plain in his address "To the Public," published January 7. "I do not intend to enter into the lists" with "Common Sense," Morris wrote, but he did so "purely to remove the force of his insinuation." That said, Morris delivered in close review his commercial engagements with Deane, and his management of the Secret Committee books. For readers throughout the colonies, these were startling revelations, laying bare material that had been the stuff of rumor and conjecture, now delivered in taut and precise prose. Morris detailed the three ventures in which he had partnered with Deane, the amount of tobacco he'd shipped to cover his end, the success of one venture (no tally of profits, just "a valuable ship and cargo") and the failure of two others.

Thence to the Secret Committee books, his efforts to settle them, the instance when "some matters to my prejudice had been insinuated by a Member in Congress," and the problems Morris encountered thereafter. The ledgers kept by Thomas Morris, he said, had never been returned to him, but an accounting at Nantes showed a debt in favor of Willing & Morris of fifty thousand livres, or about £2,200.

Having laid out small facts, he spoke to the question of two million dollars. "Some people may be led to imagine that I stand accountable for that sum. The fact is thus. . . . Many gentlemen from New Hampshire to Georgia entered into contracts for procuring supplies, for which they have accounted or are to account, and in like manner is my late house and myself to account for all monies by them and me received." Morris said many of his own ventures were still in transit, but "it clearly appears that a considerable balance is due to us."

Morris then made a declaration for the record. "I do not conceive that the state I live in has any right or inclination to inquire into what mercantile connection I have had or now have with Mr. Deane, or with any other person. As I did not, by becoming a Delegate for the State of Pennsylvania, relinquish my right of forming mercantile connections, I was unquestionably at liberty to form such with Mr. Deane." He added later, for emphasis, "Whether in consequence of my good opinion of Mr. Deane as a man of honor and integrity, I have been led to form any and what new concerns with him since his arrival here, is a matter which the public are in no ways interested to know."

It was a forceful performance, striking in its disclosures, but also powerful in tone. Morris was direct, he was specific, and though he was under attack, he managed to assert his prerogatives without sounding defensive. His sense of his own integrity rang through to his closing line: "I will only add, that it is in my power to prove, by papers in my possession, papers and records in the public offices, or by living witnesses of unquestionable character, every fact and circumstance I have laid before the public."

Paine considered this bracing reply something of a triumph. He answered it promptly, as was his wont—Paine was rarely at a loss for words. "I have been endeavoring, by occasional allusions, for these three weeks past, to force out the very evidence Mr. Morris has produced," Paine wrote two days later. Morris might have asserted his rights, but to Paine, the record was clear: this was "a confessed private partnership between a Delegate of Congress and a servant of that house." Here Paine was being facile, or ignorant, or both. From his seat as committee secretary, Paine must have been aware of the wide participation by members of Congress in munitions and supply contracts, particularly the connection between the Lee brothers, and of the Spanish trade directed from Arthur Lee to Elbridge Gerry. But this was not a forum for splitting hairs.

"To what degree of corruption must we sink, if our Delegates and Ambassadors are to be admitted to carry on a private partnership in trade?"

Paine asked. "Such a connection unfits a Delegate for his duty in Congress by making him a partner with the servant over whose conduct he sits as one of his judges. . . . Only let this doctrine of Mr. Morris' take place, and the consequences will be fatal to both public interest and public honor."

As a statement of principle, this had to be satisfying to Paine. There was no room for defense, no need to quibble over the exigencies of secret operations, over the actual success of the munitions ventures, over the personal and financial sacrifices that Morris and his agents had made, and were continuing to make. Certainly, it endeared Paine to his friends and allies in the Eastern faction of Congress.

But Paine could hardly feel that he had prevailed. Early on in his crusade to expose Deane and Morris, he'd felt public opinion swing sharply against him. Several writers had denounced him, and one angry reader, an officer on leave from the army, delivered a beating when he encountered Paine on the street, knocking him into the gutter. Moreover, in his pronouncements on the "gift" of arms from the King of France, he made specific reference to secret correspondence, violating his privacy oath and exposing the covert support effort of a valuable ally.

Forced to defend the integrity of his sovereign, Conrad Gerard lodged a formal request that Paine be reprimanded. This was taken up by Gouverneur Morris, who denounced Paine in Congress as "a mere Adventurer from England, without Fortune, without Family or Connections, ignorant even of Grammar," and moved that he be fired. When that motion died on a split vote, Paine upped the ante by submitting his resignation. But Congress was in a mood to bicker; it took a week of hot debate before they accepted his offer.

Paine was now out of a job, but his pen remained a potent force; in the week his status was debated in Congress, Gerard and Juan de Miralles got together to offer him a bribe: one thousand dollars a year to laud the Franco-American alliance—and to leave Deane alone. Paine proudly declined; he continued trading printed barbs with Deane's defenders for the rest of the spring and into the summer.

Robert Morris took the dustup over Deane pretty much in stride. True, he'd been calumniated in a fashion that he had never before encountered, denigrated by name before a skeptical public. But he also found his adherents—Thomas Mifflin, the former quartermaster and early Philadelphia radical who engineered the plots against Washington, wrote Morris to denounce "the rascally & ill-managed attack against your character."

"The attention you have given to the public business for the three last years and the commercial sacrifices you have made to your country I believed would have placed you out of the reach, at least the attempts, of every censorious scoundrel," Mifflin wrote. "Paine, like the enthusiastic madman of the east, was determined to run the muck—he sallied forth, stabbed 3 or 4 slightly, met with you but missing his aim fell a victim to his own stroke, and by attempting too much will enjoy a most mortifying and general contempt."

Morris reached much the same conclusion regarding Paine. "We have been passing a most jolly merry winter here in spite of all the enemies external and internal could do to disturb us," he wrote to a friend. "You will see by the Public Prints that my reputation has been attacked, but thank God my conduct will bear the strictest scrutiny and I have not a doubt of putting the shame of reproach intended for me, on the heads of those it belongs to, who have attempted most wantonly to injure an unblemished reputation to answer political purposes."

The triumphant tenor of this note rings a bit premature. In the coming months, Morris would find himself challenged again and again. He would survive, certainly, but the animus raised in the Silas Deane affair and the dramatic events that followed would leave all parties wounded, and the revolutionary movement in shards.

Chapter 8

BACKLASH

Henry Laurens was one of the first casualties of the Silas Deane affair, but in resigning the presidency he won for himself more freedom to engage in the partisan feuds racking Congress. And while Paine focused most of his animus on Deane, Laurens was convinced the source of corruption and mismanagement in the government was Robert Morris.

It was Laurens, it turned out, who now had possession of the books of the Secret Committee, and who provided Paine with the material he published on the committee accounts. After Morris parried Paine's thrust with his public defense, Laurens decided to take Morris on himself. Morris, after all, was Deane's sponsor on the Secret Committee, and Morris held the largest of the committee contracts. Moreover, Laurens believed Morris was profiting illegally off his work in the munitions trade.

On Friday, January 9, 1779, the day Morris's reply to Paine was published, Laurens took the State House floor to dispute Morris's printed account. He referred specifically to the debate over committee books that took place in Congress at York a year before. Laurens said he had not just made "insinuations" against Morris for retaining the books, as Morris had reported; in fact, he had made a specific allegation of misconduct. The charge was that Morris had shipped a Willing & Morris cargo of 470 hogsheads of tobacco to France aboard a frigate called the *Farmer*. The vessel was captured soon after it sailed, and Morris had allegedly altered the lading orders to show that his firm owned only eleven of the hogsheads; the rest of the lost cargo belonged to the public. This was the mode of fraud that Francey had described to Beaumarchais; here was an actual instance.

Laurens said at the January session he was offering the anecdote not to embarrass Morris but to set the record straight; he said he had shared his suspicions at the time with John Penn, delegate of North Carolina. Why he invoked Penn is unclear, as the two southern delegates detested each other. True to form, Penn refused to corroborate Laurens's story, which Laurens took as a personal insult. A week later, Laurens and Penn settled the score with dueling pistols. Each fired a single shot and both escaped injury. This was not as extraordinary as it might appear; duels were a feature of political life at the time. But it illustrates the depth of passion that charged the hearings in January.

In the meantime, with Morris absent from the debate in Congress—he was no longer a delegate—two of his political allies stood to his defense. William Paca of Maryland and Gouverneur Morris said that whatever Laurens's intent, he had now charged Robert Morris with fraud, and together they moved that he "reduce the above relation to writing." Laurens promised to comply, and the next day produced two documents. One was a letter he intended to be published in the newspapers; the second was a formal charge that he presented to Congress on Monday, January 11. Before that document was submitted, however, Laurens apparently decided against publishing his statement, and instead sent it directly to Morris.

Laurens opened his letter by suggesting, as Morris had with Paine, that he had been forced to step forward by Morris's published reference to "insinuations" by a member of Congress. The difference was that Morris had not mentioned Laurens by name, but Laurens glossed the point; it's hard not to conclude that, having seen the other combatants' exploits in print, Laurens was spoiling to get into the fight.

Laurens recounted to Morris the charges he'd offered the day before, in Congress, relating to the *Farmer*. He asserted that Morris had known of his suspicions for some time, and was surprised Morris had not contacted him to refute it. Likewise with the committee books; "I think you a little faulty" in holding them for months and returning them unsettled, Laurens wrote. Continuing, Laurens said he would examine examine the books himself, and render a more conclusive verdict. "I do not mean to draw too hasty conclusions to your detriment," Laurens promised. "If . . . there shall appear no fault on your part I shall be among the foremost to 'do justice to your Character' and to remove every groundless suspicion from the minds of others by declaring in public & in private that you have not merited censure."

If Laurens sought some accommodation by sending his column to Morris instead of to a printer, Morris's response put that prospect to rest. In a sharp rejoinder he sent the next day, Morris could barely contain his ire. "I shall say nothing as to the propriety of vindicating yourself in the news paper, nor pretend to determine whether there is or is not a better Method," he wrote icily. "Your own feelings must prompt and your judgment direct you." Morris challenged in every detail Laurens's version of how the committee books were handled. But what rankled him most was Laurens's suggestion that Morris had known of, and failed to answer, the allegations relating to the *Farmer*. Morris asserted he had heard the story for the first time on Saturday, after Laurens's speech in Congress. "I have here to add that no circumstance could have given me greater pleasure than to learn that matters which had so long been the groundwork of private Conversation against me, were now publicly investigated." If Laurens wanted a brawl, he had found one.

Morris concluded by dispensing with any further pretense to civility. "When I have received the acquittal which I am confident of and placed in that light which I know myself to deserve, it will be time enough to speak of private Friendships. I have a better opinion of you than to believe you would prostitute that term by a Connexion with me whom you seem to consider as a dishonest Man."

Morris must have understood this would not be the end of the dispute. But he could not have realized, as the coming weeks and months would show, this was just the first in a wave of charges, tribunals, and investigations. The glaring spotlight that had so long focused on Silas Deane now was shifting to him.

The same day Morris sent his letter to Laurens, Laurens was back in Congress making his case against Morris. Laurens explained that he first heard rumors of fraud involving the *Farmer* from Francis Lewis, a delegate from New York and a member of the Secret Committee. Laurens then turned to Lewis for corroboration, but Lewis, like John Penn two days before, declined to back up Laurens. This time, however, the other delegates intervened, and Lewis was required to prepare a written statement.

Lewis presented his affidavit two days later. It did little to forward Laurens's case, but much to illuminate the nature of political gossip. Late in 1777, Lewis reported, Laurens had been complaining at York about the "confused state" of the government's commerce, and sharing rumors he'd heard in Charleston about public vessels engaged to ship private goods. Lewis then volunteered a conversation he'd had in Baltimore with the captain of the *Farmer*, then preparing to ship out. Lewis had asked to captain to carry a packet of official mail, but the captain demurred; he'd been chartered as a private venture by Willing & Morris, the captain said.

This was little more than hearsay, and far short of the conclusive proof Laurens had been touting. At a hearing that followed presentation of Lewis's statement, Laurens managed to backpedal and press his case at the same time. Laurens denied spreading rumors from Charleston, and asked everyone to remember how mischievous memory can be. He then introduced the results of his own review of the Secret Committee files: the contracts, the shipping orders, and the insurance for the *Farmer* were all in the name of Willing & Morris. He did locate two bills of lading, signed by Morris, noting that the cargo was shipped "on Account of the United States," but these, he said, were written "ex post facto."

Having laid out his evidence, Laurens asserted, "I do not charge Mr. Morris with fraud. I never did charge him with fraud, nor did I ever intend to do so from bare appearances. . . . It will rest with Mr. Morris, unless the Commercial Committee can now give us satisfaction, by clear, explicit, unambiguous proofs to convince this house that his conduct was honest and justifiable." Laurens concluded with a flourish. "The best friend Mr. Morris has in the world will not more sincerely rejoice than I shall, at the sight of such evidence." With that, the statements of Laurens and Lewis were referred to a special committee for investigation. Morris and Laurens had each called for an inquiry; now they would have one.

The committee reported back February 11. This was a remarkably efficient performance in an assembly where proceedings so routinely bogged down, but there was an explanation: Robert Morris, as he had vowed, had produced witnesses and documents to thoroughly refute the charges made against him. All the transactions involving the *Farmer* had been made at the order of the Secret Committee. The captured cargo had correctly been charged to the public. The voyage had been disguised as private trade on purpose, a ruse "adopted to prevent the rising of prices of produce and hire of vessels, which generally happens when it is known that purchases and contracts are making on the public account."

The select committee took depositions, reviewed the documents, and issued its findings. "Upon the whole, your committee are of the opinion that the said Robert Morris has clearly and fully vindicated himself"; that Morris "has acted with fidelity and integrity, and an honorable zeal for the happiness of his country."

Nor was this all. The day the committee reported, Henry Laurens took the floor to announce that the statement Morris submitted to the committee had jogged his memory. Thus prompted, he himself had located yet another document affirming "beyond all doubt" that the *Farmer* had been

loaded on public account. It gave him "the highest pleasure to be an instrument in doing justice to Mr. Morris." That had to be a bitter sentence
for Laurens to utter. He'd resigned his seat, schemed with Tom Paine, and
been called to fight a duel, all to bring Morris to account; now he was forced
to proclaim Morris's innocence.

After all the buildup to its deliberations on the *Farmer*, Congress moved
on quickly in the weeks that followed. It was immediately plunged into a
new scandal when Joseph Reed and the Pennsylvania assembly demanded
prosecution of Benedict Arnold on charges of corruption. And the after-
shocks of the Silas Deane affair reverberated through the summer. Each of
the principals took their turns before the public tribunal—albeit many in
absentia—in debates described by Conrad Gerard as "incited to the last degree of animosity and indecency." Benjamin Franklin was retained in office,
but only after a series of close and contested votes. Arthur Lee prevailed as
well, but the margin was even more narrow; a motion to recall resulted in a
tie vote, and died there. William Lee and Ralph Izard both saw their commissions revoked in June.

As the summer wore on, the toll mounted. Deane appeared in person
to be grilled again and again, until he was finally dismissed and given leave
to return, without appointment, to France. Finally in September, John Jay
was named ambassador to Spain, leaving Arthur Lee without commission. "Your enemies have triumphed at last," Richard Henry Lee wrote
his brother. "Wicked persevering and under no restraint they have fairly
worried out the friends of virtue and their country."

This internecine warfare took its toll within Congress as well. Gouverneur Morris, the leader of the Deane faction, lost his appointment to Congress in September, and rather than return home to New York, opened
a legal practice in Philadelphia. Of the Eastern faction, Samuel Adams
headed back to Massachusetts, and both Richard Henry and Francis Lightfoot Lee resigned their seats in the national legislature and returned to
their plantations. There were no winners in the Deane affair; his accusers
and his defenders all were wounded, and the Congress as a whole lost pres-
tige and gravitas that it would never recover.

Without a seat on the national council, Robert Morris was spared this long
and unpleasant melodrama, but only to be caught up in the even more turbulent, and ultimately more violent politics of the state. The forum was
more parochial than Congress but no less consequential; with the most radical of all the new state constitutions and the most dynamic economy in the

nation, Pennsylvania in 1779 became the testing ground for the extremes of the revolutionary movement.

The old conflict over the constitution broke out again as soon as the state Assembly resumed its sessions in February. Over the Christmas break the radicals had been busy, collecting more than ten thousand signatures opposing the plebiscite and convention that President Joseph Reed and the full Assembly had agreed to in late November.

Meeting in refurbished and freshly painted quarters on the second floor of the State House, the radical majority of the Assembly—joined, this time, by many of the moderates—seized on these petitions to rescind the November vote. Robert Morris, Thomas Mifflin, and George Clymer questioned the validity of the signatures and put up a "spirited protest," but even their fellow moderates deserted them, and the planned referendum on the constitution was defeated by a vote of forty-seven to seven. Seeking to soften the blow, President Reed invited Morris and his cohort to treat over cups of rum at City Tavern. Little was resolved, however, as Reed combined a "rather weak explanation" for his about-face with threats of legal action against his critics.

Thwarted once again in their bid to put the constitution to a democratic test, the Philadelphia moderates decided to organize. In a series of meetings in March, Morris and James Wilson laid plans for a new political club, the Republican Society, that would serve as the nexus of the moderate opposition. They chose their name artfully—cynically, even—appropriating the term the militants used to signify all the social and political ideals they had invested in America's unexpected and epochal revolution. The message was clear; the moderates wanted everyone to understand that they too were Republicans, that they embraced the principle of democratic self-rule but differed over the ways and means. They were not Tories, not seeking a return to king and Parliament, but they could not abide the establishment of what they called the "despotic Aristocracy" of an unfettered, unicameral Assembly.

The Republican Society made its public debut with a long tract in the March 24 edition of the *Pennsylvania Gazette*. Their "first and principal" objection to the 1776 constitution was "that it vests the whole legislative authority in a single body." By dispensing with institutional checks on the will of the majority, the constitution had introduced "the same monster, so destructive of humanity" as the monarchial tyranny they were fighting to overthrow. In particular, the Republicans sought a second, elected house, an independent judiciary, and an end to oaths of allegiance to the government. They would later endorse as well a single executive with veto power, but this plank was too controversial for the initial debates.

The society sought to emphasize its broad political base. "We have and can have no common interest with one another, but that which we have with you," the statement avowed. "Some of us have been honored with seats in your Councils, and in the Councils of the Continent; and in the darkest seasons have neither betrayed nor deserted our trusts, when we sat with halters around our necks." All that was true, but it was also clear that the new society spoke for the commercial and political elite that had been sidelined in the radical Assembly. The published statement included a roster of eighty-two prominent citizens, including Morris, Wilson, and Thomas Mifflin, the popular General John Cadwalader, and onetime radicals like Clymer, Benjamin Rush, and Charles Thomson, the secretary of Congress. The chairman of the society was Richard Bache, Ben Franklin's son-in-law, but Robert Morris was the hub.

The public initiative taken by the moderates brought a prompt rejoinder from the radicals. The leaders of the old Whig Society re-formed as the Constitutional Society, and on April 1, published a statement of their own. The painter Charles Willson Peale was again the chairman; now he was joined by key state officials including President Joseph Reed, Chief Judge Thomas McKean, and Timothy Matlack, a disowned Quaker who had served for a time as assistant to Thomson in Congress but was now secretary to the Supreme Executive Council.

The Constitutionalists' statement was more concise than the Republicans', but also more inflammatory. It opened with a fairly innocuous reference to the old debates of 1776: "The original promoters of this Society are among the first, and have in every instance been among the foremost to promote . . . the Independence of the United States in general, and of this state in particular." It then renewed the class critique that had been largely dormant since the early days of the rebellion. "The public wealth is plundered by defaulters, and the whole country imposed on by forestallers and monopolizers." Now came a direct gibe at the Republicans. "We wish no one to be a member of this Society, who doth not feel for the public as for himself, and who will not exert his utmost service to remedy the evils and punish the aggressors."

This sharp language set the debate over the constitution squarely in the moralizing context of the Silas Deane affair, which was still the subject of vitriolic exchanges between Thomas Paine, Deane, and a host of anonymous scribes in the public press. And it came at a time when the continuing collapse of the Continental currency threatened to overwhelm the entire project of the Revolution. In the weeks to come, the debate over political theory would shift to an angry contest over class and economic rights. All the resentments against the opulence of the successful merchants now came into focus, and as the city's leading trader and spokesman for the establishment, Robert Morris found himself at the center of the storm.

Because of its central location, because it was the nation's largest city, and because it was the clearinghouse for supplies for both the army and the French navy, Philadelphia became the epicenter of America's growing fiscal crisis. As early as January 1779, sailors went on strike for higher wages, unrigging ships and driving stevedores and other tradesmen from the waterfront. By February, local prices for basic commodities had increased fivefold over the year before.

The fundamental question was why. The obvious answer was that there were simply too many bills in circulation; printing wildly to keep its army in the field, the Congress had doubled spending in 1777, tripled it in 1778, and was now cranking out dollars at a rate of ten million a month. Once prices started to rise, every participant in the market became, in some respect, a speculator, holding out for the highest price or the strongest currency. In fact it was the farmers who did the most to undermine the value of paper money, refusing to send their produce to market until the merchants met their price. But these were the cold facts of an intractable dynamic; more satisfying, more amenable to the impulse to righteous indignation, was to blame the price spiral on the wealthy merchants who profited off the misery of the populace.

In May, after the Republicans and the Constitutionalists had staked out their ground, the rage over rising prices finally crested. The immediate occasion was an assembly of the city militia called for the afternoon of Friday, May 23. The night before, an anonymous broadside was posted on street corners throughout the city. Under the headline "For Our Country's Good," the printed sheet called for action. "In the midst of money we are in poverty, and exposed to want in a land of plenty. You that have money, and you that have none, down with your prices, or down with yourselves . . . We have turned out against the enemy and we will not be eaten up by the monopolizers and forestallers."

The sheet was signed "Come on Coolly," but it generated real heat in the streets of Philadelphia the following day. In the morning, as the rising sun burned off the Delaware haze, knots of militiamen gathered on street corners and soon began dispensing their summary judgments. Several people spotted tearing down the broadsides were grabbed and beaten, and dozens of merchants hauled out of their stores. The unfortunate vendors were paraded through town and then hauled to the London Coffee House for impromptu interrogation. Some were released and others, at least eight in number, were jailed, the prison patrolled by armed guards.

At four in the afternoon the militia rallied at the State House yard. After a series of speeches, they marched out in ranks, three thousand strong, up to Market Street and then down to the Coffee House where they rallied again. The next morning the militia resumed the street protests, dragging more accused monopolizers to jail. That afternoon, another crowd gathered at the State House yard, this time for a town meeting, the first such mass assembly in two years. The chairman was Daniel Roberdeau, a merchant, a brigadier general of the state militia, and a leader of the Constitutionalist party.

Roberdeau delivered an emotional speech asserting that some leading merchants were "getting rich by sucking the blood of this country." He then proposed the remedy. "I have no doubt but combinations have been formed for raising the prices of goods and provisions, and therefore the community, in their own defense, have a natural right to counteract such combinations, and to set limits to evils."

With this preamble, Roberdeau proposed a series of resolutions that were passed by acclamation. One was formation of a committee of twenty-six to reduce prices, rolling them back immediately to the levels of May 1, and thereafter ratcheting them down month to month until they returned to the state of prices on January 1. The Assembly had several times sought to restrict prices by laying an embargo on exports; now an independent committee would take on the business. Once again, as during the struggle over the final break with Britain, power was shifting away from the formal government and into the hands of the popular committees.

Next, Roberdeau invoked a specific instance of the "increasing evils" behind the price inflation. There was a French merchant ship, the *Victorious*, lying in the river, its cargo consigned to Robert Morris. It had sat there for a month under army guard, part of its freight sold but the rest sitting untouched as prices steadily rose. The longer it sat, the more people talked; one rumor that gained currency was that Morris held the ship in secret partnership with Silas Deane. Surely this was an instance of forestalling, there for all the public to see, with two of the city's premier "engrossers" culpable and at hand. On Roberdeau's motion, a special committee of five was appointed to demand an explanation from Morris and report back to the next town meeting. The committee roster betrayed the political nature of the inquiry; it included Charles Willson Peale and Timothy Matlack; David Rittenhouse, a renowned astronomer and mathematician serving as state treasurer; J. B. Smith, twice appointed to Congress by the radical Assembly; and Thomas Paine—all Constitutionalists. Convicting a Republican leader of economic skulduggery would secure them a handsome political scalp.

In the week following the town meeting, bands of militia continued to roam the streets, breaking open warehouses, commandeering ships on the river, and jailing suspected Tories. Against this tumultuous backdrop, the committee called on Robert Morris. They proposed a meeting at City Tavern, but Morris demurred; his eyes were acting up again, but they'd be welcome to call at his home. The committee arrived at Front Street to find Morris in company with his brother-in-law, William White, and John Nixon, the army veteran who gave the Declaration of Independence its first public reading back in 1776. These two close friends may have attended as witnesses or, considering the circumstances, to supply moral support.

Once the group was seated, Morris unwound the full story of the *Victorious*. She had been consigned by her owners to a French agent in Baltimore named Sollekoff; he had approached Morris and asked him to handle the sale of the entire cargo and to procure tobacco for a return trip. An agreement was drafted, which Morris signed, but as the terms were in French he did not know the actual details. Morris sold a quarter of the freight at what the Continental purchasing agents called "very moderate" terms, but then learned from the ship's master that the owners had stipulated a higher price in the contract. This occasioned new negotiations and unavoidable delay, besides which part of the cargo was "unsuited to this season and this country," and thus had not been sold.

In short, Morris did not have control of the cargo, he had good reason for the delayed sales, and Silas Deane had nothing to do with the *Victorious*. Sollekoff corroborated the entire account, and the case against Morris collapsed. Once again, as with the *Farmer*, Morris's inquisitors found themselves foiled by the intricacies of his affairs, and thwarted in their hopes of a clear and compelling indictment. At the close of the meeting the militant leaders left his house bemused; they promised a return visit, but none took place.

· · ·

The five Constitutionalists remained silent for several weeks. Finally, the committee issued a report that displayed more frustration than resolution. The best they could muster in the way of impeachment was the following: "However unwilling Mr. Morris may be to acknowledge the term engrossing or monopolizing, yet as he did not import the cargo, and did, in partnership with Mr. Sollekoff, get the whole into his possession, we are at a loss to find any other name, though the expedition with which he entered on the sale abates the rigorous sense generally applied to these words."

Here the committee had touched the problem inherent to any effort to identify and condemn "monopolizers": it was exceedingly hard to define, in the normal operations of an actual market, where commodities are bought and sold for profit, just what constituted a crime against the public interest.

The one criterion upon which everyone seemed to agree was that holding back produce to let the prices rise constituted "forestalling." But Morris and Sollokoff had provided ample explanation for delays related to the *Victorious*, leaving the committee little to work with. Their predicament was reflected in a remarkably diffident conclusion. "As we are not authorized to condemn, so neither can we justify," the committee wrote. They were "persuaded that when Mr. Morris reflects on the uneasiness which such a mode of purchasing has occasioned, that he will take measures in future to prevent the same consequences; for though, as a merchant, he may be strictly within rules, yet when he considers the many public and honorary stations he has filled, and the times he lives in, he must feel himself somewhat out of character." The committee report was sent to Morris and to a printer, and was published three days later, on July 24.

Having waited nearly two months for his critics to make their case, Morris drafted a reply the day he received it. His response was measured and civil, but Morris would not let stand even the qualified condemnation the committee had pronounced. "I cannot help differing from you in [your] opinion that the transactions in question have any thing in them of engrossing or monopolizing." He now ventured into the semantic puzzle presented by the allegation: "I may not be a judge of the legal sense affixed to these terms, but in reason and common sense they seem to mean the purchasing a large quantity of any commodity, and keeping possession of it until the consequent scarcity enables the holder to extort the from the public necessities an unreasonable profit. . . . But it will be admitted on all hands that I made as speedy a sale as possible."

Here Morris was tailoring his argument to suit the circumstances and dissembling as he went. The fact was that, as with most successful merchants, price was always a factor for Morris in deciding when and where to sell nonperishable goods. In early 1778, for example, he advised Jonothan Hudson, a Secret Committee contractor and sometime business partner in Maryland, to withhold salt—a critical strategic commodity—from a depressed market. "It's best to wait patiently [as] importations will now cease," Morris counseled. "I confess I would rather see [the price of] salt fall than rise but I fear it will take another turn."

Such maneuvers were just the sort of practice the committee was seeking to prohibit. But it did not occur in the case at hand, and Morris was fortunate that he could mount a direct defense to the committee's charge. In his argument, however, he was compromising the principled integrity that he so often espoused, a tacit acknowledgment of the pressure the committee was bringing to bear.

Morris disputed, as well, the suggestion that he had acted out of character. In this case as in all others, Morris wrote, he had acted as a merchant, no more and no less. "If I have otherwise erred in my conduct, it has been because the line in which I have moved as a merchant, precluded me from the study of those subjects which are necessary for a political life."

Morris closed with a gentle thrust directed to the committee members by name: "I regret it as a great misfortune that I have been so often forced to claim the public attention to vindicate my own character and conduct. I wish to live a quiet private life, under the protection of good laws wisely administered." His greatest concern, he added, was not personal, but for the state of civic discourse. "Ill-founded accusations tend not only to destroy the confidence absolutely necessary for the conduct of our affairs, but they weaken the effect of those which may at any time be made with justice and truth."

It was a polished, muted performance, one befitting a prominent public figure who felt confident he'd been exonerated. It was especially restrained in light of the much sharper tone Morris employed in an early draft of the letter. There he denounced the motives of his accusers as "the Effects of Envy, private malice or political opposition." He also slammed Daniel Roberdeau, noting that the radical leader had himself recently speculated in bills of exchange. Such practices undermined the currency and "would no doubt be classed Criminal in me," Morris groused, "however it might be proper in the righteous chairman of the Town Meeting." These expressions of pique were deleted in the final draft.

· · ·

Morris recognized that he had to be careful. At a time when bread was scarce in the markets and the militia angry in the streets, baiting his foes would be foolhardy. And as Morris well understood, he had become a lightning rod for popular discontent. Even while the inquiry from the special committee was pending, he was the subject of a second accusation, this one even more explosive.

The charge was that Morris was purchasing flour for export in violation of state and Continental embargoes. This would implicate him not just in raising prices, but in contributing to the scarcity of a basic foodstuff at a time when hunger was driving people to real desperation. The accusation came from the price committee appointed at the town meeting.

Once again, Morris had an answer. He had indeed been purchasing flour and exporting it in great quantities, but had done so on behalf of John Holker, agent for the French forces in America. Holker, in turn, had obtained special dispensation from Congress to make the buys in order to provision the French fleet at Philadelphia and in the Caribbean.

This was delicate business. Like his American counterpart Silas Deane, Holker was widely perceived to be trading on private as well as public account. But unlike Deane, who operated in concert with the French court, Holker's private trade would have run afoul of American law; specifically, the embargo on exports. The suspicions were unproven but widespread, and Morris several times attempted to extricate himself from handling Holker's business. He was prevailed upon, however, when commissary Jeremiah Wadsworth declined to assist Holker in his search for flour.

Holker's export operations came to light when agents for the city of Philadelphia, seeking grain in Delaware, came across 182 barrels of flour in Wilmington being held in Morris's name. The agents seized the flour, shipped it north to Philadelphia, and charged Holker and Morris with violation of the embargo. Morris answered by referring the inquiries to Holker; in turn, Holker appealed to Conrad Gerard, and Gerard appealed to Congress. The whole tangle landed in the lap of a committee that included Gouverneur Morris and Henry Laurens; they promptly found in favor of Holker and issued an apology to Gerard. Thus was Robert Morris treated to the delectable amusement of seeing Laurens forced once again to vouch for his conduct. Seething, Laurens was left to comfort himself with pieties. "Reduce us all to poverty and cut off or wisely restrict that bane of patriotism, Commerce, and we shall soon become Patriots," the wealthy planter mused to a friend. "But how hard is it for a rich, or covetous man to enter heartily into the Kingdom of Patriotism?"

Morris's handling of the Holker affair won him the effusive thanks of Gerard, but did little to allay the suspicions of the Philadelphia militants. Even after the price committee learned that the seized cargo was destined for the French fleet, members continued to give out that Morris was sitting on a hoard of flour. Morris learned of this bit of slander one morning when "four or five poor women with Sacks under their arms" came knocking at the door of his countinghouse. Morris turned them away hungry. "It must be known I could not deliver it to any person," Morris told the committee in a curt note, "but by orders of my employers."

With dozens of lesser merchants in jail or under public condemnation, Morris emerged as a lone outpost of opposition to the price-fixing committee. But as the edict on prices began to take hold, the resistance began to spread. Farmers outside the city stopped sending produce to market, and declined making any transactions in paper currency. Commissary agents took to seizing provisions that they could not buy. In town, tanners, cordwainers, and other artisans took to the streets to protest the limits placed on what they could charge for their services.

Nobody doubted the urgency of the situation. "The hope of the enemy appears to be principally fixed on what they would style the bankruptcy of the Continent, occasioned by a failure of the currency," the price committee warned in a public statement in July. But as the summer wore on, the idea of setting prices by fiat began to lose its charm. "We regulated the price of flour until there was none in the market," Tom Paine admitted later. The economist Pelatiah Webster described the impasse in more graphic terms: "It is no more absurd to attempt to *impel faith* in the heart of an unbeliever by *fire* and *faggot*, or to whip love into your mistress with a *cowskin*, than to force value or credit into your money by *penal laws*."

This was more than just ideological invective. The economic historian Richard Buel concluded in a recent study of the Philadelphia price wars that the efforts of the committees to regulate prices created shortages in the market and actually accelerated the rate of depreciation in Continental money.

By the end of July, with popular support fragmenting, the price committee called for another town meeting. It was intended as a show of strength, but two days before, a crowd of radicals accosted Whitehead Humphreys, an ironmonger who had the temerity to publish a tract defending Robert Morris and denouncing Thomas Paine as a Tory. Finding his house surrounded, Humphreys drove them off with brandished pistols, but not before his sister was "dangerously wounded . . . in the head."

With the streets of the city verging on "anarchy and confusion," a crowd of several thousand turned out for the town meeting, with Morris, Silas Deane, James Wilson, and Benjamin Rush leading a strong Republican contingent. Daniel Roberdeau again took the chair and under lowering skies opened the assembly by commending the efforts of the price committee. He asserted that the "enemy"—it was not clear here if this was a reference to the British or to the Republican Society—was "exceedingly alarmed at the revival of Town Meetings." He then invited the committees to make reports.

Not surprisingly, the select committee investigating the cargo of the *Victorious* declined to make a statement. Their report had already been published, and their findings were too muddled to bear recounting. But Morris remained on the agenda; the next report concerned the affair of Holker and his flour.

After the committee chairman delivered his account of that complicated transaction, Morris stood to offer his version. He confirmed, as the committee reported, that the Holker flour had been consigned to him. But Holker was the agent of their ally in arms, and purchasing only for the sustenance of their fleet. Neither he nor Holker, Morris declared, had exported "a single barrel of provisions, except on account of His Most Christian Majesty," the king of France.

Much to the chagrin of Roberdeau and the militants, this declaration drew loud cheers from the crowd, and a motion by John Cadwalader to endorse Morris's conduct. This unscripted intrusion "created considerable uneasiness and threw the meeting into some confusion." As if on cue, thunder rumbled across the yard, and a sudden downpour forced a hasty adjournment.

When the town meeting reconvened the following day, the militants set a new and more menacing tone. As the crowd assembled, "a body of about 100 men, armed with clubs, marched in array, under their officers, with fife and drum, and placed themselves near the stage." After Roberdeau opened with a call for "strict observance of order and decorum," the meeting approved a plan to elect a new, larger price control committee. Members of the current committee then began to read off a list of citizens accused of violating the price controls. After about ten names had been called out, Morris, Wilson, and Cadwalader rose to object and climbed onto the speaker's platform.

Cadwalader, a veteran of several pitched battles against British regulars, gave little shrift to the glowering militiamen, but after he launched into a vigorous denunciation of price controls, the militants shouted him down. Seeking to restore order, Roberdeau moved that Cadwalader be allowed to speak. The motion passed, but the uproar continued until the moderates, comprising more than half of those in attendance, withdrew en masse.

Rather than disperse, the dissidents moved across the street to the college yard and held a meeting of their own. With Morris sitting as chairman, this rump session denounced the muzzling of Cadwalader as "a violation of the LIBERTY OF SPEECH"—the capitalized emphasis was supplied by a partisan newspaper account—and gave explicit endorsement to Morris and Holker. They also, in an apparent show of civic spirit, approved the efforts of the price committee, but this did little to dispel the clear impression of a divided people. Silas Deane, who was present on both days, reported on the turmoil to his brother. "There are few unhappier cities on the Globe," Deane wrote, "than Philadelphia."

The radicals scored a resounding victory in the election of the new price committee on August 2, and their success was replicated throughout the country. In Lancaster and Reading, and on up through New Jersey to Rhode Island, Massachusetts, and New Hampshire, independent, nongovernmental committees were established to set limits on prices and force supplies into the markets. In its sweep and its spontaneous, local origins, the movement reprised the nonimport movement of the early years of the Revolution.

But prices across America continued to rise through the months of August and September. In Philadelphia especially, where the price control movement was most advanced, efforts to identify culprits were consistently frustrated. Instead, intellectuals and market participants began to question the whole concept of setting prices by fiat. The artisans issued a startling public challenge to the price control system in July, a sweeping statement of market principles that bore the rhetorical stamp of Pelatiah Webster, but was subscribed by a committee of tanners, curriers, and cordwainers. "By limiting the price of country produce, [the Price Committee] have prevented its coming to market; by lowering the prices of imported goods, they have damped the spirit of the adventurer; and if they persist in limiting the prices of tradesmen, their shops will be shut, their journeymen discharged, and want, with a train of intolerable evils, will await us all."

Here the tradesmen issued an explicit call for an end to all price controls. "Trade should be as free as air, uninterrupted as the tide, and though it will necessarily be sometimes high at one place and low at another, yet it will ever return of itself sufficiently near to a proper level."

Robert Morris joined the debate in August, after the price committee election. Pelatiah Webster was active here as well, composing with Morris a second treatise that was published in the name of eighty of the city's leading merchants. This rendition reprised the virtues of a free market, arguing that "the most effectual way to turn a scarcity into plenty is to raise the price for the article wanted." Trade brought profits to the merchant, but also to the community at large; embargoes and price controls would injure everyone. "Like him who owned the goose which laid golden eggs, you will cut off the source of all future supplies, and like him too, when you repent, you will repent in vain."

Now venturing beyond the bounds of market theory, Morris and Webster settled their claim on the grounds of political liberty. "Let every man make the most of his goods and in his own way, and he will be satisfied. Let every man taste and enjoy the sweets of that liberty of person and property, which was highly expected under an independent government."

Like the debate over the state constitution, this argument went to the core question of what the Revolution was about and where it might lead. "It is a sad omen to find among the first effects of independence, greater restraints and abridgments of natural liberty, than ever we felt under the government we have lately renounced and shaken off."

This appeal to reason and rights only incited the city's militants. Days after its publication, a new broadside exhorted the "Gentlemen and Fellow Citizens" of Philadelphia to "Rouse! Rouse! Rouse!" "The time is now arrived to prove whether the suffering friends of [our] country are to be enslaved, ruined and starved, by a few over-bearing Merchants, a swarm of Monopolizers and Speculators, an infernal gang of Tories. . . . I call upon you all, in the name of our Bleeding Country, to rouse up as a Lyon out of his den." Signaling the advancing sense of desperation, the sheet was signed "Come on Warmly."

This time, however, the city answered with silence. Soon the committee itself began to flag, its project too vexing, the members "too various in their ideas to concur in all measures expected from them." On September 24, the committee notified the Assembly that it planned to disband.

The delegates in Congress felt the pressure of rising prices just as keenly as the Philadelphia committee movement, and in September announced a new plan to restore the value of the currency. Key to the plan was a vow to cap Continental emissions at two hundred million dollars; any further expenditures would be funded through taxes raised by the states and paid in to the national treasury.

These steps toward fiscal restraint were accompanied by a renewed pledge to support the dollar by funding the Continental debt. It was a matter of national honor. "A bankrupt faithless republic would be a novelty in the political world, and appear among reputable nations like a common prostitute among chaste and respectable matrons," the Congress declared in a circular letter to the states. "The pride of America revolts from the idea; her citizens know for what purposes these emissions were made, and have repeatedly plighted their faith for the redemption of them . . . knowing the value of national character, and impressed with a due sense of the immutable laws of justice and honor, it is impossible that America should think without horror of such an execrable deed."

Robert Morris took some comfort in this declaration. "It seems as if the Continent were to go mad at one Season or other & show it by acts of injustice & oppression against one another," he mused to a friend. "Revolutions such as ours cannot be effected without violence but still I hope soon to see our Finance change for the better and that people will grow less turbulent. Congress have passed resolutions which lay the corner stone for appreciation [of the currency], it behooves every state to clap her shoulder heartily to the plow and if they do their duty all will go well our money must recover its value."

Patience, Morris counseled. "Spain having joined in the war it seems impossible but that that old tyrant Britain must have her hands full, our Independence is sure. Peace and a glorious one must come, and our money must and will be paid off by Taxation."

But the Philadelphia radicals and their allies in the militia were in no mood to await the outcome of still another congressional initiative. With the price committee defunct and every legal recourse exhausted, their resentment finally boiled over.

• • •

On the morning of Monday, October 4, a handbill called all the militia in the city to assemble on the commons across 10th Street from Byrne's Tavern, a half-mile northeast of the State House. The idea was "to drive from the city, all disaffected persons, and all who supported them." The same morning, a messenger went to ask Charles Willson Peale, who was a militia captain as well as a Constitutionalist leader, to come out and take charge of the action.

Peale made the trip along with several other sometime militia officers, but by now a breach had opened between the rank-and-file militia and their officers. Peale wrangled with the angry soldiers for more than an hour, but found that "to reason with a multitude of devoted patriots assembled on such an occasion was in vain." Peale returned to the city to alert President Reed, whom he found ill and confined to bed.

By this time most of the city was aware the militants were planning to march. Several of their likely targets assembled a small brigade of their own at the City Tavern. Robert Morris was on hand with other leaders of the Republican Society, including James Wilson and George Clymer. Wilson appeared to be a particular focus of militia resentment—the legal defense he mounted for the accused Tories a year before had not been forgotten, or forgiven.

There were also a number of seasoned soldiers in the group—Stephen Chambers, a militia officer and member of the state Supreme Executive Council; Wilson's brother-in-law Mark Bird, who had raised a militia battalion under his own command; Major David Franks, an aide to Benedict Arnold; and Lieutenant Robert Campbell, a veteran who had lost an arm fighting with the Continental Army on Staten Island. Weapons were passed around and two men sent off to obtain ammunition; soon after, General Mifflin, as Thomas Mifflin was universally called, arrived to direct the novices in handling their arms. If the militia came for them, they would encounter a spirited resistance.

Word of potential strife had also reached the members of the First City Troop, a volunteer cavalry brigade founded in 1775. Known derisively as the "Silk Stocking Brigade," it was composed of sons of the city's most prominent families and commanded by John Cadwalader. These mounted soldiers felt little affinity for the hardscrabble militia, and agreed to stay close by their stables, ready to muster should an alarm be sounded.

The militia made its first foray from the commons soon after Peale left them. They marched into town, two hundred strong, drums rattling and fifes piping, crossed Market Street, and halted outside the Friends Meeting House on Fourth Street. They were standing there at noon when the Friends' Yearly Meeting let out, and grabbed Jonathan Drinker, a prominent Quaker. Moving on, they seized Buckridge Sims, Thomas Story, and Mathew Johns, all supposed Tories.

The triumphant militia marched their quarry to Byrne's Tavern, stopped to quaff a cup or two, and then headed back into town, this time on Arch Street, a block above Market, driving the hapless prisoners before them, drums beating the "Rogue's March." When they halted briefly around Fifth Street, Thomas Mifflin caught up with them—the boisterous throng was not hard to find—and attempted to intervene. He spoke with Captain Ephraim Falkner, one of the militia commanders, until he was shoved from behind with the butt of a musket. At another point in the march, Benedict Arnold also rode up in his carriage to intercede, but was driven off with growls and a shower of paving stones.

His conference over, Mifflin hurried back to the City Tavern, while the militiamen resumed their parade down Arch Street to the waterfront. They wheeled to the south, and at Chestnut Street turned again, now into town. Reaching Second Street they saw, a block away, the conclave of well-dressed and well-armed men on the cobblestones before the City Tavern; at the same moment, the Republicans spied the marching militia.

Wilson, Morris, and their cohort now retreated a block east to take shelter in Wilson's house, on the corner of Third and Walnut. The militia shouted out three huzzahs, and then began a leisurely but deliberate pursuit. Arriving in front of City Tavern, they raised another cheer, then made their way up Walnut.

James Wilson's house stood three stories tall, with smaller, single-story wings facing both Third and Walnut Streets, all built of brick. There was a main entry on Walnut, a door opening onto Third, and another door at the rear. By this time there were more than thirty men inside, Morris among them. The doors were barricaded and the windows shuttered. Wilson had sent his pregnant wife, Rachel, and their three children off to find shelter with Mary Morris.

The militia column reached Wilson's house and paused to raise another cheer. The last of the marchers had just passed by when Lieutenant Campbell, posted at a third-story window, threw open the shutters and shouted down to the throng. Here the several eyewitness accounts differ; some say Campbell fired a pistol, others assert positively that the first shot came from the street below. What is clear is that Campbell was immediately struck dead, the one-armed veteran becoming the first casualty of what came to be known as the battle of Fort Wilson.

Once the shooting started, both sides opened up full blast. Gunfire echoed off the cobblestones, and within minutes five bodies were sprawled in the street. The rioting militia scattered, but not in retreat. Some circled the house to pour on fire from the rear. Others left in search of crowbars and hammers to break down the doors; a few men ran off to fetch a cannon from the city armory.

From inside the house, Thomas Mifflin shouted an order that the militia disperse. He was answered with a musket ball that smashed into the window sash close by his head. Mifflin fired off a brace of pistols and withdrew.

Now the sledges and the crowbars arrived, and a team of men sprinted to the back side of the house. They broke through the rear door and surged inside, only to be met by withering fire from the stairs and basement "which dropped several of them." The closest of the defenders, Stephen Chambers, was slashed with a bayonet, but the intruders were repulsed.

Out in the street, a squad of militia was just turning the corner with a piece of field artillery when President Reed, roused from his sickbed by the sound of gunfire, came galloping up the street. He was trailed by several riders from the City Troop, among them Timothy Matlack, and a number of Continental cavalry. Calling out the order "Charge all armed men," Reed rode "cutting and slashing" into the panicked militia. The firing quickly ceased.

In the immediate aftermath, Reed's posse rounded up twenty-seven of the stunned militiamen and the rest of the body broke up and fled. Wilson, Morris, and the rest of the shaken Republicans made their way out of the bullet-pocked house and into the street, the warm air acrid with the scent of burnt powder. They had lost one man slain and several injured; John Mifflin, Thomas's brother, had taken a bullet through both hands. The exact number of militia casualties was never determined, but they got the worst of the action. The best estimates hold four militiamen dead and fourteen wounded, some of them "dangerously." A bystander, "a black boy" caught in the crossfire, was also killed.

The defenders of Fort Wilson, feeling relieved and perhaps a bit gallant, now formed a parade of their own. With Robert Morris in the lead, they marched up Second Street, past the City Tavern, and across Market Street, as if to prove that they had survived the fiery seige. The populace made clear where their sentiments lay; the clutch of burghers "were insulted everywhere," especially in the poor, rough, northern district of town. The

City Troop, detailed to patrol the streets that evening, fared even worse, as restive citizens lobbed bricks and "large stones" from upper-story windows. Meanwhile, after the captured militia members were escorted to the city jail, a mob formed to try to break in and free the prisoners. As evening fell, armed guards were stationed outside.

After their foray through the streets, Wilson and Morris huddled with Reed and several city officials. Wilson, it was determined, was not safe in the city. He was reluctant to leave, but at Morris's prodding he retreated to The Hills, which was still under repair. Several other Republican stalwarts also decided to flee. "God help us—Terrible times," wrote Samuel Patterson, an officer of the Delaware militia, then mustered in Philadelphia. "The poor are starving here and rise for redress. Many flying the city for fear of Vengeance."

In the wake of the violence, with the jail crowded and the taverns rife with rumors, the city spent a restive, anxious night. Over four years of war Philadelphia had been garrisoned, invaded, and occupied by the enemy, but the first pitched battle to occur within the confines of the city had taken place between factions of her own citizens.

The aftermath of the Fort Wilson Riot was marked by grief and anger. The next day, a Tuesday, Joseph Reed was called out to Germantown, where a band of militia intended marching on Philadelphia to avenge their fallen brethren. Reed managed to deter them, but in the meantime Timothy Matlack, faced with an irate crowd outside the courthouse, ordered the imprisoned militia released; upon exiting the prison gates, they drew up in a line and gave three defiant and "very loud" cheers. Hours later, as Robert Morris recorded in a letter to Wilson, "The poor unfortunates that lost their lives yesterday [were] buried this evening with the honors of war—a circumstance not calculated to allay the passions of men in a ferment."

In the days that followed, President Reed did his best to administer justice with an even hand. On Wednesday, he decreed that the Fort Wilson defenders should appear and post bail. He then called a meeting of "both parties," attended by Robert Morris along with several militia commanders. There Reed harangued everyone involved and threatened to resign his office if peace and order were not restored. In an address to the Assembly, Reed regained his composure, describing the episode "as the casual overflowings of liberty."

Morris left the conference reassured that "upon the whole there seems to be a sort of compromise . . . a fair hearing shall be given to both sides."

This, he wrote to Wilson, was all he could hope for. "I am well satisfied being always ready to submit to the same Laws that I look up to." But that did not mean the storm was over. "The militia officers are to call out the battalions this afternoon"—October 6, two days after the riot—"but without arms." The militia would then draw up memorials to the Assembly to state their grievances. "This measure I don't much like because I fear the men's minds are just now too much heated," Morris worried. "Should they get liquor this may be an afternoon or night of danger wherefore I think to stay Home."

Morris reported to Wilson that his wife and children were safe, but advised him to remain at The Hills. "You may depend that the rage is great and general against you at present, therefore you must not by any means venture into Town this night." As for himself, Morris was relieved to find that, "I have assurance from many quarters that no injury is intended against me." Morris then dispatched a domestic slave named James to bring to Wilson a parcel of food, the latest news, and the key to the wine cellar.

The next day Morris wrote again, advising Wilson to leave the state. "Retreat until the ferment is over, you may then be heard patiently and have justice done to you." For one who had just endured such a fearsome ordeal as the siege of Fort Wilson, Morris wrote with a surprising degree of composure. "In the present state of things the passions of men might do you injustice that their own judgments would hereafter condemn or their humanity regret."

Wilson was not so sanguine. Replying to Morris he insisted that the Republican Society and their allies organize to "give some stability to our defense of the first rights of man," a measure that would "unite and strengthen us, and will awe the insurgents." But Morris counseled patience, and Wilson stayed away.

The annual elections for the state Assembly took place in late October, and as Pennsylvania historian Robert Brunhouse put it, "The fury against engrossers, Tories, and well-to-do Republicans in general presaged only one result." The Constitutionalist slate scored a clean sweep. With Morris and his cohort turned out of office the militants had secured, at long last, undisputed control of the government.

But the prospect of open warfare between patriot factions shook many observers to the core. Henry Laurens, no friend to the Republicans, felt the episode boded nothing but ill for the Revolution. "We are at this moment on a precipice," he wrote John Adams the night of the riot. "What I have long dreaded and often intimated to my friends seems now to be breaking forth—a convulsion among the people."

One distinct result was a rapid retreat from the politics of confrontation, and from any attempt to control prices by legislation. Prices continued their fearsome rise throughout the fall and the winter, but the Philadelphia price-fixing committee was never revived, and the parallel movement in the states to the northward soon collapsed.

In Philadelphia itself, despite the resounding success of the Constitutionalists at the polls, the events at Fort Wilson opened a breach between the radicals and their elected leadership that never quite healed. It was the Constitutionalist stalwarts Reed and Timothy Matlack, after all, who had arrived "cutting and slashing" to deliver the Republicans from the marauding militia. For Charles Willson Peale, the Fort Wilson Riot marked the end of his dalliance in the councils of militant politics. He remained an ardent patriot, however, and returned to his brushes, rendering over the next several years a remarkable set of portraits of the leaders of the American rebellion—including among his subjects Robert Morris, George Clymer, and several others who had taken cover inside the walls of the Wilson house.

It was Benedict Arnold, of all people, who first perceived the dilemma that would come to haunt the leaders of the popular movement in Pennsylvania. Arriving soon after the shooting had stopped, Arnold had limped out of his carriage and muttered to a bystander, "Your president has raised a mob and now he cannot quell it." A week later, the Assembly salted the wounds of the militia by voting unanimously to salute Reed for putting down the riot. "This House will at all times support him and the executive authority in suppressing all such dangerous and disorderly proceedings." The radicals might control the legislature, but the legislators would not condone the idea of a violent revolution at home.

Thomas Paine expressed the anguish and the ambivalence of the militants in a letter to the *Pennsylvania Packet*. "Those who unfortunately fell on either side have paid a martyrdom to mistake, and distinguished themselves as the lamented victims of wasted bravery." Despite what appeared to be universal umbrage at James Wilson, Paine suggested the assault on his house had been beyond the pale. "That Mr. Wilson is not a favorite in this state is a matter which, I presume, he is fully sensible of, yet the difference is exceedingly great, between not being in favor, and being considered an enemy."

· · ·

For Robert Morris, the election of 1779 was a watershed event. A private man until the dawn of the Revolution, he had since served continuously in public office, on the Committee of Safety, in the state Assembly, and in the Continental Congress. Now he was returned to private life, the station he so yearned to reclaim.

But Morris departed public office a changed man from the one who had joined the protests against the Stamp Act. Then, he was a popular merchant in the middle course of a rewarding career, a friend to the governing Penns but politically independent and socially admired. Now he was, whether holding office or not, a public figure, the leader of a faction with a stake in the governance of the state and the course of the nation. The progress of the Revolution had greatly expanded the public sphere; as the Quakers learned, the very act of disengagement rendered them suspect. Nobody enjoyed a truly "private" life.

Moreover, the revolutionary movement was itself divided. The early, broad support Morris enjoyed as the consensus candidate for the Committee of Inspection and the Committee of Safety had since fallen sacrifice to the strife between Constitutionalists and Republicans. Likewise within the Congress, the deep divisions over the Silas Deane affair had cost Morris the near-unanimous endorsement he received during the tribulations of 1776.

Morris's reputation for honesty and fair dealing had suffered as well. He had prevailed in his defense against a succession of charges, but the stain of accusation remained, as it would against Silas Deane. The incomplete Secret Committee ledgers were a factor, of course, but it seems unlikely that Morris could ever satisfy ardent Whigs like Henry Laurens and the Lee brothers. For them as for their allies among the Pennsylvania radicals, Morris was marked by his wealth and status as an enemy of virtue.

But as Morris understood, nobody could expect to glide quietly through the unpredictable and sometimes violent turns of the Revolution. One day's popular hero might soon find himself denounced; even Washington had his detractors. Morris could take consolation in the counsel of those who faced the same sort of trials. "You have done too much for your country not to create Enemies," William Livingston, patriot governor of New Jersey, wrote in a friendly letter. "Indeed in these times so chequered with corruption and patriotism, with public Depravity and public Virtue, to have no Enemies rather diminishes than increases the luster of one's character."

PART II

THE FINANCIER

— *Chapter 9* —

PRIVATE FORTUNE, PUBLIC PENURY

The winter of 1779 found Morris happy at home, surrounded by friends and operating at the height of his entrepreneurial powers. His wife, Mary, had grown into her role as hostess and a trendsetter in the fashions of dress and entertainment. The couple now counted five children, the oldest aged ten years and the youngest, Maria, born in April.

Morris had relinquished his last public post—his seat in the Assembly—soon after the Fort Wilson Riot, but he remained the dominant figure in the city's commercial fraternity. And in this period, after France and Spain had joined the war and despite the disruptive spiral of currency depreciation, the commercial class was growing. After years of wartime privation, the American economy was booming again, and Philadelphia led the way.

That is not to say trade had resumed its prewar dimensions. But from the nadir of the British occupation, farm output and demand for artisans had increased steadily. The millions of dollars spent by Congress in support of the army had spawned a whole new class of businessmen, a hustling array of "merchants, monopolizers, farmers, sharpers, forestallers, mushroom traders" as one wry patriot put it, "outdoing one another" in a manner bewildering to those who yearned for the staid pace of prewar life. This commercial class was matched by an equal proliferation of government functionaries, described by the Pelatiah Webster as "commissioners, quartermasters, purchasers . . . multiplied offices of so many different names that one has need of a dictionary to understand them." Like many others, Webster disdained these petty officials as a drain on the treasury and a public blight. "I wish that they were struck off the list at one dash of the pen, that their rations and clothing might be stopped . . . and that their horses might be taken away from them, that they might not be able to parade through the country on horseback, or in carriages, as they do now, with a gayety of dress, importance of air, and grandeur of equipage, very chagrining to the impoverished inhabitants who maintain them."

Amid this crowd of merchants, speculators, and civic servants, Robert Morris stood apart, his deals larger, his interests more diversified, his capital seemingly inexhaustible. To the wordly Marquis de Chastellux, visiting Philadelphia and introduced to many of its leading citizens, Morris appeared "a very rich merchant, and consequently a man of every country . . . or if you will, a citizen of the universe." Chastellux gave a rare contemporary estimate of Morris's estate: "It is scarcely to be credited, that amid the disasters of America, Mr. Morris, the inhabitant of a town just emancipated from the hands of the British, should possess a fortune of eight millions (between three and four hundred thousand pounds sterling). It is, however, in the most critical times that great fortunes are acquired."

It's hard to say where Chastellux got his figures for Morris's wealth, or to verify them, but they certainly should be placed in context. That Morris was prosperous goes without question, but the demands on his capital were nearly always equal to its supply. He spread his stock among various business partners, and in ships plying the sea, so that any given moment might find him flush or strapped, calling in debts or laying large sums out in new ventures. Morris was rich in resources, but rarely in cash.

His lifestyle reflected the tenuous nature of his fortune. For the duration of the war, his primary residence remained the house on Front Street he had occupied since his early days with the Willing firm. Typical of Philadelphia, the building presented a modest face to the street but was roomy and warm inside, a suitable showcase for fine furniture and art. Chastellux described a visit there in 1780: "His house is handsome, resembling perfectly the houses in London. He lives there without ostentation, but not without expense; for he spares nothing which can contribute to his happiness or that of Mrs. Morris, to whom he is much attached. A zealous republican and an epicurean philosopher, he has always played a distinguished part at table and in business."

Another French visitor recorded further details of the Morris home two years later. "The house is simple, but neat and proper. The doors and tables are of superb mahogany, carefully treated. The locks and trimmings are of copper, charmingly neat." In a city where the nouveau riche trumpeted their success with imported marble and cut-glass chandeliers, the Morris home was a study in decorous restraint.

Morris also continued to maintain a retreat outside the city. The repairs at The Hills went on heavily; in the interim he obtained title to Springets-bury, a villa built in the previous century by Thomas Penn. Located about halfway out on the road to The Hills, the property boasted several out-buildings, including a greenhouse that Morris converted into a cheerful dining room.

One regular visitor at Springetsbury, the man who became Morris's clos-est friend and confidant, was Gouverneur Morris. Now out of Congress himself, Gouverneur was a raconteur who loved to sit and trade stories long after dinner. The two shared the same political outlook the same salty sense of humor, and Gouverneur's law practice in Philadelphia and politi-cal contacts in New York provided ample grist for conversation. In addition, Robert and Mary had a special attraction that held Gouverneur captivated, a frequent houseguest named Catherine Livingston. The daughter of New Jersey governor William Livingston, Kitty, as she was known, was the el-dest of three sisters, all of them celebrated beauties. The youngest, Sarah, married Gouverneur's friend John Jay while still in her teens, but Kitty was not so easily conquered. Gouverneur made a passionate play for her in 1771, when he was nineteen, but she turned him away; Alexander Hamil-ton got the same answer when he fell for her six years later.

In 1779 the British staged a raid on the Livingston family seat in Eliza-bethtown. Kitty decided that New Jersey was no longer safe for her and soon after took up quarters as a guest of Mary and Robert Morris; she lived with them on and off for the next several years. By this time Gouverneur was a confirmed bachelor and notorious playboy, but he never tired of Kit-ty's company, and together they helped make the Morris home a center of gossip and society.

William Duer was another regular guest. The New York lawyer and del-egate would stay with the Morrises for a week at a stretch; when Duer's son William was born in September 1779, Morris became his godfather. Also on hand was William Bingham, the enterprising Continental agent, just returned from his post in Martinique. Bingham, then twenty-eight years old, was courting Ann Willing, eldest daughter of Thomas Willing. She was twelve years younger than her suitor, but the difference in age was no im-pediment, as the pair was wed in the fall.

This friendly circle was shaken in May 1780 when Gouverneur was maimed in a freak accident. Clambering aboard his chariot for a Sunday visit to a friend in Maryland, Morris startled the two horses in harness and they jumped before he could grab the reins. His leg caught in a wheel and was broken in several places. Doctors immediately decided to amputate, and severed his leg just below the knee.

Still just twenty-eight years old, Gouverneur survived the surgery with his health and his jovial spirits intact. When a friend wrote to suggest that the accident might actually benefit him by restraining his pursuits of pleasure, Morris answered, "My good sir, you argue the matter so handsomely, and point out so clearly the advantages of being without legs, that I am almost tempted to part with the other." Morris wasn't the only one to find humor in his misfortune. John Jay, who was informed erroneously that the accident occurred when Gouverneur leapt from the window of a married lover, wrote Robert Morris to share his concern. "Gouverneur's leg has been a tax on my heart," Jay wrote of their mutual friend. Then, in an off-color allusion to Gouverneur's amorous exploits, Jay suggested, "I am almost tempted to wish he had lost *something* else."

Freed now from the obligations of public office, and released, as well, from the cautious business practices of Thomas Willing, Robert Morris set about augmenting his fortune. It was a period of astonishing activity and initiative, a parallel to his early work with the Secret Committee, where Morris projected his vision and his credit on a scale inconceivable in the days of imperial rule. He established, in effect, the first national conglomerate, even as the new nation was taking shape.

Morris accomplished this remarkable expansion through partnerships. He began at home while still in the government, enlisting Peter Whitesides to handle some of his regional business affairs. Whitesides was not yet thirty years of age but an able entrepreneur and a friend of George Washington's. The new firm was called Peter Whitesides & Company, the name helping Morris to keep his business interests obscure, as was his practice.

Other Philadelphia partners included Isaac Hazlehurst, who sent trading ventures to Europe, and the firm Samuel Inglis & Company. Inglis, a Virginia merchant who was wiped out by the British raid on Norfolk, was managing partner; Morris and Thomas Willing provided the capital. Also in Philadelphia, Morris continued to invest in privateering ventures that brought in unpredictable but sometimes fabulous returns.

Outside his hometown, Morris extended his trading network by exploiting his government connections, though many of those derived from former associations with Willing & Morris. The most important was Jonathan Hudson, the Continental agent in Maryland. Capitalized by contributions of ten thousand pounds each by Morris and Hudson, the new firm of Jonathan Hudson & Company ventured in salt, shipping, land, rum, and large purchases of tobacco. Typically, Morris left the primary decisions to Hudson, a mode he sometimes regretted; in his correspondence he frequently upbraided Hudson for exceeding his means. "By eternally pushing beyond your strength you harass and distress all your Friends and Connections," Morris chided at one point.

To the south, Morris partnered with Benjamin Harrison and Carter Braxton, both old friends and both sometime delegates to Congress, in tobacco purchasing, and with Virginia merchant Samuel Beall in powder ventures and, in early 1780, in land investments. In South Carolina, Morris joined with Stacey Hepburn in shipping ventures to the Caribbean and to France. These comprise the most important of his new partnerships; there were dozens of others involving both trade and investment.

Key to Morris's success was the confidence he vested in his various partners. He gave advice, suggestions, and price information, and he committed his capital, but he often left final decisions to the people on the spot. Thus, writing to Hepburn in late 1779, Morris couched his directives in the most courteous terms: "I offer it to your consideration whether it may not be advisable . . ." Similarly, when a deal went sour, Morris always sought reconciliation before resorting to litigation. "I make no doubt we shall be able to settle the matter amicably," he wrote an associate regarding a trade dispute in 1780. "My disposition lies entirely that way [and consequently] I have had very little concerns in the law during the whole course of my life."

Morris was, in short, the perfect partner for commercial enterprise—affable, square-dealing, knowledgeable, and well connected. In addition, he would usually provide funds, either in equal shares or fronting the entire supply himself. These qualities helped him take advantage of the confusion brought on by the war and to emerge as the leading business figure on the continent—nimble, sagacious, and, on paper at least, rich.

But this was not the limit of Morris's commercial activities in this fruitful period. His largest enterprises were the ones he engaged in with the international figures who congregated in the capital of the upstart new nation. Far from home, determined to secure the best possible terms of trade, these foreign agents gravitated to Morris, all but insisting that he accept their propositions. The best known of these, the partnership that got the most attention at the time, was his alliance with John Holker.

From the time Holker arrived in Philadelphia in July 1779, he drafted Morris to handle his accounts and to manage extensive purchasing operations for the French armed forces. At the same time, Holker engaged Morris in a private partnership with several French firms to ship indigo and rice to France, or if commodity prices were too high, to invest in land. Much of this private business, along with the discretion on mode of investment, was directed to Hepburn in South Carolina.

The public contracts Morris managed for Holker were large, complicated, and as we have already seen, controversial. They were also not especially remunerative, as Morris was paid by commission and not in shares of profit. Accordingly, Morris accepted these terms reluctantly, but Holker pressed, plying Morris with fine wine and the prospects of more profitable speculations. When Morris finally agreed, he convinced Holker to combine public and private funds in a single account under Morris's control. Morris thus secured easy access to yet another deep pool of capital.

The business with Holker led in turn to further connections. As early as July 1778, William Smith, a prominent Baltimore merchant, resigned his seat in Congress to partner with Morris and Holker in purchasing and shipping flour from Maryland. By January 1780, the business had grown to the point that Morris drafted William Turnbull to take over day-to-day management of the Holker contracts in Philadelphia. Turnbull was another youthful merchant like Peter Whitesides, a Scot who immigrated in 1770 and found work as a purchasing agent for Pennsylvania and for the Secret Committee. With Holker and Morris as partners, William Turnbull & Company enjoyed two years of steady growth.

The most important of these new mercantile partners, the one who formed the strongest personal bond with Morris and also proved the most profitable of his connections, was Juan de Miralles, the emissary from Havana.

Miralles, or Don Juan, as he came to be known around Philadelphia, combined in one person all the various duties of a full-fledged embassy—diplomacy, espionage, and trade. He did so in a manner that Morris wholeheartedly approved, by hosting grand parties, cultivating social connections, and entering into quiet partnerships. Miralles purchased a town house on Third Street, down the street from Thomas Willing and around the corner from Morris, and secured a lease to Mount Pleasant, the largest and finest of all the country seats outside the city center. Here Miralles competed with Conrad Gerard and later his successor, the Chevalier de la Luzerne, to throw the most lavish balls and dinners on Philadelphia's social calendar. Robert and Mary Morris were a fixture at these events, Robert at Miralles's side and Mary as the belle. After attending one French affair, Chastellux noted that "Luzerne presented his hand to Mrs. Morris and gave her precedence—an honor pretty generally bestowed upon her, as she is the richest woman in the city, and all ranks here being equal, men follow their natural bent by giving preference to riches. The ball continued til two in the morning."

Key to Miralles's diplomatic mission was to maintain steady and secure communications to his superiors in Cuba and in the Spanish court at Madrid. He achieved this in the same mode adopted by the American commissioners at Paris, but to better effect; he established a private shipping channel between Philadelphia and Havana. His partner in these multifaceted ventures was Robert Morris.

In this trade Morris reversed his customary manner of doing business; here, Miralles put up capital and the official connections while Morris attended to the details, outfitting the ships, assembling cargoes, and managing sales of the returns. The first vessel they sent out, the *Greyhound*, was owned in partnership between Morris and Miralles; afterward, Morris rented ships to the Spanish envoy. Morris was careful to avoid violation of the embargo on flour, sending cargoes of beef, pork, lard, soap, and fish, and receiving returns in sugar, rum, and fruit.

At the outset, Morris enjoyed exclusive access to Havana through his association with Miralles, as Spanish trade regulations barred foreign traders. But late in 1779, after Spain officially entered the war, Miralles sought to expand the operation. No longer was the trade designed primarily to provide cover for communications; the Spanish now needed all the provisions the Americans could provide. When Pennsylvania partially suspended its own trade restrictions, flour became the primary staple in this trade, helping alleviate critical shortages in the Caribbean.

Miralles realized only modest returns from his joint ventures with Morris, as much of the funds he invested actually derived from the Spanish court and had to be repaid. Morris, however, reaped "huge profits." It was a reprise of his lucrative prewar Spanish flour trade, but this time Morris's key contact resided in Philadelphia, and was a partner and personal friend.

Besides Morris and several prominent members of Congress, Miralles cultivated a relationship with George Washington, commissioning several portraits of the general and sending gifts of fruit, nuts, and chocolate to the general and his wife. Washington embraced the attentions of the worldly Spaniard, and reciprocated by inviting Miralles to visit his camp at Morristown, New Jersey. Miralles and Luzerne made the trip in April 1780, and were received five miles from camp by an escort of two hundred mounted dragoons and "a vast concourse of spectators."

After they had spent a week in residence, Baron von Steuben staged a military review for the foreign dignitaries, but Miralles was unable to attend. He was confined to his quarters with a "pulmonic fever"; his condition deteriorated daily despite the personal ministrations of Martha Washington, and on April 28, he died. "Poor Don Juan," Robert Morris wrote a friend to share the sad news. "You cannot think how much we are shocked at the loss of that worthy creature." It was a measure of their mutual trust that, on his deathbed, Miralles named Morris, along with his personal assistant, Francisco Rendón, as executors of his estate.

Morris had lost a friend, but not his access to the Spanish market. Even as Miralles lay dying, orders were in transit from Cuba directing him to seek all the flour he could find, as a Spanish fleet had arrived just when hurricanes had destroyed the usual stocks in Mexico and elsewhere in the Caribbean. The old restrictions on foreign commerce in the Spanish islands were rescinded, and as an added incentive, customs officers would reduce import tariffs by half. More important, the Cuban governor promised to pay for flour in silver.

With Miralles's death the responsibility for Spanish affairs in America devolved on Francisco Rendón. But as he lacked the intimate ties Miralles had established with the American government, Rendón persuaded Luzerne to act as an intermediary in pressing this urgent request for flour. Congress was at the time busily working to provision French and American forces as well as the citizens of Philadelphia, but they granted special dispensation to export to Havana three thousand barrels of flour. Luzerne was concerned about disrupting the flour market with a public announcement, however, and asked Rendón to keep news of the new Spanish trade terms quiet. Rendón complied by giving Robert Morris exclusive franchise over the initial shipments.

Morris immediately set about expanding on this windfall. While preparing three vessels to sail direct to Havana, Morris suggested to Rendón that he could arrange for three more ships to load with grain at St. Eustatius and make the quick run to Cuba. Rendón was happy to comply, writing his superiors to report that he had employed "the most powerful merchant in this city and this continent." Like all shipping in the Caribbean at the time, this new flour trade ran the risk of British capture, leading Rendón to offer exceedingly favorable terms: Rendón underwrote all the expenses of the voyages, paid the salaries of master and crew, guaranteed profitable sales in Cuba, and ensured access to such primary tropical crops as sugar and fruit for return cargoes.

These measures only locked in what was already a most compelling financial incentive. A barrel of flour cost five dollars in Philadelphia, and sold in Havana for thirty or more. Even considering the risk of British cruisers and privateers, no merchant could long resist the lure of the Cuba trade.

Moving to cement his premier position in this expanding enterprise, Morris sent Robert Smith, twenty-five years old, son of his Maryland partner William Smith, to serve as his personal factor in Havana. Soon, however, Rendón expanded the circle of firms involved until most of the major houses in Philadelphia got in on the trade, and clearances for Havana climbed from thirty-two ships in 1780 to 126 in 1781, and 211 in 1782. Morris no longer held a monopoly on the Spanish trade, but he remained the leader in this wartime bonanza, shipping more than two hundred tons on his own account by early 1781. Some time later, Morris could report to a friend that, "our port is filled . . . with many, many Spanish dollars."

This survey of Morris's expanding network of private partnerships helps to illuminate the nature and extent of his commercial operations; it also provides an answer to the larger and more critical question of how he amassed his fortune. At the time and afterward, Morris's many critics assumed that he obtained his wealth through his tenure on the Secret Committee and his prominent position as a war contractor. If not illegal, his success in capitalizing on public misfortune was at least distasteful.

William Lee outlined this theory as early as 1783. Morris had begun the war in "bankruptcy," Lee wrote in his personal letter book; then, "When the American war commenced, he had the address to get the direction of the expenditure of the greatest part of the paper money issued by Congress, till at length he brought the United States of America to a public bankruptcy, while he, at the same time, amassed an immense fortune for himself." This rendering has been preserved among a certain school of historical writers; Thomas Abernethy, chronicler of early Virginia, put it succinctly in 1937: "The idea that Robert Morris financed the Revolution out of his own pocket is purely mythological. The truth is that the Revolution financed Robert Morris."

Considering the scattered accounts of the Secret Committee and the chaotic state of wartime commerce in general, a perfect verdict on Morris's business practices is probably impossible. But in light of Morris's burst of creative and successful entrepreneurial activity after leaving public office, the blanket assertions of Lee and Abernethy can be easily set aside. While it is true that Morris greatly augmented his fortune during the course of the war, it is also clear that his commercial endeavors while in office, and particularly for the Secret Committee, often were conducted at a loss. It cannot be stated conclusively which activities profited him the most, but Morris had a variety of legitimate enterprises that were each more lucrative than his government work. It was in his private capacity, and especially in his association with the emissaries of the European powers, that Morris became rich.

While Morris and many other Philadelphia merchants were enjoying a commercial resurgence, the years 1779 and 1780 were disastrous for the fortunes of the government, both state and national. Paralyzed by the collapse of the currency, the Congress pushed the crisis back on the states, calling for tens of millions in taxes, and when those appeals came to naught, requesting contributions in kind, mass quantities of flour and grain. "The different states must supply those demands," one delegate mused, "or the period will shortly arrive when the whole Continent may totter to its foundation."

The brunt of this continuing dysfunction fell on the army. Camped once again on the heights above Morristown, Washington and his men endured the coldest winter in a century by subsisting on half-rations for weeks on end. Valley Forge is famous as the scene of the army's deepest privation, but two years later, Morristown was even worse. "Our magazines are absolutely empty everywhere, and our commissaries entirely destitute of money or credit to replenish them," Washington wrote to Joseph Reed in December. "We have never experienced a like extremity at any period of the war . . . there is every appearance the army will infallibly disband in a fortnight."

The army did not disband—it subsisted on what scraps it could forage or commandeer in the surrounding countryside—but the suffering continued. Small mutinies flared up, desperate soldiers taking to the road and heading home until turned back at bayonet point by troops sent in pursuit. Interstate conventions were called to regulate prices, but after the debacle of the Philadelphia price committees, such schemes died for lack of interest.

From his unaccustomed station as a private citizen, Robert Morris watched the progress of events with some detachment, but not without interest. He applauded the decision to stop new emissions of currency, even advising his trading partners to invest in new government securities. "Money they will want," Morris said of the Congress in December, "and I think every well-wisher to the country should make it a point to supply them." He added, with his customary bravado, "I have no doubt of these bills being paid."

Lincoln Park #380
2746 N Clybourn Ave
Chicago, IL 60614
(773) 360-2053

3A Member 111851954196
648220 KSCOQ10100CT 21.99 E
SUBTOTAL 21.99
TAX 0.49
**** TOTAL 22.48
CASH 40.00
CHANGE 17.52

E 2.25% TAX 0.49
TOTAL TAX 0.49
TOTAL NUMBER OF ITEMS SOLD = 1
08/01/2016 13:43 380 13 119 100
OP#: 100 Name: KANEISHA
Thank You!
Please Come Again
Whse:380 Trm:13 Trn:119 OP:100

Morris was willing, as well, to pitch in to the cause directly. Richard Peters, president of the Continental Board of War, recalled one such occasion in a memoir. Peters was attending a ball given by Juan Miralles, but found himself preoccupied with a problem of logistics. For weeks he'd been unable to get hold of any quantity of lead to supply the army with bullets; he'd scoured the city, even sending his agents to pull downspouts off private houses, until every local supply was exhausted. At the party, Peters encountered Morris, whom he'd known for years.

Morris "discovered [in me] some casual trait of depression," Peters recalled later. "He accosted me in his usual frank and disengaged manner, saying, 'I see some clouds passing across the sunny countenance you assume; what is the matter?' " Peters described his predicament, and Morris made light of the problem, teasing his old friend. "He played with my anxiety," Peters wrote.

"At length, however, with great and sincere delight, [Morris] called me aside, and told me that the *Holker* privateer had just arrived at his wharf, with ninety tons of lead, which she had brought as ballast. . . . 'You shall have,' said Mr. Morris, 'my half of this fortunate supply.' " Morris then pointed out his partners in the venture, who were also attending the ball. Peters confessed to Morris that he was "already under heavy personal engagements as guarantee for the department" to Morris's friends, and could not expect they would extend him credit to purchase the balance of the lead. " 'Well,' Mr. Morris rejoined, 'they will take your assumption with my guarantee.' I instantly, on these terms, secured the lead, left the entertainment, sent for the proper officers, and set more than one hundred people to work during the night. Before morning a supply of cartridges was ready and sent off to the army. I could relate many more such occurrences."

In March 1780 the free fall of the currency and the destitution of the army forced the Congress into a drastic act. Without funds and fast losing public confidence, the Congress voted to devalue its bills then in circulation at a rate of forty to one.

This was a distinct about-face, precisely the "wanton violation of the public faith" that Congress had forsworn just six months before. But three years of sporadic price legislation and appeals to patriotic virtue had failed to dampen the pace of inflation; something had to be done to jolt matters out of their perilous course.

Devaluation of the currency was the most dramatic feature of the March resolution, but not the most ambitious: the idea was to launch a new funding system that would replace the disgraced Continental dollar with a new, sound paper currency. The old dollars would be retrieved by taxation at a rate of fifteen million dollars a month; as the states sent these funds in to the treasury, the old bills would be destroyed and new bills issued that would draw 5 percent interest. Six tenths of the new bills would be returned to the states, which might then apply them toward the specific supplies required by the Congress, and the balance would be retained by Congress for its own operations. To prevent another round of depreciation, the new issue was capped at ten million; as with its prior emissions, Congress advised the states to force the new currency into circulation by making it legal tender.

It was an awkward and unwieldy plan, but that may have been inevitable in any scheme to launch a new paper medium in place of one that had already broken down. More than that, the restructuring represented a tacit acknowledgment by Congress that it had failed to function as a national government. The new currency, and with it the hopes of prevailing in the contest with Britain, now rested entirely on the states.

This decision accorded with the whole jury-rigged framework of America's revolutionary governance; the Congress had in reality never been afforded more power than a debating society, a sort of United Nations for the former colonies. But turning such critical matters over to the individual states presumed that they were in any better position than the national council to harness and direct the affairs of the people. In the months that followed the depreciation, that idea was largely put to rest.

Pennsylvania quickly emerged as the state where the new scheme for Continental administration received its most important test. Under the prodding of President Joseph Reed, the Assembly responded gamely, answering the call of Congress by collecting in taxes, through the spring of 1780, more than six million dollars in near-worthless currency and forwarding it to the Continental treasury. Then, when the official devaluation stripped the state of a circulating medium, the Assembly voted its own issue of new paper currency, one hundred thousand pounds bearing 5 percent interest.

Robert Morris had several reasons to track these developments closely. As a merchant, he was financially invested in the state of the currency. As a statesman, albeit one in retirement, he was concerned with the sinking status of the Congress. And as a leader of the political opposition in Pennsylvania, he held a partisan interest in the fortunes of his adversaries.

Morris saw the devaluation as the logical extension of poor fiscal management, another step in the misguided attempt to direct fiscal affairs by legislative fiat. But he understood that public affairs hung in too critical a balance to sustain a new and divisive policy dispute. When the Assembly announced its new emission, small traders and artisans especially bridled at the prospect of another round of dubious paper. It was left to Morris, the voice of the mercantile community, to set the plan in motion. "At first there was great opposition and clamor," Joseph Reed recorded in May, "but Mr. Morris having expressed himself in its favor, stemmed the tide, and it met with an uncommon approbation."

Whatever influence Morris was able to exert in support of the new state emission, the fund was wholly inadequate to revive the procurement program in Pennsylvania. "The neglect of the taxes has brought us to the brink of ruin," Reed wrote to a colleague in the government, "and we are daily groaning under the deplorable want of money." Despite the official devaluation, the Continental dollar continued its fall, slipping to an exchange of sixty-five to one. "Money," Reed groaned, "Money is our great object at present, and unless we can find it, we shall have no army in a little time."

Morris assayed the shattered state of American finance in a letter to Silas Deane, who was then in Virginia pending his return to France. His tone was surprisingly gentle, considering the general tenor of political discourse at the time, and his view long-term. "The affairs of finance are not well understood in Congress, and their regulations, meant for the best, generally operate badly," Morris wrote.

"That is like to be the case in the last instance"—a reference to the forty-to-one devaluation—"but the thing will bring its own remedy like most disorders in the human body that arise from repletion."

Morris elaborated on this medical analogy. "The fever that threatens destruction, brings about a purification that restores the patient to good health. So in this redundancy of paper circulation, after all the feverish palliations of restrictions, regulations, limitations etc., are found ineffectual, they will be universally condemned, cool taxation will take place, and common sense—not your friend *Common Sense*—take place in the minds of the people. Then, and not till then, will our finances be put in the train that they ought to be.

"This, I now think, is the most formidable enemy we have to contend with."

Morris was not alone in recognizing finance as the crucial factor in the struggle for independence. As early as 1778, while he was wrestling with the thankless business of the quartermaster department, Nathanael Greene declared, "It appears to me more and more probable that this dispute will terminate in a war of funds." By May of 1780, George Washington was thinking the same way. "In modern wars," the general advised Joseph Reed, "the longest purse must chiefly determine the event."

This was more than just an aphorism. Washington understood that England was not the richest nation in Europe, and claimed just a third the population of France, but that her large public debt, arranged and administered through the Bank of England, rendered her more powerful than any of her rivals. "Their system of public credit," Washington wrote, "is capable of greater exertion than that of any other nation."

Washington offered these observations as a preamble to his main point— that France was a valuable ally, but unless he was able to move quickly and concert a joint campaign, England's more resilient finances would prove decisive. Time was running short for the Revolution, and Reed must act. "Either Pennsylvania must give us all the aid we ask of her, or we undertake nothing . . . the fate of the States hangs upon it."

Faced with such a stark admonition, Reed could only stammer. He was a popular politician, but an ineffectual executive, a point he made with surprising candor in his reply to the general. "The country is much recovered from the distress of the war," Reed conceded to Washington in June. Pennsylvania "really has the three great requisites of war, men, provisions and iron . . . our difficulty is, to draw them forth." Reed had long recognized the futility of commercial laws—embargoes, price controls—which he termed "impracticable from the beginning." But now he blamed his fiscal woes on the plots of his enemies. "The parties in Congress have weakened the influence, and lessened the weight of that body"—this was a reference to the interminable public wrangle over Silas Deane—"and the internal divisions have had the like effect on the [state] governments, so that every measure, however necessary for the general good, has been timid, feeble and languid."

This was Reed's overriding preoccupation—he saw himself as a conciliator between the radicals and the moderates, and was convinced that the obstinance of the Republicans lay at the root of his frustration. "The country not immediately the seat of either party is richer than when the war began," he complained, "but the long disuse of taxes, and their natural unpalatableness, have embarrassed the business exceedingly, and Tories, grumbling Whigs, and party, have all thrown in their aid to increase the discontent."

• • •

Through the course of the spring it became apparent that the funding plan put forward by Congress, and the new Pennsylvania currency, had failed to win the confidence of the public. At the same time, continuing privation had pushed the army to the point of utter breakdown. "I assure you," Washington emphasized to Reed, "every idea you can form of our distresses will fall short of the reality. . . . All our departments, all our operations are at a stand, and unless a system very different from that which for a long time has prevailed be immediately adopted throughout the states, our affairs must soon become desperate beyond the possibility of recovery."

The same week that Washington wrote that ominous letter, still more bad news arrived from the South. Charleston had fallen, after a three-months siege, with more than three thousand American soldiers made prisoner. News of this debacle, Thomas Paine recalled several years later, "depressed the spirits of the country." One downcast member of the Pennsylvania Assembly actually suggested that "it would be in vain to contend" any longer with Britain. "How the public measures were to be carried on," Paine wrote, "the country defended, and the army recruited, clothed, fed, and paid . . . was a matter too gloomy to look at."

With Congress reeling and the state government moribund, Robert Morris stepped dramatically into the breach. If the public entities could not act, the private sector might. On June 8, Morris and several score "men of property" gathered at the London Coffee House to raise a fund "to be given in bounties to promote the recruiting service of the United States." Before the week was out, Philadelphia's merchants and traders had raised four hundred pounds in hard money and more than one hundred thousand dollars in Continental paper. The funds were immediately put to use not as bounties, but in purchasing five hundred barrels of flour for the troops at Morristown.

This was not the only volunteer scheme that flourished in this forbidding time. While their men were meeting at the Coffee House, the prominent women of the city launched a fund-raising drive of their own, going door-to-door to press for donations. Esther Reed, wife of the state president, was named the head of the group, and by June 20, Joseph Reed was able to boast to Washington that "The ladies have caught the happy contagion."

Mary Morris answered the call, along with her friends Rachel Wilson and Hannah Thomson, the wife of Charles Thomson. These right-thinking matrons pursued their charge with such enthusiasm that one loyalist visiting from New York wrote home to complain. "Of all the absurdities the ladies going about for money exceeded everything; they were so exceedingly importunate that people were obliged to give them something to get rid of them . . . nor did they let the meanest ale house escape."

The women's charity drive ended up raising about the same amount as their husbands' did, but it was the more formal association of merchants that captured the imagination of the Congress. "Our greatest hopes . . . are founded on a patriotic scheme of the opulent merchants of this city," James Madison enthused. Another Virginia delegate wrote Thomas Jefferson to praise the the idea of raising private revenue. "This patriotic fire 'tis hoped will spread both North and South."

Once broached, the idea of tapping the merchants for cash had such obvious and immediate appeal that several candidates promptly stepped forward to claim patrimony. William Livingston wrote a friend to report that he was hoisting drinks at a tavern when "I happened to drop a wish that the Merchants of this place would undertake a temporary subscription upon their own credit. . . . Upon its being broke to the merchants they appointed a committee." Thomas Paine later made a similar claim; this was supported by a letter he sent in late May to Blair McClenaghan, a wealthy merchant and an old friend. Voluntary fund-raising was commonplace in England, Paine noted, and such "subscriptions" were "far more necessary here because the depreciation has effectually disabled every government." Paine then proposed that the Philadelphia merchants "set an honorable example," and committed five hundred dollars of his own as a down payment.

More important than Paine's supposed contribution—the five hundred dollars was apparently returned to him—was the simple fact of his support for the project. A committed Constitutionalist and a public foe of Morris, Paine's early endorsement showed him to be something more than the partisan ideologue that he appeared. His thinking had evolved. His service on the Philadelphia price committee had cured him of any confidence in price controls, and, in the words of one biographer, "propelled him into the economic world of Adam Smith." In Philadelphia during the Revolution, that world was represented by Robert Morris.

Whatever the genesis of the subscription effort, the management of the fund quickly devolved to Morris. He and McClenaghan each put up the largest shares, ten thousand pounds apiece, and then helped round up the leading merchants in town to fill out the list. James Wilson, George Clymer, Jonathan Maxwell Nesbitt, John Nixon, and Thomas Willing all pitched in, as did William Bingham. Tench Francis, brother-in-law to Willing and a close friend of Morris's, was named factor for the new association.

As the funds came rolling in, Robert Morris began to reconceive the entire project. It would fulfill its patriotic mission if the money were simply collected, spent on supplies, and forwarded to Washington's army. But Morris recognized that this fund, fashioned as an institution, might be harnessed to larger goals. Since long before the war, Morris and Thomas Willing had dreamed of forming a bank; now, with the currency in arrears and the economy in tatters, that dream was suddenly within reach.

Morris presented his plan at a second meeting, this on June 17, a Saturday, at City Tavern. The "subscribers" would deposit their funds by installment, to a target of three hundred thousand pounds, and would receive in return interest-bearing notes payable in six months; at that time the donors were to be reimbursed by Congress. In the meantime the funds would be committed to the purchase of three million daily rations, and three hundred hogsheads of rum, for the soldiers of the Continental Army. The new institution was to be called the Pennsylvania Bank.

This wasn't a proper bank, collecting savings and making loans at interest, but it was a public depository for private funds, and as such unprecedented in Pennsylvania and all of America. More than that, it posed a striking alternative to the mode of supporting public currencies by force of law; the notes of the new bank would circulate at par based on the faith placed by the merchants who accepted them in the credit of the issuing institution. In a place and time where banking was a novel concept, this rudimentary form would serve as an introduction to the whole idea.

Congress immediately gave the plan all the support in its power. Less than a week after the bank was announced, the delegates pledged the faith of the United States to the "effectual reimbursement and indemnity" of the subscribers. As surety, they directed the Board of Treasury to lodge with the bank bills of exchange made out against the commissioners in Paris; these bills might be negotiated if Congress were unable to reimburse the subscribers on schedule.

While the bank project answered a long-held commercial ideal, Morris had political goals in mind as well. From the moment of its inception, the Constitutionalists had disparaged the Republican Society as self-interested and somehow inimical to the goals of the Revolution. The roster of this new patriotic association presented a firm rebuttal to that formula; of ninety-two subscribers, twenty-one were Republican founders, and several others— Richard Peters, Thomas Willing, Charles Thomson—were fellow travelers. Blair McClenaghan was a Constitutionalist, but there was no mistaking the anti-constitutionalist nature of the larger group.

Joseph Reed certainly saw the bank in a political light. "The new plan of a Bank seems to go on with great spirit; and I hope will continue to do so, as it appears to be the only system which can give timely aid," Reed wrote to Washington. "But the finger of party is so manifest that I sometimes have my doubts." Political animal that he was, Reed made sure his name appeared at the top of the list of subscribers, but that must have been a sour duty. Washington, no less political than Reed, used Reed's obvious discomfort to prod him. Answering Reed a week later, Washington noted that the bank had been established by "the party opposed to you"; he then twisted the blade. "It will undoubtedly give them great credit with the people, and you have no effectual way to counterbalance this, but by employing all your influence and authority to render services [to the army] proportioned to your station."

Washington did not let the matter rest there. In a move that demonstrated either startling indelicacy or the full measure of his pique, he wrote in July to Esther Reed to suggest that she deposit in the bank the proceeds of her fund-raising. "This, while serviceable to the Bank, and advancing its operations, seems to have no inconvenience to the intentions of the ladies. By uniting the efforts of patriotism, they will reciprocally promote each other, and I should imagine the ladies will have no objection to a union with the gentlemen."

Not surprisingly, Esther Reed deftly sidestepped Washington's advice, and immediately laid her funds out in linen that was fashioned into shirts for the soldiers. She never mentioned to her husband the general's suggestion of collaborating with the bank.

While Washington maintained a friendly tone in his correspondence with Reed, he soon concluded that Reed's skepticism of the bank was misplaced. By August, Washington informed Morris the bank was now his principal source of supplies, and suggested to Congress that similar associations be founded in all the major trading towns. Congress endorsed the plan, but no such experiments were produced.

While Joseph Reed fumed over his humiliations at the hands of the Republicans—he now referred to them as "my principal enemies"—Robert Morris took little notice of the state president or his party. He was too chagrined by his own experience of public office to celebrate the disappointments of his rivals. Writing to Silas Deane in July, Morris looked forward, taking his usual optimistic view of the prospects for America, and for himself.

The loss of Charleston came as a "shock," Morris allowed, but no more than that, as "possession of it by the enemy will advance them very little in their attempts to conquer this country." More important was the hope of launching a vigorous campaign in the north—here he was thinking on the same lines as Washington. "Most anxiously do I wish for the arrival of the French fleet and army, now daily expected to our assistance; and in order to put General Washington on as respectable a footing as our present circumstances will admit, we are setting on foot a spirit for private exertions to favor and support the public measures. The ladies have made a liberal donation to the American soldiers. A subscription is on foot for raising bounties to be given soldiers enlisting for the war. A Bank is established in this city for the purpose of facilitating provisions and rum for the army, and I need not tell you the real satisfaction I feel in being essentially useful in forming, promoting and supporting those measures."

Here Morris made a bold pronouncement:

"It is in the line of private exertions that I shall hence forward evince my attachment to my country and its interests, being determined to keep myself clear of all that public employment." Morris didn't complain of the workload, the distraction from his affairs, as he had in the past. What he wanted was to preserve his privacy. High public station "exposes an honest man to the envy and jealousy of mankind at the same time that it lays him open to the malicious attacks of every dirty scoundrel that deals in the murder of reputations." This passage was written in sympathy for Deane's long travails before the Congress; but Morris was also speaking from fresh, personal experience.

Now he turned to matters of commerce. Deane had proposed, upon his return to France, to serve as an agent locating investors interested in American lands. Morris, James Wilson, and others would syndicate to secure title to large frontier tracts, and cut out pieces to sell at a substantial markup. Such schemes had for years been tantalizing to merchants, planters, and power brokers in Europe as well as America; perhaps now, with independence just over the horizon, would be the right time to strike.

"It is my fixed intention to execute the plan in some degree," Morris wrote, "but to what extent I cannot now say; my attention is exceedingly engaged by a great variety of objects." Here Morris summarized the fruits of his season of private pursuits. "My commerce increases on my hands, and for twelve months or more much success has attended me which naturally multiplies both objects and connections.

"My assistance is still necessary to Mr. Holker, whose honesty, virtue and merit entitle him to every thing I can do for him, and I consider his country entitled to my best exertions in their service, for their liberal aid to this country. . . . I mention these things to show you cause for any delay that may happen in this land plan. Be assured that if I engage in it I shall meddle with no lands but what I have reason to believe valuable, nor transact any thing in such a way as to raise a blush in either your face or mine at a future day."

It's hard to know what to make of Morris's avowed determination to preserve his private status. The profits from his expanding enterprise certainly validated his past claims that engagement in public affairs came at cost of personal gain. And surely he was candid in the pain he expressed at public vilification. Always garrulous, accustomed to cheerful toasts and slaps on the back, he prized his reputation for hospitality and civic generosity; to find his long and sometimes arduous months of effort in government service widely attacked and disparaged had to be maddening.

But Morris must have known this pose was mostly bluster. He was too deeply engaged in a contest far too consequential for him simply to walk away. Late in the summer of 1780, Morris returned to the public lists, submitting his name to a Republican slate in the annual election for state Assembly. In October, Morris and his allies swept the field, winning Philadelphia's legislative seats by a three-to-one margin. The results reportedly surprised both sides, but it's not hard to fathom the city's shift in allegiance. The radicals' year in control of the Assembly and the Executive Council had brought them confusion and disgrace. The new bills issued in March quickly depreciated, and Joseph Reed had largely failed in his efforts to raise supplies for the army. Just as he'd feared, the popular success of the Pennsylvania Bank helped restore the standing of the Republicans. Whether expected or not, Morris had once again returned to public station.

When the new legislature sat in November, the House was politically divided and bedeviled by the continuing collapse of the currency. It was a poor prescription for legislative action, and by early December a dejected Joseph Reed reported to a friend, "Our Assembly affairs go on very badly, and slowly."

Morris's participation in the first session was limited by illness. First his wife Mary, and then he himself were all but incapacitated by a "breakbone fever" that lasted more than a month. "My dear Molly is reduced to a skeleton by constant pain," Morris related to a friend, Molly being Mary's nickname. One of the children and two longtime servants were also taken ill; one servant, a Dutch woman named Catherine Fugletesong, who lived in the household for years, died. "I have nothing but tales of woe," Morris wrote.

This gloomy period was marked by sudden and unsettling developments. In September, Philadelphia and all of America learned of the treason of Benedict Arnold. Furious at his rough handling by Reed and the radical Assembly, burdened by mounting personal debts, Arnold in July had opened a secret communication with Sir Henry Clinton, the British commander in New York. Arnold was court-martialed soon after on charges brought by Reed. After the military tribunal returned a mixed verdict, Washington sought to assuage Arnold's pride by assigning him to command of the American fort at West Point. But Arnold's loyalties had already turned, and he began plotting with Clinton to open the post to British forces. His betrayal was exposed with the arrest of his intermediary, the dashing British officer John André, who was charged with espionage, tried, and executed. With Arnold's treason America at once lost her most celebrated military hero and, upon his appointment to British command, gained a formidable new adversary in the field.

The Congress also lost some of its leading lights. John Jay was sent abroad as ambassador to Spain, and Henry Laurens, Morris's nemesis in the Silas Deane affair, was dispatched to Holland. Jay and his wife reached Madrid in August and struck up a friendly correspondence with Robert and Mary, but Laurens never arrived at his post. When he sailed for Amsterdam late in the summer, his ship was intercepted by a British cruiser. He lost his diplomatic immunity when his captors located in his papers the draft of a proposed treaty with Holland, still technically neutral. Laurens was charged with high treason, taken to England, and imprisoned in a dank cell in the Tower of London. He remained there for most of the next two years.

Laurens was gone, but Arthur Lee was back. He'd left Paris in typical fashion, intriguing with a French sea captain named Pierre Landais to usurp command of the American frigate *Alliance* from John Paul Jones. When Benjamin Franklin opposed the move, Lee composed a document proposing that Landais had the preference of Congress. With Jones in Paris, Lee and Landais traveled to L'Orient and persuaded the crew to defect. They set sail only after loading a substantial cargo on Lee's private account, leaving military stores for the American army lying on the beach.

The crossing was chaotic, as the crew and even Lee discovered Landais to be, in the words of John Adams, "an absent bewildered man—an embarrassed mind." In one of many episodes, Landais threatened Lee with a carving knife after Lee took first pass at a roast pig at the captain's table. At a subsequent court-martial, Lee testified that Landais was insane.

Arriving at Boston, Lee headed south to Philadelphia, hoping there to resurrect in Congress his feud with Franklin and Silas Deane. He fell in with Ralph Izard, also returned from Europe and now a delegate to Congress, and together they campaigned to unseat Franklin—"The political salvation of America depends on the recalling of Dr. Franklin," Izard pronounced. Fortunately for all involved, the other delegates had no interest in reviewing Lee's brief. "Arthur Lee has, I believe, been much disappointed on and since his arrival at Philadelphia," James Wilson wrote in January. "No éclat, no proceedings against those whom he dislikes."

Lee found much to dislike in the capital. Within weeks he discovered in James Duane of New York a new "Arch-Enemy." After the new Pennsylvania Assembly was seated in November, he declared in disgust, "Toryism is triumphant here." Yet he lingered on for months to press his campaign in Congress against Franklin. Finally in February he returned home to Virginia, still penning epithets about "that old corrupt Serpent."

It was during this time that Morris received a long and seminal letter from Silas Deane. The former diplomat had crossed sea trails with his nemesis, Arthur Lee, sailing for France in late June. Deane had been stripped of his political mission, but was determined to meet in Paris with an auditor appointed by Congress to settle his accounts and clear his name. He also had several business plans to pursue—the land project with Morris; a contract with William Duer, James Wilson, and others to supply masts to the French and Spanish navies; a sheaf of Continental Loan Office Certificates to sell to French investors; and several mercantile ventures, including the ship *Jane*, which he owned with Morris, that traveled in convoy on his journey east.

In addition, Deane carried a letter of commendation from Morris to Franklin. "I consider Mr. Deane as a martyr in the cause of America," Morris wrote his old friend. "After rendering the most signal and important Services, he has been reviled and traduced in the most shameful manner. But I have not a doubt the day will come when his merit shall be universally acknowledged, and the authors of those calumnies held in the detestation they deserve."

In short, Deane had set out with high hopes for recovering his reputation and his fortune. But disappointment set in even before Deane reached France—the *Jane* foundered en route. And upon his arrival, Deane learned that the devaluation of the Continental dollar had set the minds of French investors against any American ventures. His loan certificates were all but worthless.

Despite his setbacks, Deane continued in his hopeful outlook through September, when he wrote his newsy letter to Morris. He had resumed his former lodgings with Benjamin Franklin at a suburban estate outside Paris, remained confident that lands might find a market, and said he expected to settle his accounts "in a few weeks."

Especially intriguing for Morris was the profile Deane offered of Jacques Necker, the French minister of finance. Necker was a citizen of Geneva who made his fortune in the grain trade and then helped found one of the leading banks in France. As a financial consultant to the royal treasury, Necker made a deep impression on the king when he advised in July 1776 that the prospect of war with England made it "vitally necessary to strengthen the government's credit." Three months later he was appointed director of the royal treasury, a remarkable elevation for a Protestant serving a Catholic monarch.

Necker's charge was to refurbish the French army and navy through substantial new borrowing. Faced with tight lending markets, he needed to demonstrate revenue to finance the loans. But he believed taxes were already too high, so Necker focused on the bloated networks of patronage and corruption that lurked in the shadows of the French throne. Where there were six *intendants* of finance, each costing more than a million livres a year, Necker installed four salaried secretaries answering to him alone. Where there were twenty-nine financial offices in the departments of war, navy, and foreign colonies, Necker replaced them with four. And where Necker found nineteen offices of treasurer and controller in the "king's households," he abolished them all, installing a single royal treasurer. So pleased was King Louis that he called a royal audience to demonstrate his support for his minister. Holding aloft a gilded goblet, he announced, "I wish to put order and economy in every part of my household, and those who have anything to say against it I will crush like this glass," whereupon he dashed the goblet to the floor.

In his letter to Morris, Deane heralded Necker as "our great financier." After this curious lapse of national identity, Deane offered a summary of Necker's accomplishments. "This man, though a foreigner and a protestant, is become absolute in the finance department, which is the same thing as being entirely and universally so; since he who commands the purse has everything in his power at court. His furnishing money to equip the most formidable fleet France has owned since the beginning of this century, and to support the war without any new tax or burden laid on the Kingdom, is at once a striking proof of his ability, and of the dissipation of his predecessors in office.

"This renders him dear to the nation, but as this immense sum is saved out of what was formerly dissipated by the dependents, agents, and servants of the court, he must be feared and hated, rather than loved by them, but he is become so necessary that he is secure." Deane admired Necker's accomplishments, but also "the courage of the man who has dared to make such a reform in what his predecessors, even the most patriotic of them, never dared even to examine, and in which the greatest part of them probably shared."

If Deane was hinting that Necker might serve Morris as a template for his own future course, he did not let on. It may have felt too far-fetched even to contemplate. The monarchy was an obstacle to efficient administration, certainly, but it was also capable of conferring summary powers in a way that hardly seemed possible in America's disputatious new democracy.

Deane did address Morris directly, but this was in a manner of friendly estimation. "I am rejoiced to hear of your success in commerce," Deane wrote, and then he paid homage. "If knowledge and industry in business, and a generous application of the profits resulting, entitle a man to succeed, you must surpass any man I ever knew." Now Deane offered a flourish of erudition. "As 'an honest man is the noblest work of God,' so a well-informed, extensive and generous merchant is unquestionably the most beneficial to the world, and he may with great justice say:

> 'For forms of government let fools contest;
> Whatsoever is best administer'd is best.'

I hope you will not charge me with pedantry for having quoted a few lines"—the second quote was from Alexander Pope—"which express my sentiments better, and in fewer words, than I am able to do myself."

This was flattery, to be sure, but it was more than that. The verse from Pope aptly captured Morris's personal credo, and summarized everything he had brought to the Revolution. True, he had engaged in the political contest over the Pennsylvania constitution, but always on grounds of what might work. On the Secret Committee and in the full Congress he had devoted himself to administration, leaving to others the questions of principle and dogma. Now, as the war ground through its fifth long year, Morris's practical mastery would draw him back into the vortex of the struggle.

Chapter 10

THE OFFICE OF FINANCE

It was hard to conceive and harder to convey, even to their contemporaries, the sense of distress confronting the rebel Americans and their beleaguered army as the war dragged on into the 1780s. Principals in Congress, state executives like Joseph Reed, and generals like Washington and Nathanael Greene all complained that the language failed them, that words could not describe the suffering they saw around them, and their frustration in seeking out remedies.

Thomas Paine resorted to overkill. The campfire ode he wrote to the tried souls of the patriots in 1776 was published under the title *The American Crisis*; in the succeeding years, as one reversal followed another, *The American Crisis* was serialized; numbers III, IV, V, and on up to IX, a parade of crises. But in October 1780, Paine decided that even so charged a term as "crisis" would no longer suffice. Reaching for some means to amplify, to distinguish this crisis from all the others, Paine titled this piece, *The Crisis Extraordinary.*

But it wasn't Paine's prose that lit the fuse. What awakened the Americans to a new sense of urgency, what prompted them to leave off familiar assumptions and resort to radical expedients, was the mutiny of the Continental Army's Pennsylvania Line.

Sometime after nightfall on New Year's Day of 1781, ten regiments of Pennsylvania soldiers under command of the popular general Anthony Wayne mustered out from their log huts on the flanks of Mount Kemble, near Morristown, and set out on the road to Philadelphia. Wayne and more than one hundred officers tried to stop them, but the mutineers marched on, killing one captain and wounding several other officers who blocked their path, and prodding the more reluctant of their fellow soldiers at bayonet point.

The goal of the insurgents was to lay their grievances before Congress, but the sources of their discontent were known to all. Wayne had summarized them in a succession of desperate pleas for support to Joseph Reed. "We never stood upon such perilous ground," Wayne wrote in November. In December, with the winter cold settling in, Wayne's troops were "poorly clothed, badly fed, and worse paid . . . they have not seen a paper dollar in the way of pay for near *twelve months*."

The mutineers never got to Philadelphia. They marched as far as Princeton, then stopped to treat with Wayne and President Reed, who rode out from the capital escorted by the First City Troop. The soldiers were not deserters: when British general Henry Clinton made the mistake of sending emissaries to offer bounties to anyone who would defect, they were imprisoned, charged as spies, and executed. This uprising was not a failure of commitment, but a signal that the soldiery could no longer subsist on the promises and neglect of the Congress.

The talks between Reed and the disgruntled soldiers dragged on for a week. Washington, encamped on the Hudson just above West Point, decided not to intervene, fearing that in his absence the mutiny would spread to the north. A settlement was reached on January 10, the soldiers accepting Reed's promise of restitution for back pay and depreciation. No funds were available, or course, but acknowledging the mutineers' grievances as legitimate served to pacify them.

The threat had been averted, but the Congress was deeply shaken. The old mode of business had failed—the mutiny was incontestable testimony to that—and radical transformation was at hand. In February, at the prodding of James Duane, Congress at long last abandoned the committee system, voting to place the departments of war, marine, treasury, and foreign affairs under individual executives. This was the policy that Robert Morris had been advocating as far back as 1776; now all the timeworn objections to centralized authority fell away. The crisis had opened the door. "The public distress is the only friend of the public," Gouverneur Morris observed in January. "That alone will stimulate action, banish debate, give unanimity, silence jealousy, and lull to sleep the effervescence of party rage."

It was clear from the outset that the most important of these new posts, the one with the heaviest responsibility for extricating the Congress and the nation from the dangerous straits that bound them, was at treasury. The job of superintendent of finance is generally compared to the modern secretary of the treasury, but that analogy fails to comprehend the scope of the job. As the primary administrator in the executive branch of the government, he would be responsible for every aspect of governance but the disposition of the army in the field. At a time when the central government was comprised of a single legislative house, he would fill the role later reserved for the president of the United States.

It was also clear, at this time of extraordinary crisis, that there was only one viable candidate for the job—one person with the means, the will, and the political support to fill the appointment. On February 20, at the close of their session, the delegates voted without dissent to name Robert Morris superintendent of finance. The vote was unanimous, but Massachusetts delegates Samuel Adams and Artemis Ward abstained, registering a silent tribute to the eclipse of their democratic principles.

The designation of Morris as the nation's superintendent of finance was more than a simple administrative reform; it signaled the rise of a new coalition of political leaders who believed that only a vigorous central government could concert the resources of America into one coherent force. Like the Eastern faction that preceded them, this new movement had no formal organization, no founding document, no name; they later came to be called, collectively, the Nationalists.

Though they did not emerge as a power until 1781, these advocates of a central national authority were not newcomers to the scene. Their principals included the moderates of 1776, the ones who dragged out the debates over breaking with England and opposed dismantling the old state governments. The core leaders hailed from the middle states, primarily Pennsylvania, with John Dickinson, James Wilson, and Robert Morris, and New York, represented by John Jay, William Duer, James Duane, the Livingstons, and, later, Gouverneur Morris. They explicitly rejected the original idea of Congress as a mere intermediary between the sovereign states. Dickinson's primary argument against the rush to independence had been the lack of national unity; the failure, in the years hence, to ratify the Articles of Confederation only confirmed his fears.

The fact that the Articles were signed at all was another manifestation of the rise of the Nationalist faction. The Articles had been sent out for ratification at the end of 1777 but languished for years, a hostage to the jealousies and rival land claims of several individual states, principally Virginia and Maryland. Pressed from without by a majority in Congress and from within by James Madison, a budding Nationalist then just arriving as a political force, Virginia finally relinquished her extravagant claims in January

1781, and Maryland ratified eight weeks later—the same week of Morris's appointment. The union had finally been secured, though the charter that confirmed it would prove wholly inadequate to the undertaking.

The loose coalition of moderates who became the Nationalist faction had been overrun in the rush for independence, but they remained active in the government. Indeed, through the years of defeat and disappointment these reluctant revolutionaries emerged as the most capable and most adroit administrators the struggle would produce, and they came to fill most of the critical offices in the government.

The accumulated blunders of the revolutionary leadership in the early stages of the war pushed the Nationalists back to the fore, their ranks now augmented by the prime movers in the Continental Army. Some of these military men, including Washington and his aide Alexander Hamilton, remained in the field; others, like Ezekiel Cornell and James Mitchell Varnum of Rhode Island, and John Sullivan of New Hampshire, had left the army and were now delegates to Congress. They were bound by no single, overarching creed, but shared their experience in the army, the great national project that had fallen into privation and despair. They were impatient with the tautologies of Republican ideology, and the barriers raised by claims of state sovereignty to the meaningful pursuit of national goals.

Even Thomas Paine, so active in the early push for independence and with the Pennsylvania radicals, had fallen in with the Nationalists. His *Crisis Extraordinary* of 1780 appealed to Americans to support the army by accepting trade duties and shouldering the burdens of taxation, a central Nationalist theme. The broader vision of this rising faction was reflected in the first label they came to accept for themselves; they were the Continentalists, who considered the America in the whole, not in her various parts.

Some state governments were caught up in the movement as well, their parochial concerns overshadowed by the larger emergency. In New York, the state legislature voted in October that Congress should "exercise every power which they may deem necessary," and that in any state delinquent in contributions, Washington and the army should take what they needed "by military force." Virginia also shifted ground; her delegation in Congress was often divided, but the addition of James Madison in 1780 introduced a persuasive new voice for a vigorous and effective central government.

The resurgence of the Nationalists might well be pegged to the March 1780 devaluation of the currency. Having thrown the burden of the war onto the states, the Congress saw its requests for supplies largely ignored, and its new scheme for the currency rapidly collapse. The upshot was a growing consensus for new powers in Congress, a new sensibility that Ezekiel Cornell remarked on in June. "The different policy of the several states, and too many of them turning all their views to their own advantage; without consulting the Common Good, Cause some able Politicians to think that our Political Salvation in a great measure depends on a controlling power, over the whole, being lodged in some person or persons."

The most particular statement of a Nationalist agenda was produced by Alexander Hamilton. Then just twenty-five years of age, his days chock-full with his duties at Washington's headquarters, Hamilton still made time to read deeply in economics and ponder the course of the Revolution. In September 1780 he distilled the result of these inquiries into a seven-thousand-word letter to James Duane. His central precept was succinct: "The fundamental defect is a want of power in Congress," a flaw he hoped to remedy through a Constitutional Convention. And what new powers would he propose? "Complete sovereignty" to render Congress independent of the states, the power to tax, a permanent military establishment, a national bank, and administration by "great officers of state—a secretary for foreign affairs—a President of War—a President of Marine—a Financier." For that last post, Hamilton suggested that "Robert Morris would have many things in his favor."

Hamilton was precocious, but others were thinking the same way. While the young colonel was formulating his program in camp with Washington, several delegates in Congress were pushing for various elements of the Nationalist program. In August, Robert Livingston proposed a federal tax on imports, and a duty on privateering prizes, the first effort to channel revenues directly to Congress. In November a new finance committee chaired by John Sullivan proposed creation of a national bank. This was to be funded by means of a patriotic call for individuals throughout America to loan coined gold and silver plate to the government. This scheme misread the degree of faith people would place in their benighted Congress, but showed the deep impression made by the Pennsylvania Bank.

These measures arose in Congress; more drastic steps were proposed in New England, where frustration with the pace of the war supplanted the region's traditional hostility to central authority. Meeting at a convention in Boston in August 1780, delegates from New Hampshire, Connecticut, and Massachusetts urged the states to expand the powers of Congress and to place national affairs "under the superintendency and direction of one supreme head." A second convention, at Hartford in November, went further, adopting New York's prescription of handing summary powers to Washington, and that Congress be granted powers of taxation. Lastly, this convention called for appointment of a single executive to manage the finances of the confederation, a man of "Talent, abilities and integrity."

That Robert Morris should receive the crucial appointment as Financier, as the superintendent of finance came to be known, was a matter of consensus. It was he who had launched the Pennsylvania Bank, he who had led the fight against price controls. Moreover, Morris's celebrated fortune and his business savvy would immediately lend weight to the office he would occupy.

Gouverneur Morris emphasized such personal attributes in a treatise he drafted while Congress was still deliberating the question of executive departments.

> Our Minister of the Finances should have a strong understanding, be persevering, industrious, and severe in exacting from all a rigid compliance with their duty. He should possess a knowledge of mankind, and of the culture and commerce, produce and resources, temper and manner of the different states; habituated to business on the most extensive scale, particularly that which is denominated by *money matters*; and therefore, not only a regular bred merchant, but one who has been long and deeply engaged in that profession. At the same time, he should be particularly acquainted with our political affairs, and the management of public business; warmly and thoroughly attached to America, not bigoted to any particular State; and his attachment founded not on whim, caprice, resentment, or a weak compliance with the current of opinion, but on a manly and rational conviction of the benefits of independence, his manners plain and simple, sincere and honest, his morals pure, his integrity unblemished; and he should enjoy general credit and reputation, both at home and abroad.

This was a categorical description of an idealized candidate, but as Gouverneur well understood, it might also serve as a detailed sketch of his friend and mentor.

Most of the delegates in Congress shared in this generous estimate of Robert Morris's abilities and resources. Joseph Jones, the Virginian who joined Morris in his early call for half-pay army pensions, spoke for the whole of Congress when he reported the appointment in a letter to Washington. "Our finances want a Necker to arrange and reform them," Jones wrote, referring to the French financier. "Morris I believe the best qualified of any our country affords for the arduous undertaking." Hamilton made the same point in a letter to Morris that emphasized the critical nature of the job. "You may render America and the world no less a service than the establishment of American independence! Tis by introducing order into our finances—by restoring public credit—not by gaining battles, that we are finally to gain our object." Having laid out what still appeared a distant prospect, Hamilton offered his endorsement. "In the frankness of truth I believe, Sir, you are the Man best capable of performing this great work."

George Washington added his applause a few days later, but with a caveat. "I have great expectations from the appointment of Mr. Morris; but they are not unreasonable ones, for I do not suppose that by any magic art he can do more than recover us by degrees from the labyrinth into which our finances are plunged."

Morris shared Washington's reservations. He understood as well as anyone the difficulties that would face the new Financier, reprising the most formidable of them in a letter to John Jay: "The derangement of our Money Affairs. The Enormity of our public Expenditures. The Confusion in all our Departments. The Languor of our general System. The complexity and consequent Inefficacy of our Operations."

Morris might have added that the public perception of his personal wealth often exceeded the actual state of his affairs. It was true he had extensive commercial connections, but it was also true that he was subject to the setbacks and sudden losses that always attended wartime commerce. In February, Morris intimated to a friend, "Miss Fortune is fickle and coy. . . . She has played the Devil with me last Summer, Fall and Winter, but still I hope to put her in better Humor this Spring." With his own fortune under pressure, it would be harder to sustain the sacrifices of public office.

Morris recognized, too, the personal trials that resumption of high office would entail. He recorded his misgivings in a backdated entry in a diary he began keeping after he accepted the appointment. Morris was writing for himself, but also for posterity. "The appointment [as Financier] was unsought, unsolicited, and dangerous to accept of as it was evidently contrary to my financial interest and if accepted must deprive me of those enjoyments social and domestic which my time of life required and which my circumstances entitled me to." Moreover, as Morris realized, the post would cost more than just the time he would lose: "A vigorous execution of the duties must inevitably expose me to the resentment of disappointed and designing Men and to the Calumny and Detraction of the Envious and Malicious. I therefore absolutely determined not to engage in so Arduous an Undertaking."

This was a rhetorical flourish—he would indeed accept the post—but it was more than maudlin self-pity. Many, perhaps most, of the central figures in the Revolution came to view their participation in the struggle as a taxing, even painful experience, one some came to regret. Morris in particular had been buffeted in the gales of popular opinion. Certainly, he anticipated a time of trial.

Gouverneur Morris reflected on Robert's predicament in a letter to Robert Livingston. "He feels all which a good man can feel in his situation. . . . Called on by the Public, Urged by Duty, Restrained by Inclination. The contest between the Man the Husband the Father and the Citizen is continual and each by turns predominates. The Weight of the office presses sore upon his Consideration. I behold him with anxiety about to be sacrificed to the Indolence of his Sovereign, the Prejudice of his Fellow Citizens, the Arduousness of Affairs. . . . I feel for him."

As if Morris needed any prompting, Ben Franklin wrote from Paris to confirm from his own experience the tribulations that awaited the Financier. "The business you have undertaken is of so complex a nature, and must engross so much of your time, and attention, as necessarily to hurt your private Interests; and the public often niggardly even of its Thanks, while you are sure of being censured by malevolent Criticks and Bug Writers, who will abuse you while you are serving them, and wound your Character in nameless Pamphlets, thereby resembling those little dirty stinking Insects, that attack us only in the dark, disturb our Repose, molesting and wounding us while our Sweat and Blood is contributing to their Subsistence."

Others, however, were more concerned that Morris might actually turn down the appointment. The same day as the vote in Congress, Morris's trusted clerk John Swanwick addressed his employer in intimate terms. Upon hearing the news, Swanwick wrote, "I felt a sort of mixture of Joy and Pain that for some moments disqualified me for any sort of business." The joy was that the ruin of the country might be averted; the pain, that Morris might reject the office. At forty years of age Swanwick was older than many of Morris's friends, yet he regarded Morris as a father figure and begged forgiveness for presuming to offer advice.

But advise he did: "What shall I say sir? The Safety the Glory of these United States are Involved in your Acceptance or Refusal . . . either you will accept and discharge this high office with your Usual Zeal, or else that you will by Refusing, perhaps Contribute Indirectly to the Ruin of yourself and this Country. For this is my Opinion: That the Fate of this Country is so nearly tied to yours that as she rises and falls so is your Fate determined."

This was the dilemma that faced Morris. He was wealthy, the most successful and best-connected merchant on the continent, and had already paid his patriotic debt as a citizen in the popular struggle. But he may also have been, as so many of his contemporaries asserted, the only man in America capable of retrieving the affairs of the government and its ragged army.

In the end, Morris really had little choice. But he would accept the position only on his own terms. Writing on March 13, to Samuel Huntington, a Connecticut delegate and the president of Congress, Morris laid out his stipulations. They were simple enough, but they posed a fundamental challenge to the egalitarian, anti-authoritarian, Republican ideology that prevailed through the early days of the Revolution.

The first proviso was that Morris would maintain all the commercial partnerships he had formed in his capacity as a private merchant. He had formed these connections, Morris averred, in order to procure "relaxation from business without the least injury to the Interests of my Family," and had given his word to support them. "I cannot on any consideration consent to Violate engagements or depart from those principles of Honor which it is my pride to be governed by." Morris was thinking of the Silas Deane affair, when he had been held up to public derision for just such connections; this time he insisted on an "express declaration" affirming his commercial rights, "that no doubts may arise, or Reflections be cast, on this Score hereafter."

This was a brazen request, a slap at all the critics who had sniped at his endeavors during his term on the Secret Committee, and it provoked a sharp but short-lived division in Congress. When Thomas Burke of North Carolina moved "that Congress do not require Mr. Morris to dissolve any commercial connection," the broad initial support for Morris broke down. Sam Adams, the last principal figure of the Eastern faction still sitting in the house, led the opposition. Leery of Morris and of commerce in general, Adams demanded a roll call on Burke's motion, and mustered enough votes to block it, winning key support from Charles Carroll of Maryland, a wealthy landowner who looked down on the "uncultivated insolent rabble," but who also embraced Adams's credo of abstemious virtue.

But Morris found some surprising allies. Burke of North Carolina, a longtime states' rights stalwart, reversed field to support him. Likewise James Lovell, a confirmed member of the Eastern faction, broke with Adams to vote for Morris. In the event, Duane revived the motion to grant Morris his exemption; this time Carroll relented, and the motion carried. Once the permission was granted, Morris still felt obliged to place his private business in the hands of third parties to prevent "illiberal reflections equally painful to me and injurious to the Public." He had won official dispensation, but he feared the sting of popular resentment.

Morris's second stipulation was even harder to swallow. In order to rein in an overgrown bureaucracy and maintain strict controls on expenditures, he demanded "absolute power" to dismiss from government service "all persons whatever that are concerned in the official Expenditure of Public Monies," and, in addition, all government employees whom he deemed "unnecessary." This was especially audacious, posing a direct challenge to the authority of Congress itself.

This explosive question was referred to a committee that included the Nationalist James Madison and Morris's Pennsylvania ally George Clymer. They reported in favor on March 31 but here the Congress bridled. With Sam Adams again leading the opposition, the provision was rejected on a vote of five states to three, with the balance divided. For the next three weeks, the delegates wrestled with their pride, their ideals, and the urgency of the fiscal crisis. Morris did not make an appearance to press his point; this was an internal struggle. Finally in May, the Congress capitulated. Morris had everything he asked for, and on May 14 he notified Huntington that he would accept the appointment.

The concessions extracted by Morris left his critics fuming. Sam Adams departed Philadelphia for Boston "much displeased and in a temper to awaken the jealousies if not the resentments of his countrymen and constituents." Major John Armstrong, the son of one of Washington's top generals but an acolyte of Horatio Gates, wrote his father to vent his disgust. "Bob Morris sets a high price on his services," but "Congress gave him all," Armstrong scoffed. He compared the legislators to "a young man just come to the possession of a large but intricate estate, who after many virtuous and great efforts . . . in some indolent, wicked, or capricious moment grows tired of acting for himself."

Morris had the powers he sought, but still he delayed taking the oath required of his new office. To do so would require resigning his seat in the Pennsylvania Assembly, where he was engaged in a critical debate over the same fiscal questions confronting the national government. Morris realized he had very few cards to play, and he determined to use each one to its full advantage.

He was drawing out the formal procedures of acceptance, but Morris wasted no time in putting his stamp on the job. After obtaining the two key concessions from Congress, he laid out parameters aimed at trimming the scope of his unwieldy new office to realistic dimensions. First, he would assume responsibility for congressional finance from that day forward, but not for past debts. Those should be managed so far as was possible under the existing arrangements; "whatever remains unpaid may become a Funded Debt" to be settled at a future date, presumably after the war was over.

Second, Morris insisted that he be excused from the business of supporting the military for the coming campaign. That task alone would involve his new office in a "Labyrinth of confusion from which no human Efforts can ever afterwards extricate me." This was not the same labyrinth to which Washington had alluded, but it was the one Morris feared most.

Having negotiated his terms, Morris agreed to "cheerfully undertake" direction of the Office of Finance. He brought to his new post a complex and layered sense of what was involved. In its simplest formulation, Morris saw his task as "the Raising of a Revenue with the greatest Convenience to the People; and the Expenditure of it with the greatest Economy to the Public." But Morris understood further that achieving these aims would entail a fundamental shift in method and approach, what he termed "the Necessity, the absolute Necessity, of a change in our Monied Systems to work Salvation."

For all his maxims and all his self-assurance, Morris recognized the enormity of the task before him. He would be treading new ground, without precedent and without a predecessor. Morris confided his trepidation, and reached out for advice, to Jacques Necker, the French financier. Even in an era that prized complaisance, his opening line had a confessional tone: "The very high and honorable place you hold among his Most Christian Majesty's Ministers, your Confessed Utility in that place, the Dignity with which you fill it, and the Abilities you display in the management of the Finances of that Great Nation which you serve all combine to make me wish a Correspondence with a Minister so capable of advising and instructing one whose highest ambition is to promote the interest of his Country, and whose ardent wish is to tread in the footsteps of so disinterested and successful a Financier as Mr. Necker."

Having paid his homage, Morris went on to detail for Necker the succession of misadventures that had brought America to her current low state. "You will observe, Sir," Morris summed up, that "we set out in this war without arms, ammunition, clothing or stores of any kind, without money or credit (except with our own people), that despising the practices of the most experienced Nations, We determined to pursue the purest principles of Economy in our own way, until we have by dear-bought experience learned that we knew almost nothing about the matter." Morris imagined, perhaps, a long and fruitful collaboration, with Necker supplying guidance as well as loans, until the crisis had safely passed. In this he was disappointed; Necker was forced from his post soon after Morris took office.

However Morris longed for counsel, he never lacked for initiative. Three days after he accepted the post of Financier, he submitted to Congress a plan for a national bank. This would be the centerpiece of his administration, the great innovation that would at once restore the credit of the government and draw back into circulation the private resources of the nation. The title of the new institution reflected the continental ambitions of its founder; Morris called it the Bank of North America.

There had been much talk and thought devoted to the subject of a bank in the preceding months. One conspicuous product of these discussions was a lengthy proposal for a bank that Alexander Hamilton composed and sent to Morris immediately upon his nomination as Financier. Hamilton's plan was thorough and detailed, but it was the work of a student more than of a practitioner: it took for a model the Bank of England and transplanted it to America without accounting for the pronounced practical differences between the two settings. Hamilton called, for example, for an initial capitalization of ten million dollars—far more than what could be raised. Hamilton also proposed that bank loans be guaranteed by the faith and credit of the Congress, a surprising misstep considering the disgraced state of the government's affairs.

Morris thanked Hamilton in a polite note and set about formulating a plan of his own. He did so in collaboration with Gouverneur Morris, by then well recovered from his carriage accident and anxious for a voice in the national forum. Like Hamilton, Gouverneur had been drawn early on to the theoretical aspects of economics, and in the spring before his injury had published in the local press a series of essays on public finance under the pseudonym "An American." Gouverneur did not have Robert's practical experience, but he had the refined education that Robert lacked and was, like Robert, a tireless worker. Besides, the two men were by now fast friends.

Robert and Gouverneur hammered out the plan for the bank in the interval between Morris's election as Financier and his acceptance. The initial capital would be modest—just four hundred thousand dollars. This was "far short of what it ought to be," as Morris explained to Hamilton, "but I am confident if this is once accomplished the Capital may afterwards be increased to almost any amount; to propose a large sum in the outset, and fail in the attempt to raise it might prove fatal." Shares were to be four hundred dollars apiece, payable in gold or silver, and investors would receive a single vote per share in the election of the bank board; their investment would yield an annual dividend projected at 6 percent.

The bank would be a private institution. It would lend to and receive deposits from the Congress, and banknotes would be receivable in taxes, but its lifeblood would be commercial loans payable in thirty or sixty days. The loans would be issued in notes payable on demand that would circulate as an independent paper medium, their security based on public faith in the bank, not the government. The bank would be independent, governed by its investors. The first named officers were George Clymer and John Nixon, chosen by virtue of their status as directors of the Pennsylvania Bank, the subscription fund Morris had helped launch in Philadelphia a year before. Morris might hold shares in the bank but no seat on the board; as director of the Office of Finance, he was charged under the charter with inspection of the books.

It was a bold proposal, to create a bank in a country where none had existed before and at a time when every medium of exchange save for hard coin had failed. More fundamental, it represented a startling reversal of conventional wisdom about sovereignty and value. The state wouldn't set the value of the bank's paper; its value would derive from public confidence in the bank. Morris was seeking to introduce private credit as the foundation for public exchange.

Despite broad support for Morris and the growing pressure for new financial arrangements, the idea of the bank was controversial. James Madison, though a Nationalist, held that the Congress did not have the authority to sanction a corporation, and he led the opposition. In the final vote, Morris's home state of Pennsylvania was divided, and Massachusetts voted no, but seven states gave their assent and the plan was approved.

Morris sought to present this new institution to the widest possible audience. Three days after Congress endorsed the project he published the "Plan for the Bank" and a separate address over his own signature in the *Pennsylvania Packet*, and on broadsides handed out on the street. In the weeks that followed, they were reprinted in New York, Boston, and Providence. Formally a prospectus for potential investors, the articles also served to introduce Morris to Americans as their first minister of finance.

Morris was explicit in stating the purpose of the bank. By the collapse of the currency, "the public credit has received the deepest injury." The bank offered an alternative by pooling the resources of individual citizens. As he explained: "The use, then, of a bank is . . . to gain from individuals that credit, which property, abilities and integrity never fail to command. To supply the loss of that paper money which, becoming more and more useless, calls every day for its final redemption, and to give a new spring to commerce, in the moment, when, by the removal of all restrictions, the citizens of America shall enjoy and possess that freedom for which they contend." In this elliptical fashion the Financier announced that, so far as he was concerned, the era of money supported by price controls and tender laws was over. Henceforth, value would be set by the market rate of exchange, not by legislation.

In soliciting investors for the bank, Morris pointedly eschewed the calls to public sacrifice that always accompanied emissions of government paper. "It might be expected that some address should be made to the patriotism of the public on this occasion; but this is needless," Morris told his readers. "Let the measure be examined, and let it be supported only so far as it is reasonable, useful and just." Morris wanted nothing to do with the cant about duty and virtue; the key here was to acknowledge the facts of human nature, and let self-interest drive the enterprise. Here he was in accord with Gouverneur; as the younger Morris had put it in one of his "An American" essays, public policy, and especially financial policy, should "be founded in the nature of man; not on ideal notions of excellence."

Robert Morris went into closer detail about his plans, and the obstacles he faced, in a letter to John Jay in Madrid. The national debt, he said, had "swelled beyond all reasonable bounds," including not just the state obligations to Congress, but the scrip passed out by military officers in requisitioning supplies. These "certificates" represented a whole parallel currency, often issued to reluctant vendors in lieu of outright confiscation, and comprised an additional debt load later estimated at one hundred million dollars—enough to swamp any effort to clear the books of Congress.

The only way to cover the debt was through taxes, but with obligations so extensive, commensurate taxation would "injure every order of men." Morris said he had no doubt of the ability of Americans to pay the debt in the long run—"a few years of peace would bring it within the bounds of a revenue very moderate when compared with the Wealth of our Country." But in the interim, foreign loans—the primary object of Jay's mission to Madrid—and the paper medium issued by the bank would have to suffice.

This was not all. To Jay, and to Benjamin Franklin, Morris projected his larger ambitions for the new bank. In the process of reviving the American economy, he hoped to forge a new, national identity of what was still a fractious, disparate people. It was the ultimate Nationalist institution, to be anchored in mundane transactions of daily life. "One very strong motive which has impelled my conduct," he explained to Jay, "is to unite the several states more closely together in one general Money Connection, and indissolubly to attach many powerful Individuals to the cause of our country, by the strong Principle of Self Love, and the immediate sense of private Interest." Here again was the voice of the realist, proposing that the government of the new republic rest its claims to allegiance on the inherent self-interest of its citizens, rather than their virtue or their fealty. Morris distilled his thinking still further in a letter to Franklin, posing his viewpoint in a single sentence. "I mean to render this [bank] a principal Pillar of American credit so as to obtain the money of individuals for the benefit of the Union and thereby bind those individuals more strongly to the general cause by ties of private interest."

As the affairs of the Office of Finance got under way, these larger plans had to compete for attention with the daily concerns of governance that soon came rolling in. The first emergency in the new office developed even before Morris had accepted the job. It came via George Washington in yet another appeal from the general for support from Congress. On May 8, Washington reported from his camp at New Windsor that without immediate new supplies of flour, it would be "next to impossible to keep the Army together."

The letter was referred to a committee, which proposed on May 28 that Washington be authorized to seize whatever provisions he needed. Impressments under various guises had become fairly commonplace during the lean winters of the previous two years, but this edict would establish Washington as a de facto military dictator.

Morris saw this as a disastrous step. "I found myself immediately impressed with the strongest desire to afford you relief and also to avoid such measures," he explained to Washington, "being calculated like so many others that have been adopted to procure immediate relief, at the same time sowing seeds that never fail to produce plentiful crops of future distresses and disappointments." But the Treasury had no money to fill the orders for flour, and no funds anticipated.

With no other resources at his command, Morris drew on his own. On May 29 he wrote to two old friends: Thomas Lowrey, a miller in New Jersey; and Philip Schuyler, a merchant, Continental Army general, and sometime delegate to Congress from New York. Of both he requested they use their "best Skill, Judgment and Industry" to immediately secure one thousand barrels of flour, obtain wagons and teams, and send them on to Washington's camp. To make purchases on good terms would require these vendors to commit their personal credit; consequently, Morris wrote, "I must also pledge myself to you, which I do most solemnly as an Officer of the Public but lest you like some others believe more in private than in public credit I hereby pledge myself to pay you the cost and charges of this flour in hard money." Morris then dispatched Gouverneur to New Jersey to deliver his messages and look after the deliveries.

So much for Morris's vow to steer clear of army procurement. Within a week of accepting his new office he had resumed his practice, from Secret Committee days, of committing his own credit to the supply of Washington and his men.

Morris understood that this jury-rigged mode of business could not long be sustained. What he needed was revenue, and that before either taxes or the bank might be in operation. The obvious resource, distant but more likely than the others, was foreign loans. Morris was already on intimate terms with the French and Spanish embassies in Philadelphia, and the most important American diplomats in Europe—Franklin in Paris and Jay in Madrid—were close personal friends. With the new post secretary for foreign affairs yet unfilled—Congress was divided over the candidacies of Robert Livingston of New York and Arthur Lee—the management of these relations naturally devolved to Morris and the Office of Finance.

French funds were already in place. Through 1780, France had provided to Congress grants and loans of ten million livres—about two million dollars. Shipments from Beaumarchais added another four and a half million livres. This had been enough to outfit the army, but now, with the Congress insolvent, the Americans needed substantially more.

Congress in December had sent John Laurens, son of the former president, to Paris in hopes he might spur Franklin, or, better, the French court, to release additional funds. The move was instigated by Arthur Lee as another slap at Franklin, and it worked, though not in the fashion Lee intended. Vergennes, who detested Lee, decided to preempt the Laurens mission by pledging a new grant of six million livres. Moreover, fearful that Congress would squander the proceeds, Vergennes stipulated that the funds should be drawn only by General Washington and would be spent only in France.

The key figure dispensing these funds in America was the Chevalier de La Luzerne. A former major general and now the leader of the French delegation in Philadelphia, Luzerne was a subtle politician and a great ally to the American Nationalists, whose agenda he believed was essential to winning the war. Luzerne spent liberally to push the Nationalist program, hiring writers to steer public opinion—Paine was on his payroll for a time, but proved too hard to control—and paying a sinecure to John Sullivan for reports from inside the closed sessions of Congress. Morris needed no such inducements; he and Luzerne were friends, and shared their concern over the lethargy of the army.

Even before word of the new loan arrived, and even before he formally accepted office, Morris had prevailed on Luzerne to advance him forty thousand dollars in bills drawn against France to support his operations and those of the army. Once the loan was in place, Luzerne committed the new funds to Morris's management as well.

But the pledge of funds was the simplest part of the transaction. Turning them into useful cash required the sale in America of bills that the French would pay off in Paris. The price of these "bills on France" fluctuated sharply depending on demand—usually from American traders who needed French funds—and supply. With the French fleet and army buying supplies in America, French bills glutted the market, and the price of the bills sank. This worked to the advantage of the American merchants, but eroded the value of the French grants and loans to Congress.

Morris sought to retrieve the value of these funds by assuming management of all government sales of French bills. He also sought to segregate the funds committed to him from those already loaned to Congress. For two years now, Congress had been anticipating loans in Europe by drawing drafts on Franklin, sending them to Paris, and hoping the French would honor them. The drafts frequently exceeded the available revenues, leaving Franklin to juggle the funds and plead with Vergennes for more.

Upon assuming office, Morris moved to sidestep those entanglements by having the new French funds deposited with his own personal bankers in France, Le Couteulx & Company, a prominent firm operated by three brothers with offices in Paris and Cádiz, subject to his drafts alone. Luzerne approved this arrangement, and the funds became Morris's primary resource in his first months in office.

Spain presented a different case. The Spanish king had contributed money and supplies early in the war, but was more fearful of antagonizing Britain any further, and more skeptical of the American rebels. Morris sent a series of letters to Jay touting the commercial and strategic advantages Spain would realize by subsidizing the Revolution, but Jay's entreaties were rejected; like Arthur Lee, he failed even to gain an audience at the Spanish court.

The other potential resource available to Morris lay close at hand; that was the state of Pennsylvania. But drawing out a meaningful contribution from his home state would require the same sort of revolution in finance that Morris was executing at the national level.

The problems facing the Pennsylvania Assembly were much the same as those of the Congress—fiscal failure and the consequent breakdown of the government. In the spring, after his successful intervention to defuse the mutiny of the Pennsylvania troops, Joseph Reed was forced to preside over the final collapse of the state currency. The precipitating event was the spring thaw: with the river free of ice, the first returns came in from the Havana trade, the ships laden with Spanish silver. "At once," Reed recorded, "as if by that force which, in days of ignorance, would be ascribed to enchantment, all doings in paper ceased."

The state legislature responded in typical fashion, voting in April for a new issue of five hundred thousand pounds in paper money. From his seat in the Assembly, Morris rallied his Republican allies in a bid to block the move. It was not the new emission they objected to so much as the tender laws requiring traders and vendors to accept the new currency at face value. To establish the new paper as legal tender ignored fundamental tenets of economic theory that had been demonstrated through the first years of the war.

Morris made his argument in an eleven-point protest that marked out his views in plain language. Backing the new emission was destined to fail, "Because the value of money, and particularly of paper money, depends upon the public confidence, and where that is wanting, laws cannot support it, and much less penal laws."

As in the contest over price controls, he cited both economic and moral grounds. "Penalties on not receiving paper money must from the nature of the thing be either unnecessary or unjust. If the paper is of full value, it will pass current without such penalties, and if it is not of full value, compelling the acceptance of it . . . is iniquitous." Tender laws represented a "violent remedy" to fiscal ills; it was "inconsistent with the principles of liberty to prevent a man from the free disposal of his property."

To Morris, this was the crucial issue of the moment, the reason he delayed formal acceptance of his congressional office. If he could not derail the state's latest plunge into the vagaries of paper funds, his efforts in the national government would be pointless. He outlined his strategy in a letter to Washington in June: "I am Financier Elect, but that is all, for had I taken the oath and my Commission my seat in the Assembly must have been vacated, and I think it of the utmost consequence to preserve my right of appearing there, until the Tender and Penal laws are totally repealed, for I consider those laws as destructive of all Credit" both private and public. Credit was critical; "in our circumstances the war cannot be carried on without it."

Morris found seventeen other representatives to sign his protest, but the radicals retained a slight majority in the Assembly, and the new currency emission, with the attendant tender laws, went forward.

This setback proved temporary, however, as events soon brought the futility of the new paper issue into sharp focus. The currency began to depreciate as soon as it was printed, sinking to a value of five for one and forcing Joseph Reed to halt further emissions after just a quarter of the fund had been laid out. Reed then called the legislature into emergency session to reform the entire fiscal apparatus. He posed the quandary of the government in stark terms: "It cannot be denied . . . that the exportation of the produce of the country is great, the returns quick and profitable, that Providence has blessed us with plentiful crops, and that present prospects are unusually rich; and it must equally be admitted, that the army, the government, and public creditors, feel all the effects of real, undissembled poverty." The only solution, Reed asserted, was that the state's financial structure "must be wholly laid aside."

This notice set the stage for Morris. He opened the emergency session with a sweeping statement on the nature of credit and the means of restoring it, denouncing tender laws, and pressing for new and more systematic taxation. No text of the speech Morris made to the Assembly survives, but he outlined his thinking in another letter to Washington. Morris noted proudly that, with the repeal of the embargo on exports, flour was plentiful in the city and the price had sunk by half, just as he had predicted. The point, Morris said, one "which I think should be impressed on the minds of all persons in power," was that "Commerce should be perfectly free, and property Sacredly secure to the owner.

"Whenever these Measures have their proper force in our Governments, the United States will abound with the greatest plenty of their own produce of perhaps any nation in the world; the people are by Nature and habit industrious; feeling themselves secure in the possession of their property they will labor incessantly; that labor lays the foundation for Commerce." This free market prescription was tough medicine for assemblymen accustomed to seeing these issues through the prism of party affiliation, but now they found both Reed and Morris joined in an uncomfortable but firm alliance.

The lawmakers dithered for three long weeks, prompting another stern message from Reed. "The public necessities compel us to address you in a language more serious and decisive than any we have ever yet adopted," Reed began. Weeks of debate had left the Assembly "in the same state of imbecility and distress as when the session began."

This scolding apparently struck a nerve, as the following day saw the surrender of radical resistance to Morris's fiscal reforms. The Assembly voted that day to enact the three central planks of his program for the state: the repeal and repudiation of all tender laws respecting either state or Continental paper, the repeal of all embargoes or other restrictions on trade, and the levy of two hundred thousand pounds in taxes, to be collected in hard money. The sole point held by the radicals was a proviso allowing citizens who had signed the loyalty oath to pay half their tax in the new state money.

A week later, after a series of meetings with Morris, the legislature completed its capitulation by appointing him its sole agent for all financial dealings with Congress, and by committing to Morris the unspent balance of the new emission, a sum of four hundred thousand pounds. These funds were due to Congress as the state's portion of the March 1780 emission, and to purchase supplies ordered for the army, but in the meantime they were his to manage. With these measures in hand, Morris resigned his seat in the Assembly, took the oath that confirmed him as Financier, and brought in Gouverneur Morris as his trusted assistant. Robert Morris was now the chief financial officer for both the national government and for the strongest state in America. He was, in Reed's estimation, a "pecuniary dictator."

Reed supported Morris at this critical juncture, but he never abandoned his suspicions of Morris's motives, or his resentment for the Republican opposition to his administration. Reed offered a sour appraisal in a letter he wrote Nathanael Greene: in pressing his agenda, "Mr. Morris was inexorable, Congress at his mercy." The same could be said for the state of Pennsylvania.

Morris now had funds, but to spend them was to see them immediately sink in value. The trick was to preserve their value and still put them to work. He did so through several adroit maneuvers.

First, he drafted his clerk John Swanwick to act as "cashier" in the Office of Finance. This would ensure that current accounts were kept separate from all the paper money transactions still operating under the authority of Congress. The Financier wanted to start with a clean slate.

Next, Morris recruited Haym Salomon to help coordinate the sales of foreign bills. Salomon was one of the more colorful figures in the Revolution, a Polish Jew who emigrated to New York in 1772, became a patriot activist, was imprisoned by the British, escaped, and arrived destitute in Philadelphia in the summer of 1778. Slight and infirm but fluent in several languages and versed in the European credit markets, Salomon opened a small office on Front Street, near Market, and entered business as a broker. Most of his afternoons he spent at the Coffee House, buying and selling bills of exchange and helping dispose of privateering prizes.

By 1781, Salomon had become the leading bond broker in the city, handling business with dispatch and charging the lowest commission fees around. Early in the year, Luzerne retained him to sell bills to fund the French forces in America. Thus, by retaining him in June, Morris achieved two goals—reliable management of his foreign assets, and efficient coordination of the sales of French bills, allowing him to prop up the rate of foreign exchange.

Now came a bit of fiscal alchemy: a plan designed to *appreciate* the value of the Pennsylvania currency—actually to reverse the cycle of depreciation. Since too much paper in circulation caused the value to sink, reducing the volume of paper in circulation would cause the value of each note to rise, and build the total worth of the funds at his command. The plan required several distinct operations. First, Morris would keep his own stock of Pennsylvania paper off the market. Second, he would borrow depreciated Continental paper to pay off the state obligations to Congress. Third, he would soak up more currency, and reap the gains as it appreciated, by manipulating some of the proceeds of the funds loaned by France.

This last step drew Benjamin Franklin into the plan. Morris outlined his scheme in a letter to his old colleague. Morris would sell bills against

Franklin in the amount of four hundred thousand livres, for which he would accept depreciated paper. These bills would be due in six months. Then he would draw bills to the same amount in Franklin's favor, against Le Couteulx, but payable in sixty days. The four-month difference in due dates left the funds in Morris's hands for that interval. This represented, in the words of one early Morris biographer, "the most vulgar kind of bill-kiting." But it helped Morris establish his office at a time when the finances of the state were all but paralyzed.

Morris, Swanwick, and Gouverneur Morris carefully tracked all these transactions for their influence on the price of the state currency. "An operation of this kind is so delicate," Morris wrote later, "that the least derangement or interference proves fatal." His efforts bore fruit within weeks as the value of the currency began to recover; by August, after sinking to seven state dollars for one in silver, it had risen to two for one. Morris couldn't spend the funds—that would defeat his strategy—but he could leverage them to raise troops and purchase supplies.

While he was building up a reserve in state funds, Morris was at the same time experimenting with private contracts as a means to secure the supplies for the army. This was another sharp departure from established practice; previously, purchases were made piecemeal by commissary officers and state agents, sometimes at auction and often in competition with each other. The new contracts were to be awarded on the basis of sealed competitive bids, ensuring the lowest price for the government. The first request for bids, promising deferred payment in hard money, was published in two Philadelphia papers the first week in July.

Morris was acting here in several capacities, separate but intimately related to each other. The funds for his contracts flowed from his office as state agent for Pennsylvania, but he spent them in compliance with requisitions of Congress. In negotiating the deals he was agent for both the state and, in the case of the initial army flour contracts, for the Office of Finance. He established a personal stake as well when he pledged his credit to support the army contracts.

None of these roles was closely defined by precedent or statute, and Morris was shaping his powers as he went along. By this time he had already outstripped the sweeping grants of authority he'd obtained six weeks before, but the oversight was quickly rectified. On July 10, at the request of the Board of War, Congress specifically authorized Morris and his deputies to negotiate for army supplies, and all prior and future contracts under his name were declared "binding on the United States."

This new mode of working through private contractors would also supplant the system of "specific supplies," the unwieldy program allowing states to provide the army with actual goods rather than funds. Adopted after the collapse of congressional buying power in 1780, this quasi-barter scheme had failed utterly. With the states just as strapped for money and reluctant to impress supplies by force, most requisitions from Congress were ignored. When they were answered, the stocks raised rarely reached the widely scattered camps of the army. Thousands of barrels of flour or meat spoiled for lack of funds to hire transport wagons. By October, Morris had concluded that "specific supplies are at once burdensome to the public and almost useless to the government." Even before that, he introduced still another new wrinkle when he began selling the supplies raised in remote locations to finance more convenient purchases made close by the army camps.

As in the days of the Committee of Safety, Morris was using his state office to try out strategies he would soon introduce at a national level. In a time of political and social turmoil Morris easily kept pace. Innovation and risk came naturally to him, the fruit of twenty years in the shipping game. Morris brought the same drive and creativity to every public office he held, always anticipating, always looking forward.

Morris was experimenting, but not for the sake of novelty. The full range of ideas and reforms Morris introduced, from the bank to the repeal of tender laws, can be readily bound together under the rubric of laissez-faire, free market economics. This was still a new conception, given its first comprehensive treatment in 1776 by Adam Smith in his *Wealth of Nations*. Morris rarely cited sources, but he made the connection tangible when, during the first debates over the bank, he presented one delegate with a copy of Smith's work.

In the early days of the Revolution, Morris had done all he could to maintain ties to England and preserve the old order of Britain's mercantile empire. Now thrust into the vanguard, Morris had developed his own conception of what a new political order might mean. He saw dynamic potential in the combination of individual liberty and economic freedom, a vision that posed a radical challenge to the familiar conventions of the American Whigs and the old regime alike.

That is not to say Morris entered the office of Financier with a single, coherent plan for reformation. He made that clear in a letter to Jay in July: "I would gladly give you now Details of our situation and Plans for reforming it. But I have not yet sufficiently obtained the one, nor matured the other."

But the Congress had selected Morris based in large part on his business experience and financial acumen; now he would bring that sensibility to bear on the central questions of governance raised in the Revolution.

Beyond the radical implications of the policies he championed, Morris brought to his office the broad vision of the Nationalists. His mission was premised on the ability to coordinate and direct the efforts of the states, a feat that had eluded the Congress. Success would enable America to achieve "power, consequence and grandeur"; failure would leave her internally divided, vulnerable to invasion and possible reconquest.

Morris was not alone here; he was speaking for a faction in Congress, the group responsible for creating his office. But as the chief executive in the government, Morris emerged as their leader, the embodiment of their goals, and the sponsor of their program.

Morris carried this national agenda to the states through a series of circular letters addressed to the governors. The first, sent July 6 to spur the return of military supplies, set the tone of his new administration. Morris was precise, formal, and direct. He cited the acts of Congress as his mandate, and pressed for "the most speedy and punctual compliance on the part of the several states." He spoke with the authority of conviction and in a voice of assured command, at once personal and impatient. "Your excellencys good sense will render it unnecessary for me to dwell on this subject and your regard for the Public Interest, will I am confident interest you most deeply in facilitating a compliance."

A second circular, issued two weeks later, was even more bracing. "Your Excellency must be sensible of the Impracticality of carrying on the War unless the States will cheerfully furnish the Means," Morris told the state executives. "Whatever they grant will I trust be faithfully applied so as to produce the greatest Good to the Whole, but if the Means be withheld those and those only who are instrumental in it must be Chargeable with the Consequence."

By late July, Morris was moving beyond the simple matter of state supplies and addressing the larger question of acquiring a national revenue. The first source of funds would be state payment of the debts accumulated in the course of the war. These had been incurred by the Congress on the premise they would be apportioned later among the individual states, and while that division had yet to be made, some of the accounts were clearly stated and already overdue. Those payments had stalled, in part because the states were reluctant to levy taxes, and in part because some states were already raising doubts about the fairness of the ultimate apportionment.

Morris addressed the delays sharply. "If once an opinion is admitted that those States who do the least and charge most will derive the greatest benefit and endure the smallest Evils, Your Excellency must perceive the shameless inactivity which must take place. . . . I take therefore this early opportunity to assure you that all the accounts of the United States shall be speedily liquidated [that is, verified and stated in terms of hard money] if I possibly can effect it and my efforts for that purpose shall be unceasing."

Here Morris affirmed that there were two forms of debt—those arising from Congress, and the much more confused array of warrants and certificates issued by quartermaster deputies and purchasing agents in the field. The latter obligations awaited the appointment of "proper officers" to establish their value, but the first category was due and payable. Morris promised that "Justice shall be the rule" in his future management of the state accounts; in the meantime, the governors were obliged to make timely contributions. "To suppose this expensive war can be carried on without joint and strenuous efforts is beneath the wisdom of those who are called to the high Office of Legislation," Morris cajoled. "It is by being just to Individuals, to each other, to the Union, to all; by generous grants of solid Revenue, and by adopting energetic measures to collect that Revenue; and not by complainings, vauntings, or recriminations that these States must expect to establish their Independence."

The Financier acknowledged the high-handed style of this circular letter, but he made no apology. "I speak to your excellency with freedom because it is my duty to so speak, and because I am convinced that the language of plain sincerity is the only proper language to the first Magistrate of a Free Community."

Morris was no less stern, but a bit more expansive, in answering a letter from Connecticut governor Jonathan Trumbull, father of the former commissary general and a close associate of Washington's. Trumbull had written to assure Morris of his state's efforts to support Congress and the Army; Morris was writing to explain that good intentions were not enough.

"As to the complaint made by the People of a Want of Money to pay their Taxes it is nothing new to me, nor indeed to any body. The Complaint is I believe quite as old as Taxation and will last as long."

This was a curious disquisition, coming from a newcomer to government who had spent most of his life in trade, but that may be the source of his worldly sagacity. Certainly, his statement has the ring of real insight, even to modern ears. "That Times are hard, that Money is scarce, that Taxes are heavy, and the like are Constant themes of Declamation in all Countries and will be so. But the very generality of the complaint shews it to be ill founded."

Here Morris bared his teeth. "The Fact is that Men will always find a Use for all the Money they can get hold of, and more. A Tax Gatherer therefore will always be an unwelcome Guest because his demand must necessarily interfere with some pleasurable, or profitable Pursuit. Hundreds who cannot find Money to pay Taxes, can find it to purchase useless Gew Gaws, and expend much more in the Gratification of Vanity, Luxury, Drunkenness, and Debauchery than is necessary to establish the Freedom of their Country."

Morris composed yet another circular in this time of brisk initiative, this one dedicated to the one source of revenue Congress had actually claimed to itself—a 5 percent duty on imports. This was the "impost" first raised by Robert Livingston the previous fall. Congress had approved the measure in January, just before creating the Office of Finance. Soon after that, however, the states had at long last ratified the Articles of Confederation, which expressly reserved to the states the power to tax. Thus, immediately upon adoption of the Articles, Congress and the Financier were seeking to amend the new charter. And according to the Articles, that meant obtaining the endorsement of every single state.

So far, six states had approved this crucial grant of taxing authority to the central government. But some had laid restrictions on how the money could be used, and others had tendered their approval only if the remaining states signed on. Massachusetts argued that the impost was unfair to commercial states, as they would produce most of the funds, and postponed making a decision. Morris tackled these limited endorsements, and the flat refusal of several states, in his circular of July 27.

He offered a stark choice: If the impost were approved, "it is possible the public Credit might be restored." If no revenues were forthcoming, "our Enemies will draw from thence strong Arguments in favor of what they have so often asserted: that we are Unworthy of Confidence, that our Union is a Rope of Sand, that the People are Weary of Congress and that the Respective States are determined to reject its authority."

On the question of equity, Morris held that the impost was intrinsically fair: "Articles imported into the Country are Consumed in the Country. . . . The tax will fall equally on all and therefore ought in Justice be carried to the general Account." As to the partial endorsements made by some states, approvals "fettered with Restrictions" were "pernicious," Morris wrote, only serving to undermine the Congress.

In his address on the impost, he took the opportunity to survey the progress of the war and of America's experiment with democracy. "Despotic Governments are in War superior to others by the Union of Efforts, the Secrecy of Operations and the rapidity with which every Wheel may be moved by one Sovereign Will. This superiority is however amply compensated to free Governments by the Ardent Attachment of their Citizens and the general Confidence. . . . Hence the Existence of that Paper [currency] which bore us thro the conflict of five years Hostility." But public zeal could sustain paper emissions only so far; the abundant public confidence was now gone, and Congress would have to recover by degrees the "precious jewel" of public credit. Here Morris was paying homage to the ethic of patriotic virtue so beloved of the early revolutionaries, but he was also laying it to rest. Its time had passed.

Looking forward, Morris anticipated a rising threat to the Nationalist program. "I have also heard it suggested that the Public Debts ought to be divided among the several States and each be called on to provide for its Proportion." Such a scheme would render Congress a mere bystander, undermining the whole idea of America as a nation. "This Measure would be sufficient to destroy the Credit of any Country," Morris warned. "The creditors trust the Union and there can be no Right to alter the Pledge which they have accepted for any other than even a better one without their free Consent. But this is not all. There is in it a Principle of Disunion implied which must be ruinous. Even at this late period the States may be singly subjugated; Their Strength is derived from their Union; Every thing which Injures that Union must impair the Strength which is dependent upon it."

This opened a whole new arena in the nation's political dialogue. The immediate issue was who should answer for the debts of Congress, but the larger question was what shape the new nation might take. No longer were Americans contending for independence from England or the rights and obligations of Republican governance. All that was assumed. At stake now was the stature of the central government, and whether the states would yield to a sovereign authority that could project their collected power on a higher plane than they might separately.

Until now the tension between Congress and the states had been the subject of debate among factions; here it had been decided, and presented as the firm policy of the central government. More than that, it was the policy of Robert Morris. He had served them in an array of important and sometimes critical offices in the course of the Revolution, but now he emerged as the dominant figure in the government, a new force on the national scene. He was the reigning chief executive, the primary voice in diplomatic affairs, the sole arbiter on matters of personnel, funding, and expenditure. By August, writing from the Pennsylvania frontier, General William Irvine observed that "the most trifling thing cannot be done in any department but through Mr. Morris."

Joseph Reed considered Morris's rise to prominence as a mark of weakness in Congress. By placing Morris at the helm, Congress had forfeited "all business of deliberation and executive difficulty with which money is in any respect connected, and they are now very much at leisure to read dispatches, return thanks, pay and receive compliments, etc." Morris might consult Congress "to receive a sanction, but it is the general opinion that it is in form only."

Yet even with his jaundiced eye, Reed could see the distinct benefits of the energy and administrative dexterity Morris brought to the job. "It would not be doing justice not to acknowledge that humiliating as this power is, it has been exercised with much advantage for the immediate relief of our distresses, and that the public have received a real benefit from Mr. Morris' exertions."

As the central figure in the government, Morris was now the most powerful man in America, save only for George Washington. But Morris understood as well as anyone the limits of his influence. As much as he wanted to focus his attention on larger priorities like the bank, administrative reform, and settlement of the congressional debt, he found himself constantly caught up in the immediate demands of office. As early as June, Morris complained that "The multiplicity and Variety of Objects that I am *doomed* to be constantly occupied by do not permit any part of my time to be spared to things not absolutely necessary."

These were the routine pressures of the chief executive; Morris was subject, too, to the larger imperatives of the war. In early August, Morris was forced to put all his various projects on hold and travel to New York to confer with Washington. The demands of the army could no longer be ignored.

— *Chapter 11* —

YORKTOWN

On the morning of Tuesday, August 7, 1781, as the heat of another searing summer day settled over Philadelphia, Robert Morris headed out on the hard, dusty road to Trenton. He was traveling on horseback in company with Richard Peters, representing the Board of War, and James Wilson, then employed as counsel and "advocate general" for the French forces in America. It was the first leg of a three-day trek that would take them to Washington's camp at Dobbs Ferry, on the east bank of the Hudson.

Morris had been looking forward to a conference with Washington since the first days of his administration. The army was the single greatest drain on the treasury, and Morris was hoping to achieve meaningful savings through consolidation, reform, and, ultimately, reductions in force. Washington was impatient for a meeting with Morris as well, but for distinctly different purposes. He was considering a major offensive against the British, and Morris would be instrumental to his plans.

Over the past two years, the war had sunk into a dismal and enervating standoff, with the main British force garrisoned at New York, and Washington hovering nearby, close enough to keep them in check but too feeble to mount any genuine threat. The British had moved in 1780 to open a new southern theater. First came the siege of Charleston; from there, General Charles Cornwallis ventured forth to scourge the Carolinas. Congress countered by sending Horatio Gates, the Hero of Saratoga, to challenge Cornwallis with a combined force of four thousand militia and Continental regulars. When the two armies met at Camden, South Carolina, in August, Gates blundered badly, and virtually his entire force was annihilated.

This dismal episode was balanced in some degree by the arrival in July 1780 of a French expedition of five thousand troops under command of the Comte de Rochambeau. Taking up quarters at Newport, which the British had evacuated just months before, the French force fell into the same tor-por as the other armies on the continent. Washington hungered to find some means of concerting a joint action, but his limited resources, and the sea power of the British, precluded any major confrontation with the enemy.

Another year was slipping away. Washington sent Nathanael Greene south to rally the rebel forces there, and then Lafayette, in April 1781, at the head of a column of twelve hundred light infantry. Washington himself traveled north, to Hartford, for his first face-to-face meeting with Rocham-beau. The two generals found an immediate affinity, and agreed to the com-bined operations that had been in prospect since the arrival of the French army. Together, the generals sent word to the French fleet in the Caribbean under Comte de Grasse to set sail for the American coast; Rochambeau then marched his main force to join Washington's army in New York.

The primary strategic question was where this combined force might strike: against New York, the citadel of British power in America, or in the South, where Cornwallis led his ten thousand troops in the most active and punishing campaign of the war. New York appeared impregnable, but marching half the Continental Army 450 miles to the south would repre-sent the largest shift of men and matériel yet attempted during the war, a feat of endurance and a daunting logistical challenge.

All this was in play when Morris and his companions made their trip to New York. On the second day they were joined by Ephraim Blaine, a wealthy merchant from the Pennsylvania frontier who'd accepted the un-forgiving position of commissary general for purchases during the hard winter of 1780. Making their way across the rugged highlands of western New Jersey, Morris, Peters, Blaine, and Wilson carried with them all the complexities of the looming campaign—the scarcity of funds, the problems of transport, the competing demands of supplying the French and Ameri-can forces.

Morris and his party crossed the Hudson the morning of August 11, ar-riving at Dobbs Ferry, saluting the guard sentries, and entering the Ameri-can camp. Washington greeted them with a "cheerful and hearty Welcome," and invited them to attend his levee, a daily gathering where the com-mander in chief entertained anyone seeking an audience—"All the General Officers of the American and French Armies," Morris recorded in his diary, "The Commanders of Regiments, Heads of Departments, and such Strang-ers as Visit Camp." They dined at Washington's table that afternoon, and got down to business the next day.

In conference with Washington, Morris and Peters presented their plans to cut the size of the army the following year. Washington would have none of it; he firmly believed that maintaining "a superior army" was "the surest and only means of forcing [the British] to a Peace." Morris tested several other plans on Washington over the next two days and reached accord on a few small matters, but no large savings were achieved. Washington was, after all, a general in wartime; he was more interested in what Morris could do for him.

In the meantime, planning went forward for the assault on New York, Morris meeting with local contractors to spur deliveries of flour and other supplies. Early forays had been launched against enemy outposts, but the British were alert to every movement, and well entrenched on Manhattan. Peters, for one, felt that "our success in the contemplated attack on New York was far worse than doubtful; but that was the plan of the campaign." Yet one primary objective of the thrust against New York had already been achieved; the British commanders, convinced now that New York was Washington's sole objective, had issued orders to Cornwallis to send half his force north for reinforcement. This prompted Cornwallis to leave off his marauding and head for the Virginia coast to rendezvous with a transport fleet.

On Wednesday morning, their fifth day at Dobbs Ferry, both the military situation and the mission to camp were radically altered. Word had arrived the night before that De Grasse was approaching American waters with a fleet of twenty-nine warships bearing a complement of three thousand troops. They were sailing for the Chesapeake, not New York, and must return to the Caribbean in just two months. Suddenly, the southern strategy became the only viable option.

Morris and Peters were awakened "at the beat of reveille" by a messenger calling them to headquarters, where Washington convened a council of war to consider the news. "We were surprised at the circumstance," Peters recorded later. Washington was furious; he'd set his heart on New York; now De Grasse was forcing his hand, and the Americans had no choice but to follow the action to Virginia. Washington denounced the French "with expressions of intemperate passion," which Peters modestly declined to repeat. "Mr. M. [Morris] and I stood silent, and not a little astonished."

The meeting broke up, and later that morning, when the command staff and their visitors sat down for breakfast, Washington had regained his composure. He pressed Peters for an assessment of what kind of supplies and support he could expect on the long march south, and Peters equivocated.

"I can do everything with money," he told the general, "nothing without it." Both men then turned to Morris. The Financier begged for time "to consider, to calculate." Soon after, Morris delivered his assessment. The states had promised much aid but delivered little; there was no reason to expect that to change. That left his personal credit, which Morris agreed to commit so far as it might extend. He had performed similar service in the critical hours before the assault on Trenton in 1776; this was a larger engagement, but Washington could only hope Morris would come through again.

On Thursday, Morris made the short trip to the French camp, located across a small valley from their American allies. Meeting with Rochambeau and his high command, Morris made an audacious proposal: the French should put all their supply operations under his management, as well as all their foreign exchange. The competing demands of the French and American forces had driven up prices across the board; combined purchasing through competitive contracts would benefit both armies. Similarly, placing the sale of French bills in his hands would allow him to control their price and restore their value in the Philadelphia market.

Rochambeau considered all of this, but he raised one particular concern. That was the conduct of John Holker, whose multiple operations as agent for the French marine and as factor for private commercial interests had raised suspicions of where his loyalty lay. Moreover, his independent sales of French bills had glutted the market, eroding the buying power of the French forces in America. Holker retained the confidence of Luzerne, but Rochambeau was unimpressed; as he told Luzerne, "He [Holker] is a selfish merchant and not a loyal servant of the King."

As Holker's friend, his agent, and his partner in a number of private ventures, Morris spoke up in his defense, pronouncing Holker to be "as Honest a Man and as Zealous for the King's Service as any that ever came from France." Should the French appoint Morris their agent, however, "Holker would have no concern unless they chose." As to his own services, Morris asked Rochambeau "to consider everything that came from me as flowing from a pure desire to serve the general cause, that I sought no commission, profit or advantage."

After weighing these representations, the French command staff decided against having Morris intervene in their purchasing operations. They did, however, agree to his proposal that the French lend Washington the flour they had on hand in New York in return for supplies Morris would later provide "to the southward," on the march to Virginia. Morris also prevailed in his bid to handle the sale of French bills. From then on, managing relations with French diplomats and armed forces would be a primary project of the Office of Finance.

Returning to the American base, Morris was caught up in a round of meetings with officers who would be his primary contacts in the army—the quartermaster, the clothier general, the paymaster. All of them requested funds, and all got the same answer: "I could only recommend the strictest frugality and economy in their expenditures, that I might thereby be the better warranted in making reasonable requisitions to the several States." This satisfied no one, of course, but it might at least channel the pressure for money back to the recalcitrant states that were the ultimate cause of his thin resources. Morris was in fact carrying 150 guineas—about 750 Spanish dollars—in hard coin, but with demands so great he decided to keep his purse to himself.

Morris closed out his sojourn at camp on Saturday and said a quick goodbye to Washington. Orders had already been issued to prepare half the American force—two thousand men—and the entire French army for the long march south, leaving General William Heath in charge of the garrison at West Point. Secrecy was critical so as not to alert the British of the change in plans. Time was a factor as well; Morris and his party elected to take a quicker route home. As this would lead them close by the enemy lines, they were escorted the first day by a troop of twenty light horse.

Morris had much on his mind. He had set out in hopes of finding economies for the next year's budget. Instead he had learned that all his energy and available funds would be consumed in helping to supply the combined French and American armies in their epic trek from New York to Virginia. By the time Morris reached Philadelphia, Washington, Rochambeau, and six thousand hungry soldiers were already on the road.

As his first act the morning after his return Morris met with Thomas McKean. He was the chief judge of the Pennsylvania Supreme Court; he was also a delegate to Congress from Delaware, and had recently replaced Samuel Huntington as president of Congress.

In theory, Congress was to be the primary source of money and support for the campaign, but the reality was quite different. Just months before, after years of wrangling, Maryland had become the last of the states to endorse the Articles of Confederation, and Congress had finally achieved formal organization under a written charter. Yet that very charter ensured that Congress would remain a government in name only. The Articles granted to Congress alone the right to declare war and make foreign treaties, but reserved "sovereignty, freedom and independence" to the individual states. Critically for Morris, the Articles specified that "all charges of war . . . shall be defrayed out of a common treasury, which shall be supplied by the several states." But there was no provision to compel contributions from those states, and Congress was proscribed from levying taxes itself. Rather than resolve the division of powers that had produced chronic shortages of funds and supplies for the war effort, the new Articles codified them.

Morris made no record of what passed during his meeting with McKean, but it could not have been good. The states continued in arrears, laggard both in funds and the specific supplies that had been requisitioned with increasing urgency. Morris was on his own.

Leaving McKean at the State House, Morris huddled with Gouverneur Morris, John Swanwick, and a handful of clerks to sort out their prospects. The new Office of Finance was located, sensibly enough, in a building Morris had rented next door to his town house on Front Street. What Morris found there was only more bad news. Despite the efforts of Gouverneur and Haym Salomon, the price commanded by bills on France had continued to fall; even if Morris were willing to absorb the discount, the market was so glutted that bills might not find buyers at all. This meant that the proceeds of the French loan were, for the time being, useless.

Morris's control of the Pennsylvania state funds was no help either. The value of the new issue was appreciating, but only because Morris had kept them off the market. To spend those notes now, Morris wrote, "would destroy in embryo all my hopes from that quarter, cut off the only resource which I have the hope of commanding, and shake a confidence which has been reposed in me, which the public interest calls upon me to cherish." In short, as Morris reported to Washington the following day, "I find money matters in as bad a situation as possible."

Morris was without revenue but he was not without resources. He could, and did, continue to commission supplies with contracts based on his personal credit, primarily for flour but also for horses, boats, wagons, and other key supplies.

When people or vendors needed immediate payment, contracts wouldn't suffice. With cash scarce or useless, and with the new bank authorized but not yet in operation, Morris began to print and circulate a new paper issue of his own. These bills were formally drafts on John Swanwick, the cashier at the Office of Finance, but were backed by Morris's promise to pay—his personal credit. Morris first laid plans for this hybrid currency in late July when he hired an engraver named Robert Scott, previously employed by the state of Virginia, to cut copper plates for use in printing the notes. The notes were issued in several denominations, and payable on sight or at differing lengths of time.

Inevitably, the new currency came to be identified with its author—known collectively as "Morris notes"; the terms of redemption were distinguished as "short Bobs" and "long Bobs," a colloquial, first-name reference to the Financier. The Morris notes soon entered circulation as cash among the merchants and shopkeepers of Philadelphia. This was the most direct means by which Morris committed his own fortune to the demands of the national cause. "My personal Credit, which thank Heaven I have preserved through all the tempests of the War, has been substituted for that which the Country had lost," Morris explained to a friend. "I am now striving to transfer that Credit to the Public."

The Morris notes, the contracts on credit, and whatever barter Morris or Gouverneur could arrange were useful expedients, but the bulk of the supplies for the army would still have to come from the states. In the days after his return from camp, Morris badgered the state governors with increasingly stern demands. "We are on the eve of the most active Operations," Morris wrote the governors of New Jersey and Delaware. "Should they be in any ways retarded . . . the most unhappy Consequence will follow," he warned, and then he turned up the pressure: "Those who may justly be chargeable with neglect will have to answer for it to their Country, to their Allies, to the present Generation, and to all posterity." Concerned, perhaps, that his tone might offend, Morris closed with what might be termed a bit of gallows humor: "While I assure you that nothing but the urgency of our affairs would render me thus Importunate, I must also assure you that whilst those affairs continue so Urgent I must continue to Importune."

As the source of all the urgency, George Washington did what he could to pitch in, sending his own letters to the governors "to enforce in the warmest Terms, the application of Mr. Morris." But Morris would not be outdone for a dramatic display of indignation. Writing Caesar Rodney of Delaware on September 1, Morris noted that he had previously "pressed upon you as urgently as I could the Necessity of a Compliance" with the requisitions of Congress. "The moment is now arrived when that Compliance must be insisted upon."

Morris reiterated to Rodney his specific demands—hundreds of barrels of meat, two thousand gallons of rum, and five hundred bushels of salt. Then he made his argument. "It is needless to say that a Body of Soldiers will not starve in the midst of a plentiful Country." This was at once an appeal and a threat, implying that if supplies were not provided they would be taken by force. "I hope most ardently that your timely endeavors will have spared the necessity of military collection. If not I still hope that the military Force will be exerted with all possible Mildness. But at any rate the public Service must not Suffer."

While Morris scrambled to secure provisions and funds, Washington, Rochambeau, and their armies approached steadily, the French trailing two days behind the Americans. The generals, traveling ahead of their troops, reached the capital early on the afternoon of Thursday, August 30. Morris joined a festive throng that rode out to meet the commanders and escort them to the City Tavern, where they sat down to a feast shaken at intervals by the boom of broadside salutes from ships in the river. With no lodgings available and his family out at Springetsbury, Morris opened his Front Street home to Washington, Rochambeau, and their combined entourage. Mattresses were strewn on the floor, and for the next week the house served as temporary headquarters for the allied high command.

On Friday morning, with all the officers conveniently at hand, the generals convened a council of war. The southern strategy was shaping up nicely. Cornwallis, unaware of the forces moving to meet him, had led his army to the Virginia tobacco port of Yorktown, where they could meet the British transports. Lafayette was trailing him with a much smaller force, not strong enough to challenge Cornwallis, but enough to keep him in check until reinforcements arrived. Two elements remained for a successful assault: the arrival of the French fleet, and the movement of the troops from New York.

The allied commanders hoped to end their march at the riverfront town of Chester, ten miles below Philadelphia, and forward the troops from there by water to Virginia. It was left to Morris to disabuse them; there were not enough ships or seamen to provide the flotilla. In the end the generals decided to split up; the French would make their way overland, while some Americans and most of their equipment would embark at Chester. The rest would cross the peninsula to the head of the Chesapeake, and continue under sail to the York River.

The American army arrived in Philadelphia two days later, marching to fife and drum in a column two miles long, trailed by a wagon train and a cloud of dust that hovered "like a smothering snowstorm." Clad in a ragged patchwork of hunting shirts and linen britches, tired and dirty but gratified by the cheers that hailed them, they marched at a steady gait through the city and on toward Chester. It was a day of celebration for the city, but it only brought more headaches for Morris; the New England troops in particular were grumbling about the forced march in the oppressive heat. They wanted a month's pay—their first wage in more than a year—or they would march no more.

When Washington put the request to Morris—"the troops . . . have upon several occasions shown marks of great discontent"—Morris demurred, pleading his usual want of funds. But the situation was critical; promised pensions would no longer suffice. Nor would paper money—the soldiers were insisting on hard coin. Washington was insistent, and then he was gone, headed south to arrange embarkation of his army at the head of the Chesapeake, leaving Morris to conjure some sort of fund for the troops.

With his own reserves nearly exhausted, Morris turned to the only man in the city who could access substantial quantities of hard money—General Rochambeau. Morris made his pitch to the French general staff during a meeting at Luzerne's house on September 5. Rochambeau was sympathetic, but he was strapped for funds himself. De Grasse was expected to bring Spanish silver with him on his flagship, but he'd not yet been heard from. Ultimately, the French commander deferred a decision; his treasurer, who knew the state accounts better than he, was out on the road to Chester.

Seizing on this slender reed, Morris went and found Gouverneur, and the two of them set out on horseback at three that afternoon. They were looking for the treasurer and looking, as well, for some respite from the constant demands for money that found their way to the Office of Finance. Riding was a favorite recreation for both men; perhaps a change of scene would bring inspiration.

Out on the road, freed from the press of business, the two companions rode through the lush countryside, passing mills and granaries, making way for the occasional farm wagon. There was no sign of the French treasurer, but up ahead appeared a lone rider, making haste and raising a cloud of dust. As he approached the two friends hailed him and asked his purpose. He was an express rider, sent by Washington to find Robert Morris. Well, he had found him; what was the news? The rider handed Morris a packet of letters; one gave him just the report he'd been hoping for: Comte de Grasse had arrived in the Chesapeake, sailing at the head of a fleet of twenty-eight ships. The last, critical piece of the Yorktown campaign had fallen into place; more important for Morris, the French funds were on board.

Buoyed by the good news, Robert and Gouverneur continued on to Chester, where they caught up with Rochambeau, who had made the trip by water. Another conference, and a deal was struck: the French would provide Morris twenty thousand dollars in coin on his promise to repay it by October 1. Their business concluded, Robert and Gouverneur found a room for the night. Rising early the next morning, Robert dashed off a quick note to Washington. He celebrated their good fortune, but could not resist a dig at the source of so many frustrations. "I wish the states had enabled me to do more, but it is to be lamented that the Supineness of the several Legislatures still leaves the servants of the public to struggle with unmerited Distresses. It shall however be a Part of my Business to rouse them into exertion and I hope soon to see the Army better paid than before."

The two Morrises then got back on the road, this time finding it jammed with French troops making their way south, their fitted white uniforms and black gaiters a marked contrast to the tattered Americans. Arriving at Philadelphia around noon, the Financier and his assistant dove back into business. Letters went out to the army paymaster, directing management of the French loan; to Rochambeau, confirming terms of the deal; to a merchant in Baltimore soliciting more flour; and to Governors Clinton of New York and Livingston of New Jersey, asking help in driving cattle south for the army. It was 1776 all over again, Morris stepping in at the critical moment to direct all the key functions of the government.

Morris heard from Washington the next day. He'd not yet learned of the French loan, and now the protests of the soldiers presented the primary threat to the whole campaign. "Every day discovers to me the increasing Necessity of some money for the troops," Washington emphasized. "I wish it to come on the Wings of Speed."

The French funds arrived that afternoon, kegs of silver dollars that the paymaster played to best effect, knocking in the heads of the barrels and spilling the silver on the ground as the soldiers looked on. It was the first time in the war they had received any hard money for their service. It heartened the troops, but it wasn't enough; on September 8, with Washington already gone, General Benjamin Lincoln reported to Morris that the funds had run out before all the soldiers had received their money. "It will be difficult if not impossible to keep the men quiet who did not receive their pay," Lincoln warned; he needed six thousand more.

This produced sheer exasperation. Appeals for funds came from every direction—drovers, sailors, soldiers, state officers, express riders. "It seems as if every person connected in Public Service entertain an opinion that I am full of money," Morris groused in his diary; they "give me infinite interruption so that it is hardly possible to attend to Business of Consequence."

Many of the supplicants he turned away, but somehow he found six thousand more in coin for the army. Reading the text of his letter to Lincoln, you can almost hear Morris's sigh of relief: "I supplied the Pay Master General with Six thousand two hundred Dollars in preference of the many other demands that came on me," Morris wrote, "and I wish it may always be in my power to answer your desires as expeditiously as in the present Instance."

The urgent demands of the southern campaign had been satisfied, but the effort forced Morris to call in every available resource. One more shock would leave him undone.

Such a shock was not long in coming. Word arrived on September 11, the same day Morris sent the last supply of silver to General Lincoln, that the British were considering an attack on Philadelphia to relieve the pressure on Cornwallis. State authorities immediately called up three thousand militia, and applied to Morris for funds to provision this new force. Morris doubted the gravity of the threat, and warned Joseph Reed against plundering the treasury any further. "The late Movements of the Army have so entirely drained me of Money, that I have been Obliged to pledge my personal Credit very deeply, in a variety of instances, besides borrowing Money from my Friends; and advancing, to promote the public Service, every Shilling of my own." Should the emergency arise, Morris wrote, "all I can promise is the use of my Credit."

Much as Morris discounted the threat, it prompted Reed to call a council of war at his city home on September 21. Morris attended, as did members of the congressional Board of War and three generals of the state militia. While the military men talked of militia musters and entrenchments, Morris talked finance. In particular, he touted a plan proposed to him by Thomas Paine, that a quarter of the city's property rentals be diverted into a defense fund. "I need not mention to you," Paine wrote to Morris, "the great difference between giving up a quarter's rent and losing the whole rental together with the Capital" in the event of an invasion. This scheme was not effected, but it represented another step in Paine's evolution from Morris's public antagonist to his close collaborator.

In the meantime, new demands on Morris crowded in. In early September, Congress named him agent of the marine, thus conferring on him the second of the four executive positions it had created in February. Morris was a natural choice, both for his extensive maritime experience and by virtue of the personal bond he formed with the sea captains who sailed under him. John Paul Jones, for example, so revered Morris that he made him executor of his will, and upon his death in 1792 bequeathed to Morris the gold-mounted sword given him by the king of France in recognition of his daring exploits off the coast of England.

The navy post represented as much burden as it did honor, however, as efforts to create an American fleet had met with little success but much expense. Morris accepted reluctantly, "contrary to my Inclinations and inconsistent with the many Duties which press heavily upon me," and only because he believed he could "at least save Money to the Public." Part of those savings he realized on September 24 when he closed the office he'd set up next to his town house and moved his clerks and his books to the Marine Office, a few blocks up Front Street.

Even as they settled in to their new quarters, Morris and his staff had to field continued, pressing appeals from armies north and south. In New York, the garrison at West Point was out of flour and becoming desperate for food. In South Carolina, Nathanael Greene's southern army was subsisting, and only barely, on what they could forage from the countryside. "When I tell you I am in distress don't imagine I mean little difficulties," Greene wrote to Morris, "but suppose my situation to be like a ship's crew in a storm where the vessel is ready to sink and the water gains ground in the hold with every exertion to prevent it." Morris did what he could; in New York, where he had strong commercial ties, he prevailed on William Duer to purchase an additional two thousand barrels of flour based on an advance of coin and the balance in Morris notes, while reminding General Heath that, "I by no means hold myself responsible for feeding the Army . . . on the contrary, when I entered into Office, I made an express stipulation on the subject with Congress, to prevent that Responsibility." To Greene, Morris was able to send only a few hundred dollars, along with "the fullest applause to an Officer who finds in his own Genius an ample resource for the want of men, money, clothes, arms and supplies."

Morris knew this was inadequate, but he'd run out of options. In closing his note to Greene, Morris confessed that the only real chance for a reprieve lay with Washington. "I hope and trust that the arrival of the French fleet and the operations which are now commencing in the Chesapeake will greatly relieve you from the Embarrassments which you have hitherto labored under." What was true for Greene was also true for Morris, for the Congress, and for the American Revolution: everything depended on Yorktown.

Through these anxious weeks of marches and maneuvers, despite all the distractions and demands on his office, Morris managed to keep in mind and to press forward with key elements of his larger agenda for reviving the national economy and restoring the strength and authority of the Congress. His full program was still amorphous, but some of the separate components impressed him as clearly necessary, and in each case, time was a critical factor.

As always, there were setbacks, complications, and disappointments. The heaviest of these came in connection with his first and favorite project— the launch of the Bank of North America.

Morris's fond hope in founding the bank was to fund it by subscription—that enough wealthy Americans would answer his initial appeal to supply the four hundred thousand needed to commence operations. But early returns were uniformly disappointing; the southern states were in turmoil and New England too distant to place trust in such a novel institution. Morris tried an appeal to his Nationalist allies in the army, but got a sobering response from his longtime friend Tench Tilghman, Washington's senior aide-de-camp. "I am afraid I shall be a very unprofitable agent, for I believe it may with truth be said that there is not an Officer in the Army from the Commander in Chief downward who is at this time able to pay in a single subscription," Tilghman wrote Morris in June. Washington himself was "desirous . . . to patronize and support the scheme," Tilghman added, but "so far has the income of his estate for several years fallen short of his family expense and Taxes that he has lately been obliged to sell part of his real Estate."

Morris would have to improvise. Even before he heard from Tilghman, he asked Congress for authority to transfer to the new bank the bills of credit previously lodged as loan guarantees with the Bank of Pennsylvania. This plan was approved on June 22; a week later, the directors of the old bank agreed to the transfer. The bills were based on dubious claims of Congress to anticipated Spanish and Dutch loans, but they formed at least the appearance of capital.

With domestic funds in hiding, Morris cast about for foreign sources. The most promising supply lay in Havana, where Spanish silver collected in large quantities pending shipment to Madrid. These funds, Morris proposed, would be safer in the new bank than dodging British patrols during transit across the Atlantic.

Morris used all his arts in this bid to lure the support of Spain. He spent Morris notes to outfit the thirty-two-gun *Trumbull*, one of the frigates built for the Continental Navy, for a trading venture to Havana. She would sail with five hundred barrels of flour on account of the Congress, with proceeds returned in silver to Morris. She would also carry bills drawn by Morris on his French bankers, and those from the Bank of Pennsylvania that had been drawn against Madrid; sale of those bills would raise additional silver. Lastly, Morris included the plan for the new bank, which he hoped would interest private subscribers in Cuba.

To manage sale of the bills and to contact prospective investors, Morris had Congress appoint Robert Smith, his commercial agent in Havana, as a Continental agent; as with many of the agents for the Secret Committee, Smith was to receive no pay, but would earn a commission on any transactions he made for the government. Writing Smith to inform him of the appointment, Morris said he had recommended him on the basis of "your Character, Situation and Attachments to your Country"; now, Morris wrote, "I shall put your Talents to the Proof." Morris also drew on his Spanish contacts in Philadelphia, asking Francisco Rendón to endorse the bank project. Rendón complied with letters to the Spanish court and the governor of Cuba touting the bank and praising Morris as "a man full of spirit, knowledge and enterprise," and owner of "the largest fortune on the continent."

Morris placed the bills and the letters in the hands of James Nicholson, captain of the *Trumbull*, along with sealed orders directing him to Havana. Nicholson put to sea in early August, but he never reached the Caribbean. The *Trumbull* was spotted as she cleared the Delaware capes by the British warship *Iris*, which trailed her until dark. That night, the *Trumbull* was caught in a storm and dismasted; the next morning the *Iris* found her again and took Nicholson and his crew prisoner.

Reports of the capture reached Philadelphia when Morris was at camp conferring with Washington. Gouverneur Morris relayed the news to Robert in New York, along with a draft letter advising John Jay in Madrid to reject the captured bills if they found their way to Spain. These letters were themselves captured in transit, and landed in the hands of a Tory printer in New York. Morris's chagrin was complete when Gouverneur's intercepted note was published in the New York *Royal Gazette* along with the mocking comment, "Admirable Financing this, truly, Mr. Morris! But what else can be done by the Financier of a Bankrupt Commonwealth."

It was France that finally came up with the funds to launch the bank. John Laurens had spent two months in Paris seeking to expand on the grant of six million livres Franklin had secured in the spring. Young Laurens "brusqued" Vergennes and the court exceedingly, to use Benjamin Franklin's disapproving term, but not without effect; the court declined to advance any new funds but, after much prodding, agreed to guarantee payment on a prospective loan of ten million livres from the bankers of Holland.

As America's man on the spot in Paris, Franklin was custodian of the French loans, and he parceled out the funds carefully. He retained 5.5 million livres to cover bills drawn against him by Congress, and assigned 2 million to Laurens to purchase arms. That left 2.5 million—$450,000—for shipment to America. On the first day of June, Laurens boarded a seventy-two-gun French frigate laden with silver coin packed in reinforced barrels.

The voyage west, in convoy with several other warships and two supply frigates, took longer than expected, and was diverted to Boston to avoid British patrols off Philadelphia. The squadron finally arrived on August 26 after a passage of nearly three months, and Laurens made his appearance in Philadelphia on September 2.

Learning that the French silver had arrived at Boston, Morris decided these funds would afford the necessary foundation for the bank. On September 4 he wrote the state governors to announce that bank directors would be selected November 1, and to request that the banknotes be made receivable for taxes and debts due to Congress. That same day, George Clymer and John Nixon set October 1 as the closing date for subscriptions to bank stock. All that was left was to get the crucial coin from Boston to Philadelphia.

This would be a demanding task. Still smarting from the loss of the *Trumbull*, Morris determined not to ship the bullion by sea, but instead to move it overland. Morris pondered for days whom to place in charge of the project until he chanced across Tench Francis, the family friend who had served as factor for the Bank of Pennsylvania. Francis had been accused early in the war of Tory sympathies, and jumped at the chance to repair his reputation through patriotic service. Morris sent him to Boston with typically detailed instructions, minute down to the age of the oxen to be used hauling the French hoard, and a false route that Francis should disclose to decoy possible British patrols.

Alert as ever to any means that might extend the value of his funds, Morris commissioned Francis to invest part of the French coin in bills of exchange, which were selling at a steep discount in Boston; these bills would fetch a better price in Philadelphia, with the profits augmenting the value of the French grant. At the conclusion of the journey, Morris advised, the ox teams could be sold for a profit as well.

Francis arrived at Boston in late September and fitted out fourteen customized freight wagons, reinforced to carry a ton apiece, laden with strong-boxes packed with coin and welded shut. He set out in early October and for the next two months wended his way south, escorted at various points by militia, infantry, and mounted Continental dragoons. To the farmers tending their fences and stocks on an autumn afternoon, the passing wagons looked like just another army supply train; little did they suspect it carried the richest hoard of silver that had ever traversed the American countryside.

The bank would be central to Morris's effort to revive the economy and fund the operations of the government, but it was perhaps the simplest of the many projects confronting his still young administration. More daunting, and if possible, more important, was to address the great mass of debt that had been created by the Congress in the course of the war. This would help facilitate the business of raising revenue and, more broadly, help to restore credit to the government.

Upon first accepting his office, Morris had expressly stipulated that he would not be responsible for funding debts incurred prior to his administration. But at the same time he was convinced that sorting and assigning those debts for future payment was an urgent and immediate priority. Lacking such a settlement, the individual states came to adopt the view that each had done more for the cause than their neighbors. As a consequence, the states had collectively grown "more and more negligent, a dangerous Supineness pervades the Continent, and Recommendations of Congress, capable in the year 1775, of rousing all America to Action, now lie neglected."

Morris in July had promised the state governors that he would provide a firm accounting of their obligations to Congress, and that "my efforts for that purpose shall be unceasing." Now, even as he was scrambling to collect the supplies and funds to keep Washington's army on the march to Yorktown, Morris composed a detailed and comprehensive plan. He laid out his policy in a letter to Congress dated August 28, but realizing that the delegates were already overburdened, Morris delayed presenting the proposal for more than two months. His early formulation of the plan showed both his sense of urgency and his remarkable capacity to think ahead even in the midst of current crises.

The first step, Morris said, was to define and reduce to hard numbers the various requisitions Congress had charged to the states, both collectively and individually, and to assign them on an equitable basis, adjusted for inflation. Individual states would be credited for the contributions they had sent in, and billed for whatever deficits remained. Assigning the proportionate burdens would necessarily be an arbitrary process, as the relative financial strength of each state had never before been assayed. Yet further delay would only make the process more arbitrary. Moreover, Morris insisted this division of debts should be final, putting to rest the disputes and "jealousies" between the separate states.

"I have thought much on this Subject, and feel very anxious about it," Morris wrote. Without clear and final accounts, the states would continue ignoring the requisitions of Congress. In that case, "the Precedent of Disobedience once established, our Union must soon be at an End, and the authority of Congress reduced to a metaphysical idea." State settlements, Morris wrote, represented "the Corner Stone of the whole Fabrick."

So far, Morris's prescription followed closely the basic outline laid down in the Articles of Confederation, where the central government served mainly as a clearinghouse to coordinate the actions of sovereign, independent states. But now Morris proposed a crucial innovation—a separate category of "public debt" incurred by Congress as a whole. These obligations, comprising domestic and foreign loans, along with the mass of certificates issued by agents of the commissary and quartermaster departments, should be addressed by Congress alone, and funded through a new regime of federal taxes.

The certificates presented a special case. Having often been issued in lieu of outright seizure, the certificates usually exceeded the actual value of the goods "purchased"; in other cases, vendors engaged in outright fraud, a practice widely tolerated by government agents grasping for any available supplies. Rather than pay the certificates at face value, Morris wanted each one examined by a federal commissioner and adjusted to real value in hard dollars. The certificates would then be replaced by new bills payable at future dates with interest.

All of this debt, together with the loans incurred by Congress, would accrue to the central government instead of the states. The interest would be funded by the national impost Congress had proposed to the states in February. Now Morris suggested for the first time that Congress levy, in addition to the impost, land, excise, and poll taxes. The tax rates could be modest or even nominal, but together with the impost they would be sufficient at least to secure new loans. In the meantime these taxes would set in motion the independent operations of a central government.

Certainly Morris was aware that the power to impose such taxes was expressly reserved to the states by the Articles of Confederation, but he quietly ignored that prohibition in his letter. Not content simply to referee the claims on the various public creditors, Morris was pressing to establish Congress as a truly sovereign entity. This was the Nationalist agenda, a new and more grandiose conception of the central government.

Such forward thinking, at a time when the demands of the moment seemed all-consuming, was a hallmark of the Nationalists. We have already seen how Alexander Hamilton studied economic policy during breaks from his duties as Washington's aide; Nathanael Greene, commanding a beleaguered army in South Carolina, was similarly preoccupied with the larger affairs of state. In August he opened a wide-ranging dialogue with Morris that echoed the concerns of the Financier and served to confirm his vision.

"No Nation ever had greater resources in the confidence of the people, than Congress had at the beginning of the war," Greene mused ruefully, but tender laws and the fear of imposing taxes had squandered that confidence. "Credit and reputation are much alike either in public or private life," Greene wrote. "Once lost they are very difficult to be regained."

As to politics, Greene was also in accord with Morris. "I lament exceedingly that Congress have given up so much of their just and necessary prerogative into the hands of the different States; and I am apprehensive we shall want that force and vigor in our National character which is necessary to our security." Greene was concerned about internal division as well as external threats. "I am not less apprehensive that intestine broils and feuds will frequently convulse the [American] empire for want of a sufficient respect and dependence of the States upon Congress."

These lines so closely matched Morris's views that they might appear the result of some sort of groupthink, the product of some surreptitious cabal. But Morris and Greene were separated by circumstance and experience, one entrenched in his Philadelphia countinghouse, the other camped under the southern stars. What they shared was an outlook, one shaped by mutual frustrations in the service of the Revolution.

As much as Morris looked forward, he also had to reckon with the obligations and connections he had formed early in the war. The Secret Committee was gone, but the agents and the arms traders were still out there, presenting Morris with problems and demands that he could not ignore.

One of the more delicate cases involved William Bingham. Already wealthy when he accepted his appointment as Continental agent in Martinique in 1776, Bingham returned three years later as one of the richest men in Philadelphia. It's hard to say just how Bingham had built up his fortune—aside from private trade with Morris, Bingham had important partners in Maryland and in the Carolinas—but it appears that little of it derived from government business. His letters to the Secret Committee included frequent pleas for funds, and his advances to support government contracts stretched his personal credit to the limit.

Bingham's appointment included no salary—he was to make his living by commissions and in private trade—but he was to be paid his expenses. These totaled more than one hundred thousand dollars, funds Bingham said he needed urgently, in part to fulfill government contracts. Bingham's claim was first reviewed by a committee of Congress in 1780 and gained tentative approval with an advance payment of seven thousand pounds sterling in bills on Spain. Bingham was still seeking the balance when Morris was named Financier the following year, and his claim was referred to Morris in August. On September 7, Morris responded with a letter to Congress.

As Bingham was known to be his friend and sometime business partner, Morris had to state his case carefully. He acknowledged that Bingham's charges "amount to more money than at the time of his appointment I had any idea of," but noted as well, "It is very certain that the emoluments arising to Mr. Bingham from the Commercial business of Congress fell short of what was expected, and it is equally certain that the inconvenience arising from his constant advances and consequent distresses must far outbalance the commissions he drew." Morris left the final decision to the committee, which ruled in Bingham's favor.

Morris tried to keep Bingham's case at arm's length but the grant of funds, combined with Bingham's obvious wealth, led to much grumbling about Morris favoring his committee agents. He made a similar exception for John Ross, another former agent and business partner. Ross had presented his claim in 1779 and, like Bingham, saw it approved before Morris took office, but it fell to Morris to produce the funds. This violated his policy of rejecting debts incurred prior to his assuming office, but Morris reasoned that failure to cover the debts of government agents would damage American credit abroad. Morris doubtless also felt a personal obligation to agents who had served at his direction.

Whatever his motivation, charges of favoritism dogged the Financier for years. One disgruntled sea captain voiced the sense of the merchant community when he complained that "Mr. Morris has taken a number by the hand in the course of the war and they have acquired wealth." The captain's dispute was not with Morris directly, but he felt the Financier should have intervened to support his claim against another Secret Committee merchant. Morris did not, the captain said, "because I would not fall down and worship the Golden Politician."

But while many regarded Morris as Philadelphia's King Midas, few Secret Committee agents actually gained by their connection to the Financier. If Ross and especially Bingham profited by their work for the government—and it is not clear that they did—they were the exception. Most foreign agents commissioned by the Secret Committee paid dearly by their service.

Two of the more unfortunate Secret Committee agents were Samuel Curson and Isaac Gouverneur. Both were engaged by the committee early on, Curson posted at St. Eustatius and Gouverneur at Curaçao. Curson suffered the common fate of Secret Committee agents when failed remittances left him deep in debt, but his real travails began when he and Gouverneur were captured during a British raid on St. Eustatius in early 1781. Both were "stripped of every thing but their wearing apparel" and sent to Britain in chains, where they were imprisoned as spies. "Special Severity, it is supposed, has been shown to them in Consequence of their acting as Agents to Congress," the Foreign Affairs Committee noted in May.

Another Caribbean agent, Stephen Ceronio, was driven so deeply into debt that in 1778 he seized a cargo shipped by another congressional agent to cover his bills. When his creditors brought suit for payment, Ceronio made his way to Philadelphia in 1781 to seek settlement. Congress granted him fifty-five thousand livres—about ten thousand dollars—but he was to collect his money back at Hispaniola. After Ceronio set out in June, his ship was captured by the British, and during his absence his post was filled by a Frenchman, Bernard Lavaud. When Ceronio finally arrived at Cape François, Lavaud refused to honor Morris's order to pay Ceronio, and the dispute festered for years.

Oliver Pollock also suffered for his services to the Secret Committee. As the agent in New Orleans for both the Congress and the state of Virginia, Pollock had advanced three hundred thousand dollars from his own funds to support James Willing and George Rogers Clark in their raids against British outposts on the western frontier. By 1781, Pollock lamented, "When I undertook the Agency of the United States and conceived it my duty to act for Virginia also, my credit was extensive, my fortune equal to $100,000. At this date my credit as a merchant is injured, my fortune annihilated, and my numerous family become pensioners on the Bounty of my Friends."

As with Bingham and Ross, Pollock's claim was approved by Congress in early 1781, but in November a committee barred Morris from paying the claim until separate obligations between Pollock and the Spanish governor of New Orleans were settled. Pollock had much the same experience with Virginia, which voted him thirty-five thousand dollars—a fraction of his claim—but had no funds to pay him. Finding his own hands tied, Morris wrote in support of Pollock to his old friend Benjamin Harrison, then sitting as governor of Virginia. Speaking of Pollock but also for the rest of the agents, Morris said, "I have remarked in the course of this revolution that some men who would not trust the country a farthing have obtained rewards in Money for Supposed Services whilst others who made actual advances have found the utmost difficulty to obtain even acknowledgments of the Justice due to them." Public bodies "very soon grow tired" of financial appeals, Morris observed, "until the Individual is ruined and his bitter complaints are constantly injuring Public Credit."

Having yet to be paid in 1783, Pollock accepted appointment as agent for Congress in Havana, but when he arrived at his post he was arrested for debt and jailed for eighteen months. Congress finally paid his claims in 1791.

Of all the agents deployed abroad by the Secret Committee, Silas Deane was the most important, the most productive, and ultimately the most disappointed in his dealings with Congress. Upon his return to France in 1780 Deane set about settling accounts that he expected would return a large balance in his favor. He met on and off for weeks with an auditor appointed by Congress, a merchant in Nantes named Joshua Johnson, but in the end Johnson refused to render a verdict.

As the months dragged by, Deane was forced to borrow from friends for subsistence and became deeply embittered. In the cafés and salons of Paris, he muttered darkly about the weakness of Holland and France and the inexorable power of Great Britain. America was "already conquered," Deane said, and "Congress a mere cipher." To his enemies Deane's grumbling confirmed disloyalties they had long suspected; even his friends worried that he was losing his bearings. "Poor Mr. Deane," Beaumarchais wrote after one gloomy visit. "He shows a bitterness that borders on something worse. . . . I am uneasy, observing his profound emotion."

Deane gave vent to his growing disaffection with a series of eleven letters he sent to some of the leading figures in the Revolution, including Morris, James Wilson, William Duer, and Benjamin Harrison. The letters all covered roughly the same ground—the decision for independence had been taken hastily (Deane supported the move at the time, but was in Paris and not on hand for the debate), and rested on "erroneous ideas of our own importance." The war would leave both Britain and America drained and vulnerable to the other powers of Europe.

Deane dwelt at length on the prospects for postwar commerce, and whether Americans would do better within the British Empire, or without it. "I have examined the question as thoroughly as I am capable," Deane wrote, "and am convinced we must be losers." Americans would face hostile markets abroad and be swamped with British imports at home, with no way to earn the hard currency to pay for them. Just as troubling, the political culture of the Revolution boded ill for commerce and economic growth. "You, who are perfectly acquainted with the disposition of those who form the Congress and the Assemblies of the several states, know that it is very far from being favorable to commerce," Deane observed to Morris.

Deane disdained the rustic ideal of yeoman husbandry that had come to dominate the early years of the Revolution. "I hear men reputed as the wisest and most enlightened of American patriots, advance that commerce is rather injurious, than beneficial," Deane wrote. These true believers could not recognize that "agriculture and commerce mutually depend on, and support each other," holding instead that "the whole attention of America as an independent nation should be turned to agriculture. . . .

"When I hear such doctrines advanced, and by men whom America has been taught to look up to revere . . . I become doubtful, whether our commerce would not suffer as greatly from internal checks and embarrassments, as from external."

So far, Deane's argument appeared reasonable enough—at least as far as Morris was concerned. Deane's position on independence echoed that of Morris and his allies in 1776. And his summary of American revolutionary ideology would have struck a chord with any Philadelphia entrepreneur. But Deane did not stop there. With enthusiasm for the war waning and with Britain showing unexpected stamina, now was the time—perhaps the last chance—for the rebels to seek a negotiated settlement.

This was apostasy, a call for capitulation. It was also a case of bad timing. The letters were written in May and June, when the Congress was bankrupt and the Continental Army moribund. Deane could not have expected—nobody did—the early success of Morris's administration, the mobilization of August, the arrival of De Grasse, and the momentous drive against Cornwallis in Virginia. By the time Deane's letters arrived in October, talk of submission was not just traitorous, it was ludicrous.

And it was delivered in the worst possible fashion. The ship bearing Deane's letters was captured at sea, the sensational documents forwarded to New York, and the letters published in October in the *Royal Gazette*. Deane never intended his letters to be confidential—he addressed them to too wide an audience for that—but their garish exposure left his friends in a most embarrassing situation. Fortunately for Morris, the wave of loathing the letters unleashed was limited to Deane himself. "Strange as it is," Joseph Reed complained to a friend, "it seems that shame and disgrace reach no farther than the party immediately detected." To Reed this was just another proof of loose morals, flagging patriotism, and the undue influence of Morris, Deane's friend and collaborator. "It is a melancholy proof," Reed wrote, "what money, expectation of office, entertainment, good wine, and fear of offending great men, will do."

But if Morris escaped opprobrium, the letters doomed any chance that Deane would obtain a timely settlement from Congress. Despondent but still defiant, Deane departed Paris for less costly lodgings in Flanders. By March 1782, Franklin reported to Morris, "Our former friend Mr. Deane has lost himself entirely. He and his letters are universally condemned. . . . I see no place for him but England. He continues however to sit croaking at Ghent, chagrinned, discontented, and dispirited."

Deane did indeed proceed to England, in 1783, and died in penury in 1789. His heirs pressed his claims, as much to restore his reputation as to profit by his estate. A Senate Committee on Revolutionary Claims revisited the matter half a century after Deane's death, and issued a warrant for thirty-seven-thousand dollars. The original audit of his accounts, the committee found, was "ex parte, erroneous, and a gross injustice to Silas Deane."

It was not until late August when the British high command got the first reports that De Grasse was headed for the Chesapeake, and not until the 28th that Admiral Thomas Graves departed the Hudson to challenge him. By then it was too late for Cornwallis, too late to unhinge the trap that had been laid for him.

Sailing at the head of a fleet of nineteen warships, Graves rounded the Virginia capes the morning of September 5 to find De Grasse already there. Graves had superior position, but De Grasse had a stronger force, and in battle that afternoon the fleets fought to a standstill. Four of Graves's ships sustained heavy damage, while De Grasse maintained possession of the bay. The British admiral hovered off the coast for another week, but the French had a decided advantage in firepower, and on the 14th, Graves headed back for New York.

The battle of the Chesapeake capes all but decided the fate of Cornwallis. His position at Yorktown had been chosen for easy access to the British fleet; as a defensive position it left him trapped, hemmed on three sides by water. Cornwallis might have broken out with a sortie against Lafayette, who commanded the only enemy force on the spot, but he chose instead to buttress his defenses and await relief from Graves. It was a rare failure to act by the enterprising British commander, and a fatal one.

It took the balance of September for the French and American forces to assemble for the final assault, but during the last week of September 1781, the months of planning and frantic activity by Washington, Morris, and Rochambeau came to fruition on the banks of the York River in Virginia. By October 1 the allied armies had massed twenty thousand men, more than half of them French soldiers, sailors, or marines. Cornwallis had less than half that number. His forces were entrenched on high ground in the village of Yorktown, but with De Grasse commanding the harbor, they had no avenue of retreat. For once, after all the marches and maneuvers of the war, Washington enjoyed numerical and tactical superiority.

Washington commenced siege operations against the British positions on October 6. Fighting and bombardment continued for the next ten days, but the outcome was never really in doubt. Cornwallis attempted to ferry his men across the river in a last bid to escape on the night of October 16, but a sudden storm turned them back. The next morning, a drummer boy appeared at the parapet of the British defenses, followed by an officer waving a white handkerchief. Cornwallis was vanquished, and for the second time in the war an entire British army capitulated.

Rumors of the victory at Yorktown reached Philadelphia on Monday, October 22, but official word took another two days. The messenger, Washington's aide Tench Tilghman, arrived in the predawn hours of the 24th, exhausted and feverish from a long, hard ride. Tilghman reported to Congress later that morning. Finding that their messenger had arrived penniless, the delegates each contributed a hard dollar to fund his room and board—one requisition Morris did not have to answer.

That evening, responding to a proclamation from the Supreme Executive Council, the windows of the city were illuminated to celebrate the victory of allied arms. As usual on such occasions, the Quakers and other conscientious objectors left their windows dark. And, as was also usual on such occasions, the city's radical militants took the opportunity to smash every window they found without a lighted candle. It was a visceral demonstration that, while the Americans had found the pluck and vigor to challenge their enemies in the field, they had yet to peaceably settle their differences at home.

The next afternoon, Robert Morris sat down with Tilghman for a more sober assessment of the ramifications of Yorktown. True, it was a signal victory that could well mean the end to British plans for subjugating her former colonies. But there were more immediate considerations—thousands of American and French soldiers still in Virginia, and thousands of new British prisoners to feed. In addition, as a reward to his victorious troops, Washington had agreed that his officers might have their pick of goods being offered by British traders who had followed Cornwallis to Yorktown—and that Morris would pick up the tab, "a very considerable debt incurred upon you as Financier," as Washington confessed soon after.

Morris would have to juggle these expenses with the crying needs of the American armies at West Point and in South Carolina, both beset by chronic shortages of food and clothing. At the same time, Luzerne had informed Congress that America could expect no further grants in aid from the court of France. Peace might be at hand, but for Robert Morris, his travails as Financier had only just begun.

Chapter 12

EXECUTIVE ACTION

The celebrations of the victory at Yorktown were already a month past when George Washington made his way back to Philadelphia. He'd spent a week close by the battlefield, arranging the disposition of his troops and the vanquished British, and then a hiatus at Mount Vernon, lingering there to mourn the death of Jack Custis, the last surviving offspring of Martha Washington's first marriage. Now he had come to the capital to confer with the civil administration on the next campaign. It was too soon to leave Martha to her grief; she accompanied him along with his military "family."

The general and his staff entered town quietly. Cornwallis had been captured, but the British still held Manhattan, Georgia, and the Carolinas—Washington was in no mood for pomp and display. Instead he made his way to the Robert Morris house on Front Street. Mary Morris had hosted Martha Washington in the past; she would do her best to make the matron of Mount Vernon comfortable.

That evening Morris sat down with Washington and the Marquis de Lafayette to consider the most pressing question facing the American government: the prospects for future aid and funding from France. With funds from the states coming in at a trickle, France was the sole source of revenue Congress could rely on. Lafayette had been conferring with Morris for weeks on the same subject and was intimately familiar with the thinking of the French delegation. He would depart within days on a return voyage to France, acting as a diplomatic emissary for his adopted Revolution.

Morris had much news to impart—and none of it good. In September, even as the troops were massing in Virginia, Chevalier de la Luzerne, the French ambassador, had informed Congress that no new funds could be expected from the French court. Soon thereafter, Luzerne had opened a series of exchanges with Morris seeking to curtail any further drafts on France.

The discourse began cordially, Luzerne complimenting Morris on "the advantageous use which you make of the public resources," but it soon grew testy, the amity forged at banquet tables giving way to the clashing priorities of their separate stations. Desperate for funds, Morris alternated between appeals to mutual interest and argument over the specific accounts in question. Luzerne, ordered by French foreign minister Vergennes to halt further drafts, became exasperated.

For once, the poor and delayed communications between America and Europe worked in Morris's favor. When word first arrived of the six million livre grant, the four million loan, and the prospective ten million livre loan from Holland, Luzerne had magnanimously extended Morris's initial line of credit. It took weeks to learn that Benjamin Franklin had claimed much of the first ten million livres in Paris, and that the Holland loan had yet to be filled. At that point, Luzerne tried to backtrack, but Morris had already issued drafts beyond his initial limit.

Rather than antagonize Luzerne, Morris tried to enlist his sympathies in the projects of the Office of Finance. He was seeking to raise taxes, he told Luzerne, but Americans "have neither been accustomed to them, nor have the Legislatures hitherto adopted the proper Modes of laying and levying them. . . .

"Taxation requires Time in all Governments," Morris lectured Luzerne. "America, divided as it is into a Society of free States . . . cannot suddenly be therefore brought to pay all which might be spared from the Wealth of her Citizens."

While he temporized with Vergennes, Morris adopted a much sterner tone with the recalcitrant states. In mid-October, in another circular letter to the state governors, Morris announced that the French subsidies were suspended, and further, that without those funds he was forced to terminate interest payment on the domestic loans issued by Congress early in the war. He wrote in the rousing personal style that was becoming the signature of his administration.

"I am now to address you on a subject of very great Importance," Morris wrote. "Whatever may be the Fate of my Administration, I will never be subjected to the Reproach of Falsehood or Insincerity. I therefore take the earliest possible moment . . . to make those Communications which will give insight into our real situation." With that, Morris presented a detailed breakdown of the French loans, the expenditures that had consumed them, and the paltry balance that remained. He then dismissed any future reliance on new foreign funds.

"People have flattered themselves with a visionary idea that nothing was more necessary than for Congress to send a Minister abroad, and that immediately he would obtain as much money as he chose to ask for. . . . But without the clear prospect of Repayment, People will not part with their property." This meant raising funds at home, at least to support loans abroad. "Sir," he wrote the governors, "I must speak to you most plainly. While we do nothing for ourselves, we cannot expect the Assistance of others."

Lest the point be lost, Morris reiterated: "It is high time to relieve ourselves from the Infamy we have already sustained, and to rescue and restore the national Credit. This can only be done by solid Revenue." Now Morris laid open his twofold strategy to bring pressure on the states, deploying the holders of Loan Office Certificates, whose interest payments he had shut off, to amplify his own appeal to the dignity of the sovereign states. "To the public Creditors therefore I say, that until the States provide Revenues for liquidating the Principal and Interest of the public Debt, they cannot be paid; and to the States I say, that they are bound by every principle which is held sacred among Men, to make that Provision." The fate of America, Morris intoned, was in the hands of its citizens, and not the monarchs and bankers of Europe. "We may be happy or miserable as we please."

Morris enclosed this circular in a November 3 letter to Luzerne as "an additional proof of my desire to draw from among ourselves the necessary resources, and therefore to become truly independent." Then Morris invoked the idea of French self-interest. "When we consider that the object of the [American] war is of the last Consequence to the Commerce of His Majesty's dominions, and especially to his Marine, and when we further consider, that his Honor stands pledged to our Support, to doubt his further assistance would imply a reflection both on his Wisdom and Integrity."

The French ambassador answered the next day. To Luzerne, the surrender of Cornwallis should be regarded as a turning point. "After the great success which has just crowned the allied armies, the King has a right to expect some extraordinary efforts on the part of the United States and if he ordered me before to declare to them that they should count only on their internal resources it is in no way probable that he will change his opinion." Morris could only wince as Luzerne threw his own reasoning back at him. "If in these circumstances the people did not show their devotion to independence by some extraordinary effort," the ambassador wrote, "one would almost be in a position to regret successes which instead of arousing their energy would throw them into inaction."

Luzerne closed by dismissing Morris's rash reference to the king's honor. "As to the integrity of the King you know as well as I, Sir . . . that His Majesty has surpassed by far the measure of his obligations toward his allies."

This last, sharp rejoinder prompted a quick answer from Morris. He was contrite, but he did not give ground. "It is impossible that I can doubt the Wisdom and Integrity of his most Christian Majesty," Morris wrote, "or that you can doubt his desire of giving further assistance to the United States."

Morris wisely let matters lie still, until a chance encounter with Luzerne the week before Washington came to town. Luzerne at that point asked Morris for a written accounting of what funds he had received from France. Morris complied, adding a note detailing his efforts to ensure profitable sales of the French bills, and the commitments he'd made based on those funds. "If those foundations on which I built are removed," Morris pleaded with Luzerne, "my past labors will have been thrown away, and my future utility absolutely destroyed."

Luzerne was unmoved. Any future bills drawn by Morris against France, he warned, would be rejected.

Morris reviewed all of this correspondence in his conference with Washington and Lafayette. Clearly, there was little more to be done with Luzerne. It was up to Lafayette to hasten to France and join Benjamin Franklin in lobbying Vergennes for yet another grant of aid. Perhaps the fame Lafayette had acquired in America, his youthful dash enhanced by his exploits in Virginia, would soften the hearts—and open the coffers—of the French court.

Lafayette was to sail from Boston aboard an American frigate. With his departure from Philadelphia set for later in the week, Morris sat down to compose a comprehensive statement that Lafayette would deliver to Franklin in Paris. This was a critical performance. Franklin himself had grown irritated with Morris's incessant demands; Morris needed to persuade his old friend that he was doing everything he could to restrain spending and raise taxes at home, while providing arguments Franklin might use in appealing for new funds.

Morris opened with a review of his efforts to settle accounts with the states, his machinations in Pennsylvania, and his calls for new revenue. "Notwithstanding my pressing Instances very little hard money has been obtained from the states . . . as to the paper money it is of no use.

"The picture I have already given of this country will not be pleasing to you," Morris wrote. But instead of the moralizing tone he'd adopted in his letters to the states, to Franklin he pleaded for sympathy. "What else could be expected from us? A Revolution, a War, the Dissolution of Government, the creating of it anew, Cruelty, Rapine and Devastation in the midst of our very Bowels, these Sir are circumstances by no means favorable to Finance. The wonder then is that we have done so much, that we have borne so much, and the candid World will add, that we have dared so much."

Morris then led Franklin through the whole of his exchange with Luzerne, enclosing copies of every letter. As Luzerne would surely forward the same letters, and the same arguments, to Vergennes, Morris offered Franklin his best rebuttal. Luzerne "takes it for granted that the People will make extraordinary efforts in Consequence of their successes, and I will readily admit that they have the Ability, and ought to have the Inclination; but they must differ much from former Experiences if they really do exert themselves."

Here Morris opened to Franklin his personal views on the problems raised by democracy, a political system new to the modern world, and in its unfettered operations virtually unique to the rebel governments in America. "I will admit that their Rulers ought to urge them into Activity, but it must be remembered that those Rulers are themselves of the People, that their ideas and views are limited, and that they act like the People, rather from Feeling than from Reflection."

This wasn't to cast aspersions on the operations of the popular will. Through all his skirmishes with the radicals in the Assembly and the factions in Congress, Morris wrestled gamely with the changeable gusts of democratic governance, but he never suggested reverting to any other political format. Still, he could catalogue its shortcomings. "Our general System has not yet grown into that Form and Vigor which can communicate the Impulses of a Sovereign Mind to the remotest Members of subjected Power," he observed to Franklin. "I will admit that a Monarch would on so brilliant a Success [as at Yorktown] call into Action all which his kingdom possessed of strength and Resources, but America is not under Monarchial Government."

Gouverneur Morris, writing around the same time, went further, suggesting to Nathanael Greene that "I have no hope that our Union can subsist except in the form of an absolute monarchy," adding that, "this does not seem to consist with the Taste and Temper of the People." Here as on other occasions, Gouverneur showed himself to be more impetuous, more impatient, than his mentor, but the question of governance troubled them both.

Besides the problems that came with democracy, the Financier said the sheer size of the former colonies—"this immense Republic," as his assistant termed it—tended to dissipate the sense of urgency required to support the war effort. "America is so extensive that a shock given in one extremity, is lost before it reaches the other," Robert Morris wrote. The long distances only reinforced mankind's essentially parochial nature. "The inroads of the enemy create opposition . . . but when the inroad ceases, when the enemy retreats, the Storm subsides, each man returns to his domestic pursuits and enjoyments."

Such intrinsic obstacles might be overcome in time, Morris suggested, but America's allies must be patient. "It is certain that America ought to do everything in her power . . . but it is in vain to think of breaking the Bounds of Possibility, and equally vain to think of changing the Nature of Man." Here was Morris the realist. "There is little propriety," he wrote, "in reproaching Americans with the Faults inseparable from Humanity."

Recall, Morris added, that many sacrifices had already been made. Set moral strictures aside, he urged, and give the new nation time to get her bearings. "The exertions of this Country have really been very great, and as soon as more consistency shall have been put in the Administration, they will again be great; but this is the Period of weakness between the convulsive Labors of Enthusiasm, and the sound and regular Operations of Order and Government."

Morris had made his pitch. It was addressed to Franklin but was really a brief for the French court; it was also a candid summary of his current outlook, views he shared and developed in a continuing dialogue with Washington. Morris delivered the letter to Lafayette, who was traveling overland to Boston in company with his brother-in-law, the Comte de Noailles. Morris had a letter for Noailles, too, this one including a list of shoes and clothes that the count had agreed to purchase for Mary in Paris. "Remember that if this commission proves troublesome it was voluntary on your part," Morris wrote playfully; "your only reward will consist in the approbation no doubt your Taste in the Choice will meet with, and the Thanks of Mrs. Morris and myself."

As Lafayette and his entourage rode north, Morris returned to the relentless demands of the Office of Finance. At the same time, he pressed his thankless effort to steer the country through its "Period of Weakness," and rally Americans to what he conceived to be their duty.

Morris did so in partnership with a small coterie of like-minded and influential public officials. Principal among them was George Washington, who stayed in Philadelphia through the following March, marking the first time in the war that the general spent the cold season away from the main army's winter camp. His itinerary was unformed when he came to the city; Morris sought to anchor him in the capital by securing him lodgings, which were much in demand at the time. He did so through the offices of his friend Francisco Rendón, the unofficial Spanish ambassador. Rendón was quartered in a mansion on Third Street, on the same block as Thomas Willing and just a short walk from Morris's home. Rendón was "perfectly disposed" to host the illustrious general. Morris took Washington to look at the place the afternoon of Friday, November 30, and the deal was struck. "This house will answer well for the General," Morris noted in his diary, "and no other can be got."

Another key player in what soon evolved as a Nationalist circle was Robert Livingston. A wealthy member of one of New York's dominant political clans, Livingston was an occasional delegate to Congress who opposed independence in 1776 but was called away before the decisive vote. He studied law under his uncle William Livingston, Kitty's father, and was close personal friends with the New York moderates John Jay, James Duane, and Gouverneur Morris.

Livingston was nominated as secretary for foreign affairs at the same time Robert Morris was named to finance, but he was opposed for the position by Arthur Lee. The choice was a clear one; Livingston was friendly with Luzerne and the rest of the French delegation, while Lee regarded France with suspicion. The question divided Congress for months, and was finally settled in August, when Livingston prevailed on a split vote. Lee, hungry for a new role to play after losing his post in Europe, saw his defeat as a product of a cabal involving Luzerne and the Deane faction in Congress, led by Robert Morris. After visiting Philadelphia to press his case, he returned to Virginia seething as usual. "The plot is deep," he grumbled in a letter to the president of Congress.

Robert and Mary Morris were both friendly with Livingston, Mary helping to find Livingston lodgings in the city much as Robert did for George Washington. Soon after his appointment, Livingston named Gouverneur's nephew Lewis Morris as his undersecretary, cementing his ties to the Office of Finance.

Rounding out the corps of Nationalist leaders was Benjamin Lincoln, named in October as secretary of war. Lincoln was nobody's first choice for the post, but Philip Schuyler of New York had too many enemies, and

Nathanael Greene could not be spared from the field. Lincoln was a suitable compromise: as a general he'd been wounded at Saratoga, led the doomed defense of Charleston, and held command at Yorktown. He had demonstrated administrative skill during the long march south, and enjoyed Washington's high regard.

When Lincoln accepted his new office November 26, Congress had filled the last of the new departments it had drawn up in February. The government now had officers in charge of Finance, War, and Foreign Affairs, but with no director, no named chief executive. Morris immediately, instinctively, stepped into that role. The Monday after Lincoln's appointment, Morris contacted Washington, Lincoln, and Charles Thomson, the secretary of Congress, calling them to a meeting at his office that evening. There they were joined by Robert Livingston and Gouverneur Morris.

This was, in essence, the first session of an executive branch of government operating under the auspices of the Congress. There was a degree of political elegance to the roster Morris drew up—he would have a second in Gouverneur, as Washington would with Lincoln. Livingston didn't need one—he was on intimate terms with Gouverneur, and much of the initiative in foreign affairs lay with Finance, anyway. Inviting Thomson would defuse any suspicion of keeping their actions hidden from the legislature.

Robert Morris opened that first session by proposing that the group meet at the same time each Monday, "for the purpose of Communicating to each other whatever may be necessary and for Consulting and Concerting Measures to promote the Service and Public Good." No minutes were kept of these meetings; just the bare notations Morris made in his diary—at the first conference, for example, Morris presented the latest letters from Franklin in Paris, and led "a General Conversation as introductory to the business." The business, that is, of pulling the country out of the dangerous course it was on.

The particulars of their discourse are obscure, but we know the people in the room, and can infer the workings of this nascent revolutionary cabinet. The meetings took place on the second floor of the Marine office, the clerks from Finance having retired for the day. We don't know the dimensions of Morris's quarters, but the group who assembled would have filled any room. Save for Thomson, who was slim and wan, each of the men was physically large—Robert, Gouverneur Morris, Livingston, and Washington all stood six feet tall. Robert Morris was known for his girth, but he was probably matched by Lincoln, who was marked by "his great bulk and his loose jowel." Each had an ego to match, and skills of address and command honed in legislative debate or under enemy fire. They were distinguished as well by their industry. Both Morrises, Washington, Livingston, Thomson, and Lincoln each had ably performed key offices in the course of the national crisis.

Robert Morris would have set a warm, collegial tone, probably augmented with a ready supply of Madeira. Washington was by nature earnest and taciturn, but Gouverneur Morris, famous for his wit and his arch humor, provided a degree of leavening. None of the group was bashful, but if they disagreed over tactics, their priorities were in close harmony. They were Nationalists, none more so than Livingston, the initial sponsor of the Continental impost. Even before Yorktown, Livingston was convinced Congress must assume larger powers, "or some daring Genius, with necessity for his plea, shall seize what they dare not give." Now, with all of America celebrating the defeat of Cornwallis, the assembled Nationalists feared that transitory conquest "may have the pernicious tendency of lulling the country into inactivity."

Washington was without question the dominant public figure in the group. In the weeks after Yorktown his fame had crested—it was in this period that a Philadelphia newspaper termed him, for the first time, "The Savior of our Country." That Homeric encomium may have lent him a certain preeminence in this ad-hoc cabinet, the sort of last-word authority he would exercise years later as president. But in the evening sessions at the Marine office, there is little question but that it was Morris who set the agenda, who offered programs and threw out strategies. Pressing as were the needs of the army—and they were always pressing—it was Morris who had to come up with answers.

The meetings continued through December and on through the spring, with Morris continuing to work closely with Washington until the general left the city in March. This was a period of creative burst for Morris, as if the nation might embrace his vision of the future if he could only sketch it in fast enough.

The area where Morris could cover the most ground through executive action independent of the other departments was in reducing the expenditures of the government. Key here was to expand the contracting program Morris had instituted on a trial basis in Pennsylvania early in the year. Those contracts had realized substantial savings along with real flexibility in modes of payment; it was time to apply them throughout the army.

Early in December Morris placed newspaper ads calling for contractors to supply rations for Continental Army troops at "the lowest prices and longest terms of payment." The contracts were divided geographically, and would be awarded on the basis of sealed competitive bids.

The savings involved in this process were enormous. No longer would the government be liable for transporting supplies from state to state, for the spoilage of goods that could not be moved, for the salaries of the commissariat and the quartermasters, or for the premiums paid by government agents when bidding for supplies. Gone as well would be the army-operated magazines where the food and clothing for the troops were stored and often pilfered. All those costs, and all the responsibility of getting stores to the troops at camp, would be assumed by the contractors.

To Morris's great satisfaction, the contracts drew a wide range of bidders, and by the end of December, most of the army's scattered divisions were accounted for. The winning bids promised delivery of rations at a rate of about ten cents per soldier per day. Disputes over quality were to be settled on the spot by impartial referees, with the contractors liable for substandard provisions. Supplies captured by the enemy would be charged to the government provided the vendors could produce vouchers for what was lost.

The largest contract, to supply West Point, went to Comfort Sands, a wealthy New York merchant who held the post of auditor for that state during most of the war. Another important contract, covering army posts in New Jersey and western Pennsylvania, went to Tench Francis, recently returned from his mission to Boston.

Morris had alerted several other long-standing friends when the contracts were let, including William Duer and Philip Schuyler, who had answered his first, urgent calls for provisions at the outset of the Yorktown campaign. But in a testament to the integrity of the process, both found themselves underbid. Duer in particular had begun buying cattle and packing beef in anticipation of success; Morris managed to soften the blow by agreeing to buy Duer's beef at a set price.

In the months that followed, the resourceful Duer worked through Sands to land a piece of the West Point contract, in partnership with the ubiquitous John Holker. In February, Duer and Holker added a second contract to their portfolio, this to supply posts "Northward of Poughkeepsie." On this occasion, Morris invoked his friendship with Duer to "Urge in the most pressing manner" strict compliance with the terms of cost and delivery.

Concern over the military and economic problems to the southward barred Morris from extending his contracting system there. But by February, Morris was able to claim that, from Philadelphia to Boston, he had installed "the cheapest, most certain, and consequently the best mode of obtaining those articles which are necessary for the subsistence, covering, clothing, and moving of an army."

This amounted to bare maintenance, but it was all that Morris could accomplish. The soldiers and officers got their provisions, but they would receive no pay. This policy—patently unfair but fiscally inescapable—strained relations between the army and the government, and even between Washington and Morris. Relaying to Morris news of widespread desertions and another aborted mutiny in May, Washington cited the disparity between unpaid soldiers and the government's salaried civil employees as a source of much resentment. Morris answered directly, proposing that "your Excellency must be of opinion with me that without the civil List is paid neither civil nor military can exist at all." Washington answered tartly: "If the military should disband for want of Pay (while the War continues to rage) a period will very soon be put to the Civil Establishment."

Morris did make exceptions. A lieutenant ill with cancer received sixty pounds cash, after Benjamin Lincoln certified him as "an exception from the general Rule." On occasion, as in the case of General Arthur St. Clair, Morris reached into his own pocket. "This gentleman's distress is beyond description," Morris noted of St. Clair. "Not a dollar in his possession when his duty calls him to camp and a starving family to remain behind him." But Morris turned away most of the appellants, however heartfelt, advising them to add their voices to the demands of the public creditors.

While implementing the contracts on a large scale, Morris also hastened to advance his important innovations in the area of public credit and finance. The central objective here, as it was from the moment he took office, was the bank.

The drive to raise private subscriptions had fallen well short of expectations, bringing in an estimated seventy thousand dollars through sales of about 175 shares. Also disappointing to Morris, who had hoped to draw capital from throughout the former colonies, most of the subscribers were from Philadelphia. The main exceptions were Jeremiah Wadsworth and John Carter, Connecticut entrepreneurs doing business as contractors for the French navy, and John Langdon of New Hampshire, the former congressional ally and occasional business partner of Morris's.

But the arrival of Tench Francis and his train of wagons packed with French silver breathed new life into the plans for the bank. Morris had many demands for the funds—foremost among them, paying off the loan from Rochambeau—but he managed to sequester two hundred thousand dollars in silver to invest in six hundred bank shares. This brought the total bank capital to two hundred seventy thousand dollars, plus the foreign bills deposited by the old Bank of Pennsylvania. It was short of the four hundred thousand projected for initial capitalization, but for Morris, it was close enough.

On November 1, at Morris's direction, John Nixon called a meeting to select the bank's first board of directors. Convening at City Tavern, the subscribers consisted largely of longtime friends and associates of Robert Morris: James Wilson, William Turnbull, John Ross, and Thomas Fitzsimmons, a rising merchant who was head of the Philadelphia Chamber of Commerce. Most had been founding investors in the Bank of Pennsylvania; most, save for the radical officeholder Timothy Matlack, were critics of the state constitution and members of the Republican Society.

Concerned that this conclave was too parochial for what he continued to see as a national institution, Morris on the eve of the gathering pressed Samuel Osgood, a new delegate to Congress from Massachusetts, to attend the meeting and run for the board. When Osgood demurred for lack of funds, Morris offered to lend him four hundred dollars against a draft on his home state. Agreeing to this "kindly, & at present I am of opinion very judicious" offer, Osgood purchased a share and stood for a seat on the board.

The organizational meeting lasted all day, with several of the officers elected in absentia. The new board included Fitzsimmons, Wilson, William Bingham, and John Maxwell Nesbitt. Osgood and Matlack were also selected, allowing the board to claim at least a modicum of geographic and political diversity. Morris's longtime partner Thomas Willing, staid and solid, was named president.

One last hurdle remained before the bank could commence operations—final approval from Congress. The first endorsement in May had been conditional on the raising of funds; now a formal charter was required. Members of Congress generally recognized the utility of the bank, but some, led by James Madison, saw as well that the Articles of Confederation made no provision for granting corporate charters. Better the bank should seek charters from the states in which it would operate.

At a meeting of the bank directors with a committee of Congress, Morris pressed his case: that investors in the bank had been assured of government sanction, that soliciting legislation from individual states would take too long, and that as Financier he would need support from the bank to honor the army contracts already struck. Despite misgivings over "a want of power and an aversion to assume it," Congress went ahead and granted the charter. At the same time, it encouraged the bank to continue seeking the sanction of the states.

The Bank of North America opened for business January 7, 1782, in a three-story building rented from Tench Francis on Chestnut Street, across from Carpenters' Hall. (Francis was also named cashier for the bank.) That same day, Morris took out a hundred thousand dollar loan in the name of the Continental treasurer.

"When the bank was first opened here," Willing recounted to friends in Boston several years later, "the Business was as much a novelty to us, who undertook the management of it, as it can possibly be to you. It was a pathless wilderness, ground but little known this side of the Atlantic." Yet, because they knew the directors, and because of their prior experience with the Bank of Pennsylvania, the merchants of Philadelphia readily embraced the bank and its bills. Before two weeks were out, Samuel Osgood could report to a friend, "The Bank Notes succeed beyond our most sanguine expectations. People seem fully satisfied with and fond of them."

Winning acceptance for the banknotes outside Philadelphia was more difficult, but Morris was able to establish their value through careful oversight. He forbade federal officers from paying more in notes than the stated hard money price, and withdrew the notes from circulation in areas where they depreciated. By his vigilant management, the notes gradually acquired currency at par throughout the union.

Aside from the bank, Morris chose the turn of the year to present yet another major fiscal innovation, his plan for an American mint. This was a hobbyhorse "which has employed my thoughts very frequently," Morris told the Congress; he might have said the same for Gouverneur Morris as well. In October, before any mention of the business in Congress, the Financier had retained the services of a skilled metallurgist to assay the metals in various coins and to draw up plans for fabrication.

The wide array of coinage and currency in the colonies had befuddled commerce in America since the beginning, with the result that, as Morris observed, "the commonest things become intricate where Money has any thing to do with them." The solution Morris proposed was to establish for the first time a single currency for all the former colonies, a unit of exchange based on the Spanish silver dollar and, for ease of calculation, denominated in decimals. This would facilitate trade, and also tend to "banish all other [coin] from circulation." It was not the first time such a scheme was proposed to the Congress, and it would not be the last; the plan was well received but soon set aside to await a more stable time in the affairs of the nation.

The contracts, the bank, and the other elaborate plans Morris laid for restoring credit and trade in America might mitigate, but could not obviate, the underlying lack of funds for the central government. Morris was daily issuing drafts on Swanwick—Morris notes—and now drafts against the bank, but these all rested on anticipated revenues from the states that had yet to materialize.

The fund on which Morris placed his fondest hopes was the impost. All but three states had approved the measure; in January, Morris addressed the holdouts—Massachusetts, Maryland, and Rhode Island. "Let me once more entreat, that this great object be seriously considered," Morris wrote to the governors. "Let me repeat that the hope of our Enemy, is the derangement of our Finances, and let me add, that when revenue is given, that hope must cease." Morris posed the question in the most graphic terms. "He therefore who opposes the grant of such revenue, not only opposes himself to the Dictates of Justice, but he labors to continue the War, and of Consequence to shed more blood, to produce more Devastation and to extend and prolong the Miseries of Mankind."

Morris returned to the governors a month later, this time to focus on the sole existing source of revenue to Congress, the requisition on the states. He sounded the same themes he had staked out in October—the dearth of credit, the end of aid from France—but he introduced new ones as well. "Many people flatter themselves with the Hope of Peace," Morris observed, and consequently shrugged off the demands of Congress. Yet Britain had shown no inclination to end the war. Even if it did, a robust military campaign would ensure peace on the best possible terms. "The only way to secure peace is to prepare for war," Morris intoned. "And depend on it, that if we neglect the present moment, we shall have bitter cause to regret our Negligence."

His communications to individuals were more acerbic. Informed by one Maryland revenue officer that his state would fail to answer its latest requisition, Morris shot back, "I am so habituated to receive apologies instead of Money, that I am not surprised at [your letter]. If Complaints of Difficulties were equivalent to Cash I should not complain that the quotas are unpaid. But unluckily that is not the case."

Aware that by now the drumbeat of his incessant appeals was blunting their influence, Morris turned to the other members of his cabinet and demanded their support. Meeting with Washington and Livingston, Morris showed them his draft circular and an ancillary letter to Congress. "I told them plainly that I shall hold them bound to avow their approbation of these letters and the measures proposed and to support me therein," Morris recorded in his diary.

Washington needed little persuasion. Already in January, he had written his own circular lending his voice to Morris's call for funds. Washington was usually careful to avoid questions of a civil nature, but he could no longer skirt the issue. Matters of finance were "somewhat out of my province," the general confided to the governors, "yet I consider it so nearly connected with, and so essential to the operations under my direction, that I flatter myself, my interference will not be deemed impertinent."

While his manner was steeped in courtesy, the general was just as trenchant as any of the dispatches from the Office of Finance. After close consultations with Morris, Washington wrote, "I entirely concur" in the October requisition for eight million dollars in new taxes. He then recalled the mutiny of the previous year, and "the ferment into which the whole army was thrown." The contracts Morris had drawn up to supply the army would prevent another season of discontent, but only if funds were forthcoming.

"Enabling the financier to comply with his contracts is a matter of utmost importance—the very existence of the army depends upon it. Should he fail in his payments, the contract ceases, and there is no alternative left, but to disband, or live upon the seizure of the neighboring property." Washington had been forced to rely on impressments at Valley Forge and again at Morristown; he wished never to resort to such measures again.

Some might protest that the tax was too high—"beyond the ability of the country to pay." Washington offered "a plain answer," and a stern one. "If the war is carried on, a certain expense must be drawn from the people, either by a partial, cruel, and I may say illegal seizure of that property which lays most convenient to the army, or by a regular and equitable tax."

Washington had done his part; Livingston weighed in three weeks later with his own address to the states. As foreign minister, he focused on the situation in Europe—the continuing strength of England, the ambivalence of Holland and Spain, the "determination" of France to end her subsidies. "What, then, is to be done?"

He answered himself with a review of the makeshift means by which the war had been prosecuted so far, with the states that were the theater of action contributing soldiers and supplies—often involuntarily—while those spared the fighting were also spared the burden. As a consequence, Americans had been reduced to fighting "a weak defensive war with an unpaid army."

To Livingston the conclusion was inescapable. "Every motive, then, national honor, national interest, public economy, private ease, and that love of freedom which pervades every legislature on the continent, call loudly . . . for a compliance with the requisitions of Congress."

Morris had gotten everything he'd asked from the fellow members of his cabinet—the explicit endorsement of the key agencies of the government, in formal address to the governors of the sovereign states. But he needed something more. He knew that the governors, powerful as they were in their own right, were beholden and attentive to the prevailing currents of public opinion. Morris wanted to expand the dialogue, to address the people at large, not just their elected leaders.

This conviction brought about one of the more unlikely alliances to be found in the annals of the Revolution—the political partnership of Robert Morris and Thomas Paine.

Through all the debates over independence and the turmoil over the Pennsylvania constitution, Paine had opposed Morris at every turn. Defiant by nature, he had fallen in with the Philadelphia militants, denouncing Morris and his allies as Tory sympathizers, "men whose political principles are founded on avarice." During the Silas Deane affair Paine censured Morris by name; in the months of recrimination that followed, he sat on the committee formed in Philadelphia to investigate Morris's business practices.

Yet with the passage of the seasons, as the militants stood their terms in state office and the Continental currency went into its death spiral, Paine began shifting his ground. His experience on the price committee convinced him that the paper money policies of his allies were in error. And as with so many of the Nationalists, Paine's close engagement with the Continental Army led him to mistrust the direction of the separate states, and wisdom of the people at large. "The people of America understand *rights*, better than *politics*," Paine proposed to Joseph Reed in 1780. "They have a clear idea of their object, but are greatly deficient in comprehending the means." Here Paine was speaking specifically on the question of taxes to support the army. "They want to have the war carried on, Lord knows how."

By 1781 Paine reached something of a crossroads. Unemployed and nearly destitute, he felt abandoned by the movement he had helped ignite. In a grand gesture at the outset of the war, Paine had directed that all revenues from sales of *Common Sense* go to support of the army; now he wanted some sort of compensation for his toil. But Paine no longer enjoyed the universal acclaim his early works had gleaned; recent publications had alienated members of the Eastern faction who had formed his core constituency. "There never was a man less beloved in a place than Paine is in this, having at different times disputed with everybody," Sarah Franklin Bache wrote to her father in January. "The most rational thing he could have done would have been to have died the instant he had finished his Common Sense, for he will never again have it in his power to leave the world with so much credit."

Moody and frustrated, Paine decided to leave the country. He considered a furtive return to England to produce a sequel to *Common Sense* that would fire a peace movement in Britain, but abandoned the scheme on the advice of his friends. Instead he joined John Laurens on his mission to France. The two had become close during Laurens's service on Washington's staff, and Paine agreed to assist with Laurens as an unofficial secretary.

Returning to Philadelphia in late August, Paine arrived broke, lonely, and disillusioned. "I now felt myself worse off than ever," he mused later. But if Paine was abandoned by his former friends, his arrival drew the attention of the Financier. Never one to hold a grudge, Morris had been impressed by Paine's performance with the *Crisis Extraordinary*. Now he asked his former antagonist to drop by the office.

Paine came as bidden, and Morris made a proposition: "that for the Service of the Country he should write and publish such Pieces respecting the propriety, Necessity and Utility of Taxation," particularly in support of the army. This led to Paine's proposal that Philadelphia landlords be dunned for a quarter of their annual rents, a scheme that won Morris's endorsement but was rejected by the Assembly.

Morris's overture in September led to a series of meetings and, improbably, a genuine friendship. While they differed markedly in circumstances, the two men shared much in common: both had emigrated from England, both enjoyed conversation over cups, and both were convinced that the fortunes of America depended on drawing political and economic power into the hands of the central government.

Their newfound amity underwent a test of sorts when Silas Deane's letters were published later that fall. Paine, who had been Deane's leading public tormentor, took the letters as proof of Deane's perfidy, and gleefully called on the Office of Finance to savor his triumph. To his great satisfaction Paine found both Robert and his assistant were ready to renounce their former friend. "Robert Morris assured me that he had been totally deceived in Deane; but that now he looked upon him to be a bad man, and his reputation totally ruined," Paine wrote to a friend. Gouverneur Morris completed the capitulation, Paine reported. The Financier's assistant "hopped around on one leg, swore they had all been duped, himself among the rest, complimented me on my quick sight—and by God says he nothing carries a man through the world like honesty."

This exercise in submission had to be painful for Gouverneur, who had excoriated Paine in print and on the floor of Congress for the attacks on Deane. It was probably less so for Robert; having already sacrificed his fealty to his brother in the wrangling over the munitions trade, he was not about to embarrass himself with a continued defense of so distressed a soul as Deane.

As much as Paine enjoyed his new access to the highest officials in the government, it did nothing to alleviate his pressing financial problems. At the end of November he wrote a long letter to Washington dilating on "the secret of my own situation." He had given his all to the Revolution, Paine wrote; now he needed the Revolution to give something back. He was again considering a return to Europe. "I have literary fame, and I am sure I cannot experience worse fortune than I have here."

Washington had always liked Paine, and he had seen the dramatic results Paine's writings could produce. Over the next few weeks Washington canvassed friends and connections to drum up some kind of sustenance for Paine; one who responded was the French ambassador. Luzerne "engaged Paine to write a few articles on the advantages gained by the United States through the Alliance," and paid him more than three thousand livres over the next two years. Now it was Paine's turn to taste embarrassment; just four years before he had sneered at "the wretch" who lowered himself to write "on any subject for bread, in any service for pay."

The stipend from France was welcome, but for his pride and for his purse, Paine wanted something more meaningful from his adoptive home government. He raised his grievances several times with Morris, but the Financier had to plead poverty. Finally, in January, Morris suggested to

Paine that "Something might turn up, and I should have him in mind."
Days later Morris posed to Gouverneur Morris, and then to Washington,
the idea of establishing a secret fund for Paine.

After both readily endorsed the plan, Robert Morris ran it by Livingston, with the suggestion that the Foreign desk provide Paine material by
sharing with him the contents of diplomatic messages from Europe. Here
was another rich irony; it was Paine's disclosure of just such sensitive material that got him dismissed from the Foreign office during the Silas Deane
affair. But Livingston signed on, even agreeing that Paine would be paid
through a "secret service" account Morris would set up for the office of
Foreign Affairs.

The plan was settled at a Tuesday evening conference attended by
Washington, Livingston, Paine, and both Morrises, and memorialized over
the signatures of Robert Morris, Livingston, and Washington. The memorandum cited "the important situation of Affairs," "the Propriety and even
necessity of informing the People and rousing them into Action," and "the
Abilities of Mr. Thomas Paine as a Writer." Paine would receive eight hundred dollars per year; the payments would be secret, as "a Salary publicly
and avowedly given . . . would injure the Effect of Mr. Paine's Publications,
and subject him to injurious personal Reflections."

Morris drew up a second memo to state in explicit terms the message
they wanted to see from Paine. "We wish to draw the resources and powers of the country into action." That meant funds from the states and "permanent revenues" for Congress, money to field the army and pay the debts
of the war. Ultimately, Morris and his cabinet sought "To extend by a new
confederation the powers of Congress, so that they may be competent to
the government of the United States." This was, in short form, the Nationalist agenda.

All of this was agreeable to Paine, who was already on record endorsing
new powers for Congress. As for his status as a "hireling writer," Paine ra-
tionalized the deal as grounded in newfound amity. Publication of Deane's
letters "has proved me right," he wrote to Morris, while adding graciously,
"it has at the same time proved no one wrong." With their past differences
behind them, "I am therefore under no difficulty of accepting the proposal,
because I will know that it is not only out of friendship to me, but out of
Justice to me."

Paine was immediately energized by his new secret sponsorship. Even
before the deal was signed, Paine informed Morris he had a column ready
for print—his first publication in fourteen months. This opening salvo

would return to ground first covered in *Common Sense*, berating King George for his "sniveling hypocrisy" in prosecuting the war. Soon to come, Paine told Morris, was a piece "on the subject of revenue."

In the event, Paine opened this second installment with one more attack on Silas Deane, recalling how "every man, almost without exception, thought me wrong in opposing him." Having indulged once more his sense of vindication, Paine turned to the business of taxation. The initial efforts to finance the war had plunged Americans into a "wilderness of error" rooted in paper money and other "temporary expedients." Now that confusion had been cleared away, the obligations tallied by the Office of Finance, and the proper taxes levied, failure to pay "would be a blot on the councils, the country, and the revolution of America."

To those who said the country could not bear the load, Paine offered the flat declaration, "The doctrine is false. There are not three millions of people, in any part of the universe, who live so well, or have such a fund of ability, as in America."

Moving past the question of funds, Paine addressed the critical question of union, and the role of the central government. "Each state is to the United States what each individual is to the state he lives in," Paine proposed. "It is on this grand point, this movement upon one center, that our existence as a nation, our happiness as a people, and our safety as individuals, depend."

More than simply tout the idea of Congress as an independent entity, Paine specifically endorsed Morris's program of separating state revenue from national. "It has been our error, as well as our misfortune, to blend the affairs of each state, especially in money matters, with those of the United States," Paine advised. "The expenses of the United States for carrying on the war, and the expenses of each state for its own domestic government, are distinct things, and to involve them is a source of perplexity and a cloak for fraud."

A week after the essay was published, Paine invited Morris to join him and George Washington at Paine's cluttered apartment "to eat a few oysters or a crust of bread and cheese." They made for a motley trio—Morris with his fine clothes and gold-tipped walking stick, Washington in his blue-serge uniform, and Paine disheveled and threadbare. Certainly there was wine on the table as these three friends whiled away the evening, ruminating over the remarkable progress and uncertain future of a revolution each had done so much to bring about.

· · ·

With his propaganda machine in full swing, Morris turned his attention to the mechanics of collecting the revenue. Until now, Congress had relied on the states to impose taxes and forward their share out of the total. This system failed on a number of levels: tax collectors usually were elected locally, rendering them beholden to local interests; what revenues did arise were claimed by the states, leaving little surplus to send to Congress.

Morris sought to circumvent the whole process by establishing a separate, parallel system of receivers who would answer directly to the Office of Finance. These receivers comprised a new class of public officials in America, named by authority of Congress to represent the interests of the national government in the individual states. They were empowered to collect federal taxes separate from state accounts, to sue local tax collectors for nonperformance, and to press the state legislatures to answer to requisitions of Congress.

These receivers would also serve the specific aims of the Financier. They would support the circulation of banknotes and Morris notes by receiving them for taxes and by redeeming them on the spot, paying for them out of whatever tax revenue had come in. They would also report to Morris on prices of goods and of bills of exchange, and on political developments in their home states. Critics of the Financier and his program derided the receivers as "licensed spies."

One more key function of the receivers was to advance Morris's propaganda campaign by posting in the local papers a specific, monthly account of their receipts, naming who had paid and, more important, who had not. Morris might be leery of democracy, but he understood how it worked. "Public opinion is always a useful reinforcement to the operation of laws," he advised one appointee. "When a part of the community have paid punctually they feel a degree of resentment excited against the negligent and unwilling. Those half Tories who want to be considered as Whigs will not suffer the public to know that they do not pay taxes and in very little time they feel that payment interesting them to make others pay. Thus the Cords of Government get wound up by degrees to their proper Tone."

Aware of the critical role they would play in the operations of the Finance office and as harbingers of the Nationalist program, Morris selected his new corps of receivers carefully. Some were chosen for their local stature, some for national reputation. The only one derived from his familiar mercantile network was John Swanwick, but he was named receiver for Pennsylvania only after Morris made a personal appeal to David Rit-

Walter Stewart, a colonel in the army whose role in defusing the January mutiny of the Pennsylvania line won him a reputation for a cool demeanor. Stewart held a "very considerable" stake in the domestic loans, he told Morris; loss of the interest would leave him and other creditors "much distressed." Morris was sympathetic, but said he was constrained by "the general interest of the country" to support the new policy.

Stewart then proposed organizing the public creditors to press their claims. This was just what Morris was looking for. He proclaimed himself "very desirous to serve and support . . . their claim to Justice," but then advised Stewart on just what that claim should be. Congress had "done their duty" in attempting to fund the debt, Morris explained, but appeals to the states for revenue had been futile.

Philadelphia's public creditors moved quickly to prepare their case. Led by Blair McClenaghan, a Constitutionalist merchant and early investor in the bank, and Benjamin Rush, the onetime radical and former member of Congress, the creditors held several meetings with Morris and several on their own. Morris continued to encourage and to steer them. "I advised these Gentlemen to make one common cause with the whole of the public creditors of every kind to unite their interest so that they might be able to have influence on all the Legislatures in the several states." They should "avoid the language of Threats," he warned, but "I assured them of my concurrence."

But it was Congress, not the states, that controlled the interest on the loans, and it was to Congress that the creditors addressed their protest. They presented their "Remonstrance" on July 8, claiming "the Merit of being among the earliest Promoters of the glorious Revolution in America." They included among their ranks "The Widow, the Orphan, the Aged, and Infirm, whose only hope to screen them from the most wretched Poverty, depends on the Payment of the Stipulated Interest."

Aside from their personal loss, the creditors pointed out the critical effects of the suspended payments on public credit. For authority they cited the statement of Congress itself in a circular letter of September 1779. "Let it never be said that America had no sooner become Independent than She became Insolvent," Congress had declared, "or that her infant Glories and growing Fame were tarnished by broken Contracts and violated Faith."

The creditors' petition was referred to Robert Morris. He had no quarrel with the creditors, nor did he dispute the decision to suspend the payments. But to his mind, the petition had arrived at a critical time for the

tenhouse, the mathematician and ardent Constitutionalist who was then serving a term as state treasurer. Rittenhouse, exhausted with the state's political wars, declined the job and resumed his scientific pursuits.

Nor did the new receivers share a single political outlook: James Lovell, named for Massachusetts, was a strong adherent of the Eastern faction, though he had a high regard for Morris and his administrative skills. Alexander Hamilton, on the other hand, was a confirmed Nationalist; at the time Morris offered him the post in May, Hamilton was just completing a series of important essays calling for taxes and an impost, and denouncing "the fatal mistakes which have so deeply endangered the common cause, particularly . . . a want of power in Congress." These arguments were published under the title "The Continentalist."

Hamilton proved to be the most active and effective of the receivers appointed by Morris. Traveling to Poughkeepsie to meet with committees of the state legislature, Hamilton drafted critical bills revising the state tax code, providing for collection of back taxes, and committing the state to raise eighteen thousand pounds in hard money to the order of the Finance office. Hamilton prevailed as well in pushing key elements of the Nationalist program, including a call for "a Convention of the states to enlarge the powers of Congress"—the first step on the road to the Constitutional Convention.

Hamilton made a powerful impression on the lawmakers at Poughkeepsie, so strong that they voted to send him to Congress in the fall. But if he was persuasive, Hamilton was also realistic. Writing Morris to report on his progress, Hamilton warned that even if the legislature approved a grant of funds, "I cannot hope that it will produce in the treasury half that sum; such are the vices of our present mode of collection."

It was apparent by May that such an estimate was wildly optimistic. The first quarterly installment on the state requisitions fell due in April, and the results were dismal. Far from sending to Congress a fraction of the funds requested, most states were sending in nothing at all. "The habitual inattention from the states has reduced us to the brink of ruin," Morris informed the Congress May 17, "and I cannot see a probability of relief from any of them." Congress referred this alarum to a committee, and in conference with the Financier decided that still another circular would be pointless. Instead, they deputized four delegates to travel out from Philadelphia—two to the southern states and two to the northward—to proselytize in the name of domestic taxes. Before they departed, the envoys were invited for an evening session with the cabinet, where Morris, Livingston, and

Lincoln—Washington was by now with the army at West Point—offered them "every information possible" in order to "spirit up their exertions."

The delegates got on the road, and in the course of the next month completed their tour of the states, though John Rutledge and George Clymer, the emissaries to the South, did not get further than Virginia. In all the states they visited, the delegates found the legislators "generally to be convinced" of the need for funds. Their message delivered, the delegates rode on. They returned to Philadelphia with no new revenues, but with bills for expenses that they presented to Morris for payment.

In the meantime, the nation's financial outlook went into a steep decline. After the defeat at Yorktown, the British had abandoned their land-based strategy, pulled their soldiers into defensive positions, and intensified their naval campaign. The idea was to cut off American provisions for French and Spanish forces in the Caribbean, but the effect was general strangulation of American commerce. As Morris informed De Grasse in May, "It is only by a Kind of Miracle that any vessel can get in or out."

The freeze on American commerce had dramatic implications for Morris. It dried up the primary streams of revenue to the states, effectively eliminating the source for any taxes they might have raised for the Congress. With American merchants unable to access foreign trade, demand for European funds evaporated, eroding the value of the French bills Morris was selling to finance his operations. And with merchants unable to make payments, the Bank of North America was forced to curtail any more loans, cutting off an important source of credit for Morris.

The blockade had a direct effect on Morris as well, effectively knocking out all his personal shipping and privateering operations. "What I had afloat has all been lost," Morris reported in July to a friend seeking a private loan. Morris added demurely, "the amount of that loss I will forebear to mention as there might be in it an appearance of ostentation."

As with so many of the problems confronting the confederation, the onus of responding to the trade crisis fell to the Office of Finance. Issuing a flurry of diplomatic correspondence, Morris pleaded with France and Spain to provide convoys, but the allied fleets were fully occupied in other theaters. As an alternative, Morris proposed to Congress reviving the American navy, but here as usual, the lack of funds precluded any meaningful action.

In desperation, the merchants of Philadelphia took matters in their own hands, obtaining a loan from the Bank of North America to purchase and outfit the armed vessel *Hyder Ally*. Named to command was Joshua Bar-

ney, the young sea captain commissioned by Morris in 1776, who had since been captured four times by the British and four times had escaped. Barney promptly achieved a sensational victory, taking the better-armed warship *General Monk* after a hard-fought action. But while the victory earned lasting fame for Barney, it did little to break the British stranglehold. Emboldened by Barney's exploits, Philadelphia merchants sent ten ships to sea the following week; all were captured and sent to New York as prizes.

Morris got one bit of good news in April, when he learned from Luzerne that the appeals of Franklin and Lafayette had been answered, France agreeing to a new loan of six million livres. But this firm promise of new funds came with assurances just as firm that no additional loans would be forthcoming. Luzerne emphasized in particular that, contrary to past arrangements, France would not make separate payments to cover the interest on American Loan Office Certificates.

This put Morris in a quandary. His first reaction was to keep the news secret, fearing that the states would cite the loan as an excuse not to raise tax revenues. By May, however, Livingston learned of the new loan in a letter from Franklin, and both Livingston and Luzerne insisted that Congress now be informed.

Morris did so, seeking at the same time to turn it to his advantage. Notifying Congress of this latest French loan, he observed that "every sous we can command during the year 1782 is already anticipated"—that is, already committed to one essential expenditure or another. In early June, Morris took it a step further, advising Congress to end its reliance on France for the interest on domestic loans.

This was a necessary step, but also a strategic one. Congress had relied on domestic borrowing early in the war to supplant, and in some cases to retire, the Continental currency. In 1777, with sales of Loan Office Certificates lagging and France committing to secret grants of aid, Congress moved to sweeten the deal by paying interest on domestic loans in bills drawn against the French funds. Morris had for some time been convinced that the "public creditors"—those Americans who had purchased the bonds issued by Congress—could provide the sort of local political pressure to which the state legislators might respond. It was a costly gambit for Morris, as he personally owned substantial holdings in the domestic debt, but cutting off interest payments would spur the public creditors into action.

This strategy soon began to bear fruit. Morris's report on French funds was referred to a committee, which on June 26 concurred with him in favor of ending the drafts on France. That same day, he received a visit from

Revolution and for his administration. The government was in arrears and its treasury was bare, but if they acted now, if they embraced his program and followed his lead, they might yet realize the "Interest, happiness, freedom and Glory of the United States." Resolved not to let the moment pass, Morris gathered himself to present in one sweeping statement his summary view of the financial crisis confronting the new nation. The product of close deliberations with Gouverneur Morris, this was the crescendo of their first year in office.

The broad outlines of Morris's "Report on Public Credit" were familiar enough: America must do justice to its creditors, and afford itself access to future loans, by raising revenue to pay the interest and eventually the principal on its debts. But in this lengthy document—seventeen printed pages, accompanied by two detailed numerical estimates—Morris went further than ever before in exploring and explaining the subtleties of public finance. In the process he laid down a series of assumptions on the nature of debt and credit that would serve as a touchstone in the gradual evolution of the American state.

As he opened his piece, Morris took up the two fundamental means by which Americans were funding the war: debt and taxes. It is critical to keep in mind, as Morris did in composing his report, that neither of these means could be assumed. Many Americans believed the Revolution was a war not just against improper taxation, but against taxation itself; just as many decried all debt as a moral failure of the political leadership, and funding of the debt as a sop to the "moneyed interest." In contrast, Morris found virtue in both.

Even apart from the utility of public projects and national defense, taxes served to increase national wealth, Morris theorized. "First they stimulate Industry" by requiring individuals to produce the wherewithal to pay their share. "Secondly, they encourage Economy so far as to avoid the purchase of unnecessary things, and keep money in readiness for the tax gatherer." The habits of industry and frugality, exercised over time, would purge the natural inclination to "waste or extravagance," and help raise up the nation as a whole.

But there was a limit. "When taxes go so far as to intrench on the Subsistence of the People, they become burdensome and oppressive. The expenditure of money ought in such case to be (if possible) avoided; and if unavoidable, it will be most wise to have recourse to loans." Later in his essay, Morris introduced a second element of equity to his critique. "Taxes fall heavy on the lower orders of the community," he wrote, while money raised through loans relieved them of that burden.

Loans had their own obvious utility, allowing individuals and institutions to engage in projects that yielded profits above and beyond the cost of the funds. This was especially important in regard to foreign loans, as they provided access to capital beyond what Americans might raise from each other. Foreign credit had been crucial in carving a society out of the American wilderness, and would continue so long as entrepreneurs found projects worthy of investment.

Domestic borrowing by the government carried a special, ancillary benefit. Loans from private parties "give stability to government, by combining together the Interests of moneyed men for its support." This was the same logic Morris had invoked in support of the bank; he wanted to harness self-interest to the public weal. Domestic borrowing entailed a cost as well, as government demand for capital would raise the cost of money as reflected in the rate of interest. Private individuals, then, would have to pay more for loans. That cost would be offset, however, by the relief deficit spending afforded to taxpayers. In addition, easy access to funds would "induce men to engage in Speculations which are often unprofitable"; higher rates of interest would discourage such speculation. Here Morris was advocating what today would be called a tight money policy.

Underlying all this thinking, but unstated, was Morris's subtle, intuitive understanding of capital. It was more than just money; in Morris's mind, capital was the great mechanism by which a society organized itself and pursued its endeavors. The free flow of capital meant trade, production, and enterprise; blocked capital markets meant stagnation and "indolence." Morris made this point most directly in discussing the cost of failing to fund the debts of the Confederation. By allowing the principal lenders of the nation to stand neglected, the community lost the benefit of "the full Exercise of their Skill and Industry. . . . Whereas if these Debts which are in a manner dead, were brought back to existence, moneyed men would purchase them up, and thereby restore to the Public many useful members who are entirely lost." The key here, Morris said, was to restore the value of invested capital, and put such value "into those Hands which could render it most productive."

The idea was not simply to enrich the capitalists—that would be a vulgar and simplistic reading of his scheme. To Morris, capital flowed naturally to those who could demonstrate "character," attributes he defined in another forum as "persons possessed of knowledge, judgment, information, integrity, and having extensive connections." Such distinctions arose naturally in any society, and capital would afford those who possessed them the means by which they could orchestrate the endeavors of the larger community.

All of this depended on the restoration of public credit. Morris divided this process into two parts. First was to close out the business, long overdue, of retiring the mass of paper currencies issued by Congress and the states over the course of the war. Morris did not oppose paper money per se—after all, the bank issues and his own Morris notes were paper money he himself had fostered. But the paper issues of the Revolution had run their course. At this point, he said simply, "all paper money ought to be absorbed by taxation (or otherwise) and destroyed before we can expect our credit to be fully reestablished." Whatever devalued paper remained, Morris said, would be worthless to those who held it and a bane to those who received it—"a monument of national Perfidy."

The next step was to fund the debt, not by new loans, but by grants of revenue. Here Morris saluted the petition of the public creditors, "not only because I wish well to a righteous Pursuit, but because this success"—that is, the success of the government in paying off its creditors—"will be the great groundwork of a Credit which will carry us safely through the present just, important and necessary war, which will combine us closely together at the conclusion of a Peace, which will always give to the Supreme Representative of America the means of acting for the general defense on Sudden Emergencies, and which will, of consequence, procure the Third of those great objects for which we contend, *Peace, Liberty, and Safety.*"

Morris then rehearsed his familiar prescription for funding the debt— settling accounts with the states, setting in hard figures the value of the certificate debt, raising funds from the states, and imposing new federal taxes. The critical point here was that the numbers were high, but manageable: Morris estimated the debt at roughly thirty million, with annual interest charges of two million. If the states would provide for current costs, new federal taxes would answer the interest. The impost had now been approved by every state but Rhode Island, and as "there is reason to believe that their compliance is not far off, this revenue may be considered as already granted." Land, poll, and excise taxes would make up the difference.

From this calculation, Morris looked forward. Taking the new federal taxes as a given, Morris proposed that they be used as security to establish new issues of public debt. "Thus the Money would be paid out of the Treasury as fast as it came in . . . and return speedily the Wealth obtained by Taxes into the Common Stock."

A new and expanded market in public securities, Morris acknowledged, "would enable Speculators to perform their Operations." But this was not to be feared: "Even if it were possible to prevent Speculation, it is precisely the thing which ought not to be prevented; because he who wants money to commence, pursue, or extend his business, is more benefited by selling stock of any kind, than he could be by the rise of it at a future Period; Every Man being able to judge better of his own business and situation, than the Government can for him." This was Morris the laissez-faire modernist, tilting at the mercantile conventions of the Old World.

This ambitious formula led Morris to one more critical stipulation: the public debts should be paid in full. This might seem obvious, but it was not at the time; many of the original securities issued by Congress had since changed hands, often purchased at a steep discount from the original holders. "It is not uncommon to hear," Morris noted, "that those who have bought the public debts for small sums, ought only to be paid their purchase Money. The reasons given are, that they have taken advantage of the distressed creditor, and shown a Diffidence in the public."

Morris addressed each of these objections in turn. "As to the first, it must be remembered that in giving the creditor money for his debt, they have at least afforded him some Relief, which he could not obtain elsewhere; and if they [the purchasers] are deprived of the expected Benefit, they will never afford such relief again. As to the second, those who buy up the public debt show at least as much confidence in the public faith as those who sell them; but allowing (for Argument's sake) that they have exhibited the Diffidence complained of, it would certainly be wiser to remove than to Justify it. The one mode tends to create, establish and secure public credit, and the other to sap, overturn, and destroy it. Policy is therefore on this (as I believe it to be on every other occasion) upon the same side of the question with Honesty."

The questions raised in the "Report on Public Credit"—federal versus state taxes, full funding for the public debts—would divide the leaders of the Revolution for another ten years. Morris would play a central role in that debate, never veering from the cogent position laid out here. In this seminal document, Morris distinguished himself by his discernment, his insight, and his relentless certitude. At a time when America was torn and confused by a war whose duration few had anticipated, Morris offered clear and firm direction.

Chapter 13

FIGHTING FOR FUNDS

B y the end of his first year in office Robert Morris was operating at the height of his powers as the top civil executive in the American government. His state papers set the agenda for the Congress, his banknotes and the drafts against his own office provided the circulating medium for the nation's major business entities, and his circulars to the governors drew the disparate states into his orbit. In the weeks after Yorktown, when civil affairs displaced military matters as the chief concerns of the nation, Morris was the man of the moment. "Mr. Morris has become a new star in our American hemisphere," Benjamin Rush declared in September.

This was more than just a reflection of Morris's commanding personality or the gloss of his legendary fortune. In Philadelphia and across the sea in Europe, officials and diplomats marveled at the change he had wrought in the operations and fiscal administration of the government. Robert Livingston summarized the prevailing view in a letter to John Jay. "Order and economy have taken place in our finances. The troops are regularly clothed and fed at West Point and most of the other posts, at the moderate rate of ninepence a ration when issued; so that the innumerable band of purchasing and issuing commissaries is discharged. . . . Our civil list, formed upon plans of strictest economy, after having been many years in arrear, is now regularly paid off, and the departments in consequence of it filled with men of integrity and ability. Embargoes and other restrictions being removed, our commerce begins to revive, and with it the spirit of industry and enterprise. And what will astonish you still more is that public credit has again reared its head."

Benjamin Franklin echoed the same sentiments when he reported to Morris from Paris that "Your conduct, activity, and address as a Financier and provider for the exigencies of the State are much admired and praised here, their good consequences being so evident, particularly in regard to the rising credit of our country and the value of bills. No one but yourself can enjoy your growing reputation more than I do."

Morris himself, in the occasional moments when he set aside the frustrations of scarce revenues and laggard legislators, exulted in his growing stature. "You may very truly tell your antagonists," Morris wrote to Gouverneur in April, "that from one end of this Continent to the other I can obtain Whatever is wanted for the public service by a *Scrip* of the pen." This was not simply a boast; Morris was emphasizing to Gouverneur the stance he should take in talks with British commanders in New York. It was a fair statement of the powers he'd assembled.

But as much as Morris savored his accomplishments, he could never forget the fundamental weakness of his position as Financier of a destitute and overburdened government. The day after New Year's in 1782, Morris issued orders to his clerks requiring that people seeking funds put their requests in writing, rather than badger the Financier in person. "The greatest part of my time since in office has been consumed in hearing the Tales of Woe . . . which I cannot prevent in any other way than by declining personal interviews."

The new rule engendered "great wrath" among the creditors, and in the end made little difference. As the final arbiter in any government transaction, Morris found himself virtually under siege. He began his days early, arriving at his office before breakfast, and spent the daylight hours parrying demands for money and huddling with Gouverneur to draft correspondence and state papers. Important meetings and conferences with his cabinet were conducted in the evening, and often ran past midnight.

In June Morris tried another tack: "Finding that the daily interruptions which I met with by persons making applications on various matters that chiefly relate to themselves, prevents my getting through the business of this Office . . . I have now determined to set aside three days in the week wherein I will receive from the hours of ten to twelve all applications that are Personally made."

When they did finally manage an audience with the Financier, these myriad petitioners usually went away disappointed. Morris employed a range of measures to delay or redirect their claims—requesting documentation, sending them to Benjamin Lincoln or to Congress for authorizations—until an ultimate reckoning was inescapable. These final encounters might be quick or drawn out. To James Smith, a purchasing agent being dogged by creditors for hundreds of thousands of dollars he'd committed on his personal credit to support the army in 1777, Morris could only advise that "he must have patience," and confided in his diary, "This poor gentleman I pity very much." Smith did not receive a settlement for another six years. More common was Morris's encounter with the quartermaster general on May 7: "Col. Pickering applies for Money which he says is absolutely necessary for the use of his Department, but he must wait."

There was little else Morris could say. There was virtually no money coming from the states, his drafts on France were exhausted, and his personal credit fully committed in supporting the contracts to supply the army. The one ready resource at his command was the bank.

In its first months of operation, the officers of the bank went to extraordinary lengths to convince the public of the sound, hard money value of its notes. This was tricky business: before they would accept paper notes, borrowers and depositors had to believe there was enough hard money on hand that they could claim their balances in coin anytime they wished. Bank officers achieved this feat by ruses that appear almost comical today. One contrivance, the brainchild of cashier Tench Francis, was to set up a system of pulleys by which clerks would raise and lower boxes of silver from the loan office to the vault below, a procedure calculated to "dazzle the public eye by the same piece of coin multiplied by a thousand reflectors." Another ploy was to acquiesce in a demand for silver, and after the borrower in question left the building, to send an agent to plead that he return the critical coinage and accept banknotes instead. Morris threw the weight of his office behind the bank as well, authorizing his Continental receivers to accept banknotes for taxes in lieu of hard money.

These maneuvers worked remarkably well, and for the first few months of 1782 Morris was able to rely on bank loans to answer his most pressing calls for cash. But by late May, after Morris had borrowed three hundred thousand dollars for the government, the bank directors informed him they could make no more advances "until some of the former engagements are discharged."

Morris accepted this ruling "because it appears right and consistent with that Prudence and Integrity" required in keeping the bank afloat. In fact, with Philadelphia commerce frozen by the British naval blockade, many merchants were unable to answer calls on their loans, and the bank was facing its first liquidity crisis. Morris intervened by persuading Luzerne to secretly deposit a store of hard money he'd received to cover the payroll of the French army, thereby averting the first run on the fledgling institution. But while this saved the bank, it did nothing to solve Morris's own credit crunch. In this instance Morris was reduced to borrowing "on his Private obligation" twenty thousand in silver from John Chaloner, a local merchant and agent for the American contractors supplying the French.

By July, Morris's seemingly limitless ebullience had begun to wear thin. An appeal from a colonel in the 5th Pennsylvania Regiment who pleaded for back pay pushed him to a rare display of temper. "How I am enabled to do that or any other thing you can never know unless you were a witness to my distressing situation. . . . The [state] Legislatures not only unjustly and ungratefully neglect their Creditors and their Servants but they madly risk the Existence of the Country by Inattention to the Calls of Congress which from the Importance of the Consequences becomes deeply criminal. There is the Source of all our Misfortunes."

The heaviest demands levied against Morris, and the ones he worked hardest to meet, were the claims of the contractors hired to supply the army. Morris had put the entire contracting operation into motion with substantial advances made in hard currency in January. That deposit kept him ahead of the game until the spring, when his system began to unravel. When bills came due in April he paid a week late; in May he paid in banknotes that were immediately returned for collection in hard money, a transaction that stalled actual payment for a month. By June he was ten thousand dollars in arrears to Comfort Sands.

The delayed payments caused multiple problems. Flour was plentiful and cheap early in the season, but by the time funds arrived it had doubled in price when it could be found at all; rival purchasers from the French fleet, always armed with ready cash, had bought up most of what was available. The price of beef rose even more.

The brunt of these funding problems fell on the army at West Point. The troops supplied there by Sands and his partners saw the quality of their rations sink steadily—the flour infested, the meat spoiled, the whiskey watered down. Just as aggravating, Sands refused to place his magazines close to camp, as stipulated in the contract, but several miles away, leaving the soldiers to haul their food on foot, their drudgery tabulated by the commissary at a cost of four thousand pairs of shoes.

George Washington was convinced the problem lay with Comfort Sands—"wrongly named," was the general's grim quip. By June the general and his lead contractor were in open breach. "Mr. Sands," Washington asserted to Morris, "is determined to make all the money he can by the Contracts. Herein I do not blame him . . . but his thirst for Gain leads him in my opinion into a mistaken principle of Action."

Sands may indeed have been the culpable profiteer Washington suspected him to be, but Morris could not so easily disparage the character of his good friend William Duer, who by now had become a full partner with Sands. In a heartfelt letter penned in early August, Duer pleaded with Morris for payment. He was losing money on the contract and putting his credit at risk, Duer said; unless future payments were made in full and on time, he would "instantly quit the execution of the contract." More than that, Duer advised Morris to withdraw from any personal commitments as well, leaving the states, and the army, to fend for themselves. "I write you in haste, with an Anxious Mind, and a trembling hand," Duer confided. "Nothing but the critical situation I am in could have drawn from me the letters I now write to you."

The standoff between Washington and the contractors put Morris in a most delicate position. To Washington he vowed that the contractors were being paid; to the contractors he pleaded for performance based on promises and partial payment. Washington took the Financier at his word— "[Sands] cannot I presume charge these neglects to a failure on your part," he wrote Morris in June. Morris did not correct him, but instead sought to enlist the sympathies of his august friend.

"It is impossible for me to state the Trouble and Distress I go through," he wrote Washington in early July. "I am tied here to be baited by constant, clamorous Demands, and the Forfeiture of all which is desirable in Life, and which I hoped at this moment to enjoy, I am to be paid by Invective. There is scarce a day passes in which I am not tempted to give back into the Hands of Congress the Power they have delegated, and lay down a Burden which presses me to the Earth.

"What may be the Success of my Efforts God only knows, but to leave my Post at present would I know be ruinous. This candid State of my Situation and feelings I give to your Bosom, because you who have already felt and suffered so much will be able to sympathize with me."

Washington did answer with empathy. "It is not my wish or design to wound you with fruitless complaints, of which I know you are not the cause," he wrote Morris from New York. But the general did not leave off pressuring the Financier, enclosing an ominous letter he'd sent to Benjamin Lincoln, warning that "the patience and long sufferance of this Army are almost exhausted."

By this point Morris was so hemmed in that even good news carried bad portents for the Office of Finance. Talk of peace, which began with the victory at Yorktown and grew in volume over the months that followed, raised spirits from Boston to Savannah, but only hamstrung the operations Morris tried to effect.

One direct result was a dramatic reduction in trade, even beyond that wrought by the British naval blockade. Recognizing that peace would mean lower rates of insurance and, most likely, the resumption of trade with Britain, merchants along the American seaboard suspended all imports, especially those from France. This meant weak demand for new loans and slower payment on existing loans for the bank, which in turn restricted the funds Morris could borrow. At the same time, there was little need for French bills, depressing the value of the French funds Morris relied on. Thus, Morris observed in a note to Washington, two of his primary means for raising funds had been rendered "useless by the total Stagnation of Trade, owing to the expectations of Peace."

More broadly, and just as discouraging for the Financier, the approach of peace relieved the states of any sense of urgency in prosecuting the war or supporting expanded powers in the central government. Morris was convinced—with good reason—that news of peace talks hampered all his efforts to collect revenue from the states. Why pay taxes to Congress when Congress was no longer necessary? The conflict with Britain had been the single bond that drew the states together; the end of the war could sever that bond, leaving the states to go their separate ways.

Morris was not so brash as to lament publicly an event that all Americans had hoped for since the war began, but he offered a candid summary of his outlook in a letter to a friend in Europe. Speaking from his personal interest, he wrote, "I wish most sincerely and ardently for Peace," but only because "I may get rid of a most troublesome office and spend the Remainder of my Days with more ease and in less hurry than those which are past.

"But was I to confine myself to the language of a Patriot, I should speak in another manner and tell you that a continuance of the War is Necessary until our Confederation is more strongly knit, until a sense of the Obligations to support it shall be more generally diffused amongst all Ranks of American Citizens, [and] until we shall acquire the Habit of paying Taxes (the means we possess already)."

The prospect of peace had a distinct influence in France as well. As Luzerne had made clear in the weeks after Yorktown, the French court expected Americans to shoulder their own burdens once the threat from Britain was withdrawn. Now, almost a year later, Luzerne ridiculed the idea that French subsidies should continue in peacetime. His stance was confirmed by Vergennes, the French foreign minister, in October. Luzerne should be cagey in his dealings with Congress, Vergennes directed, "but do not conceal from Mr. Morris that we are astonished at the demands which they continue to make on us, while the Americans obstinately refuse to pay taxes."

A second piece of news that was hailed in Congress but was double-edged for Morris and his allies was a loan from Holland that John Adams secured in June. This substantial loan of five million guilders—about two million dollars—represented the first meaningful loan from Europe to originate outside France. But the money came in only after the loan was funded through a private Dutch syndicate, which took more than a year. In the meantime, word of a new European sponsor undercut everything Morris was trying to assert about credit and taxes. For months he had warned that without the impost, without specific funds to cover at least the interest on a loan, no foreign lender would entertain such a risk. Now the recalcitrant states could point to Holland and say that Morris's fears were overblown.

Nor did the Dutch loan relieve the financial pressure on Morris in the critical summer of 1782. In his dispatches announcing the new loan, Adams specifically asked that it not be drawn against until he gave further notice on the size of the drafts available. Desperate for funds as he was, Morris ignored this proviso and secretly incorporated drafts on Holland in a new seagoing venture to raise hard money in Havana. These funds he hoped to devote specifically to pay for the army. Still he was disappointed: in this case the ship he sent out made it to Cuba, but the bills drew little interest from investors, and the return of silver dollars raised by sale of the cargo was delayed in port for months by the threat of capture. When critics in Congress questioned the venture months later, Morris cited their 1781 resolution authorizing him to import money and goods for the government.

Even as he was pushing every expedient to keep his office and the government afloat, and despite the broad support he enjoyed in the capital, resistance to Morris was growing. The opposition was sharpest in states that had suffered from British occupation, where legislators felt Morris failed to account for the economic problems they confronted in answering his constant demands for money.

Outside the deep South, New York had sustained the heaviest losses; its largest city was under British occupation, and in the hinterlands, the American army had supported itself by widespread, forced confiscations. Continental receiver Alexander Hamilton saw little prospect for tax collections; other Morris allies felt he was asking too much from the beleaguered state. "Strange that the Financier, in spite of every Remonstrance, should persevere in the Idea that this state is able to pay the tax assessed upon it!" wrote James Duane in June, "and more unaccountable that he should find a Native of this state [a reference to Gouverneur Morris] to encourage that Opinion, probably to beget as well as to foster it!"

Governor Benjamin Harrison of Virginia was another old friend who questioned Morris's authority and disputed his initiatives. Upon his election in December 1781, Harrison had written Morris to commiserate over the "Anarchy and Confusion" that reigned in his state, and to make a personal request that Morris procure for him on credit a supply of "best Madeira and one of Sherry." "I know you don't deal in this way," Harrison admitted, "but I have no other friend from whom I can ask such a favor."

Within weeks, however, Harrison had changed his tone. At issue was the agreement Washington had struck at Yorktown to pay the British merchants for goods sold to the victorious army. Washington had passed the bill off to Morris, and Morris to the state of Virginia, to be paid in tobacco owed under the old requisitions for specific supplies. Harrison took this as a violation of the Articles of Confederation, which allowed Congress to call for funds, but not to say how they should be paid. Moreover, Harrison asserted that Virginia owed nothing to Congress, having satisfied its obligations by supporting the army during the fighting there. Congress "have no right either by themselves or those acting under them," Harrison wrote, "to lay their hands on any property of the State." At the same time, Harrison called on the Virginia delegates at Congress to suggest that Morris was discriminating against their state by refusing to extend there the contract system used to supply the army in Pennsylvania and New York.

This led to a meeting with the Virginia delegates at the Finance Office. Morris won the support of the delegates by pointing out that until taxes were levied in Virginia he could not support the contracts there. But in writing to Harrison, Morris took exception to the governor's "passion," leading to a sharp exchange. Harrison sought to patch their differences with a personal letter assuring Morris that "I did not intend to give offense," and reprising the sufferings of his state at the hands of the British.

Opposition from the states was to be expected, but the contest was carried into Congress itself when Arthur Lee was added to the Virginia delegation. The year he'd spent at home after his return from Europe had done little to soothe his disputatious nature, and the rise of Robert Morris only confirmed his conviction that Congress was rank with corruption. Lee expounded his views in a letter to his old ally Samuel Adams. "The accumulation of Offices in this man"—this a specific reference to Morris—"the number of valuable appointments in his gift, the absolute control given him over all the Revenue officers, his money & his art; render him a most dangerous man to the Liberty of this Country, as his excessive avarice does to the treasure of the public so much in his power."

Lee ran for Congress and lost, but then secured appointment to fill a vacancy in the delegation in December. Arriving at Philadelphia in February, he was soon agitating for investigations into any commercial contracts Morris might have authorized, into the distribution of funds from France, and for any other measures that might rattle the Financier. To Lee, Morris and his plans weren't the solution; they were the problem. "Our embarrassments for money are great," Lee explained to a friend in Europe, "not because there is any real want of it, but because by the constitution of the Bank, & until lately a most prosperous commerce, in this tory city, has accumulated all the money here & consequently disenabled the other States from paying taxes to support the war." As this letter suggests, Lee had by now added Philadelphia to his list of targets for scorn. "The residence of Congress in the bosom of toryism & the encouragement given to them is as impolitic as it is unjust."

Fortunately for Morris, Lee's influence was tempered by the other Virginia delegates, who knew Lee well enough to fear him. James Madison was alluding to Lee when he wrote on July 2, "The prevailing temper of the present delegation is too little flexible to the factious and vindictive plans of a particular member of it to be relished by him and his adherents. No delegate who refuses to league with him in the war against the financier must expect to be long at ease in his post."

Madison was the junior member of the Virginia delegation, socially awkward, wan, and small—"no bigger than half a piece of soap," one wag described him—but he had a firm mind and resisted the strong prejudices against Morris that reigned in his home state. "My charity I own cannot invent an excuse for the prepense malice with which the character and service of this gentleman are murdered," Madison wrote of Morris in June. "I am persuaded that he accepted his office from motives which are honest and patriotic. I have seen no proofs of misfeasance. I have heard many charges which were palpably erroneous; I have known others somewhat suspicious vanish on examination; every member of Congress must be sensible of the benefit which has accrued to the public from his administration."

Despite his support for Morris, Madison inadvertently opened a door for Lee and his rancor when he proposed, in mid-June, that Congress establish five standing committees to monitor the departments of finance, foreign affairs, war, marine, and the post office. This was a good-government measure, designed to "expose to just censure" any misconduct, but also to "shelter in some degrees the faithful officers from unmerited imputations & suspicions." Morris embraced the plan "from a conviction that the more they know of my proceedings the more they will be convinced of my constant desire and exertions to promote the Honor and Interest of the United States."

Morris and Madison were both disappointed to find, when the rosters were issued in Congress, that Arthur Lee had been named to the finance oversight committee. Under his influence, it appeared the committee might be just another avenue for Lee to attack his perceived enemies. "All the movements of the Doctor," Madison wrote in reference to Lee, "are pointed directly or circuitously either to Morris or Franklin."

Here again, however, Lee was baffled by the composition of the committee. The other members—Samuel Osgood, Abraham Clark of New Jersey, and Thomas McKean of Delaware—were all lukewarm in regard to Morris, but the chairman was the New Yorker James Duane, a stalwart Nationalist. With Duane at the helm, Lee decided "that Congress did not mean the inspection should be productive of public good. Nor have I any reason to think it will."

With the investigative committee divided, Lee found other avenues to bedevil the Financier. The most brazen turned, conveniently enough, on collecting funds for himself from Morris's meager supply.

Lee made his application in a memorial to Congress July 12. He had previously applied for his salary and expenses in Europe, and had been paid in Loan Office Certificates. Now he wanted to exchange those certificates for bills drawn on Franklin in Paris. In making his argument, Lee averred that "every other" American diplomat had been paid in full, leaving him "the sole object of neglect." Moreover, he observed "that not only foreign ministers have been paid, but even Agents & Factors"—these would include John Ross and William Bingham—"who had profits on large sums of public money advanced to them, have also been paid considerable Sums out of the invoices borrowed in France."

This was classic Lee, self-pity combined with a sharp dig at Morris for the payments he'd made to the Secret Committee contractors. More than that, filling Lee's request would force both Morris and Franklin, ever the objects of Lee's wrath, to tap their precious French reserves. Charles Thomson, in recording the debate, observed one further irony—that Lee had submitted his accounts upon "his word of honor," without any of the vouchers or receipts he had so haughtily demanded of Silas Deane and the other agents in Europe.

Lee's request was approved by Congress and referred to Morris for payment. Not surprisingly, Morris let the matter lie until pressed by Lee in October. At that point Morris declined to act, contending that he could not in propriety pay Lee until all the loan certificates issued by Congress were funded. Lee answered with his customary indignation, complaining of "Manifest injustice." Morris, probably enjoying Lee's frustration, stalled some more, explaining to Lee that "I cannot dispense with what I conceive to be my proper Line of Conduct to obtain your good opinion on which nevertheless I pray you to be persuaded I have set the proper Value." This last bit of barbed ambiguity was gratuitous, as Morris had already obtained a new authorization from Congress. He provided Lee the French bills he sought in November.

In the meantime, Lee was doing his best to make hash of Morris's efforts to acquire domestic revenues. Appointed to a committee weighing Morris's call for poll, land, and excise taxes, Lee, flanked again by Osgood and Abraham Clark, deemed such measures "exceptionable." No steps should be taken until the disorder in state and certificate debts was sorted out, the committee advised; at that point, new revenues "may become necessary."

In July, while Congress was weighing his request for French bills, Lee finally found a vehicle for his inquests. During his evenings away from the State House, he informed Congress, he had "looked into" Robert Morris's May report on foreign aid, and found that "large sums of money are reserved in France for certain purposes; that in his opinion some of these purposes did not require so large a sum as was reserved for them, and that others were not proper." Considering "the situation of our treasury," Lee said, the matter "required an examination."

One can imagine Lee, closeted in his candlelit room on a hot summer's eve, fired by glowing ambers of wrath as resentment, ignoring the shouts of tavern goers in the street below as he pored over the ledgers and correspondence submitted to Congress from the Office of Finance. Here were the letters between Franklin and Morris, his two nemeses; here were the transactions of Deane and Beaumarchais. Many of the delegates who had engaged in the bitter feuds of 1779 were long gone from the capital, but Lee would outlast them, stalking his quarry like a hungry wolf.

Upon Lee's presentation, Congress formed a committee to report on "the application of the moneys of the United States in France." The committee would include Lee, his anti-Franklin acolyte Ralph Izard, and Samuel Wharton of Delaware. This last appointment reflected Congress' sense of fairness—or sense of humor—as Lee detested Wharton. And when Wharton quit the committee soon after his appointment, he was replaced by James Duane. Undeterred, Lee stayed on the offensive; in September, Madison recorded, Morris was "the object of almost daily attack" by Lee.

As it turned out, in the case of the French funds, Lee's insinuations of misconduct went much further than what he could prove. The committee did not report until September 27, and its findings were not taken up by Congress until late November. Very little was produced except Lee's long-standing contention that Caron Beaumarchais, the man behind the shadow firm Hortalez & Company, deserved no compensation. His critical supplies to the American army had been a gift from the king, Lee argued, and the funds he claimed were pure graft. Based on this report, Congress halted all further payment to Beaumarchais until a new, full accounting was made.

This result, of course, played directly into the hands of Robert Morris. As early as May, Morris had suggested to Franklin that the claims of Beaumarchais might be put off. He would not declaim on the merits of the case, Morris wrote, but he ventured to observe "that if the very considerable sum which is now payable to that Gentleman forms a deduction from the pecuniary aid afforded us [in the king's six million livre grant] the remainder will be extremely incompetent to the purposes intended by it." In other words, Morris simply could not afford to pay Beaumarchais out of the French grant. A week later, Morris had warmed to the idea. "There is a misteriousness in this transaction arising from the very nature of it," he wrote to Franklin. Perhaps the king would step in again—secretly, of course—and settle the matter for them.

This reflected a change of heart in Morris, probably grounded in necessity. He'd stood with Deane and Beaumarchais when both had been accused of malfeasance, but now, with an army to feed and a government to fund, he eased up a bit on his principles. Besides, Deane was in disgrace, and both he and Beaumarchais were across the sea in Europe. More than that, Beaumarchais had lost his influence at court; in July, Luzerne had told Robert Livingston that "Congress should not pay any attention to the Claims and demands of Monsr. De Beaumarchais." The Beaumarchais funds were up for grabs, and Morris was taking his money where he could find it.

By the time Franklin received these letters, he'd already paid Beau-marchais 2.5 million livres. Unfortunately Morris, apparently considering his wish to be fact, had already spent that sum, and thus was overdrawn to Franklin by that amount. Still, Beaumarchais was claiming another three million livres. On this score Morris formed an alliance of convenience with Arthur Lee and convinced Congress to suspend payment until another audit of Beaumarchais's accounts, one to be attended by the "strictest Scru-tiny," could be conducted.

Another character arrived in Philadelphia at this time who, while he never cut so menacing a figure as Arthur Lee, would do more damage to Morris and the Finance Office than the entire Lee family. That was David Howell, a new delegate to Congress from the state of Rhode Island.

Robert Morris met Howell in early July when Howell and another Rhode Island delegate, the Nationalist and former Continental Army gen-eral Ezekiel Cornell, stopped by the Office of Finance to discuss recent news from their home state legislature. The two delegates assured Morris that "the Impost Law will at length be passed in that state," and went on their way. What Morris didn't know, and what Howell didn't tell him, was that Howell was already an implacable foe of the impost.

A linguist and mathematician, learned, voluble, and ambitious, Howell was the first tutor hired to teach at Rhode Island College, the school later known as Brown University. In 1770 he married into the school's found-ing family, the mercantile Brown brothers of Providence, and became a devoted champion of their interests. The dominant figure here was John Brown, the leading merchant in town and a man of consuming passions who in 1772 had personally led a fleet of longboats in a midnight raid on the British revenue ship *Gaspee*. Steeped in Rhode Island's fiercely indepen-dent political tradition, John Brown and his brothers Nicholas and Joseph saw the impost as a threat to local autonomy.

Despite his political connections, David Howell was twice defeated in elections for Congress, in 1778 and again in 1781. The controversy over the impost provided him a new platform, one he made the most of. The debate opened in earnest in March 1782 with the return from Congress of James Mitchell Varnum, a celebrated orator, a former brigadier general in the Continental Army, and an avid Nationalist. Dismayed to find his home state standing as one of the few holdouts against the impost, Varnum pub-lished a series of articles in the *Providence Gazette* calling for broad grants of power to the Congress, including the impost. The Articles of Confederation had failed to include such powers, Varnum conceded, but they were implied by the existence of the central government—a doctrine favored by the early Nationalists, but rarely to good effect.

Howell responded with a series of articles under the pseudonym "A Farmer" that struck against the impost as a harbinger of despotism. Recalling "that fatal day when the Stamp Act was hatched by an infernal junto of British Ministers," Howell vowed to oppose any tax imposed from outside the state, and the "foreign officers"—Americans, of course, but foreign to Rhode Island—sent to collect it. The Articles of Confederation were explicit and sufficient, he said, and contained no "magic charm" of extended powers. This was states' rights ideology in full flower, the language of independence now turned against the central government in America.

Along with the fundamental question of self-rule, Howell had several specific points to make. A duty on imports would unfairly burden Rhode Island, he argued, as the state economy rested principally on maritime trade. The bleak financial outlook for Congress posed by Varnum was "a high colored painting" construed only to pressure the state into submission. And once the impost was granted, other taxes would follow. This was indeed Morris's design, but Howell put it in stark terms. Once granted, the impost "will be like Adam's fall, unalterable."

Howell's arguments struck a chord in Rhode Island, which had been founded by the banished preacher Roger Williams as a "lively experiment" in religious and political liberty. Populated by hardy mariners and hardscrabble farmers, the colony had a long tradition of piracy and smuggling, and at the outset of the Revolution was the first colony in America to renounce allegiance to the king. Capitalizing on Howell's newfound popularity, the merchants of Providence drafted him to oppose Varnum as a candidate for Congress, and on May 1, Howell scored a "smashing" victory.

Traveling overland to join Congress at Philadelphia, Howell felt confirmed in his pride of place. "As you go Southward," Howell wrote to Welcome Arnold, scion of another Providence merchant clan, "Government verges toward Aristocracy. In New England alone have we pure & unmixed Democracy & in Rhode Island & Providence Plantations"—the full name of the state, then and today—"is it in its perfection." To Howell this only sanctified his sense of mission. "Should our little State have the credit of preventing the 5 percent [impost] from taking effect it would be to us an additional gem."

However firm he was in his convictions on the question, Howell was at first careful not to broadcast them. Arriving in the capital, he found that "all the members of Congress, as well as the Inhabitants, were universally in favor of the Impost, and concluding that my single voice would be unavailing against the current I cautiously avoided entering unnecessarily into the subject." This explained his silence in his initial meeting with Morris.

Howell was drawn into the open toward the end of July, when he and Ezekiel Cornell were called before a committee of Congress to explain why Rhode Island had yet to approve the impost. Cornell supported the tax, so it fell to Howell to step into the role of spoiler. "I embraced it with pleasure," he noted later.

Morris sat in on the hearing, and listened intently as Howell reprised the arguments he'd made in the press—that as the commerce of his state depended on maritime trade, import duties would cost Rhode Island disproportionately; that direct taxation by the central government would violate the sovereignty of the individual states; that establishing a federal tax on trade would rob the individual states of a key source of funding; and that an external tax on trade would erode the "morals" of the community "by increasing temptations to perjury both in officers of the customs & in citizens, & by nourishing in idleness & Luxury a numerous train of Collectors, Comptrollers, Searchers, tide-waiters, Clerks etc."

Morris did not debate Howell at the hearing; he recognized that his quarrel was with the state, not with its delegate. Instead he asked Howell for a written summary of his speech. At least now the objections to the impost were on the record; perhaps Rhode Island would entertain a response.

With Howell's memo before him, Morris composed a rebuttal addressed to Rhode Island governor William Greene. It was technical and a bit scattered—not his strongest performance—but it laid down some of the basic principles that made duties on trade the most palatable mode of taxation. He took as a given that some sort of revenue must be raised; the question was one of fairness and proportion. The burden of the impost did not fall on the merchant, Morris argued, but on the consumer. And since a consumer could always opt to buy local productions in place of foreign articles, "the Tax is voluntary, and cannot be considered as disproportionate."

Allowing individual states to impose their own trade duties would be "unjust in itself," as "commercial" states like Rhode Island and Pennsylvania would siphon revenue from their "uncommercial" neighbors. As to the "numerous train" of collectors and tax officials, Morris answered that trade duties would require a smaller corps of collectors than any other mode of taxation.

Having worked his way through Howell's arguments, Morris closed with one of his own. "As all taxes are unpleasant, some state will be found to oppose any which can be devised, on quite as good ground as the present opposition. What then is the Consequence?"

The reckoning for Morris arrived in late August when the contractors supplying the army demanded their oft-delayed funds. Morris notes and issues from the bank would no longer suffice; they must have hard money, and they must have it on time.

Tired of dealing through intermediaries, Comfort Sands traveled to Philadelphia with his brother Richardson Sands in early September for a face-to-face meeting with the Financier. Their plan was to collect twenty thousand dollars due them under contract or to quit the business on the spot. Meeting with Morris in the evening, they engaged in "a long conversation" but got little satisfaction. "I assured them of my entire disposition to supply Money to them as fast as possible," Morris recorded in his diary, "and if at any time it is detained longer than it ought I begged they would exert themselves and support [me] instead of plaguing and Distressing me with importunity."

Returning to New York, the Sands brothers sat down with William Duer and the other partners in the contract and drew up an ultimatum for Morris. They would continue to supply the army through the first of October, but if new funds were not immediately provided, "we shall on that day be reduced to the painful necessity of surrendering a trust too hazardous for us to continue."

Here, at least, the contractors and Morris were in agreement; he could no longer support the provisioning of the army. Morris laid out his position in an anguished letter to Washington that he drafted at the end of August. After a quick review of the yawning gap between costs and revenues, Morris advised Washington to "consider how your army is to be subsisted or kept together if I am obliged to dissolve the contracts. I pray that Heaven may direct your mind to some mode by which we may be yet saved. I have done all that I could and given repeated Warnings [to the states] but it is like preaching to the Dead."

Fearful as he was of the import of this message, Morris kept the letter secret even from his own clerks, and sat on it for another week. On September 9, with no relief appearing, he wrote an addendum, confessing that, "at present I really know not which way to turn myself." Washington answered two weeks later. If he was to revert to the "ruinous system" of seizing supplies, the decision had to be made soon, before winter set in.

Fortunately for both of them, Morris won a reprieve that same week when a merchant named John B. Carter stopped by his office seeking to collect on a loan. An emblem for those tumultuous times, Carter was a man of mystery, a Londoner living under an assumed identity—his true name was John B. Church—who had emigrated in the first year of the Revolution to flee, depending on which rumor was to be believed, gambling debts or a vengeful Tory politician. In America he attained high marriage—to Angelica Schuyler, daughter of the New York general Philip Schuyler and sister of Alexander Hamilton's wife Eliza—and high station, becoming partners with former Quartermaster General Jeremiah Wadsworth as contractors supplying the French forces in America.

The debt Carter sought to collect was the twenty thousand dollars Morris had borrowed in May from Carter's agent John Chaloner. Though at the time the loan was meant to be repaid "in a few days," Morris still did not have the funds. But Morris recognized in Carter the solution to a much larger problem. Carter and Wadsworth were doing a handsome business by catering to the French—and routinely outfoxing their American counterparts—perhaps they would take on the Comfort Sands contract as well.

Over the next two weeks, Morris and Carter worked out the basic terms of an agreement. This new contract would extend only to the end of the year, but it would stave off the crisis in provisions, and provide the added benefit of ending the destructive competition between the French and American supply operations. Crucially, Carter agreed to extend Morris three months credit before the first bills would come due. But there was a price—Morris would have to pay Wadsworth and Carter a full third more than he did to Comfort Sands. In addition, Carter needed immediate payment of the outstanding twenty thousand dollars.

For this last proviso, Morris called on William Bingham. Morris had backed Bingham's claim before Congress; would Bingham now come to his aid? Bingham bridled, but finally came through with a twelve thousand dollar loan. It wasn't all Morris wished for, but he made it suffice.

With the new contract in place, Morris broke off his talks with Comfort Sands. "I confess to you Gentlemen," he wrote the contractors in October, "that these events give me Pain." Here at least, the feeling was mutual. "Our feelings, Sir," Sands and his partners wrote back, "as well as our interest, are deeply affected by the manner in which the contract for the moving army has been precipitously wrested from our hands." Not surprisingly, the whole transaction ended in litigation, against the government and between the contractors themselves. The case remained open until 1834.

As soon as Wadsworth's interim contract was in place, Morris solicited new bids for supplying the army in 1783. Unfortunately, word had spread of the government's problems in paying on the contracts and few offers came forward. Morris was able to secure favorable terms—under ten cents per daily ration—for posts in Pennsylvania, but Wadsworth, the sole bidder for the Northern Army contract, held fast to his minimum of fourteen and a half cents. Convinced he could get a better price, Morris called in his friend William Duer, who had expressed interest but feared he could not manage the deferred payments Morris proposed. Morris finally relented, agreeing to advance one hundred thousand dollars via a bill on France, provided it be negotiated in Boston, as the market in Philadelphia was glutted. Duer agreed, and promptly drafted the Boston merchant Daniel Parker, and the French entrepreneur John Holker, to join him as partners. Duer considered his last-minute acquisition of the contract something of a coup. "I didn't bid for the contract," Duer confided to Parker, "nor have I time to tell you the extraordinary manner by which it became mine."

While the bridge contract with Wadsworth and Carter prevented a total breakdown in provisions, it did nothing to address the deepest sources of discontent in the army. The soldiers and officers still served without pay, and in the South, Nathanael Greene's forces were continuing to live off what they could wrest by whatever means from the states they occupied. "For upwards of two months more than one third of our men were entirely naked with nothing but a breech cloth about them," Greene wrote in August. "Our beef was perfect carrion, and even bad as it was, we were often without any." Secretary of War Benjamin Lincoln was convinced that change must come, and soon. "It does not require a very penetrating eye to discover, that a heavy cloud is gathering over the United States, nor a prophetic spirit to foretell, that unless the greatest precautions are taken, and those speedily, it will burst and sweep away our feeble confederation, and endanger, if not overturn, the union of these states."

The collapse of the Comfort Sands contract spurred Morris to make one more drive to collect revenue from the states. Disclosing the terms of the new, more expensive deal, Morris told the new president of Congress that matters had taken a discouraging turn. "The negligence of the several states . . . has at length brought on the Evil which I had long apprehended, and attempted (in Vain) to guard against." That same day he addressed a new circular to the state governors. "How long is a Nation who will do nothing for itself to rely on the Aid of others?" Morris demanded. "How long will one Part of a Community bear the Burdens of the whole? How long will an Army undergo Want in the Midst of Plenty? How long will they endure Misery without Complaint, Injustice without Reproach, and Wrongs without Redress?"

This appeal was sincere enough, but from the performance of the states to date Morris knew not to expect any sudden infusion of tax revenue. His one real hope for funds rested on the impost; consequently he addressed a separate summons to Rhode Island. Patiently, forcefully, Morris walked through the logic of his circumstances. "It must be remembered that the Duration of the War does not depend on Congress. This is an invaded Country. . . . The idea of submission is and ever ought to be rejected with Disdain. Opposition therefore becomes a Matter of Necessity; and that Opposition involves expense." Those expenses would have to be raised by taxes, but as those had proven deficient, the government must resort to loans. "They cannot obtain loans without Credit, and they cannot have Credit without funds." This brought the question back to Rhode Island, and the impost. "This, Sir, is an Object of great Magnitude, and one which directly or indirectly concerns every inhabitant of the United States." Now was the time for decision. "The Evil presses hard," Morris warned. "Public Credit is at the last Gasp."

Morris had one other card to play, and at this critical juncture he reached for it, calling Tom Paine to meet him for a conference. Paine was on Morris's payroll, of course, but he was also in complete accord with the Nationalist agenda, and readily set about composing a new series of columns on Rhode Island and the impost.

In Congress, the Nationalist majority needed no prompting from the Financier. Even before his report on the failure of the West Point contract, a "grand committee" on finance had recommended pressing Rhode Island for an "immediate definitive answer" on the impost. In voting October 10, the delegates approved the motion by a tally of nine states to one. The only opposition came from Georgia, which had just one delegate and was thus not counted as present, and from Rhode Island.

As hard as Morris and his congressional allies pushed for ratification of the impost, Rhode Island representative David Howell pushed back just as hard. He sent a stream of letters to political leaders back home exhorting them to hold their ground, and wrote numerous articles for the Providence press trumpeting local sovereignty. Howell did not deny the gravity of the funding problems facing the nation, but he continued to hold out requisitions on the states as the only legitimate means for securing a national revenue. This was contradicted by puny tabulations reported each month by the Continental receivers, but Howell saw the question in strictly ideological terms. "The liberties of America," Howell wrote, "the interests of the present & all future generations are suspended on a single resolve of our little State."

These convictions were buttressed by a personal sense of melodrama, even martyrdom, that trumped any logic or appeal that Morris and his allies could make. Howell delved into his internal dialogue in a letter to a friend back home. "If ever there was a Cause in which I have felt myself disposed to suffer as well as die, and in which I have suffered as well, it is this." Howell didn't harbor the same rancor toward Morris that animated Arthur Lee—at one point he praised the Financier for "candor and prudence"—but he did see the struggle over the impost as one of right against might. "Nothing affords more Satisfaction in Life or lays a better foundation for hope in Death," Howell sermonized, "than the Consciousness of having maintained the rights of the poor, the Weak and the Ignorant against the Rapacity, the Violence and the Intrigue of the Rich, the powerful, and the Subtle."

However strained Howell's reasoning might appear, his dispatches from the capital resonated in Rhode Island, where they were matched by an outpouring of defiant declarations from local scribes. Writing in the *Providence Gazette*, "A Freeholder" advised that passage of the impost would shred the protections of local rights embodied in the Articles of Confederation, "at once destroying all the liberties of the several states, reducing them to so many provinces of Congress, and tending to the establishment of an aristocratical or monarchial government."

The question was called before the state Assembly on November 1. There John Brown, Howell's principal sponsor and an Assembly delegate from Providence, spent an entire week marshaling his allies and leaning on the laggards. After a final day of hearings, with the State House "the most crowded with respectable spectators I ever knew," as Brown recorded later, the impost was rejected on a unanimous vote.

The decision in Rhode Island led to a dramatic erosion of public confidence in the central government. In Pennsylvania and Maryland, public creditors immediately pressed their state legislatures to step in and assume the financial obligations of Congress, if necessary by diverting tax revenues from Congress directly to the creditors. On December 2, unwilling to treat any longer with an insolvent Congress, Robert Livingston submitted his resignation. It appeared that, just as the war was drawing to a close, the new American republic was splitting asunder.

These appearances of impending dissolution stimulated a renewed sense of mission among the Nationalists in the Congress. Their leading voice was James Madison, now augmented by a new delegate from New York, the energetic and willful Alexander Hamilton. They made an odd couple— Madison shy and socially awkward, Hamilton vocal, brash, and cocksure— but they worked in tandem to rally the other delegates in support of Morris and his program. Teamed with South Carolina's John Rutledge, the pair met with Pennsylvania legislators December 4 to stall the Assembly's bid to take over the Continental debts, arguing that such a step would undermine "our system of administration, and even our bond of Union would be dissolved."

Two days later Hamilton called on Congress to dispatch a delegation to Rhode Island and press for a new vote on the impost. This plan encountered little opposition but "considerable debate," a discourse that helped to crystallize the thinking in Congress. Among the salient points Madison recorded in his notes were "the necessity of the impost, in order to prevent separate appropriations by the States, to do equal justice to the public creditors, to maintain out national character & credit abroad, to obtain essential loans for supplying the deficiencies of revenue, to prevent the encouragement which a failure of the scheme would give to the Enemy"—each step derived from the Morris playbook. The motion carried easily, with Rhode Island providing the only votes in dissent.

Conspicuous by his absence in this dialogue was Arthur Lee. Never bashful in challenging his enemies on the floor of Congress, Lee would have at least provided a second to David Howell. But Lee had his own battles to fight back on his home turf in Virginia.

Lee's problems arose in Philadelphia, where his surplus of ill temper had finally outstripped his carefully nourished reputation for moral and political rectitude. Thwarted in his attacks on Morris and Franklin—largely by fellow Virginian Madison—Lee had resorted to the public prints, airing his cynical views of local politics and the upcoming election for Assembly. This was followed by a letter from Lee to a friend in Virginia ridiculing Congress for its close relations with Luzerne and the French delegation. Both performances drew equally caustic responses. In Philadelphia, Benjamin Rush led a phalanx of writers attacking Lee for "base motives"; in Virginia, lawmakers called for Lee's censure and his recall from Congress.

With pressure mounting against him, Lee felt obliged to hurry home and confront his foes. "He left this place I believe not in the best of humors," Madison reported on October 8. "In Congress he has been frustrated in several favorite objects, and from the press he has been most rudely handled."

Arriving at Williamsburg to attend the legislature in session, Lee managed to turn back his enemies, due in part to the support of Richard Henry Lee, and in part to the absence of Patrick Henry, who never trusted the Lee brothers. Having defeated the threat to his standing, Arthur Lee took the offensive, launching an attack on the acceptance of Morris notes as payment of taxes in Virginia, and raising a challenge to the impost, which the Assembly had endorsed more than a year before. He could not strike at Franklin from his redoubt in Williamsburg, but he could at least make Morris feel his venom.

The motion to rescind approval of the impost was introduced quietly on December 4, and "hurried thro' without due consideration," winning approval of the legislature on December 7. The vote was a product of the subtle, factional politics of the Virginia House of Burgesses; Governor Benjamin Harrison did not know of the repeal until after the legislative session closed on December 28.

For weeks afterward Virginia delegates Madison and Joseph Jones, and later even George Washington, sought clarification of the decision. The best explanation they got came from Edmund Randolph, the state attorney general. "The fatal repeal [of the impost] is wrapt up in more than common mystery," Randolph told Madison. "But the opinion of an attentive observer of legislative movements is, that the situation of America was not duly reflected on, and thereby an opportunity was presented to the Lees of piquing [Robert] Morris. The tenor of their daily language justifies the suspicion"—this in reference to the Lee brothers—"their character for malice confirms it."

Word that Virginia had withdrawn its endorsement of the impost filtered out slowly. Madison learned of the vote in December, but kept mum until he could obtain corroboration and details of the decision. In the meantime, Morris pressed forward with plans to bring pressure on Rhode Island. On Saturday, December 7, Morris met with Abner Nash of North Carolina and Thomas Mifflin, two of the three delegates named to the Rhode Island expedition, and supplied them with letters and financial statements to buttress their case.

Later that day Tom Paine stopped by the Office of Finance to share "some useful hints" on the impost debate, and proposed that he also go to Rhode Island. This was in some degree rooted in Paine's inflated idea of his personal celebrity, but there was strategy involved as well; airing the dispute in the capital was only jeopardizing the gains already made in Congress. It would be "a piece of prudence to make the debate as limited as possible by keeping it to the Rhode Island papers only," Paine explained later. "The less it was blazed around the world, the less would the reputation of America suffer." Morris agreed to the plan, and Paine set out two days later, riding on a rented horse, happy once again to be engaged in critical service to his adopted country.

Paine was already in Providence before the congressional delegation finally got under way. Nash, Mifflin, and Samuel Osgood had ridden about ten miles out of the city when Nash "casually mentioned" seeing a letter to Madison reporting that Virginia had dropped its support for the impost. His fellow delegates stared back at him. If the report was true, they had lost their strongest argument—that the rest of the states awaited only the approval of Rhode Island to implement the new continental tax. "Rather chagrined," the delegates turned their steeds around and headed back to Philadelphia. When they arrived at the State House Morris pressed them to get back on the road, but the larger Congress felt the venture pointless.

Two hours later, Madison received a second report from Virginia confirming the news. The implications were inescapable: the impost was all but dead, and with it was lost any chance to effect orderly payment on the loans from Europe or to provide creditors in America with funds collected through Congress. Madison presented the letter he'd received to Congress, and recorded the reaction. "The most intelligent members were deeply affected."

The ill-starred career of the impost helps illustrate both the achievements and the failures Morris realized in his campaign to establish his funding program as a foundation for a central government in America. By the middle of 1782, on the strength of his arguments and his moral suasion, eleven of the thirteen independent states had approved the concept of a Continental duty. Such a step would dramatically enlarge the powers of the Confederation and, as both critics and advocates agreed, set the stage for additional taxes in the near future. Yet in the one holdout state, the opposition had become entrenched, and there was little prospect that Rhode Island would return to the fold.

Morris's critics, then and later, held that he overreached, demanding of the states not just what they would not give, but what they could not. This seems unfair: the impost was first proposed, after all, by Congress, not the Financier. Certainly he embraced it, but as he argued repeatedly in his circulars, it was the least obnoxious and most reliable of the revenue measures available to him. And to anyone familiar with the state of congressional finance, it was clear that something had to be done.

But in making the campaign for the impost his own, Morris allowed the question to shift from one of policy and efficacy to a referendum on Morris himself. This alternate view was first formulated by Arthur Lee but soon gained a wider constituency. By December 1782, Joseph Reed was calling Morris a "Colossus, who not only bestrides all the other officers of Congress, but even Congress itself." In the months that followed, as the approach of peace augured a new era in America, Morris loomed as a large and easy target for critics of the national government.

— *Chapter 14* —

A DESPERATE GAMBIT

I n the waning days of December in 1782 a small troop of Continental
soldiers rode south from the army cantonment at Newburgh on the
Hudson. They were cloaked against the cold but warmed by mingled
feelings of grim purpose and indignation. Their leader was Alexander Mc-
Dougall, fifty years old, a major general and commander of the New York
Line. Something of a firebrand, McDougall in his youth captained a privateer in the French and Indian War, and early in the Revolution became a
prominent organizer with the radical Sons of Liberty. A checkered military
career had seen him named successor to Benedict Arnold in command at
West Point, and later court-martialed for an altercation with William Heath,
commander of the army's Eastern Department. He spent 1781 in Congress
as a delegate from New York, and rejoined the army the following year.

That autumn McDougall had been offered a return to active command.
He declined due to chronic rheumatism, but that did not prevent his cold-
weather expedition to Philadelphia. This mission was as much civil as
military—to deliver an urgent, last-ditch appeal to the civil government.
Arriving in the capital on a Sunday afternoon, McDougall and his cohort
found lodgings at the Indian Queen tavern and set about their business the
next day. Their message was addressed to the Congress, but their first stop
was at the Office of Finance.

Meeting with Robert Morris and Gouverneur Morris the afternoon of
December 31, McDougall and four fellow officers presented their petition.
With the enemy idle for much of the past year, soldiers and officers of every
rank had watched in dismay the proceedings of Congress and the problems
of finance. "We have borne all that men can bear," their petition intoned.
"Our property is expended, our private resources are at an end, and our
friends are wearied out and disgusted with our incessant applications."

Here the aggrieved soldiers were speaking, understandably enough, in the voice of the past, echoing the long hard winters of Valley Forge and Morristown. But it was not privation per se that inspired this embassy to the Congress. In fact, by this time, the contract system the Financier had put into place had dramatically altered the circumstances of the army. Washington himself made the point in a February letter to General Heath. Washington wrote, "I have . . . the satisfaction of seeing the troops better covered, better clothed, and better fed than they have ever been in any former Winter Quarters."

What inspired the petition was not the experience of hardships endured but the dread of new, anticipated miseries. Pay had been promised, again and again, with none forthcoming. Now, with peace in the offing, they feared the prospect of being disbanded and sent home in destitution.

All they wanted was their due, but that took several forms: a final settlement—"liquidation" was the contemporary term—of the various debts owed the soldiers by the government, to be stated in hard dollars and paid at some later date; reparation for past payments made in depreciated funds; compensation for short rations. But the primary request, the one that the delegation from the army made clear had to be granted before they would depart, was an immediate supply of cash to allow the soldiers to leave the army with something in their pockets.

The petition was respectful in tone, but laced with an unmistakable, overt threat. "It would be criminal in the officers to conceal the general dissatisfaction which prevails, and is gaining ground in the army, from the pressure of evils and injuries which, in the course of seven long years, have made their condition in many instances wretched," the memorial warned. "The uneasiness of the soldiers, for want of pay, is great and dangerous; any further experiments on their patience may have fatal effects." Those ill effects were not specified, but the options open to the army were few: if the war continued, they could refuse to continue the fight, leaving the American states exposed and defenseless. And if the war ended, they could refuse to disband, leaving the new republic with a band of ten thousand hungry, mutinous men in its midst.

Either way, the petition put Congress on notice: with the end of the Revolution in sight, the army was angry and restive. The claims of the soldiery could no longer be ignored.

Just as extraordinary as the language of the petition were the signatures beneath it. Atop the list was Henry Knox, the artillery chief who had achieved lasting fame for his expedition early in the war to retrieve British cannon captured in the icebound fortress at Ticonderoga. One of Washington's most trusted generals, Knox could never be accused of rash or unwarranted insubordination. Below Knox appeared thirteen more signers, including the ranking officers of the Massachusetts, Connecticut, New York, New Jersey, and New Hampshire lines. This was no splinter faction, but a united front speaking for the main body of the Continental Army.

Absent from the roster, but fully witting of the delegation and its mission, was the commander in chief. Washington had reviewed the contents of the memorial before it was sent and made "no objection." Instead, he prepared Congress to receive it. Writing his friend, the Virginia delegate Joseph Jones, Washington confirmed that dissatisfaction in the ranks had risen to an "alarming height," and that officers had been planning to resign en masse before agreeing at the last minute to await the outcome of the memorial. Washington was especially disturbed by the "insidious distinction" under which civil officers were paid while the soldiers were not, a point he'd previously raised with Morris.

While McDougall and his delegation were clear in their goals, they and the officers at camp were divided over the means. That is, they were undecided whether to look to Congress for the funds they sought, or to direct their appeal to the individual states. Morris and his assistant gave immediate and emphatic advice. They would oppose any steps by the army to seek revenues from the states "till all prospect of obtaining Continental funds was at an end." In the meantime, Robert and Gouverneur advised, the soldiers should make common cause with the public creditors in demanding that Congress exert authority over the states.

This would lend some steel to the drawn-out debate over the impost. Certainly that was the view held by Gouverneur Morris. In a coded letter he penned New Year's Day, Morris reported to his old friend John Jay on the meeting with the delegation from Newburgh. "The Army have Swords in their Hands," Morris wrote in typically lurid prose. And he expected those weapons to come into play. "I think it probable that much convulsion will ensue," he prophesied. Yet Gouverneur embraced this explosive new development. "I am glad to see things in their present train," he wrote. "It must terminate in giving to Government that power without which Government is just a name."

More harsh than his mentor in views of politics and humanity, Gouverneur offered a commentary that betrayed his thoroughly aristocratic background. "The People are well prepared. Wearied with the War their Acquiescence may be depended on with absolute Certainty," he confided to Jay. "You and I my Friend know by experience that when a few Men of

Sense and Spirit get together and declare that they are the Authority such few as are of a different Opinion may easily be convinced of their mistake by that powerful Argument the Halter. It is however a most melancholy Consideration that a People should require so much experience before they will be wise."

This statement went well beyond anything Robert Morris ever wrote on the operations of democratic politics, but it gives us a window on the tenor of the dialogue at this critical juncture. The approach of peace was just as alarming to the Nationalists in the civil government as it was to the army. Until now, the external threat from England had been the glue that united the disparate states in America. If peace came before the establishment of firm authority in the central government, without in particular the power to tax vested in Congress, the states would drift apart. To the Nationalists, America was at a crossroads—she could be home, like old Europe, to a league of uneasy, sometimes quarrelsome states, or to one single nation, united by ties of mutual interest and their powers combined for mutual defense. For the Financier and for the Congress, the petition from the army brought the struggle to shape America's future to a head.

Congress reviewed the army's incendiary memorial on Monday, January 6, and referred it to a grand committee of one delegate from each state. As their first act, the committee set the following evening for a conference with the Financier. Madison, born amanuensis that he was, took careful notes.

Morris opened the session with a statement, speaking with candor and cautioning the Congress to move carefully. He told the committee emphatically that "it was impossible to make any advance of pay in the present state of finances," and that the army should receive no assurances "until certain funds should be previously established." This was for actuarial reasons, but also for tactical ones; if Congress should appear to be caving in to pressure from the soldiers, Morris said, it would only encourage more extreme demonstrations in the future. He had "taken some measures" to acquire funds for the army—the October expedition to Havana—but he could not disclose them without risking their success.

With that the floor was opened to debate. "Much loose conversation passed on the critical state of things," Madison recorded, as the delegates reviewed the continuing deficit, the failure of the impost, and the potential reaction of the army should its emissaries return to camp empty-handed. It was decided that the grand committee should meet again at the end of the week, this time with the soldiers from Newburgh. Morris was asked to attend.

Morris petitioned Congress the next day, again asking for a secret committee to consider the "alarming" state of his department. In December, he'd lost his favorite domestic stratagem for extending his credit when the bank called in its loans. Without funds, Morris had been forced to sell back to the bank most of the shares held by the government. Soon after, new statements had arrived from Paris showing that Morris was substantially overdrawn on the loan from the French king. Moreover, French ambassador Luzerne had informed him there would be no new loan advanced for 1783.

The new committee was appointed and met with Morris on a cold and snowbound night at the Office of Finance. Morris described his predicament; despite all his efforts to economize, and contrary to his estimates, he was overdrawn in France by 3.5 million livres, about seven hundred thousand dollars.

This disclosure represented a distinct change in direction for the Financier. No longer would he find excuses, as he had in April, to conceal from Congress when Franklin yelped that he could cover no more overdrafts. Now Morris was telling the delegates the whole ugly story, unbidden but in formal channel, with the usual injunctions of secrecy he requested when opening to outside eyes the inner workings of his financial operations.

There was never any doubt that Morris had gone to extremes in support of the nation's credit. He had manipulated markets by careful management of information, floated paper on wishful anticipations of foreign loans, extended by advances and deferred payments the reach of his credit—in short, deployed all his mercantile arts. He had rarely informed Congress of the details, but that was their pass card; during the span of his administration, the delegates had left him to tend to the shambles of their finances in any way he saw fit, with few questions asked. Now he was telling them, and he was demanding that they sign off on his overdrafts. He was no longer willing to do this on his own.

The committee reported back to the full body the next day, and Congress directed Morris to continue writing drafts against their spent French account. Their European ally would have little choice but to pay or to throw their American allies back on the mercy of Britain. When a lone delegate rose to object to such an "unwarrantable and dishonorable presumption on the ability & disposition of France," he was promptly talked down. It was, as Madison recorded, "a mortification which could not be avoided without endangering our very existence." As the delegates fully understood, this desperate policy could easily lead to bankruptcy. "In private conversation" outside the hall, Madison noted, there was "great unhappiness that during negotiations for peace, when an appearance of vigor & resource were so desirable, such a proof of our poverty & imbecility could not be avoided."

These grave concerns set the stage for the meeting between Congress and the delegation from Newburgh. McDougall opened the session by insisting on the "absolute necessity" of an immediate cash payment to the soldiers. He "painted their sufferings & services, their successive hopes and disappointments throughout the whole war, in very high-colored expressions." Only "actual distresses" would have produced such an exceptional appeal, McDougall said, but the troops were compelled by "the seeming approach of peace, and the fear of being still more neglected when the necessity of their services should be over." His fellow officers at the hearing answered questions from the delegates; if no funds were found, "at least a mutiny would ensue," and that "disappointment might throw them into extremities."

Half-pay was an especially contentious point, as two New England states had expressly barred their delegates from approving any military pensions. Here the army delegation came prepared with a compromise. Nothing that half-pay pensions had been "industriously and artfully stigmatized" in some states, McDougall proposed that the pensions be "commuted" to a single, one-time grant. This might be paid later; what was needed now was acknowledgment of the prior commitment, and the separate, immediate grant of a month's pay in cash.

A politician as well as a soldier, McDougall closed with a salute to the idea of the union. "The most intelligent and considerate part of the army were deeply affected at the debility and defects in the federal government, and the unwillingness of the States to cement and invigorate it," McDougall said, adding that "in case of its dissolution, the benefits expected from the Revolution would be greatly impaired." By now it was clear that the emissaries from Newburgh, wielding the threat of a militant soldiery in arms, were squarely on the side of the Nationalists.

Convinced now that something must be done for the army, Congress dispatched Madison, Hamilton, and Rutledge to meet with Morris. Only funds would mollify the soldiers. After "a long conference" at the Finance Office, Morris made his decision: he would issue a month's pay to the army—two hundred fifty thousand dollars—assembled via the usual mélange of bills of exchange, Morris notes, whatever cash he could pull together, and slim hopes for unforeseen relief.

The next day, Morris received word from Nathanael Greene that complicated, but also reinforced, his decision. The British had evacuated Charleston, and Greene had taken it upon himself to issue drafts against Morris for two months' pay to his officers, many of whom he had released from service. The army was already beginning to disband.

On Friday afternoon the Financier closed his eventful week by sending for McDougall and his fellow officers. When they arrived, Morris laid out his terms. He would produce the month's pay they had asked for, though he would dole it out a week at a time, in part to protect the soldiers from blowing the whole amount on a single plunge into commissary rum, and partly to give Morris a bit more time to find the money. As to the other points in the army petition, Morris counseled, "They must have patience and as they wish for Substantial Justice, so they must give time for Wise Measures."

Morris had done his part to defuse the dangerous initiative from a restless army; now it was up to Congress to take some meaningful step to secure reliable revenue. But within the confines of the State House all the pressure seemed to evaporate, dissipated by familiar factions and tired quarrels, every initiative stifled in endless byways of committee, conference, and procedure. For a week debate foundered over proper apportionment of debt between the states, while delegates bickered over land feuds between New York and Vermont, and Pennsylvania and Connecticut. The Nationalists appeared exhausted from months of crisis and disappointment. Eliphalet Dyer, an elder statesman from Connecticut who had served sporadically in Congress since 1774, captured the sense of despair. "We are all aground," Dyer wrote to the patriot preacher William Williams. "What shall be done no one knows."

On the overriding question of the impost, the arrival of a new delegate from Rhode Island did nothing to break the impasse. Writing home to Providence after attending his first session of Congress, Jonathan Arnold expressed unflagging support for David Howell, and sarcastic disdain for the opinion of the other delegates. The impost, he wrote, "was extolled as the infallible, Grand Political Catholicon, by which every evil was to be avoided, and every advantage derived." Arnold was pleased to report that with the vote in Rhode Island, "a Capital & I hope fatal stroke has been given a system which, had it prevailed, would have involved the Country in fresh & unsuspected scenes of distress."

Morris still had hopes for Rhode Island. He wrote Tom Paine, urging him once again to "impress the general utility and necessity" of the impost. By that time, however, Paine had learned the ingrained nature of politics in Rhode Island. His weekly columns in the *Providence Gazette* had focused increasingly on the small clique of merchants that dominated the legislature and reviled any tax, however worthy. This drew withering fire from the local writers, who denigrated Paine as a mercenary, a bankrupt, and a drunk. Home on leave from Congress, David Howell chortled, "Mr. Paine has been handled without mittins— His cause and his character, I think have both rather suffered by his tour this way."

Morris had seen enough stasis, enough stalemate. He had done what he could to deflect the crisis brought on by the delegation from the army; now he ignited a crisis of his own. At the close of business on Friday, January 24, Morris submitted a letter of resignation.

The move was sudden, uncharacteristically impulsive, and stunning to Congress. In a short, terse note announcing his decision, Morris offered two reasons for his startling act. The first was the approach of peace. "As nothing but the public Danger would have induced me to accept my Office, so I was determined to hold it until the Danger was past, or to else meet my Ruin in the common Wreck." With the enemy withdrawn and peace talks under way, "my original Motives have ceased to operate."

Second, he wrote, "My attention to the Public Debts . . . arose from the Conviction that funding them on solid Revenues was the last essential Work of our glorious Revolution." That motive had also lost its power, but for different reasons. "Circumstances," as Morris euphemistically put it, "have postponed the Establishment of public Credit in such a manner that I fear it will never be made. To increase our Debts while the Prospect of paying them diminishes, does not consist with my Ideas of Integrity." This was the heart of the matter. "I should be unworthy of the Confidence reposed in me by my fellow Citizens, if I did not explicitly declare, that I will never be the Minister of Injustice."

That was not all. Morris promised to stay on the job through the end of May, "lest the Public Measures be deranged by any Precipitation." If, during the interim, Congress were able to "make permanent Provision for the public Debts, of every Kind," he would consent to stay on. But that was unlikely. And without those funds, "I must therefore quit a situation which becomes utterly insupportable."

It would be easy, in light of the caveat about permanent funds, to dismiss this provisional resignation as a lobbying ploy, an aggressive gambit by the Financier to jar Congress out of its torpor. Clearly that was part of what Morris had in mind. He was convinced, along with Gouverneur Morris, along with Hamilton and the other Nationalists, that Congress was as much at fault as Rhode Island in allowing a single cantankerous state—"Perverse Sister," Madison called her—to threaten the progress, safety, and possible existence of the larger nation. This was the theory of "implied powers," the idea that the power to incur debt outlined in the Articles of Confederation carried with it an implied power to force the states, by one means or another, to pay for those debts. Here Morris was telling Congress that the game was up: he could no longer conjure up funds and credit unless they took the steps necessary to secure revenue.

But Morris also genuinely believed that his utility to the government was finished. Until now, he felt that his policies and his management might actually right the listing ship that Congress had asked him to command. The defeat of the impost, and the inability of Congress to fashion a meaningful response, put an end to that confidence. "I had no alternative," Morris wrote to Nathanael Greene of his decision to resign. "I saw clearly that while it was asserted on all Hands our Debts ought to be paid, no efficient Measures would be adopted for the Purpose." With his larger plans out of reach, the constant grind of his office—the incessant appeals for funds, the constant resort to expedients—all seemed gratuitous. "I am heartily tired of Financeering," he told another friend in the army that week.

Morris was also concerned with the toll his post was taking on his personal credit. This was a selfish interest, of course, and Morris was the first to proclaim it so. But as he had pointed out repeatedly in different ways throughout his tenure, it was also fundamental to the effectiveness of his administration. It was his personal credit, extended but not yet transferred to the public, that allowed Morris to move ships and cargoes, feed armies, and turn paper advances into hard money. Without funds, the mounting overdrafts now explicitly authorized by Congress would inevitably exhaust both his own credit and the nation's. Considered in that light, to remain in office would not just be pointless, it would be ruinous.

It appears from subsequent correspondence that Morris believed he would indeed retire. Writing to Washington at the end of February, Morris spoke in the past tense of his labors to assist the army, his disappointment at not being able to do more, and his warm feelings for the general. "I hope my successor will be more fortunate than I have been, and that our glorious Revolution may be crowned with those Acts of Justice, without which the greatest human Glory is but the Shadow of a Shade."

Whatever Morris's ultimate intent, his letter "made a deep and solemn impression" when it was delivered to Congress. Madison observed some of the dire implications; it would serve "as a source of fresh hopes to the enemy when known; as ruinous both to domestic and foreign credit; & as producing a vacancy which no one knew how to fill & which no fit man would venture to accept."

Congress had no answer, but the delegates still had their pride. So much, Madison noted, that they "could not, however anxious their wishes or alarming their apprehensions might be, condescend to solicit Mr. Morris" to stay on. The sole response they mustered was to stall: they voted to keep the letter secret.

For the next two weeks, Congress labored under the weight of two insistent ultimatums, the one from the army and the other from Morris. Both were designed to force a new consensus over funding the public debts, yet in the face of mounting pressure, the Nationalist coalition began to divide. The first to defect was John Rutledge.

A skilled lawyer who had spent two years as president of the war-torn state of South Carolina, Rutledge had worked closely with Hamilton and Madison to postpone Pennsylvania's assumption of her share of the federal debt, and to seek new sources of revenue for Congress. But in the week after Morris submitted his resignation, Rutledge split with the other Nationalists to propose a new impost devoted exclusively to funding the army and the debts in Europe—leaving the domestic creditors to plead their cause in the individual states. Rutledge was seconded by Arthur Lee, recently returned from the political wars in Virginia and always eager to slash at Morris and his funding program.

This new combination was opposed by two representatives from Pennsylvania, the merchant Thomas Fitzsimmons and James Wilson, recently returned to the Congress. If the public creditors were abandoned by the central government, Wilson declared, Pennsylvania would divert its share of national funds directly to those creditors. Wilson made his point in graphic terms; his state was willing "to sink or swim according to the common fate, but she would not suffer herself, with a millstone of six million of the Continental debt about her neck to go to the bottom alone."

Madison himself drew out the larger implications of leaving internal debts to the discretion of states. "What then would become of the confederation?" he asked his fellow delegates. "What would be the authority of Congress? What the tie by which the States could be held together?"

1

Robert Morris Senior was a business agent from Liverpool who pioneered the Maryland tobacco trade. He died at age thirty-nine.

2

Robert Morris in 1785. He was a sponsor and benefactor to the portraitist Robert Edge Pine.

3

Downtown Philadelphia: Second Street looking north from Market. The spire of Christ Church dominates the skyline.

4

The view from across the Delaware: Philadelphia was the busiest seaport in North America, a center for New World trade.

Thomas Willing in 1782. The longtime business partner of Robert Morris, "Old Square Toes" was the first president of the Bank of North America and the Bank of the United States. Separated during the Revolution, he addressed Morris as "the man I love most in the world."

Philadelphia friends: Robert Morris's political circle included [clockwise from upper left] John Dickinson, who was an early advocate of American rights but opposed the Declaration of Independence; Thomas Paine, who vilified Morris but then became his chief public advocate; Charles Thomson, an early militant activist who became secretary of Congress and a Morris ally; and Thomas Mifflin, a popular general whose term as governor was marred by rum and corruption.

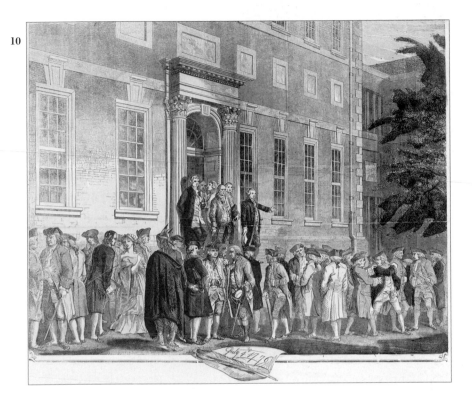

10

11

Philadelphia's patriots gather in the State House yard to hear John Nixon give the Declaration of Independence its first public reading. Robert Morris opposed the measure in Congress, but signed the document two months later. His name appears prominently, just below that of his friend John Hancock.

The Foreign Service: America's revolutionary diplomatic corps included several close friends of Robert Morris, including [clockwise from top] John Jay and Silas Deane, along with Morris's inveterate enemy Arthur Lee.

15

16

17

Friends in France: The French were America's great ally in the Revolution, the source of critical aid and funds for Robert Morris. Pictured here [counterclockwise from top] are Pierre Augustin Caron de Beaumarchais, the flamboyant playwright and arms trader; the diplomat Chevalier Anne-Cesar de la Luzerne; and Jacques Necker, the great financer who became a model for Morris.

The War at Sea: Besides his work in the Office of Finance, Robert Morris was a dominant figure in naval affairs. He sponsored the careers of great fighting sailors like John Paul Jones [top left] and Joshua Barney, and supervised construction of the Continental Navy.

The Office of Finance: The two principals are depicted here in a dual portrait by Charles Willson Peale. Gouverneur Morris [left], the loyal assistant, has a characteristic, mischievous smile on his lips; to his right, the Superintendent assumes his customary posture of command.

22

Haym Salomon was not a regular employee of the office, but performed essential service as a broker of foreign bills.

Financial instruments:
a sampling of the various media of
exchange used by Robert Morris.

Continental currency: These bills
sustained the early part of the war
but then quickly lost value.

Morris note: Signed by the Financier, these instruments provided
an alternate medium of exchange.

Bill on France: One of the bills of
exchange used to finance the debts
of the Revolution.

Bill on Boston: Morris sent this
claim to Boston, to be funded by
the Continental Receiver there.

The Nationalists of 1782. These were Robert Morris's principal allies in the drive to establish a strong central government; each played a prominent role in the Constitutional Convention five years later. Alexander Hamilton (top left) was serving his first term as an elected Representative. James Madison (top right), a born amanuensis, joined Hamilton to push the Morris funding program. James Wilson (bottom left) had a brilliant legal mind. Gouverneur Morris (bottom right) was maimed in a carriage accident but remained a figure of respect and influence.

Powerful Enemies: By his wealth and his policies, Robert Morris offended the early stalwarts of the Revolution, principally Samuel Adams of Massachusetts (top), and Richard Henry Lee of Virginia (right). David Howell of Rhode Island (bottom) led opposition to the impost in Congress.

34

Influencial Friends

Ben Franklin and Robert Morris were thrown together in the early days of the war as strategists in the secret arms trade and soon learned to rely on each other. They collaborated across the Atlantic to manage the French funds that sustained the Revolution and rejoined forces in Philadelphia as delegates to the Constitutional Convention. This portrait was made in 1785, the year of Franklin's return from France.

George Washington counted Robert Morris as his closest friend in government; the Financier supplied the general with the funds and materiel that made possible his greatest victories and hosted him at Philadelphia during the war and after. Morris displayed two busts of Washington in his home.

Robert Morris tended to wear his hair loose and let it grow out as he aged. He is depicted here during his term in the United States Senate, at the height of his influence but dogged by financial problems.

Mary Morris adopted the role of Philadelphia's leading matron, a first lady on the social circuit and friend to Martha Washington. She is shown here wearing lavish regalia in the countryside, probably at her beloved estate, The Hills.

The house on Market Street: Robert Morris moved here at the end of the war, then moved next door to make room for George Washington.

Intended as the grandest private residence in all of Philadelphia, this house cost Robert Morris a fortune and was never finished. It came to be known as "Morris's Folly."

This is a detail from the fresco "Commerce," one of six groups surrounding the central panel, "The Apotheosis of Washington," painted on the ceiling of the rotunda of the U.S. Capitol in 1865. Rendered at the height of the hagiographic period in American historiography, the fresco depicts Robert Morris, quill pen in hand, accepting a bag of gold from Mercury, the Roman god of commerce. Morris would lose his place in the popular pantheon after the turn of the century, when historians began to question the motives of the founders.

Arthur Lee dismissed these misgivings on a point of principle. "He said the States would never agree to those plans which tended to aggrandize Congress," Madison recorded, "that they were jealous of the power of Congress, & that he acknowledged himself to be one of those that thought this jealousy was not an unreasonable one." The fatal flaw lay in the Articles of Confederation; Whig political theory called for a division of powers, but with the central government composed of a single entity, there could be no such division. In Lee's formulation, "No one who had ever opened a page or read a line on the subject of liberty could be insensible to the danger of surrendering the purse into the same hands that held the sword."

With their agenda stymied in Congress, the Nationalists turned back to the army. The memorial from Newburgh had failed to break the deadlock; the army's allies in the government now pressed the soldiers for something more dramatic, more compelling. This was something of a gamble, and possibly a dangerous one. Inciting an insurgent army to assert their grievances could lead to armed strife, even civil war. But to the more ardent Nationalists, convinced that the union hung in the balance, this was a risk worth running.

The most straightforward approach was made by Gouverneur Morris, who believed from the moment McDougall and his delegation arrived in Philadelphia that the army held the key to breaking the impasse between Congress and the states. Eschewing the several intermediaries available, Morris wrote directly to General Knox on February 7. Morris made two points. First, as he had emphasized to McDougall, he warned Knox against any reliance on the states. "During the War they find you useful and after a Peace they will wish to get rid of you," Morris wrote, "and then they will see you starve rather than pay a six-penny tax." Consequently, "the only Wise mode is for the Army to connect themselves with the public creditors of every kind both foreign and domestic and unremittingly to urge the Grant of general permanent Funds" to Congress.

Second, Morris called for action. "The Army may now influence the Legislatures," he wrote. He didn't say how, exactly, and he didn't propose a resort to arms. But he saw how it might end. "If you will permit me a metaphor from your own profession," he offered to Knox, "After you have carried the post the public creditors will garrison it for you."

Gouverneur Morris's dispatch to Newburgh was carried by Colonel John Brooks, one of the officers who came with McDougall to Philadelphia. Brooks also carried with him the first installment of pay for the army—five thousand dollars in cash, a like amount in Morris notes, and three kegs of silver estimated at ten thousand dollars.

It was later revealed that Brooks was more than just a courier. He'd been assigned—by McDougall, presumably—to lend force to Morris's letter by agitating for "some manly, vigorous association with the other public creditors." But instead of fomenting revolt, Brooks divulged the import of his mission to one of his superiors, either Knox or George Washington, or both. "He betray'd it to the Commander in Chief," one militant officer groused.

Just who was involved in this effort to provoke the army has always remained obscure. Besides General McDougall and Gouverneur Morris, Alexander Hamilton appears at least to have been witting, for he wrote Washington in February to suggest that the only means for advancing the claims of the army was to press their appeal with "firmness," and that the general himself might "guide the torrent." Both Hamilton and Gouverneur had strong personal ties to McDougall, forged during their early days in New York.

Where that left Robert Morris is a matter of speculation. Gouverneur was, without a doubt, his closest confidant. And Gouverneur and Hamilton both concerted closely with Morris on the drive to secure revenues for Congress. Yet unlike either of these key lieutenants, none of Robert Morris's papers reflect any overt steps to stir the passions of the army. And of all the various contemporary accounts of this shadowy game only one directly implicated the Financier, and that came thirdhand, when Washington at one point posited that "the Financier is suspected to be at the bottom of this scheme." But the general soon corrected himself. It was Gouverneur he had in mind, Washington explained, when he pointed to the Finance Office.

In the event, these initial provocations were rejected by both Knox and Washington, but each took pains to avow their firm support for the larger goals of the Nationalists. Answering Hamilton, Washington acknowledged that to disband the army without pay would produce "Civil commotions and end in blood." His political views corresponded exactly with those of his former aide. "It is clearly my opinion, unless Congress have powers competent to all general purposes, the distresses we have encountered, the expenses we have incurred, and the blood we have spilt in the course of an Eight years war, will avail us nothing." But Washington deemed it "impolitic" to attempt throwing the weight of the army into the debate in Congress. Personally, he vowed, "I shall pursue the same steady line of conduct which has governed me hitherto."

Knox responded in the same fashion to Gouverneur Morris, assuring him that "your ideas of the general state of our affairs must be just." He confirmed the Nationalist sentiments of the troops, offering that, "It is a favorite toast in the Army, 'A hoop to the barrel' or 'Cement to the union.' " And Knox agreed on the critical point: "America will have fought and bled to little purpose, if the powers of Government shall be insufficient to preserve the peace." His only comment regarding politics was that, "As the present constitution [the Articles of Confederation] is so defective, why do not you great men call the people together, and tell them so. That is, to have a convention of the states to form a better constitution."

This was astute, of course, but obviously impractical. The restive soldiers could not be expected to await such knotty deliberations. As to bringing pressure from the army, Knox said nothing to Morris. But writing to McDougall the same day, Knox emphasized the limits of the army's influence. It "can only exist in one point, and that to be sure is a very sharp point which I hope in God will never be directed than against the Enemies of the liberties of America."

Much took place while these letters were in transit. On February 13, word reached Philadelphia that, during a speech to Parliament, King George mentioned that a preliminary peace treaty had been signed. This produced "great joy" in Congress, Madison recorded, though "the most judicious members" found their delight tempered by recognition of "the impossibility of discharging the arrears and claims of the army." The war for independence might have ended, but the struggle to found a new nation had not.

The following week, several of those "judicious" members—the leading Nationalists—attended a caucus at the home of Thomas Fitzsimmons. Madison and Hamilton were there, along with Richard Peters, former secretary of the Board of War and now a delegate for Pennsylvania. Madison's presence was fortunate, for his careful notes provide us a window on what was a pivotal moment in an escalating crisis.

It was agreed that evening, with only Hamilton dissenting, that it would be "impossible" to secure any Continental taxes besides the impost, which was itself, of course, still out of reach. This was a fundamental concession. As Morris and his foes both agreed, the impost alone was never going to generate all the revenue needed to answer the national debts. If Morris's allies in Congress were ready to abandon their larger goals, then his funding program was dead, and with it the whole project of erecting a competent central government in America.

That same night, probably in response to this painful admission, Hamilton and Peters threw new fuel into the fire. They "informed the company," Madison recorded, "that it was certain that the army had secretly determined not to lay down their arms" without provisions made for their pay. So determined were the soldiers, Hamilton averred, that plans had been laid to depose Washington, who was known to "dislike every unlawful proceeding." This was more ominous than anything McDougall had suggested to Congress.

It's not clear where Hamilton and Peters obtained this remarkable bit of intelligence; it's possible that it was a product of their own ambitious imaginations. Whatever its genesis, the proposition of plots in the army would soon take on a life of its own, leading to a momentous confrontation in the army camp at Newburgh. But that event lay in the future; the ramifications of this late-night caucus would first be felt in the Office of Finance.

Robert Morris learned of the verdict of the caucus—that the Nationalists would abandon any effort to establish federal taxes—the next day, when he was visited by Hamilton, Madison, and Fitzsimmons, now joined by Edward Rutledge. They sat in conference the entire morning, "during which," as Morris recorded in his diary, "I gave my opinion fully." Just what that opinion was can only be surmised, but it appears that Morris was now convinced to follow through with his threat to resign. Two days later, he petitioned Congress to lift the injunction of secrecy covering his letter of resignation. "The Time approaches very fast when I am to quit this office," Morris wrote to the president. Only public disclosure would provide the "due and seasonable Information" which he owed to those doing business with him on public account. In the meantime, Congress should move quickly on finding a replacement.

Congress answered the next day. Perhaps they were distracted; perhaps they were inured by the weeks in which the resignation had been pending, but the delegates agreed to make Morris's resignation public "without dissent or observation." Morris promptly spread the word, sending one copy of his original letter to George Washington, sharing another with John Dickinson, who had recently returned to state politics with his election as governor of Pennsylvania, and providing one to a local printer. The letter of resignation, with its dour forecast for the public credit and the ringing declaration that "I will never be the Minister of Injustice," was published in full on March 1.

News of Morris's resignation traveled far and fast, shaking confidence in the revolutionary government and in Morris himself. Among his friends especially, the threat to step down felt like a betrayal from a man they had come to consider indefatigable. Writing from Virginia to James Madison, Edmund Randolph offered a survey of popular reaction. "The speculations are various on the subject," Randolph reported. "Some impute the step to weariness and fatigue; others to an excess of private business; while others, whose disposition is not cordial towards him, ascribe it to a more disagreeable motive. For my part I conjecture that he must have been led to this measure by disgust, & want of due support. But even my respect for him will not suffer me to acquit him for resigning at this hour."

John Jay was thinking in the same vein when he sat down in July, in Paris, to write a scolding letter to his beleaguered friend. "Your office is neither an easy nor a pleasant one to execute," Jay told Morris, "but it is elevated and important, and therefore envy, with her inseparable companion injustice, will not cease to plague you. Remember, however, that triumphs do not precede victory, and victory is seldom found in the smooth paths of peace and tranquility. Your enemies would be happy to drive you to resign, and in my opinion both your interest and that of your country oppose your gratifying them."

Jay had a point: the high command of a historic revolution was no place to indulge in tantrums. But Morris had a point as well; it's hard to steer a ship when the crew ignores the call of its captain.

Aside from the questions of propriety raised by Randolph and Jay, Morris's resignation highlighted one feature that distinguishes the American Revolution from so many of the revolutions that would follow: its leadership almost uniformly abhorred the positions of power they came to assume. Like Washington and Nathanael Greene, like Jay and Duane in New York and Dickinson in Pennsylvania and even Henry Laurens, Robert Morris entered public life reluctantly, out of a sense of duty, and always considered it a burden. None of these prime actors fought to hold on to power the way their successors did in France, in Russia, in China, or in most of the other tumults that marked the Age of Revolution; each of them—save for Jay, a born jurist—would step down from their positions of responsibility as soon as they felt they were able. This is not to disparage the motivations of any particular, later revolutionists, but to point out one key characteristic of this first, remarkable revolution.

The most immediate result of Morris's public letter was a renewed sense of urgency in Congress. All the frustration of the Nationalists, and all the resentment of their states' rights foes, burst forth on March 4 and consumed two full days of "lengthy & warm debates." Arthur Lee and a fellow Virginia delegate, Theodorick Bland, railed against Morris and his administration, Lee declaring that "the man who had published to all the world such a picture of our national character & finances was unfit to be a Minister." Speaking up in response were Hamilton and James Wilson, who delivered "a copious defense & Panegyric of Mr. Morris." Recording the furor on the floor, James Madison found the rest of the delegates were divided. The letter of resignation was generally held to be "reprehensible," though at the same time, "in general also a conviction prevailed of the personal merit and public importance of Mr. Morris."

Aside from the act of publication, there remained the question of what would follow. Some delegates took comfort in the idea that the resignation was provisional, and even if adhered to, would not take effect for another two months. But, according to Madison, "All impartial members foresaw the most alarming consequences."

These fears prompted one more bid to fashion the plan for "permanent revenues" that Morris had made requisite to his continuing in office. This gave rise to a hodgepodge bill packed with compromises and partial measures that would neither answer the objections of the more intractable states nor secure sufficient funds to support the debt. But it did include one profound innovation—the suggestion, offered by Madison and endorsed in committee, that state moneys spent in the war effort but not sanctioned by Congress be folded into the general, national debt. This was the first proposal for wholesale federal assumption of the state debts, a plan that might remove one of the most difficult obstacles to achieving a true union of the states under Congress.

The whole package was printed and referred to the Financier, but if the idea was to placate Morris, the delegates were sorely disappointed. Feeling liberated by his impending release from office, and confident, perhaps, that he now had the army on his side, Morris answered with a harsh riposte that scored Congress for its timidity and adamantly called them to their duty. He opened with the general assertion, *"Justice requires that the debts be paid,"* underlining the maxim for emphasis. He elaborated: "Each public creditor has a complete Right to demand his whole debt from Congress, and to name the terms on which he will forgo it, and Congress have similar rights with respect to the States on whose behalf they had made themselves the Debtor." This led to another underscored maxim: *"The Right of Congress is perfect and the Duty to pay absolute.* It appears necessary that this power be exerted in the most *decisive Form."*

This was the core of his message; implied powers should be seized and exercised. The states had received requisitions for years, and had largely ignored them. Now, Morris said, they should be given a deadline: pay taxes to fund the debts, or the Congress would impose taxes of its own. "The objections heretofore raised against the impost will by this means be totally done away because each state may at its option either comply with the general plan or pay her particular share of the whole debt."

Morris then went into details. Most of them were familiar elements of his program, but here he included as well Madison's plan of assumption. Those states that had spent the most in the war would gain by credits against their share of the general debt. The sooner accounts were settled, and the sooner reliable revenues established, the lower the interest at which the whole could be funded. "It will not be forgotten," Morris emphasized, "that whether the debt be lesser or greater and whether the interest be higher or lower *the People must pay all.*"

This was, as Morris well knew, far more than Congress would accept. But the Financier was no longer quibbling about what could be done; this was his prescription for what ought to be done. Here was Morris unbound, talking straight finance and ignoring the limits of politics and faction. Besides, the turmoil in the army might change the boundaries of what was possible. That drama was unfolding, five days' ride to the north, at that very moment.

When Congress authorized Morris to release his letter of resignation, he sent it to Washington in care of Walter Stewart, a colonel in the Pennsylvania line recently appointed an inspector for the Northern Army. Playing the same role John Brooks did three weeks before, Stewart carried the Morris resignation, another missive from Gouverneur Morris to Henry Knox, and a letter to Knox from McDougall, this time signed in the code name "Brutus." But where Brooks's loyalties lay with Washington, Stewart was a former aide to Horatio Gates, Washington's longtime rival, who had joined the army at Newburgh in October. And where Brooks had declined to spread fears that Congress would abandon the army—one militant officer denounced him as a "timid wretch"—Stewart proved an able agitator.

Arriving at Newburgh Saturday, March 8, Stewart reported to Washington, delivered the Morris letter to Knox, and then visited Gates at a private house three miles from Washington's headquarters. As Stewart made his rounds, rumors trailed behind him that echoed of the report Hamilton and Peters had made at the evening caucus in Philadelphia—that secret plans had been laid to keep the army together until it was paid, and that the public creditors were looking to the army for help prying funds from Congress. These rumors, coupled with the firm report of Morris's resignation, fomented a spirit of outright rebellion. "We were in a state of tranquility," Washington recorded a week later. Then Stewart arrived, and "A storm very suddenly arose."

On Monday, "while the passions [of the army] were all inflamed," an anonymous address was circulated through the camp. Caustic and eloquent, the broadside recalled the "suffering courage" the army had shown on the battlefield, and raged at the idea they should be sent home penniless, to "starve, and be forgotten!" Instead, the soldiers should retain their weapons and press their claims. "Change the milk-and-water style of your last memorial; assume a bolder tone," the address advised. Tell Congress "that in any political event, the army has its alternative. If peace, that nothing shall separate them from your arms but death; if war . . . you will retire to some unsettled country, smile in your turn, and 'mock when fear cometh on.' "

This was the infamous "Newburgh Address," a call for an armed uprising against the civil government. A second, terse announcement was circulated the same day, calling an unauthorized meeting of general and field officers the next day to consider the latest report from McDougall on the proceedings in Congress. The author of both documents, it later appeared, was John Armstrong, an aide to Gates. Knox and Washington had both shied off the efforts from Philadelphia to rile the army but Gates had opted for sedition.

Alarmed that his army might be "plunging themselves into a gulph of Civil horror," Washington moved swiftly to intervene. He issued orders barring any "disorderly proceedings" and rescheduled the meeting to five days later. Gates would sit as chairman, and Washington asked for a report, giving the obvious impression that he would not attend. The new date fell, as it happened, on the Ides of March.

That morning the officers convened in an atmosphere "exquisitely critical" at an auditorium raised in camp during the winter. Armstrong was on hand, as were Knox and the rest of the top command. When Gates mounted the stage and prepared to open the meeting, Washington appeared and asked his surprised subordinate if he might address the meeting. He then turned to deliver a stern and passionate statement.

Washington first attacked Armstrong's "anonymous production." It was "unmilitary," he said, "subversive of all order and discipline." And what did it propose? "The blackest design. . . . This dreadful alternative of either deserting our country, or turning our arms against it." Washington recoiled at the prospect. "My God! what can this writer have in view. . . . Can he be a friend to the army? Can he be a friend to this country? Rather is he not an insidious foe?"

Congress was slow, Washington acknowledged, but it would come around. "That their endeavors to discover and establish funds have been unwearied, and will not cease till they have succeeded, I have no doubt," he said. Until then, the officers should reject any scheme that would "overturn the liberties of our country" and "deluge our rising empire in blood."

Washington paused. He looked out to the assembly and the officers stared back, inscrutable. He had a letter, from congressman Joseph Jones, which might testify to the good intentions of Congress. Pulling it from his pocket he unfolded it, squinted, and then reached for his spectacles. "Gentlemen, you will permit me," he said. "I have not only grown grey but almost blind in the service of my country."

This simple gesture broke the spell. Emotion swept the room, a few of the battle-hardened officers breaking into tears. Gates and his allies were speechless. Washington had recovered the allegiance of his troops, and the threat of an insurgency on the Hudson was over.

With the emergency behind him, Washington sought to run down the source of the near-mutiny. "There is something very mysterious in this business," he wrote to Hamilton in March. Two weeks later he was more precise. "Some men in this army are beginning to entertain suspicions that Congress, or some Members of it," were using the soldiers "as mere puppets to establish Continental funds." This was more than reckless, Washington warned: "The Army is a dangerous instrument to play with." It was here that Washington posited, "The Financier is suspected to be at the bottom of this scheme."

The general would later shift this pointed accusation from Robert Morris to Gouverneur Morris, but in the meantime, Hamilton answered Washington by describing in broad strokes the politics of the moment. "There are two classes of men Sir in Congress of very different views—one attached to state, the other to Continental politics. The last have been strenuous advocates for funding the public debt upon solid securities; the former have given every opposition in their power, and have only been dragged into the measures now being adopted by the clamors of the army and other public creditors."

Here Hamilton entered into his opposition to giving the army precedence over the other public creditors, a position he knew Washington held firmly. Part of the reason was tactical: funds for "partial purposes" would be blocked in states whose citizens had large holdings in public debt—Pennsylvania in particular. "It is in vain to tell men who have parted with a large part of their property that the services of the army are entitled to a preference," Hamilton wrote. But there was a larger issue at play. "The question was not merely how to do justice to the army creditors but how to restore public credit." That required funding all the debt, not just the debt to the army.

This brought Hamilton to an admission of sorts. "In this situation what was to be done? It was essential to our cause that vigorous efforts should be made to restore public credit—it was necessary to combine all the motives to this end. . . . The necessity and discontents of the army presented themselves as a powerful engine." Just how far Hamilton had gone to incite those discontents, he did not say. Instead, he turned to a detailed defense of the Financier.

"As to Mr. Morris, I will give Your Excellency a true explanation of his conduct. He had for some time been pressing Congress to endeavor to obtain funds, and had found a great backwardness in the business." Hamilton reprised the slow taxes, stalled loans, and incessant demands for funds. "He found himself in short reduced to this alternative either of making engagements which he could not fulfill or declaring his resignation in case funds were not established by a given time. Had he followed the first course the bubble must soon have burst—he must have sacrificed his credit & his character; and public credit already in a ruinous condition would have lost its last support. He wisely judged it better to resign; this might increase the embarrassments of the moment, but the necessity of the case it was to be hoped would produce the proper measures."

Morris's resignation might have been taken "wisely" but his decision to make it public was "ill-advised," Hamilton ruled. "This was an imprudent step and has given a handle to his personal enemies," helping to raise "a cry against him." There was more at stake here than policy. "The truth is the old leaven of Deane & Lee is at this day working against Mr. Morris. He happened in that dispute to have been on the side of Deane & certain men can never forgive him.

"But Mr. Morris certainly deserves a great deal from his country. I believe no man in this country but himself could have kept the money machine a-going."

Once again, Hamilton returned to the charge that some in Philadelphia were playing the army for puppets. And once again, he offered justification, not denial. "The men against whom the suspicions you mention must be directed are in general the most sensible, the most liberal, the most independent and the most respectable characters in our body as well as the most unequivocal friends to the army. In a word, they are men who think continentally."

Washington tarried awhile before asking Robert Morris directly what role he played in the plots at Newburgh. When he did, in May, Morris responded in the same mode as Hamilton. "By some designing men my resignation from office . . . was represented as a factious desire to raise civil Commotions," Morris wrote Washington. "It was said that the Army were to be employed as the Instruments to promote flagitious Interested Views. These insinuations found Admittance to Minds which should forever have been shut against them." This was the closest Morris came to a denial.

Instead he made a facetious reference to his efforts to secure funds for the troops. "The factious designing Man who was to have lighted up the flames of Mutiny and Sedition"—that is, Morris himself—"has undertaken a most arduous and perilous Business to save this Country from those Convulsions which her Negligence had hazarded." Morris was growing bitter.

The opposition he encountered in Congress was one source of resentment, but what really dismayed Morris was the steady beating he was taking in the public prints. And he could not escape the fact that, in large part, he had brought it on himself.

The trigger, as Hamilton had noted to Washington, was Morris's decision to publish his resignation. This had opened the door to his enemies—in particular, to Arthur Lee. Through most of his tenure as Financier, Morris had enjoyed easy treatment in the press and broad public support. Now he would taste the calumny Benjamin Franklin had predicted when Morris accepted his office.

A polemicist who had honed his skills trading printed barbs with the royalist factions in London, Lee in March launched a series of scathing attacks on the Financier. The name Lee chose to write under was "Lucius," likely a reference to Lucius Junius Brutus, who ended the rule of kings and founded the republic in Rome. The sobriquet spoke both to Lee's conception of himself, and of Morris.

Addressing his columns to Morris by name, Lee opened his campaign by disparaging the decision to broadcast in his letter of resignation the precarious state of American credit. "If what you say be true, could you not think of divulging it, without reflecting with horror on the consequences of it to your country? If it be not true, as I am convinced it is not, what can atone for such an abuse of that confidence which has been reposed in you?" Either way, Lee wrote, Morris had done damage to the very credit he sought to preserve. "In what light, then, do you place that public, which you pretend it was your object to save from danger? Without character, without credit, without justice, without resource—is it possible, sir, that you could lay us more prostrate?"

Lee's next installment played on the same theme, but with more art. " 'I Have done the deed!' you may cry out like Macbeth, and with equal horror—'I have murdered the public credit as she slept—I have murdered her, being my guest!' To your guardianship, sir, she was committed. Where is she now? Does she exist? Has not your announcement to the public . . . stab'd her to the heart?"

Now Lee introduced a new wrinkle, proposing that Morris's pursuit of funds to support the debt was rooted not in the public interest, but in his own holdings of Loan Office Certificates. Morris purchased these early on, as we have seen, in a bid to support the failing Continental currency, but Lee would brook no such caveats. "Perhaps it will be found that all this boast of honesty and patriotism is prompted solely by the interest you and your friends have in these certificates, not as *original subscribers*, but as purchasers from the *distressed possessors*, at an *immense depreciation.*"

The column was salted with mordant humor, but there was no levity in Lee's closing line. "Whether folly, or faction, or private interest, or public enmity, were the real motives of your publication, the act itself is so replete with mischief that it ought to destroy you forever in the opinion of a discerning people."

As was the mode in the Philadelphia press, these columns begat others, some defending Morris, some joining in the attack. Following his own practice, Morris remained mute, convinced that Congress was the only audience to which he had to answer. "Writers for a News Paper may indeed through the medium of Misrepresentation pervert the Public Opinion," Morris wrote to Congress, "but the official Conduct of your Servants is not amenable to that Tribunal." But this outward silence only seemed to incite Lee; he baited Morris to answer him, goading him, goring him.

"Will you condescend from your high state, so elevated above the simple citizens who were once your peers—will you deign to cease a moment from the luxurious enjoyment of that enormous power and that wealth, with which a war, that has afflicted the virtuous citizens of these United States with poverty and distress, has filled your overflowing coffers, will you deign, sir, to inform us, what possible good consequences could flow from your publication?"

Lee now left the specifics of Morris's resignation—all these fulminations referred to that single, five-hundred-word document—to declaim on its tone. "Your letter contains little else, but insolent ostentation of your own importance. You produce yourself as the Atlas on which the United States entirely rest. . . . Is then the mere superintendance of our finances, with an assistant and a legion of clerks, at ten paces from your family, so mighty a sacrifice of time—is daily rioting in Asiatic luxury at festive boards, so fatal to domestic bliss?" Lee scoffed at all the frustrations and toil that had attended Morris's term as Financier. "In fine, sir, is not the disbursement of eight millions annually in contracts, is not the profit and influence arising from this, is not the hourly offerings of incense and adulation from surrounding parasites, is not the pushing your superlative abilities and merits by pensioned dependents through all the states, sufficient to satiate your vanity, pride and avarice?"

The columns continued, evolving into a running commentary on Morris, his program, and his tenure in office. When word arrived from Newburgh that Washington had defused an uprising, Lucius returned in high dudgeon. "What a pity it is that the tempest, so labored to be excited there, has not risen; that we might have seen you ride the tempest, and direct the storm." Here Lee offered the cynic's view of Morris's resignation: it was designed and timed to throw the army "into the most desperate and dangerous commotions. How it could escape your sagacity, that your publication was pregnant with this most destructive consequence, is not to be conceived."

By late April the Lucius columns were beginning to lose their shock value, but Lee felt compelled to deliver one last salvo scoring Congress for sponsoring Morris in the first place. In the process, Lee indulged in a little pride of place. Born to high station in the Virginia gentry, he'd taken degrees in medicine and law during his long sojourn in London. Now in his adopted role as spokesman for the "simple citizens" of a virtuous republic, Lee sneered at Morris as a parochial rustic, unfitted for the national stage. "I confess myself to be one of those who always doubted your talents for the department you occupy; notwithstanding the splendid promises of your friends. That you were a good accountant, and an adventurous merchant, I had no doubt; but from whence, in your confined sphere of education and action, you could have drawn that liberal, vast, and extensive knowledge of the interests of nations, and the most approved systems of taxation, of the various sources of revenue, and the productive powers of the state, all which, together with a mature and able judgment, are necessary to constitute a capable financier; was to me utterly incomprehensible."

Through all of this barrage Morris maintained his stony public silence, but it is clear Lee succeeded in vexing his target. Morris complained in his diary when the first column appeared of a "virulent attack on my Public and private Character . . . replete with the most infamous Falsehoods . . . and insinuations as base and infamous as Envy and Malice could suggest." Morris put his hopes in the idea that Lee's reputation for distemper might blunt the influence of his censures. "I think I know the author and if my Conjecture is right, he is of that baneful Character which brings dishonor to those whom he means to befriend and the reverse to those whom he opposes." But this was wishful thinking. Lee had already proven, in the case of Silas Deane, that insinuation and unfounded attacks could destroy the career and reputation of even the most earnest public servant.

With the Lucius columns, Lee succeeded where Tom Paine had failed, establishing an indelible caricature of Morris in the public mind. At the outset of the war, Morris had enjoyed universal support for his work on the Committee of Safety and in the early Congress. During the battles over the state constitution that support had fractured, but Morris remained a figure of substance, his counsel valued, his financial acumen unquestioned, a force to be reckoned with in the public lists. From now forward, the very underpinnings of Morris's success—his wealth and his worldly financial vision—would identify him as an object of suspicion and sometimes derision.

While the blasts from Lucius reverberated through the streets and coffee houses of Philadelphia, inside the Office of Finance Morris struggled to meet the claims of the army. The notes and coin that he'd sent to camp with Colonel Brooks in January were just an initial deposit. Ever since, he had been working to produce the balance of that quarter-million-dollar commitment. This evolved into complex and continuing negotiations in Philadelphia, with Secretary of War Lincoln and Paymaster General John Pierce, with Pierce's deputy in New York, with George Washington, also in New York, with Continental tax receivers there and in Boston, and with the contractors and their suppliers.

The trick was to turn the Morris notes and the bills on France into cash without glutting the thin market in the region near the army encampment. "There are certainly not Merchants, not moneyed men enough in this Wild Country, to negotiate so many Bills," Pierce's deputy reported in February. "For the Regimental Paymasters to have to hazard obtaining the avails from Philadelphia is an unwieldy business." One plan, to sell the bills on the Boston market through William Duer's partner Daniel Parker, was vetoed by Morris as too expensive. Then in March, with notes still unfunded and the troops "quite out of patience," Washington stepped in, striking a different deal with Parker. The contractor would fund the notes on the spot in New York, partly in cash and partly in kind, offering clothing and other supplies— but not liquor—to the troops for their long journey home. Parker would then send the Morris notes to Philadelphia to be redeemed at the bank.

This agreement gave Parker an unsettling degree of leverage over the soldiers, but after the performance of Comfort Sands, Parker proved a capable and reliable replacement. Writing to Morris, Washington described Parker as "a Gentleman of amiable manners and dispositions . . . a Man of great integrity and capacity in business." Parker later traveled to Philadelphia to work out the details with Morris in person.

Morris had to make separate arrangements—and separate payments— to cover smaller bodies of troops in Pennsylvania and elsewhere. The timely arrival in March of a ship bearing $120,000 in coin from France, and of Captain John Barry, who fought his way through British patrols to deliver $75,000 from Havana, helped to keep the payments to the army in motion.

But every success Morris had in making these payments only whetted the appetite of the army. In April, with the drama of Newburgh behind him, Washington informed Congress that it was now "universally expected," and "absolutely indispensable" that, in addition to the one-month grant, the soldiers receive three months' pay before they head home. "To be disbanded at last," Washington wrote, "without this little pittance, like a set of beggars, Needy, distressed and without prospect, will not only blast the expectations of their Creditors . . . but will drive every man of Honor and Sensibility to the extremest Horrors of Despair." The advance would total seven hundred fifty thousand dollars.

Congress forwarded this new request to the Financier. This confronted Morris with an excruciating dilemma. He was weeks away from his announced retirement, his funding plan had been abandoned by Congress, and "Lucius" was hounding him in full throat. He had answered Washington's pleas in the darkest hours of the Revolution, at Trenton and again at Yorktown; what would be his answer now?

The first response was unequivocal. There was no money in the treasury, Morris explained in a letter to Congress, and the states offered "but little Hope." The only available option was another issue of paper, Morris wrote, "and it is essential to the Success of it that my Credit should be staked for the Redemption." Here Morris betrayed the pain he was feeling at the snide treatment he was getting in the press. "Do not suppose Gentlemen that this Declaration is dictated by Vanity. It becomes my Duty to mention the Truth."

He had weighed the question carefully, Morris said, and had decided it was simply too much to take on. The long-term notes he would have to issue would put him on the hook for half a million dollars when he left office—a staggering sum, easily exceeding Morris's available funds—and leave it to his successor to find the money to pay him back. "I am willing to risk as much for this country as any man in America but it cannot be expected that I would put myself in so desperate a situation." It was simply beyond his means. "Though I would sacrifice much of my property yet I cannot risk my Reputation as a Man of Integrity nor expose myself to absolute Ruin."

This letter bore a distinct tone of finality, and when Congress sent a committee to plead for reconsideration, Morris was adamant. "I wish for Nothing so much as to be relieved from this cursed Scene of Drudgery and Vexation," he told the delegates. But the pressure continued—more committees, and a visit by Daniel Parker, sent by Washington to propose new terms of payment. Morris began to waver.

Finally on Saturday, May 3, Hamilton, James Wilson, and Thomas Fitzsimmons called on Morris at his office. These were his closest allies in Congress, the men who had rallied to his side and who looked to him as their leader. Morris found them "so extremely Anxious" that he could not turn them away. After all the opprobrium he had endured, these entreaties were gratifying; Morris was also painfully aware of the straits of the army, and the need for his personal management of the notes he'd already issued. All things considered, Morris seemed to have little choice.

He decided that morning, against his inclination, to issue the three months' pay. The notes would be redeemable in six months and rest on his personal credit; he would remain in office long enough to fulfill this new commitment. That afternoon Morris wrapped up his current business "as fast as possible," closed the office for the weekend, and headed out to the country. A long gallop on a spirited horse might help clear his mind.

The following Monday, Morris moved quickly to issue the new round of notes. He ordered up fifteen thousand sheets of paper and drafted Benjamin Dudley, the engraver retained for the mint, to work up copper plates that would stamp the paper with "National Debt" in watermark, a measure to stave off counterfeiters. The paper was delivered on June 6, and for the next week, stealing time from the other duties of his office, Morris inscribed his signature on six thousand individual notes in denominations from $5 to $100.

That had to be a most loathsome chore. After all his efforts to erect a foundation for an efficient and durable system of national finance, the fortunes of the new nation had withered to this. Late into the night, Morris sat at his desk, scratching his quill over the printed notes, each one drawing his personal fortune deeper into jeopardy, each one promising to extend even further his tenure in an office that had become a personal purgatory.

— Chapter 15 —

FINAL SETTLEMENTS

T here is no single date that marks the end of the American Revolution. The last great battle against the British took place at Yorktown in 1781, but hostilities continued through April 1783, and formal articles of peace were not signed and exchanged until May 1784. In between, for those who lived through eight years of epic and often dubious struggle, the end came in different ways, at different times. Few had expected the war to last so long, and many doubted to the end that the British monarch would actually release his grip on the lands and people he claimed as his birthright. "We have many reports for and against Peace," Robert Morris wrote in February, "which occasions many people to doubt if the blessing is so near at hand as others persuade themselves it is."

For Morris, the moment of recognition—that the war was over, that independence was assured—probably came on March 24, 1783. Morris was hosting friends at his town house for a Sunday afternoon dinner when a sea captain strode up to announce news from the waterfront: a mail ship had arrived from Cádiz, Spain, bearing word that preliminary articles for peace had been signed January 20 in Paris. The same ship carried dispatches from France recalling her warships.

John Carter, partner with Jeremiah Wadsworth in some of the major army contracts, was among the company on hand. Hearing the news, he left immediately to share the report with John Chaloner, his factor in Philadelphia. Having done this duty, Chaloner related in a letter to Wadsworth, Carter immediately "returned to Morris' to Get Drunk." The toasts must have lasted well into the night.

After his head cleared the next morning, Morris recorded in his diary his "infinite Pleasure" at the news. But for all the speculation and all the anticipation, the end of the fighting only added to the confusion that beset the government. "We are now in the ecstasy of anticipation," Morris wrote in April, "but peace has, so to speak, so abruptly pounced on us that we find ourselves thrown into a state of disorder."

George Washington had his moment of recognition on April 17, when an express rider trotted into the army camp on the Hudson with a copy of a proclamation from Congress suspending all hostilities against Britain. As with so many others, the news caught Washington by surprise and unprepared. In the four weeks since the climax of the Newburgh affair, the general had been negotiating with Morris and several committees of Congress to obtain firm commitments for pay and terms to allow an orderly discharge of his fighting men. He wanted all back accounts settled, and four months' pay in hand, before disbanding the army. Those talks were still under way; Morris had agreed to seek the funds, but nothing had been finalized.

The sudden onset of peace threatened all those arrangements. Most of the men under Washington's command had enlisted "for the war"; if the fighting was over, there was nothing to hold them in camp, nothing to restrain them from "Acts of excess."

Washington's first instinct was to withhold the proclamation from his troops. He gathered his generals to propose this measure, but they dismissed the plan as "impractical as well as impolitic." The soldiers would have to be told.

The announcement was scheduled for noon on Saturday, April 19. The soldiers and officers on duty were called to the parade ground, where a field officer read the proclamation from Congress, and an extra ration of rum was passed around. But there was no word of discharge, no time set for the men to return home.

For the next several weeks Washington implored Congress and Morris to set terms for demobilization. The first answer came from Congress: hold the army together until a definitive treaty was ratified and all accounts settled. Morris spoke next: Congress and Washington must choose between keeping the army in camp and sending them off with pay. They could not have both. With foreign funds exhausted the only resource was revenue from the states, and while some states had at last begun making payments to the treasury—$260,000 for the first quarter of the year—the revenue could not keep pace with expenses. "If your army is kept together they will consume as much in one month as taxes will produce in two and probably much more," Morris explained in May. "Unless they are disbanded immediately the means of paying them even in paper will be gone."

This report forced Congress to alter its plans. On May 26, the delegates approved a halfway measure: the army would officially remain intact, but the troops would be released on "furlough" pending recall and a final settlement. The order was sent to camp in custody of Secretary of War Benjamin Lincoln, along with a letter from Morris to Washington promising his best efforts to raise three months' pay.

By the time Lincoln reached camp a week later, the army was already fragmenting. Many soldiers had departed, trading IOUs written against the pay they'd been promised for high-priced supplies at the commissary. Speculators drifted into camp to buy up promissory notes at steep discounts. Those troops still on hand grumbled darkly that officers were conspiring to profit off these ad hoc transactions. Riots broke out in the barracks, and Washington maintained order only by having instigators punished at the whipping post.

The calm that followed was unstable and uncertain. "They are more quiet, but not the less dangerous," one veteran general reported to Washington. "I should not be surprised if some secret machinations of the soldiery bursts upon us like a Clap of Thunder."

Upon Lincoln's arrival, Washington felt he could no longer hold his men in camp. He issued orders granting voluntary furloughs, while assuring his officers that warrants for three months' pay were on the way. At the same time, Washington sent an express rider to Philadelphia to collect whatever funds Morris could produce. "Pray do not delay him for a single instant," the general implored the Financier.

Morris answered two days later. The notes were still with the printer. "I am to sign them and as fast as that can be done they shall be sent forward . . . you will be the best judge whether to detain the troops a little while longer or not." Morris worked frantically, but time was against him. The first batch—one hundred thousand dollars—was delivered to the paymaster June 7, but it took another week before it arrived at Newburgh.

For most of the soldiers the Morris notes got there too late. Fed up with delays, beset with rumors, and distrusting any commitments made by Congress, the troops opted for the furloughs and marched out of camp "starved, ragged and meager," "without a shilling to assist themselves . . . many of them having several hundred miles to go in this very distressed situation." Despite all the efforts of Washington and Morris, the Continental Army, whose trials included the wretched winters of Valley Forge and Morristown, would end as it had fought, in destitution and neglect.

. . .

Dismay over furloughs without pay reached Philadelphia June 12, carried by disgruntled troops from Maryland as they made their way home. The soldiers of the Pennsylvania Line barracked in Philadelphia, a corps of about three hundred men, immediately determined to reject the terms proffered at the main army camp. They issued a sharply worded manifesto to Congress: they would not accept the furloughs, and they would not disband until they had received their pay.

Events moved rapidly. On June 16, Colonel Richard Butler announced the furloughs at the army post in Lancaster, and got the same defiant response. The next morning, a column of eighty soldiers set out from there to join their brethren in the Philadelphia barracks. They would "obtain Justice" by demanding their pay in full or, better yet, raid the Bank of North America and take their arrears in cash.

Officials in the civil government scrambled to devise a response. John Dickinson, Robert Morris's onetime political mentor and now the governor of Pennsylvania, stopped by the Office of Finance to ask advice. Morris advocated a hard line: call up the local militia to face down the rebels from Lancaster. That same morning, Congress appointed a committee headed by Alexander Hamilton to manage the crisis. Hamilton sent the assistant secretary of war to turn the troops back, but his orders were ignored. This was open mutiny.

In the afternoon, Hamilton and his committee sat down at the State House with Dickinson and the Supreme Executive Council. Like Morris, Hamilton believed the insurgent soldiers should be "checked with energy and punished severely," and advocated calling out the militia. But the state council balked. The troops on the road had yet to commit any violence, they reasoned, and their claims were supported by most of the populace. Besides, if the militia were called they might not answer. Better to invoke "the language of invitation, and good humor . . . than any immediate execution of authority."

The soldiers from Lancaster arrived in town the next morning, marching to fife and drum, bayonets glinting under a bright sun. They paraded to the army barracks, heartened by the applause of citizens in the streets. Rumors swirled in their wake: the soldiers were taking direction from the Constitutionalist faction in Philadelphia, or from the Nationalists in Congress; they were "ready to strike a desperate blow." The consternation at Newburgh, quelled in dramatic fashion by Washington in March, now settled over the capital.

As the rebel ranks swelled, the government fell into confusion. An assistant paymaster announced that soldiers who refused their furloughs would forfeit their pay. This was countermanded by Robert Morris. All soldiers would receive their notes, but—at the suggestion of Colonel Butler—those from Lancaster must first return to their base. The soldiers only scoffed.

That night, Hamilton and Gouverneur Morris visited the barracks to assure the insurgent troops that they would receive all the pay Congress had promised them. This embassy quieted the resentments of some soldiers, but the leaders of the mutiny were busy that night as well, and produced a new strategy. Congress had no funds, the pledge of the Financier's assistant notwithstanding; they should bypass Congress altogether and press their demands on the state Supreme Executive Council, scheduled to meet at the State House the next day.

Early Saturday John Dickinson stopped by the Office of Finance for another conference with Robert Morris. With him was an officer from the barracks, who reported continuing unrest, and more threats against the bank. After Dickinson departed for the council meeting, Morris sent for bank president Thomas Willing, "and informed him of the dangerous Temper of the soldiery."

Nearby, on the second floor of the State House, the Executive Council had just convened when it was interrupted by the arrival of thirty soldiers, marching in formation, who drew up outside the front door. A note was delivered: the council had twenty minutes to enter negotiations, "or otherwise we shall let in those injured soldiers upon you." The council, continuing its policy of stasis, ignored the ultimatum. While they conferred, another 250 soldiers arrived

Jarred at the spectacle of a mutinous body of federal troops arrayed outside the Pennsylvania State House—"an armed banditti," Hamilton called them—the Congress decided it had to respond. No formal session was scheduled, but President Elias Boudinot issued an emergency call and delegates soon began to arrive. They found a raucous atmosphere outside, soldiers milling about in brilliant sunshine, quaffing liquor served up by local taverns, a growing crowd of bystanders cheering them on. The rebels had sentries posted at the doors, but the delegates entered the hall unimpeded.

There was not much they could do. Too few delegates responded to form a quorum of Congress, while upstairs the state council continued to resist any effort to raise the militia. The lawmakers tarried for several hours, peering out the windows to find the soldiers below jeering and taunting them. The members of Congress departed that afternoon without incident, and after the state council agreed to a later parley, the soldiers returned to their barracks.

Robert Morris did not stick around for this placid denouement. The bank was a target; he might be one as well. The march of a throng of mutinous soldiers, unopposed, down the center of Market Street, felt too much like the early hours of the Fort Wilson Riot. When the soldiers approached the State House, Morris hurried home, collected his family, and took them to the house of a friend outside the city.

With Mary and the children at a safe remove, Morris returned to town. Boudinot had called Congress together again that evening, this time acquiring a quorum. The delegates were dismayed by the conduct of the soldiers, but angrier still that the state council had failed to act in their defense. Two resolutions were approved that night; one ordering Washington to send troops to put down the mutiny, and another proposing that, should the council continue to ignore "the dignity of the Federal Government," the Congress would leave Philadelphia altogether. Morris ended his long day by consulting with Boudinot and then stopping for one last conference with Dickinson, where he "strongly urged the calling out of the Militia to quell the riot."

Dickinson and the council vacillated for the next two days. Their stance was dictated by circumstance—militia officers confirmed that if called, their men would not answer—but also by politics. Dickinson, timorous in the best of times, had been elected in a tough contest and was leery of raising the ire of the Constitutionalist opposition. His hesitation may also have revealed something of his core character. He had been an early advocate for American rights but had balked at signing the Declaration of Independence. And he'd been among the first to call for a union of the colonies; now, when the national government asked for the protection of his state, Dickinson faltered again.

Dickinson's indecision put Hamilton and the other Nationalists in a quandary. They wanted to stay in Philadelphia—as the metropolis of the new nation, it was the logical seat for the central government—but they considered Pennsylvania's management of the crisis an insult that could not be ignored. "The conduct of the executive of this state was to the last degree weak & disgusting," Hamilton fumed later.

With Congress officially in recess, the Office of Finance became a clearinghouse for news, rumor, and decision. The French ambassador, the secretary of Congress, bank cashier Tench Francis, Hamilton, and the members of the Pennsylvania delegation all came by to trade gossip and consult with

Morris. The public demonstrations were over, but according to Madison, "the Barracks were in constant vibration," and a flash of violence appeared imminent. "In this state of things what can Congress do?" wondered a North Carolina delegate. "Without the means of paying those debts constitutionally contracted for the safety of the United States, responsible for every thing, and unable to do any thing, hated by the public creditors, insulted by the soldiery and unsupported by the citizens?" Beset and indignant, the delegates arrived at the fateful decision to remove from the wartime capital.

Toward the end of Tuesday, June 24, President Boudinot stopped by Morris's house to inform him that Congress would depart immediately. Morris returned to his office that night and briefed his chief clerk, Samuel Lyon, on the state of affairs. Lyon was to "keep constantly in the office during my absence," guarding the state papers and fending off any sallies by the rebellious soldiers. No public business should be conducted until further orders. Morris then ordered an armed guard posted at the bank, joined with Gouverneur Morris, and headed out on the road to Trenton.

Riding north in the cool of a starlit night, the two friends had a chance to reflect on this extraordinary turn of events. Twice before in its short history, the Congress had been forced to flee Philadelphia, each time under threat of an invading army. This time peace was at hand, the enemy sequestered in its last redoubt on Manhattan. The threat now came from within, posed by angry soldiers and the indifference of the state that had been its home. This was certainly not the launch of the "rising empire" the Financier and his assistant had so long envisioned.

The departure of Congress took the air out of the Philadelphia mutiny. Dickinson held conferences with the rebel soldiers, but before any resolve was struck, two ringleaders fled, slipping aboard a ship for passage to Europe. Most of the mutineers surrendered the next day. Force was not a factor—Dickinson did finally call on the militia but, as he'd predicted, only a handful responded.

The tempest had subsided, but the chaotic breakup of the Continental Army caused continuing problems for Robert Morris. As the ultimate authority in disbursing pay to the troops, Morris caught blame and resentment for the furloughs and the delays in getting his notes to paymaster. Worse, many soldiers suspected Morris had delayed those payments in order to profit by their distress.

There were at least two versions of this story. One held that Morris secretly funded a broker to buy up the discharge notes of the soldiers at steep discounts, thereby securing thirty thousand dollars in profits for the government. Another version proposed that Morris was in league with the army contractors, and by holding back the soldiers' pay forced them to accept inflated prices at the commissaries. Still another rumor held that Morris was speculating in his own notes. This was probably rooted in the continuing efforts by his office to maintain the value of Morris notes by purchasing them on the open market.

Morris answered these hazy allegations as they arose. In June he was able to invoke the findings of the oversight committee charged with examining the Office of Finance. This committee, now chaired by Thomas Fitzsimmons, found that "the order and economy which has been introduced since the establishment of this office has been attended with great savings of public money." Release of the report prompted a public letter by Benjamin Rush proclaiming that "Mr. R. Morris has lately triumphed over all enemies," but the letter, printed in newspapers from Connecticut to South Carolina, was easily discounted as just another partisan salvo.

In July, Morris addressed the governors regarding "a Slanderous Report that I have Speculated on this very paper which I urge the redemption of"—the Morris notes. "Most solemnly I declare," Morris wrote, "that I have never been concerned, directly or indirectly in any such speculation. If there be a Man in the World who knows any Instance to disprove what I say let him step forth with an Accusation." Here Morris was attempting a feat that has eluded public figures in every age—to disprove a negative. His avowals may have heartened his friends, but they made scant impression on his enemies. And in the summer and fall of 1783, those enemies were ascendant.

Since his appointment as Financier two years before, Morris had personified the ideals of a strong central government and a firm union of the states. The defeat of the impost had thrown that project in doubt, and as the advocates of state sovereignty gained the initiative in Congress, they trained their sights on Morris. Arthur Lee, once a lonely contrarian, now enjoyed the support of several key allies—Theodorick Bland of Virginia, Howell of Rhode Island, and Stephen Higginson, a cantankerous new delegate from Massachusetts. At the same time, some who had aligned themselves with Morris early on, like John Rutledge and Samuel Osgood, now began backing away from the Nationalist program.

The new alignment of delegates became more pronounced after Congress left Philadelphia. Robert and Gouverneur Morris were among the first to arrive at Princeton, the provisional capital, but finding few delegates in town, returned to Trenton for the weekend. They were back in Princeton on Monday, June 26, to find Congress comprised of a bare seven states. Anxious now to return home, Morris advised President Boudinot that "the Public Service may be materially injured unless I should speedily return to Philadelphia." With the president's assent, Morris left that afternoon.

The departure of the Financier completed the severance of Congress from its longtime base. "I conceive great hopes that things will take a different turn in Congress now it is removed from the unhealthy and dangerous atmosphere of Philadelphia," David Howell exulted. Arthur Lee was thinking the same way. "Robert Morris' undue and wicked influence . . . has manifestly diminished since the removal from Philadelphia, & the fixing of Congress in any other place will I hope restrain it within due bounds." Lee had his wish; determined to avoid Philadelphia, but divided on where to make its new home, Congress agreed to become itinerant, moving between Princeton, Annapolis, Trenton, and finally New York.

Alexander Hamilton bucked the new mood in Congress for three weeks before deciding his time was being wasted. The centerpiece of his efforts was a draft resolution calling for a convention that would revise the Articles of Confederation and invest the national legislature with powers to levy taxes and establish a peacetime army. It was Hamilton's last bid to persuade government to reform itself. When the plan was ignored, Hamilton quit the Congress and returned to New York.

It was a good time to leave. With Hamilton gone and Morris in Philadelphia, Arthur Lee and his allies embarked on a concerted campaign to drive Morris from office. Harking back to the Silas Deane affair, Lee launched a new investigation into the contracts of the Secret Committee, and a separate inquiry into why clothing shipped from Europe failed to reach the troops for whom it was sent. By September, Madison reported to Thomas Jefferson, "The department of finance is an object of almost daily attack."

It got to the point where virtually every issue to come before the delegates became grist for a partisan skirmish. In one ugly display, the delegates spent a full day in heated debate over pensions for three foreign seamen who lost limbs in fighting under the command of John Paul Jones. The stipends would have won routine approval had their petition not been submitted by Morris as agent of marine. "This recommendation was sufficient to excite the opposition of those whose malice seems so inveterate that they would risk their salvation to ruin the man," Charles Thomson wrote his wife in disgust. Higginson and Bland led the opposition, but in the end "the grant was made, and the poor fellows prevented from starving in our streets."

Stephen Higginson might object to the hues in Thomson's portrait, but there was no disputing the motives ascribed to him. "Things seem to be working right; the great man and his agents are very uneasy," Higginson wrote in August, using his favorite sarcastic moniker for Morris. "The members [of Congress] act with much more independence than they ever did or will do in Philadelphia," he wrote. "I have great hope that we shall yet catch him on the hop, and perhaps get rid of him." Like Lee, Higginson saw Morris as formidable, and diabolical. With the ouster of the Financier, "we should stand a much fairer chance of having our Government settled on right principles. . . . The spider's web is so nearly finished, so many of our members have got entangled in it, and so artful are the maneuvers made use of to draw others into it, that I see no way of getting rid of the danger, of shaking off the fetters, but that of destroying him who has the management and placed it at his will."

Higginson appears to have misread Morris's reaction to Congress' move to Princeton. Morris thought it was mistaken, but there is little indication that he was "uneasy." He was, after all, looking forward to leaving his office, not fighting to hang on. Upon his return to Philadelphia, finding that no official observances had been arranged to celebrate Independence Day, he hastily called together forty of his friends—government officials, foreign diplomats, fellow merchants—"and spent the afternoon and evening in great festivity and mirth."

When Lee brought his charges, Morris answered each in formal detail, though not without a touch of umbrage. On the activities of the Secret Committee, he enclosed a copy of his contracts with Deane, and then invoked the stance he'd adopted from the outset of the dispute, stiffly asserting that, "the Superintendent of Finance has no *Official* Knowledge of the private concerns of Mr. Robert Morris." Likewise with the clothing shipments: in concluding a detailed report to Congress, Morris advised that "the frequent applications from Congress, from their committee, and from individual Members" for past accounts and statements had so burdened the comptroller that the official books were now several months out of date. "As there is no man either in Congress or out of it who can suppose that have the least Desire to withhold information," Morris wrote, "I feel myself perfectly at ease in laying this matter before Congress."

Lee was, predictably, galled. "The superintendent has answered, that he does not know what has been purchased, & that he thought it was more proper to sell the clothing than distribute it to the soldiers," Lee reported to James Warren, the Massachusetts patriot and confidant of Sam Adams's. This much was true—as Morris explained in his report, no clothing had been ordered under his administration, what arrived from prior orders had come without invoices, and all the supporting documents remained in Europe. Moreover, most of the shipments that came in landed after the peace accords; the troops were already marching home.

All of this Lee ignored, and instead reprised for Warren his original conception of the case: "In laying out the public money Commissions accrue to [Morris's] friends, in selling the things so purchased, new commissions arise to the sellers. . . . Thus while fallacious reports on this man's conduct are published in all the papers"—a reference, presumably, to the commendations of the oversight committee—"the public money is lavished away, the Soldiery, defrauded & the public plundered." It was clear that Morris would never satisfy Arthur Lee.

The rounds of accusation and enmity raining down from Princeton only confirmed Morris in his plans to leave the Office of Finance. For his first two years in office he'd been engaged in formulating the broad fiscal program that would lay a foundation for economic growth and international stature as the new nation stepped onto the global stage. With the onset of peace and the defeat of his program, Morris turned his attention to the private pursuits that he'd reluctantly set aside. Unlike his earlier exploits with the Secret Committee, however, Morris was careful to keep this new round of business endeavors separate from his activities in the government.

He began exploring new opportunities in March, soon after Congress agreed to make public his plans to resign. Grander and more ambitious than any of the projects he'd undertaken in the past, they reflected his growth and evolution over two years at the head of the American government.

The first concrete commitment Morris entered into, and one that forecast the most important of his future engagements, was made with John Vaughan, a wealthy British entrepreneur who traveled to Philadelphia in 1782 to invest family funds in American lands. At Morris's instigation Vaughan returned to Britain in March 1783 to solicit up to four hundred thousand dollars from European investors to purchase land in America. The agreement was signed March 20 between Vaughan, Morris, and Gouverneur Morris, who would segue easily from the Financier's assistant to his partner and agent in the years to come.

The funds were to be borrowed at 5 percent interest with the principal coming due in ten years. Vaughan held a half-interest in the venture, with the Morrises claiming a quarter-share each. The lands would be bought in New York, New Jersey, Pennsylvania, Delaware, or Maryland—not Virginia, where local authorities and prominent families like the Lees had been disputing the claims of out-of-state speculators for generations.

Upon arriving in England, Vaughan won the enthusiastic endorsement of his father and brothers, but found the capital markets in England and Holland already exhausted from financing the belligerent armies of Europe. Numerous objections were raised—the term was too long, the interest too low, and the landed security too distant. "But the real truth of the matter seemed to be," Vaughan reported from London, "that the rich were rich enough, and also old and distrustful; the young would have been sanguine but too poor." Vaughan added that he kept all his inquiries confidential, "least we should make the credit of the parties stale, as well as blow the scheme."

This was much the same reception Silas Deane had received in France when he pitched a land scheme backed by James Wilson. But Morris was convinced that the end of the war would bring a rush of immigration from Europe, and that American lands would prove a bonanza for anyone in position to reap the spoils. From this conviction Morris sought in November to revive the scheme. "A very considerable treasure" had just been landed in Spain; with the powers of Europe "now in perfect peace," the infusion of hard coin might loosen up the capital markets. By then, however, Vaughan's ardor for investing abroad had cooled.

A more romantic commercial adventure, more visionary yet ultimately more practicable, presented itself in the person of John Ledyard, a hawk-nosed seaman and adventurer who had sailed with Captain James Cook on his last trip around the globe. At home in Connecticut in 1783, Ledyard conceived of a trading voyage to China. Unlike the conventional route taken by most Europeans, Ledyard would take a westward route, sailing around Tierra del Fuego and into the Pacific, stopping in the wilds of northern California to acquire furs that might be traded for tea, silks, and other exotic goods across the sea.

Ledyard sought backers in New England and New York but all shied away from his extravagant scheme. In June, discouraged and nearly broke, Ledyard tried his pitch in Philadelphia. He shared his story with anyone who would listen, on the waterfront and in the taverns in town, and eventually found his way to the Office of Finance.

Ledyard was not the first to propose a trip to China. With America now free of the British Rules of Trade, several prominent members of Morris's mercantile circle had considered challenging the monopoly position of the East India Company by staging independent ventures of their own. The leader here was John Holker, the French enterpriser and military contractor. Holker had been casting about for partners in a China venture for two years, but at this point Morris was keeping Holker at arm's length. "Holker is full of schemes," Morris wrote to a mutual friend in the fall of 1782. "I cannot pass much time with him or enter into his Plans and Views."

But this plan of Ledyard's struck a chord with Morris. It was bold and unexpected—to sail west instead of east, to open the markets of the Pacific Northwest, as well as those of the Orient. And it could not have come at a better time. With peace on the horizon, both Britain and France had closed their Caribbean colonies to American trade, drastic measures designed to shore up their mercantile economies. American merchants desperately needed new outlets for their ships and their capital.

Morris invited the young sailor to come back a second time, and then asked him to commit his plans to paper, with the route, ship specifications, and a detailed budget. Ledyard was elated. "Ye beneficent!" he wrote to a cousin in July. "What a noble hold [Morris] instantaneously took of the Enterprise!"

Ledyard was scheduled for one more meeting with Morris the following day, and would then head for New England to round up a crew. By then Gouverneur had been introduced to the circle; he and Morris were both convinced that "Yanky Sailors" should man the ship. "Tomorrow is a day big with the fate of Josephus and America," Ledyard enthused ("Josephus" was the pen name Ledyard used with his cousin). "I take the Lead of the greatest Commercial Enterprize ever embarked on in this country."

Of course, it was not so simple as Ledyard might hope. Morris would provide seed money for the venture, but he could not stage such a novel and risky project on his own. Capital would be tied up for a year or more, awaiting very speculative returns. He needed partners, he needed a cargo, and he needed a ship.

The partners he found close at hand. The first to sign up was Daniel Parker, the army contractor so warmly recommended by George Washington. Parker had funds, ambition, and avid interest. He was, as well, an active, hustling enterpriser, constantly on the move, always alert to new investors and opportunities. He dealth with all comers—in New York, after securing the contract for the American army at West Point, he had opened talks with the British at New York to supply their forces as well.

Parker joined the China venture soon after Morris's meetings with Ledyard. In turn, he brought in William Duer, his partner in the army contracts. Parker was to be the active manager of the enterprise; Duer would sail as the "supercargo" to manage the trading on the Pacific coast and in the Far East. At first, Parker and Morris were each to put up a third of the capital, and Parker would offer the final one-third interest to investors in Boston. By July, the plans were snowballing. There would be multiple ventures—as many as six ships setting out for China—with some sailing west, and some east.

Parker set about buying vessels in July. This was tricky business as the government was just then offering ships for sale under the auspices of Morris as the agent of marine. This put Morris in a most sensitive position, a conflict of interest he sought to finesse with only partial success.

The Continental Navy was a source of real disillusionment to Morris. In July 1782, when he still had the confidence of Congress and was looking to the future, Morris had proposed a major strategic shift toward naval as opposed to land forces. The first fleet of American frigates had been largely shattered in encounters with the enemy, but two substantial vessels remained. Two more, the seventy-four-gun *America* and the twenty-eight-gun *Bourbon*, were under construction at shipyards in New England, but work on both was stalled for lack of funds. Morris outlined a new program that would build six ships a year, a force that would relieve the pressure on the army, occupy the British fleet, and help free American commerce from the shackles of the blockade.

This was one case where Congress exercised more fiscal caution than Morris. The delegates slashed his proposed navy budget by 90 percent, and the small size of the loan advanced by France rendered any further debate on the question moot. In the months to come Morris had to accept the idea that reducing costs took priority over keeping a naval force afloat.

One major savings was achieved in August, when a seventy-four-gun French ship, the *Magnifique*, struck a rock and sank in Boston harbor. Congress, at Morris's behest, offered the still unfinished *America* as a replacement. This came as a huge disappointment to John Paul Jones, who'd been named to command the new ship, but it was a chance to both trim expenses and curry favor with their principal ally, an opportunity too good for Congress to pass up.

By May, already having announced his plans to resign as Financier, Morris asked Congress to relieve him of duty as agent of the marine. When that request was ignored, Morris formally abandoned his quest to develop naval power under the Confederation. "Until revenues can be obtained," Morris wrote to Congress in July, "it is but vain to talk of Navy or Army or anything else. Every good American must wish to see the United States possessed of a powerful fleet but perhaps the best way to obtain one is to make no effort for the purpose till the People are taught by their Feelings to call for and require it. They will now give Money for Nothing."

With that, Morris recommend the sale of the frigates *Hague*, being out-fitted at Boston, and *Bourbon*, recently launched but still awaiting rigging, crew, and cargo. The *Hague*, Morris noted, was sluggish under sail and would likely sell at a low price, but considering the costs involved in getting her ready for sea, "we should gain by giving her away."

As soon as he received authorization from Congress, Morris noti-fied his marine agents in New England to place advertisements solicit-ing bids for both ships. Thomas Russell, the agent at Boston, expected a poor sale there, and suggested sending the ship to Philadelphia for auc-tion. Morris declined for practical and political reasons. "She will sell for but little at either place," he wrote to Russell. Besides, such a maneuver would only excite suspicion. His critics believed he was constantly seek-ing to give advantage to his friends in Philadelphia, Morris wrote, "and of Consequence every thing which may serve as a Scaffolding to raise Objec-tions must be avoided." He advised Russell to give wide notice of the sale, and to ensure a minimum price by offering the first bid himself, on public account.

As the date of the auctions approached, Morris had second thoughts on this strategy as it applied to the *Bourbon*. Concerned that public purchase "would doubtless be converted to an ample source of Calumny," he ordered his Connecticut agent to get the best price possible, but to refrain from bid-ding himself. This left the door open to Daniel Parker, partner with Morris in the China venture. Two weeks before the auction Parker reported to one of his partners—not Morris—that he believed the *Bourbon* could be ob-tained for a "*very small*" sum.

When the sales took place in September, both ships went to Morris's associates. Russell's opening low bid took the *Hague*, and Parker obtained the *Bourbon* for eight thousand dollars. In the weeks that followed, Con-gress declined to accept Russell's purchase on public account, and Russell became the owner. Morris confirmed the terms in October, telling Russell,

"Your purchase has been fair, your offer is disinterested, Congress ordered the ship to be sold, you have bought her, she is yours." Soon after, Russell joined forces with Parker in the China venture and proposed the *Hague* for one of the voyages.

As Morris anticipated, and despite ample public notice of the auctions, Morris's critics pounced on the transactions as evidence of collusion. The principal accuser was Stephen Higginson, then sitting as chairman of the oversight committee for the navy. "I find that the most scandalous conduct has been practiced in the Marine Department," Higginson wrote from Boston to Arthur Lee. The ships had sold for less than half their book value, the sales not amounting to the cost of repairs and upkeep. "The reason for this is very plain, when we attend to the Terms of Sale, and the Persons who purchased them. Mr. Morris' agents purchased both of these ships. . . . This conduct is so extraordinary as to require a particular explanation."

Higginson reported his suspicions to Benjamin Hawkins, a fellow delegate on the navy committee, and asked him to conduct an inquiry. But Hawkins was sympathetic to Morris and the Nationalists, and no action was taken by the committee or in Congress.

It's hard to form any conclusions about the propriety of the ship sales from this exchange. There's no question that, as Higginson was so keenly aware, the vessels were taken by men involved with Morris on both public and private account. But Morris engaged his partners and contractors for the very reason that they were active and successful entrepreneurs; it comes as little surprise that they should put up the winning bids. To Morris's mind, the sales were the best result the government could hope for. Once he learned the outcome, Morris made a point of applauding Russell for his "Manly and disinterested Conduct" in the purchase of the *Hague*.

In any event, contrary to Higginson's suspicions, Morris never acquired direct interest in either the *Hague* or the *Bourbon*, and neither vessel found its way to China. By November, financial and other issues forced the partners to scale back their plans. William Duer was firmly opposed to the Pacific route and had declined to sail on such "a dangerous Experiment in Navigation." Still, the project remained alive, the hopes of the partnership resting on a speedy new vessel Parker purchased at a Boston shipyard. Morris, as was his wont, took a large view of the venture. "I am sending some Ships to China," he advised John Jay in November, "in order to encourage the adventurous pursuits of Commerce and I wish to see a foundation laid for an American Navy."

• • •

As he was ramping up his private commercial concerns, Morris worked to close down his government operations and settle his public accounts. He was what we would call today a lame-duck president—the chief of the executive branch whose legislature had rejected his initiatives, and who had decided not to seek a second term. The date of his departure had not been set, but it would come as soon as Morris could fulfill his obligations. The greatest of these, the millstone that would anchor him in office for another full year, was the three months' pay to the army.

As we have seen, the notes Morris issued did not reach the main army cantonments in time for delivery to the departing troops. Instead, Morris put his notes in the hands of John Pierce, army paymaster, who distributed them through officers in the soldiers' home states. Pierce also took on the business of "settling" accounts—determining what each soldier was owed—and issued roughly eleven million dollars in government notes as payment. The difference was that these were undated promissory notes to be funded, like the loan office certificates, at some unstated future date. The Morris notes were due in six months, secured by his personal bond, and payable in cash.

With this obligation hanging over him, Morris was compelled to engage in the most protracted and precarious financial maneuvers of his tenure as Financier. They taxed his personal connections, his bankers in Philadelphia and in Europe, and the wits and resources of the American ambassadors abroad.

There was little question the funds to back the Morris notes would ultimately have to come from Europe. But how much was available, and how much Morris could devote to redeeming his notes, was always in doubt. Part of the uncertainty rested on the structure of the loans from Holland. Instead of a lump sum like the loans from the French king, the Dutch raised funds by a "subscription," an offering from bankers in Amsterdam that had to be sold to individual investors who bought shares priced at a thousand florins apiece. The loans "filled" over time, with the sales influenced by the progress of the war, news of peace, and the varying prospects that Americans would actually pay off the obligations as they came due.

On the American side, Morris accessed the proceeds of the Dutch loan as he did with the French, by selling bills of exchange that drew against his bankers in Europe. He could extend the time before such notes came due by drawing the bills against third parties—merchants or bankers elsewhere in Europe—who would then pass the drafts on to the principal bankers handling the loans. These "circuitous negotiations" might be extended further by the terms specified in the bills; they would be paid thirty days after presentation to the corresponding merchants or banks, or ninety days, or more.

By the summer of 1783, Morris was already overdrawn on the loans from France, and much of the funds from the first Dutch loan, the one guaranteed by the French court two years before, were being used to cover that overdraft. His sole resource, then, was the loan for five million florins—about two million dollars—that John Adams had secured in 1782. Adams and Franklin used this fund to defray the prior French loans, the army contracts negotiated by Morris, old bills dating from before Morris took office, and their own expenses. By July, the initial proceeds of the Dutch loan had been exhausted. From that point on, Morris was banking on funds that had yet to be raised.

In doing so, Morris indulged in a bit of wishful thinking, an attitude he was diligent in sharing with the bankers handling the American loan. In May he proposed that peace would prove a boon to American commerce and thus her credit, and that the makeshift funding plan approved by Congress—which he had vigorously denounced—might "establish American credit with you." In July, after learning from Amsterdam that the loan was filling slowly, Morris continued to voice optimism. As he had with John Vaughan, Morris suggested that peace in Europe would spur new interest from investors. And while he conceded that the revenue plan in Congress had not yet attained the requisite "solidity," he proposed that "there is a Basis of national Wealth which like a new and rich Mine must yield profusely to the first well-directed Efforts of Taxation."

In fact, at this point, with demands from the army mounting and tax receipts from the states continuing to lag, Morris was becoming desperate. "Being in great distress for want of money," Morris consulted with Gouverneur Morris and Haym Salomon, "considering ways and means but as yet unsuccessfully." Salomon, at least, had some promising information; in anticipation of peace, the merchants of Philadelphia were placing large orders for imports, leading to heavy demand for bills on Holland. With the price as high as it had been for years, Morris decided to forge ahead, selling drafts on Holland far in advance of the current loan subscription.

These maneuvers were threatened in October by a proposal in Congress to end all drafts against loans from Europe. This bid to economize was supported by some Nationalists, but others recognized it as "one more rascally attempt" to "break" the Financier. Morris managed to turn this internal threat aside, but did not await the event, moving in the meantime to make his deepest plunge yet into the market for foreign funds.

On October 21, Morris called to his office three of his closest commercial associates—John Ross, Peter Whitesides, and Isaac Hazlehurst, all current or past partners in business—and made them a proposition. They would each put up notes of $100,000, payable in 120 days. In return, Morris provided each with drafts on Holland of 250,000 florins, payable 150 days after presentation to the bankers in Amsterdam. That these sales were done as a favor to the Financier is indicated by the unusually long terms involved, and by the additional provision, requested by Morris, that the buyers would exact no penalties if the notes were rejected by the Dutch bankers.

Morris did not expect his friends to risk any more than he did himself. A day before the conference, pressed by officers of the bank to clear a long-standing loan to the government of one hundred thousand dollars, Morris put up one hundred thousand of his own funds against the Dutch loan, and deposited his note for that sum in the bank to clear the government debt. Thomas Willing, president of the bank and Morris's longtime partner, supervised the transaction.

Morris kept the notes from Ross, Whitesides, and Hazlehurst in hand until December, when large quantities of his notes to the army came due. Now he brought them into play, depositing them in the bank as security for cash advances which he then used to pay the obligations to the army. In the meantime, Morris resumed his old practice of sending cargoes of tobacco to Europe on public account, the proceeds in this case to be applied to the Dutch loan. The shipments were not enough to substantially reduce the balance, but helped build confidence in Morris's commitment to repay the loan.

By stretching, pulling, and teasing every asset he could reach, Morris had found the money, but it remained for the diplomats in Europe to cover his bills on Holland and salvage his thin-stretched credit. By November, even before the Dutch bankers learned of Morris's final drafts of a million florins, they had written to Franklin seeking French funds to cover the previous overdraft. John Adams, working with Franklin in Paris to hammer out the final details of the peace treaty with the British, feared nothing less than a "catastrophe to American credit."

Franklin now engaged in the same game at which Morris was so adept, shifting termed debts to avoid the final reckoning. Finding "Money in general extremely scarce," Franklin met with the French banker Ferdinand Grand. He agreed, as Franklin explained to Morris, to "lend his credit in the way of Drawing and Redrawing between Holland and Paris, to gain Time till you could furnish funds." But there were no funds to furnish, just further extensions before the claims fell due, which Morris obtained from Hazlehurst, Whitesides, and John Ross.

It fell to John Adams, already weary from years of isolation and negotiation in the capitals of Europe, to cajole one last loan that would cover Morris's drafts. When word arrived from Holland that "an immense flock of new bills had arrived," Adams set out once more for Amsterdam, his coach drawn by a team of six horses over the frozen flatlands that lay between. Meeting with the Dutch bankers, Adams learned that they were reluctant to return the bills drafted against them unpaid, but that investors were no longer interested in the 5 percent American loan. Adams and the bankers together petitioned the Amsterdam Town Council to take up the outstanding balance; when that appeal was rejected, the bankers proposed a new loan of two million florins at a new rate of 7 percent. Adams reluctantly agreed, and the bankers opened the new loan for subscription in March. Adams reported the news to Congress with an almost audible sigh of relief: "With a great deal of difficulty and at a dear rate I have at last obtained money to save Mr. Morris' bills."

Adams later boasted to Arthur Lee that he had been the sole support for Morris in the closing years of his administration. That was true to some degree, but it was also true that Franklin and the French bankers played instrumental roles. And it was true as well that Morris's own measures—the stream of letters he sent the Dutch bankers assuring them of his fidelity, and the long terms he arranged with his creditors—supplied the confidence and the flexibility necessary to keep his drafts afloat.

As much as Adams and Franklin were put to extremes to support Morris in his high-wire measures to answer the demands of his office, neither ever protested the Financier's methods or disparaged his performance. They shared his views of Congress, and deplored as much as Morris did the laggard response of the states to calls for taxation. Morris took great satisfaction when Adams wrote him in May 1783, "I wish I were in Congress, that I might assist you in persuading our Countrymen to pay taxes and build ships." Adams amplified on that sentiment in July: "Creditors at home and abroad, the Army, the Navy, every man who has a well founded Claim upon the Public, has an unalienable Right to be satisfied"—that is, paid—"and this by the fundamental Principles of Society." Like Morris, Adams rejected the talk in Congress of partial payments, or discounting loans made early in the war. "To talk of a sponge to wipe out this Debt, or of reducing or diminishing it below its real value in a country so abundantly able to pay to the last farthing, would betray a total ignorance of the first Principles of national Duty and Interest."

Ben Franklin took an even harder line. He wrote Morris in December to report himself "hurt and afflicted by the difficulty some of your late bills met with in Holland." But he directed his umbrage at the citizens of America. "The Remissness of our People in paying Taxes is highly blameable, the Unwillingness to pay them is still more so. I see in some resolutions of Town Meetings, a Remonstrance against giving Congress a power to take, as they call it, *the People's Money* out of their Pockets. . . . They seem to miss the Point. Money justly due from the People is their Creditors' Money, and no longer the Money of the People who, if they withhold it, should be compelled to pay it by some law."

Civilization, Franklin wrote, conferred benefits that also carried obligations. "All Property, indeed, except the Savage's temporary cabin, his bow, his matchcoat, and other little Acquisitions . . . seems to me to be the Creature of public Convention. Hence the Public has the right of Regulating Descents and all other Conveyances of Property." All "superfluous" property, he insisted, "is the Property of the Public, who by their Laws have created it, and who may therefore by other Laws dispose of it, whenever the Public welfare shall demand. . . . He that does not like civil Society on these Terms, let him retire and live among the Savages."

Franklin was a philosopher, inclined to reduce matters of state to fixed principles. Morris was more the pragmatist, but in this case, their different approaches led to the same conclusion—personal liberty was a worthy ideal, but that it could not take precedence over the responsibilities and the obligations of citizenship.

In May 1784, Morris learned to his great relief that the second Dutch loan had issued. He promptly asked Congress for his release, but at this point, the Congress was itself on the verge of utter breakdown. With the Nationalists and their program defeated, the delegates who remained were more concerned with restricting the powers of the central government than with operating it. It took a month for the delegates to compose an answer for Morris; when they did, it was to propose appointing a three-member board to administer finance, a reversion to the old format the preceded the Office of Finance. They asked Morris to stay on until the committee was formed.

The next day Congress adjourned for the summer, leaving its business to the management of a Committee of the States, a sort of shadow legislature with sharply proscribed powers. The committee did not achieve a quorum of nine states until July, then immediately adjourned. Efforts to revive the "phantom" committee, as the French consul glumly termed it, ended in failure. With the Nationalists in eclipse, the Congress was rapidly disintegrating.

Against this backdrop, Morris wound down his administration. His diary, for years the log of frantic and momentous activity, now slipped into doldrums—"Nothing material this day," Morris wrote on July 10. The lassitude stretched on for months. "Sundry applications of little consequence," read an entry in August.

With no pressing business, Morris turned to a project he had long anticipated—a statement of the accounts of his administration. Here he was following in the mode of Jacques Necker, the French financier, who broke the obscurantist tradition of previous royal ministers by publishing his accounts for all to see. Morris was thinking as well of the cloud of suspicion that still trailed him from his days on the Secret Committee. This comprehensive financial statement would be a preemptive strike against critics present and future, offering a close review of his endeavors from the beginning of his term to his final day in office. Morris submitted this final statement to the Congress, but had the document printed, bound, and addressed to his "Fellow Citizens" with the inscription, "The master should know what the servant has done. To the Citizens of the United States of America, therefore, the following pages are most humbly submitted."

The statement comprised a five-thousand-word preamble and actuarial tables that fill two hundred printed pages, an enormous undertaking that detailed his revenues, his expenditures, the shortfalls, and the loans that helped him get by. All of the exhortations to the states had not been without effect—by the end of his term, Morris raised more than three quarters of a million dollars from the states, the largest share coming by his own hand, from Pennsylvania. This did not amount to a tenth of the budgeted requisitions, but by limiting expenditures and close management of assets, Morris was able to close his accounts with a balance of $21,986 in the treasury.

Perhaps even more satisfying to Morris was an advertisement he published in October, while awaiting the return of Congress. Printed under the dry heading "Note Respecting the Redemption of Robert Morris' Notes," the announcement assured anyone holding his paper that he would soon be leaving office, but "he hereby pledges himself personally" to pay the amounts in full. This was one paper issue that would hold its value to the end.

Throughout this period of retrenchment, the debate continued over Morris's tenure and his service. Arthur Lee maintained his customary snarl. Unless the Financier was quickly run out of office, Lee wrote in May, "he and his immoral Assistant have malignity enough to endeavor to ruin where they can no longer plunder." But the prospect of Morris's departure was sobering even to some of his critics. In February, answering Stephen Higginson, who wanted Morris removed at any cost, Samuel Osgood offered a measured defense of the Financier.

"I will tell you very freely," Osgood wrote Higginson, "that in mere Money Transactions, he has saved the United States a very large sum. . . . I am also of Opinion that much more Regularity has been introduced in Keeping the Accounts than ever before existed. This is a Matter in my Mind of very great importance. And without the strictest attention to it, the several states ought not to trust Congress with a single Farthing of their Money."

Osgood's dispute with the Financier was political, not practical. "I lay it down as a good general Maxim, that when a person is to be attacked, it is wise not to endeavor to depreciate his real Merit. . . . If you suppose that [Morris] has rendered the Public no valuable services, I acknowledge there is a very considerable Difference in our Sentiments. If you suppose that he may have rendered valuable Services, but that his Notions of Government, of Finance & of Commerce, are incompatible with Liberty, then we shall not differ. I think therefore the Fort to be raised against him ought to stand on this Ground."

Morris formally resigned his commission in November. It was accepted by Richard Henry Lee, the new president of Congress, named in November to preside over just the sort of insipid central government that he had so long championed. Eight years later, looking back almost wistfully on Morris's tenure, James Madison attached no caveats to his assessment of the Financier. Morris, he told a friend, had "with five million dollars carried on the War to more effect, paid & clothed a large army & rendered more services than his predecessors in office had done for four times the amount."

Morris was out of office, but he toiled another five months in completing his final "Statement of Accounts." He considered it his magnum opus, and submitted five hundred copies to Congress in March 1785. Morris no longer had any formal role in the government, but he took the occasion to point out once more the means by which the new nation might shoulder the debt that was the legacy of eight years of war.

"No treason has operated, or can operate, so great an injury to America, as must follow from a loss of reputation. The payment of debts may indeed be expensive, but it is infinitely more expensive to withhold payment. The former is an expense of money, when money may be commanded to defray it; but the latter involves the destruction of that source from which money can be derived when all other sources fail. That source, abundant, nay almost inexhaustible, is public credit."

Funding that debt would not only preserve the ability to borrow, Morris emphasized, but would put the debt itself to work. "A due provision for the public debts would at once convert those debts into a real medium of commerce. The possessors of those certificates, would then become the possessors of money." And that money would provide the seed capital to set the American economy into motion.

Having declaimed from his area of expertise, Morris could not resist a brief excursion into politics. America had won its liberty from Britain; now it must preserve it. "The inhabitant of a little hamlet, may feel pride in the sense of separate independence," Morris wrote. "But if there be not one government which can draw forth and direct the combined forces of united America, our independence is but a name, our freedom a shadow, our dignity a dream."

PART III

THE NEW REPUBLIC

— *Chapter 16* —

THE GREAT
BANK DEBATE

O n a sunny Saturday afternoon on the first day of May 1784, a large
group of men gathered on a grassy lawn overlooking the placid waters of the Schuylkill River. They included some of the more prominent citizens of Philadelphia, but they had painted their faces and wore
rawhide and loincloths, the garb of the Delaware Indians. These were the
Sons of Saint Tammany, one of the more colorful of the town's many social
clubs, this one founded in 1772 as a patriotic and benevolent society and
named after King Tammend, the Delaware chief who granted William Penn
much of the land on which the city was raised.

In hindsight the club looks like a sort of precursor to the Bohemian Grove,
a venue for well-heeled city folk to get in touch with the occult spirits of the
American wilds. May Day was the date for their annual feast, a boisterous carnival of ritual drinking and antic dance performed around a ceremo-
nial fire. This particular year, with peace declared and the British departed,
three of the thirteen official toasts were raised to George Washington.

Toward evening word circulated around the "council fire" that Washington was in town, there to preside over the first meeting of the Cincinnati, an
honorary society organized by veteran soldiers upon the dissolution of the
Continental Army. As had become his custom when visiting Philadelphia,
Washington was staying at the home of Robert Morris.

Loath to let the party end, the Sons of Saint Tammany decided instead to
pay homage to their hero. They set out on the road into town, musicians at
their head—fife, fiddle, and drum—singing and dancing as they made their
way to Morris's town house. Hearing the commotion in the street, Morris
opened his front door and presented the general to the crowd below. Washington looked wan and a little feeble, his arm in a sling from a bout of ar-

thritis, but he smiled gamely as the ersatz Indians raised thirteen hearty cheers.

There would be many more celebrations in the years to come, larger, more formal, more splendid, but none that captured so well the spirit of the new nation, the optimism and the sense of possibility. It marked a turning point for Morris and for Washington, the end of their wartime collaboration and the beginning of a genuine friendship that would continue through the years of debate and decision that lay ahead.

Washington spent a week in Philadelphia, his wife making social rounds with Mary Morris while Robert showed George the progress being made in restoring The Hills, including an icehouse that so impressed Washington that he ordered his own rebuilt on the same design. The general departed a week later, returning to his Virginia plantation as a private citizen for the first time in eight years. For Morris the transition to private life was not so seamless. He retained his office for another six months, and while he threw himself wholly into personal business concerns, affairs of state would color his engagements long after.

The breakup of winter ice that had choked New York's East River for two long months at last cleared the way for the ambitious venture to China. On February 22 the *Empress of China*, a sleek, copper-bottomed vessel built in Boston on the order of Daniel Parker, weighed anchor, eased down the Narrows, sounded a thirteen-gun salute to the battery at the southern tip of Manhattan, and set sail for Canton. Her cargo was deceptively simple— twenty thousand dollars in silver, and two hundred fifty casks of ginseng.

Prized by the Chinese for medicinal uses, ginseng resisted cultivation but grew profusely in the wilds of the Appalachians. In September, Parker had commissioned a physician and naturalist named Robert Johnston to scour the region; four months of trekking and barter produced thirty tons of the exotic root. It would trade in China for tea, silks, and, of course, porce-lain, commodities formerly available in America only through the medium of the British East India Company. This voyage would expand the horizons of American commerce and match the global reach of the British Empire.

At the helm of the *Empress* was John Green, an Irish seafarer who sailed for Morris for ten years before the war, and then under his direction as a captain in the Continental Navy. His supercargoes were Samuel Shaw and Thomas Randall, former officers who fought together in the Revolu-tion under Henry Knox. Newspapers hailed the captain and crew as "young American adventurers . . . instruments in the hands of Providence, who have undertaken to extend the commerce of the United States of America to that distant and to us unexplored country."

For all the fanfare, the partnership behind the venture barely survived long enough for the voyage to launch. William Duer had dropped out the autumn before, too ill to make the journey and dissatisfied with the terms of his contract. John Ledyard was out as well, Morris having reluctantly agreed with his partners that the Pacific route was too speculative and too expensive. And Parker had failed to find the funds he sought in Boston, forcing him to turn to John Holker, his silent partner in the army contracts, for additional financing. The terms were redrawn; Robert Morris now held half-interest, with Parker and Holker dividing the other half.

The entry of Holker was most unsettling to Morris. He and the free-wheeling Holker had become partners and boon friends for two years after Holker arrived in America in 1778. Morris established some distance in 1780 by forming the firm Turnbull, Marmie & Company to handle Holker's business, but continued to partner with him separately in a variety of shipping ventures. The relationship began to sour after Holker came under pressure from the French government to account for his activities as agent for the French army and marine. Unfortunately for Holker, he'd left all the management of his early activities to Morris, and in January 1783, he asked Morris for a statement of his government accounts.

Morris was fully engrossed at the time in his efforts to raise money for the army, and he largely ignored Holker's request. Months later, prodded by the French consul Luzerne, Morris assigned a member of the comptroller's office to prepare an estimate, which found Holker owing $160,000 to the United States. Holker and Luzerne set this ruling aside pending a review of French claims against the United States stemming from naval operations in the Caribbean. In the meantime, with Luzerne planning to depart for France, Holker pressed Morris for a general settlement of their affairs.

This time Morris responded vigorously, taking weeks out from his official business to sit down with John Swanwick and draw up a full report of all his public and private transactions with Holker. While this work was proceeding, however, Holker and Morris engaged in an escalating dispute over the records upon which the accounts were based, and over who would be held responsible for losses owing to the depreciation of Continental funds during the early phase of their joint operations. By the time Morris presented his statement to Holker—an account that showed Holker deeply in debt to Morris—the two were no longer speaking. At the end of March they severed all joint concerns between them—except for the China venture.

These two primary backers were feuding, but it was Daniel Parker, the managing partner in the consortium, who was struggling, and failing, to keep up with his obligations. Some of the pressure came from Morris, who was seeking as Financier to recoup some unspent advances made to Parker on the army contract, and some from Holker, who with William Duer was pressing Parker for one hundred thousand dollars in proceeds from that same contract. At the same time, Parker was pleading with both Holker and Morris to cover his expenses in procuring ships—besides the *Empress*, he'd bought at least two others, which eventually sailed on more modest trading ventures—the ginseng, and the twenty thousand silver dollars freighted on the *Empress*.

On the day the *Empress of China* sailed, Parker was desperately short of funds. So short, in fact, that he pilfered $2,300 from the casks of silver sent aboard as cargo. In the spring, with the ship safely at sea, Parker traveled to Philadelphia and spent several months meeting with Holker in an effort to settle his accounts. In May Parker announced the dissolution of his partnership with Holker and Duer, and brought in Thomas Fitzsimmons as a trustee to oversee any settlements. Finally in August, Parker absconded, setting sail for Europe and leaving Holker to answer for hundreds of thousands in unpaid debts. A clerk from Parker's countinghouse later testified that Parker had diverted most of the advances on the China venture to personal use; his books were, as Holker termed them, "a downright swindling statement."

By the time the *Empress of China* returned a year later, the fortunes of her various sponsors served as a case study for the risks and vagaries of post-revolutionary finance. Far from sinking into obscurity, Daniel Parker had set himself up in Amsterdam as a successful broker in American government securities. Holker was embroiled in litigation and had mortgaged his interest in the China venture to several investors in Philadelphia. And Morris, ever nimble, had established a new partnership in New York with Gouverneur Morris, William Constable, and John Rucker, all then residing in Manhattan.

The deal was set up by Gouverneur. He and Robert would hold a third interest each, with Constable and Rucker serving as the public face of the firm. The Morrises' primary contribution was capital, though in fact it was Robert Morris who put down the payment for himself and Gouverneur, an advance of ten thousand pounds in New York currency. The firm would be involved in shipping, but also in financial speculations and any other promising investments. Constable was at that time the most prominent merchant in Manhattan, but he was a surprising character to find in league with either Morris, especially Robert.

A native of New York, Constable entered the fur trade before the war, moving to the frontier outpost of Detroit and establishing himself as "considerate sober and esteemed—by much the cleverest young man" in town. Upon the outbreak of hostilities with England, Constable sailed for London, then returned to occupied New York to help a well-known Tory trader set up a store. In 1778 he moved on to occupied Philadelphia. He remained when the British evacuated, and in October 1780 was arrested in connection with charges brought against Benedict Arnold, months before his famous defection. Constable soon after enlisted in the Continental Army to cover for his collaboration with the British, but neither Robert nor Gouverneur Morris could have been ignorant of his story. Both had a flexible attitude in regard to political fealties, but in Constable they had lowered the bar of what sort of "character" they might require in a business partner.

Part of Constable's allure might have been the fourth partner he brought to the table, John Rucker. He was the son of a wealthy Prussian merchant whose family had connections in the British Parliament and mercantile and banking offices in London, France, and Germany. He had come to America in the service of the Philadelphia merchant John Nesbitt, and soon fell in with Constable. He would soon return to London, lending the new firm international standing and immediate clout in European finance.

In this case, however, the duties of Constable, Rucker & Company were more prosaic. Upon the return of the *Empress*, they disposed of her cargo— she returned a relatively modest profit of 25 percent after all costs—and then put the ship up for sale. Bidding was tepid, and in the end Constable bought her outright for the firm, collected a new cargo, and sent her back to Canton.

The success of this first American voyage to China shone all the brighter against the gloomy backdrop of postwar commerce. Beginning in early 1784, the American economy slipped into recession. Imports from Europe surged while available cash evaporated, pushing prices up and hard money into hiding. Bankruptcies claimed major houses on both sides of the Atlantic, with Philadelphia as an epicenter. In March 1785, during a business trip through New York and Pennsylvania, Connecticut businessman Peter Colt observed that "everything seems at a Stand . . . except that the Merchants are going *downhill* very fast." That summer, Morris remarked, "there seems to be a more general want of money both in Europe and America than I ever knew."

With other avenues of trade closed down, the success of Morris's China venture spawned many imitators. Some shipowners adopted John Ledyard's plan and headed west, others stuck with the traditional route. Morris remained a principal in the trade for years, operating through Constable and other partners. At a time when the European powers were hoping to bottle up the commerce of the American upstart, China became, as Morris had predicted, an important vent for seafaring enterprise. At the height of the season in 1789, sixteen American ships rode at their moorings in the harbor at Canton.

The dispute between Holker and Morris only intensified in the months the *Empress* was at sea, growing in scope until Congress, the French ambassador, and the Pennsylvania Assembly all joined the fray. Morris had talked for years of a return to "private concerns," but it soon became apparent that the high profile he attained in public office would stick with him, for better or worse, in whatever station he assumed.

John Holker had also achieved a rare degree of prominence in his years in Philadelphia. Buoyed by his early profits as a military contractor, he had bought a large town house and a country estate, had enlisted business partners in most of the major ports in America, and become prominent in the same social circle as Morris. Their clash was a battle of financial titans involving two of the wealthiest and best-connected entrepreneurs on the continent, and the falling out between these two powerful friends became the source of public sensation and private gossip.

With his fortune and his reputation in jeopardy, Holker turned to the French legation for assistance. Fortunately for him, Luzerne, who never trusted Holker, had sailed home in June. His replacement, François Barbe-Marbois, was as lean and severe as Luzerne had been affable and rotund. Marbois took a quick dislike to Morris based on his suspicion that Morris planned to avoid, in his capacity as Financier, making payments on the debts due to France. Marbois had little love for Holker either, but sided with him in his claims against Morris.

In December 1784, Marbois wrote Congress to complain that French agents in America—he avoided mentioning Holker by name—were having trouble settling accounts because of "the Slowness of the usual forms of Justice." Congress was responsive, writing the states to request "remedial" laws that would expedite settlements.

This threw the contest between Holker and Morris before the Pennsylvania Assembly. Here Holker enjoyed two distinct advantages. First, the pendulum of Pennsylvania's politics had swung once more, the Constitutionalists gaining sway in the October elections. Second, Marbois had recently wed the daughter of a leading Constitutionalist politician. Despite dogged opposition from Morris's allies in the Assembly, a bill was proposed ensuring "speedy trial" for any suit brought in the name of the French king. The proposed bill was published in March, pushing the Morris-Holker imbroglio to the front of the public agenda.

This legislation, coming on the heels of Morris's arduous service in the government, came as a shock to Morris, his friends, and his family. Mary Morris was so distressed that she proposed leaving Philadelphia altogether and moving the family to New York. Robert opposed such a removal as "letting my enemies triumph over me," but he was clearly shaken. "This business I am told appears to hang heavy on Mr. Morris' spirits," a friend reported to Kitty Livingston. As to Holker, "it is said he is not in his right senses."

Morris attempted to maintain a front of dignified reserve, declining the advice of friends to address the Assembly in person, but on at least one occasion he lost his composure. Running by chance into Charles Pettit, a brother-in-law to Joseph Reed and a leader of the Constitutionalist majority in the Assembly, Morris exploded in a rare display of temper. "Mr. Pettit," Morris bellowed, "By God if you pass that bill, which if you are not all damned rascals you cannot do, I will be revenged on you and all your party!"

Morris's threat notwithstanding, the bill passed handily, and Holker quickly filed suit before the state Supreme Court. But the case did not come to a hearing for months—delays that allowed Gouverneur Morris, now working as Robert's attorney, to assemble documents for a compelling argument. Ruling in October, the court found that Morris was accountable only to Holker, not to the French king, and ordered all parties to submit records and documents to a panel of five arbitrators. The case dragged on for three more years but the crucial decision came early, when the arbitrators accepted Morris's argument that as Holker's agent, he had acted only under specific instructions from Holker. The final verdict, issued in April 1789, found Holker indebted to Morris for fifteen hundred pounds Pennsylvania currency.

Not content to bedevil Morris with the Holker bill, the Constitutionalists in 1784 resurrected another long-standing claim against the Financier, this involving his management of state contributions to Congress. The question first arose in 1782, when public creditors were pressing both the state and the federal government to pay off the bonds issued by Congress. This prompted a call on Morris to settle the state accounts.

He responded with a detailed statement of his expenditures, and a proposal that the state seek cash credit from the Congress for the supplies requisitioned to support the army. Upon receiving this report, state president John Dickinson applauded Morris for presenting "such accurate accounts of such large sums of public monies rendered so quickly." But three years later the new state comptroller, an ambitious young accountant named John Nicholson, decided that Morris's management had benefited Congress over the interests of the state. Nicholson disputed Morris's application of state funds to federal purposes, and in May 1785 filed suit seeking to hold Morris personally liable for one hundred thousand dollars of such funds.

This was, simply put, a spurious claim, and was dismissed in Morris's favor after several years of litigation. But it consumed time and energy, and combined with the Holker affair, tied Morris to his desk and left him sputtering. "I have been prevented from paying you a visit," he wrote a friend in June, "in part by a fresh party attack." Morris never doubted the eventual outcome of the case. "I have just mentioned the matter lest false reports make you uneasy." But he did not intend passively to absorb the blows aimed against him. "I shall get the better of all these Sons of Darkness," Morris vowed, "and in the end oblige them to acknowledge the Services they try to Traduce."

Nicholson's unprovoked attack and Holker's wretched effort to reclaim his fortune combined to tax Morris's energy, his time, and his resources, but he could shrug them off as the price he paid for his high public stature. More disturbing to Morris was a far-reaching challenge raised at this time by Pennsylvania's militant democrats, a campaign to revoke the charter of the Bank of North America.

This struggle over the bank came to dominate the political life of the state in 1784 and for the following two years. For its proponents it was a crusade against the prerogatives of commerce in general and against the power of Morris and his mercantile circle in particular. More than that, it was a fearful reaction to the advancing postwar recession, rooted in a yearning for the simpler days of the early colonial economy. For Morris it represented a threat to a signal achievement of his administration, an institution that had already assumed a central role in the American economy. Morris marshaled all his resources in his effort to save the bank, and ultimately felt compelled to return to a public arena he had so long planned to renounce.

The first stage of the campaign against the bank opened, ironically enough, with a bid to launch a second, competing institution. This was a response to the early success of the Bank of North America—in 1782, the first full year of its existence, the bank paid shareholders dividends of 8 percent, and the year following, 14 percent. These high returns, combined with the general scarcity of capital, led directors to announce plans to expand. New shares would be offered, at five hundred dollars each, and the bylaws revised to limit the influence of those with larger holdings. The directors were seeking to broaden their base.

Two weeks after the new subscription was announced, however, a rival syndicate stepped up offering shares in a new bank. The sponsors were a mix of Quakers, Tories, and Constitutionalists, principally bound by their desire to compete with the Bank of North America in the business of finance.

This was not surprising. At the same time this bank was being organized, two other new banks were being projected for New York and Boston. The idea of commercial finance was catching on with merchants throughout the new nation. But to Morris and the other directors, the prospect of a second bank in Philadelphia represented a mortal threat that put all private credit in the city at risk. The only object of the rival sponsors, Morris said later, was "the destruction of the Bank of North America." The investing public had no such qualms, however, and the new bank sold more than seven hundred shares in ten days. Directors were chosen, bylaws adopted, and the new board applied to the Assembly for a charter.

At this point the directors of the Bank of North America intervened, requesting a hearing to present arguments in opposition. The Assembly agreed and a hearing was set for March 2, 1784, setting the stage for a lively and contentious debate.

James Wilson and Gouverneur Morris spoke for the established bank. Their argument was simple: a single bank would be more secure, operating with a larger capital stock and consequently able to lend at lower rates of interest. This opened the door to a pointed rejoinder from the sponsors of the new bank. The Bank of North America, they observed, was a monopoly, protected by the state in the same fashion that monopolies in Britain were established by royal edict. This created a privilege; to deny a charter to a second bank would subvert democracy and equality, the primary objects of the just fought Revolution.

These were powerful arguments for the most radical legislature in the union, and it was apparent the Assembly would grant the new charter. Anticipating this result, bank president Thomas Willing called an emergency meeting of the stockholders to propose a new strategy: reduce the price of the new stock offering and invite the sponsors of the rival bank to buy in. The proffer was made, the terms accepted, and the new bank withdrew its request for a charter. This solved the immediate problem of an upstart challenger, but the episode had awakened the citizenry, and especially the Constitutionalists, to broader questions of finance, and to the growing power of the bank.

Robert Morris took no direct role in this stage of the contest. This was in part because he had no official position at the bank—he was a shareholder, but not an officer—and in part because he recognized that by now his presence would only incite the opposition. By his high position in the government and his extensive trading connections, Morris's name had become synonymous with power and wealth in a country enamored of the newfound idea of social equality. The point was made emphatically a week before the March debate, when "Septimus" railed in the *Freeman's Journal* that the true motive driving the Bank of North America was that "all power may be centered in the hands of one man—Robert Morris and his Creatures."

But while Morris stayed in the background, he played a key role in formulating the defense of the bank. He was routinely consulted by the directors, he fully endorsed the position of the board, and it was his lieutenants—Gouverneur was his partner in government and business, and Wilson a political ally and his sometime attorney at the Office of Finance— who spoke at the Assembly.

The state's deepening recession forced the bank back before the Assembly two weeks after the charter debate. With commerce in a free fall for lack of money, the Assembly considered setting up a loan office. This was the prevailing form of state finance that operated before the Revolution, whereby the state issued loans on landed security, much like the latter-day savings and loan associations. In this case, however, the Assembly proposed that the Bank of North America float the loans.

Thomas Willing reported to the State House to answer this request in person. The bank did not offer loans against real estate, he pointed out, and besides, the response to the new stock offering had been sluggish and at present the bank had no funds to lend. The lawmakers then asked if the bank would accept paper issued by a state land bank, and Willing again answered in the negative. After the dismal wartime performance of state and federal paper emissions, the bank directors were determined to deal only in hard money.

Rebuffed by the bank, the Assembly voted to issue fifty thousand pounds in paper to be lent against landed security. The bills were not made legal tender, but were receivable at face value at any state land office. This concluded the action for that session, but generated a surge of popular resentment at the bank's refusal to float the paper issue.

This anger culminated in October 1784, when the Republicans, now closely associated with the bank, were trounced at the annual Assembly elections. The Constitutionalist majority promptly set about expanding its new financial project. They approved the issue of four hundred thousand dollars in new state paper. This fund would serve two purposes: two thirds would go to pay interest on the federal debt held by Pennsylvania citizens—obligations that Congress had been unable to meet—and the balance to the land office. The paper was to be supported by new taxes.

The bill passed easily, and in the weeks that followed the Assembly once again turned to the bank. The question this time was not a prospective new bank, but the status of the old one. The militants in the Assembly wanted to revoke its charter. Considering the uncertain standing of the original charter granted by Congress, this thrust by the Assembly could be fatal.

The arguments against the Bank of North America were both economic and political. The specific economic allegation was that the bank had created a shortage of money. This was clearly a reaction to the bad economic times, and was easily refuted. By its very operation—accepting deposits that then became the basis for loans—the bank multiplied the funds lodged in its vaults. Money might be short, but the bank was not the culprit.

More fundamental, and harder to answer, was the political charge that the bank was too powerful. An Assembly committee put forth the indictment. "The accumulation of enormous wealth and power in a society"— here "society" referred to the bank—"will necessarily produce a degree of influence and power which cannot be entrusted in the hands of any set of men, whatever, without endangering public safety. . . . We have nothing in our free and equal government capable of balancing the influence which this bank must create, and we see nothing which in the course of a few years, can prevent the directors of the bank from governing Pennsylvania."

This went to the heart of the matter, and posed a critical challenge for Pennsylvania and for the nation. In the Old World, questions of license and privilege had always been answered in the context of a state dominated by a monarchy, where the king could grant and withdraw favors as he saw fit. America, by its Revolution, had introduced a new form to the world, a democratic republic governed under principles of equality and liberty. What would be the standing, under such a framework, of an independent institution, of a corporation? The question was all the more pressing in the case of the bank. Heretofore, all questions of money and credit had been the province of the state.

To Morris and the directors, the operation of the bank was value-neutral; their project was to establish a lasting font of capital, and to make credit available to any party, private or public, whom they warranted a reliable risk. Here, as Morris put it, "the interest of the state and of the bank are the same." But for the Pennsylvania militants, the bank possessed what they called "the money power," an awesome faculty that influenced the life of every citizen. With this attack on the bank charter, the Constitutionalists were seeking to recover a key element of state power that had been ceded to the bank, and to Robert Morris.

The move against the bank was so radical, so potentially disruptive in an economy already in recession, that some Constitutionalists backed away from it. Charles Pettit, the Joseph Reed acolyte Morris had upbraided for backing the Holker bill, proposed a compromise that would "alter and amend," but not repeal, the bank charter. Likewise, George Bryan, one of the authors of the radical state constitution, worried that repeal "would hurt our merchants much." But Bryan saw that the flame of his party was too high to be quenched. It was the bank's own fault, he believed—their "opposition to the second bank . . . to the funding, or money bill etc. etc. were all foolish provocations."

Thomas Willing, surprisingly, thought the whole episode would blow over. "Our Assembly," he wrote to William Bingham in August, "have attacked us with all the violence of party rage—but I believe they'll drop the attack before the session is over." Willing proved a better banker than pundit.

The bill came up for a final vote in September 1785. At the request of the bank, one last hearing was held, with a single speaker arguing for each side. James Wilson spoke for the bank. He possessed a fine legal mind, but the points he made were abstruse and technical, and did little to advance his cause. Moreover, he conceded a critical point—that the bank was abetting the surge of imports that was destabilizing the economy. It remained for other, later voices to make the case for the utility of the bank.

The rebuttal was delivered by Jonathan Dickinson Sergeant, the state attorney general, a Constitutionalist stalwart, and an early sponsor of the rival bank. Sergeant was more persuasive than Wilson, and more illuminating. He focused on the change the bank had wrought in the economic life of the state. This had several permutations.

The sector hit hardest by the bank, according to Sergeant, was agriculture. Pennsylvania farmers had prospered for generations with the land banks, which issued notes for a term of as long as sixteen years. This long-term credit, as opposed to the forty-five-day notes issued by the bank, was better suited to the annual cycles of agricultural production. In addition, Sergeant said, the high dividends paid by the bank attracted so much of the available private capital that farmers could not rely on private lenders to underwrite their operations. The bank's opposition to state paper, he said, made the land bank infeasible. The two could not coexist.

Sergeant didn't rest his argument there. The short terms of the bank loans, he said, and its strict rules on punctual payment had changed the character of daily life in Pennsylvania. In the past, a borrower could invoke his good reputation and extract easier terms for a loan. Now, a debtor had to pay on time, "or his character, fortune, and everything near and dear were lost. Let him give what interest he would, his note must be taken up [paid off], or his credit would be blasted—this made even the most opulent tremble."

It seems unfair to fault the bank for holding borrowers to their word, but to Sergeant, the strict terms imposed by the bank had generated the "current of bankruptcies" plaguing the state. In its few short years of existence, the bank had undermined the amiable ethic of the people. It was "no longer a question with many, how to EARN money, but how to GET it, by any means, however iniquitous."

This was stern language coming from the champion of a rival bank. But Sergeant was something of a zealot, and the campaign against the bank had become a personal mission.

As to the question of right, Sergeant said the needs of a chartered institution could never take precedence over the right of the people "to make laws for themselves." The specter of the bank now threatened to negate everything the Revolution had been fought for. "Consistent with the duty I owe my country," Sergeant declared, "I cannot behold this dreadful engine working such horrid mischiefs, without raising my voice aloud, and crying out to you, Exterminate the bank!"

Sergeant's performance, and Wilson's, only confirmed the Constitutionalists in their animus. The vote was put, and the charter revoked by a two-to-one margin.

The loss of the state charter pushed the bank into an existential crisis. Without official standing, what kind of entity was the bank; how could its debts and obligations be enforced?

James Wilson offered one answer, in a pamphlet published before the September debate, asserting that the charter granted by Congress was perfectly competent and grounded in the sovereignty of the national legislature. But that was just the problem—with the war over, the standing of Congress was itself precarious, and without a state charter, there was no authority to which the bank might be held to account.

This was more than a theoretical question. As word of the repeal spread, confidence in the bank rapidly receded. Deposits shrank, the price of the bank stock slipped below par for the first time, and major stockholders began looking for ways to get their money out. All the directors could do was hunker down and shore up the bank's capital; money lending was suspended, and all outstanding notes were called in.

But if the bank was wounded, it was not without resources and it was not without friends. As much as the backcountry farmers resented the bank and its success, the urban traders and artisans of Philadelphia had shared in that success and were alarmed to see the institution under attack. In the months between introduction of the bill to repeal the charter and the final vote, the newspapers were filled with tracts defending the bank. Public sentiment was beginning to turn.

Just as significant, the repeal of the charter forced Robert Morris to abandon his chosen position of detached reserve. In October 1785, less than a year after he stepped down as Financier, Morris ran for a seat in the state Assembly.

Morris first considered a bid for president of the state, but this was rendered moot by the arrival in September of Benjamin Franklin, returning from his long tenure as ambassador to France. Franklin was immediately hailed as the catalyst who might unite Pennsylvania's divided polity, and was solicited by both Constitutionalists and Republicans as their candidate for the Executive Council. To both he gave his assent.

Franklin's happy arrival did not end the political rivalry, however, and in October the Republican slate edged the Continentalists, bringing the warring parties to virtual balance in the Assembly. Morris was elected along with Thomas Fitzsimmons and George Clymer, each of them integrally associated with the bank. Unable, apparently, to engage by half-measures, Morris took a leading role in the Assembly, sitting as chairman of Ways and Means and several other key committees. His primary interest was the bank, but here he moved with deliberation. He took his first step in December, at the close of the winter session, when he presented a memorial from the bank protesting the repeal of the charter as a violation of right. The appeal would not be heard until the following spring.

In the meantime, Morris and Thomas Willing had to cope with an uprising within the bank itself. This was led by Jeremiah Wadsworth and John Carter, the Connecticut business partners whose adroit handling of contracts to supply both the French and American armies helped them emerge from the war as two of the richest men in America. Both had speculated heavily in bank stock; they were alarmed at the attack on the bank charter, and the suddenly uncertain status of their investment. The attorney for both men was Alexander Hamilton, now practicing law in New York.

Wadsworth informed Hamilton in November that he had "determined to take the first favorable opportunity to withdraw" from his stock holdings. This decision was encouraged by Arthur Lee, the ever-present enemy of all things Morris, who had purchased shares in the latest offering and was now "exceedingly anxious & determined to withdraw his." The dissident shareholders were confounded, however, by the low price of the stock; they could not sell without incurring a substantial loss.

Hamilton agreed that "To leave so considerable a sum in a Company of this kind not incorporated is too dangerous." He advised Wadsworth that the Republicans' strong showing in the last election might yet result in a new charter, and "it would be prudent" to await the next session of the Assembly. Should Morris and his allies fail, however, Hamilton proposed legal action to test the status of the dubious congressional charter. "Get some person to refuse to pay a note to the bank," Hamilton advised, and force the bank to sue for performance. If the bank prevailed, "it must be on the principle that the Bank still subsists [as] a corporation in Pennsylvania." If the action failed, "you can then insist that your money be returned to you and may compel its being done."

This was a dangerous plan for the bank—a court finding in the negative would almost certainly doom the entire enterprise. But Wadsworth was impatient. He wanted to put the charter to an immediate test, and he collected proxies from several other prominent shareholders, including the ambassador from Holland, who represented a consortium of Dutch investors, to lend heft to his views.

Wadsworth carried these proxies to Philadelphia to attend the bank's annual shareholder meeting in January. Arriving in the city early, Wadsworth held several conferences with Robert Morris. At the outset Morris adamantly opposed the legal test as precipitate and, considering that the courts were stacked with Constitutionalist judges, destined to fail. But in dialogue with Wadsworth, Morris "softened down much," and when the meeting convened gave his full endorsement to Hamilton's gambit.

Wadsworth raised a second concern with Morris and at the shareholder meeting. This pertained to James Wilson, the lead counsel for the bank and also a director, who had run up close to one hundred thousand dollars in loans to support his speculations in land. Contrary to customary practice, some of those debts had been extended for years. Besides the potential liability, the loans to Wilson opened the bank to charges of favoritism and inside dealing.

With his proxies in hand, Wadsworth carried the day at the shareholder meeting. He won an explicit resolution "to have a legal opinion as soon as possible," and unanimous agreement that should the decision go against the bank, the corporation would dissolve and pay stockholders the par value of their shares. Further, he obtained guarantees from Morris and others to underwrite Wilson's debt. With Wadsworth mollified, the shareholders voted to retain Willing and the other bank officers and adjourned for the year.

This was a tactical victory for Willing and Morris. The fact was, neither one had any intention of putting the fate of the bank in the hands of a judge. With Wadsworth neutralized, they could now enter the political arena to wrest a new charter from the Assembly. This involved a systematic, all-out campaign to enlist public opinion in the cause of the bank. Morris was often arraigned for his disdain for democracy, but at this critical juncture he chose the court of public opinion over the courts of Pennsylvania.

Morris and Willing were old friends and longtime partners, and together they staged a masterful campaign. Their first move was to apply for, and obtain, a corporate charter for the bank from the neighboring state of Delaware. This was certainly a ruse—there was little chance they would forsake the commercial citadel of Philadelphia for a sleepy farm town in the "lower counties"—but it awakened fears that the bank might actually depart, and take its business with it.

Next came a petition drive. These were standard fare in the political campaigns of the time, but in this affair the petitions carried extra weight. The bank was denounced as an elite institution that served a small coterie of moneyed men; mass signatures would undermine that construction. The first petition, circulated in Philadelphia, garnered more than six hundred signers and was presented to the Assembly on March 3; petitions from more distant counties drifted in for weeks after.

While those signatures were being gathered, Morris wheeled out his big guns—Pelatiah Webster and Thomas Paine. These were the two leading pamphleteers of the time, and in February 1786 each produced a major statement on the bank. Until then, for all the public controversy, the whole idea of banking remained arcane, remote, and somewhat mysterious. Few citizens had actually engaged in transactions with the bank, and fewer still understood its function in commercial life.

Webster, by now well known as a prolific essayist on economics, provided a sort of primer on the history and function of banks. He linked the rise of banking in Genoa, Amsterdam, London, and Paris to the strength and prosperity of their national governments, and contrasted that experience to the debate in Pennsylvania. "It must, therefore, be very absurd, to suppose that such an institution can be hurtful or even useless."

Webster then went into the minutiae of bank operations—personal checking, the virtues of thrift and savings, the multiplier effect of bank loans, the efficiencies of private management. From this foundation, Webster offered a daring defense of the bank's wealthy backers—daring in that few voices were raised, now but especially then, in defense of the rich.

"There is no doubt but wealth creates influence, but it is that sort of influence that has ever been found safe to the state," Webster wrote. He explained: "The parson lives on the sins of the people, the doctor on their diseases, and the lawyer on their disputes and quarrels. But the merchant lives on the wealth of the people. He never wishes for a poor customer or a poor country. . . . The merchant has every inducement to seek and support the wealth of the state.

"I think it absurd to banish wealth from a state, for fear it should gain too much influence in government . . . it would be much more politic to make a leveling act [a steep tax on estates, presumably], to prevent the great wealth of individuals, who are much more likely to become dangerous to the State, than any aggregate bodies of men."

Webster made another point that flew in the face of conventional wisdom. There was no clash, he wrote, between commercial and agrarian interests. "The richer the merchants are, and the greater their trade, the better market they afford for the produce of the country." This was of critical importance to the farmers of Pennsylvania. "Their husbandry is animated and supported by their market: indeed, the husbandman and the merchant ever mutually support and benefit each other."

Paine's essay was more personal, and more emotional. Harking back to the early disputes over the radical state constitution, Paine acknowledged his long association with the Constitutionalists who had engineered the revocation of the charter. "I feel myself now entering on unpleasant and disagreeable ground," he confessed, because he was now breaking ranks with his old friends. He did so in his usual uncompromising fashion. "The attack of the late Assembly on the bank, discovers such a want of moderation and prudence, of impartiality and equity, of fair and candid inquiry and investigation, of deliberate and unbiased judgment, and such a rashness of thinking and vengeance of power, as is inconsistent with the safety of the republic. It was judging without hearing, and executing without trial."

Not only was the decision against the bank an abuse of power, Paine argued, but it was also wrong. He himself had helped launch the bank—the Bank of Pennsylvania, that is, forerunner to the Bank of North America—and he was proud of the result. "The sudden restoration of public and private credit, which took place on the establishment of the bank, is an event as extraordinary in itself as any domestic occurrence during the progress of the Revolution." Coming from the man who had first given voice to the rebellious spirit of 1776, this was itself nothing less than extraordinary. Thomas Paine, leader of the price committees and chief accuser of Robert Morris in the Silas Deane affair, was now holding up Morris's singular contribution as the most profound achievement of the era.

There was more. "Ingratitude has a short memory," Paine scolded. "It was on the failure of the Government to support the public cause, that the bank originated." Now that the war was over, "the whole community derives benefit from the operation of the bank. It facilitates the commerce of the country. It quickens the means of purchasing and paying for country produce, and hastens the exportation of it. The emolument, therefore, being to the community, it is the office and duty of the government to give protection to the bank."

Nor did Paine confine his remarks to the bank. Paper money, the darling of the bank's critics, was an "airy bubble" that "depends for support upon accident, caprice and party." Tender laws, the ultimate support of unfounded paper issues, "operate to destroy Morality," Paine wrote, "and the punishment of a member who should move for such a law ought to be *death.*"

Turning to the fundamental political question of the time, the radical Pennsylvania constitution, Paine made his conversion complete. "My idea of a single legislature was always founded on the hope that whatever personal parties there might be in the state, they would all unite and agree in the general principles of good government. . . . But when party operates to produce party laws, a single house is a single person, and subject to the haste, rashness and passion of individual sovereignty. At least, it is an aristocracy.

"The form of the present Constitution is now made to trample on its principles."

This was a startling declaration, echoing the original line taken by the Republican Society in their long campaign against the constitution. Paine elaborated in a subsequent public letter, seeking to reconcile his early support for the radicals with his newfound convictions. "In the winter of 1778, a very strong opposition was made to the *form* of the constitution. As the constitution was then on experiment, and the enemy in full force in the country, the opposition was injudicious. To this may be added another reason, which is that the constitution, by having only a single house, was the best calculated form of civil government that could be devised for carrying on the war; because the simplicity of the structure admitted of dispatch, and dispensed with deliberation. But that which was then its blessing is now its curse. Things are done too rashly."

This was more than just apostasy. Paine remained a towering figure in the political life of the state and the nation, and his condemnation represented a heavy blow to the stature of his former allies. By the time the repeal of bank charter came up for debate in the Assembly in March, the foes of the bank retained a slim majority of votes, but they were on the defensive.

The petitions supporting the bank were presented to the Assembly in early March and referred to a committee of five headed by Morris's ally, the merchant and onetime radical George Clymer. This lent the Republicans an opening edge in the coming debate.

Clymer's committee delivered a report three weeks later that leaned heavily on a point made by Tom Paine, that revoking a charter grant was to act in a judicial, not legislative capacity, and in taking such a step, the Assembly "exceeds its powers." The committee focused its ire on Robert Whitehill and John Smilie, two frontier-county assemblymen who had authored the original legislative indictment of the bank. Neither had bothered to visit the bank in preparing their "preconceived" report. The vote against the bank arose from a "predetermination to condemn," and "has its foundation deeply laid in injustice."

The Republicans on the committee felt bound to add a prideful note on the petitions they had gathered. Among their signers were "the most respectable characters among us . . . best experienced in the effects, good or bad, produced by the operations of the bank."

This report sparked a stormy floor debate when Smilie, a sharp-tongued Irishman, rose to defend his vote and his character. Smilie denied "totally" any failure to consult the bank directors, and scornfully dismissed the petitions submitted in their relief. "I believe the influence and terrors of the bank have been exerted to procure" those signatures, he said. The signers from the country had been duped, and the idea that the friends of the bank were "respectable" smacked of class pride. "This is holding out an aristocratical idea," Smilie declared. "A democratical government like ours, admits of no superiority. . . . If we inquire what constitutes respectability meant in the report, we shall very probably find it riches. They have more money than their neighbors, and are therefore more respectable." Smilie was playing his trump card first. The debate over the bank was a question of class rivalry, not simply a matter of policy.

Now he took up the charter, and the right of the Assembly to revoke it. No charter was sacrosanct, Smilie said, and certainly not a monopoly, which represented a "monster in the face of the constitution." The legislature had no obligation to prove misconduct on the part of the bank. It could be condemned "on higher ground," by "a conviction of its dangerous tendency." Dangerous how? In its "influence," its wealth, and particularly, in its ability to supplant the state currency. "The paper money of the state cannot exist with the bank." There was no room for accommodation.

The debate continued over the next three days, drawing into its vortex all the currents of social and political conflict that had been in contest since the early days of the Revolution. It was the culmination of years of strife between Constitutionalists and the Republicans, and would settle fundamental questions of power, setting the bounds between state authority and private prerogative.

There would be no more reports, no more referrals to committee. This would be played out in full-throated oration on the floor of the Assembly before an avid audience packed in the public galleries. In this instance it was fortunate that Congress had departed the city, allowing the Assembly to take over the larger, downstairs hearing room at the State House. "No subject of debate that has been agitated before the legislature of Pennsylvania," Thomas Paine recorded, "ever drew together such crowded audiences as attended the House during the four days that debate lasted."

With the critical question now at hand, with so much personal vision and toil vested in the outcome, Robert Morris did not leave this moment to his proxies. He had allies who rose to speak on occasion—Clymer, principally, and Thomas Fitzsimmons—but it was Morris who held the floor for hours at a stretch, speaking for the bank and for the Republican faction, always mindful that he was addressing the public as well as the lawmakers. "I rejoice that so many of my fellow citizens are present at these debates," he said, "as they will probably, from the explanations respecting the bank, become better acquainted with the nature of it." Morris was convinced that the operations of the bank would provide its best defense. "It only wants to be understood, to make it fully and clearly seen how much the interest of every man in the state may be or is benefited by it."

Morris dominated these long days of polemic, not by eloquence or learning, but by force of character. None but Morris could offer with such authority the offhand confession, made during his first extended tour of the floor, that "As to the theory of commerce, I do not pretend to be deeply versed in it; but I have had some experience in the practical part." Morris was supremely confident, confronting his foes with easy poise, his eyes and his temper alert to every insinuation. His marathon performance cemented a reputation that was recorded a year later by a visiting statesman from Georgia: "I am told that when he speaks in the Assembly of Pennsylvania, that he bears down all before him."

Morris offered only procedural remarks in the first full day of debate, but took the floor in earnest on Thursday. He opened by challenging Smilie's suggestion that the defenders of the bank were "interested in it personally," while its critics had "no private interest to serve." This represented, Morris said, "a kind of solicitation to pay little regard to what falls from us. . . . This is neither fair nor candid." Morris acknowledged holding stock in the bank, but he noted that he was not a director, and claimed a deeper concern. "I had some hand in forming the institution—or brat, as it is called out of doors—now, so far as I had a hand in the formation of this brat, I esteem myself bound in honor to support it." More serious, and more broad, Morris asserted that his support for the bank arose from "a perfect and thorough conviction, that the institution, in its operation, far from being injurious to the state, is of service to every individual in it."

This was an important point to establish. Nobody in the room that day doubted that Morris had a vested interest in the fortunes of the bank. But by invoking a more personal, even parental connection, Morris established his expertise and his sincerity. In a debate over the continued existence of the nation's first bank, who better to speak in its defense than its author?

Morris proceeded to take up the specific challenges raised against the bank. The most damaging was the idea promoted by champions of virtue everywhere—that the bank undermined the yeoman farmers of the countryside. "By what means can the bank injure agriculture?" Morris asked. In fact, short-term loans were often issued "for the express purpose of encouraging agriculture."

Pursuing the question, he sketched in plain language the role of credit in the Philadelphia market. "Let us suppose a ship arrives here from the West Indies" laden with imports for sale. The cargo might be unloaded, but unless credit were available, the ship would lie empty and idle until enough cargo was sold to finance a return voyage. "I have frequently experienced it myself," Morris said. Without credit, "the farmer would have his wagons waiting in Market Street, and no sale; while the [merchant] would have an abundance of rum, mahogany, logwood, dry goods, etc. in his stores. . . . By means of the bank, the merchant is enabled to purchase, and the farmer to return home." It was the simplest of allegories but it illustrated Pelatiah Webster's crucial point—that when it came to finance, the interests of the farmer and the trader were the same.

Morris returned repeatedly to the question of the bank's usefulness. Hard money was not sequestered by the bank, he said, but was put into motion—"the bank being, with respect to the circulation of specie, as the heart to the circulation of blood."

Every class of people benefited by that circulation, Morris insisted. The farmer and the miller were mentioned again, along with the mechanic, and the journeymen he employed; "every description of men that have any thing to do with money."

Morris was on shakier ground when addressing fears that concentrated wealth would "necessarily produce a degree of influence and power" that would "endanger the public safety." His answer here was oblique. "How is this accumulation of enormous wealth to take place?" Not among individuals; the profits of the bank were diffused among the stockholders. The bank itself might grow larger, but this would only make it "more useful." Here Morris was seeing with the trusting eyes of a parent. Even in this new era of popular democracy, it was apparent that economic power carried political clout. But it was also true, as Morris pointed out, that whatever influence the bank might wield, it had failed so far to preserve its standing before the Assembly.

On the question of the bank's freedom from state control, Morris was more direct. "The report goes further to say, 'That the bank is not dependent on government,' " Morris observed. "I am very glad it is not.

"The moment it becomes dependent on government, that moment it is destroyed." This maxim went to the original motives in launching the bank. It had been established explicitly in order to supplant that credit that the government had squandered. To restore the power to regulate the circulating medium, as by the tender laws and new issues of currency, would vest too much power in the hands of the government. This was Morris's key insight, the principle he had pursued in Congress and through the price wars in Philadelphia: to separate the public sphere from the private, and leave the market to function on its own.

The bank had proven its effectiveness in the darkest of times, and now, "the utility of the bank is experienced by every man in the state. . . . Is it possible, then, that we shall pursue measures for the destruction of an institution so useful?"

While Morris sought to focus on the mundane operations of commerce, the Constitutionalists emphasized questions of equity and power. Opening the third day of debate, Robert Whitehill said he had heard nothing to change his opinion, nor did he expect to. The crux of the matter was axiomatic, resting on the inherent nature of the bank: "The institution having no principles but that of avarice, which dries and shrivels up all the manly, generous feelings of the human soul, will never be varied in its object, and if continued, will . . . engross all the wealth, power, and influence in the state."

His critique was not grounded in "facts of doubtful credibility." His conclusions, Whitehill said, "are drawn from the nature of things, the principles of nature. . . . They carry their evidence with them, with a certainty like that of sparks flying upwards, or the waters running to the sea."

To Whitehill, the contest over the bank was simply a struggle for power. "Shall we support this engine of destruction, and enable a few men to take advantage of their wealth. . . . The question at present is, whether the state shall give way to the bank, or the bank give way to the state?"

Resuming the floor that afternoon, Morris expressed a degree of exasperation. Whitehill had retained his original views? "I have never heard any declarations from that gentleman's lips, which obtained more credit with me than this," Morris said. "I do sincerely believe, that he does and will retain his opinion. Even were an angel from heaven sent with proper arguments to convince him of his error, it will make no alteration with him." Yet Morris persisted, defending the petitions presented in favor of the bank, criticizing the reports against it, and challenging the motives of the Constitutionalist critics "whose suspicions have been roused by the dread of phantoms presented to their imagination through the medium of envy and jealousy."

By now personal attacks were assuming as much influence in the debate as reasoned argument. John Smilie, the most artful of the Constitutionalists, turned his sights on Thomas Paine, deriding him as "an unprincipled author, who lets out his pen for hire." Morris stood in his defense. "He is not in my pay, nor do I know any who do pay him." As Paine was not a member of the Assembly, he could not take the floor to defend himself. "I feel for his situation," Morris said. "I do not reproach [Smilie] for using the freedom of speech, but I wish more delicacy had been used."

Morris was not above such indelicacy himself, however. In the afternoon of the third day of debate, he turned on one Constitutionalist to demand, "If wealth be so obnoxious, I ask this gentleman why is he so eager in pursuit of it?" Morris alleged he'd seen the assemblyman stopping by the land office to transact business as an agent. The charge was emphatically denied.

Underlying all the rhetoric was the unspoken assumption that, aside from the challenge to the institution, the attack on the bank was aimed at Morris himself—it was his power, and his "influence," that so concerned the Assembly majority. The Constitutionalists were too politic to make this point directly, so Morris brought it up himself. "I have frequently been told, out of doors . . . that the opposition to the bank is in part leveled at me personally," Morris said at the close of the third day of debate.

"If any oppose it in that view, and suppose that my interest would suffer by the annihilation of the bank, they are grossly mistaken." This was arrogance, but it was also conviction. "Be assured, sir, that if this [bank] be destroyed, another shall rise out of its ashes—one that will be of great advantage to my interest . . . and so far from doubting its success, I do not hesitate to pronounce that even my enemies (and God knows I seem to have enough of them) will deal with and trust me; not that I expect they may like me any better then than now, but they have confidence in me; and for the sake of their own interest and convenience, they will deal with me."

As the argument slipped into invective, it became clear, as Whitehill had said, that the parties were entrenched. At the close of the debate the factions stood as they had at the outset. When the resolution to restore the charter was called, it failed by a vote of twenty-eight to forty-one.

The Constitutionalists had won the battle, but the war was going against them. Soon after the Assembly vote Tom Paine remarked on "the great change in sentiments that is spreading through both the city and country." Paine did his best to keep the heat on, elaborating the case for the bank in a stream of public letters through the summer of 1786. Quietly, Benjamin Franklin weighed in as well. He had no appetite for controversy, but the economic advantages of the bank were too obvious to ignore.

The full extent of the shift in public opinion was registered at the annual Assembly elections in October. Robert Morris led the Republicans to a clean sweep in Philadelphia city and county, and his party made strides in the rural districts as well. The Constitutionalists were now a distinct minority, and while Whitehill returned, John Smilie lost his seat. The results fulfilled—at least in part—a brazen prediction Morris had made at the outset of the Assembly debate. "I venture to pronounce," he said in his first extended monologue, "that as the utility of the bank comes to be more generally known, and the subject better understood, every member who voted against it, will be discarded by his constituents."

To the Republican partisans, this was a watershed moment, a turning point in the political wars that had dominated the state since the overthrow of the old Assembly. "An important revolution took place on the 10th day of this instant in favor of the wisdom, virtue, and property of Pennsylvania," Benjamin Rush wrote in late October. "Mr. Robert Morris, the late financier of the United States, is at the head of the party that will rule our state for the ensuing year." Rush was a man of changeable fealties but always brought fresh enthusiasm to his latest convictions. Now it was Morris's turn to enjoy his unalloyed encomiums. "This gentleman's abilities, eloquence, and integrity place him upon a footing with the first legislators and patriots of ancient and modern times."

With his party in control, Morris moved swiftly. The bank charter was referred to committee in November, and a favorable report issued in December. This time, the only real division was among the Republicans: Morris wanted a bill declaring the revocation of the charter null as an illegal attack on a vested right. Thomas Fitzsimmons found this too drastic, and legally risky. Better, he said, to draw up a new charter, one that mollified the bank's critics by accepting restrictions on its total capitalization and the duration of the charter. Morris assented, and in March 1787 the new charter easily won approval.

The Constitutionalists never gave up their fervent opposition to the bank. Unable to block the final decision, they exacted their wrath on Hugh Henry Brackenridge, a new state representative from Pittsburgh. A country lawyer who had studied at Princeton, Brackenridge traveled to Philadelphia with full intent to support the platform of his fellow frontiersmen. But he was impressed with Morris's financial mastery, and became his ally in the floor debates.

Brackenridge sealed his political fate when he joined a small gathering of frontier delegates at the home of state chief justice Thomas McKean. When he overheard one of the assemblymen grumbling that Morris was pushing the bank out of personal interests, Brackenridge exploded. "The people are fools," he declared to anyone within earshot. "If they would let Mr. Morris alone, he would make Pennsylvania a great people, but they will not suffer him to do it!" This outburst earned contemptuous play in the partisan press, "A Farmer" deriding Brackenridge for having "sold the good will of his country for a dinner of some stockholder's fat beef." Brackenridge went on to a career as a writer and a jurist, but was never again elected to public office.

From that time forward, Robert Morris remained a divisive figure, his wealth and power marking him as an enemy of the common man. But that could not diminish his singular achievement in the Pennsylvania bank debate. Relentless, resourceful, convinced that he was right, Morris had persuaded a skeptical public to look past the attacks on his wealth and status and to weigh their own interest in establishing private markets for credit. In public forum he'd turned the tide of popular opinion against state intervention in the market, opening the door to free operation of credit and capital.

The bafflement of the bank's foes spelled the end of concerted political opposition to banking throughout the former colonies. Following the charter grant in Pennsylvania, legislatures in New York, Massachusetts, and Rhode Island all sanctioned the launch of new private banks—New York's founded by Alexander Hamilton, William Constable, Jeremiah Wadsworth, and several others from Morris's immediate orbit. In the formative years immediately following the Revolution, with the national government still creaking along in the rickety framework of the Continental Congress, America was firmly committed to the path of laissez-faire capitalism.

There was a paradox here. In their opposition to the bank charter, the radical democrats, the militant defenders of the state constitution, had invoked the old economic order of pre-revolutionary Pennsylvania. It was Morris and the Republicans, the financial and social elite of Philadelphia, who had opened the door to a new era of commerce, limited state sovereignty, and social mobility. Historians ever after have labeled Morris and his allies as conservatives, but at this critical juncture it was Morris who saw the future, and who embraced it.

— *Chapter 17* —

THE CONSTITUTION

The end of the Revolution and his release from the Office of Finance allowed Robert Morris to turn his attention to personal affairs. He was the unabashed commercial and political leader of the largest city in what he referred to with some pride as "a rising empire." He believed in appearances and the trappings of status. He needed an upgrade.

The first claim on his interest was a new residence. Morris had lived in the same house he first occupied when he partnered with Thomas Willing two decades before the war; now he sought a home that would reflect his standing. He found it in 1781, a three-story brick structure at the corner of Market Street near Sixth, two blocks north of the State House. Reputed to be the largest private residence in the city, the building came with a distinguished legacy. Erected by a wealthy widow in the late 1760s, it was home to Governor Richard Penn for several years before the Revolution. Upon the British occupation the house was taken over by General William Howe, and after his withdrawal by General Benedict Arnold; it was there he married Peggy Shippen. When Arnold defected to the British, John Holker, then Morris's friend and now his nemesis, rented the place and moved in, but it was gutted by fire soon after. Morris bought what was left of the mansion, but did not clear title until 1785.

Besides basic renovations, Morris made substantial additions—an icehouse, a second story over the kitchen, a free-standing, three-story bathhouse, and stables for twelve horses. The finished house had two dining rooms—one for the family, another for formal affairs—a drawing room described by one visitor as "brilliant beyond anything you could imagine," six bedrooms, and quarters for a household staff that now included a confectioner and a French chef.

Once they took up residence, Robert and Mary filled the house with furnishings that marked their wealth and their sense of style. The walls were hung with tapestries and paintings, including likenesses of the Morris's elder sons and family friends Gouverneur Morris and John Jay. There was a bust of John Paul Jones and two of George Washington. The front parlor featured a harpsichord where Morris's friend Francis Hopkinson, jurist, humorist, and signer of the Declaration, played the minuets that won him added fame as America's first published composer. And there was a "musical clock & guitar" valued at two hundred fifty pounds—the most expensive item in the house.

The tables, bureaus, bedsteads, and bookcases throughout the house were all made of mahogany. The dishware was silver plate and gilt china; the wine decanters of the "best cut flint glass." Entertaining was clearly a priority: an inventory listed a dozen dining tables, 98 glasses for wine and 21 for champagne, and ten armchairs gathered in a clubby upstairs sitting room. The inventory was composed years later, but most of the family's accumulation happened around this time, and it captured the flavor of the Morris household. This was evidence of the "Asiatic luxury at festive boards" that Arthur Lee had denounced in his "Lucius" columns. Morris would answer that, in a city that hosted the foreign embassies and global trade, he was just keeping up appearances.

Robert and Mary now had the space and the setting to put on the sorts of dinners and balls befitting a social circle that soon came to be called the "Republican court." He entertained, one frequent guest recalled, with "a profuse, incessant, and elegant hospitality." Mary decked herself in the latest fashion—gauzy, flowing dresses, elaborate bonnets, and hair coiffed in tight ringlets. Robert presided with "gentlemanly deportment," but without airs; his convivial nature imbued his gatherings with "festive mirth."

Outside the home, Morris patronized the arts and engaged in intellectual pursuits ranging far beyond the bounds of his prewar interests. He sat for a portrait by the British émigré painter Robert Edge Pine—and then became his sponsor, recommending him to Washington and building him a house to live in and show his works. In 1784, after hot-air balloons became a sensation in Paris, Morris gathered friends to launch one from the garden of his new, yet unfinished house. Fired by burning straw, the paper vessel filled, rose, and drifted over the spires of the city, "to the great astonishment of the populace."

Rather than join another banquet club, Morris helped launch, in early 1787, a new club called the Society for Political Inquiries. At its organizational meeting, at City Tavern, the group elected Benjamin Franklin as its president, though it's unclear whether this reflected an organizational role, or simply Franklin's status as its most popular associate. The group included among its forty-four members leaders of both the Republican and Constitutionalist parties, and comprised some of the foremost intellects of the era—Franklin and his grandnephew and assistant Jonathan Williams, Morris and his constant companion Gouverneur Morris, Thomas Paine, David Rittenhouse, James Wilson, John Nixon, Franklin son-in-law Richard Bache, and Philadelphia's longtime mayor Samuel Powel.

The society set out with verve, meeting twice a month, usually at Franklin's house, to discuss topics ranging from prison reform and freedom of the press to commercial and tax policy. Attendance soon waned and the society expired after two years, but for Morris it was a rare excursion into the realm of social theory. Nor does it appear Morris was putting on airs; invited, in 1786, to join the prestigious American Philosophical Society, he modestly demurred. "My avocations thru life not having permitted an attention to the proper studies," he informed the secretary of the society, "I must beg leave to decline the acceptance of a station I do not find myself qualified to fill."

The Morris family that moved in to the refurbished mansion on Market Street had changed in recent years. In 1781, with the local schools thrown into disorder by the war, Robert and Mary had sent their two eldest sons to Europe. The boys were put under the charge of Matthew Ridley, a friend and business colleague, and enrolled at a school in Geneva where Benjamin Franklin Bache, Franklin's grandson, was a classmate. Morris wanted them trained in the classics, Romance languages, mathematics "and every science," but above all, as he wrote to Ridley, "I think it of infinitely more consequence that they should be good Men, than learned or great Men." Ridley, Franklin, and John Jay all reported to Morris on the progress of his sons, the discourse forming a friendly backdrop to their weighty letters on affairs of war and finance.

With young Robert and Thomas abroad, the Morris brood included William, Hetty, Charles, Maria, and Henry, born in July 1784. Robert doted in particular on Maria, "a charming creature and very independent," but he and Mary ran a strict house. Morris tried to make sure that his children did not take their future—and his wealth—for granted. "It is a very dangerous lesson to teach boys," Morris wrote to one of his sons' tutors, "that they are dependent on their father or any other's Fortune. I pray you teach them economy as a leading virtue. I don't mean parsimony, but . . . extravagance leads to ruin not only of Fortune but of good principles."

With Mary, however, Morris stinted on little. He ordered her shoes from

Paris, tea from China, and encouraged her every enthusiasm. "My dearest," he wrote her at one point, "I am never so happy as when you partake the enjoyments of life." Robert's feelings for his wife had, if anything, grown stronger over time. He was convinced, he said, that "our existence on this earth is very necessary to each other's happiness."

Morris's engagements at this time extended well beyond the limits of Philadelphia. He was spending lavishly to rebuild The Hills, which he had expanded through purchase to encompass three hundred acres. Besides the hilltop residence overlooking the Schuylkill, foundations were laid for two farmhouses, one of stone and the other of brick, and another brick residence for a gardener. There were barns, stables, a coachhouse, a small brewery, and greenhouses for raising citrus, pineapple, and other tropical fruits. His herds were restocked with sheep, fine cattle, and a "celebrated" stock of pigs.

Morris purchased a second rural estate during the war, a tract of 2,500 acres fronting the Delaware opposite Trenton. This investment was probably based on the tentative designation of the site by Congress in 1783 as the nation's future capital, based on its central location and easy access to the river. But Morris did not let the land lie fallow; he raised a self-contained settlement that would eventually comprise farms and basic industry, including a quarry, a gristmill, a forge, ironworks, and a hat manufactory. A dam seven feet high, reaching to an island in the river that was part of the estate, supplied power to the mills. At the center of the property, Morris built a mansion surrounded, as at The Hills, by stables, outbuildings, and manicured gardens. He called the place Morrisville.

All of this Morris funded on credit. His trading ventures to China were profitable, but not on a scale to support such large and growing commitments. While the China trade was winning plaudits in the popular press, Morris was venturing on a much greater scale into an exclusive franchise to deliver tobacco to France. It was here that Morris would truly do justice to his reputation as the leading merchant in America. The deal would also stretch his credit, strain his personal and political connections, and push him to the brink of bankruptcy.

The French tobacco contract arose toward the end of Morris's tenure as Financier. It came about in part for the same reason he landed the Spanish flour contracts before the war: the Europeans sought him out. His extensive credit and capacity to manage international shipping ventures set him apart from any other merchant in America. State entities in particular wanted to partner with Morris because he operated on their scale. His tenure as Financier only enhanced his standing; he'd been the linchpin for Spain through the agency of Don Juan de Miralles and Francisco Rendón, and for France through Silas Deane and then John Holker. The key player this time was his old friend and official liaison in Paris, Benjamin Franklin.

The primary motivation of the French court in the struggle against Britain was always their ancient enmity for England. But they were also eager to cash in on the ancillary benefits, and as Franklin well knew, the one commodity produced in America that the French wanted in quantity was tobacco.

The French public consumed tens of thousands of tons a year, mostly in snuff—smoking became a national passion only later—and they preferred American leaf to any other, import or domestic. Until the war they had been forced to rely on British trading houses who imposed a heavy surcharge for their services; the French were entranced by the idea of a direct connection.

Tobacco thus became the asset Americans dangled before their closest ally from early in the war. The munitions shipped by Beamarchais and the other French arms traders had been secured with promises of tobacco, often to be shipped through Willing & Morris and the firm's agent at Nantes, Thomas Morris. Robert Morris was charged with arranging the remittances, but most of the cargoes never arrived, driven back or captured by the British blockade. With peace, the French could finally get the tobacco they craved straight from America, supplanting a British monopoly dating back two hundred years.

The planters of the South, in Maryland and especially in Virginia, looked toward the direct trade with France with equal enthusiasm. Before the war tobacco had been the single largest export of North America, but because their product went through Great Britain, English and Scottish factors had a stranglehold on the traffic. The Revolution brought visions of a free market, higher retained profits, and debt relief.

The rulers of France, however, had different ideas. True, they detested their prewar dependence on the great British trading houses that controlled the American market. But the French trade was governed by a quasi–state monopoly known as the Farmers General. These were not farmers, in fact, but a syndicate of privileged aristocrats who "farmed" public revenues through control of trade in critical commodities like salt, wine, and tobacco. The Farmers had entered the wartime trade alongside Beaumarchais, advancing a million livres on their account to underwrite Silas Deane's purchase of war supplies, but their remittances had been lost with the rest.

As monopolists, the Farmers were accustomed to dealing through selected intermediaries, not free markets. In 1783, with the war ending and
the blockade coming down, the Farmers asked Franklin to recommend an
American factor who could handle a sole-source contract for the French tobacco trade. Franklin proposed Robert Morris.

It seemed like a good idea. The Financier—Franklin's reference came
while Morris still held that office—could act in both official and private
capacities, sending tobacco under government auspices to help clear the
American debt to the Farmers, and filling the balance of their order through
private trade. But at this point Morris's hands were tied. He was already
sending all the tobacco he could obtain on public account to Holland, to
help fund the Dutch loan. And he was fully engaged in frantic maneuvers
to cover the notes he'd issued to pay the army.

The best Morris could do for the Farmers was to refer their proposal
to Congress, then sitting at Princeton. He did so in September; Congress
answered with an emphatic no. Ever since the Silas Deane affair the delegates had renounced any mixed-use ventures, and they reiterated their policy here, the Dutch tobacco shipments notwithstanding: "It will be highly
improper for the United States to engage in any commercial plans of any
Kind on any Account whatsoever."

Still, Morris found the Farmers' proposal tantalizing. His father, after
all, had found success in tobacco. The French contract would allow Morris
to ply that trade on a scale grander than anything his father had ever conceived. Morris mulled over the project for a time, and finally in November
proposed to the Farmers a first step toward a major commitment. He would
send a private cargo of several grades of leaf from different quarters of the
Tidewater; from these samples they could decide what kind to buy, and at
what price. But no such shipment could be prepared before spring, and by
that time the Farmers, and Franklin, had moved on.

Not long after sending his proposal to Morris, Franklin had struck upon
a different scheme, one that would keep the tobacco trade under his direct
control. For the length of the war Franklin had kept his grandnephew on
retainer, sometimes as his assistant and then, after the miserable failure
of Thomas Morris, as the supervisor of American contracts at the port of
Nantes. Jonathan Williams had proven an able and conscientious businessman; Franklin now proposed to put him in charge of the tobacco contract.

For this venture Franklin paired Williams with William Alexander, an
old friend and the father of Jonathan's wife. Alexander was uniquely qualified; he was a banker in Edinburgh and had served, like his father be-

fore him, as the tobacco factor for the Farmers General in Scotland. As the senior member, the partnership was organized under his name, and on Franklin's recommendation, the Farmers in September 1783 entered a non-exclusive contract with William Alexander & Company to accept delivery of fifteen million pounds of tobacco per year at a low, fixed price. This was a major order, but it was not the sole-source deal the Farmers ultimately planned on. It was a trial run.

Steering this business to his relatives was a case of nepotism on Franklin's part, clearly, but it was more than that. Two major British trading houses had recently made serious proposals to supply the Farmers. The French foreign minister, Comte de Vergennes, forbade any deal with the English, but he needed Franklin to come up with a viable alternative. Williams and Alexander presented a plausible solution close at hand.

The new partners appear to have had the necessary skills and experience, but they were thin on capital and credit. Though he had extensive commercial connections, Alexander had a tendency to overreach, and his tangles with creditors had landed him in debtor's prison as late as 1776. As to Williams, his primary holdings consisted of American bills of exchange on which the French government had stopped payment. He could make claims on his debtors in America, however, and was able to obtain a modest line of credit from a small bank in Paris. Armed with these assets and the imprimatur of the French contract, Alexander sailed for America in November.

Landing at Virginia, Alexander was distressed to learn that the end of the war had failed to depress the price of tobacco, a factor he counted on in negotiating his contract with the Farmers. He also learned that his credit was wholly inadequate to the massive purchasing and shipping operation he had undertaken. Franklin had suggested to him a backup plan should events turn against him, and toward the end of February, he took it. Making his way through heavy winter snow, he traveled to Philadelphia to meet with Robert Morris.

Morris was intrigued by Alexander's story, but he had to move carefully. Arthur Lee and his allies in Congress were sure to challenge any hint that Morris was mixing private and public business. More important, Morris knew the long shadow he cast over the mercantile world. Word of his entry into the tobacco market—in any capacity—would immediately cause prices to rise. By a contract signed on March 3, Morris agreed to become a silent partner with William Alexander & Company, sharing in all profits and losses. He would do no buying, selling, or shipping, but would extend credit to Alexander and back his bills. Morris would take a one-third interest in the contract, and his participation would be kept strictly secret.

While these terms were being settled in Philadelphia, deliveries to France were lagging, and pressure mounted on the Farmers to satisfy the national taste for tobacco. They appointed a special agent, Simon-Emmanuel-Julien Le Normand, to arrange further purchases outside the William and Alexander contract. He bought some domestic tobacco, but this drew immediate protests for its poor quality. And he secretly circumvented Vergennes's prohibition to buy some Virginia tobacco through houses in Britain and Holland. But Le Normand knew he must eventually establish a direct channel to America.

In May Le Normand made his own approach to Robert Morris, asking him to revive the plan to ship a cargo of samples. Morris weighed the proposition warily; the postwar fall in tobacco prices that many had anticipated had failed to materialize, and Alexander was already having trouble finding product at the low figure set in the Farmers contract. But prices were bound to moderate sometime, and when they did, whoever held the French franchise would become the biggest single player in America's largest commodity market. In September, with his duties as Financier all but behind him, he decided to accept.

Now Morris had two major tobacco ventures under way, both of them secret. He ran his end of both operations through Tench Tilghman, the former military aide to George Washington. Now established in a merchant house in Baltimore, Tilghman had contacts throughout the tobacco districts of Maryland. At Morris's suggestion, Tilghman accepted agency commissions from Alexander and all other prospective buyers. This gave Tilghman the strongest possible position in the market, allowing him to keep his bids as low as possible.

Unfortunately for Morris and for Alexander, tobacco prices remained at their wartime peak. This was due in part to a limited harvest, but also to the surge of British exports into American ports. With hard currency scarce, import merchants from Boston to Savannah were buying tobacco to send to England to pay off their debts. Until this demand bubble subsided, prices would remain artificially high. Through the fall of 1784, Tilghman and Alexander trolled the plantations for bargains, but Alexander could secure only a fifth of the leaf called for under his contract, and much of this at a loss. In the process, Alexander incurred the wrath of both the planters in Virginia, who complained that he was depressing prices, and the French factors in America, who wanted to service the Farmers themselves and alleged that

Alexander was paying too much. Witnessing all this consternation, Morris had to be glad that he'd managed to keep his role quiet.

At first Morris kept his deal with Le Normand confidential from Alexander, but in the fall he let his half-partner in on the deal. This occasioned another visit by Alexander to Philadelphia. The cagey old Scot had a proposition. Jonathan Williams was thoroughly compromised by his financial problems in France, and the low price called for in the original contract ensured that any further purchases of tobacco on those terms would carry a loss. Instead Alexander proposed that Morris negotiate new terms for a new partnership, this between just Morris and Alexander, but this time with Alexander holding a third interest as the silent partner. Morris would provide financing in America, and Le Couteulx, his banker in Paris, would supply credit in Europe.

Morris liked the idea. Prices in Virginia were still too high, but the import boom was waning, and a long-term contract might yield healthy profits at the back end. Morris pitched a three-year deal to Le Normand in late October, proposing a base price 20 percent higher than that secured by Alexander. The Farmers General, strapped for supply by the failure of the experiment with William Alexander & Company, eagerly signed. The only sticking point was Le Couteulx; concerned about mounting political pressure on the Farmers, the banker held out for a 5 percent commission on his services.

Morris received the final terms from Le Normand early in April 1785. He hesitated again. The price offered by the Farmers was still below the current market, cash and credit were increasingly scarce in America, and the Bank of North America, Morris's mainstay, was under serious attack. But Le Normand had sweetened the deal with an advance of a million livres from the Farmers—about two hundred thousand dollars—to underwrite the early purchases. Morris signed on April 10 after stipulating an option to extend the contract for another year. With a total value of more than twenty million livres, it was the largest single contract ever issued under France's ancien régime.

Aside from the sheer size of the commercial operation involved—Morris and Alexander would be buying millions of pounds of leaf, packing it in tens of thousands of hogsheads, and sending as many as thirty ships a year to France—Morris was faced with two major tasks if the contract was to be accomplished. The first was to somehow bring prices down until he could realize a profit at the limits set by the Farmers General. Second, he had to find the credit to back his purchasing until his cargoes could be delivered in France.

Morris devised a daring solution to these problems. The Virginia price stayed high due largely to the demand for remittances to England, but Morris could realize a savings of 10 percent or more by paying cash. Hard money and bank loans were scarce, however, and transporting cash through rural Virginia was exceedingly risky. Morris's solution was to issue notes, much as he had done through the bank and through the Office of Finance. Those issues were both backed by the government as well as Morris's reputation; these new notes would rest strictly on his personal credit.

As his contract with the Farmers was still secret, Morris could not issue these notes directly. Instead he wrote them in the name of his purchasing agents, Tilghman in Baltimore and Benjamin Harrison, Jr., in Virginia. Once countersigned, they guaranteed payment on sight at Philadelphia, either in hard coin or in bills of exchange on London. And since bills got a better price at Philadelphia than in the rural plantations of Virginia and Maryland, the notes were actually worth more than silver. They soon caught on.

More complex, and more risky, was funding these notes through Europe. This required correspondent agents on the continent who would accept the bills drawn by Morris and keep them afloat—through third-party loans or on their own account—until tobacco arrived in France and payment was issued by Le Couteulx. The house Morris used for this delicate business was his own—Constable, Rucker & Company in New York.

The firm continued to engage in transatlantic mercantile ventures, but financial operations of this sort were by now taking precedence. Here Rucker was the key. When bills of exchange came due Morris would send his drafts, not directly to Le Couteulx in Paris, but to Rucker in London, who would fund them on his credit there. He would then wait for shipments to arrive in France and dun Le Couteulx for the payments owed to Morris, thus extending by months the float, or the time of final reckoning for Morris's drafts. This gave Morris enormous flexibility in managing his debts.

This was just part of the load Rucker shouldered in London. His firm was engaged in a separate but similar foreign-funds operation, this on behalf of the national government. The scheme involved obtaining advances in New York from the federal Board of Treasury, for which the firm agreed to cover in Europe the interest payments due on the Continental debts to Holland and France. This gave the partners in Constable, Rucker & Company still another source of funds to leverage in shipping operations and financial transactions.

Since John Rucker was still fairly new to this sort of legerdemain, Gouverneur Morris wrote him in early 1786 to offer some tips on how he might manage his accounts. The letter provides us a rare window on the dizzying subtleties of international finance in the eighteenth century, a game in which Robert Morris was an acknowledged grand master. "Suppose," Gouverneur counseled his young associate, "Constable will draw on you for five thousand pounds sterling payable at six months sight, and he will obtain from our friend Robert Morris in Philadelphia a credit on you in Paris to the amount. You will draw on Amsterdam and assign a credit to Paris to redraw. This double usance from London to Paris through Amsterdam gives four months—and we pay here to Robert Morris the value of the livres payable in Paris on the day when the bills are payable by you in London respectively, this gives at least seven months. The operation will be chargeable with the commissions (one of which you pocket) and the exchanges— whatever all this may exceed legal interest will be a loss and whatever it may fall short will be a gain. But the eventual payment always being certain renders it a desirable business to our friends and when occasion offers may be useful to us." This was one of several scenarios drawn by Morris, each exploiting the float and requiring long extensions of credit.

Soon after Morris put his private notes into circulation, in the fall and winter of 1785, his tobacco operations ran into political trouble on both sides of the Atlantic. In France, the opposition was led by Thomas Jefferson, recently appointed to replace Ben Franklin as American consul in Paris. A planter himself, Jefferson was convinced that open trade with France would yield the best prices in Virginia. And as a revolutionary, he saw the Farmers General as a crucial prop to the French aristocracy. In August 1785, even before he knew Morris had obtained the tobacco franchise, Jefferson proposed to Vergennes the dissolution of the Farmers. He supported his position with a memorial showing the huge profits the Farmers were reaping off the tobacco trade.

This was a remarkably forward position for a new ambassador to take, and it soon backfired. Vergennes himself was sympathetic, but he knew, as Jefferson apparently did not, the firm support the Farmers enjoyed inside the French bureaucracy. It also turned out that in his financial estimates, Jefferson had failed to take into account routine factors of spoilage, trimming, and other standard losses entailed in shipping tobacco, and his estimate of the Farmers' revenue consequently landed quite wide of the mark.

With his calculations discredited, Jefferson's initial thrust was easily parried by the Farmers and their allies. Jefferson quietly withdrew, but

he returned in early 1786, this time in league with the Marquis de Lafayette, recently returned from America. At this point word had surfaced
that Morris held the exclusive franchise with the Farmers. Lafayette was
personal friends with Morris, but like Jefferson he despised the privileges
enjoyed by the Farmers General, and he was convinced as well that free
markets would better encourage trade with America. Morris, too, had long
advocated free trade, but in his view, France was a special case. That is,
the Farmers would pursue a sole-source contract regardless of American
policy. If they could not find a viable American contractor, they would simply revert to prewar practice of buying through England, and the tobacco
growers of the South would have gained nothing by the war.

Lafayette, however, was hoping to bring reform to France by building
on its wartime union with the new citadel of liberty in America. Encouraged by Jefferson, Lafayette set as his goal "nothing less than the destruction of the tobacco farm, the greatest obstacle to Franco-American trade."
In February, working through his friends at court, Lafayette won the first
round—the creation of a state panel to conduct a broad investigation into
the tobacco trade.

In the meantime, in Virginia, news that Morris was the secret mover behind the French tobacco franchise spurred his longtime enemies there into
action. In December 1786 the Virginia legislature passed a law barring the
circulation of private banknotes, a stab both at the Bank of North America
and at Morris's tobacco notes.

Morris viewed these reverses with remarkably good humor. Regarding
the Virginia prohibition, he wrote to Tilghman in February, "I am unwilling to place myself in opposition to the laws of any country; and as I imagine these measures are leveled at me, I will be beforehand with them, and
therefore request that you will not pass any of the notes you have by you."
Two weeks later, however, Morris got his dander up. "Upon reflection," he
told Tilghman, "I do not see how it is possible for the Virginia law or any
law in a Commercial Country to prevent me from giving my note of hand to
any body that will take it." With that, Morris resumed issuing his notes; his
only concession was to make the bills payable to specific individuals, and
not to the bearer.

As to the agitation against the French monopoly, Morris only scoffed. To
whom should such a protest be addressed, he wondered. "To the Farmers
General? They are interested to support it. If to the King he must support
the Farmers for they support him. If to the Tobacco Planters, they will sell
to those who want to buy and will pay."

By early 1786, Morris's insights into the dynamics of the tobacco market began to pay off. For months he'd been watching price movements in Europe and holding to his limits in America, waiting for the tide to change. It did so in May, when remittance orders finally sated the continental demand. Prices fell to the point that Morris's competitors could no longer afford to ship to any port in Europe without a loss; suddenly, buyers who had outbid Morris months before were selling those stocks to him at his price. Over the first year of his contract, Morris had fallen well behind his shipping targets; now, in the spring of 1786, he was sending out every vessel he could find, and drawing "immense" advances on Le Couteulx to purchase all the tobacco he could lay hands on.

The fall in prices and Morris's prominent role in the market seemed to confirm the worst fears of Virginia tobacco planters, and many of them, Jefferson included, blamed Morris for their troubles. Their resentment was misplaced, however. While Morris held a monopoly position in the French trade, France represented just a fraction—about 20 percent—of the entire export market for American tobacco, with Britain still claiming the lion's share. As Morris knew all too well, he was subject to the price movements in the international market just as the planters were. The mite he added to "falling" the price by staying his purchases was a minor factor, though the hostility he encountered when he finally did enter the market was genuine enough.

Once again, Morris's fortunes were rising at a time when those of the nation were sinking. The economic doldrums that set in after the peace deepened steadily, spurred by new British trade rules that punished their former colonies by taxing American grain and prohibiting imports of American fish, beef, and whale oil. Spain joined the protectionist circle in 1784 by closing New Orleans to American traders.

These measures combined with the lingering effects of wartime debts and destruction to bring on what one eminent historian termed "the most serious economic setback suffered by Americans since the earliest days of colonial settlement." The depression was most severe in New England and the deep South, which lost their prewar export markets, but were felt as well in the commercial centers; commodity prices sank, and Philadelphia witnessed a "parade of bankruptcies" extending through 1790. Only the subsistence farmers of the frontier escaped the general decline.

Legislators in the individual states battled the downturn with a rash of laws designed to retaliate against Britain and encourage their local economies. Eight states imposed new trade duties, and seven sponsored fresh issues of paper money. Coming at different times from different places, however, these measures had mixed and often counterproductive results. The spotty import duties had little impact on British policy, and American merchants recoiled at the shifting values of the paper money issues. In 1785, New York augured new divisions within the Confederation when it authorized a duty on any imports arriving from other states. And the larger political question of how to treat with Spain threatened to cleave the new nation.

With trade policy in shambles and regional tensions rising, commercial and political leaders naturally looked to Congress for a response. But after the departure of the Nationalists the itinerant Congress was all but moribund. Delegates failed to attend, resolutions were ignored, and state payments dwindled to nothing. Richard Henry Lee sat as president for a year; thereafter, successive delegates passed through that thankless office in a matter of months.

Nowhere were the debilities of the Congress so glaring as at the Board of Treasury. After Morris departed the government in November 1784, it took seven months to select three members to serve on the board. William Livingston and Samuel Osgood consented to accept the post at the end of January, but the delegates took another four months to confirm the most avid candidate, Arthur Lee. The case against Lee was summed up by Thomas Jefferson, writing from Paris to register his dissent: "He has no talents for the office and what he has will be employed in rummaging old accounts to involve you in eternal war with [Robert] Morris. . . . He will in a short time introduce such dissentions into the Commission as to break it up." In his defense, Lee's backers could only offer, "The fact is we can get none better." Lee assumed the post in July.

Having assumed the responsibilities formerly shouldered by Morris, the new board now adopted his policies. The board called for an impost, berated the states for ignoring their requisitions, and lamented the "Embarrassed situation of Finances." Unable to perform even basic functions of the office, the board suspended payment of interest on the debt to France in 1785, and farmed out to private parties the transfer of funds to Holland. Most of these contracts went to Constable, Rucker & Company; in effect, Morris was now providing on a commission basis the services he and Haym Salomon had formerly handled in-house.

Lee was eloquent as ever in casting blame. The states were "shamefully defective" in providing revenues to Congress; Americans "do not have the public virtue and private temperance which are necessary to the establishment of free Republics." To Richard Henry he confided deep misgivings about the future. "We have independence without the means of attaining it; and are a nation without one source of national defense . . . we don't seem to feel these things are necessary to national existence. The Confederation is crumbling to pieces." None of this should come as any surprise; what is remarkable is that after all the carping about Robert Morris, Lee never acknowledged the paradox of his new outlook.

Outside the Congress, the incapacity of the central government was becoming inescapable. Writing to his uncle from Baltimore, Tench Tilghman voiced the general sense of malaise. "It is a melancholy truth, but so it is that we are at this point in time the most contemptible and abject nation on the face of the earth. We have neither reputation abroad nor union at home. We hang together merely because it is not in the interest of any other power to shake us to pieces, and not from any well-cemented bond of our own."

The political allegiances of the American states had always been tenuous; the one sinew that remained was the one Morris had nurtured so carefully—the federal debt. Even after he was forced to suspend interest payments on the domestic debt, Morris as Financier had systematically drawn in to Congress new debts represented by commissary certificates and army pay, confident that these domestic obligations would persuade the states to support the central government. But by 1786, that last tie was beginning to fray. With Congress clearly unable to make its payments, public creditors around the nation pressed the states to assume the federal debt. And as the state with the largest share of these federal bonds and certificates, Pennsylvania emerged as the focus of this movement. From his seat in the state Assembly, Robert Morris found himself once again fighting to preserve the union.

Pennsylvania's movement to assume the federal debt got under way in 1783 at the height of the Newburgh affair. With the government in crisis, Morris and the Nationalists in Congress had persuaded the Assembly to back off until the larger questions of a national funding system could be settled. In 1785, however, during a lull in the debates over the bank, the question arose again, and two thirds of a new paper money issue was assigned to pay interest on federal obligations held by Pennsylvania residents. In 1786 the redemption was expanded again when the Assembly formally assumed all federal securities held in the state, exchanging them for "new loan" state securities. Still another means of retiring federal debt was to issue state certificates to compensate veterans for pay lost to depreciation. These certificates, and the new loan securities, were made payable for large tracts of land on the state's western frontier, which were immediately dubbed "depreciation lands." By 1787, Pennsylvania had retired more than six million dollars in the debts of the Confederation.

Morris opposed these measures for two basic reasons. First, he rejected all experiments in paper currency because their uncertain valuation tended to undermine trade and credit in general. And he feared any move by the states to take over the federal debt would only hasten the demise of the union. But here Morris found himself divided from the major public creditors, who were ready by now to accept funds for their certificates from whatever entity might take them. As Financier, Morris had helped organize the public creditors into an effective lobby; now that influence was working against him.

The same forces were at work throughout the union. New York, prodded by its public creditors, called in all state *and* federal securities in early 1787, replacing them with state notes redeemable for land; the same act issued two hundred thousand pounds in new paper money. A similar measure in New Jersey lost on a close vote. It was apparent that, just a few years hence, the Confederation would simply dissolve.

The question, then, was whether America was better off with a national government or without one. Thomas Paine, never modest in his claims to foresight but sometimes correct nonetheless, cogitated years later on the origin of the move to replace the Continental Congress with a true federal government. "It so happens," Paine recalled, "that the proposition for that purpose came originally from myself." He had raised it, he said, in a letter to Robert Livingston in the spring of 1782 when the impost had failed in Rhode Island and the limits of the Confederation were all too apparent.

The letter prompted a meeting of what was then the core of the executive cabinet—Robert Morris, Gouverneur Morris, Livingston, and Paine—at Morris's house on Front Street. There was no dissent over the goal that evening; the only question was how to get there. His position, Paine said, was that there was no point in pressing. "I considered it as a remedy in reserve, that could be applied at any time *when the states saw themselves wrong enough to be put right.*" By 1786, with the economy in recession and the Congress in remission, that time had come.

The catalyst, unmarked at the time but now registered in every history of the founding era, was a dispute between Virginia and Maryland over who would collect duties from ships entering the Potomac River. The question was settled amicably by delegates from the two states during a conference at George Washington's Mount Vernon estate in March 1785. But the conference raised broad issues of interstate commerce that could be addressed only by policies expressly barred in the Articles of Confederation. The Virginia delegates returned to the House of Burgesses and proposed a larger conference, a convention to consider "regulations of trade." Invitations went out to all twelve of her sister states.

The convention was set for Annapolis, but early reactions were inauspicious. Even Maryland, the host state, declined to send delegates for fear of insulting the Congress. Pennsylvania was more enthusiastic. Ben Franklin, the president of the Executive Council, had long advocated a strong central government, and in April 1786 he appointed five delegates, including Robert Morris, Thomas Fitzsimmons, George Clymer—all leading Republicans—and Tench Coxe, a young merchant who had been a prime sponsor of the upstart Bank of Pennsylvania.

By the time the convention met in September, it was clear no major decisions would take place at Annapolis. New England and the southern states would not be represented at all, prompting one Delaware representative to ask, "How ridiculous will all this parade appear?" Only Tench Coxe made the trip from Philadelphia. But the week-long session served one critical purpose: it reunited Alexander Hamilton and James Madison, the two leading Nationalists from the Congress of 1783. At Madison's behest, Hamilton drafted an address to the states that cited "important defects in the system of the federal government" that had given rise to "the embarrassments which characterize the present state of our national affairs, foreign and domestic." To remedy those "defects," the delegates called on Congress and the governors of the states to assemble and empower a new convention that would "render the constitution of the Federal Government adequate to the exigencies of the Union." This convention, Hamilton proposed, should be held in what the Nationalists still considered the nation's true capital—Philadelphia.

Congress, as was its wont, wavered. It might be ineffectual, but it was still jealous of its prerogatives, and it let the Annapolis address lie in committee for five long months. Finally, late in February 1787, it endorsed a convention, to be held in May, "for the sole and express purpose of revising the Articles of Confederation" and reporting the results back to Congress.

The states were more eager. Five, Pennsylvania among them, named delegates even before the call from Congress. The delegation, named in December by an act of the Assembly, read like the guest list for an intimate dinner at The Hills: Robert Morris, James Wilson, George Clymer, and Thomas Mifflin. Gouverneur Morris, now residing in Philadelphia to manage Robert's legal affairs, and Jared Ingersoll, a London-trained attorney who served in the Continental Congress in 1780, were added later, perhaps to bolster the delegation's legal credentials. Benjamin Franklin, overlooked in the first ballot only because it was believed he would decline serving, was added in March by a special act.

Franklin's unaligned status notwithstanding, this was a clean sweep for Morris and his allies. Several Constitutionalists sought nomination, but the Assembly was by now solidly Republican. After his umbrage over the Holker bill and the assault on the bank, Morris had made good on his vow to Charles Pettit, "to be revenged on all your party."

Any reluctance in the other states to tamper with the framework of the national government was swept away in the fall by Shays's Rebellion, an armed uprising against taxes imposed by the state legislature in Massachusetts. To some it was a sign that the state governments could not on their own manage the legacy of debt run up during the war; to others, it confirmed their fears that some central authority was needed to rein in the extremes of pure democracy. But all agreed that, as South Carolina's Pierce Butler put it, a revised constitution was "the only thing at this critical moment that can rescue the states from civil disorder." By the time the convention was set to begin, twelve of the thirteen states were sending representatives—all save the obstreperous little republic of Rhode Island.

The delegates straggled into town, tardy, perhaps, from the dilatory custom of the Congress. On May 11, the scheduled opening date, only Pennsylvania and Virginia were on hand; a quorum of seven states was not achieved for another two weeks. As they came in, Morris was gratified to see many of his old allies from the political wars of the Congress—Madison, Hamilton, John Rutledge, John Dickinson, now representing Delaware, and, though he arrived late in the deliberations, John Langdon of New Hampshire.

Just as telling were those who didn't show up. The old radicals who had led the push for independence back in 1776 and persecuted Silas Deane two years later had fallen silent, stepped away. Sam Adams, pillar of the Eastern faction, was now sixty-five years old and president of the Massachusetts Senate. Shays's Rebellion had knocked him off balance and he overreacted, declaring that "the man who dares to rebel against the laws of a republic ought to suffer death." With his faith in the Revolution shaken, he found no words to challenge the gathering of Nationalists in Philadelphia.

Arthur Lee was busy as well, attending Congress in New York; he, too, kept his counsel, straining along with the delegates to catch any word of the proceedings. Richard Henry Lee was invited to join the Virginia delegation, but cited failing health and declined. He'd spent less time abroad than his brother, more time in Congress, and had come to a grudging acknowledgment that the Articles of Confederation, the document that most embodied his conception of the Revolution, was deeply flawed in its premises and ought to be revised. He felt comfortable with the Virginia delegation, and claimed a "disposition to repose with confidence in their determination." The firebrand Patrick Henry, also invited, also declined, though he was less politic. He would not travel to Philadelphia, he said, because he "smelt a rat."

The sole voices of the old Eastern faction at the convention were Elbridge Gerry of Massachusetts and Roger Sherman, the stern, stilted, puritanical Connecticut delegate who never did trust his countryman Silas Deane. Sherman had been there at the beginning, and here he was at the end, one of only two members of the convention to have signed both the Declaration of Independence and the Articles of Confederation. The other was Robert Morris.

The visiting delegate who meant the most to Morris, and to the convention, was George Washington. Famously retired from public life, deeply engaged in the operations of Mount Vernon, Washington actually took ill at the prospect of returning to service. But come he did, arriving after four squally days on the road to find generals Thomas Mifflin, Henry Knox, and James Mitchell Varnum, and the First City Troop riding out to meet him. They escorted him to the boardinghouse run by Elizabeth House, a favorite haunt of the Nationalists when Congress was in town, but in the crowd that received him there he found Morris, and accepted his invitation to room with him at Market Street. He sent his baggage over, and after stopping to pay respects to Benjamin Franklin, retired to join Morris for the night. The next afternoon, he dined "in a family way" with Robert, Mary, and the children.

For the convention, Washington was essential. More than Congress, more than all the politics and the pamphleteers, he embodied the Revolution, commanding popular allegiance and defining, in his strict deference to civil rule, the moral tenor of the new republic. For Morris, he completed the circle. With Hamilton, Madison, and Gouverneur Morris, Washington was integral to the Nationalist core that had backed Morris in the critical months of 1782 and 1783. They had failed then, thwarted by Rhode Island and then Virginia in their quest to establish a central government worthy of

the name. Now they were back, charged to begin anew the project of trans-
lating into written law the ideals and achievement of their daring, unprecedented Revolution.

The Nationalists at the convention shared a fraternal sense of elation,
a clubby camaraderie that helped leaven the endless sessions of debate
and sustain the delegates through spring and into a long, hot summer. One
undated anecdote helps capture that spirit; it arose during a conversation
among Hamilton, Robert Morris, Gouverneur Morris, and several other
friends. Hamilton, whose bond with Washington had been strained during
the war, pronounced his opinion that the general's austere character would
not brook familiar relations even among intimate friends. Gouverneur rose
to the bait, offering that he could be as easy with Washington as with any of
his acquaintances. Hamilton, never one to back down, dared Morris to support his words by clapping Washington on the shoulder in greeting.

Gouverneur soon got his chance. Hamilton was hosting a large gathering with Washington as the guest of honor. On cue, Gouverneur strode up
to the general, bowed, shook hands, and then laid a hand on Washington's
shoulder and announced, "My dear general, I am very happy to see you
look so well!" Startled by Gouverneur's physical familiarity, Washington recoiled and "fixed his eye on Morris for several minutes with an angry frown,
until the latter retreated abashed, and sought refuge in the crowd." Afterward Gouverneur sat down with Hamilton, Morris, and the others who
were in on the game. "I have won the bet," Gouverneur said to guffaws,
"but paid dearly for it."

Hovering over all the proceedings, as much in spirit as in person, was
Franklin. Then in his eighty-third year, Franklin had lost his vigor, and was
absent for the tavern banter and the evening salons when delegates were
at liberty from the State House. But he attended the sessions assiduously,
enjoying what he called the "daily exercise" of the three-block walk to the
State House—though on many days he opted for the ease of a sedan chair.
He rarely spoke during the debates, but his tacit endorsement lent gravity
to the proceedings.

Franklin carefully avoided taking sides in the Pennsylvania schism between Constitutionalist and Republican, but he and Morris shared a separate, special bond. Franklin had lived through a generation of political
wars before he ever knew Morris, but he came to rely on the younger
man's entrepreneurial wiles in their days on the Committee of Safety, on
the Committee of Secret Correspondence in Congress, and through their
bi-continental management of the Revolution's French connection. This

convention would crown their long partnership, the culmination of twelve years of labor in the councils of the Revolution.

When the federal convention finally got under way, on Friday, May 25, Robert Morris opened the proceedings. He was selected for this symbolic role because he was a delegate from the host state, and because Franklin was too ill to make it to the State House that day. His inaugural act was almost pro forma. He called for the election, by ballot, of a president, and then he nominated George Washington. John Rutledge offered his second. There was no question, no rival, but the delegates went through the formality, and the election was unanimous. After the results were read, Morris and Rutledge joined Washington on the floor and walked him to the raised dais from which he would observe the proceedings—by rule, the president took no part in the debate.

This was, to large degree, the full extent of Morris's contribution to the federal convention—it would not acquire the name "Constitutional" until after its work was done. He attended consistently, sitting at one of the felt-covered tables arrayed in an arc before the president's chair. But he was content to let the lawyers and the more experienced lawmakers hammer out the bargains that led to the final document—compromises on representation, court jurisdiction, separation of powers, and the awful dilemma of slavery. He was never comfortable, Morris said, with the "science of law." He hadn't hesitated taking the floor in the Pennsylvania Assembly, but in this case, Morris was little concerned with the details under discussion. The point was to have the convention itself; for him, that alone was enough.

There were, of course, several matters under consideration that would have brought Morris to his feet. But the power to tax—the central plank of the fiscal program he'd sponsored in Congress—was taken as a given at the convention. Several other of his primary objects were likewise the subject of consensus: the states were barred from emitting paper money or making laws impairing private contracts, and the power of coinage was reserved to the national government, all without debate. Just as Morris had envisioned, all of America would now be united through a single medium of commercial exchange. Also crucially, the new Congress expressly assumed responsibility for the wartime debts run up under the Confederation. This measure drew little comment in this predominantly Nationalist forum; it would generate much more controversy later.

Nor was there any debate in the convention over the other question dearest to Morris—the status of commercial banks. At one point Morris was tempted to propose that Congress be expressly empowered to issue bank charters, but Gouverneur Morris headed him off—better to say nothing than hazard an open discussion. It probably helped that the debates were kept strictly secret, allowing the delegates to leave popular passions on such controversial subjects at the door. And so, in the final draft, there was not a word about banks, which was the best Morris could hope for, and all that he really expected.

From his station on the periphery, through a stifling summer that some wise heads said was the worst since 1750, Morris looked on as Gouverneur Morris, James Wilson, and James Madison took their tours of the floor, setting the pace and defining the terms of debate. Morris himself was content to play the part of host to George Washington and monitor of the proceedings. He shared his outlook and his sense of pride in a letter he wrote in June to his sons in Europe: "General Washington is now our guest, having taken up his abode at my house during the time he is to remain in the city. . . . There are gentlemen of great abilities employed in this Convention, many of whom were in the first Congress, and several that were concerned in forming the Articles of Confederation now about to be altered and amended. You, my children, ought to pray for a successful issue to their labors, as the result is to be a form of Government under which you are to live, and in the administration of which you may hereafter probably have a share, provided you qualify yourselves by a proper application to your studies." A proper grounding in law and history, Morris said, "are essentially necessary to entitle you to participate in the honor of serving a Free People."

Washington was, for both Morrises, a most genial guest. He made a point, soon after his appointment as president, of escorting Mary to a concert at the City Tavern. This was a glorious moment for Mary, whose standing as Philadelphia's leading lady had been threatened by the recent return from London of Thomas Willing's daughter, now Ann Bingham. Her beauty, European fashions, and lavish entertainments had created a social sensation. Washington also shared with Mary an affinity for cards—she was reputed "one of the best cardplayers in Philadelphia"—and their contests filled quiet hours at home.

For his first few weeks in town Washington spent afternoons and evenings making the rounds of his many friends and contacts, visiting with John Penn, John Ross, Thomas Willing, George Clymer, William Bingham, Thomas Mifflin—whose efforts to undermine the commander during the war had been buried, if not forgotten—and Mayor Samuel Powel. But as the weeks wore on and his social obligations had been answered, Washington spent more of his time with Morris and his family, the two friends sharing their hopes and fears in the evenings after the debates at the State House were adjourned.

On most Sundays, Washington joined Robert, Mary, and their children in attending services at Christ Church, where Mary's brother William led the services. Robert held lease to a box pew near the front of the congregation, as did Ben Franklin; George would later do the same for himself and Martha. Morris and Washington appear to have shared a respectful but distanced regard for religion. Like Washington, Morris rarely invoked his creed in his correspondence; when he did, it was in the most generic fashion, as when he wrote, to John Jay, "God bless you & grant success to America." William White never remarked on his brother-in-law's religious practice, but he did on Washington's, observing that, while Martha Washington always took communion on Sacrament Sundays, her husband never did. "I do not believe," White recalled years later, "that any degree of recollection will bring to my mind any fact which would prove General Washington to have been a believer in the Christian Revelation."

Though Morris and Washington both kept their own counsel during the sessions of the convention, their spirits rose and fell with its progress or the lack of it. One dark hour occurred early in July, when the delegates appeared stalemated over the question of representation, the small states threatening to walk out if they were not accorded equal weight in the Senate with their more populous neighbors. The impasse looked so intractable that Franklin proposed the delegates pray for divine counsel, but this pacific gesture was refused.

That night Gouverneur Morris, who had taken leave for several weeks to attend business matters in New York, returned to Philadelphia to resume his attendance. Arriving after dark, he stopped at Market Street to find Robert Morris and Washington commiserating over "the deplorable state of things . . . animosities were kindling, some of the members were threatening to go home, and at this alarming crisis a dissolution of the convention was hourly to be apprehended." The two revolutionary chieftains briefed Gouverneur on the stalemate, and at the convention the next day he delivered a passionate speech that "painted the consequences of an abortive result . . . in all the deep colors suited to the occasion." Gouverneur did not renounce his partisan position on the issue at hand, but he "spoke with such eloquence and power on the necessity of union . . . that he effected a change in the feelings of the members which was the means of restoring harmony." The deadlock had been broken.

In the weeks that followed Gouverneur Morris's return, the delegates reached—over Gouverneur's objections—the "Great Compromise," allowing for proportional representation in the House but designating two senators for each state, thus balancing the prerogatives of the small states with the large. With this breakthrough in hand, the convention voted to put its deliberations into a Committee of Detail, which would sort through the twenty-three resolutions passed so far and present a coherent document that would form the basis for a final settlement. Here James Wilson played a pivotal role, securing his enduring claim as a primary architect of the federal union. In the meantime, the delegates took an eleven-day adjournment.

The weather had broken, the searing heat of early July lifted by a northwest breeze, and Robert Morris and his coterie decided to exploit the convention hiatus by getting out of town. On Monday, July 30, Gouverneur Morris and Washington climbed into Morris's four-wheeled phaeton and headed west, following the course of the Schuylkill until they reached the dilapidated remains of the army camp at Valley Forge. There, under the shadow of Mount Misery, the two friends cast lines into the stream that formed the eastern bound of the old encampment.

The pair spent the night at the home of Jane Moore, owner of a two-hundred-acre farm who had provided what forage she could during the army's desolate winter there ten years before. The next evening, after another day of sport and soulful reminiscence, Washington and Morris returned to find that "Robert Morris & his Lady" had arrived in the afternoon. The friends dined together, spent the night, and after waiting out a morning rainfall, headed back to the city.

The four spent a quiet evening closeted at the house on Market Street. Two days later, extending their retreat from politics and from the demands of Philadelphia society, the little clutch of friends headed out again— Gouverneur, Robert, Mary, and George—this time up toward Trenton, for another round of fishing and a visit with Samuel Ogden, an ironmonger and brother-in-law to Gouverneur. They made their way back on the evening of Sunday, August 5, clattering along the darkened road, thinking, certainly, about the political labors that lay ahead, but sharing as well a sense of intimacy that never deserted them.

· · ·

As much as he celebrated the event of the convention, Morris's delight was not unalloyed. Early in the spring Carter Braxton, a sometime partner in trade and privateering ventures and once his closest confidant in Virginia, sued Morris to settle their extensive accounts. In April, Tench Tilghman, Morris's good friend and his most reliable ally in the tobacco trade, died at age forty-two of hepatitis, probably contracted during his service in the army. And on June 12, in New York, Arthur Lee fulfilled Jefferson's prophecy by opening a new investigation into the long dormant accounts of the Secret Committee. Morris, of course, was the target.

Around the same time, Morris received the worst of all possible news from Europe. Early in the spring, while attending the business of his partners, John Rucker had received an unexpected call for payment of bills written by Morris and Constable. Under the plans laid by his partners, Rucker was to fund them on his own account and await the arrival of warrants from Constable or tobacco ships from Morris. Instead, Rucker panicked, sailing first to London and then back to New York, leaving the bills to be protested.

Rucker's failure of nerve, it turned out, stemmed from his uncle John Anthony, head of the family's mercantile operations in London. After learning of the troubles the Bank of North America had encountered at the Pennsylvania Assembly, John Anthony warned his nephew he would be disinherited by his family if he accepted any more bills from America. Forced to choose between his partners in America and the more immediate threat from his uncle in London, Rucker meekly acquiesced.

Learning of this debacle, William Constable was aghast. Besides scrambling Morris's tobacco engagements, Rucker's withdrawal meant the firm's contracted interest payment of the American debt in Holland would not go through. As Constable explained to a business associate, "When we had just got matters in train Mr. Rucker writes that his Uncle in London has forbad him to accept American bills. . . . This has blasted the fairest prospect."

The government managed the failure of the Constable payment in the usual way—the Board of Treasury relayed the news to John Adams, still serving as ambassador to Holland, and Adams arranged one last loan to cover the shortfall. Morris, however, had no such backup, and the call on his bills threw his tobacco operations in disarray. "What a foolish piece of work Rucker has made for the sake of obliging his uncle," Morris wrote Constable. "I have drawn above £100,000 on him, he will be supplied with Funds to pay punctually his acceptances and that alone would have given him credit—but it is over."

In fact, it was far from over. The process for rejecting of claims on third-party institutions took several steps; these notes had been stopped at the first stage—protested for nonacceptance—but had not yet been returned under protest for nonpayment, in which case Morris would have to pay damages to his creditors and fund the bills anew.

Sorting through the tangled affairs Rucker had left behind in London would take the next several years, but the initial shock, and the injury to Morris's reputation and credit, was already accomplished. Nor was there any containing the damage; word of his protested bills got out on June 27, the night before Morris was to host a large dinner party. When the guests assembled, news of the misfortune befalling the "great man" of Philadelphia commerce dominated the dinner-table gossip. It was all, as Washington recorded in his diary, "a little Mal apropos."

It was a huge setback for Morris and his partners, serious enough that Gouverneur had to leave the federal convention to spend two weeks in New York conferring with Constable. But it did not diminish Robert Morris's pride in the final product of the convention, printed and signed by the delegates on September 17 after four months in continuous session. The business done, the delegates sat down to one last dinner at City Tavern, and then headed back to their home states to seek the endorsement of their constituents.

The critics, and there would be many, would denounce the Constitution for its centralization of powers and its deliberate dilution of direct democracy. Morris had his own misgivings. "This paper has been the subject of infinite investigation, disputation, and declamation," Morris wrote to a friend that winter. "While some have boasted it as a work from Heaven, others have given it a less righteous origin. I have many reasons to believe that it is the work of plain, honest men, and such, I think, it will appear. Faulty it must be, for what is perfect? But if adopted, experience will, I believe, show that its faults are just the reverse of what they are supposed to be." Whatever qualms he had, Morris set them aside in giving his full endorsement to the new national government. This had been his goal since he first assumed the title of Financier, and it would be the vehicle for implementing, at long last, the full breadth of his national program.

— *Chapter 18* —

THE FIRST
FEDERAL CONGRESS

The day after the Constitutional Convention closed its affairs, the Pennsylvania Assembly resumed its sessions in the room the convention had vacated. That morning Franklin, Morris, and the other Pennsylvania delegates filed in to the State House to present the fruits of their labors. At that moment, the nomenclature of the legislature changed. The Republicans, organized in opposition to the Pennsylvania constitution, became the sponsors of the new national charter—they were the Federalists. And the Constitutionalists, who saw the federal Constitution as a threat to state sovereignty, were in that instant robbed of their preferred moniker. They became the Anti-Federalists.

The lines were already drawn. The Republicans hoped to see their home state take the lead in ratifying the new framework for a national government, but the opposition was already caucusing at the home of Judge George Bryan, a Constitutionalist standard-bearer. Even before the work of the convention became public, an Anti-Federalist writer had denounced it as "the most daring attempt to establish a despotic aristocracy among freemen the world has ever witnessed." More to the point for the Pennsylvania partisans, Bryan voiced his fear that the federal charter "will annihilate our own [state] constitution."

At first, the two parties in the Assembly observed a tacit truce while they awaited formal referral of the new Constitution from Congress. A week later, however, with no word from New York, the Federalists decided to forge ahead. The legislative session was slated to adjourn on September 29, and the backers of the new Constitution didn't want to hazard its ratification on the results of the October election for Assembly. On the morning of Friday the 28th, George Clymer moved to schedule a ratifying convention. The motion passed by a two-to-one margin—a measure of Federalist strength in the Assembly—and consideration of the date and rules for the convention was scheduled for that afternoon. The Assembly then broke for lunch.

When the lawmakers reassembled, around four P.M., the Federalists realized they had been had. Recognizing they could not block the vote, nineteen Anti-Federalist assemblymen simply did not return to the State House, leaving the body two votes short of a quorum. This tactic had been employed by both parties in the past, most memorably by the radicals in 1776, when their boycott brought down the old charter government. It worked again; a sergeant-at-arms was sent out to collect the Anti-Federalist holdouts, but they gruffly spurned his summons. The Assembly was done for the day.

That night an express courier arrived from New York with the formal referral of the Constitution from Congress, setting the stage for a Saturday showdown at the State House. A crowd of onlookers turned out the next morning to watch, but when time came for the Assembly to convene, only the Federalists appeared. Now the State House spectators stepped in to settle the question. John Barry, one of Morris's favorite sea captains, led a rowdy gang from the Assembly gallery to a nearby boardinghouse where the Anti-Federalists had holed up the night before. They smashed the windows, broke down the door, seized the two radical assemblymen they found there, and dragged them back to the Assembly. This was not the sort of street action the militants were accustomed to; "none but gentleman mobs have been active in Philadelphia," George Bryan sniffed later.

Arriving at the State House, the two shanghaied delegates demanded their release. But Barry and his followers blocked the door, a quorum was declared, and a ratifying convention set for late November. Balloting to name delegates was set for November 6. It was election season in Pennsylvania.

The weeks that followed saw the most spirited and contentious public contest in Philadelphia since the debates over independence. James Wilson, Benjamin Rush, and the redoubtable Pelatiah Webster penned tracts for the Federalists, while Samuel Bryan, George's son and a former clerk for the Assembly, won fame for scathing Anti-Federalist essays published under the sobriquet "Centinel."

For all the bombast, the results of the annual Assembly election in October proved surprisingly tame, with fewer seats changing hands than in any vote since the Revolution began. The Republicans—running as "Friends to the Federal Constitution"—retained a comfortable majority in the Assembly, and on November 6 they scored an equal, commanding margin in the election of delegates to the ratifying convention. Robert Morris, however, did not run; nor would he be on hand for the state's verdict on the Constitution.

With the election returns still coming in, Morris began packing chests with clothing and legal papers for an extended road trip. The outcome of the balloting was not much in doubt, and Morris's business concerns could be put off no longer. In early November, Robert Morris and Gouverneur Morris set out for Virginia to sort out the long-standing dispute with Carter Braxton, and restore the tangled affairs of Robert's massive tobacco operation.

Along the way, the two companions stopped in Baltimore for a visit with Robert's oldest child, Polly, the daughter he'd sired out of wedlock. In 1781, Polly had married Charles Croxall, a Baltimore native who'd fought in the Continental Army and spent several years as a prisoner of war. Morris had placed funds in trust for Polly long before, but had seen her rarely during her adult life. Now she was pregnant with her second child, and at that point just recovering from a persistent fever. The two Morrises passed several days with Polly and her family.

There was, as usual with Morris, a business as well as a social purpose to their visit. Croxall was something of a ne'er-do-well and Morris had advanced him a series of loans, few of which Croxall had managed to repay. Croxall had tried his hand at farming and in shipping, but failed in both. This led to some tense moments around the kitchen table as Robert and Gouverneur each went over Croxall's engagements and his future prospects. More pleasant was a morning jaunt to the Baltimore market where Morris bumped into Matthew Ridley, a friend and trading partner recently returned from Europe, who pressed his old chum to stop by his house for breakfast. Ridley had married Kitty Livingston, Robert and Mary's close friend and wartime tenant, and Morris was delighted to find her pregnant, like his daughter, and "very cheerful."

This venture southward was the first time in years that Robert had spent an extended period away from Mary. The last time was in 1776, when Robert sent her out of the city for fear of a British invasion. He felt this latest separation keenly, and his letters home displayed a level of intimacy in their marital bond not present a decade before. "You frequently are the subject of my meditations whether I am in or out of company," Morris wrote from his room at the Croxalls'. "I will not make love to you at this time of day," he wrote coyly, "but I shall never fail to feel more Esteem and affection than I can express." In closing, Morris addressed Mary by her nickname. "I am my dear Molly ever yours."

Departing from Baltimore in the morning, Robert and Gouverneur continued south, jostling over the rough country roads in Robert's two-bench, four-wheeled phaeton, each with his own servant perched on the driver's bench up front. They made their next stop at Mount Vernon, where they stayed three days with George Washington. There was talk of politics, of course, and of the French tobacco contract, which was a paramount concern to Washington and many of his tobacco-growing neighbors. But this was primarily a chance to savor the pleasures of a southern fall in the shade of Washington's white-columned veranda overlooking the broad reach of the Potomac.

The two Morrises got back on the road on Sunday, making their way to Richmond, a commercial and political center that had replaced Williamsburg as the state capital in 1780. The travelers took up residence with Benjamin Harrison, the former governor and, as with so many others, a sometime business associate of Morris's. Harrison's plantation, known then and now as Berkeley, covered eight thousand acres anchored by a three-story brick mansion set in a stand of sculpted mulberry trees. The two Morrises shared a bedroom and used a second room as a study and office. The pair worked constantly. "We live well as to eating and drinking," Robert informed Mary, "but being closely engaged in business we do not mix much with society."

The dispute with Braxton dated back to the Secret Committee, when Braxton served as agent and partner with Willing & Morris in purchasing tobacco for remittance to Beaumarchais and the other French arms traders. Willing & Morris had put up much of the financing, and Braxton had never refunded their advances.

Morris had sent Gouverneur to Virginia in 1785 in hopes of getting those accounts settled. Braxton had recently suffered a series of reversals, and Robert was reluctant to add to his burdens. "Poor Braxton," he wrote to Gouverneur at the time. "What a situation is his; I am sorry for him and for his family." Gouverneur wrote back to assure Morris he had managed to "settle accounts in the most Amicable manner, holding out always the Hope of Relief and of putting off the Evil Day" of a final collection.

Two years later, Braxton had been forced by creditors to sell his plantation. Desperate for funds, he filed suit to challenge the settlement with Morris, alleging that Morris owed him substantial sums due in part to losses attributed to currency depreciation. Morris had by now lost sympathy with his onetime friend. "I have at last got Mr. Braxton's accounts with a specification of all his rascally claims," Morris wrote to Ridley in Baltimore. "It is well I came down on this business, for I have the Documents to prove in the fullest & most satisfactory manner the Villainy & Folly of his attempts to plunder me, in which he has not the smallest chance of succeeding." In this Morris was correct, but it would take a team of lawyers and twelve years of litigation before Morris was awarded a judgment of twenty thousand pounds in Virginia currency. By then Braxton had died insolvent.

Toward the end of November, while Robert and Gouverneur were preparing court filings in the Braxton lawsuit, word arrived from New York that the protested bills served on John Rucker were being returned to America. This was a moment Morris had feared for months, and he sat down to unburden himself by writing to his wife. "This letter my dear Molly is the messenger of bad news," Morris began. He had learned that "the next British Packet will bring back a parcel of my ill-fated bills."

The physical return of a bill was the final step in the long round-circuit traveled by a protested note. There could be no more appeals, no chance that some correspondent house in London or Amsterdam had been found that might yet honor his credit. Morris now had to raise the cash to cover his original tobacco purchases, plus charges for damages that ran as high as 20 percent. Worse was the blow to his credit, which made new borrowing more difficult and more expensive.

The prospect shook Morris's celebrated self-confidence to the core. "I am exceedingly hurt in my feelings," he wrote Mary, "notwithstanding that my mind was previously prepared for this event." Morris confessed his weakness, then vowed to battle against it. "There are men in the world who would be tolerably easy in similar circumstances to mine but I am not one of that class. I shall summon all my fortitude and meet my fate with the best grace in my powers, but I now lay my account in being very uncomfortable for months to come."

Speaking as much to himself as to his wife, Morris asked Mary to persevere until he could restore their fortune. "My greatest consolation is the certainty of being able to pay every farthing and of having sufficient left for my family. This being certain, you must compose yourself on this occasion and make yourself easy, leaving to me the vexation, mortification & struggles which it is my part to sustain, and I shall use every exertion to clear myself of this situation the soonest that circumstances can possibly admit.

Keep up your spirits, live as usual and the less you say or hear of these affairs the better for the present."

This was a rare display of emotion for a man accustomed to the vicissitudes of mercantile trade and party politics. "I cannot add to this letter as it awakens my feelings too much," Morris wrote. "God bless you and my children. I hope to make you happy as you can wish and that before any great length of time shall pass away."

Mary Morris responded to these poignant letters with attentive sympathy and useful observations on life at home. She wrote in December to let him know that the Constitution had won ratification. "As you know that I am something of a politician I therefore could not forebear informing you that the federal government is agreed to by our convention." Mary made a point of telling Morris he'd been acknowledged during the festive demonstrations that greeted the news. "They did not forget *you*," she wrote. The mob in Market Street had stopped to raise a salute to Morris. "We had three cheers."

In January Mary wrote to ask her husband for more information on "the fatal event of your bills." She let Morris know that word of his problems was circulating around town, but that his reputation might still be restored. Some friends had assured her that he would soon recover, and that "You would find the stroke nothing like so heavy as it first threatened." Mary also told Morris that Louis Stephen Le Couteulx, one of the three principals in his French banking firm, was in Philadelphia. Considering the state of his debts, Robert may have been relieved not to be on hand for Le Couteulx's arrival, but for Mary the banker's visit presented a social predicament; Ben Franklin, receiving the Parisian financier, had suggested that Mary would be glad to host Louis and his wife "for several days." Mary spoke no French and managed deftly to pass on the engagement. She would be, she said, "very careful in future of giving those French friends of ours an invitation."

Mary did not confine herself to news. She reciprocated Robert's warmth, and assured him of the depth of their connection. "O my dearest partner," she pined at one point. "How my heart yearns for you to return to enjoy with me the amiable society of our children."

However reassuring were these letters from home, Morris had to wrestle on his own with the anxiety brought on by the failure of his credit in Europe. This was new ground for him. His fears startled him awake at night. He contemplated leaving business for good, and vowed upon his return home "to make a great reform in our expenses." He asked Mary to press the children to their studies, since they would have to "make their own way in the world."

In May, Gouverneur Morris crashed the phaeton while driving too fast down the main street in Richmond—his earlier accident had failed to reform his reckless streak. After helping Gouverneur out of the wreck, Morris faced a small crisis of conscience. Should he buy a new carriage? He decided against it, explaining to Mary that "I cannot bear the idea of insulting my creditors by making a show in any way whilst I am in debt and not able to pay as fast as I ought."

But this newfound modesty had to contend with traits of pride and status that were deeply ingrained in Morris's outlook. The same week as the carriage accident, he counseled Mary not to skimp on a purchase she and her mother were contemplating for the house. "Mrs. White and you must choose the handsomest chintz for the new furniture," Morris wrote, "for although I am not so rich as I thought myself, yet I hate to do anything by halves."

During breaks in the legal conferences over the Braxton case, Morris had a chance to review in person the functioning of his Virginia tobacco operations. He did not like what he found. Alexander, it turned out, had been spending the advances from Morris on speculations in state and federal securities, and using that paper to purchase tobacco. This drove up the price he paid for leaf, expanded the amount of his calls for advance funds, and further undermined Morris's credit.

Especially galling was that, among his financial speculations, Alexander had bought up many of the original bills Morris had written for tobacco purchases. Now that those bills were being returned unpaid, Alexander was charging Morris full damages, "although he purchased them at an under rate of exchange from those to whom they were passed in the first instance, and paid for them with my money." Further, Alexander was now refusing to pay for tobacco he'd contracted to buy, instead holding the funds advanced by Morris as surety against the protested bills.

Convinced he was being swindled by Alexander, Morris opened a full inquiry into his activities, interviewing third-party vendors and seeking to assemble a documentary record of Alexander's conduct. Alexander himself was no help, refusing to open his books to Morris and instead offering statements that inflated the advances he made to subagents who may or may not have spent the money to purchase tobacco.

This new and unexpected imbroglio forced the Morrises to extend their stay in Virginia by several months. Robert and Gouverneur now had two protracted legal actions to manage—the defense of Braxton's charges and a new case they prepared against Alexander. Gouverneur was serving as Robert's personal lawyer, but each lawsuit would require a team of local attorneys to collect evidence and attend hearings. At the outset, Morris's principal lawyer was Benjamin Harrison, Jr., the son of the governor, but in the end the management of both cases devolved to John Marshall, a veteran of Valley Forge and a friend of Washington's who later became the dominant chief justice in the early life of the U.S. Supreme Court.

While he was attending these legal problems, Morris was at the same time seeking to maintain his tobacco shipments. The price in Europe had fallen to the point that every cargo he sent out yielded a profit, and those profits were the only way he would be able to pay off his dishonored bills. Moreover, in consequence of the campaign by Jefferson and Lafayette, the Farmers had agreed to accept shipments on the open market, though at the same price stipulated for Robert Morris. To Morris, this was a signal to ship more tobacco and soak up the excess demand. "I am on a sure footing and shall keep on," Morris wrote when the new terms were announced. "I am determined not to sit tamely & see the bread taken out of my mouth."

But Morris now faced major new obstacles. The return of his bills meant he could no longer buy on his personal credit, and the falling out with Alexander deprived Morris of his primary purchasing agent in Virginia. Forced to innovate, he began relying on intermediaries whose purchases and shipments could not be traced back to him. Among these was Robert Cary, who had taken over Tench Tilghman's Baltimore firm after Tilghman's death. Morris hardly knew Cary but did not hesitate to take him into confidence; with so many of his contacts burned, Morris had little choice.

Writing Cary in February, Morris laid out a scheme to ship a cargo of half a million pounds of tobacco as soon as the winter ice pack broke up. Cary was to issue bills against a new correspondent mercantile house in London, making them payable at sixty days after presentation. The cargo should be purchased on Cary's account, landed at Le Havre, and directed to Le Couteulx, with the bill of lading sent to the London house. "You will see that my name is not to appear at all in this transaction," Morris explained. "I mean to guard against attachments should any of the Bill Holders be so ill natured or impatient as to attempt it either on this or the other side of the waters." Morris was not attempting to defraud his creditors, but he had to keep his trade going in order to revive his funds. Attachment of his cargo, he clarified, "would not answer any good purpose to them as I shall take up the protest much sooner than they can possibly recover by Law."

Staging major shipments through new partners was tricky business, but here Morris was in his element, and he pursued new ventures with obvious relish. "As it is probable we may make better music by going together I will strike it and play my part," Morris cajoled one prospective factor. "You will therefore go on with the purchases at the current price for any amount until you make the cargo proposed."

Remarkably, Morris was able not only to sustain his purchasing operation, but to exceed the pace he'd set the previous year. In 1787 and early 1788, he shipped to France 33 million tons of tobacco, satisfying his contract with the Farmers General at a price that returned him a handsome profit. But most of those funds would remain tied up in Europe for years, and in the meantime, his legal battles dragged on through the courts, draining his resources and sapping his spirit. Holker and Braxton in particular had been good friends before their affairs led then into dispute; Morris could not resist feeling betrayed and disillusioned. "I hope to be done with them all by and by," Morris confided to a friend. "But I confess to you that the ingratitude and ill usage which I have experienced from these men is nearly sufficient to deter me from ever again entering into extensive dealings with mankind."

As much as Morris was consumed with his legal and financial problems in Virginia, he could not escape the political rumblings emanating from Philadelphia. Far from settling the question of the Constitution, the endorsement of the ratifying convention in December had only stoked the resentments of the Anti-Federalists. After all the years of pitched political battles in the Assembly and in Congress the Pennsylvania militants were not about to let the vote of a popular convention sit as the last word. In the angry press battle that ensued, Robert Morris became a primary target.

His chief antagonist was Samuel Bryan, whose initial volleys as the Centinel had become a running calumny against Morris and his cohort. Washington had been duped, Bryan opined, and Franklin was too old to resist the machinations of "James [Wilson] the Caledonian, lieutenant general of the myrmidons of power, under Robert the Cofferer"—a new epithet for Morris—and "his aide-de-camp Gouverno, the cunning man." Arrayed against this clique, in Bryan's formulation, were the frontier politicians Whitehill, Smilie, and William Findley, "that bright constellation of patriots," who had opposed Morris in the bank debates, and now stood firm against the federal Constitution.

In February, after Massachusetts had ratified the Constitution and adoption of the new frame of government by the states seemed assured, Sam Bryan returned with a new and more specific challenge. The ban on ex-post-facto laws, the Centinel proposed, had been included in the Constitution in order to "screen the numerous public defaulters," ensuring that "the unaccounted millions lying in their hands would become their private property." Writing in a tone of leering sarcasm, Bryan averred that the "immaculate convention" included among its delegates "a number of the principal public defaulters," including "the late Financier."

A month later, in his seventeenth installment, Bryan expanded his attack on Morris. Here Bryan assembled all the charges ever raised by the Lees, Henry Laurens, and Theveneau de Francy—that Morris was bankrupt at the outset of the war, that his position with the Secret Committee "afforded unrestrained scope to peculation and embezzlement of the public property," and that by charging losses to the public account, and successful ventures to his own, he had become wealthy. "When we add to these considerations the principles of the MAN . . . and the immense wealth he has dazzled the world with since, can it be thought unreasonable to conclude, that the principal source of his affluence was the commercial agency of the United States, during the war?—not that I would derogate from his successful ingenuity in his numerous speculations in the paper moneys, Havana monopoly and job, or in the sphere of financiering."

The Centinel was, surely, another of the "bug writers" Franklin had warned of back in 1781, "who will abuse you while you are serving them, and wound your character in nameless Pamphlets." Bryan's accusations were grave, some made publicly for the first time, and they stung. Writing Mary in April, Morris said the columns brought to mind a friend who had recently taken the field for a duel of honor. "If I was to fight it should be with the authors of that abuse so freely lavished on me in the Prints," Morris fumed.

Instead of pistols Morris took up his pen, writing a defense of his conduct for the printers in Philadelphia. But it was a weak performance, suggesting that his remove from office and his legal entanglements had dulled his enthusiasm for public debate. He asserted that, in Congress and as Financier, he never touched "one shilling" of public money, but then conceded that as a contractor, he received "considerable sums of money." He had executed his contracts, he wrote, but they remained unsettled because vouchers were scattered and key papers were lost at sea. Congress had been slow to pursue a settlement, but so had he. "I have indeed been less solicitous on this subject than otherwise I should have been, from the conviction that there is a balance in my favor."

This was a surprisingly tame argument for the man who had scolded the state governors and floated the Confederation on his own personal credit. Instead of indignation, Morris could only muster diffidence. "I think it necessary to apologize for having written this letter, to all who may take the trouble of reading it," Morris wrote. "A newspaper is certainly an improper place for stating and settling public accounts."

Part of his timidity lay in the fact that, on the score of his unsettled accounts, Morris and the Centinel were largely in agreement. As Financier, Morris had introduced new and exacting standards of accounting; the state of his own Secret Committee records was a continuing embarrassment. He had struggled with them for months in 1778 and then surrendered them to Henry Laurens, but Laurens had no more success than he in sorting them out.

The papers had lain dormant until 1786, when Arthur Lee took them into custody of the Board of Treasury. In perusing the documents, Lee fell upon the work of a prior committee, which had approved payments made under the Secret Committee. "For the honor of the committee," Lee wailed in a private memorandum, "for the honor of Congress, for the honor of human nature, it is to be hoped none of them drew up this false and foolish report—it must have been Robert Morris himself who wrote it!" Yet Lee made no more progress than his predecessors in reaching a verdict on Morris's accounts, and the whole business was left unresolved, a source of chagrin to Morris and fodder for his enemies.

Morris had hoped to return to Philadelphia by May, but the spring came and went, and still he was in Richmond, consulting attorneys, drawing up legal briefs, and securing new factors and new tobacco deals throughout the Tidewater. In June, Gouverneur took time out to attend the state ratifying convention in Richmond, which approved the new federal Constitution by a narrow vote, but Robert could not spare the time from his business concerns. He finally got free in July, and wrote Mary to rendezvous with him at Mount Vernon. Washington wrote as well, encouraging Mary to bring her children along, "for with much truth we can assure you of the pleasure it would give us to see them all under this roof with you and Mr. Morris."

The family gathering took place on July 12, a warm, sun-drenched Saturday; Robert and Gouverneur arrived from the south, and Mary from the north, in company with Robert Jr. and Thomas, just arrived from their years of schooling in Europe, and Hetty, their elder daughter. It was a reunion for Robert and Mary and for Robert and his sons, and a festive afternoon for Martha Washington. Her marriage with George had never produced children, so she was always gratified by the presence of young people in her home.

For Robert, George, and Gouverneur this summer dalliance was a rare moment of carefree relaxation. So many times in the past, their encounters had taken place amid crises of war and state, the fate of entire armies and the course of the Revolution hanging in the balance. For once the pressure was off. Yet at the same time, each of this trio recognized that, however Washington treasured his status as a private man, a farmer attuned to the land and the seasons, the time was fast approaching when the new government they each had done so much to erect would commence. Inevitably, inescapably, Washington would be called back to assume the mantle of command, and soon after, in some capacity, each of the Morrises would join him. Ambling among the gardens of Washington's graceful estate, or down the shady trails to the slow-moving Potomac, these three friends would have talked of business and politics, of family and friends, but there was a lightness, a buoyancy and an optimism. Their trials were behind them, the future appeared full of promise.

The interlude lasted through the weekend. On Monday, George and Martha escorted their friends for the first few miles of their homeward journey, a cavalcade of carriages, coachmen shouting, teamed horses racing along the well-tended river road. They traveled in train as far as Alexandria, where they all sat down "in a large company" to an afternoon banquet hosted by William Hunter, a Scottish merchant and the mayor of the town. After the meal the friends took their leave, the Washingtons heading back to Mount Vernon, and the Morrises north, through Fairfax County and into Maryland.

Arriving back at Philadelphia, Morris found that the Centinel had less influence than his columns had bite. The state remained divided over the Constitution, but the Federalists retained their strong influence in the city and their dominance over the Assembly. Moreover, it had been decided in the Constitutional Convention that while the seats in the House of Representatives and the Electoral College—a newfangled institution designed to blunt sectional interest in the election of the president—would be elected at large, the delegates to the Senate would be chosen by the state legislatures. The candidates for Senate, at least, would be spared the rigors of another campaign.

The selection of Pennsylvania's two senators was taken at the end of September, when the Federalists in the Assembly convened after hours at Hassell's Tavern, one of the watering holes across the street from the State House. As the dominant figure in their faction, Robert Morris was a natural choice. The second was a more tactical pick; cognizant of the complaint that their party was rooted in and favored Philadelphia, the Federalist politicians settled on William Maclay, an acerbic, land-rich surveyor and lawyer from Harrisburg who described himself as a "rigid republican." Maclay was a consistent critic of the radical state constitution, but as his colleagues in the Senate would soon discover, he found much to criticize in the new federal charter as well. Still, he was a confirmed Federalist, and emerged as the consensus candidate who could bridge Pennsylvania's east-west political divide. The decisions made at the tavern were confirmed by a formal vote of the Assembly a week later. Maclay received sixty-seven votes, and Morris, the Federalists' partisan favorite, thirty-one.

Soon after his selection to the Senate, Morris joined Gouverneur for another business trip, this time to New York, the current seat of Congress and the head office of Constable, Rucker & Company. Robert had unpleasant business pending with both entities.

In Congress, Morris sought the appointment of commissioners to settle once and for all his outstanding accounts, but he found that body languishing in its twilight, unable to muster a quorum. Instead, to his dismay, he learned that among its last acts was approval of a committee report finding that much of the business of the Secret Committee, more than two million dollars, "remains to be accounted for."

This verdict was based on the probe staged by the Board of Treasury—chiefly Arthur Lee and Samuel Osgood—who had dismissed the statements filed by Morris, William Bingham, John Ross, and the other primary contractors in the secret arms trade as self-interested and unsupported by vouchers and other receipts. Lee's own accounts from the same period had been approved on just such a basis, but Lee was not one to let consistency get in the way of self-righteous judgment. Lee assured the committee he was conducting "a full enquiry" into the contracts and the funds expended in France, but in its last report, on September 30, the committee could only conclude, "the subject of this enquiry seems to be involved in darkness."

The murky state of the Secret Committee contracts was consistent with most of the other departments of the government from the early stages of the war; accounts and records had been scattered or lost, and those that remained were, in the words of one federal auditor, "involved in impenetrable intricacy and irregularity." What distinguished the accounts of the Secret Committee was the avid interest of Arthur Lee, and his burning determination to settle, at the distance of more than a decade, the scores of the Silas Deane affair. It was, in fact, his last harangue. Displaced under the new government, he returned to Virginia, failed in a bid for Congress, and lived out his days in gloomy resentment. All his years in politics, Lee was convinced, "have only ruined myself without benefiting the public," and now he was "cast off with as much disgrace as they can fix upon me." Lee retired to an estate he purchased overlooking the Rappahannock River and sought, unsuccessfully, for a wife to reside there with him. He died alone, at the age of fifty-one, in 1792.

Lee's last thrust at Morris bore fruit in November, when Samuel Bryan got hold of the committee report on finances. In the twenty-third—and penultimate—installment of the Centinel, Bryan cited the reference to two million dollars in unsettled accounts as proof of the transgressions of "the Cofferer."

"What conclusion must every dispassionate person make of this delinquency?" Bryan asked. "Is it not more than probable that he has converted the public money into his own property, and that, fearful of detection and reluctant to refund, he has, and will as long as he is able, avoid an investigation and a settlement?"

Morris responded quickly, and in more cogent fashion than his first reply in April. He had traveled to New York expressly to straighten out his accounts, Morris said in a public letter, and he was doing "everything in my power to obtain a final settlement." Here, at last, Morris offered an affirmative argument in his defense. The sheer volume of the sums in question, Morris wrote, only went to "prove the extent and vigor of my exertions in the public cause." Any public judgment must await the result of the official inquiry. "Till that settlement shall take place, no candid citizen will draw an inference against me merely from the importance of the trusts which have been committed to me by my country." Morris did not mention that Congress had failed to take up his request; to him, it was enough that he had made the effort.

Stymied in Congress, Morris turned his attention to business, sitting down with Gouverneur Morris and William Constable to see what could be salvaged of their firm's credit and finances. It was an ugly story. After leaving his partners' bills to bounce, John Rucker had returned to New York to consult with Constable, then sailed back to London to face his uncle, and at last turned about again and sailed back to New York. There, exhausted and disgraced, he died. Rucker was not a drunkard like Thomas Morris, but there was something akin to Thomas in his tragic demise; it appeared that, for both young men, the pressure of handling the demands on Robert's credit in Europe had overwhelmed and finally crushed them.

Constable was sure, when he met with Robert, that had Rucker held his ground Morris's engagement could all have been answered. But by now there was no retrieving the credit of the firm. They agreed to re-form the partnership as Constable & Company, with Morris remaining a silent partner, and the affairs of the firm under Constable's direct control. This did little, however, to restore Morris's wounded credit in Europe. Toward the end of October, he settled on a new approach. He would send Gouverneur Morris to Europe.

Gouverneur would have plenty to do. He would attend to the final settlements on the tobacco contract, which had now run its course. He would negotiate extensions of credit with Le Couteulx & Company, which had imposed new limits pending negotiations with the Farmers. And he would seek to revive the land speculations that had stalled under the management of John Vaughan. After obtaining letters of introduction from George Washington, Gouverneur sailed from New York in December, bound for Paris.

Taking leave of his closest friend and adviser, Robert returned to Philadelphia to prepare for the first meeting of the new national government. More than a routine legislative session, this would be, in effect, an extension of the Constitutional Convention. The new federal charter had been drawn in broad strokes; it was up to the House and Senate to fill in the details and work out the balance between the various branches and departments of the government. There were no precedents, no guidelines. The very idea of republican government was still a novelty to the world. As the initial expression of the new Constitution, the first federal Congress would determine whether America's Revolution would sink into confusion and anarchy, or had opened a new epoch of democracy and self-rule.

Morris set out on the 1st of March, traveling in his coach past Trenton and up through New Jersey. At Princeton he fell in with the other Pennsylvania delegates, and William Maclay accepted his offer to ride with Morris the rest of the way. It was the beginning of a wary, often testy relationship between the two senators.

They could not have been more different—Morris was corpulent and affable while Maclay was slim and peevish; after hours, Maclay liked to retire early, while Morris tended to eat, drink, and tell stories late into the night. One evening, when Maclay sat down with Morris and the other Pennsylvania delegates and the wine began to flow, Maclay was appalled to see Morris and his friends throw off the formalities of their legislative decorum. From four in the afternoon, when the plates were cleared, until nine that night, "I never heard such a scene of bestial badney kept up in my life," Maclay recorded in disgust. "Mr. Morris is certainly the greatest blackguard in that way I ever heard open a mouth."

There were tactical differences as well; on the question of compensation for senators, Maclay endorsed a flat fee of five dollars per day of attendance at Congress, while Morris proposed eight dollars for senators and supported on principle a differential between senators and representatives. This was an old saw for Morris, who had long held that only generous salaries would draw men of talent into public service. This maxim offended Maclay's republican sensibilities; Morris offended them further when he announced that he cared not a whit for "the common opinions of people," but would follow his own counsel. Maclay would record the rocky course of his association with Morris, and the inner workings of the Senate, in a diary that became a prized resource for historians of the founding era.

Morris and Maclay arrived in New York at six A.M. on the day appointed for the inaugural session of the Congress. They were greeted by chiming church bells and an eleven-gun cannonade—one for each state that had ratified the Constitution. The City Hall on Wall Street had been remodeled at great expense by the French architect Pierre L'Enfant to serve as the new capital, and crowds gathered to gawk at the arriving delegates. There were too few delegates on hand to make a quorum, but the false start failed to dampen Morris's spirits. After settling in to a guest room at William Constable's house on Great Dock Street, Morris wrote Mary to share his sense of excitement. The preparations in the city "gave the air of a grand Festival to the 4th of March, 1789," Morris wrote; the date "will be celebrated as a new Era in the Annals of the World."

Later that evening Robert's son Thomas, in New York studying law, learned of his father's arrival and came by to visit. Thomas would be his frequent companion during his stay in New York, and would soon become a collaborator in his father's business affairs.

The House of Representatives finally got under way on April 1, and the Senate achieved its quorum a week later with the arrival of Richard Henry

Lee. As much as he detested the ineptitude of the Continental Congress during the year he spent as president, Lee had been among the first to resist the new Constitution when he sought, in September 1787, to block its referral to the states. Now he and his Virginia colleague, William Grayson, formed the core of a small Anti-Federalist bloc in the new Senate.

In their first test of strength, Lee and Grayson teamed with their allies in New England to deny Charles Thomson, the inveterate secretary of the Confederation Congress, the post of Senate secretary. Robert Morris sought to rally support for Thomson, but could muster only six votes—enough for a tie, but not enough to prevail. This did not indicate the intensity of Anti-Federalist feeling in the Senate so much as Lee's ability to revive the old Eastern faction in the new national legislature.

As it happened, Thomson was not on hand for the vote. He'd been dispatched, in April, to Mount Vernon, to formally notify George Washington that he'd been elected president. Washington set out soon after, traveling with Thomson in the general's great, cream-colored coach, their progress quickly taking on the tone of an inaugural holiday as throngs turned out to salute America's national hero. In every hamlet and every town—Alexandria, Baltimore, Wilmington—church bells pealed, speeches were delivered and answered, and mounted cavalry and uniformed militia turned out to escort the new president on his way.

Robert Morris hurried down from New York to be on hand for Washington's arrival in Philadelphia. This time, however, Washington felt constrained to decline the offer of lodging at Morris's home; as president, he would carefully avoid showing partiality to any friend or faction. Instead, he accepted the seat of honor at a banquet for 250 guests at City Tavern, and there he spent the night.

Washington did, however, take Morris aside for a political consultation. He proposed, as his step-grandson George Washington Parke Custis later recorded, that Morris take the post of treasury secretary in the new administration. Morris declined, probably out of concern that his troubled personal finances would occupy too much of his attention. But he offered an alternative: "I can recommend a far cleverer fellow than I am for your minister of finance," Custis quoted Morris, "your former aide-de-camp, Colonel Hamilton." The dialogue is undoubtedly reconstructed, as Custis was just eight years old at the time, but the timing of the meeting appears correct, and the story lived on within Washington's intimate circle.

At this point Morris had not spoken with Hamilton about stepping in at the treasury; they were political allies but not confidants. Nor, apparently, had Washington yet considered Hamilton for the job. Hamilton was still in his early thirties and had never held an important administrative post. Washington was startled at the suggestion, telling Morris that he never supposed Hamilton "had any knowledge of finance." But Robert had no qualms; he was exercising his instinct for young talent. "He knows everything," Morris told Washington. "To a mind like his nothing comes amiss."

The next day Washington continued his triumphant progress toward New York. Morris tarried in Philadelphia for another two weeks and was not on hand for the inauguration, a scene of pomp and celebration that drew the largest crowd ever assembled in Manhattan. Robert Livingston administered the oath on the second-story balcony of what was now dubbed Federal Hall. Washington seemed awed by this novel ceremony, speaking in such low tones that few could hear his brief statement, but Livingston provided an appropriate flourish. When the new president closed his speech by kissing the Bible, Livingston gravely pronounced, "It is done," then turned to the throng in the street and shouted, "Long live George Washington, President of the United States!"

Morris returned to New York on Monday, May 11. The next morning he took a long stroll with Maclay, who filled him in on the proceedings of the Senate. The two were still friendly at this point; they had drawn straws to decide which would serve for two years and which for six, and Morris had won the longer term, but as neither senator liked being away from home, there was no resentment on that score.

Morris hadn't missed much over the past two weeks. Most of that time had been spent in a curious, sometimes comical debate over how the president should be addressed. It was an indication of the embryonic stage the new government was in, and of just how far they had to go.

Old-world precedent called for elaborate titles to signify the dignity of rank, but the egalitarian rhetoric of the Revolution seemed to supersede those formalities. Surprisingly, it was the members of the Eastern faction, Richard Henry Lee and Vice President John Adams, who clung to the ancient modes; these early enemies of monarchy insisted that any reference to the president should be preceded by "His Highness," or "His Serene Highness," as were the princes of Europe and antiquity. Adams's predilection earned him only ridicule, and the backbench title "His Rotundity."

Arriving at Federal Hall to find this farcical debate still under way, Morris joined in with evident glee. The proposed title "Protector of the Liberties of America" was redundant as it was ridiculous, he advised; that responsibility accrued to the Congress as a whole. Two days later, as the discussion dragged on, Adams asked earnestly if it would be proper to receive a missive addressed to "His Excellency the Vice President." With the Senate breaking up in laughter, Morris offered that "the majesty of the people would do as they pleased."

By his layover in Philadelphia, Morris was absent when Washington began holding his levees, formal audiences for friends and visitors that were a holdover from his days as a military chieftain. These were dour affairs, the president stiff and distant—bows were exchanged, but not handshakes—and the conversation minimal, but they were obligatory and often the only way that members of Congress or the various petitioners to the government could have access to the president. Morris would attend plenty of these functions in the future, but at this point he and Washington had occasion for a more familial rendezvous. On May 27, a Wednesday afternoon, the two headed down to the waterfront, boarded a barge, and were rowed over to Elizabethtown, where they met their wives.

Martha Washington had followed her husband's route from Mount Vernon, enjoying the same ebullient reception in the towns along the way until she reached Philadelphia, where she stayed three days as Mary's guest at the Morris home on Market Street. From there Mary and Martha continued on together, Martha with her grandchildren Eleanor and "Wash," as young George Custis was called; and Mary with daughter Maria, then eight years old, all riding in Martha's capacious coach. Finding their husbands waiting on the Jersey bank of the Hudson, the two families were ferried to New York and greeted with a booming cannonade.

Mary stayed in town for a month, serving as a sort of attaché to Martha as she shouldered the social duties of the first first lady—teas, dinners, and levees of her own. Mary was always seated at her right, and helped guide her slightly homespun hostess through the latest fashions and customs of the urban gentry. Mary was affectionate with Martha, but she could also be a bit catty. At a dinner Robert hosted for several Pennsylvania delegates, William Maclay happened to mention how difficult it was to find good cream in New York. This prompted Mary to tell a story of dining at the president's house two nights before; when a large trifle was served for dessert, Mary had tasted it and found it rancid. She declined taking another bite, she told Maclay with a giggle, "but Mrs. Washington ate a whole heap of it!"

Mary returned home in July, followed by another round of heartfelt letters from Robert. She was, he wrote, the "Goddess whom I most adore on this earth," the object of his "first devotions." Aside from their separation, Morris continued to be haunted by his financial problems. All hopes now rested with Gouverneur in Paris. Morris wrote ominously that he had dreams of letters arriving from France, "but not agreeably if I am to interpret as the matter appeared to me." Until something turned up, Morris asked Mary to conserve her expenses. This need for thrift was a new experience for them both. Sending her one hundred dollars "for family expenses" in July, Morris wrote simply, "Your prudence will make it go as far as possible knowing as you do my embarrassments and the difficulties I must meet with in collecting money." A week later he advised her to raise money by selling a pair of prized Virginia horses, "for I must avoid expenses in time to come."

With the ceremony of its commencement now accomplished, the Congress got down to the pressing affairs of national legislation. Morris took a prominent role in the Senate, his colleagues relying on his mercantile and administrative expertise much as they had in the early years of the war. He sat on forty-one committees, more than any other senator, and reported for sixteen. And he coordinated with his longtime political allies Thomas Fitzsimmons and George Clymer in the House to press the broad agenda that he had proposed, and seen defeated, under the Confederation—the impost, the bank, the mint, and funding the debt—as well as a broad array of measures dealing with commerce and navigation. Morris was, as Maclay recognized early on, a force in his own right.

Yet, to the mystification and occasional annoyance of Maclay and some of his colleagues, Morris did not achieve his influence through assiduous attendance, in the manner of, say, James Madison, or by dominating the floor like Richard Henry Lee. Morris often failed to show for critical debates; at other times he would sit in silence. On one occasion he startled Maclay by confiding his plan to sit quietly while his foes made their speeches, to "attend with the utmost attention to all their arguments, fully determined to give them their utmost weight."

Maclay took this as vacillation, but Morris was heeding his long experience in public councils. He explained his legislative philosophy in conversation with a Dutch visitor in 1784: "When I was in the Assembly some members used to come to my house and ask me, 'What is your opinion on such a matter?' I told them, 'When I come to the House, I'll hear what they have to say and determine. Do you the same. Keep yourselves open as I do.' If I had given my opinion, and any circumstance brought me to a change, they would not have known how to reconcile it to my honesty, and would no more have trusted me." Like a seasoned, high-stakes gambler, Morris liked to keep his cards close to his vest.

Morris was not so consistently reserved in the Senate, however, as at the Constitutional Convention. He made occasional speeches on the floor and worked the hallways outside the Senate chamber, usually in pursuit of elements of the Nationalist agenda he'd outlined in his tenure as Financier. One early challenge drew Morris into a full display of his emotions and his skills. The question was the impost; there was consensus in Congress in favor of this first federal tax, but division over variances proposed for specific articles. In particular, the Senate was weighing a reduction in the tariff on molasses, which was a trade staple in the New England states where it was distilled into rum for domestic or export use.

The discussion was civil enough until Caleb Strong of Massachusetts took the floor. "Facing himself to the right of where Mr. Morris and I sat," Maclay wrote, Strong "fell violently on the members from Pennsylvania, with insinuations that seemed to import that we wished to overcharge New England with an undue proportion of the impost." This was a largely spurious argument; while Massachusetts imported molasses to make rum, Pennsylvania imported about the same quantity of other spirits. The tax burden was basically equivalent. More disturbing to Morris, Strong was introducing that spirit of sectional rivalry that had doomed the impost under the Confederation. Morris would not brook lightly another such division in the new forum of the Senate.

Sitting next to Morris, Maclay watched him physically recoil at Strong's accusation. "When this attack was begun, I could see his nostrils widen and his nose flatten like the head of a viper," Maclay wrote when he retired to his room that night. Fortunately, he noted, Morris had to sit through another speech before he could stand in response to Strong. "This gave him time to collect himself," Maclay observed. "He rose . . . and charmingly did he unwind all their windings. It is too long to set down, but he was clear and conclusive."

This debate over tariffs was sometimes contentious, but it demonstrated just how far the political center had shifted over the past five years. The taxing power of the federal government had been expressly endorsed in the Constitution, and the impost, that great stumbling block of the Confederation, was among the first measures approved by the new Congress.

There were factions within the new Federalist consensus, but the alliances were fluid, shifting at the margins depending on the issue at hand. Many of the members were new to each other, and few were of a mind to compromise. Each had his own sense of priority, and all felt the significance of the precedents that were being laid. Friends often felt obliged to divide; on several key issues Morris even tested his bond with George Washington.

Their first outright breach came over the balance of powers between the executive and the legislative branch. Morris had supported giving Washington authority to fire members of his cabinet; the president needed consent from the Senate for appointments but he could, it was decided, dismiss them at will. When it came to foreign treaties, however, Morris sided with the Senate.

Washington put the "advice and consent" clause of the Constitution to test in August when he made a rare personal visit to the Senate chambers, accompanied by Henry Knox, his secretary of war, to press for quick endorsement of five new treaties Knox had negotiated with the Indians of Georgia and South Carolina. After John Adams read the treaties aloud, Washington asked "bluntly" for an immediate endorsement. There was a restless stirring among the delegates, and then Morris stood to request a second reading—the banging of carriages on the street below had rendered Adams inaudible. Adams read the bills over again and promptly asked, "Do you advise and consent?" Morris leaned over to Maclay and whispered playfully, "We will see who will break the silence first." That distinction went to Maclay, who took Morris's challenge and stood to suggest that such a hasty proceeding "ravished" the intent of the consent clause.

As Washington glared down from the dais, several senators raised questions of information on the treaties that could not be answered immediately. The implication was clear; Washington was forcing a decision that the Senate did not feel ready to render. Then, with Washington growing visibly more irritated, Morris stood and moved that the treaties be referred to committee. The president was incensed. He "started up in a violent fret" and declared, "This defeats every purpose of my coming here." Here was his secretary of war; his answers, and the presidential imperative, should suffice. But Morris and the Senate refused to back down, and as Washington spoke, Maclay observed, "he cooled . . . by degrees." In the end he agreed to table the discussion to the following week. "I can not now be mistaken," the prickly Maclay wrote in his diary. "The President wishes to tread on the necks of the Senate." When debate resumed the next Monday, however, amendments were made and the president conceded in excising some elements from the treaties. One of the key prerogatives of the Senate had been established.

There were other policy rifts between Morris and Washington, but none so acute as to damage their underlying friendship. Through hard-earned experience they had laid too strong a foundation of trust, in each other's character and in their shared vision for America, to be shaken by the particularized divisions they were bound to meet along the way.

Through its first year in existence the Congress busied itself with fashioning the shape and tone of the government that had been outlined in broad strokes in the Constitution. The taxing authority, the regulation of commerce, the structure of the judiciary, the management of foreign affairs, all had to be designed, debated, and implemented. Morris took all this seriously; he gave less shrift to the Bill of Rights. They had been drawn up to answer the critics of the Constitution, and Morris dismissed them as pure politics. "Poor Madison got so cursedly frightened in Virginia" during the ratifying convention, Morris wrote to a friend, "that I believe he has dreamed of amendments ever since." Morris lost no energy opposing them, but he considered them trivial distractions from the great work at hand.

The administrative measures were important—fundamental, even— but they were overshadowed by two larger questions that hung over all the rest, tempering relations between the representatives and influencing every major decision. These two principal concerns were "residence"—the ultimate location of the nation's capital—and the federal debt.

That they were related at all seems a little strange. Residence was an essentially parochial question, as the location of the capital would yield benefits—yet unknown—to just one jurisdiction, while the fate of the debt was an intrinsically national issue that carried ramifications for every citizen and district in America. Yet they were two issues that raised the most intense feelings in the Congress and among the public, and both could be decided only in the national council.

These two questions were similar, as well, in their intricacy. Each had permutations that would complicate their progress through Congress, and ultimately lead them to be linked; passage of one could not be accomplished without approval of the other. Residency was really two questions: besides a permanent seat of government, the lawmakers needed to choose a temporary residence, the place where Congress would meet during the ten to fifteen years it would take to erect a proper capital. The question of the debt was divided as well, between the debts run up by the Continental Congress—obligations to Europe and to the domestic creditors—and those run up by the states during the war. The additional debt of the states, which came to be known under the rubric "assumption," proved much more controversial, as some states emerged from the war under heavy obligation while others were relatively free of debt.

Every representative and every official in the government felt the weight of these two impending decisions. They were, as Washington wrote at the time, "the most delicate and interesting" issues facing the Congress; more than that, "they were more in danger of having convulsed the government itself than any other points." That is to say, these two dilemmas presented the true test of the new government formed under the Constitution. Unless it could produce some sort of agreement on both, the consensus behind a national government would "burst and vanish," Thomas Jefferson warned, "and the states separate to take care of everyone of itself."

Robert Morris played a pivotal role in the debate, the deal making, and the ultimate resolution of both these questions. He did so by virtue of his status and his influence in the Congress, but also because he was deeply, personally interested in the outcome of each. Through most of the war, of course, Philadelphia had been the de facto capital of the rebel nation, and Morris took it as his charge from the opening session of the new Congress to secure the return of that body to what he considered its rightful seat. As for the debt, it had been his vision in the first place to establish that obligation as the bond that would tie the states together, "an express national Compact between the United States and each Individual State." During his tenure as Financier Morris had used every available means to collect the debts of the war under the authority of the Congress, and in March 1783 he expressly called for assumption as the means by which "a Degree of Simplicity would be introduced into our Affairs and we might avoid the Horrors of intestine Convulsions."

Morris was thwarted at the time by the states' rights faction in Congress and the unanimous consent provision in the Articles of Confederation. The revival of the debate in the new Congress provided him another chance to put his agenda into action; he would not let it pass.

— *Chapter 19* —

THE COMPROMISE
OF 1790

T he question of where the nation's capital should stand was first
raised in earnest when Congress fled the mutinous soldiers of the
Pennsylvania Line in 1783. Robert Morris, James Madison, Alexander Hamilton, and the other Nationalists sought a quick return to Philadelphia, but the old-school radicals—principally Arthur Lee and David
Howell of Rhode Island—considered the escape from the metropolis a
stroke of fortune. They would accept almost any destination rather than return to environs dominated by Morris and his allies.

Certain what not to do, but unable to settle on an alternative, the Continental Congress turned vagabond in its final years, assembling at Annapolis, Trenton, Princeton, and finally New York, always temporarily, its
stature waning with every move. All the while, local promoters from New
York to Virginia laid plans and arguments to claim the title of the future
capital.

The one principle that all agreed on was some degree of "centrality," that
the national government should be placed at a site accessible to all. This
consensus eliminated New England and the far South; within that range,
the debate over residency raised questions of the nature and character that
the new nation that would emerge from the Revolution. Would Americans
be an agrarian or an urban people? Settling the capital in a major city, the
champions of Republican virtue agreed, would subject the government to
the baneful influence of wealth and commerce; a more rural setting would
be more wholesome. But which would be favored, the industrious North,
or the export-oriented, slave-based economy of the South? Every potential
location, from New York to New Jersey, through Philadelphia and down to

Baltimore and the Potomac, was freighted with ideological scores and sectional allegiances.

Still another wrinkle, odd in hindsight considering the rapid expansion that followed, was the prospect of future settlement. Would the capital sit on the familiar shores of the Atlantic, or should it straddle, as some proposed, a river opening on the heartland, "gateway to the west" that would help foster bonds of union among generations to come? These were the terms of a debate undertaken with the utmost gravity, under the threat that the wrong choice would hasten dissolution of the still fragile union, North dividing against South, or East against West.

Underneath this high-toned debate lay more unseemly but probably more powerful motives of parochial and personal self-interest. Anyone harboring romantic notions of the nation's founders as selfless idealists should avert their eyes from the orgy of huckstering that attended the ultimate selection of the capital. George Washington, Benjamin Franklin, James Madison, Alexander Hamilton, Thomas Jefferson, Gouverneur Morris, the Lee brothers, and Robert Morris each had a hand on the wheel; each sought to steer the decision toward his home state, and most of them with an eye toward their own personal fortunes. Gouverneur entered the sweepstakes early on, proposing his family estate just above Manhattan as the best site for a national capital back in 1783; but he was gone to Europe before the question neared a decision.

New England had no horse in the race, but her representatives, voting in a bloc, set the terms. Ever watchful for the encroachments of "corruption," they felt a connection to any established city—especially Philadelphia— would "tend to concentrate power, aristocracy and monarchy." But that did not necessarily preclude Pennsylvania. Centrally located, with waterways opening to the West as well as the East, it was always a leading candidate for sectional compromise, and if Philadelphia was unacceptable, there were plenty of other sites in the Quaker state. Franklin himself laid the groundwork when he presented the new Constitution to the state Assembly in 1787; that same day he proposed setting aside a district ten miles square to offer the Congress as the site of their future home.

By the time the delegates to the first federal Congress assembled in New York, the newspapers were already calling for quick resolution to "that great question" of residency—"otherwise it will prove the cause not only of disputes," the *Federal Gazette* warned, "but of such jealousies as may lay the foundation of *dissentions* that may prove fatal to the Union." But those very jealousies made the matter too ticklish to admit of quick resolution. Alexander Hamilton and Robert Morris each sought a prompt decision on temporary residency, at least—Hamilton to stay in New York and Morris to remove to Philadelphia—but neither could secure a decisive vote. In the protracted negotiations that ensued, James Madison took the lead in the House, and Morris in the Senate.

Two basic versions of a deal emerged. The first would leave Congress in New York for a decade or more, and set the permanent capital somewhere in Pennsylvania. The second, southern, option would remove Congress temporarily to Philadelphia—this was a sop to the interests of the middle states—and fix the permanent seat of government on the Potomac. The New England delegates would prefer no vote at all—that would leave Congress in New York indefinitely—but if forced to choose, they leaned toward Pennsylvania.

The Pennsylvania delegation, however, was divided within itself. Robert Morris supported a capital at the falls of the Delaware, opposite Trenton, where he happened to own property; William Maclay wanted a site situated on the westerly coursing Susquehanna, which flowed by his estate at Harrisburg, down through Maryland, and emptied into the Chesapeake. This Maryland connection made Maclay's position appealing to the South; Morris countered by pressing Hamilton and John Jay, his strongest allies in New York, to swing the New England delegates into the Trenton column.

Various coalitions formed and re-formed through the summer of 1789 until, toward the end of the first session, it appeared a deal was at hand. On August 27, Thomas Scott, a representative from western Pennsylvania, stood to call the House to a decision on residence, as further delay would imperil the harmony of the entire Congress. To Morris's disappointment, Scott supported the Susquehanna.

Now the maneuvers began in earnest. Fearing that an immediate vote would doom the Potomac option, James Madison led the southern members in seeking a postponement to the next session of Congress. He was surprised to find his motion supported by a succession of New England representatives. This was not according to script; New England was supposed to be aligned with Pennsylvania. Seizing the moment, Madison turned the tables, deserting his new northern allies to join Pennsylvania in backing a hearing on Scott's motion the following week.

At this point Pennsylvania was aligned with the South against New York and the North, leaving Morris and Trenton out of the picture. This forced a rearguard action by Morris, who left a Senate hearing on the federal judiciary to attend the House debate. With the situation suddenly in flux, Morris called a morning meeting of the Pennsylvania delegation, and sought to revive the North-Central coalition by offering new proposals from Hamilton. Maclay and his allies recoiled at the "deceitfulness" of New England, however, and decided to stick with their new southern allies.

At the same time, the specter of Pennsylvania collaborating with the South spurred the northern interest—New York and New England—to a caucus of their own. There Senator Rufus King, a Massachusetts transplant representing New York, revived the plan to support permanent residence in Pennsylvania in return for temporary residence in New York. To Morris's renewed frustration, however, the Pennsylvania site they settled on was the Susquehanna.

Now the horsetrading reached something of a crescendo. On Tuesday evening, September 1, Morris invited King to meet with the Pennsylvania delegates and settle the terms for a coalition. Just as the talks began, James Madison showed up to present a deal of his own. Startled, Morris hustled King upstairs while Madison made his pitch. Notes were passed upstairs and down. Morris obtained from King a commitment to the Delaware, but in his finagling, lost his grip on the Pennsylvania delegation; Clymer, Fitzsimmons, Scott, and the rest declared against any treaty with the northern bloc. Maclay, confined to his room by a lingering illness, viewed all of this with disdain; "here I could give an advantageous lecture on scheming," he chided in his diary.

A full debate in the House got under way the next morning, and for the next three weeks Madison contested with the northern representatives—principally the famed orator Fisher Ames of Massachusetts—over the relative merits of the Potomac and the Susquehanna. Madison wound on heavily, endangering his status as "first man" of the House and even jeopardizing support for his cherished Bill of Rights. In the end, he could not overcome the basic numbers of the sectional divide, and on September 22 the House endorsed the Susquehanna by a margin of thirty-one to seventeen. As the debates progressed and the Delaware slipped off the agenda, Morris dropped by Maclay to fill him in. "Well," Morris muttered in disappointment, "I hope you are gratified." And of course Maclay was.

Madison had lost, but master of legislative procedure that he was, he got a poison pill attached to the bill, an amendment requiring Pennsylvania and Maryland to make major improvements to navigation of the Susquehanna. This rider sounded innocent enough, but threatened to divert trade from the Pennsylvania interior away from Philadelphia and down to Baltimore and Annapolis. The "proviso," as this clause was termed, fomented a new rift in the Pennsylvania delegation. Heeding the dismay of powerful interests in Philadelphia, Fitzsimmons, Clymer, and several other representatives moved back into the Morris camp. They would vote for Trenton.

Monitoring all these maneuvers, his consternation mounting with every vote, was George Washington. Like most of the other contenders for the capital, Washington believed the public interest coincided with his private interest; he saw the Potomac as a potential "gateway" to the Ohio valley and the western frontier, and felt that Virginia needed a major port to liberate the Tidewater planters from the merchants of Baltimore and Philadelphia. Washington's preference for the Potomac was well known, but he felt constrained to stay out of the debates.

Morris had the temerity, during the House debates, to sound Washington on the matter directly. It proved to be another test of their friendship. "I had a long talk with a Great Personage last night on this subject," Morris wrote Mary in September. "He was very cautious in expressing himself, but I received that he is much dissatisfied with what is doing in this business and I think not a little angry at my agency in it, which I suppose has been represented to him as proceeding from interested motives but as I know my motives to be pure, and as I believe that I am promoting the public interest, and faithfully discharging my duty, I shall go on let who will dislike or like it."

On the day the House voted for the Susquehanna, the residency bill was forwarded to the Senate. As the debate got under way, Morris was in constant motion, "running backward and forward, like a boy," Maclay sniffed, calling senators out of the debates, forging new alliances, speaking from the floor. His first object was to strike the proviso, but it was popular with southern members and with all of Philadelphia's many rivals, and Morris could secure only four votes, besides his own, against it. Maclay then moved to confirm the House selection of the Susquehanna, but Morris found the votes to block it. Now Morris proposed Germantown, close to Philadelphia but outside the city limits. To sweeten the deal Morris vowed that Pennsylvania would ante up a building fund of one hundred thousand dollars—and that if the state failed of this pledge, he would put up the money himself. Morris won the support of every senator from Delaware to New Hampshire; every vote to the South was against him, along with a Connecticut delegate who was determined Congress should remain in New York, and Maclay, who was just as committed to the western part of the state as

Morris was to the east. This left the Senate deadlocked; on September 24, Vice President John Adams broke the tie with a vote for Germantown.

Morris reported to Mary the next day. "I am exceedingly plagued and harassed, fretted and vexed, & pleased alternately in the proposals of this business of the permanent residence," he wrote. He'd won Germantown, but the larger question remained in contest. "So far as we have gone I have carried my points but I doubt a good deal whether I shall be able to hold what I have got."

Morris's judgment was sound as ever. The Senate bill was sent back to the House on Friday, and over the weekend, Madison did everything he could to kill it. He failed in the House, which approved the Senate bill on Monday, September 28. But he succeeded in planting new fears in the New York delegation, warning them that federal buildings could be erected in Germantown within a few short years, that the temporary residence would then become permanent, and that Congress would be lost to them forever. When the bill returned to the Senate that afternoon, the New Yorkers deserted Morris and the Senate voted to postpone the whole affair. All of Morris's machinations had backfired, leaving the Delaware option in doubt and the "great question" still hanging in the air.

With the Senate in recess Morris returned to Philadelphia in October. He found that much in the city had changed during his extended absences in Virginia and New York. A new elite was emerging, social and political, and Morris was no longer at the center. What made this evolution more disconcerting was that many of the rising new characters were men who'd once labored in his shadow.

William Bingham was the most conspicuous of these arrivistes. He'd done well during the war, sailed for England in 1783, and done even better there. Returning toward the end of 1786, Bingham served a brief stint in the Continental Congress, and then settled back in Philadelphia. He announced his new stature by building a mansion in town that was the largest and most opulent anyone could remember, attended with a full retinue of transplanted European customs.

One guest of the Binghams recalled his bafflement upon his first visit to their new estate. "Each visitor on entering the hall at the foot of the staircase, had his name called out by a servant in livery, when another servant on the stairs took it up in a loud voice, and passed it on to the man in waiting at the entrance to the drawing room; the large folding doors of which were covered with glass reflectors, and caused such a bewildering and optical illusion, that the images of the assembled company, seated on the left, appeared to occupy the right side of the door within the room, so that unsophisticated and untraveled visitors, already confused by the repetition of their names, made themselves objects of ridicule, by making low bows and curtsies to the looking glass with their backs to the company."

William Bingham paid the bill, but it was Ann Bingham who set the tone. Already considered among the most beautiful women in Philadelphia, she now was the most fashionable, a distinction that Mary Morris could not ignore. At a time when Robert was asking Mary to curb household expenses, Ann Bingham "blaz'd upon a large party at Mr. Morris' house in a dress which eclips'd any that has yet been seen. A Robe a la Turke of black Velvet, Rich White satin Petticoat, body and sleeves, the whole trimm'd with Ermine. A large Bouquet of natural flowers supported by a knot of Diamonds, Large Buckles, Necklace and Earrings of Diamonds, her Head ornamented with Diamond Sprigs interspers'd with artificial flowers, above all, waved a towering plume of snow white feathers." Next to Ann Bingham, Mary Morris must have felt as dowdy as Martha Washington.

Another upstart was John Swanwick, who had emerged from his partnership with Morris and, free from such entanglements as the French tobacco contract, had made a fortune in bank stock and mercantile trade. Like Bingham, Swanwick courted one of Thomas Willing's daughters, and had launched a political career as well. His diminutive stature and his foppish airs earned him the tag "Our Lilliputian, with his dollars," but the rise of his former clerk had to be at least unsettling to Robert Morris. State controller John Nicholson and Tench Coxe, a new star in the financial world, were two more newcomers to Philadelphia's elite who respected Morris, but did not follow him.

The state political scene had undergone its own postwar reformation. The Federalists were ascendant, but this was not the same circle that Morris had gathered when he launched the Republican Society in opposition to the state constitution. James Wilson remained active and effective, but the other party leaders included Thomas Mifflin, Thomas McKean, and William Maclay, none of whom maintained more than a dutiful connection with Morris.

Through the spring and summer of 1789, with Morris in New York, the Pennsylvania Federalists capitalized on the momentum generated by the federal convention to lead a new assault on the radical state constitution. Morris encouraged their efforts from a distance, writing Richard Peters in August that, in his view, Philadelphia was "Ripe for a Change." Now was the time to strike, Morris advised. "There is nothing to fear . . . you must therefore push on boldly for it will not do to look back." By the time of Morris's return in October, the Assembly had approved a convention to revise the state constitution.

This was the goal Morris had been working toward since the unicameral legislature was installed in 1776, but he played no active role in the debate. Nor would he be on hand for its culmination. The details took more than a year to iron out, under the direction of James Wilson, who worked in collaboration with the frontier radical William Findley. Together they managed to keep strife to a minimum, and by the end Wilson had effected all the changes Morris and his allies had asked for—a bicameral Assembly, executive powers invested in a single governor with veto power over the legislature, life terms for judges—along with a specific Bill of Rights. The final document was approved in convention on a vote of sixty-six to one.

This closed the state's great political wars, a bitter struggle for economic and political supremacy that had been ushered in by the break with England and climaxed in the Fort Wilson Riot. After swinging wildly for more than a decade, Pennsylvania's political pendulum had come to rest very close to where it began.

The most popular of the triumphant Federalists was Thomas Mifflin, the inveterate intriguer who had survived the debacle of the Conway Cabal; he was elected the first governor under the new constitution. A gifted orator, Mifflin was also notoriously corrupt and often drunk, and many of his fellow Federalists, particularly James Wilson, began searching for a replacement. They turned to Robert Morris as the one man with the contacts and the influence to displace Mifflin, but Morris declined. He was deeply preoccupied with his business concerns; the only political affairs he could devote any time to were federal. Indeed, the question of residency was so pressing that during the congressional recess some of the principal players in the debate followed Morris to Philadelphia to continue the wrangle there.

Among these itinerant politicians was William Grayson, one of Virginia's senators. Laying over on his long journey south, Grayson found that the failure to decide the location of the future capital, in whatever location, Pennsylvania or the Potomac, "is much reprobated in this City"; much of that opprobrium, naturally, fell on Morris. As it happened, Grayson encountered Morris on the street and they struck up a discourse which they decided to continue over dinner. Morris was "very much irritated" with the whole affair, and said he would press again for Germantown when the Senate resumed. Grayson was guarded, offering only that "New York and the Eastern people"—the faction that had deserted Morris in the final vote—possessed no "*real* sentiments than those that were *frustratory*." They would be satisfied to stall until someone forced their hand.

Grayson concluded, "Morris with all his prudence I find has a great deal of resentment" against New York, and consequently, the Potomac option was "gaining friends daily. . . . I would now (though never sanguine before) bet her against the field."

Days later, Morris bumped into another key figure in the Virginia delegation, James Madison. They had been the principal rivals in the debates in New York but were also longtime Nationalist allies; now they sat down to a meal. As with Grayson, Morris railed against the Northern faction, but by now his thinking had progressed. He wanted to punish New York with the prompt removal of Congress, even to the point of accepting Virginia's plan of trading temporary residence in Philadelphia for a permanent capital on the Potomac. Morris would not commit, however; as much as he resented New York's defection, he felt honor-bound to stand by their agreement for one more vote. Madison had little to add. Morris had the edge if he could corral the votes; until then, as Madison confided to George Washington, he and the Virginians would have to bide their time.

Thus the matter stood, on razor's edge, North pitted against South with Pennsylvania in the balance, when Congress resumed in January. But Madison and Morris were both late in rejoining their respective assemblies, and a final resolution would have to wait. In its place, dominating the attention of the delegates, the press, and the public at large, was Alexander Hamilton's plan for funding the federal debt.

Hamilton had been appointed secretary of the treasury in September, the last of the key cabinet positions filled by Washington. It had taken that long to draft and sign into law the bill creating the Treasury Department—Elbridge Gerry of Massachusetts tried, but failed, to retain the three-member Board of Treasury favored by the old radicals—but in the end, Hamilton's selection was confirmed without incident.

Hamilton had been preparing for the post, in one fashion or another, since he wrote his detailed letters on economic matters in 1781. The autumn recess of Congress gave him a few more weeks to fashion his official debut. And he had help—five assistant secretaries were confirmed the day he was installed in office. The first of them was William Duer, the war contractor who had partnered with Morris but dropped out of the first China venture. Duer was a personal friend of Hamilton's and had served as secretary to Osgood and Arthur Lee on the last Board of Treasury, he would provide a degree of continuity in the operations of the new department.

Attacking his task with youthful energy and an exacting mind, Hamilton soon had a staff of thirty-nine operating at full throttle. But his most important performances, the state papers that outlined the ways and means of his administration, he composed himself.

If there was any doubt about what pressing national priorities Hamilton ought to address, the public creditors of Philadelphia offered an emphatic answer a week before the treasury secretary took office. This was the same group Morris had marshaled in his failed bid to break the impasse over the impost, and they remained a potent force in the key states of Pennsylvania, New York, and Massachusetts. In August, several of the Philadelphia creditors with the largest holdings in government paper renewed their claims in a memorial sponsored in the House by Representative Thomas Fitzsimmons.

The petitioners recalled the contributions they'd made to the cause by purchasing bonds "in the hour of extreme necessity, when complicated Want enfeebled, and impending Ruin agitated, their Country." They applauded the new Congress for the achievements of the first session, especially "the Foundations that have been laid for the Production of an efficient Revenue." But now, the creditors said, it was time to address the next major step in restoring the public credit—funding the federal debt.

This did not require immediate payment, which was acknowledged to be "if not impracticable, greatly inconvenient," but arrangements for "punctual Payment of the interest" would raise the debt to par and afford its holders "all the advantages of the Principal, without injuring the Credit of the Country, or straining her resources." Under such provision the debt would become "a National Benefit" by fostering investment and enterprise; "public Credit," the petition averred, "is the vital Spark of modern Policy."

The sixteen signers of the memorial included two Continental Army officers, the privateering chieftain Blair McClenaghan, and several prominent Pennsylvania politicians, including Charles Pettit and Thomas McKean. These were not political allies of Robert Morris's—some, in fact, were longtime foes—but they had embraced his program, and were now pressing it before the Congress and the public. Their memorial was published in the *Congressional Register*, in newspapers in Philadelphia, New York, Massachusetts, and the Carolinas, and submitted to the House a month before it adjourned. Upon Hamilton's confirmation, the matter was referred to his charge.

The memorial made its point with some force, but the question was more complicated than that. Most of the public debt—estimated by Hamilton at $54 million, foreign and domestic—had been sold and resold in the years since it was issued. Many of the signers of the Philadelphia memorial were original creditors, allowing them to make a more principled argument, but they were the exception. By far the larger share was now in the hands of brokers and investors who had bought the government obligations for as little as twenty or even ten cents on the dollar, the price reflecting the public faith—more precisely, the *lack* of it—in the government's willingness to pay.

The question now was whether to fulfill those low expectations by reneging on some or part of the debt, or to fund it fully. Viewed strictly in terms of the state of public credit, full funding was the obvious answer. But the moral implications of full funding were much more ambiguous. Paying face value for bills bought at steep discounts would mean a windfall for speculators and make a cruel mockery of the soldiers, farmers, and other creditors who had parted with their nearly worthless scrip under conditions of duress and sometimes destitution.

For Hamilton there was really no question. As director of the treasury, as an economic theorist operating on a national scale, he considered restoration of public credit as the first priority. Such provision would restore the faith that had been shattered by the forty-to-one devaluation of 1780, permit future borrowing at reasonable rates of interest, and provide capital to underwrite the progress of manufactures, agriculture, and commerce. More than that, it would "cement more closely the union of the states." This was the trail blazed by Morris, of course, and Hamilton hewed to it in the "Report on Public Credit" that he submitted to Congress in January. Public credit being essential, Hamilton wrote, it could be restored only by "good faith," and "the punctual performance of contracts." Not only was this required "by the strongest inducements of political expediency," but also by "the immutable principles of moral obligation." Here Hamilton might have profited by borrowing the simpler maxim Morris had laid down in 1782, that policy was on the same side as honesty.

These principles should apply not just to the federal debt, Hamilton wrote, but to the obligations of the several states, which should be folded into the larger national debt. This was "assumption," another policy previously asserted by Morris, the step by which the federal government would "assume" an estimated $25 million in state debts, bringing the total federal debt close to $80 million. Assumption would forward every element of the larger strategy—enhancing public credit, binding the states to the union, freeing up frozen capital—while rescuing deeply indebted states like Massachusetts and South Carolina. It would also resolve the potential for damaging competition between the states and the central government over tax revenues.

Having offered a new estimate of the federal debt, Hamilton now proposed the means for funding it. But here especially his plan was more intricate and more convoluted than anything Morris had projected. For domestic loans in particular, Hamilton drew up several different modes of payment that creditors might choose from, some offering partial payment in funds and part in land, others paying part in cash and part in new issues of debt; still others involved long-term annuities at interest rates ranging from 4 to 5 percent. Ultimately most of the debt was to be redeemed with new issues of government securities bearing set terms and fixed rates of interest. The key was to pay the interest, which would raise the value of the government certificates to par. Paying off the principal could follow at some later date.

This was something less than the simple commitment to full funding that Hamilton espoused in the opening stanzas of his report, but the new treasury secretary was careful to distinguish these partial measures from the popular proposition that the government make full payments to original holders, but only partial payments to the investors and speculators who purchased debt certificates down the line. Such "discrimination" was unworkable, Hamilton observed, but more important, would be "inconsistent with justice" and "ruinous to public credit."

The various and Byzantine formulations for payment led to much confusion, memorialized in the *Federal Gazette* of the United States in an irreverent rhyme:

> *The Secretary makes reports*
> *Whene'er the House commands him;*
> *But for their lives, some members say*
> *They cannot understand him.*

Still, the general thrust of Hamilton's policy was clear—the public debt should be funded in full, and the state debts assumed by the federal government, all with an eye toward restoring the credit and revitalizing the capital markets of the new nation.

As the "Report on Public Credit" had been ordered by the House, that is where it was introduced. The broad outlines of Hamilton's funding policy won quick endorsement from the Federalist majority, but progress bogged down in the face of opposition from James Madison. He had paired with Hamilton in support of the Morris program in 1783, but now Madison altered his stance, leading a Pyrrhic campaign against full funding that left Hamilton, his erstwhile comrade, aghast. Madison called for a full payment to holders of original debt and only a fraction to subsequent purchasers. He had expressly opposed discrimination in the past, and had been the first to put forward the doctrine of assumption, but his "continental" views on finance had placed him at odds with his constituents in Virginia; now he was mending fences back home.

Madison's change of heart was driven as well by the dramatic surge in speculation that attended Hamilton's appointment at Treasury. From the time the federal Constitution was ratified, prices on securities had begun to rise on expectations that the new government would honor the Revolutionary War debts. But in the months Hamilton labored over his report, the hunt for undervalued securities accelerated and, in the words of one southern delegate, "a spirit of havoc, speculation and ruin" swept the nation.

Unfortunately for Hamilton, his assistant William Duer was leading the charge, assembling a huge personal portfolio and advising his friends to do likewise. Duer was also the "governor" of the Society for Establishing Useful Manufacturers, a private development project founded by Hamilton that Duer used as a personal slush fund. Duer ran his side-door fiscal manipulations on a large enough scale that he became known as "King of the Alley," and his reputation for shady dealings cast suspicion over all of Hamilton's administration.

One of Duer's friends and collaborators was William Constable, who matched Duer's plunging in government securities. Constable invited Robert Morris to join in his speculations, but Morris declined; during this period of frantic, risky investment the former Financier avoided any significant engagements in securities. This was a tactical position, not a moral one. In fact, during this time Gouverneur Morris had opened talks with the French on a proposal that he, Robert Morris, Le Couteulx, and the ever-enterprising Daniel Parker purchase at a discount the American debt to France. The scheme was wildly ambitious and never came to fruition; in the meantime, in March, at the height of the House debate over Hamilton's plan, Duer's efforts to profit by his public office came to light and he was forced to resign. Tench Coxe was named assistant in his place.

Duer's downfall appeared to confirm Madison's moral critique of the funding program, but the fact remained that, despite the acrimony of the House debate, the basic goals of the Nationalist agenda had already been achieved. The adoption of the Constitution and formation of a true national government had revived credit markets in the major coastal cities, boosted agricultural prices, and restored American credit in Europe. The economy was swiftly pulling out of its postwar doldrums, and state tax receipts were rising steadily. All this derived from the stability and public confidence engendered by the new government, and from the prospect of a funded debt—precisely the outcomes Robert Morris had predicted when he pressed for tax authority under the Confederation.

Against this backdrop of rampant speculation but also renewed prosperity, Madison's maneuvers were only partially successful. His plan for discrimination in debt payments was defeated handily, but his campaign to bar assumption prevailed by a narrow, two-vote margin. Assumption was just one plank in Hamilton's program, but some Nationalists considered it the key to maintaining the union. "I almost begin to despair of the assumption of the State debts," Jeremiah Wadsworth, now a representative from Connecticut, mused as the critical vote loomed, "and with that I shall despair of the National Government."

The House bill for federal but not state funding was now referred to the Senate. For the next four months it shared time with a continuing, seesaw debate over residency. This was a period of kaleidoscopic political formulations, with deals made and broken on a weekly basis. Pennsylvania, holding swing votes on both residence and assumption but also divided internally, was in the thick of the bargaining, with Thomas Fitzsimmons working the House and Morris the Senate. Here Morris was in his element, up and down from his seat, in and out of the hall, sometimes "laughing heartily" as he proposed motions and amendments, sometimes displaying "a violent disposition of anger." Observing these gyrations close at hand, Maclay could only marvel. "Never," he ruminated in his diary, "had a man a greater propensity for bargaining than Mr. Morris."

For all his giving and taking, Morris never lost sight of one primary objective. That was full funding of the debt at the original, promised rate of 6 percent. This may have been a tactical position, staked out to balance the calls for partial repudiation, but Morris defended it with vigor, "blazed away," as Maclay put it, whenever the question reached the floor. Morris had spent too long fighting for federal funding to see his program shredded in last-minute haggling.

In May, with both houses of Congress thoroughly flummoxed in their legislative gridlock, the delegates were sobered by an incident that threatened to render all their quarrels irrelevant: George Washington was gravely ill. At the first onset of a fever he had gone out to Long Island, "on purpose to get room for exercise and to change the air," as Morris reported to Mary, but this vigorous mode of therapy was poorly chosen. For two weeks the Congress and the city were enveloped in a "universal gloom" that lifted only when Washington recovered. Less startling but no less distressing was the death, on April 17, after lingering illness, of Benjamin Franklin. In her correspondence, Mary informed Robert of Franklin's large and socially minded bequests, and of the public funeral that drew a throng of twenty thousand mourners. Robert thanked her for the reports, but did not dwell on his long association with Franklin, the schemes they concocted, and the triumphs they shared. He lamented him simply as "the Old Gentleman."

None of this dire news prompted Hamilton to pause in his drive to win approval for his funding program. All through April he pressed his campaign, packing the House gallery with his supporters and accosting senators outside their closed sessions, but his pressure only seemed to galvanize the opposition. By early June, distraught and on the verge of despair, he changed gears. If he couldn't persuade, perhaps he could exercise some leverage.

On Friday, June 11, Hamilton sent Tench Coxe, his new assistant, and William Jackson, personal secretary to the president, to offer a deal to the Pennsylvania delegation. They could have the permanent residence if they would throw their support behind assumption. There'd been plenty of talk of swapping temporary for permanent residency, but this was the first time that assumption had been placed in the scales. It was a serious offer, delivered by an embassy from the administration. And it could work: by unifying Pennsylvania with the Northern bloc, the South could be by passed on both the key issues facing the Congress.

But Morris had been sideswiped by the New Yorkers once before on residency. Rather than negotiate with intermediaries, Morris scrawled out a note: early the next morning he'd be taking a stroll along the Battery, a fortified embankment at the southern tip of Manhattan. If Hamilton wanted to talk he should meet him there, "as if by accident."

Morris headed out at dawn, and sure enough, down by the waterfront, he found Hamilton—"on the sod before me," he told Maclay. In silhouette and in character, the two wary allies were a study in contrast. At fifty-six years of age, Morris was old enough to be Hamilton's father, and he looked the part, wearing a top hat and carrying a walking stick, jowls at his neck, his hair gone snow-white, worn loose and hanging nearly to his collar. Morris's manner, like his features, was large and soft, while Hamilton was taut and precise, his coiffed hair swept back.

They walked and they talked. Hamilton reiterated the offer from his deputies: he would swing the New York votes to place the capital on the Delaware at Germantown or opposite Trenton—Morris's preferred location—in return for one more vote for assumption in the Senate and five in the House. Morris countered. He recognized that, regardless of what Hamilton might offer, permanent residency on the Delaware was out of reach. But if Hamilton would support temporary residency in Philadelphia, Morris would deliver the votes on assumption. Hamilton agreed, and the two departed to round up their votes.

Morris teamed with Thomas Fitzsimmons to nail down the senator he needed when the two joined George Read, a moderate Delaware Federalist, for a long Sunday ride outside the city and persuaded him to switch his vote. Two days later, however, Hamilton told Morris the deal was off; he couldn't deliver the House votes for Philadelphia. It was the final betrayal of the first session all over again.

Now Thomas Jefferson entered the picture. He stopped by Morris's lodgings late on a Friday evening and proffered a new deal on residence: fifteen years at Philadelphia, followed by permanent residence on the Potomac. This was the original southern scheme, several times buried but now finding new life. The link to assumption went unspoken.

Jefferson had the advantage of being new to the game. After his long diplomatic sojourn in France, he had returned to America and accepted the appointment as secretary of state, but did not arrive at New York until March. He was shocked, he said, to find the Congress embroiled in such a "bitter and angry contest" over funding that it threatened "a dissolution of our Union at this incipient stage." Jefferson was personally close to Madison but also loyal to Washington, and on the critical question of funding he took direction from the president and his treasury secretary.

Having made his overture to Morris, Jefferson now sought an accommodation between Madison and Hamilton. He invited them both to his house for dinner. They came, probably on June 20, a Sunday evening, and with

Jefferson playing moderator, an agreement was struck: Madison would not have to vote for assumption, but he agreed to temper his opposition; in return Hamilton would deliver a permanent capital to the Potomac.

This dinner meeting, memorialized by Jefferson, is often cited as the beginning and the end of the critical and convoluted negotiation over the weighty issues that threatened to stalemate the first federal Congress. It was not; by Jefferson's own account, the principals parted with tasks assigned—Madison to swing two Virginia votes (though not his own) for assumption, and Hamilton to settle residency "with the agency of Robert Morris." But the anecdote captures the flavor of the negotiation; with the very survival of the government at stake, high-flown principle gave way to political pragmatism.

For Morris the key concession to come out of the dinner was not permanent residency or assumption—in his view these elements of the bargain were already in train—but obtaining consent of the New Yorkers to move Congress to Philadelphia while the capital was being built. This was the import of a conference he held with Hamilton after the fateful dinner, and he reported the news to Maclay during another Senate hearing on tariffs on the China trade. "Morris was often called out," Maclay recorded. "He at last came in and whispered me: 'The business is settled at last. Hamilton gives up the temporary residence.' "

The key votes trailed out for another month. The first decision came in the Senate; on June 30, after a flurry of last-ditch bids from Baltimore and New York were turned away, the Philadelphia-Potomac combination prevailed, fourteen votes to twelve. Thence to the House, which passed the residence bill by thirty-two to twenty-nine. Assumption reached the Senate floor July 19. Morris led the debate, reminding his colleagues of the importance of avoiding another delay, demanding the roll be tallied on every amendment, and finally dropping his insistence on a full 6 percent. "Half a loaf," he declared, "is better than no bread." Funding of the federal debt, with the state debts folded in, was approved by the same narrow margin as residency. The House signed off a week later, and the Compromise of 1790—funding for residency—was accomplished.

There were many authors of this monument to legislative contrivance, with winners and losers on both sides, but nobody could take more satisfaction from the outcome than Robert Morris. The funding plan fulfilled the vision he had outlined ten years before; he'd seen it scorned and defeated, and now it became the law of the land. As for residency, Morris failed to secure the site that would have made him rich—the lands he owned on

These cartoons were published in New York to denounce the Compromise of 1790, which removed Congress to Philadelphia pending completion of a new capitol at Washington, D.C. Both depict an oversized Robert Morris—Robert Coffer, in one rendition—as the architect of the move.

the Delaware opposite Trenton—but still he had the distinction of wresting Congress from Philadelphia's principal rival.

Certainly the New Yorkers saw it that way, and in the weeks that followed the Congress and Morris were disparaged on the streets and in the local press. Morris was the special target for a spate of political cartoons that were published as handbills and hawked around Manhattan. One tagged Morris as "Robert Coffer," and showed him oversized, with bags of money in his hands as he leads Congress to Philadelphia. Another depicted him with Federal Hall strapped to his back; a black devil with curly horns leads the procession, calling over his shoulder, "Come along, Bobby!"

While he was deeply engaged in politics of the residency and funding bills, Morris was pressing again, in the spring of 1790, to close his accounts with Congress. He broached the subject in February by composing a petition that he made out in triplicate and sent to the president, to the speaker of the House, and to Vice President John Adams for submission to the Senate. Its tone was solicitous but far from obsequious.

The memorial began by recalling the appointment, in June 1785, of a committee of three assigned by the Continental Congress to review the performance of the recently resigned Financier. No action had resulted; nor had Morris received, as did the other department heads who served Congress during the war, any thanks or commendation at the close of his term. What probably hurt even more, though Morris did not mention it, was the final slap delivered by his enemies in Congress at the end of Morris's term in the government—they had never released to the public the five hundred copies of his "Statement of Accounts" he'd delivered to the Treasury in 1785. That an investigation had been announced but never conducted, Morris said in his petition, left him "exposed to the surmises" prompted by such an inquiry—the "surmises" of the Centinel likely ringing in his ears—without the opportunity to clear his name.

Three years later, and again in 1789, Morris had appealed for a formal inquiry in hopes of "rescuing his reputation," but still without result. The Board of Treasury, Morris noted, had in the meantime launched a separate inquiry into the accounts of the Secret Committee, a process he hoped "will be speedily accomplished," but that was a separate matter. His performance as Financier had yet to be acknowledged; Morris wanted a "strict examination . . . in order that if he has been guilty of Maladministration it may be detected and Punished, if otherwise, that his Innocence may be manifested and acknowledged."

As with so much of the business before the first federal Congress, Morris's petition had no precedent; it was the only one submitted in the first session by one of the members themselves. With no protocol to follow, each legislative house fashioned its own response. In the Senate, a committee chaired by Ralph Izard called on the president to appoint commissioners to inspect the accounts of the Office of Finance, and the full Senate voted to pay the examiners' salaries. Washington maintained his customary silence, however, and no commission was ever formed.

The House named a committee with James Madison as chair. Madison was at odds with Morris on all the great questions of the moment—funding, assumption, and residency—but unlike many of his colleagues from Virginia, he harbored an abiding respect for the magnate from Philadelphia. Having fought for Morris's funding scheme in 1783, he credited Morris's motives, probably more than he did Hamilton's. And he never forgot the dramatic improvements Morris had wrought in the administration and finances of the government in the darkest years of the war. He wasn't now going to derail a series of delicate negotiations by smearing the former Financier on grounds he believed baseless.

Madison first collected documents, including Morris's final, published statements, and announced in March, "it appears to the Committee that the regular official examination has already been made," and that it would be "inexpedient to incur the expense of a re-examination." After debate in the House, however, a new committee was named, with Madison still in the chair, and the inquiry was reopened under supervision of Joseph Nourse, a top government accountant. Nourse reported August 30, and his statement was promptly published. It did not amount to much more than a rehash of Morris's own figures, however, as critical records in most departments of the government had been lost or never composed in the turmoil of the war. The statement provided Nourse by Henry Knox, secretary of war, was typical: the regular troop strength could be reliably estimated, but no return existed for militia enrollments in many key states. As for ordnance and stores supplied by the states, Knox said, "There are not any documents in the War Office from which accurate returns could be made."

To Madison and his committee, there was not much more to be said. It was, they reported, "evidently impossible for the Committee to examine in detail the public accounts . . . and unnecessary." There would be no accusation against Morris, but no exoneration either, and no commendation. In a perfectly value-neutral conclusion, the committee promised to make its records available as "the best practicable means of appreciating the Services of the Superintendent."

More troubling to Morris was the continuing probe into the accounts of the Secret Committee. After the new government was formed, the Board of Treasury inquiry was handed off to an auditor from South Carolina and Oliver Wolcott, Jr., a judge and son of the former congressman from Connecticut. Morris met with them repeatedly through the summer, poring over a patchwork of records and trying, with little success, to convey the chaotic disorder that attended the business of the secret arms trade. The auditor in particular, Morris worried in a letter to Mary, "is a good Officer and a sensible man but was not bred a merchant." This led to disputes that continued "until I have become so fretted and vexed as to be obliged to quit for a time to prevent me from venting improper expressions." Morris managed to restrain himself, but the conferences continued throughout the summer, sometimes on a daily basis.

The other private concern that Morris pursued during these hectic days in New York was land. His fixation on real estate left him out of the government securities sweepstakes that engaged so many of his colleagues in and out of the Congress, but Morris was convinced that the unsettled lands of the American West—that is, the far reaches of New York, Pennsylvania, Virginia, and the deep South—were vastly undervalued and would soon appreciate as waves of European immigrants sought room for homes and farms. He was right, of course; it was only a matter of time.

The prospect of buying and selling great swaths of the western frontier had tantalized the elites of colonial America for generations. Washington, Franklin, the Wharton brothers of Pennsylvania, Patrick Henry, the Lee brothers, and many others had all invested in large-scale but highly improbable land ventures, their hopes tied to parliamentary alliances and royal charters that never materialized. Indeed, some historians ascribe the internal tensions of the Continental Congress to rivalries over land, though such scenarios are often overwrought. With independence, Americans no longer had to seek their deeds and titles abroad. The future of the frontier belonged to Congress, and to whoever could raise the capital first.

Morris had thought deeply on the proper course of western development. In 1782, in his landmark state paper on public credit, he devoted two separate sections to a typically sagacious exposition on land tax and policy. "Land," Morris pronounced, was "the ultimate Object of human Avarice," and combined with its immutability, "stands foremost as the Object of Taxation." In America especially, where so much terrain lay fallow, a land tax could serve a social as well as a fiscal purpose. Morris divided American lands into two classes, "that which belongs to the great Landholder, and that which is owned and occupied by the industrious Cultivator." Here Morris joined with his sometime critics in Virginia to designate "the Husbandman" as "the most Valuable part of a community . . . the natural Guardian of his Country's Freedom." A flat tax on acreage, Morris advised, would tend to break up large holdings and encourage a more equal—and more useful—distribution. It would, he said, "have the salutary Operation of an Agrarian law"—redistribution of land by fiat—"without the Iniquity." This incisive formulation was rejected at the time by the Virginians in particular, in part due to their committed opposition to Morris's national program, but also because their professed fealty to pastoral virtue clashed, in this instance, with their true interest as proprietors of the great plantations.

Morris returned to land in the conclusion of his report, dismissing the notion, favored by the anti-tax faction in Congress, that the government could pay off its debts by quick sale of western lands. "If these lands were to be sold for the public debts they would go off for almost nothing," he warned. "Very few moneyed Men would become possessed of them, because very little money would be invested in so remote a Speculation." A better course, he suggested, would be to mortgage the back lands as security for European loans. If necessary, smaller pieces could be sold off to pay the interest on those loans. This course, too, was passed over by Congress.

A decade later, Morris believed that the renewed strength of American and European capital had altered the market for land. As to public policy, his thinking had not changed, but his station had. In regard to land, at least, his primary concern was his personal prosperity. He was looking toward, as he had put it a decade before, "the Ultimate object of human Avarice," and how it might salvage his fortune.

Speculation in land was particularly suited to Morris's financial circumstances. It required substantial credit both in America and Europe, but if handled adroitly, little in the way of up-front capital. On a more personal level it demanded a determined optimism and a steady hand in the face of unnerving levels of risk, qualities Morris had long relied upon. Ultimately, Morris believed he had little choice; he could always make incremental profits in trade, but only windfall gains on land sales could at last free him from his entanglements in Europe.

Up to this time Morris had purchased discounted lands on a relatively modest scale. Before the war he'd partnered with Thomas Willing and James Pollock to buy a plantation in Mississippi. They stocked it with slaves, but it never got into production. And after the peace he bought tracts at Morrisville, opposite Trenton, and in rural Northampton County. He'd discussed much larger schemes with Silas Deane and others, but held back because his credit was already encumbered by wartime endeavors. He'd also seen his friend and political ally James Wilson plunge deeply into debt with ill-conceived investments in land, but while Wilson possessed a brilliant legal mind, he was never much of a businessman. Morris was convinced he could prosper where Wilson had foundered.

Morris stumbled across his first major land deal in the summer of 1790, at the peak of the wrangling over residency and assumption. Or, one might say, the opportunity stumbled into Morris. It arose in the form of a visit to Congress by Nathaniel Gorham, a Massachusetts native and former delegate to the Continental Congress who had recently purchased a tract of two million acres of unsettled Indian land below Lake Ontario and reaching west from Fort Stanwix to Lake Erie. The land had been subject to conflicting claims from Massachusetts and New York, and at its western edge, Pennsylvania, under grants from the British crown dating back more than a century. In 1786, Congress split the difference on the two primary claims, awarding title to the land to Massachusetts and jurisdiction to New York. The Massachusetts legislature put the land up for sale, subject to simultaneous purchase from the native tribes.

At that point Gorham stepped forward with a partner, Oliver Phelps. Both were prominent in Massachusetts politics and both were acquainted with Robert Morris, Gorham from Congress and Phelps through service in the commissary during the war. Gorham and Phelps obtained the tract by paying Massachusetts £300,000 in its own state securities—less than three cents per acre—and £2,100 New York currency to the Six Nations of the Iroquois, with an annual annuity of £500.

The deal closed in 1789, but a year later Hamilton's funding program had raised the price of state securities to the point that Gorham and Phelps could no longer swing the purchase. The pair traveled to New York in 1790 seeking to finally resolve the claims of Pennsylvania, and looking for a partner. Robert Morris provided the answer to all their problems.

William Maclay, deeply concerned with the Pennsylvania's territorial claims in the West, was away from New York when Gorham and Phelps arrived in town; upon his return August 16 he learned, to his relief, that Morris was already in conference with Gorham, and had tabled the question of jurisdiction until his arrival. Over the next three days Morris and Maclay succeeded in establishing Pennsylvania's claim to what is now known as the Erie Triangle, ensuring the state's access to the Great Lakes. But Maclay was mystified at the depth of Morris's engagement in the matter. "It is strange," he mused in his diary, "that Gorham should be so often calling him out and holding conversations with him."

What Maclay did not realize was that Gorham and Morris were hammering out a deal of their own. Rather than join in partnership with Gorham and Phelps, Morris bought out half their interest, purchasing one million acres for thirty thousand pounds in Massachusetts currency. Even before the deal was struck, Morris wrote Gouverneur Morris in Paris to share the news and ask his old friend to serve as agent in selling off tracts in Europe. Robert described his new property, much of it rolling arable terrain drained by the Genesee River, as "the best tract of Country now remaining in a body (unoccupied) within the limits of the United States of America for settlement of Foreigners who wish to live contiguous to each other." This "bargain," Robert wrote exuberantly, "will not only be the means of extricating me from all the embarrassments in which I have been involved, but also the means of making your Fortune and mine."

With the close of the second session of the new Congress in August, Morris returned home feeling buoyant, his confidence restored and his optimism confirmed. The great questions of residency and finance were finally settled, he had a signed agreement with Gorham and Phelps packed among his papers, and when the government resumed business in December, it would do so in Philadelphia. To cap it all, before leaving New York, Morris had agreed to offer his Market Street house to the president as his official residence in the new, temporary capital. Washington would arrive sometime in November. Morris had much to do.

His first task was to move his family, though this step he had prepared in advance. Soon after he purchased his house on Market Street, he had bought the neighboring property, a smaller but still handsome residence formerly occupied by Joseph Galloway, a loyalist politician and former Franklin ally who had served the British authorities as mayor during the occupation and who fled to London upon their evacuation. Three stories tall and located on the corner of Market and Sixth, the Galloway house was separated from the Morris home by a garden wall. For the final six years of Washington's presidency, Morris would be his neighbor.

While this circumstance rendered the move as easy as possible, Morris still considered his offer to make room for the president a "sacrifice . . . both of interest and convenience," as he wrote to Gouverneur. "I think there is no other man for whom I would have done it." Considering that he had a new house empty and waiting nearby, and servants enough to effect the move, it's hard to see why Morris resisted the idea so strongly—unless that resistance arose with Mary. The Market Street house was the largest and best home she had occupied during their marriage; it may be that, with all their recent financial problems, she wanted to hold on to what she had.

But there was no getting around it. Morris's home was not the largest house in Philadelphia—that distinction belonged to William and Ann Bingham—but it was in Washington's estimation "the best single house in the City." Even so, it would require extensive—if hasty—renovations, which Washington detailed in September during a layover on his trip from New York to Mount Vernon.

Even his proximity to his friend was little consolation to Morris. "It will have the effect of keeping me at a greater distance from him, even though I live next door," Robert groused to Gouverneur. "If I am seen much there it will create envy, jealousy, and malice, and I do not see why I should expose myself to such passions."

Here Morris was being a bit melodramatic; Washington arrived to take up residence in November, and when he resumed his twice-weekly levees, beginning on Christmas night, he did not hesitate to make Morris his guest. Whatever jealousies Morris might have detected, he learned to live with.

For all the housekeeping that was going on, Morris didn't neglect to set in motion the sales of his new landholdings in the Genesee Country. Gouverneur already had his hands full in Paris, with Robert's affairs and his own; Morris decided to send another agent to Europe who would devote his full attention to selling his lands.

The agent he settled on was William Temple Franklin, grandson of Morris's late, great friend. Temple, as he was known, had spent his youth as Franklin's personal secretary in Paris; now thirty years old, he had attended his grandfather's bedside and burial, and was looking for something to do. Morris approached Temple Franklin in September and proposed to retain him on remarkably generous terms. This was typical of Morris's business practice but also indicated the urgency he felt to effect a sale—the only way he could gain by the lands he'd bought was by moving them.

Morris promised Franklin six hundred guineas annual salary, a 10 percent commission on all sales, and all expenses including travel and banker's commissions. In addition, Morris would buy out Franklin's interest in three farms in New Jersey, paying 10 percent down and the balance in eighteen months. Franklin was to set up shop in London; he should consult with Gouverneur in Paris, but the final decision on sales would be his. As to the price, Morris stipulated a minimum of two livres per acre, though he should aim for five or even six. Franklin should seek "ready money," but if no buyers appeared he might consider offering the whole property in a lottery, the sale to go forward when the fund reached three million livres. At this price, Morris would have increased his investment fivefold.

Franklin agreed to the terms and prepared to sail in October. Before his departure, Morris added another sheaf to his portfolio—deeds to the ten thousand acres of timberland Morris owned in Northampton. His title to the property was clouded by Indian unrest and squatters from Connecticut, depressing the value of the holdings by about two thirds. Morris would rather hold the lands until they appreciated, he said, but he needed the money now. Any sales that went through should be credited to Gorham and Phelps with a banking house in London.

Casting his net as wide as possible, Morris retained still another agent that September, a Flanders native named Benedict Van Pradelles. A soldier and adventurer, Van Pradelles had come to America at the end of the war and had spent two years exploring the New York frontier, including the Genesee watershed. The terms in this case were a bit more modest—8 percent commission and a retainer of six hundred silver dollars. Van Pradelles was to operate on the continent and lodge the proceeds of any sales with Morris's bankers in Amsterdam; he was to coordinate his efforts with both Franklin and Gouverneur Morris. Van Pradelles left Philadelphia for Baltimore in September, and sailed for Europe the following month.

Having done all he could to put his land operations in motion, Morris returned to the business of politics. Congress would assemble in Philadelphia in December, but many of the principals were already arriving.

With residency and funding already settled, one great concern remained in which Morris had a primary interest—paternal, even, he might say—and that was Hamilton's proposal to establish a national bank. There were now several private banks operating in America, but Hamilton wanted one that would be answerable to the government. Such an institution, styled after the Bank of England, would help underwrite his funding projects; it would also, by virtue of close government supervision, bring a degree of stability to the largely unregulated world of American finance.

Morris supported the idea of banks in principle, of course, and he wanted to endorse Hamilton's initiatives. But he was skeptical of establishing a bank as a quasi-governmental institution. He'd launched the nation's first bank expressly to establish credit that the government had squandered, and he didn't see the need to alter that formula now.

Hamilton arrived in Philadelphia in November. He was using the congressional recess to develop his bank proposal, and several times he called on Morris to consult with him. The content of these meetings was not recorded, but there was little question that Morris would support Hamilton's plan.

The bank proposal was taken up by the Senate soon after it convened in December and promptly referred to a committee that included Morris as a member. When it came up for debate the members didn't delve into the nuances of public versus private banking, but instead reprised the pro- and anti-banking arguments of the earlier debates in the Pennsylvania Assembly. Maclay, skeptical of all of Hamilton's financial stratagems, took the "agriculturalist" position: he considered banks "as an aristocratic engine . . . operating like a tax in favor of the rich, against the poor." But as with the funding program—not to say assumption—a majority vote for the bank was assured, and Morris spent little time on the floor. He considered at one point making a motion requiring government holdings in bank stock to be treated in the same fashion as private shares, but in the end decided to defer to the treasury secretary.

The one real stumbling block for the bank, it turned out, was the continuing jealousy of the southerners over the ultimate location of the capital. If the national bank were established in Philadelphia, as Hamilton proposed, it might serve to make the government's temporary residence there permanent. This led to a genuine North-South schism in the House, and the prospect that Washington might exercise his first veto to block the bank bill. James Madison and Thomas Jefferson both leaned heavily on the president to kill the bank, but Washington gave Hamilton the last word and, on February 23, signed the bill into law.

Preparations for opening of the bank were attended with avid public interest. Hamilton selected the ever-reliable Thomas Willing, "Old Square Toes," as president, drafting him from his post at the Bank of North America. When shares in the new institution were finally put up for sale, at four hundred dollars apiece, demand was overwhelming, and the stock was sold out in the space of an hour.

Here was a critical instance in which any suggestion of a financial cabal involving Morris and Hamilton can be put to rest; Morris and his friend

Thomas Fitzsimmons, another political ally of Hamilton's, were not informed that the sale was taking place and neither was able to obtain a single share. Morris was reportedly so angry at being left out that he threatened a lawsuit.

There's no reason to doubt that Morris's indignation was genuine, but his anger over the bank stock fiasco was short-lived. Morris was pleased, after all, to see the bank in operation; it confirmed his conception of national finance and reinforced his earlier triumph in the great Pennsylvania bank debates. Besides, while many of America's "moneyed men" were staking their future on bank stock and government securities, Morris was committed to speculations in land. It was there that Morris would see his fortunes rise or fall.

— Chapter 20 —

RUIN

Through the autumn of 1790, Robert Morris negotiated the details of the renovations of his Market Street house with Tobias Lear, personal secretary to the president. The work was often delayed because most of the skilled artisans in town were already occupied making alterations and repairs elsewhere. Eight years after the government had fled its original home, all of Philadelphia was caught up in preparing for the return of Congress.

There was no edifice so grand as the Federal Hall in New York, but there was a new county courthouse, raised just a few feet west of the State House, which the Assembly readily committed to the use of the federal government. There would be renovations here as well; a gallery for three hundred spectators in the House chamber, and mahogany desks, wool carpeting, and Venetian blinds for both the House and Senate. The result, in the eyes of one representative, was "neat, elegant & convenient."

Nor were the preparations strictly architectural. The City Tavern announced that members of Congress could order private dinners at any hour of the day. And one anonymous poet exhorted the women of the city to "put on your best; in all the colors of the bow be drest. Procure clean linen—if you can—For every maid shall have her man."

Once the government convened, the anticipation gave way to what Tobias Lear called "a frenzy" of parties, dinners, card games, and other diversions. Lear's boss, the president, was at the center of it. Washington arrived in Philadelphia at the end of November and spent the first month moving his family, his personal secretaries, and his servants and slaves—more than thirty people in all—into their new quarters. But by Christmas the president was ready to shoulder his public duties, which included a relentless schedule of entertainments: the stiff and formal levees, every Tuesday afternoon at three o'clock, state dinners for as many as thirty guests

490

every Thursday, and Martha Washington's own levees, more convivial than George's, on Fridays.

Robert and Mary Morris were fixtures at these affairs, Robert always seated at the president's right hand, and Mary enjoying the same status with Martha, confirming her station as "the second lady of the so-called Republican Court." Robert had vowed to Gouverneur he would avoid this sort of intimacy, but Washington made his preferences clear. One of the chief duties of his steward, upon setting the table for dinner, was to pour a glass of wine chosen for Morris, and then step over to the Morris house and deliver formal notice that the president "expects your company as usual." Morris was in no position, and had no real inclination, to decline.

It's no great leap to suppose that Morris took enormous satisfaction from this close association with Washington. They had a genuine personal bond, and they had been close collaborators—partners, even—in an uncertain struggle that lasted close to twenty years, from the darkest hours of the war to the long debates at the Constitutional Convention. To see their shared dream of American sovereignty under a single, national government become a tangible reality, to participate in that government and help shape its institutions, had to carry a sense of political accomplishment that has been experienced by just a handful of men in all the annals of history.

But as was so often the case with Morris and Washington, this sense of grandeur and fulfillment could only rarely be separated from the crosscurrents and turbulence of daily life, political and otherwise. Always, there were dissenters and critics, political rivals fighting for an alternate vision or merely for their share of power. Here, as had been the case with Morris throughout the war, the opposition was both local and national—the remnants of the old Constitutionalist party in Pennsylvania, along with the more inchoate but no less avid Anti-Federalist faction in Congress. These two constituencies fed off each other in the political hothouse of postwar Philadelphia.

George Washington was particularly susceptible to the barbs directed his way. He was renowned for his fearless courage on the field of battle, but political attacks pierced straight to that dark core of his spirit which gave an air of gravitas to everything he did. One such attack was a newspaper column published in 1793, at the height of popular fascination with the mayhem of the French Revolution. Titled "The Funeral Dirge of George Washington and James Wilson"—Wilson had been appointed a justice on the first Supreme Court—it described Washington being executed on the guillotine for his aristocratic ways.

The column appeared during a flaring public controversy sparked by Edmund Charles Genet—"Citizen" Genet—a brash, barrel-chested new envoy from the revolutionary government in France, which was then at war with England. In his first weeks in America, Genet had challenged Washington's determined neutrality, even to the point of arming a captured brig, manning it with a crew of American volunteers, and sending it out from Philadelphia to raid British shipping, all in defiance of express orders from Washington.

The president convened a marathon session of his cabinet to review this diplomatic crisis. During the second day of meetings, Secretary of War Henry Knox brought up the "Funeral Dirge," prompting a sudden outburst from Washington. He became, as recounted by Jefferson, "much inflamed, got into one of those passions when he cannot command himself," and complained at length of the "personal abuse which had been bestowed on him." With the members of his cabinet looking on—Knox, Hamilton, Jefferson—Washington delved deep into his sense of resentment and personal anguish. Every day, he said, every hour, the thought of submitting his resignation hovered in his mind. He'd rather be at home on his plantation, Washington said, than be emperor of the world.

Worse, in Jefferson's view, was Washington's statement, repeated twice in the cabinet meeting, that he had dined recently with Robert Morris, and that Morris had offered to "engage for all his connections" in a campaign against the insolent French diplomat. To Jefferson, who championed the French revolutionists, this was an indication of weakness far more disturbing than Washington's display of distress. To rely on Morris, Jefferson wrote, "shows that the President has not confidence enough in the virtue and good sense of mankind to confide in a government bottomed on them." Here was the old, southern dichotomy—"virtue" versus commerce, true "Republican" righteousness against the worldly wiles of the commercial class.

Jefferson was not the tortured soul that was Arthur Lee, but he shared Lee's suspicions of Morris and his mercantile friends. They represented, Jefferson wrote, "a host who are systematically undermining the public liberty and prosperity." And Jefferson shared Lee's tendency to project the shadows of his own psyche in his conception of others. Sitting with Morris at dinner, which he did occasionally during his time in Philadelphia, Jefferson felt conflicted, convinced of Morris's "hatred . . . even in those moments of conviviality when the heart wishes most to open itself to the effusions of friendship and confidence."

This was the beginning of Jefferson's abiding enmity for the Federalists, a split in the national leadership that would define American politics for generations. It was not new—the foundations had been laid in the original Congress and the debate over independence—but the banners of leadership had been handed off. Franklin and John Dickinson and the Lee brothers had passed from the scene, leaving the contest to younger men whose ambition still burned. Washington had no appetite for this struggle; he served out his term dutifully, but treated his post, and the members of his cabinet, with growing reserve.

Robert Morris did the same. Once the Compromise of 1790 was effected, once those central dilemmas of the first federal Congress had been settled, Morris took less interest in the affairs of the government, and a less active part. As during the Constitutional Convention, the primary role he played in politics was to serve as Washington's collegial friend. Morris had seen enough of faction and political strife. Besides, his new incarnation as a land baron was consuming all his attention. Before long, it would consume all of his fortune as well.

Morris can be forgiven for what later appeared a reckless plunge into the volatile and largely untested market for lands on the American frontier. With the new constitutional government in place many of America's leading men were caught up in the mania for lands—aside from James Wilson, political figures like Henry Knox, Arthur Lee, Robert Livingston, James Duane, and even George Washington, as well as business tycoons like William Bingham, William Constable, and Jeremiah Wadsworth all tested their credit and resources to purchase huge tracts of virgin land. In this scramble for fortune, Morris was among the first, and took the largest share.

It helped, too, that Morris's first great speculation was a success. Soon after William Temple Franklin arrived in London as Morris's agent, he made contact with Sir William Johnstone Pulteney, a former member of Parliament and the premier land speculator in Britain. Pulteney was interested, and combined with William Hornby, a former governor of Bombay, to strike a deal with Franklin.

The terms were decided by March 1791. Everything would take time— the Pulteney Associates would pay in annual installments, beginning that year and running through 1797, while Morris was to clear title to a million acres of land in the Genesee country, "notwithstanding any Law which now exists concerning Alienage or other Disabilities." New York, in fact, did have a law baring aliens from holding land, which Morris dodged by lodging title with a third-party trust. It was an excellent sale, for a total seventy-five thousand pounds sterling, about three times what Morris had paid for the property. Morris spent the next two years completing the transaction. After paying a separate, handsome commission to Franklin, and allowing discounts to Pulteney for advance payments, Morris by 1793 cleared $165,000 in the deal.

As had long been his practice in trade, however, Morris did not sit on these profits, but immediately plowed them back into new land operations. His first move was to purchase the balance of the original Phelps and Gorham tract, roughly four million acres divided into five unmapped tracts. Morris proceeded artfully, concealing his position by making his offer through Gouverneur's brother-in-law, Samuel Ogden. Massachusetts accepted his offer of about $350,000 at the same time the Pulteney deal was confirmed.

Moving to dispose of these lands, Morris brought his two eldest sons into his operation. Thomas, now graduated from law school, he sent to the village of Canandaigua on the New York frontier to manage his holdings there, and Robert Jr. he dispatched to Europe as agent representing two of the new tracts. Meantime, in Philadelphia, Morris opened talks with Theophilus Cazenove, an agent from Amsterdam representing four Dutch banking houses. One of the five tracts, the easternmost, running south from Lake Ontario, he kept for himself, dubbing this strip of land the "Morris Reserve."

Sales again came quickly. Too fast, it turned out, for Morris's plans. In December 1792 he sold to Cazenove and the Holland Land Company one and a half million acres, though not in the clear-cut mode of the Pulteney deal. The price was seventy-five thousand pounds up front for the first million acres and half that for the rest. But there was a caveat: in the first three years of the deal, the Holland Company could withdraw from the sale; in that event, their initial cash advance would become a loan, with the mortgaged land as security. In the meantime, Morris was to commission surveys and clear all Indian claims to the land.

The price was less than Morris thought the land was worth, and he decided to hold the remaining lands off the market until the value appreciated. He sent this directive out to Robert Jr., but by the time it arrived in Europe, his son had already made his sale. He'd started in London, but finding no interest there, had proceeded to Amsterdam, where he found lively interest from the same bankers who were buying the first two tracts from his father. In December 1792, the same month Robert inked his deal with Cazenove, Robert Jr. conveyed a million more acres to Holland Company, this for six hundred fifty thousand florins, about a third less in value than his father's sale. The Dutch bankers received an additional option for eight hundred thousand acres at the same low price. The sums were substantial, but so were the costs of purchase, commissions, and surveys. "He has made a very bad bargain," Morris wrote to Thomas. After fees, and payments to the Indians, this latest land venture in New York was barely breaking even.

With expenses mounting faster than the proceeds of the sales, Morris made a dangerous move. In August 1791, he borrowed one hundred thousand dollars from the Pulteney Associates, mortgaging the Morris Reserve as security. He repaid half the loan on July 1, 1792, but when the balance came due the following January, he couldn't raise the funds. At the same time, beginning in February 1792, he began selling off pieces of the reserve. In 1795, with his fifty thousand debt still outstanding, Pulteney Associates learned that Morris was making sales out of the mortgaged tract, and obtained a court injunction barring further sales. The holdings were frozen for the next three years.

The transactions in New York were complex and financially compromising, but Morris was still ahead of the game, and after the initial sales negotiations he set his northern venture on the back burner. The fever for land speculation was by now sweeping all the former British colonies in America, and nowhere did it reach such a pitch as in Morris's home state.

The catalyst for the land rush in Pennsylvania was a new law passed in 1792 designed to open remote regions of the frontier and at the same time raise money to fund the state government without imposing taxes. The properties included all those "Depreciation Lands" and "Donation Lands" set aside years before to compensate the soldiers who served in the Revolution, as well as 26 million acres of the proprietary estates that the Penn family had relinquished to the new government. Much of this territory had been offered for sale through a state Board of Property organized in 1782, but settlement had been sluggish, giving rise to a volatile secondary market in depreciation and other warrants granted to soldiers and their widows.

Moving the land into private hands was easy enough—the Assembly simply reduced the asking price from eighty cents an acre to twenty. More difficult was enforcing a settlement policy that limited individual sales to four hundred acres and required that purchasers actually reside on and improve their new holdings—build houses, roads, farms, mills, and ultimately new towns. One especially elastic loophole suspended the settlement requirement for lands threatened with "foreign invasion"; at a time when Native Americans constituted hostile "foreigners," this provision was easily and frequently invoked.

The land act of 1792 was well-intentioned policy, but it fell sacrifice to the administration of Governor Thomas Mifflin. Always more popular than his talents warranted, Mifflin was by this time a full-blown drunkard, often arriving to meetings of the Executive Council, sometimes even before noon, "in such a seesaw situation or intoxicated state," as one fellow lawmaker recorded, "that they were obliged to break up." With Mifflin all but incapacitated, management of the state lands fell to his friend and closest adviser, Comptroller-General John Nicholson.

To go by his official résumé, Nicholson was to postwar Pennsylvania what Robert Morris had been to the early Congress—a consummate administrator, adroit in finance and possessed of broad connections in business and politics. He even helped to launch a bank—the Bank of Pennsylvania, the long-contemplated rival to the Morris-dominated Bank of North America. As comptroller, Nicholson filled a critical role at a time when state finances appeared hopelessly compromised between a succession of state and congressional issues of bonds, certificates, and paper money. Perhaps the highest compliment he received in office was a request for information from a bondholder who appealed for his counsel as the only man in the state with "perfect knowledge of all paper matters respecting Pennsylvania."

Here the similarities between Morris and Nicholson ended. Unlike Morris, Nicholson had never made his mark in the world of business; public office was the primary foundation of his fortune. And where Morris was always candid in his ambition to serve his private interest as well as the public's, he always gave priority—the accusations of the Lee brothers notwithstanding—to the public interest. Nicholson had no such compunction.

There is ample evidence of Nicholson's chicanery during his early tenure in public office, but beginning in 1792 he engaged in what might best be characterized as a crime spree, using middlemen and fictitious names to fraudulently bypass the acreage limits and amass title to hundreds of thousands of acres on the Pennsylvania frontier. His chief accomplice in this swindle was Governor Mifflin, who signed so many warrants granting land titles to Nicholson that his hand gave out—"By God," the governor cried in 1794, "I cannot write!" Too enterprising to limit his schemes to the governor's office, Nicholson brazenly bribed state surveyors, clerks at the Land Office, and judges of the district courts. In particular, Nicholson cultivated a mutually beneficial relationship with Daniel Brodhead, a military hero and an in-law to Mifflin. Appointed the state surveyor general, Brodhead routinely back-dated claims in Nicholson's favor and signed off on pseudonymous land claims for both Nicholson and himself.

Some of these shenanigans were brought to light in 1794, when Nicholson was impeached in a trial before the state Assembly. The committee that lodged charges against him conceded that "the fault perhaps laid most with the legislature, who had increased both his duties and his powers farther than any man was able to perform, and farther than any man should have been entrusted with." Nicholson prevailed in a political verdict, but resigned his office.

Robert Morris's first encounters with Nicholson were distinctly unpleasant. They were already political adversaries—Nicholson was aligned with the old Constitutionalist faction—but Nicholson had made it personal when he initiated the vexing legal action that sought to hold Morris personally liable for state funds he'd committed to congressional use during the war. By the early 1790s, however, when he shifted the focus of his land speculations from New York into Pennsylvania, Morris had come to use Nicholson as his agent.

Their first recorded association came in 1792 when, a month after the land act became law, Nicholson formed the Pennsylvania Population Company to raise capital for his speculations. Stock was sold for two hundred dollars a share, and secured by holdings of five hundred thousand acres Nicholson had assembled in northwest Pennsylvania. The directors included James Wilson, Generals William Irvine and Walter Stewart, the Dutch agent Cazenove, and Aaron Burr of New York. Morris purchased one hundred shares, and joined the board in January 1793. It was the first of six land companies Morris would engage in with Nicholson, their association growing steadily deeper and more intimate.

This might appear as just another instance of Morris's remarkable penchant for ignoring grudges in his personal and business relations, perhaps best illustrated in his friendship with Thomas Paine. In addition, Nicholson was polished, charming, and ambitious; if he was willing to bury past animosities, why should Morris object? But there was a qualitative difference involved here. All through his career in business and politics, Morris had put a premium on "character" in choosing his associations. Perhaps it was because the crisis of the Revolution was over, or possibly it was a function of his increasingly precarious financial position, but in forming his connection with William Constable, and especially here with Nicholson, Morris was forsaking a personal ethic that had always served him well. Now approaching his sixtieth year, an age when many of his peers had retired to their country estates, Morris was operating out of fear.

And with good reason. While the fundamentals of the American economy—agriculture and mercantile trade—were recovering their pre-war vigor, the larger economic picture was fraught with hazard. Early in 1793, after the French revolutionaries declared war on Britain, the Bank of England suspended hard money payments for its paper obligations, shaking the financial world. A rash of bankruptcies ensued, including a small London bank where Morris lost, by his estimate, £124,000 sterling. Closer to home, William Duer, Morris's old friend and Hamilton's former treasury deputy, failed in spectacular fashion after investments in land and securities went sour, taking scores of investors with him. Even in the China trade, so promising a few years before, profits shrank as new ventures crowded the market.

Morris and Nicholson, now operating as partners, answered these uncertain times with ever grander ventures in land. There were two basic approaches to the land business at the time; buy large tracts on credit and pay for them by turning them over quickly to second-wave speculators, as Morris had in New York, or set up land companies that would sell small lots to settlers. These ventures took longer to mature, but were better regarded by lawmakers and, at least theoretically, yielded higher end prices.

At the outset, Morris and Nicholson followed the latter, more conservative mode. They formed the Asylum Company to cater to refugees from the Terror in France led by Comte de Noialles, Lafayette's brother-in-law and a friend of Morris's from the war. The venture was stalled by conflicted land titles and impecunious aristocrats, but gave rise to a modest settlement recalled today in names like Frenchtown, Asylum Township, and Laporte. Another less successful venture offered land to Joseph Priestly, a British utopian whose flock decided not to follow him.

These were relatively modest endeavors; more expansive, and more demanding of the partnership's resources, was their engagement in the greatest single public works project of the era, the erection of the capital in the District of Columbia. From the time of the Compromise of 1790, creation of the new city on the Potomac had been something of an obsession for Washington. He'd appointed three close friends to a presidential commission overseeing its development, and installed Pierre L'Enfant as chief architect and resident visionary.

L'Enfant seemed wonderfully qualified for the task. He'd studied design and engineering in France, and had demonstrated his commitment to the American cause during the Revolution, sustaining a grave wound to his leg in the doomed defense of Charleston in 1780. After his release from a British prison he gravitated to Washington and the Nationalist circle—Morris, Hamilton, Henry Knox, and Baron von Steuben all became close friends—and helped consecrate their ascendance in his refurbishment of Federal Hall in New York.

Traveling to Virginia in March 1790, L'Enfant surveyed the rolling plain of the new federal district and drew up plans that exceeded anything yet proposed, a complex of plazas and broad boulevards that would encompass some six thousand acres, fashioned closely after the extravagant French palace at Versailles. The three members of the presidential commission balked at the extravagance of the plan but the president himself endorsed it—and his was the one vote that counted. L'Enfant, unfortunately, had none of Washington's discretion, and soon had so antagonized the commission that he was relieved of his post. His design, however, survived largely intact.

The wrangle over the scope of the project obscured one fundamental underlying problem—the question of money. Virginia and Maryland, whose boundaries the new district straddled, each committed modest sums to the project, but Congress had put up no funds at all. The city was to be financed in the fashion typical of the speculative vogue, by advance sales of lots in the new capital. Three auctions were held, each presided over by Washington himself, but the results were disappointing—of the few lots sold, several went to the president and his commissioners in an effort to support the asking price.

While the sales were dismal, the last of these affairs, in September 1793, drew the interest of a man who might just be the financial savior that Washington and his commissioners were looking for. James Greenleaf was only thirty-two years old, but he hailed from a prominent Boston family, had served a term as American consul in Amsterdam, and boasted a sizable personal fortune. Even better, he was on intimate terms with the leading bankers of Holland.

Five days after the September auction, Greenleaf cut his own deal with the commissioners, agreeing to buy three thousand lots for two hundred thousand dollars. The commissioners stipulated that Greenleaf and any secondary buyers build houses of brick or stone on every third lot within four years of purchase, but this was all downstream. Money was the key, and Greenleaf appeared to have plenty.

Unbeknownst to the commissioners, Greenleaf had two silent partners in the deal, prominent land speculators he'd recently met in Philadelphia—John Nicholson and Robert Morris. Greenleaf made the initial approach to Morris, and Morris bade Nicholson to join with the ebullient prediction that "Washington building lots will continue rising in price for one hundred years to come!"

In December, feeling confident and flush, Morris and his two young partners agreed to double their holdings in Washington. At the same time, these three ambitious speculators plunged into huge new commitments in the West and South—hundreds of thousands of acres in Pennsylvania and Kentucky, a million acres in Virginia and in the Carolinas, and more than two million acres in Georgia. Most of the land they bought in partnership, but each also snapped up deeds and titles on their own—in Morris's case, more than a million additional acres. Much of the land they had never seen, and many of the titles they obtained were suspect or contested, but none of this gave them pause. These lands were not bought for settlement, but for quick resale, and here speed was of the essence. There were other opportunists in the field, snapping up territory for pennies on the acre, many of them longtime friends and sometime partners of Morris, men like Wilson and Bingham and Wadsworth. The game was to get the most the fastest.

At the scale they were buying, the debts mounted rapidly, but always on credit, and with the prospect of fabulous sales just over the horizon. In the confidence game that was the underpinning of this first American land rush, these three partners inspired confidence in each other and in their lenders—Morris, the former Financier; Nicholson, the Pennsylvania comptroller; and Greenleaf, with the banks of Amsterdam at his back. They endorsed each other's notes, thereby multiplying their credit but also their obligations. They didn't always agree—Morris declined joining Nicholson in one particularly dubious investment in Tennessee—but together they felt invincible.

Not everyone was convinced. Gouverneur Morris, trying to manage Morris's debts in Paris, and George Washington both implored Morris to cease his desperate spending. "In the name of Friendship and of common sense," Gouverneur wrote his former mentor, "let me ask you to what purpose all this accumulation of property with so much Trouble and Labor and Anxiety?"

Morris answered with a show of bluster, declaring to Washington, as his step-grandson recalled it, "My dear general, I can never do things in the small. I must be either a man or a mouse." But it may be that, by then,

Morris had no choice but to keep moving. His debts soon reached the point that windfall sales were his only way out.

The French aristocrat Charles-Maurice de Talleyrand, touring America in search of investment opportunities, described the dynamic in 1794. "It is true these lands increase in value by the sole effect of the passage of time, but to benefit by this increase it would be necessary to be in a position to postpone resale for several years and most of them are bound by engagements which make it necessary to resell soon, failing in which, they experience constant demands for money, and . . . have soon exhausted their credit. Mr. Morris especially is in this position and as he is more enterprising than anyone he has also experienced more difficulties."

Three years later, however, Talleyrand revised his forecast, proclaimed the potential for "huge profits" in wild lands, and arranged to purchase one hundred thousand acres from Morris. It was hard to resist the lure of this earliest American real estate bubble.

It did not take long before the coalition of Nicholson, Greenleaf, and Morris experienced its first serious setback. The shock came from Amsterdam, where the rippling impact of the French Revolution spurred the monarchs of Europe to field armies financed by heavy borrowing. In May 1794 the Dutch government had approved Greenleaf's plan to float a subscription loan for a million florins secured by American lands, but with credit markets all but frozen, the scheme raised just 10 percent of the projected fund. Greenleaf's backing, it turned out, was nearly worthless.

In Washington as in New York, however, a key early sale convinced Morris and his partners their dreams would soon be realized. The buyer was Thomas Law, a British nabob from Bengal who moved to America in 1794 with a small family and a large fortune. After meeting Greenleaf in New York, Law caught the "Potomac fever" and agreed to buy from Greenleaf and his partners 445 lots at three hundred dollars apiece—triple the original price. This allowed Morris, Nicholson, and Greenleaf to make their first payment to the district commissioners and commence work on the homes they were obliged to build.

George Washington, keeping a close eye on the progress of his favorite project, viewed the sale to Law with some trepidation. "Why are speculators to pocket so much money?" the president queried his commissioners. But there was no effort to block the sale; with the Greenleaf group strapped for funds, it was the only money keeping the nascent capital city afloat.

It was during this period, buoyed by his few sales and the prospect of many more, that Morris commissioned the now unemployed Pierre L'Enfant to build for him a new mansion that would eclipse William Bingham's as the most opulent in town. He sold his lots on Market Street to the city—it became Washington's landlord—and acquired a lot of open ground the size of an entire city block between Chestnut and Walnut Streets on the western edge of town. He moved into a rental property across the street with Mary, the family, and their furniture. From there they and the rest of the city looked on bemused as L'Enfant directed work on a massive structure—"the grandest ever attempted in Philadelphia for the purposes of private life." For two years, workers excavated a basement two stories deep, a catacomb of brick arches and stone vaults, and then commenced work on the superstructure, another two stories high and clad in imported marble.

Costs soared as the structure rose and Morris fell to squabbling with L'Enfant, whose price estimates proved as fanciful as his neoclassical design. Furnishings arrived on every inbound ship—furniture and tapestries from Paris, glass from England, tableware from China—with no place to put them. Passersby strolling on summer afternoons reported sightings of Morris standing by the curb, silently contemplating the hulking, hollow manor. Intended as a monument to his worldly success, the palatial project came to be known in the taverns and coffeehouses as "Morris's folly."

The travesty across the street seemed to mock him as his debts crowded in. "I am in want of money," he confided to Benjamin Harrison, Jr., in 1795, "and when that is the case every plague follows. I cannot raise wind fast enough during this calm in the circulation of money."

Morris had plenty of company in his misery. After all the exultation at the return of the national government, the 1790s were a dark time for Philadelphia. In the summer of 1793, the city was swept with yellow fever. By August, anyone with a place to go had departed; those who remained burned fires on street corners and sparked powder charges in their homes, hoping to smoke out the mysterious and lethal malady. Benjamin Rush worked tirelessly to care for the afflicted, but his treatments—bloodlettings, purgatives, and icy baths—were often fatal. Thousands died, city offices were shuttered, and the officials of the federal government retreated to Germantown. The plague abated with the first frost, but the fever returned the following summer, and again in 1797.

Trouble came in waves. The wars in Europe brought seizures of hundreds of U.S. vessels, first by the British and then by the French, and the powers demanded that America choose sides. Washington clung to a principled neutrality, but at the cost of turmoil in the streets and in his cabinet. Armies were sent out against the Indians, and against the backcountry farmers of the Pennsylvania frontier whose refusal to pay the new federal excise tax gave rise to the Whiskey Rebellion. Seventeen ninety-four brought Nicholson's impeachment; 1795 saw a committee of Congress declare that Morris owed the government ninety-three thousand dollars for his transactions with Secret Committee—a verdict he blamed on depreciation and always disputed. Morris paid the bill with a note secured by land he'd already sold. In 1796 it was discovered that the president of the Bank of Pennsylvania had diverted one hundred thousand dollars to his own account; the scandal resulted in a run on all banks, with "very injurious effects upon credit generally." The following year, more than a hundred Philadelphia business firms failed.

For Morris, Greenleaf, and Nicholson, already dangerously overextended, such shocks to the credit markets came as mortal blows. They couldn't sell the land they had bought, and they couldn't pay for it either. In 1795, the three partners concocted a last, desperate scheme to raise funds—a new company that would sell stock secured by more than six million acres in land they claimed from New York to Georgia. As testimony to their probity, the partners retained as trustees the speaker of the U.S. House of Representatives, the state attorney general, and the mayor of Philadelphia.

Brimming with bravado, they printed a florid brochure and sent copies to Europe in the hands of a dozen agents funded with thousand-dollar stipends and bountiful commissions. The salesmen included Morris's son William and his new son-in-law, James Marshall, brother to the attorney John Marshall, recently betrothed to Morris's daughter Hetty. Morris was committing every personal and financial resource in trying to move his lands, but the investors of the Old World were unmoved. The only receivers of the overamped stock were involuntary—the creditors of Morris and Nicholson, who received shares of the company instead of cash.

While their agents were still making their way to Europe, the partnership was racked by a new, internal crisis. James Greenleaf, who had arrived promising unlimited financial backing from Holland, was broke. Worse than that, it turned out he had appropriated to his own use all the paltry proceeds of the Dutch loan, and there was no money left to fund the required improvements in Washington.

In May, Greenleaf dropped out, relinquishing title to his Washington lots for notes from Morris and Nicholson totaling more than a million dollars. The notes were all but fictitious, based on sales of land and stock that would never take place. This was the same sort of bill kitting Morris had used to such good effect in supporting the government during the Revolution, but then he'd still had his personal fortune, and the goodwill of Britain's European rivals, to support his notes. He'd used the same mode to float his ventures in tobacco. But this time his credit was slender and his resources exhausted. It was the beginning of a rapid slide into a deep hole.

Promissory notes held the commissioners in Washington at bay for a time, but they soon began to demand that Morris and Nicholson make their payments in hard money. George Washington added his voice to the appeal, writing Morris to implore, in the name of "private friendship" as well as "public duty," that Morris make his payments. Failure to do so would force the suspension of work on the public buildings that were the cornerstone of the whole enterprise—"a disagreeable spectacle."

Also pressing for funds were the crews of workers toiling on the partnership's Washington properties. Nicholson and Morris had architects, construction foremen, and scores of stonecutters and artisans working at the site, many of them going unpaid for months. "What am I to do?" one contractor appealed to the partners. "My property gone and wasting to pay engagements for you—my Family even in want of necessaries." When funds were not produced, several of these employees began seizing building materials for resale to pay expenses; others ended up jailed for debt.

The year 1796 brought a fresh burst of optimism from Morris. The Congress finally agreed to underwrite the cost of some public improvements, and Morris was able to sell several Washington lots for more than a thousand dollars apiece—six times his initial cost—but for credit, not cash. He traveled to the district in August, proclaimed himself "delighted" at the progress of the buildings, and hosted a barbecue for two hundred workmen and visitors. Reviewing the progress of construction, Morris was torn between the pleasure of seeing his commercial instincts confirmed, and the sobering prospect of his immediate circumstances. "The property we now hold will hereafter be of a value beyond consideration," Morris wrote home to Mary. "Alas we cannot continue to hold it but must sell it." That is, if any buyers could be found.

Morris stayed in the district for ten weeks, three times longer than expected, as if by his absence from Philadelphia his many creditors might forget him. They did not. Upon his return he was met by the sheriff; lawsuits were beginning to pile up, and the many plaintiffs feared that Morris had actually absconded. His debts, together with Nicholson's, were estimated at more than twelve million dollars.

The next two years were a story of spiraling decline. Morris and Nicholson tried to use their bills as Morris had his notes during the Revolution, but they played more like the Continental dollar, with speculators buying and selling bundles of them at a fraction of their face value. One broker, in 1797, offered to buy one hundred thousand dollars in notes for four thousand dollars cash. None of Morris's creditors wanted his scrip, nor titles to his land. John Baker, the Philadelphia sheriff, became a regular visitor at The Hills, notifying Morris of duns, accepting various paper obligations to deliver to creditors, and politely returning them when they were refused.

Morris's mood shifted by the day. To Nicholson, supervising their projects in Washington, Morris cried out as he had in the harried days at the Office of Finance. "Scenes of trouble open fast upon me here, every human being seems to be distressed almost to frenzy, universal distrust has taken place . . . Notes that were current when you left this place will not now go at *shaving* discount." A week's time brought no improvement. "The hue and cry for money here exceeds all description," Morris wrote. "My engagements come too fast for my needs and I am dreadfully harassed and a little discouraged."

Yet when he closed his doors to the incessant demands, Morris still assumed the prerogatives of the merchant prince and the pleasures of the epicurean life. Writing to an agent in Bordeaux, he placed an order for a hogshead of the finest vintage available. "I want these wines for my own use, and therefore you must send the best or none." From another Bordeaux merchant he ordered a hundred bottled cases, warning him to "Remember, if the wines are good we shall drink your health; if not, we drink none of them."

In moments that can only be called delusional, Morris even continued buying land—thirty thousand acres in Ohio, in 1796, and 44,000 acres in the Shenandoah Valley the following year. For this last tract he assigned a debt due him for the sale of lands in New York. Both holdings were soon mortgaged to Thomas Fitzsimmons, who lost much of his fortune in dealings with Morris and Nicholson.

By 1797 all of Philadelphia knew of the troubles of the former Financier, but Robert and Mary maintained their cheerful, hospitable mode. John Marshall, Morris's attorney in the complex Virginia litigation that was still ongoing, described the scene during a visit in July. "That family receives me with precisely the same friendship & affection as formerly & seems to preserve in a great degree its vivacity," Marshall wrote in a letter to his wife, "but it must be discernable that a heavy gloom hangs around them which only their good sense restrains them from showing." Soon after, following a visit to the Bingham estate on the Schuylkill, Marshall couldn't help but draw comparison. "The entertainment was elegant" at the Binghams', he said, but he then felt obliged to add, "I like nobody so well as the family of Mr. Morris. There is among them throughout a warmth & cordiality which is extremely pleasing."

Morris kept up the same brave front in his faltering efforts to salvage his affairs. When John Marshall's brother James, now in London with Hetty, wrote to report dismal results from a sales expedition to several European capitals, Morris counseled patience and faith. "I think I can perceive a little symptom of despondency in your letters," Morris wrote soothingly. "I beg you not to give way to it. Keep your expectations alive." It was the inner voice of a born salesman, a personal credo that had guided Morris through a storied career. "Cherish with confidence the expectation that you are to succeed, make every attempt you can think of, and one day or other, perhaps when expectation is at its lowest ebb, you will succeed."

This time, however, unfortunately for Morris and his many creditors, that day never came. In December 1796, James Wilson was removed from his august position on the bench of the Supreme Court and clapped in jail, the first of the great Philadelphia land speculators to land in debtor's prison. The implications for Morris were obvious. "I am seriously uneasy," he wrote to Nicholson, "for Mr. Wilson's affair will make the Vultures more keen after me." But what could be done? "Money is not to be had, good notes are equally scarce. . . . I will do everything I can and then bear my fate like a man."

By the summer of 1797, with creditors stopping by daily with their duns and their threats, Morris retreated to The Hills. It took the pressure off his family, who remained in the rented house on Chestnut Street, and removed him from the immediate jurisdiction of the sheriff. The more aggressive or more desperate of his creditors followed him there, but Morris barred the door, accepting written communications only via a bucket lowered from a second-story window. Only half-joking, he dubbed his redoubt "Castle Defiance."

With Nicholson similarly sequestered in his own home—"Castle Defense"—the beleaguered partners devised ever more improbable schemes to win their reprieve—new land companies, debt swaps, more notes—through a frenzied correspondence that at times reached twenty letters a day. "Another inundation of notes from you is just powered in upon me," Morris wrote one winter morning. "I have enjoyed a little more comfort this day by adhering to my plan and begin to think that perseverance in it will stop the torrent."

Through these months of self-imposed confinement, Morris saw his prospective empire fall to shards. Large swaths of terrain were lost to tax hearings, and squatters took possession of much that was left. "By Heaven!" he exclaimed after one tax sale. "There is no bearing these things; I believe I shall go mad." Just as vexing was the parade of creditors who made their way out to The Hills, built campfires on the grounds, and kept night-long vigils in hopes of finding Morris outside his doors. On one occasion they came in force; just after Christmas in 1797 a constable named Dunwoody showed up with six men bearing pickaxes and sledgehammers. Fortunately for Morris he had several visitors that day and a ready stand of small arms. As Morris informed Nicholson, "They would have had me in five minutes if every pistol and gun in the house had not been manned and fixed at them, for we could not have killed all."

It was not pikes that would pry Morris loose, of course, but legal action, and by 1798 his creditors had finally gotten themselves organized. In February, Morris realized the game was up, and sent a note asking Sheriff Baker to come take him in. That night he scrawled out one more note to Nicholson: "My money is gone, my furniture is to be sold, I am to go to prison and my family to starve. Good night."

On the morning of Friday, February 16, Robert Morris was escorted from The Hills to his house in Philadelphia where the sheriff made a formal arrest. This two-stage procedure conformed with the legal norms of the time, but led to an unfortunate, final confrontation. Harrison Gray Otis, a young congressman from Massachusetts, relayed the story to his wife: "I am told that his family exhibited a dreadful scene of distress, that Mrs. Morris was almost frantic, and flew upon the people who brought him to town and would have committed violence but was prevented."

With Mary distraught and under restraint, Sheriff Baker walked Morris the two short blocks from his rented house to the entrance of the city's debtor's prison, a two-story brownstone known as the Prune Street Jail. It stood across an open yard from the New Gaol, four stories high, a civic improvement opened just before the war; the whole prison complex was enclosed by a twenty-foot stone wall. A block north, past its own walled yard, lay the State House where Morris had delivered some of his greatest performances.

The spectacular fall of a figure so central to the life of the new nation generated surprisingly little comment in the press or the correspondence of the day. This was in part a reflection of the hurly-burly nature of politics in the young republic; Americans had seen so many heroes rise one day only to fall the next—Horatio Gates, Silas Deane, Benedict Arnold—that they'd become inured to the luster of fame. Only Washington and Franklin had managed to navigate the vicissitudes of war and independence with their reputations intact, and even they had felt the lash of popular odium enough to fear its sting. The formal lexicon of the day was gracious and sentimental, but the hearts of the public were not.

More immediate, the public turned against Morris because of the nature and scope of his delinquency. Scores of Philadelphians, especially those personally close to Morris, had bought into his stock offerings or accepted his notes; many had lost their all. And for those fortunate enough to stand on the sidelines, there was the age-old satisfaction of seeing the mighty brought low. "What an example of the folly and vanity of human grandeur," Otis mused in his letter home. "But a few years since he was in wealth and honor, the most considerable man in the United States, and she ruled the world of fashion with unrivalled sway. He will now probably moulder away a few remaining wretched years in prison." Elizabeth Hewson, sister of a prominent physician, was more succinct. Shortly before Morris was arrested, Hewson wrote to her brother, "I think he should be in jail. He deserves to be there if ever any man did."

But if popular opinion deserted Morris, the political classes did not. For all the enemies he made over the years, none came forward to gloat over his demise. After Thomas Jefferson was elected president, he remembered Morris only to lament that he could not bring him into his cabinet. "What a misfortune to the public that R. Morris has fallen from his height of character," Jefferson wrote to Madison. "If he could get from confinement, and the public give him confidence, he would be a most valuable officer. . . . But these are two impossibilities in the way."

The Prune Street Jail was located in the heart of the city where Morris had spent most of his life, but within its confines he encountered a new and different world. Inmates were generally at liberty and could receive visitors from daylight until nine at night. The criminal residents were separated from the debtors by a low wall that traversed the large exercise yard, but this barrier did little to prevent bands of ruffians from climbing over to rob the debtors or avail themselves of the prostitutes turned in by their land-lords. Despite their penury, debtors were required to pay their jailers for room and board; the more destitute were crowded ten to a room, hungry and half-naked. One historian described the scene as "a purgatory worthy of Hieronymus Bosch."

In the first days of his confinement, Morris drifted in hazy uncertainty. "Having no particular place allotted to me," he reported to Nicholson, "I feel myself an intruder every place into which I go. I sleep in another person's bed. I occupy other people's rooms, and if I attempt to sit down and write it is at the interruption and inconvenience of someone who has acquired a prior right to the place."

Within a week, however, Morris got his bearings and established his presence. Somehow, Mary obtained some money, and with it Morris secured his own room—"the best in this house," as he termed it. Within its whitewashed walls, under a window barred with an iron grate, Morris soon assembled his furnishings: three writing desks, a borrowed mahogany table, "an old Windsor settee and eight old Windsor chairs," six chests stuffed with correspondence and business papers, a mirror, a trunk of clothes, and a bed. Among the other inmates, Morris encountered several friends and not a few enemies; James Greenleaf resided just down the hall, while Daniel Allison, an acquaintance fallen on hard times, "fitted up a room . . . where a dozen of them play cards from morning til midnight."

Morris resumed his correspondence and soon recovered his sense of humor. He teased Nicholson about his fears of the prison, and invited him to join him for dinner at the "Hotel with Gated doors." Morris assured Nicholson the warden had no claim upon him. "Come therefore my friend as early in the forenoon as you can that we may have some conversation before as well as after dinner."

As time passed, Morris settled into a routine. He rose early and took his exercise by long walks around the perimeter walls, carrying pebbles that he dropped to count his laps. William Wood, an impecunious actor, met Morris during his own period of confinement. "His person was neat," Wood recorded, "and his dress, although a little old-fashioned, adjusted with much care." In their first encounter, in the yard, "Mr. Morris appeared cheerful, returned my salutation in the politest manner, but in silence, continuing his walk. . . . For some mornings the same silence prevailed, until at length, observing my languid deportment, he suddenly stopped, inquired whether I was ill, and added, with something like severity: 'Sir, this is but an ill place for one so sickly, and apparently so young.' From this time on he spoke to me with almost daily, and always with great kindness."

Sitting in his cell, surrounded by papers and ledgers that only confirmed the blasted state of his fortune, Morris lamented his lot but did not protest it. "A man that cannot hear and face misfortune should not run risks," he wrote to his son Thomas. "But I have been too adventurous and therefore it is my duty to meet my Fate with Fortitude and I do it." His primary concern, Morris told Nicholson, was the impact on his wife and children. "The punishment of my imprudence in the use of my name and loss of credit is perhaps what I deserve but it is nevertheless severe on my family and on my account, I feel it most tormentingly."

Mary did her best to support Robert through his incarceration, visiting Prune Street every afternoon, usually in company of their younger daughter, Maria, who was still in her teens and living at home. But the fall of her husband robbed Mary of her station in society, and she could not conceal her distress. Abigail Adams could only sympathize when she paid Mary a call during her husband's first year as president. "She received me with all that dignity of manners for which she more than any Lady I ever saw, is distinguished," Adams wrote to a friend. "She endeavored to smile away the Melancholy which was evident on her whole countenance. . . . I requested her to come and take Tea with me! I took her by the hand. She said she did not visit, but would not refuse herself the pleasure of coming someday when I was alone. She then turned from me, and the tears burst forth. I most sincerely felt for her."

Robert Morris remained in prison for three and a half years. He never ceased in his efforts to revive his fortunes and extricate his estate, but the land market failed to rebound and his debts, estimated at the end of his term at three million dollars, remained beyond the reach of his means.

No formal effort was ever made to win his freedom, but Morris was not forgotten by his friends. Gouverneur Morris visited several times after his return from Paris, and George Washington, called once more into service in 1798 during the diplomatic crisis with France, stopped by one evening to break bread in Morris's cell. It was the last meeting of the two chief architects of America's improbable Revolution; Washington died in December 1799, with Morris still in prison.

On Gouverneur's first visit to Prune Street he found Morris "strongly affected" by his imprisonment, and held that Mary "puts on an air of firmness which she cannot support and was wrong to assume." But it was not in Robert's nature to despond, nor in Mary's. On a later occasion Gouverneur reported that "Morris and his family are in high spirits, and I keep them so by a very lively strain of conversation."

Gouverneur did more than talk to raise the spirits of what was in truth his adoptive family. As the agent in Robert's ongoing dealings with the Holland Land Company, Governeur set as a condition for transfer of title the assignment of an annuity of fifteen hundred dollars per year to Mary Morris for the duration of her life. This sum, a pittance in comparison to the extravagance of years gone by, allowed Mary to rent a small house on Twelfth Street, so far from the city center that the streets were not yet paved.

Inside the prison, life took on its own rhythms, its own highs and lows. Morris had the chagrin to see James Greenleaf released, having found the wherewithal to pay nine million dollars to his creditors—though none to his former partners, who took to blaming him for their ruin. In August 1799, John Nicholson finally joined Morris at Prune Street after mounting a tenacious but futile defense in the courts. Ever industrious, Nicholson published a newspaper that was distributed outside the city walls under the title *The Supporter*; his subscribers included President John Adams and two major banks, and the subscriptions helped pay the bills for Nicholson, his wife, and their eight young children. But Nicholson did not bear up well under the burdens of disgrace and confinement. He died in prison in December 1800; some said he'd gone insane.

Morris bore his own share of tragedy in Prune Street. During his first summer and the one that followed, the scourge of yellow fever returned to the city, and dozens of prisoners died. At the height of the plague permission was granted for inmates to remove to quarters in the countryside, but Morris declined, content to remain in his cell and tend to his plot in the prison garden. "I feel no kind of apprehension," Morris recorded at the time. "My only anxiety is for my wife and daughter and these poor sick people."

Morris was spared but not so his family; his son William, twenty-seven years old, was stricken in September, and after being "bled, blistered, purged, sweated," finally succumbed. William had been profligate in his youth and desultory in his father's service, but Morris felt his death keenly. He thought of him constantly, Morris told Nicholson; "his value to his family I never counted until he was lost, and now I see its magnitude, and that it is irreparable."

Through all these travails Morris continued to spar with his creditors and judicial authorities to secure his freedom, but when his release finally came it was through no cause of his own. In the spring of 1800, spurred by the string of failures that swept the country—Morris's being perhaps the largest—Congress passed the nation's first bankruptcy law. Designed to limit fraud and equalize competing claims, it allowed for the release of major debtors upon the petition of their creditors. In Morris's case, as might be expected, the negotiations were protracted, but on August 26, 1801, he walked once more through the gates of the Prune Street Jail. "I embrace the first opportunity to tell you," Morris wrote his son Thomas the next day, "I obtained my liberty last evening, and had the inexpressible satisfaction to find myself again restored to my home and family."

He'd been released from prison, but not from his debts. The next three months Morris spent in hearings before a panel of bankruptcy commissioners appointed to manage the claims of more than ninety creditors. At the commissioners' direction Morris composed his last great treatise, an "Account of Property," which laid out in painstaking—and undoubtedly for Morris, painful—detail his vast holdings, how they were acquired, what had been disposed of, and what remained. Morris professed to the end his good faith in these acquisitions; he observed wistfully that, had he limited his land speculations to his initial purchases in New York, "I have every reason to believe that at this day I should have been the wealthiest citizen of the United States." He then added an aside that could have afforded little solace to his creditors: "That things have gone otherwise I lament, more on account of others than on my own account, for God has blessed me with a disposition of mind that enables me to submit with patient resignation to His dispensations as they regard myself."

Morris's sole admission of misconduct was in issuing his notes, which he conceded to be so numerous that he'd completely lost count. "It is well known that Mr. Nicholson and myself owe a very large debt by Notes drawn and endorsed by each," Morris wrote. "The issuing of these notes is the blameable part of our conduct, which we have both felt and acknowledged. But as no use can arise to the holders of such Paper from any Reflections I can now make, I will forbear any attempt to justify that Business; altho' circumstances might be adduced that would at least soften the disposition to censure."

Armed with this "Account," the bankruptcy commission closed its books on December 4 and the claims against Morris were put to rest. "My business was finished in the district court without opposition," he wrote to Thomas. "I now find myself a free citizen of the United States without one cent that I can call my own."

It's hard to resist moralizing over the collapse of a vast financial empire established on credit by a man who always claimed character and integrity as his primary personal asset. But Morris's story was always more complicated than what lay on the surface, and that was the case here as well. His land speculations were no Ponzi scheme. He believed to the end that his lands would find buyers and that his creditors would be made whole. His titles were often iffy, but no more so than those of his rivals. By and large, the underlying value was there.

What failed Morris in the end was overconfidence. He exceeded his credit. This was a function of economic conditions—the general shortage of money—but also of his miscalculation. His great operations for the government he had always supported on the strength of his personal credit; his tragic error was to actually conflate his credit and that of the government. The bills against Franklin, and the Dutch loans that had bailed out Morris's notes to the disbanding army, had been paid against the nation's credit, not Morris's, a distinction the Financier couldn't seem to recognize. When he sought personally to exercise that same degree of leverage, in the tobacco market and especially in land, he overreached.

Viewed in light of his career in public office, Morris's downfall takes on operatic, even mythic dimensions. His trajectory follows that of Icarus, but in place of the sun, Morris was dazzled by gold. He felt he had mastered the arts of finance, and as a matter of state policy, he may have. But when lucre became his personal obsession, it consumed him, and the higher he flew, the more he shed the plumage of strict principle and personal integrity that had first carried him aloft. He abused his credit, betrayed his reputation, and forfeited all that he had achieved.

The hubris that brought him down confirmed the righteous tone of the critics who dogged him over the years, the Lee brothers and the other arbiters of virtue who preached against avarice. But it could not obviate the enduring contributions Morris made to America's founding and his indelible impact on the life of its people. His secret agents had supplied the armies of the Revolution, his credit had salvaged its finances, and his faction had fashioned its Constitution. More than that, Morris installed his pragmatic, realist, modernist vision of a free people united by the principles of economic self-interest and not by bonds of state or political authority. For better or worse, that is the feature that distinguished America from every other nation established in the New World, and set America on its course to becoming the economic powerhouse we know today.

· · ·

Upon his release from prison Morris attempted a return to commercial life but he found the business climate daunting and his own reputation too much of an impediment. "I am on the lookout for something to do that will give me bread," Morris recorded; "I will not be idle." Though it was the dead of winter he exercised his freedom by taking to the road to renew contacts and assay what remained of his lands. He headed south to Washington, where he dined with President Jefferson and James Madison, then secretary of state. They were, Morris wrote to his son, "very polite, very attentive, but that is all."

Morris found a warmer reception when he went north, in June, this time in company with Mary, to visit Gouverneur Morris at his New York estate. Gouverneur described his old friend as "lean, low spirited, and as poor as a commission of bankruptcy can make a man whose effects will, it is said, not pay a shilling on the pound." Robert and Mary stayed several weeks. The couple made social calls in New York and Robert took meetings with Gouverneur, reviewing the papers of their defunct partnership with William Constable and sorting out the details of Mary's annuity. Upon their departure, Gouverneur was pleased to report, "I sent him home fat, sleek, in good spirits, and possessed of the means to live comfortably for the rest of his days."

The following year Morris was gratified when a group of merchants asked him to serve as president of a new bank they planned to launch. The sponsors got so far as to issue stock, but the plan stalled in the face of a rival offering. It was his last genuine business opportunity.

In the spring of 1804, Morris busied himself in preparing his will. It was a document that reflected his poverty, but also the warmth of his sentiments. To his son Robert he left a gold watch that had belonged to his father before him, "left to me at his death and carefully kept and valued by me ever since." To Thomas he bequeathed his gold-headed walking stick— "The head was given to me by the late John Hancock esq. when President of Congress, and the cane was the gift of James Wilson whilst a Member of Congress." Henry, then just starting out in business, received a copying press, a gift from one of Morris's London factors. To his daughters, Hetty and Maria, now both married, he conferred pieces of family silver that he'd managed to repurchase from the bankruptcy court.

Gouverneur Morris was the only person Robert memorialized who was not a member of the immediate family. He received a "telescope spying glass" that Morris had bought from a French refugee during the war. The rest of his estate, such as it was, Morris left to "my dearly beloved wife Mary."

Morris felt obliged, at the close of his will, to offer something of an apology. "I have to express my regret at having lost a very large fortune acquired by honest industry, which I had long hoped and expected to enjoy with my family during my own life and then to distribute amongst those of them that should outlive me. Fate has determined otherwise and we must submit to the decree, which I have done with patience and fortitude."

It was, in effect, his epitaph. Morris died the following spring, in his seventy-first year. There were no public ceremonies, no parades to mark his passing. He was buried quietly in the yard of the Christ Church. Mary survived him another twenty-one years.

EPILOGUE

I n the century after his death, the memory of Robert Morris acquired
the stature that his exploits during the Revolution secured for him at
the time. He never overshadowed his friends and colleagues George
Washington and Benjamin Franklin, but he was closely associated with
both, and was given credit, in Philadelphia especially, for the critical role
he played in America's triumph in arms and in the formation of the new national government.

In the modern era, however, Morris all but disappeared from the roster of the founding fathers. His seminal contributions continued to be acknowledged by scholars, but his labors, his achievements, and his influence
on the life of the republic were all lost to popular conception. The facts of
his life and career remained the same, of course; what changed was the
nature of how Americans viewed their history. Much as a close reading
of Morris's life tells us a great deal about the trials and complexity of the
founding era, the story of his posthumous reputation illuminates the shifting basis of American historiography, and the meaning of history itself.

Morris was little lamented at the time of his death. This was a consequence of his ultimate financial failure, and of the press of events in the
new nation, where revolutionary unity quickly gave way to a bitter partisan
division between the Federalists and Thomas Jefferson's pastoral populism.
But in the years after the Civil War, Americans turned to the mythos of the
Revolution as a touchstone of national identity, and Morris enjoyed a full
restoration.

The first full-length treatment of Morris was a two-volume study by William Graham Sumner published in 1891. Sumner spent his career at Yale,
where he built a reputation as an early social Darwinist and also as an ardent foe of American imperialism. Dry and poorly structured—a hazard
in any effort to encompass so eventful a career—*The Financier and the Fi-*

nances of the American Revolution offered an extended tour of the obstacles Morris encountered in office but failed to capture the drama and arc of his life saga. Moreover, Sumner's analysis was necessarily incomplete, as he lacked access to critical papers—several volumes of the Morris diary, his letterbooks, and other documents—that surfaced in Europe toward the end of the century.

Those papers found their way to the Library of Congress in 1901, where they drew the attention of Ellis Paxson Oberholtzer, a Philadelphia historian with a penchant for economics. Oberholtzer published his *Robert Morris: Patriot and Financier* in 1903, four years before a two-volume set, *Jay Cooke: Financier of the Civil War.* Appearing at a time when hagiography was the historian's primary pursuit, Oberholtzer's work settled comfortably in midstream, giving us Morris as the embodiment of public virtue whose "patriotic exertions" had salvaged the revolutionary government. In this mode, florid language served to illustrate simple points: in shrugging off the attacks of his enemies, Morris "did not dwell with small spirits, and what they meant to be sword thrusts were mere pin pricks to this Brobdingnagian character."

Oberholtzer worked during the heyday of hero worship, but even as he was composing his ode to Morris the national consensus idealizing the founders and their achievements was beginning to splinter. The outbreak of the Spanish-American War and the long reign of the robber barons shook American confidence in its political and economic model and led to a new, more critical appraisal. This was the Progressive Era, epitomized in the historical arena with the publication in 1913 of *An Economic Interpretation of the Constitution of the United States*, by Charles A. Beard. Trained at Oxford and at Columbia University in New York, Beard asserted—not for the first time, but in a more systematic fashion than any before him—that the founders were best understood as motivated by self-interest, especially in the fabrication of the Constitution. Rather than a pristine exercise in political philosophy, Beard said, the new frame of government was the product of a "deep-seated conflict between a popular party based on paper money and agrarian interests and a conservative party centered in the towns and resting on financial, mercantile, and personal property interests generally."

This was a bracing new formula that had broad appeal at a time when Marxist social analysis was sweeping the globe. Together with fellow Progressive historian Carl Becker, who famously suggested in his study of the Revolution in New York that the war was fought to determine, not just "home rule," but "who should rule at home," Beard enjoyed a period of enormous popularity. Beard and Becker each took turns as president of the prestigious American Historical Association, and the idea that the Revolution was grounded in class conflict became the focus of a new generation of historians.

Robert Morris was not an explicit target of either Beard or Becker, but he neatly fit the thesis of an American oligarchy hijacking the spoils of an incipient democracy, and soon went into eclipse along with Washington, Hamilton, Gouverneur Morris, and the other crypto-aristocrats of the new republic. As the nation's intellectuals tried to make sense of unprecedented hard times and the rise of global communism, the familiar, heroic version of the founding was discarded as a two-dimensional fairy tale.

The new historical consensus did not well survive the rigors of academic scrutiny, however. Fissures appeared as archivists delved into the early debates over nonimport and price controls to find that economic circumstance served as a poor indicator of political outlook. The movement to refute Beard culminated in a book-length rebuttal, *We the People: The Economic Origins of the Constitution*, published by Forrest McDonald in 1958. Using Beard's methodology as a starting point, McDonald surveyed the financial holdings of every delegate to the Constitutional Convention and found that every class, faction, geographic sector, and "all shades of political opinion" were represented within each group. A simple class analysis simply did not conform to the facts.

There was much quibbling over the facts cited by McDonald, but within a decade the argument was deemed settled. "Today Beard's reputation stands like an imposing ruin in the landscape of American historiography," the historian Richard Hofstadter declared in 1968. "What was once the grandest house in the province is now a ravaged survival."

Yet even as successive rounds of research eroded the foundations of the Beardian thesis, Beard's disciples branched out, unearthing disputes as old as the nation itself—the division between the Articles of Confederation and the Constitution, the quarrel over state issues of paper money, the contest between "Republican" virtue and the corrosive influence of commerce. Here Morris emerged as an easy mark for academics convinced that the Revolution had been usurped by a small coterie of moneyed men.

The leader in this field was Merrill Jensen, a revisionist historian at the University of Wisconsin who shied away from strict economic determinism, but posited that the entire dynamic of the revolutionary period in America boiled down to a struggle between radicals and conservatives. I chose to avoid the latter designation entirely in this book from a conviction that even

the most reluctant of the revolutionaries—Morris foremost among them—
had still chosen to join and abet an armed uprising against the traditional
power structure, a course that could hardly warrant the term "conservative." But Jensen and his followers drew no such distinction. Jensen saw
"fundamental divisions in American society," with "the masses in the towns
and the farmers of the backcountry" pitted against "the ruling class."

This facile, neo-Beardian construction soon ran into some fairly obvious obstacles. One primary problem was that, while certain aspects of class
were firmly established—the subjugation of blacks, women, and Native
Americans, chiefly—American society was still relatively fluid, as Robert
Morris's own rise to prominence illustrates nicely. Moreover, the artisan
mechanics who comprised the nation's tiny "working class" often aligned
themselves with Morris and the merchants, making it difficult for latter-day
Marxists to make their paradigm stick.

The changeable nature of politics in the Revolution posed another vexing problem for Beard, Jensen, and their adherents. Benjamin Rush, for
example, began the Revolution as a leading Pennsylvania militant but soon
became a committed critic of the radical state constitution. Similarly, the
migration of America's most famous radical, Thomas Paine, from antiestab-
lishment militant to champion of the bank and Morris's Nationalist funding
program appears to confute any simple taxonomy of class allegiance.

Yet while factual problems arose to blunt the primary thrust of Beard's
economic determinism, his radical rejection of the heroic mode of American historiography had opened the gates of academia to wholesale, "Progressive" revision of the revolutionary era. In the South, and particularly
in Virginia, that meant a renewed interest in the anti-commercial critique
of the Lee brothers. For Julian P. Boyd, an archivist at Princeton who
broke ground with his exhaustive edition *The Papers of Thomas Jefferson*,
that meant fierce new attacks on Silas Deane and Benjamin Franklin. For
Thomas Abernethy, distinguished historian of the South, it meant a savage
treatment of anyone who threatened the righteous claims of the Virginians.
That included Franklin and especially Robert Morris.

Following closely the fears and suspicions first enunciated by the Lees,
Abernethy resurrected their themes in his 1937 opus *Western Lands and
the American Revolution*. Like the Lees, Abernethy saw Morris as a stalking horse for the Lees' rivals in Virginia, Carter Braxton and Benjamin
Harrison. And like the Lees, Abernethy saw the moderates in Congress—
Morris, Franklin, James Wilson, and John Dickinson—as corrupt and self-
interested practitioners of "political expediency." It was Abernethy who

formulated the enduring claim that "The idea that Robert Morris financed the Revolution out of his own pocket is purely mythological. The truth is that the Revolution financed Robert Morris."

Ben Franklin's fabled career and towering reputation were more than adequate to survive these posthumous challenges, but Silas Deane was a far more obscure figure, and despite some recent attempts at restoration, he has lately come to be viewed as the rogue the Lees alleged him to be.

Robert Morris's case is more complex. He was too important an actor in the revolutionary drama to be written off with a caricature, and in 1952 his tenure as Financier was the subject of a brilliant study by the economic historian Clarence L. Ver Steeg. Working through a range of widely scattered letters and documents, *Robert Morris: Revolutionary Financier* made a powerful argument for Morris as the pragmatic architect of the American financial system whose program "resembled that of Hamilton's a decade later not only in general design but also in precise detail." Ver Steeg was no apologist, but his careful rendering put to rest some of the more outlandish claims set forth by Boyd and Abernethy.

Ver Steeg's work was recognized with a book prize from the American Historical Association, but it was essentially an academic treatise and failed to resurrect Morris as a central figure among the founders. That project fell to E. James Ferguson, one of Merrill Jensen's first graduate students at Wisconsin.

Ferguson made his inclinations clear in one of his first major papers, titled "Business, Government, and Congressional Investigation in the Revolution." Published in 1959, Ferguson opened with the breezy observation that "A normal aftermath of war is the exposure of the inefficiency and graft that occurred in waging it." The Revolution was no exception, Ferguson wrote, particularly as "procurement services were staffed with merchants who remained in private trade."

With this preamble, Ferguson sketched out the general operations of the Secret Committee, and lodged a circumstantial indictment against Robert Morris as "the merchant whose career owed the most to the fertile linkage of public office and private business." Morris dominated the committee system in Congress, obtained the largest of the committee contracts, and "was in the enviable position of negotiating contracts with himself or his associates." Ferguson conceded that it was "impossible to know" whether Morris had diverted public funds to his own account, and acknowledged that Morris prevailed in a series of investigations. But Ferguson was satisfied that "it is clear that Morris took an improper advantage of his position," and cited the disputed finding, reached well after the end of the war, that Morris owed eighty thousand dollars in unreturned advances from the Secret Committee.

It was a one-sided portrait of Morris and the committee, making no mention of their success in arming the rebel army or the toll the arms trade took on the merchants who engaged in it. But it was a brash and confident piece that marked Ferguson as an important new voice in the field of early American history.

Ferguson carried this reputation, and his critical outlook, into several more articles and then a major book—*The Power of the Purse: A History of American Public Finance, 1776–1790*. This was a seminal production, the first major modern study of the most persistent and divisive problem facing the leaders of the Revolution.

Here Ferguson continued to regard Morris with suspicion, but his critique now extended well past the question of personal peculation. The subtext of *The Power of the Purse* was to provide new ammunition for Merrill Jensen's central thesis—that the Nationalists in Congress had used the economic problems confronting the Congress to usurp the democratic aspirations of the American patriots and impose the oppressive central government that was embodied in the Constitution.

Ferguson was more than just an ideologue. He was an avid researcher and developed a subtle understanding of the myriad issues involved in financing the war—the brief reign of paper money, the several strains of military certificates, state currencies, domestic debt instruments, and foreign obligations—and the various phases of political response to the mounting financial pressures. On fiscal matters *The Power of the Purse* represented an important advance in explicating the practical problems the Revolution had to surmount.

This, of course, accrued to Morris's credit. Ferguson saluted Morris as "the inescapable choice for the Department of Finance," "expert and full of expedients," whose "mastery of Continental business was virtually unsurpassed." Of his performance in office, Ferguson said, "Morris was supremely competent, even brilliant."

But Ferguson's political formulation was just as important to his message, and on this score he could not help but regard Morris as scheming, conniving, even Machiavellian. Morris was "grimly determined" in pursuit of his goals—as if that distinguished him from anyone else in those grave and portentous years—he "operated through henchmen," he displayed a "high-handed disposition . . . to strike boldly and crudely at his main objectives."

These were qualities of leadership, the marks of any executive faced with protracted warfare and extraordinary political turmoil. What most disturbed Ferguson was his perception of Morris as a "conservative," committed to replacing paper emissions and price controls with laissez-faire policies emphasizing capital formation and a free market. Ferguson could not accept these as fiscal strategies grounded in Morris's experience as a world-scale capitalist, but as political measures that he interpreted through the lens of Progressive Era class analysis. Morris was "the leader of the first conservative movement in national politics," "a national alliance of conservatives," which achieved its design in the writing of the Constitution.

This was an apt enough description, given the framework within which Ferguson was working, but there are other formulae that might serve just as well. Stripped of the ideological baggage, Morris and the Nationalists might be viewed as they saw themselves—leaders of a national liberation movement who answered crisis with innovation and gloomy prospects with unflinching resolve. Their timely intervention in 1781 had come at the urgent request of a Congress that had squandered the moral and financial capital of the Revolution, and the charter they crafted in 1787 laid a sound foundation for the operation of the world's first constitutional democracy. What part of this epic undertaking, one might ask, should be termed "conservative"?

Ferguson felt obliged to answer this question directly. Fiscal reforms like budget cuts, sound-money policies, and the launch of the bank were "the proper work of a financial administrator," he conceded, but were just the window dressing for Morris's "larger goal of recasting the structure of the Union." This underlying agenda had to do with raising a nation of "power, consequence, and grandeur," in Morris's words, which Ferguson elaborated as "a break with the agrarian past and the growth of commercial and industrial enterprise."

Here was the same paradox Morris presented in his effort to win a renewed charter for the Bank of North America—he is the "conservative" who wants to leave the past behind and open the doors on a new era of economic development. What, exactly, qualifies such a forward-looking orientation as conservative? Ferguson's answer is that Morris and the Nationalists were anti-democratic. "In their private letters," Ferguson writes, "Morris and his associates avowed their contempt for the people and their impatience with popular government."

It is telling that, in this instance, Ferguson invokes Morris's "associates" as well as Morris himself, because, in fact, in all his correspondence public or private, Morris never once cast aspersions on "the people" as a body. Gouverneur Morris did, and so did Hamilton, but they were more reckless in their language, and did not share Morris's easy and enduring connection to "the people" that Ferguson says he despised. Just as comfortable in a dockside tavern as in a paneled drawing room, Morris often sparked controversy in Philadelphia, but he always retained his popular standing, and was to the end a political force in the most radically "democratic" state in the nation.

Recognizing, perhaps, that he was on shaky ground, Ferguson cites Morris directly, quoting a letter Morris wrote Hamilton deriding "vulgar souls whose narrow optics can see but the little circle of selfish concerns." But here Ferguson is taking Morris out of context. It was not "the people" that Morris was disparaging in his letter to Hamilton, or "democracy" per se, but the leaders of the New York legislature, and particularly Governor George Clinton. That Clinton was a demagogue and a grasping power broker few would presume to deny; here Ferguson is raising Clinton up as a paragon of democracy and the people's champion.

Continuing, Ferguson asserts that Morris and the Nationalists pressed their agenda, especially in the critical years from 1781 to 1783, in the face of a spirited, principled, and broadly popular opposition: "Morris and his associates were quite aware that the United States was a singularly democratic country and that the majority of the people did not subscribe to their aims." This is central to Ferguson's thesis and echoes the rhetoric of Arthur Lee, David Howell, and the other critics of Morris's program at the time, but it grossly misstates the historical record. The fact is that the impost— the crucial first plank of the Morris program—was endorsed by Congress, won the support of all but one of the legislatures in the union, and failed only because of the intransigent opposition of a tiny mercantile clique that dominated local politics in the smallest state in the new nation. There were no polls to establish the true sentiments of "the majority of the people" at the time, but there is no question that the Nationalist program was embraced by the vast majority of the democratically elected lawmakers from New England to the Carolinas.

That so acute an observer as Ferguson would stake his position on such flimsy ground was not an error in judgment so much as a reflection of the depth of his commitment to a particular historical construct, one he termed, on a different occasion, "neo-progressive." This school of thinking held that, while Charles Beard might have been refuted in his particulars, his larger idea, that the Revolution was shaped by "competitive forces within society," and not "social cooperation in adapting to external circumstances," retained its force. To the end, Ferguson was convinced that a neo-progressive analysis was the only paradigm that conformed to "the dominant materialism of our age, which tends to regard ideas as subservient to desire, not the source of it, and to give priority to socio-economic factors."

This was a most revealing statement. Ferguson was explicitly locating himself in place and time, establishing himself as an exponent of what he considered the newfound insights of "our age." In effect, he was acknowledging what another historian posited as the hazard of his profession—that most "schools" of history "form a commentary on the ages that propose them" as much as they illuminate the subject at hand.

Ultimately, Ferguson was torn over how to assess the career and character of Robert Morris. As a student of the trials and the triumphs of the American founders, Ferguson found Morris to be an exemplary administrator and a man of almost mystical powers, the "presiding genius" of the Nationalist faction, "a controversial figure about whom legends clustered." But as an ideologue, the student and the defender of Merrill Jensen, Ferguson regarded Morris as a class adversary, an enemy of liberty and democracy, and possibly a crook.

His ambivalence was reflected in his restatement of Thomas Abernethy's indictment of Morris. "The myth still persists that Robert Morris financed the Revolution out of his own pocket," Ferguson averred. "If it is rather the other way around—that the Revolution financed Robert Morris—he was nevertheless one of the great men of his time."

To Ferguson's credit, his deep engagement with Morris in the course of his research for *Power of the Purse* only whetted his appetite and sharpened his focus. Morris became the whale to Ferguson's Ahab, a subject of endless fascination and the quarry of all his future scholarly endeavors. Soon after publication of his financial opus, Ferguson launched the central project of his professional life, the collection, annotation, and publication of *The Papers of Robert Morris*.

It was a huge endeavor, part of an archival movement among twentieth-century American historians to assemble new, comprehensive editions of the state and personal papers of the leading founders. Boyd started the trend with his Jefferson compilation; soon Hamilton, Madison, Franklin,

John Adams, and, of course, Washington each had a new collection in the works.

The Morris project was similar, but more closely targeted. Rather than assemble a lifetime of correspondence, as with the other founders, Ferguson limited his scope to the years Morris spent as superintendent of finance. It was probably a good idea. Spanning less than four years—from February 1781 to the end of October 1784—the collection fills nine weighty tomes, the sheer volume providing ample testimony to the extraordinary scope of Morris's responsibilities and the extent of his energy and industry. The fourth volume, for example, covering just the first four months of 1782, runs more than six hundred pages.

Ferguson got the project under way in the late 1960s, assembling a team of experts and producing the first volume of the Robert Morris papers in 1973. The work continued for the next twenty-five years, and in the interim, lives and careers unfolded. John Catanzariti, Ferguson's chief assistant, moved on to join the team working on the Jefferson papers. Ferguson himself sustained a head injury in 1980; by the end he was replaced as chief editor by Elizabeth Nuxoll and Mary Gallagher, who had assisted on the first edition as graduate students. They acquired skills and finesse as they went; as one reviewer observed, "The quality of the product improves with each successive volume."

For Ferguson, who died in 2002, the work on the Morris papers had to be satisfying but also exasperating. He never quite let go of the preconceptions that he brought to the project—that Morris was politically opportunistic and ethically suspect—but he never found evidence for the perfidy that he was seeking. Like Arthur Lee two centuries before, his painstaking review of Morris's official and private correspondence failed to produce a single instance of self-dealing or subversion of the public interest. In time, though he never conceded it publicly, Ferguson's critique of Morris softened.

It had to be a bittersweet moment for Ferguson when the reviews came out on the first installment of the Morris papers. Writing in *The Pennsylvania Magazine of History and Biography,* Paul H. Smith, manuscript editor at the Library of Congress, hailed the collection as "an awesome practical increase in the information now available on the economic and administrative development of the United States." That was gratifying, certainly, but as a committed critic of the early Nationalists, Ferguson must have cringed at Smith's conclusion: "In the long run, I believe we can confidently predict, the work will provide the foundation for a new era of an ascendant nationalist interpretation of the American Revolution, for by comparison to Morris' activities the contributions of state officials will appear miniscule and will derive significance only as they relate to the larger programs and purposes of the Superintendent."

Fortunately, perhaps, for Ferguson's peace of mind, no such new era arrived. The Morris papers did supply a missing keystone to the annals of the Revolution, but the interests of the academy were no longer focused on the core dynamic of the nation's founding. Instead, historians were at the time embarked on a new project of rescuing the stories of those marginalized during the long march of western civilization—women, slaves, Native Americans, the poor. Serving these constituencies—the historiographical equivalent of the "identity politics" vogue—may carry a certain moral value, but it does little to advance our understanding of the chaotic events and pivotal decisions that gave rise to the first democracy of the modern era. The founders, it is true, were exclusively white men, most of them wealthy in some degree, most of them accomplished in law or commerce, all of them subject to the prides and prejudices of their time. But that does not diminish their centrality in the great and sometimes astonishing drama and achievement of the founding. When the credits roll, every gaffer, grip, and catering truck driver may deserve to see his or her name on the screen, but top billing will still be reserved for the stars of the movie.

Robert Morris is today remembered best by a small coterie of historians who, energized by the political debate over globalization, have sought to devise new and more serviceable permutations of the class-based Progressive analysis. Among the leading voices here is Terry Bouton, an associate professor of history at the University of Maryland. Bouton laid out his thesis in *Taming Democracy*, a slim but contentious volume published in 2007 and dedicated to the proposition that the America's democratic Revolution was followed by a counterrevolution that used the Constitution to restore social and fiscal power to the prewar elites. Fellow professors hailed the book, predicting that *Taming Democracy* "will have a major impact on early American historians and further the reevaluation of the entire Revolutionary period."

Bouton places Morris as the central figure in the elite's unseemly bid to "grab power." "One of the iconic figures of the Revolution"—among the ironies of Morris's story is that his critics are the first to credit him with power and influence—"Morris envisioned gentlemen taking control of the government, using it to enrich themselves, and then scaling back democracy so it did not threaten their interests." Bouton presents this scheme as hatched fully formed, making scant reference to the failure of the Continental dollar or the desperate economic straits that forced Congress to draft Morris into the powerful new office of Financier.

More than that, Bouton suggests that Morris actually created the economic crises that he managed so effectively. In his formulation the Bank of North America was the *cause* of the credit crunch besetting the rebel government, not a response to it. By launching the bank and issuing his private notes to finance the operations of the government, Morris was executing "a larger plan to privatize finance by removing powers once held exclusively by government and turning them over to private corporations." This was true to a degree—the failure of public credit forced Morris to establish a medium of exchange founded in private finance. But Bouton moves on to paint a scenario entirely at odds with the record established in the Morris papers and a dozen other studies of the period, asserting that "privatization"—here he invokes the loaded lingo of today's culture wars— was "a disaster for most Pennsylvanians," and not the masterful stroke of policy that salvaged the finances of the Congress and the nation.

Bouton doesn't just rewrite the record, he mangles it, pulling quotes far out of their original context to suit his purposes. Following Ferguson's lead, he misquotes the letter to Hamilton to assert that Morris "viewed the common people"—a phrase Morris never wrote—"who forced the Revolution on gentlemen like himself, as 'vulgar souls.' " Later, discussing the resistance of Pennsylvania farmers to new taxes imposed by Congress, Bouton quotes Morris acknowledging "in private moments" that "it would be as difficult to pay your tax Quota without Money as it would be to make bricks out of straw." Morris goes on to lament the scarcity of cash which he had purportedly created. "Few persons even here," Morris writes, "are aware of the Extent of this Calamity which is now only in its Commencement." A check of Bouton's footnotes reveals that these quotes are accurate enough, but have nothing to do with the money supply or the farmers in Pennsylvania. The reference to straw and bricks is paraphrasing the statement of a correspondent from New Hampshire—one that Morris goes on to dispute—and the calamity Morris refers to concerns the effects of the British blockade.

If Bouton were a journalist working in a newsroom, such egregious manipulation of text could cost him his job. But in today's academia it appears that everything can be reduced to a question of ideological allegiance.

Among historians thrashing out issues that have been argued for centuries, such misrepresentation passes for argument.

Bouton's factual transgressions are more than technicalities; he applies them in broad strokes to distort the whole of Morris's career. He contends that Morris "used government positions to make a killing from the war," a blithe bit of shorthand that echoes Arthur Lee but is largely contradicted by the facts. He then compounds the alleged crime, asserting that "Morris hoped to use his government-supplied wealth to gain political power needed to bypass democracy," and attributing his motivation to "his past failures to persuade the public." Here Bouton flatly ignores Morris's long tenure as a committeeman, an elected official, and the leader of a political faction that engaged gamely in Philadelphia's vital political scene. Far from subverting democracy, as Bouton would have it, Morris led a successful popular movement to introduce the system of checks and balances that has become the hallmark of modern democracy.

In the end, the more familiar one is with the story of Morris in the Revolution, the more it appears that Bouton is simply making up the story as he goes along. When Karl Marx mused that history would unfold "first as tragedy, the second time as farce," he was talking about actual events; Bouton has taken that prescription to a new level of abstraction, where historiography trumps history itself.

This, then, was the tortuous course of Robert Morris's road to obscurity. From the ignominy of his final days he was raised up to the pantheon, then swept out by the theoretical sea change of the Progressive Era. He found his greatest student in E. James Ferguson, but also a great skeptic, and by the time Ferguson's toil had laid the foundation for a new appraisal of Morris and the Nationalists, the academy was no longer interested.

Some of the founders had enough cachet or personal charm to survive the scorn of the scholars, and have enjoyed a recent popular resurgence. John Adams serves as one example, borne in part on the strength of his long and intimate correspondence with wife Abigail, and later with his one-time nemesis Thomas Jefferson. And Jefferson himself, whose soaring expressions of democratic ideals managed to survive the apparent hypocrisies of the life he lived. Morris, however, was too rich to be a folk hero, and the ultimate failure of his personal fortune robbed him of any Midas-like mystique.

Thus we find Joseph Ellis, one of our leading writers on the period, presenting in 2007, in his *American Creation*, many of the key contests in which Morris played such a prominent role—the debate over independence, the prosecution of the war, the contest between the states and the central government, the Nationalist funding program, the bank—without once mentioning Morris's name.

I'm generalizing here, addressing the foundations of the popular conception of the founders. There are important exceptions. In the economic sphere, historian Richard Buel, Jr., has acknowledged Morris's contributions in the larger context of wartime decline and peacetime recovery. And in their careful studies of the shifting factions dividing the early Congress, political historians Jack Rakove and H. James Henderson have introduced a fresh view of the pressures and dilemmas that brought Morris and the Nationalists to the fore, and a new appreciation of their achievement. But such works gain influence only slowly; in the larger consensus, Morris remains a marginal figure.

This is more than oversight; it robs the story of critical context. Without Morris in the picture, Hamilton's funding program looks more like a putsch than the culmination of a years-long effort to place the nation's finances on a sound footing. If we never saw Morris "blazing away" in the Pennsylvania Assembly, we'd never understand the democratic evolution of America's treatment of banks and public finance. Had we not learned of the subtle operations of the Secret Committee, we couldn't recognize the level of international intrigue that attended the break with England. Morris was the most powerful figure in the government, the leader of the faction that wrote the Constitution, but the way the story is being told today, it's as if he never existed.

ACKNOWLEDGMENTS

One by-product of the twenty-odd years that E. James Ferguson spent producing the nine-volume *Papers of Robert Morris* was the team of historians and archival researchers that he assembled to complete the project. The principals in that group have long since moved on, but two of them continue to write on Morris, to study the influence of Morris and his faction on the life of the new nation, and to look after the rare assemblage of primary documents that comprised the foundation of the Morris Papers collection.

Those two historians made critical contributions in my effort to research and tell the story of Robert Morris. Elizabeth M. Nuxoll, editor of a new collection of John Jay papers being assembled under the auspices of Columbia University in New York, and Mary A. Gallagher, adjunct professor of history at Queens College and an associate editor on the Jay project, answered questions by phone and email, made time for in-person interviews, and helped me gather printed materials that were crucial to production of the manuscript.

In addition, Mary Gallagher gave me unrestricted access to the photo-copied original documents used in the Morris collection. This voluminous archive has been relegated to a couple of locked and forgotten file rooms in the undergraduate library at Queens College, a satellite campus of the City University of New York. I was able to read and make copies for my use any of the documents published in the collection, as well as many letters dated before and after the parameters of the Morris collection, which were limited to Morris's tenure as superintendent of finance.

Gallagher and Nuxoll's assistance saved me the time and expense of trips to the many far-flung repositories where the original papers reside, and their guidance helped me navigate thickets of complex relationships and long-ago business deals. As usual in such cases I am grateful for their support but must claim all errors of fact and interpretation as my own.

Mary-Jo Kline, another accomplished historian and archivist and the author of an important study of the career of Gouverneur Morris, shared with me her insights and a copy of her manuscript.

Thanks go also to my lifelong friend Peter Lowe and his wife Amanda, who graciously agreed to take me on as a boarder during the time I spent combing archives in New York City. My stepsister, Dianne Montague, was my host for a second stay in New York. Just as genial were Don and Gaye Kimelman, friends of a friend, who opened their home to a stranger and gave me the run of the place for several weeks of research in Philadelphia. Such instances of unfeigned generosity provide a source of real pleasure in the sometimes arduous business of tramping the documentary trail. It was my mother's old chum Ruth Pruecel, who provided my introduction to the Kimelmans. And the Kimelmans' son Sam kindly agreed to make follow-up visits for me to the Historical Society of Pennsylvania. I thank them as well.

Aside from these personal assists, I was the beneficiary of the various collections maintained and made available to the public by libraries and historical societies on the east coast and in California. I am indebted to the staff and the trustees of the Massachusetts Historical Society, the Houghton and Pusey libraries at Harvard University, the New York Historical Society, the New York Public Library, the Historical Society of Pennsylvania, the Library Company of Philadelphia, the American Philosophical Society, the Pennsylvania Historical and Museum Commission at Harrisburg, the Library of Congress, the Huntington Library in San Marino, California, and the Doheny Library at the University of Southern California.

In the same vein I want to salute the people at Wikipedia for providing a consistently reliable and often the only online source for information on obscure dates, events, and people. I frequently checked the facts I found there, and always found them to be accurate. Hats off as well to Google Books; by a quirk of timing and corporate strategy, my research coincided with their effort to digitize and post a healthy sampling of historical writing going back two centuries, allowing me to access a range of useful texts from my desk at home. Some writers and publishers have fought the Google Book project, but in my view it serves the same role that libraries have long filled. Unfortunately, Google appears to have since changed course, and many of the titles I found there are no longer available.

The people and resources named above were important to my research; I also must thank the friends and family who encouraged me to take on, and to stick with, a daunting and sometimes overwhelming project. They include my mother Ann Crompton, her steadfast husband Fuzz Crompton, my brothers Bill and Tim Rappleye, my cousins Felicity Blundon and Sarah Sargeant, and my children, Dexter and Kelly Rappleye. All contributed their enthusiasm and their unstinting love. My father Willard Rappleye was equally enthusiastic and consulted closely at every stage of the manuscript, giving me the benefit of a life spent practicing journalism at the highest level. My friends David Cogan, Mark Cromer, and John Seeley here in Los Angeles, and Shippen Page of Cambridge, Massachusetts, served as brothers in arms, if not in fact.

My editor Alice Mayhew continues to surprise and to gratify with her unswerving confidence in me and in this book. Her editorial team, including senior editor Roger Labrie, associate editor Karen Thompson, and copy editor Fred Chase, were helpful and professional. And my agent in New York, Paul Bresnick, served as an editorial sounding board as well as a font of sage and reliable advice.

But of all my friends and advisers, none contributed more or endured more through the duration of this project than my wife Tulsa Kinney. She is a fine editor and a tough critic; she is also a wonderful cook, a soulful companion, and a continuing source of delight. Tulsa put up with my moods, pressed my deadlines, shared my fears and then swept them away. This book is dedicated to her; she certainly earned it.

Notes

INTRODUCTION

PAGE

4 *"the most powerful man in America":* Bouton, *Taming Democracy*, p. 72.

1. "A CHARACTER I AM PROUD OF"

PAGE

8 *"the first who introduced the mode":* Wagner, *Audacious Patriot*, p. 3.

8 *Morris was remembered:* Biographical information on Robert Morris, Sr., is derived from "The Worthies of Talbot," available at www.tcfl.org/mdroom/worthies/morris.html#twelve.

8 *Philadelphia rivaled Boston:* Bridenbaugh, *Cities in Revolt*, p. 5.

9 *a district known as Helltown:* Kelley, *Colonial Philadelphia,* p. 167.

9 *"the Art, Trade, or Mystery of Merchandize":* From the Indenture of Jeremiah Wadsworth, in Platt, "Jeremiah Wadsworth," p. 2.

10 *Morris longed to return to his home in England:* Samuel Bean to RM, 5/30/61, Levis Collection, HSP.

11 *"I took charge of this brother":* LDC: Robert Morris to Henry Laurens, 12/26/77.

12 *Robert promptly purchased all the flour:* Oberholtzer, *Robert Morris,* p. 5.

12 *"its peculiar precariousness":* Doerflinger, *Vigorous Spirit of Enterprise,* p. 44.

12 *"Our damned creditors":* RM to John, 11/29/59, HL.

13 *Charles Willing contracted the fever:* Horle, ed., *Lawmaking and Legislators in Pennsylvania,* III:1428.

14 *"drunk I shall be today":* Samuel Bean to RM, 5/30/61, Levis Collection, HSP.

14 *"twelve o'clock punch drinkers":* Thompson, "The Friendly Glass," p. 556.

15 *They breakfasted at eight:* "From the well-known English player Bernard," in Platt, "Jeremiah Wadsworth," p. 73, n. 1.

15 *Underwriting insurance was one typical innovation:* Horle, ed., *Lawmaking and Legislators in Pennsylvania,* III:1432.

15 *Willing took a direct hand:* Wright, "Thomas Willing," p. 549.

16 *"Cash is monstrous scarce":* Schlesinger, *Colonial Merchants,* p. 58, n. 4.

16 *"partial schemes of private men":* PA, Series VII, Vol. VIII, p. 5953.

17 *But the official opinion:* See Ernst, *Money and Politics in America,* pp. 122–24, cited in Bouton, *Taming Democracy,* pp. 38–39; see also Wright, "Thomas Willing," p. 537.

18 *"The spirit or flame of rebellion":* Morgan and Morgan, *Stamp Act Crisis,* p. 247.

18 *boys were sent out with muffled drums:* Hutson, "An Investigation of the Inarticulate," p. 4.

18 *Speaking for the committee:* Hart, "Robert Morris, A Sketch."

19 *The episode marked a turning point:* The Philadelphia demonstrations against the Stamp Act, and the negotiations with John Hughes, are treated in Morgan and Morgan, *Stamp Act Crisis,* pp. 238–57; Oberholtzer, *Robert Morris,* pp. 9–12; Schlesinger, *Colonial Merchants,* pp. 61, 67; and Ryerson, *Revolution Is Now Begun,* pp. 26–27.

19 *There was a distinct element of self-interest:* Egnal and Ernst, "An Economic Interpretation of the American Revolution," p. 21.

20 *huge bowls of punch:* Thompson, "The Friendly Glass," p. 554.

21 *he usually went along:* Ryerson, *The Revolution Is Now Begun,* p. 78, n. a.

21 *"a real playhouse":* Repplier, *Philadelphia,* p. 74.

22 *master of ceremonies, was Morris:* Scharf and Wescott, *History of Philadelphia,* II:1467.

22 *the town's gentry would retreat:* Baker, "The Camp at Schuylkill Falls," p. 29.

22 *"aristocratic":* Description from Scharf and Westcott, *History of Philadelphia,* II:1437.

22 *by the middle 1760s, Robert Morris:* "The Mount Regale Fishing Company of Philadelphia," *PMHB* 27 (1903).

22 *"fishing societies"*: The Philadelphia fishing societies are treated in Bridenbaugh, *Cities in Revolt*, pp. 163, 363.

23 *"to instruct him in the profession"*: LDC: RM to Henry Laurens, 12/26/77.

24 *"I dine at The Hills every Sunday"*: LDC: RM to Benjamin Harrison, 12/29/76.

24 *"an embarrassment to itself"*: Johnson, "Where Has All the Flour Gone?," p. 17; see also Johnson, "El Niño, Environmental Crisis, and the Emergence of Alternative Markets," p. 365; and Doerflinger, *Spirit of Enterprise*, p. 113.

25 *"Mr. Bob Morris, the head man"*: "The Journal of Miss Sarah Eve," p. 198, n. 1.

26 *"It is the profession to which I have been bred"*: RM to the Philadelphia Committee, 8/5/79, in *Deane Papers*, IV:34.

26 *"very simple in his manners"*: Marquis de Chastellux, in Sumner, *Financier*, II:222–23.

26 *"more gaudy, but less comfortable"*: Scudder, ed., *Recollections of Samuel Breck*, p. 203.

26 *Morris's was assessed:* Oaks, "Big Wheels in Philadelphia," p. 361.

26 *"Poor Bostonians"*: RM to Jas Parker at Norfolk, Virginia, 6/1/74, Queens.

2. SUING FOR PEACE, ARMING FOR WAR

PAGE

27 *"The tumult and disorder"*: "Early Days of the Revolution in Philadelphia: Charles Thomson's Account," p. 411.

28 *"I recommend constantly"*: RM to James Duff at Cádiz, 2/26/75, RM Papers, NYPL.

29 *Abashed and deflated:* For the Philadelphia committee movement, see Ryerson, *Revolution Is Now Begun*, pp. 39–61, and Schlesinger, *Colonial Merchants*, pp. 341–56.

30 *"The individual who declines"*: RM to Joseph Reed, in Force, *American Archives*, V, I:467.

30 *"We are so taken up"*: Reed, *Reed*, I:75.

30 *"mighty feasts"*: Burnett, *Continental Congress*, p. 27.

30 *hosting him for a weekend retreat:* Jackson, "Washington in Philadelphia," p. 126.

30 *"plain as a Quaker"*: Kaminski, *Founders on the Founders*, p. 278.

31 *Even the Virginia delegates:* JCC I:52, n. 1.

31 *"that all such foes"*: Text of the Continental Association, *JCC* I:79.

32 *Robert Morris was named on both tickets:* The rival slates are listed in Ryerson, *Revolution Is Now Begun*, Appendix K, p. 270.

32 *Quakers, loyalists, and the disaffected stayed away:* See ibid., p. 96.

32 *"I have pushed freely and boldly"*: RM to James Duff at Cádiz, 2/26/75, RM Papers, NYPL.

33 *"the finest ship in America"*: McCusker, "The Continental Ship Alfred," p. 228.

34 *As the story goes:* The St. George's Day feast is recounted in Fisher, "Revolutionary Reminiscences," and in Oberholtzer, *Robert Morris*, p. 17.

34 *"The martial spirit"*: LDC: John Adams to James Warren, 5/21/75.

34 *every bell in the city chimed:* Ward, ed., *Journal of Samuel Curwen*, p. 29.

36 *Morris . . . requested compensation:* Secret Committee Minutes, in Force, *American Archives*, IV, I:498.

36 *enough to outfit half a dozen outgoing voyages:* Estimates for expenses in Doerflinger, *Vigorous Spirit of Enterprise*, p. 100.

36 *one shipment of powder:* Secret Committee Minutes, in Force, *American Archives*, IV, II:504.

36 *another two tons of powder:* Ibid., IV, II:511.

36 *Congress was seeking gunpowder at the same time:* Nuxoll, *Munitions Merchants*, p. 27.

37 *"What does this matter":* LDC: John Adams Notes of Debates, 9/24/75.

37 *"The spirit of commerce":* Maier, *Old Revolutionaries*, p. 187.

38 *"watchful to prevent":* "Account of Transactions with the Secret Committee," no date (c. 1778), RM Papers, HL; see also Nuxoll, *Munitions Merchants*, p. 166.

38 *"Mr. Duncan must have perished":* Undated (c. 1778) "Statement of Accounts," RM Papers, HL.

38 *all of them together secured less than half:* Stephenson, "The Supply of Gunpowder in 1776," p. 277.

39 *"jolly tars, market people and others":* Graydon, *Memoirs*, p. 111.

40 *Morris signed the order:* Committee of Safety Minutes, 10/7/75, in Force, *American Archives*, IV, III:1815.

40 *the ugly riot before the Coffee House:* For more on the Kearsley affair, see Graydon, *Memoirs*, p. 111; Christopher Marshall, *Diary*, pp. 42, 46; Ryerson, *Revolution Is Now Begun*, p. 131; Bell, *Patriot Improvers*, p. 379; and *Leigh Hunt's New World Forebears*, at www.lib.uiowa.edu/spec-coll/Bai/leigh-hunt.htm.

40 *the radical ticket prevailed:* Ryerson, *Revolution Is Now Begun*, pp. 128–31.

41 *Morris sent his half-brother, Thomas: LDC*: Robert Morris to Henry Laurens, 12/26/77.

41 *"the most hotly contested in Philadelphia":* Ryerson, *Revolution Is Now Begun*, p. 135.

41 *the Assembly moved its meetings:* Eisenhart, ed., *Historic Philadelphia*, p. 23.

43 *"fearful, timid, skittish":* Burnett, *Continental Congress*, p. 46.

43 *"timid members":* Ibid., p. 90.

43 *"traveled almost from one end of the continent":* Walker, "Life of Margaret Shippen," p. 423.

43 *Congress directed them to arm the populace:* Jensen, *Founding of a Nation*, p. 606.

43 *"We have been obliged to act":* Ibid., p. 488.

44 *"We strictly enjoin you":* PA, Series VIII, Vol. VIII, p. 7353.

44 *"I am unhappy to tell you":* LDC: RM to Unknown, 12/9/75.

45 *The committee handled its contracts:* Details of Secret Committee operations can be found in Nuxoll's magisterial study, *Congress and the Munitions Merchants*.

47 *"call on the several persons appointed": JCC* III:378.

3. INDEPENDENCE

PAGE

48 *"very eligible"*: Hedges, *Browns of Providence Plantations*, pp. 229–39.

48 *Morris named agent for their account:* For further notes on Penet and Pliarne, see Price, *France and the Chesapeake*, p. 702; and Nuxoll, *Munitions Merchants*, pp. 121–29.

49 *Uniformed troops from Pennsylvania's Continental contingent: JCC* III:396.

49 *handbills were posted at taverns:* Miller, *Sea of Glory*, p. 84. For ship crews, see Morison, *John Paul Jones*, p. 38.

49 *Morris would emerge as the navy's de facto commander:* For RM's influence on naval strategy, see Morison, *John Paul Jones*, pp. 93, 126.

50 *The committee was the State Department of the nascent national government:* For notes on the Committee of Secret Correspondence, see Burnett, *Continental Congress*, p. 118.

51 *"harassed the whole time by much public business": LDC:* RM to Charles Lee, 2/17/76.

52 *Plan of 1776:* See Bemis, *Diplomacy of the American Revolution*, pp. 45, 61.

52 *"For heaven's sake what is meant by a Chamber of Commerce?":* RM to William Hooper, 1/18/77. No copy of this letter has been found, but a transcript made by Clarence Ver Steeg is located in the Queens collection. Ver Steeg quotes the letter in his *Robert Morris*, p. 38.

52 *"You ask what you are to think of Robert Morris?": LDC:* Adams to Horatio Gates, 4/27/76.

53 *The exploits of Thomas Mason:* Drawn from the Affidavit of Thomas Mason, Pleasants Collection, HSP. See also *LDC:* Caesar Rodney to Thomas Rodney, 2/4/76, n. 3.

54 *Half the ships were captured:* Nuxoll, *Munitions Merchants*, pp. 124–26.

55 *the British were alerted early on:* See ibid., pp. 161–63. See also Augur, *Secret War*, pp. 86–87.

55 *"the Adopted Father": PRM* 1:172, n. 1.

56 *"capable and faithful to the last degree":* RM to Silas Deane, 8/11/76, in *Deane Papers*, I:176.

56 *His first task was to receive shipments:* Minutes, Pennsylvania Committee of Safety, in Force, *American Archives*, V, VI:662 (Ceronio is spelled "Caronio").

57 *"reckoned a good man":* James, *Silas Deane*, p. 7.

57 *Morris arranged for Deane's passage:* RM to Silas Deane, 3/30/76, Queens.

58 *"useful hints": LDC:* RM to Silas Deane, 6/5/76; see n. 2.

58 *"I am about to enter on the great stage of Europe":* Silas Deane to Elizabeth Deane, 3/3/76, in *Deane Papers*, I:121.

58 *"since our enemies themselves are hastening it":* Samuel Adams quoted in Jensen, *Founding of a Nation*, p. 650.

59 *"sound doctrine and unanswerable reasoning":* Washington quoted in Foner, ed., *Writings of Thomas Paine*, I:2.

60 *Morris received an anonymous packet of papers:* Details from the Bristol packet

are related in *LDC*: Robert Alexander to the Maryland Council of Safety, 2/27/76.

60 *A second letter advised:* The note on Rockingham is from Richard Smith's Diary, *LDC*: 2/27/76.

60 *he shared the news:* Robert Treat Paine learned of the Prohibitory Act that night; he also notes the weather. *LDC*: Alexander to Maryland Committee, 2/27/76, n. 2.

60 *"The bill is very long":* Richard Smith's Diary, *LDC*: 2/27/76.

60 *"Act of Independency":* John Adams to Horatio Gates, 9/23/76, in Burnett, *Coutinstal Congress*, p. 138.

60 *But he was just as sure that outright war would be ruinous: LDC*: RM to Robert Herries, 2/15/76.

61 *"Where the plague are the commissioners?":* *LDC*: RM to Horatio Gates, 4/6/76.

61 *"friends of America":* Marshall, *Diary*, p. 57 (January 20, 1776).

63 *"the dark and untrodden way of Independence":* "Civis," reproduced in Force, *American Archives*, IV, IV:802.

63 *"They get all the profit":* Lincoln, *Revolutionary Movement in Pennsylvania*, 94.

63 *"an aristocratical junto":* Foner, ed., *Writings of Thomas Paine*, p. 125.

63 *"Several persons have formed a cruel design":* Lincoln, *Revolutionary Movement*, p. 259.

64 *"grown rich from nothing at all":* Hawke, *Midst of a Revolution*, p. 29.

64 *the message was clear:* For results and analysis of the May vote, see ibid., p. 30.

64 *"making themselves acquainted with the channel":* Ibid., p. 116.

65 *The cannonades ended at sundown:* For a detailed account of the *Roebuck* affair, see Jackson, *Pennsylvania Navy*, pp. 38–57; see also *PA*, Series I, Vol. IX, pp. 747–54.

65 *he elevated Joshua Barney:* Miller, *Sea of Glory*, pp. 89, 284.

65 *"Any government under the crown of Great Britain":* *JCC* IV:358.

66 *"It is independence itself":* Burnett, *Continental Congress*, p. 160.

66 *"Why all this haste?":* Duane quotes are from Hawke, *Midst of a Revolution*, p. 122.

66 *"In this province":* James Wilson quoted in ibid., p. 121.

66 *six states to four:* The actual tally was not recorded. For a breakdown of votes, see Carter Braxton to Landon Carter, 5/17/76, n. 2.

67 *"an Epocha, a decisive event":* Jensen, *Founding of a Nation*, p. 685.

67 *"We stared at each other":* Diary of James Allen, p. 187.

67 *the captains lashed out:* Diary of Dr. James Clitherall, p. 470.

67 *"Several of the Committee of Safety are suspected Tories":* Hawke, *Midst of a Revolution*, p. 61; see also the "Memorial of the Committee of Privates," 5/11/76, in Force, *American Archives*, V, V:421.

67 *"Address to the Public":* *PA*, Series IV, Vol. III, pp. 605–8.

68 *"We have some trade revived":* *LDC*: RM to Deane, 6/6/76.

68 *a scheme of private trade:* The extent and nature of private trade engaged in by Deane and Morris became the subject of controversy in 1779 and has remained in dispute ever after. My reading suggests Morris made his first concrete pro-

posal to Deane in the June 6, 1776, letter. For incisive comment on their private schemes, see Ver Steeg, *Robert Morris*, Chapter 1, n. 40 (p. 206).

69 *"The people behaved in such a tyrannical manner"*: Diary of Clitherall, p. 470. For the rally in the State House yard, see also Hawke, *Midst of a Revolution*, pp. 133–38.

70 *"these United Colonies are, and of right ought to be"*: Burnett, *Continental Congress*, p. 171.

70 *"the Cicero of America"*: Silas Deane to Elizabeth Deane, 9/10/74, in Kaminski, ed., *Founders on the Founders*, p. 365.

70 *"fast ripening"*: Lincoln, *Revolutionary Movement*, p. 261. The vote is given on p. 263.

71 *"for the express purpose of forming a new government in this province"*: Gibson, "The Pennsylvania Provincial Conference," p. 313.

71 *On July 1:* The dates are in dispute; I take July 1 from the account of Thomas McKean ("Caesar Rodney's Ride," *PMHB* 39, 454) and Burnett, *Continental Congress*, p. 183.

71 *it was the venerable Franklin who met Morris and Dickinson:* Gibson, "The Pennsylvania Provincial Conference," pp. 339–40.

71 *"the greatest question was decided"*: John Adams, in Burnett, *Continental Congress*, p. 184.

72 *"I have uniformly voted against and opposed the Declaration"*: RM to Joseph Reed, 7/20/76, in Force, *American Archives*, V, I:467.

4. WAR AND POLITICS

73 *"A great concourse of people"*: Marshall, *Diary*, p. 83.

73 *the polity in Pennsylvania remained:* Ryerson, *Revolution Is Now Begun*, p. 240.

73 *The Convention met almost daily:* For notes on the Pennsylvania Constitutional Convention see Hawke, *In the Midst of a Revolution*, pp. 189–195; Brands, *First American*, p. 513; and Christopher Marshall, *Diary*, pp. 85–95.

74 *"I did expect my conduct"*: RM to Joseph Reed, 7/20/76, in Ford, *American Archives*, V, I:467.

75 *Each of these agents:* Nuxoll, *Munitions Merchants*, pp. 437–59.

75 *"a young gent of good education"*: RM to Deane 9/12/76, in Augur, *Secret War*, p. 105.

75 *"keep doing something constantly"*: RM to Bingham, 10/20/76, in Ver Steeg, *Robert Morris*, p. 16.

76 *Bingham received a warm reception:* For background on Bingham, see ibid.; see also Brown, "William Bingham," *PMHB* 61, p. 54; and Alberts, *Golden Voyage*, passim.

76 *Morris had sailed the Caribbean with Pollock:* James, "Oliver Pollock, Financier," p. 67.

76 *Morris folded Pollock into his network:* Nuxoll, *Munitions Merchants*, p. 484.

76 *Deane . . . was immediately contacted by Pierre Penet:* Deane to the Secret Committee, 8/18/76, in *Deane Papers*, I:196.

77 *an audience with the French foreign minister Comte de Vergennes:* Ibid., p. 199.

77 *Gerard assured Deane that Beaumarchais would have no trouble:* Deane to Gerard, 7/22/76, in *Deane Papers*, I:159.

78 *Vergennes and Beaumarchais together had persuaded the king:* For a concise treatment of the French decision to aid the Americans, see Kite, "French 'Secret Aid,' " p. 143.

78 *"men whom I cannot trust":* Augur, *Secret War*, p. 118.

79 *"he had discarded all his follies":* LDC: RM to John Ross, 1/31/77.

80 *"improving our fortunes ought not to be lost":* LDC: RM to Deane, 8/11/76.

81 *"I am much concerned that we have been so unfortunate":* Ibid.

81 *"I have much in my power":* LDC: RM to John Bradford, 10/8/76.

82 *more than half the tobacco ventures put out by the Secret Committee were taken:* Nuxoll, *Munitions Merchants*, pp. 206–8.

83 *"I have been so exceedingly harassed":* RM to Silas Deane, 8/11/76, *Deane Papers*, I:172.

83 *"As long as your whimsical constituents shall permit":* John Jay to RM, 10/6/76, in Wharton, ed., *Revolutionary Diplomatic Correspondence*, II:164.

83 *"to direct all matters in their department":* Rolater, "Continental Congress," p. 114.

83 *"It is our indispensable duty to keep it a secret":* Wharton, ed., *Revolutionary Diplomatic Correspondence*, II:151.

84 *"be attentive to his conduct":* RM to Silas Deane, 10/23/76, in *Deane Papers*, I:332.

84 *Morris confided to Franklin:* BF to RM, 12/21/77, BF Papers, APS.

85 *the plan became the template for American foreign policy:* Bemis, *Diplomacy of the American Revolution*, pp. 46, 170.

85 *Pennsylvania became the testing ground:* For the unique nature of the Revolution in Pennsylvania, see Wood, *Creation of the American Republic*, pp. 83–90, 226–37.

85 *"honest well-meaning country men":* Rev. Francis Allison, in Brunhouse, *Counter-Revolution*, p. 13.

86 *"know ye, we despise you":* Hawke, *Midst of a Revolution*, p. 191.

86 *"That, an enormous Proportion of Property vested in a few individuals":* Ibid., p. 190.

86 *"the danger of establishing an inconvenient Aristocracy":* Brunhouse, *Counter-Revolution*, p. 15.

87 *"When the Legislative and Executive powers are united":* Force, *American Archives*, V, II:1150.

87 *"absurd democratical notions":* Hawke, *Midst of a Revolution*, p. 112.

87 *"We think it our duty to declare to you":* "Address to the Inhabitants of the City and Liberties of Philadelphia," 11/2/76, in Force, *American Archives*, V, III:483.

88 *rescinded the following day:* Brunhouse, *Counter-Revolution*, p. 21.

88 *Morris lingered on:* For RM acting as intermediary, see *JCC* VI:995.

88 *Washington was also at peak strength:* Force levels are from Boatner, *Encyclopedia*, p. 798.

89 *their efforts lagged as a consequence:* Gruber, *Howe Brothers*, pp. 95–97; see also the relevant entries in Boatner, *Encyclopedia*.

89 *"many of 'em entirely naked":* Fischer, *Washington's Crossing*, p. 155.

90 *Bands of militia roamed the streets:* Diary of James Allen, p. 193.

90 *"people of all ranks":* Marshall, *Diary*, pp. 105, 107.

90 *"Our affairs are amazingly altered":* RM to Deane, 12/6/76, in *Deane Papers*, I:408.

90 *"poisoned the minds of the people":* LDC: Samuel Adams to James Warren, 12/12/76.

90 *"Our Constitution is disliked":* LDC: RM to John Jay, 1/12/77.

91 *"Indeed, my spirits were":* Mary Morris to Robert Morris, 12/20/76, in Hart, "Mary White," p. 158.

91 *"It looks dismal and melancholy":* LDC: RM to Silas Deane, 12/20/76.

91 *"execute Continental business":* JCC VI:1032.

91 *"I believe we dispatch":* LDC: RM to John Jay, 2/4/77.

91 *"The business of this committee":* LDC: RM to John Jay, 1/12/77.

92 *"These are the times":* Paine, *American Crisis I*, in Foner, ed., *Writings of Thomas Paine*, pp. 50, 55.

92 *"If every nerve is not strained":* GW to John Augustine Washington, 12/18/76, in Force, *American Archives*, V, III:1275.

92 *"Our people knew not":* LDC: RM to Silas Deane, 12/20/76.

93 *Morris had first met Washington at the Philadelphia Jockey Club:* Jackson, "Washington in Philadelphia," p. 117.

93 *Robert and Mary had hosted Martha Washington:* RM to Joseph Reed, 7/20/76, in Force, *American Archives*, V, I:467.

93 *forwarded the critical provisions to the Delaware camp:* Fischer, *Washington's Crossing*, p. 156.

93 *the wagons started moving that afternoon:* Ibid., p. 269. See also *LDC*: RM to GW, 12/30/76.

93 *"Silver would be most convenient":* GW to RM, Fitzpatrick, ed., *Writings of Washington*, VI:457.

94 *One early biographer poses a conversation:* Oberholtzer, *Robert Morris*, p. 32.

94 *"a lady of old family in Philadelphia":* Fischer, *Washington's Crossing*, p. 534, n. 31.

94 *"The year 1776 is over":* LDC: RM to GW, 1/1/77.

5. MASTER OF THE SECRET NETWORK

PAGE

95 *"It's now as cold as I ever felt in my life":* Joseph Woods to RM, 12/14/76, in Henkels, *Confidential Correspondence of Robert Morris*, p. 176.

95 *"The Damndest Hole in the World":* Benjamin Harrison to RM, 12/26/76 and 1/8/77, in ibid., p. 12.

96 *"I have scolded the officers like a gutter-whore": LDC*: RM to RHL, 12/29/76.

96 *"Congress seems unanimously sensible":* William Hooper to RM, 12/28/76, in Henkels, *Confidential Correspondence of Robert Morris*, p. 22.

96 *"Without the least appearance of Flattery": LDC*: John Hancock to RM, 1/14/77.

96 *hosting there a circle of friends:* RM to John Hancock, 1/23/77, in Queens.

96 *"The absence of my family sits grievously hard on me": LDC*: RM to Benjamin Harrison, 12/29/76.

96 *"My dearest husband":* Mary Morris to RM, 2/28/77, in Huntington.

96 *"I wish you would inform":* Mary Morris to RM, 12/30/76, in ibid. Some Mary Morris correspondence is also available in Hart, "Mary White," *PMHB* 2:157–83.

97 *"This letter from Mr. Duff alarms me":* RM to Silas Deane, 1/31/77, in *Deane Papers*, I:476.

97 *"examine into his conduct to the very bottom": LDC*: RM to John Ross, 1/31/77.

98 *"Unhappy to the last degree":* RM to Thomas Morris, 1/31/77, in Queens.

98 *"I am entering now on a most delicate affair":* Deane to RM, 12/4/76, in *Deane Papers*, I:400.

98 *"We are sorry to say":* Wharton, ed., *Revolutionary Diplomatic Correspondence*, II:248.

98 *not mentioning his name: LDC*: RHL to RM, 12/29/76.

98 *Morris readily agreed to the measure: LDC*: RM to John Hancock, 1/6/77.

98 *"My earnest wish": LDC*: RHL to Arthur Lee, 4/20/77.

99 *a contract with the Farmers General:* Price, *France and the Chesapeake*, p. 707.

99 *made plans in February to leave Europe altogether:* Thomas Morris to Deane, 2/10/77, in *Deane Papers*, I:488.

99 *"I am Embarrassed between a desire to serve": LDC*: RM to William Bingham, 6/20/77.

99 *"He is drunk at least 22 hours out of every 24":* John Adams citing William McCreery, in Schiff, *A Great Improvisation*, p. 13.

99 *"Eight months with but two letters":* Deane to RM, 12/4/76, in *Deane Papers*, I:399.

100 *"These damn Men of War plague us exceedingly": LDC*: RM to John Jay, 1/12/77; RM to William Bingham, 2/26/77; and RM to Silas Deane, 6/20/77.

100 *"She blew up with a most terrible explosion":* Morgan, *Patriots and Pirates*, p. 36.

100 *"Mr. Morris has met":* Mary Morris to Ethan Morris, 4/14/77, in Huntington.

101 *"impossible":* Wharton, ed., *Revolutionary Diplomatic Correspondence*, II:283.

101 *Still, the smaller sum would cover the expenses of the American mission:* Bemis, *Diplomacy of the American Revolution*, p. 92.

102 *"A virgin state should preserve the virgin character":* BF to Arthur Lee, in Wharton, ed., *Revolutionary Diplomatic Correspondence*, II:298; see also Rolater, *Continental Congress*, p. 124.

102 *All three were relieved to see Lee depart:* Potts, *Arthur Lee*, p. 167.

102 *"You have considered your situation":* Thomson, *Spain*, p. 51.

103 *"Matters are returning to the old channel":* Diary of James Allen, p. 278.

103 *"too busy": LDC*: RM to James Wilson, 1/31/77.

103 *"Although his private business suffers exceedingly"*: Sumner, *Robert Morris*, I:192.

103 *"My time is so engrossed by Public business"*: LDC: RM to John Bradford, 10/8/76.

103 *"engrosses so much time"*: LDC: RM to John Langdon, 1/12/77.

103 *"Their whole time and attention"*: Secret Committee Statement of Accounts, c. 1778, HL.

104 *British merchants had lost 350 sail:* Gruber, *Howe Brothers*, p. 140.

104 *had seized 120 ships:* Patton, *Patriot Pirates*, p. 139.

104 *"extensive connections and dealings"*: RM to Deane, 9/12/76, in ibid., p. 60.

104 *"Having had several vessels taken from me"*: LDC: RM to William Bingham, 12/4/76.

105 *Ord performed brilliantly:* Alberts, *Golden Voyage*, p. 51.

105 *"My scruples about Privateering"*: LDC: RM to William Bingham, 4/25/77.

105 *a British spy counted eighty-two ships in the harbor:* Patton, *Patriot Pirates*, p. 71.

105 *"is, in fact, so accustomed to the success of his privateers"*: Chastellux, *Travels in North America*, I:200.

106 *"I wish Congress may remove back with all my heart"*: LDC: Benjamin Harrison to RM, 1/8/77; see also Burnett, *Continental Congress*, p. 232.

106 *"If the Congress means to succeed in this Contest"*: LDC: RM to Committee of Secret Correspondence, 12/16/76.

106 *"You may depend on this"*: LDC: RM to Silas Deane, 12/20/76.

107 *first to $3 million, then to $5 million every three months:* Grubb, "The Continental Dollar," p. 283.

107 *"certain monopolizers"*: Committee of Privates to the Philadelphia Committee of Inspection, 4/2/1776, in Force, *American Archives*, IV, IV:764.

107 *a more penetrating critique from Pelatiah Webster:* Webster, "Observations on Finance," 10/4/76, in Force, *American Archives*, V, II:434.

108 *"to support the Credit of our Currencies"*: Scott, "Price Control in New England," p. 453.

109 *"If the Congress do not embrace this measure"*: LDC: RM to Benjamin Rush, 2/15/77; see also Ferguson, *Power of the Purse*, p. 35.

110 *"What folly, what madness"*: LDC: Henry Laurens to John Gervais, 9/5/77, 9/8/77.

110 *"A young man borrowing money"*: Ibid.

110 *"Taxation and Economy"*: LDC: John Adams to James Warren, 8/18/77.

110 *just five delegates voting against:* JCC 8:725. See also Ferguson, *Power of the Purse*, p. 36.

110 *"I have been backward"*: LDC: RM to GW, 2/27/77.

111 *"The freedom with which"*: GW to RM, George Clymer and George Walton, 3/2/77, in LDC, VII:220.

112 *"given orders to every department"*: LDC: RM to GW, 3/6/77.

112 *"Very happy to find myself at home"*: Mary Morris to Esther White, 3/15/77, quoted in Hart, "Mary White," p. 160.

112 *Robert stole the opportunity to take a brief leave:* LDC: RM to GW, 3/15/77.

112 *"What is to become of America and its cause"*: LDC: RM to GW 2/27/77.

113 *"I have really had my hands, Head & Heart"*: LDC: RM to John Hancock, 2/21/77.

113 *"Don't you feel quite important"*: Mary Morris to Esther Morris, in Hary, "Mary White," p. 161.

113 *"The whole Race of Commissaries"*: For reorganization of the Commissary, see Carp, *To Starve the Army at Pleasure*, pp. 42–44; Fleming, *Washington's Secret War*, pp. 88–89. The quote appears in both texts.

114 *"Richard Henry Lee seized the opportunity"*: For Lee's influence in shaping the Committee for Foreign Affairs, see Rolater, "Continental Congress," pp. 124–27.

114 *Lovell had little regard for Silas Deane*: Lovell soon condemned Deane as a "weak or roguish man." See *LDC*: James Lovell to William Whipple, 7/29/77.

114 *"I must also request to spare me"*: LDC: RM to Bingham, 2/16/77; see also Burnett, *Continental Congress*, pp. 241–43.

114 *Lovell made in the basis of a formal motion*: LDC: James Lovell to William Whipple, 7/29/77, n. 3.

115 *"This gentleman speaks French very well"*: Gaines, *Liberty and Glory*, p. 65.

115 *Lafayette placed his funds with Morris*: Clary, *Adopted Son*, pp. 133, 173.

115 *"There are many faults"*: Hawke, *Midst of a Revolution*, p. 196.

115 *"The government of this province"*: Diary of James Allen, p. 282; see also Brunhouse, *Counter-Revolution*, pp. 38–46.

115 *"The clamors of the red-hot patriots"*: Judge Yates to Col. Burd, 3/29/77, in Harding, "Party Struggles over the Pennsylvania Constitution."

116 *"out of curiosity"*: Sellers, *Artist of the Revolution*, p. 156.

116 *"We have not that fond notion"*: "Address of the Whig Society," *Pennsylvania Gazette*, 3/26/77.

116 *"That the present constitution has errors"*: "To the People," 3/18/77, in Foner, ed., *Writings of Thomas Paine*, II:271.

117 *"anarchy and ruin"*: Brunhouse, *Counter-Revolution*, p. 30.

117 *"Was lost, a new invented Government"*: *Pennsylvania Evening Post*, 5/8/77, in Hindle, *David Rittenhouse*, p. 181.

117 *"If Congress had not interposed"*: Notes on the April 15 conference are from *PA*, Series I, Vol. V, p. 311. For Duer quotes, see *LDC*: William Duer to New York Convention, 4/17/77.

119 *"We intend sending off our best furniture"*: Hart, "Mary White," p. 161.

119 *"to indicate hope"*: Flexner, *Washington in the American Revolution*, p. 217.

119 *"We now have an army"*: LDC: John Adams to Abigail Adams, 8/24/77.

120 *"If Congress have not left Philadelphia"*: Fleming, *Secret War*, p. 71; see also Chernow, *Alexander Hamilton*, p. 98.

120 *"It was a beautiful, still, moonlit morning"*: Thomas Paine to BF, in Paine, "Military Operations Near Philadelphia," *PMHB* 2, p. 283.

120 *"caravan of covered wagons"*: Oberholtzer, *Robert Morris*, p. 293.

120 *members of the Eastern faction found lodging with Daniel Roberdeau*: LDC: John Adams to Abigail Adams, 9/30/77.

6. CONGRESS IN EXILE

PAGE

121 *Morris began making plans to leave the government: LDC*: RM to William Whipple, 9/4/77.

121 *"exposing me to feelings the most Poignant"*: RM to Silas Deane, 6/29/77, in *Deane Papers*, II:77.

122 *"abandoned to the most disgraceful pursuits"*: John Ross to Silas Deane, 7/30/77, in ibid., II:155.

122 *"Poor unfortunate and inconsiderate mortal!"*: John Ross to William Carmichael, 9/13/77, in ibid., II:155.

122 *he would not step aside*: John Ross to Silas Deane, 7/19/77, in ibid.

122 *"he should hereafter despise us"*: Silas Deane to RM, 9/13/77, in ibid., II:157.

122 *"the faithless principles"*: William Lee to Francis Lightfoot Lee, 8/9/77, in ibid., II:99.

123 *"strange and unhappy conduct"*: William Lee to RHL, 8/12/77, in ibid., II:102.

123 *Lee joined with Morris in demanding that Williams be replaced*: Silas Deane to the President of Congress, 10/12/78, in *Deane Papers*, III:11.

124 *"To have such a demand come upon me"*: Thomas Willing to RM, 10/1/77, in Balch, ed., *Willing Letters*, p. 41.

124 *"My good friend"*: Thomas Willing to RM, 11/3/77, in ibid., p. 55.

124 *"I lament from my soul this cruel separation"*: Thomas Willing to RM, 10/13/77, in ibid., p. 52.

125 *"a reign of terror"*: Hunt, *Provincial Committees of Safety*, Chapter 3.

125 *"The prevailing idea now"*: Diary of James Allen, p. 296.

125 *"I think it is dangerous to the state"*: *LDC*: RM to James Wilson, 10/22/77.

125 *"every thing which may tend to distract or divide"*: *JCC* 9:853.

126 *"a small token of his real regard"*: John Hancock to RM, 10/25/77, in Henkels, *Catalogue*, p. 10.

126 *"Our greatest enemies are within ourselves"*: *LDC*: Henry Laurens to John Lewis Gervais, 8/5/77; for Laurens's doubts about the Secret Committee, see *LDC*: Henry Laurens to RM, 1/7/79.

127 *he heard mutterings among the traders*: *LDC*: Francis Lewis to Congress, 1/14/79.

127 *a note from his quarters in Philadelphia to Willing, asking for a conference*: Thomas Willing memoir, 11/2/77, in Willing Family Papers, HSP.

128 *"freely spoken of"*: "Examination of John Brown," *PA*, Series I, Vol. VI, p. 345.

128 *"suspicion that he is employed by the enemy"*: "Resolution of Congress," 11/18/77, in ibid., p. 344.

128 *the delegates refused to meet with Brown*: *LDC*: Henry Laurens to GW, 11/19/77.

129 *"I am surprised Mr. Willing should suffer himself"*: GW to Congress, 11/23/77, in *PA*, Series I, Vol. VI, p. 30.

129 *"innocent in his intentions"*: RM to Pres. Wharton, 11/30/77, in ibid., p. 45.

129 *Brown was finally released in January*: Brown's release noted in Marshall, *Diary*, p. 164.

130 *the arms delivered at Portsmouth that the American forces carried into battle:* See, among many sources crediting the shipments from Hortalez, Kite, "Secret Aid," p. 151; and Stephenson, "Supply of Gunpowder," p. 281.

130 *despite the passive role he played:* Boatner, *Encyclopedia,* p. 974: "Gates' performance in the battle was entirely passive."

130 *"superstitious veneration":* Burnett, *Continental Congress,* p. 268.

131 *"I expect to have more command":* LDC: RM to Pennsylvania Council of Safety, 11/11/77; for the quote, see n. 1.

131 *"consider the best and most practicable means":* JCC 9:972.

131 *close to half his troops were barefoot:* Fleming, *Secret War,* p. 12.

132 *"mode of introducing into Society":* LDC: James Lovell to Sam Adams, 1/13/78, in *PRM* V:522.

132 *The British raiders repulsed an American vanguard:* See entry for Matson's Ford in Boatner, *Encyclopedia,* p. 686.

132 *"We have received Authentic information":* LDC: RM to Committee of Commerce, 12/17/77.

133 *"I am sorely hurt":* LDC: RM to John Brown, 12/24; 12/29/77.

133 *"I blame myself much":* RM to BF, 12/27/77, in Franklin Papers, APS.

133 *He was also officious, censorious, and a stickler for detail:* For a critical profile of Laurens's tenure as president, see *LDC:* "Charles Thomson's Statement to a Committee of Congress," 9/6/79.

133 *"No part of his conduct":* LDC: RM to Henry Laurens, 12/26/77.

133 *"very affecting":* LDC: Henry Laurens to RM, 1/1/78.

134 *"actually in a continual state of madness":* William Lee to RHL, in Ford, ed., *Letters of William Lee,* I:240.

135 *Beaumarchais had made it clear:* Beaumarchais to Lee, 6/6/76; Lee to Beaumarchais, 6/14/76, in Wharton, ed., *Revolutionary Diplomatic Correspondence,* II:97; Wharton comments on Lee's failure of memory in a note.

135 *Lee asserted the opposite:* Arthur Lee to Committee of Foreign Affairs, 10/6/77, in ibid., II:401.

135 *"you have as good a right to order your servant":* William Lee to Silas Deane, 12/17/77, in *Deane Papers,* II:275.

135 *"Arthur Lee must be shaved and bled":* Silas Deane to Ed Bancroft, 1/8/78, in ibid., II:310

136 *"an able, faithful, active":* BF to James Lovell, 12/21/77, in Wharton, ed., *Revolutionary Diplomatic Correspondence,* II:458.

136 *"He died at the last very easie":* Hilton, *Silas Deane,* p. 66

136 *"I find myself obliged to think":* LDC: RHL to Samuel Adams, 11/23/77.

137 *a dispute that dragged on for weeks:* This imbroglio is detailed in Nuxoll, *Munitions Merchants,* pp. 367–73.

137 *"conducted in the most genteel and decent manner":* Penet to RM, RM Papers, HSP.

137 *thirteen-gun salute:* Morison, *John Paul Jones,* p. 128.

138 *"He has paid the last tribute":* RM to William Lee, 5/22/78, in Queens.

138 *"every great Plumb pudding":* LDC: James Lovell to Sam Adams, 1/1/78.

138 *huddling at his estate in Reading:* Fleming, *Secret War*, p. 90.

138 *"There are open dissentions":* Lafayette to GW, 12/30/77, in Augur, *Secret War*, p. 274.

139 *"The list of our disgusted patriots":* LDC: Thomas Mifflin to Horatio Gates, 11/17/77, n. 5.

139 *"I have been a slave to the service":* Fleming, *Secret War*, p. 122.

139 *"prompters and actors, accommodators":* Burnett, *Continental Congress*, p. 280.

139 *"You must have seen and heard":* Tench Tilghman to RM, 2/2/78, in Henkels, *Catalogue*, p. 167.

140 *"I really think it a horrid thing":* LDC: RM to Richard Peters, 1/25/78.

141 *"I tried every way to get him":* Thomas Willing to RM, 4/27/78, in Balch, ed., *Willing Letters*, p. 79.

141 *"some matters to my prejudice":* LDC: RM "To the Public," 1/7/79; see also the warning from John Penn of North Carolina, "some members at times drop expressions on that subject that I do not like," in ibid., 2/4/78.

141 *"the great expenditures of Money":* LDC: Henry Laurens to RM, 1/10/79.

141 *He produced a series of reports:* Several of these reports did not survive, but are referred to in LDC: Committee of Commerce to RM, 2/21/78; see also RM to Committee of Commerce, 2/17/78.

142 *due chiefly to the opposition of Henry Laurens:* LDC: Charles Thomson, Notes of Debates, 7/24, 7/25/77.

142 *His expedition did indeed flush the enemy:* Caughey, "Willing's Expedition," p. 5.

142 *"Some of the members were dissatisfied":* LDC: Committee of Commerce to RM, 2/21/77.

143 *"perfect innocence":* Henry Laurens to RM, 4/6/78, in Henkels, *Catalogue*, p. 90; see also LDC: RM to Laurens, 4/7, 4/13/78. For Swanwick's background, see Baumann, "John Swanwick."

143 *"I do most religiously believe":* Burnett, *Continental Congress*, p. 313.

143 *"It would lay the foundation":* LDC: Henry Laurens to William Livingston, 4/19/77.

143 *"We murder time":* Burnett, *Continental Congress*, p. 317.

144 *"a little deformed":* Cornelius Hartnett to Thomas Burke, 11/13/77, in Burnett, *Continental Congress*, p. 255.

144 *"Massachusetts is against us":* LDC: GM to RM, 5/12/78.

145 *Gouverneur had been Washington's liaison:* Kline, *Gouverneur Morris*, p. 51.

145 *Their collaboration in promoting half-pay:* For votes on half-pay, see JCC 11:495, 503; for notes on the factions in Congress, see Henderson, *Party Politics*, pp. 121–24.

146 *"this insidious proceeding":* Van Doren, *Secret History*, p. 87.

146 *"unfolded to me what I suspected":* LDC: Henry Laurens to RM, 4/27/78, n. 1.

146 *"Arise then! To your tents":* Address of Congress, 5/8/77, in Einhorn, "Peace Offer of 1778," p. 201.

146 *members of the peace commission arrived in Philadelphia:* For further treatment of the affairs of this final peace commission, see Van Doren, *Secret History*, pp. 97–106.

147 *This brought to ignominious conclusion:* See Einhorn, "Peace Offer of 1778";
     Roche, *Joseph Reed*, pp. 136–37.

7. THE RETURN OF SILAS DEANE

149 *"Nothing but wanton desolation":* Marshall, *Diary*, p. 189.

149 *"The Town exceedingly Dirty & disagreeable":* Eberlein and Hubbard, *Indepen-
     dence Hall*, p. 238.

149 *bodies of deceased prisoners and starved horses:* Burnett, *Continental Congress*,
     p. 343.

149 *"my mind was much engage":* RM to John Brown, 6/26/78, Queens.

150 *Arnold secretly arranged with clothier general James Mease:* Flexner, *Traitor and
     the Spy*, p. 222.

151 *"This worthy American . . . is dejected":* Beaumarchais to Vergennes, 3/13/78, in
     Deane Papers, II:405.

152 *"absolutely taken sides":* Potts, *Arthur Lee*, p. 210.

152 *"violence to the authority":* Arthur Lee to BF, 4/2/78, in *Deane Papers*, II:448.

152 *"It is true that I have omitted":* BF to Arthur Lee, 4/4/78, in ibid., p. 451.

153 *"the storm against Deane":* Morton and Spinelli, *Beaumarchais*, p. 198.

153 *"The public or political character of the Virginians":* Breen, *Tobacco Culture*,
     p. 88.

154 *"renders them uneasy, peevish":* Ibid., p. 133. On planter debt, see pp. 125–29.

154 *"wicked," "evil," "designing":* Quotes are: RHL on "avaricious Men," from Maier,
     Old Revolutionaries, p. 182; Arthur Lee on Franklin, from Potts, *Arthur Lee*
     pp. 224, 251; RHL on Deane, from Ballagh, ed., *Letters of Richard Henry Lee*,
     II:47; Arthur Lee on Scots, in Potts, *Arthur Lee*, p. 28; William Lee on Ross,
     Ford, ed., *Letters of William Lee*, II:368, 419; and Francis Lightfoot Lee on profi-
     teers, *LDC*: Francis Lightfoot Lee to RHL, 6/17/77.

155 *"have done everything in their power to traduce me":* Arthur Lee to RHL, in
     Potts, *Arthur Lee*, p. 179, 196; RHL to William Lee in Maier, *Old Revolutionar-
     ies*, p. 179; William Lee, ibid.

155 *"an honest man, faithful and zealous":* John Adams to James Lovell, 2/20/79, in
     Deane Papers, III:377.

155 *"his smooth discourse":* LDC: William Duer to Robert Livingston, 7/9/77.

156 *"The hasty, unpreserving, aristocratic genius":* Maier, *Old Revolutionaries*,
     p. 193.

156 *Lee was vindicated:* McGauhy, *Richard Henry Lee*, pp. 80–84.

156 *he led a bizarre procession:* Maier, *Old Revolutionaries*, p. 196. McGauhy, *Rich-
     ard Henry Lee*, touches on the same ground, p. 78.

157 *"It is tempting":* Maier, *Old Revolutionaries*, p. 197.

157 *"avaricious and ambitious men":* Quote from RHL is in Wood, *Creation*, p. 420.

157 *"Your friend Deane":* LDC: Gouverneur Morris to John Jay, 8/16/78.

158 *Deane's enemies, it appeared, were stalling:* The progress of the Deane hearings
     can be followed in *JCC* 11:796–826.

158 *"on every occasion":* Morton and Spinelli, *Beaumarchais,* p. 191.

158 *"As he is the only merchant in Congress":* Francey to Beaumarchais, 7/11/78, in Bigelow, "Beaumarchais the Merchant," p. 10.

158 *"Active, zealous, a great and the most useful partisan":* Sumner, *Financier,* I:208.

159 *John Ross, venturing as a partner with Morris:* For notes on Ross, see Nuxoll, *Munitions Merchants,* pp. 380–99.

159 *"have suffered exceedingly": LDC:* RM to John Brown, 4/28/78.

159 *The Continental agents were now preying upon:* For Pollock and Ceronio, see Augur, *Secret War,* p. 209.

159 *He asked Congress to appoint a new committee:* RM "To the Public," 1/7/79, in *Deane Papers,* III:263.

160 *Miralles needed no introduction:* For Miralles and RM, see McCadden, "Juan de Miralles"; see also Cummins, *Spanish Observers,* p. 118.

160 *Morris met Holker at the July 4 dinner:* For Holker, see Sullivan, *Maryland and France,* p. 58; for RM's account of his first meeting with Holker, see RM to John Rucker, 6/18/84, in *PRM* IX:410.

161 *"I think our friend D has much public merit": LDC:* RM to John Jay, 9/8/78.

161 *"Deane had misapplied the public money": JCC* 11:927.

161 *"in the strongest manner":* William Lee to RHL, 1/9/78, in Ford, ed., *Letters of William Lee,* II:334.

161 *"You were not mistaken": LDC:* RHL to Arthur Lee, 9/16/78.

162 *"I did not pay sufficient attention":* Carmichael's testimony is available in *Deane Papers,* II:489–99.

162 *"The Doctor is old": LDC:* RHL to Arthur Lee, 9/16/78.

163 *"The avowed Tories are I think": LDC:* RM to John Jay, 9/8/78.

163 *"sundry persons, notoriously disaffected":* Rosswurm, *Arms, Country and Class,* p. 154.

163 *sentenced to death:* Brunhouse, *Counter-Revolution,* p. 50; Roche, *Joseph Reed,* p. 146. Rosswurm reports thirty-six initial cases; he agrees with Roche on the number taken up by prosecutors.

163 *"They have actually put to death":* Repplier, *Philadelphia,* p. 289.

164 *"whether the state of Pennsylvania shall be happy":* Konkle, *George Bryan,* p. 162.

164 *Committee of Congress . . . never recovered the initiative:* For a comparison of committee activities after Morris left, see Nuxoll, *Munitions Merchants,* pp. 72–73.

164 *"Mr. Morris has left the Marine [Board]":* Capt. Thomas Bell, in Clark, "John Ashmead Story," p. 26.

164 *Robert sat down with Reed: LDC:* Gouverneur Morris to Joseph Reed, 4/9/79.

164 *Morris and Thomas Mifflin underwrote the cost of a huge banquet:* For the dinner, see Roche, *Joseph Reed,* p. 151; for Morris picking up the tab, see Christopher Marshall, *Diary,* p. 211.

164 *some degree of compromise had been achieved:* For notes on the election of 1778, see Brunhouse, *Counter-Revolution,* pp. 49–58; Rosswurm, *Arms, Country and Class,* pp. 158–61; and Ireland, "Ethnic-Religious Dimension," pp. 431–34.

164 *a fourfold increase over the year before:* Budget figures in Carp, *To Starve the Army,* p. 69.

165 *Prices of flour, beef, and molasses doubled in July alone:* Price quotes from Rosswurm, *Arms, Country and Class,* p. 168; see also ibid., p. 106.

165 *"If I was to mention to you the price":* Sarah Bache, in Stone, "Philadelphia Society," p. 373.

165 *"I know of no news":* Mary Morris to Esther White, July 1778, in Hart, "Mary White," p. 162.

165 *"We are plagued to death":* LDC: Cyrus Griffin to Thomas Jefferson, 10/6/78.

165 *"To the Free and Virtuous": Deane Papers,* III:66.

167 *"It appeared terrible to me":* Adams Diary of 2/12/78, in *Deane Papers,* III:349.

167 *"for the honor and dignity of this House":* Laurens's speech is in *JCC* 12:1204.

167 *"Phantasticability and absurdity":* Burnett, *Continental Congress,* p. 365.

168 *"A picture of the times":* GW to Benjamin Harrison, 12/30/78, in Fitzpatrick, ed., *Papers of Washington,* XIII:462.

168 *"Our great Fabius Maximus":* Greene to Alexander McDougall, 2/11/79, in Freeman, *George Washington,* V:91, n. 35.

168 *"barbarous, unmanly and unsupported attack":* Thomas Paine's argument covered seven newspaper installments and thirty pages; see *Deane Papers,* beginning III:209.

169 *"I do not intend to enter into the lists":* RM "To the Public," 1/9/79, in *Deane Papers,* III:259.

170 *"I have been endeavoring":* Thomas Paine, "On Robert Morris' Address," 1/12/79, in *Deane Papers,* III:267.

171 *"a mere Adventurer":* Sparks, *Life of Gouverneur Morris,* I:200.

171 *Paine was now out of a job:* For Paine's travails in Congress and out, see Keane, *Tom Paine,* pp. 176–86.

171 *"the rascally & ill-managed attack":* LDC: Thomas Mifflin to RM, 1/26/79.

171 *"We have been passing a most jolly merry winter":* RM to Horatio Gates, 2/5/79, in Queens.

8. BACKLASH

173 *Laurens . . . had possession of the books:* LDC: "Committee Accounts," 1/7/79, n. 1.

174 *Laurens and Penn settled the score with dueling pistols:* LDC: "In Congress," 1/9/79, n. 3.

174 *"I think you a little faulty":* LDC: Henry Laurens to RM, 1/10/79.

174 *"I shall say nothing":* LDC: RM to Henry Laurens, 1/11/79.

175 *Lewis volunteered a conversation:* LDC: Francis Lewis to Congress, 1/14/79.

176 *"beyond all doubt":* For the results of the committee inquiry, and for Laurens's late discovery of an exculpatory document, see *JCC* 13:162–76.

177 *"incited to the last degree":* Potts, *Arthur Lee,* p. 232.

177 *"Your enemies have triumphed":* Ibid., p. 237. For a survey of the congressio-

nal debates over its European diplomats, see Henderson, "Congressional Factionalism."

178 *the planned referendum on the constitution was defeated:* Brunhouse, *Counter-Revolution*, pp. 59–60; Harding, "Pennsylvania Constitution," p. 381, n. 5.

178 *Reed invited Morris and his cohort to treat over cups:* For the City Tavern meeting, see Roche, *Joseph Reed*, p. 164 and n. 96.

179 *Robert Morris was the hub:* For notes on the Republican Society, see Rosswurm, *Arms, Country and Class*, pp. 176–77; and Foster, *Moral Visions*, pp. 114–19.

179 *"The original promoters of this Society":* Constitutionalist statement printed in *Pennsylvania Packet*, 4/1/79, quoted in Foster, *Moral Visions*, p. 120.

180 *sailors went on strike:* For the sailors' strike, see Brunhouse, *Counter-Revolution*, p. 69; for the strike and price increases, see Rosswurm, *Arms, Country and Class*, pp. 166, 168.

180 *ten million a month:* Spending figures from Carp, *To Starve the Army*, p. 69.

180 *it was the farmers who did the most to undermine the value of paper money:* In his study of the revolutionary economy, Richard Buel deemed the farmers to be "the principal culprit." See *In Irons*, p. 142.

180 *"Come on Coolly":* Reproduced in *Pennsylvania History* 52.

181 *others, at least eight in number, were jailed:* Rosswurm, *Arms, Country and Class*, p. 178.

181 *where they rallied again:* Marshall, *Diary*, p. 217.

181 *the first such mass assembly in two years:* Rosswurm, *Arms, Country and Class*, p. 184.

181 *"getting rich by sucking the blood of this county":* Alexander, "Fort Wilson Incident."

183 *"As we are not authorized to condemn":* Philadelphia Committee to RM, 7/21/79, in *Deane Papers*, IV:20.

183 *"I cannot help differing from you":* "Answer of Robert Morris," 7/31/79, in *Deane Papers*, IV:34.

184 *"I confess I would rather see":* RM to Jonothan Hudson, 3/29/78, in Queens.

184 *"the Effects of Envy, private malice":* Morris's original draft is discussed and quoted in Cummings, "Episode of the Polacre 'Victorious.' "

185 *Holker was widely perceived to be trading on private as well as public account:* For allegations of Holker engaging in private trade, see *LDC*: Committee of Congress to John Holker, 6/25/79.

185 *Morris several times attempted to extricate himself:* For RM's reluctance to deal with Holker, see *LDC*: Gouverneur Morris to Unknown, 5/20/79; for Wadsworth, see ibid., Committee of Congress to Jeremiah Wadsworth, 5/18/79.

185 *Morris answered:* For RM's answer to the price committee, see RM to Committee of Complaints, 6/28/79, in Henkels, *Catalogue*, p. 35. For a review of the Holker flour incident, see Kline, *Gouverneur Morris*, pp. 154–57.

185 *"Reduce us all to poverty":* *LDC*: Henry Laurens to William Livingston, 4/19/79.

186 *"The hope of the enemy":* "Address of the Committee," *Pennsylvania Gazette*, 7/7/79.

186 *"We regulated the price of flour":* Keane, *Tom Paine*, p. 192.

186 *"It is no more absurd":* Stone, "Philadelphia Society," p. 386.

186 *a recent study of the Philadelphia price wars:* See Buel, *In Irons*, pp. 131, 142.

187 *"dangerously wounded . . . in the head":* For the assault on Humphreys, see Keane, *Tom Paine*, pp. 185–86.

187 *"enemy" was "exceedingly alarmed":* Rosswurm, *Arms, Country and Class*, p. 189.

187 *"created considerable uneasiness":* Ibid., p. 190.

187 *"a body of about 100 men":* *Pennsylvania Gazette*, 7/28/79. Silas Deane described this contingent in a letter to his brother as "two or three hundred men of the lower Orders of the people armed with large staves or bludgeons"; quoted in Eberlein and Hubbard, *Independence Hall*, p. 252.

188 *the clear impression of a divided people:* Two accounts of the divided town meeting were published in the *Pennsylvania Gazette*, 7/28/79; see also Rosswurm, *Arms, Country and Class*, pp. 189–91; Alexander, "Fort Wilson Incident," p. 599; and Brunhouse, *Counter-Revolution*, p. 74.

188 *committees were established to set limits on prices:* For the national price control movement, see Buel, "The Committee Movement of 1779," pp. 157–58.

189 *"Trade should be as free as air":* *Pennsylvania Packet*, 7/15/79.

189 *"the most effectual way":* Rosswurm, *Arms, Country and Class*, p. 197; see also Nash, *Unknown American Revolution*, p. 367; and Brunhouse, *Counter-Revolution*, p. 74.

189 *"Come on Warmly":* 8/29/79, reproduced in *Pennsylvania History* 52.

190 *"A bankrupt faithless republic":* *JCC* XV:1060–61; see also Harlow, "Aspects of Revolutionary Finance."

190 *"It seems as if the Continent were to go mad":* *LDC*: RM to Stacey Hepburn, 9/23/79.

191 *"to reason with a multitude":* Statement of Peale, in Reed, *Reed*, II:424.

194 *the city spent a restive, anxious night:* This passage on the Fort Wilson Riot is based on two fine essays: Smith, "The Attack on Fort Wilson," and Alexander, "The Fort Wilson Incident," as well as Rosswurm's extended treatment in *Arms, Country and Class*, pp. 205–27. I also consulted the contemporary accounts included in Reed, *Reed*, II:149–53, 423–28, and the statement of David Conyngham, a member of the First City Troop, published in *Wyoming Historical and Genealogical Record*, VIII (1902).

194 *"The poor unfortunates":* Smith, "Attack on Fort Wilson," p. 187.

194 *"the casual overflowings of liberty":* Brunhouse, *Counter-Revolution*, p. 76.

194 *"upon the whole there seems to be":* RM to James Wilson, 10/6/79, Morris Papers, HSP.

195 *"give some stability to our defense":* RM and Wilson quoted in Smith, "The Attack on Fort Wilson," p. 187.

195 *"The fury against engrossers":* Brunhouse, *Counter-Revolution*, p. 76.

195 *"We are at this moment":* *LDC*: Henry Lowry to John Adams, 10/4/79.

196 *from any attempt to control prices by legislation:* On the failure of the committee movement, see Buel, "Committee Movement," pp. 158, 167.

196 *"Your president has raised a mob"*: Narrative of Philip Hagnez, in Reed, *Reed*, II:427.

196 *"This House will at all times"*: Assembly resolution of 10/10/79, in Reed, *Reed*, II:154.

196 *"That Mr. Wilson is not a favorite"*: Foster, *Moral Visions*, p. 124.

197 *"You have done too much for your country"*: William Livingston to RM, 2/23/81, in *PRM* I:14.

9. PRIVATE FORTUNE, PUBLIC PENURY

PAGE

201 *the American economy was booming again:* For the boom of 1779–80, see Buel, *In Irons*, pp. 173–78; Carp, *To Starve the Army*, p. 104; and Ver Steeg, *Robert Morris*, p. 55.

201 *"merchants, monopolizers, farmers, sharpers"*: Carp, *To Starve the Army*, p. 104.

201 *"commissioners, quartermasters, purchasers"*: Stone, "Philadelphia Society," p. 387.

202 *"It is scarcely to be credited"*: Chastellux, *Travels in North America*, p. 199.

202 *"The house is simple"*: Prince de Broglie, in Sumner, *Financier*, II:222.

203 *Springetsbury:* For detail on Springetsbury, see Day, *Historical Collections*, p. 554; for the greenhouse, see Kitty Livingston to John Jay, 7/10/80, in John Jay Papers.

203 *he never tired of Kitty's company:* For Gouverneur Morris and Kitty Livingston, see Kline, *Gouverneur Morris;* pp. 25–26; for Alexander Hamilton and Kitty Livingston, see Chernow, *Alexander Hamilton*, pp. 93–94.

203 *Morris became his godfather:* For RM as godfather, see RM to William Duer, 3/29/81, in *PRM* I:88.

204 *"My good sir"*: Adams, *Gouverneur Morris*, p. 126.

204 *"Gouverneur's leg has been a tax"*: Kline, *Gouverneur Morris*, p. 176.

204 *Robert Morris set about augmenting his fortune:* Ver Steeg surveys RM's new round of partnerships in *Robert Morris*, pp. 29–35.

205 *"By eternally pushing"*: RM to Jonathan Hudson, 2/9/79, in Ver Steeg, *Robert Morris*, p. 30.

205 *"I offer it to your consideration"*: RM to Hepburn, 12/10/79, in HL.

205 *"I make no doubt"*: RM to William Patterson, 5/15/80, in ibid.

205 *his alliance with John Holker:* For the Morris-Holker relationship, see Gallagher, "Private Interest and the Public Good"; and Ver Steeg, *Robert Morris*, pp. 32–34.

206 *"Luzerne presented his hand"*: Chastellux, *Travels in North America*, p. 277.

207 *Miralles sought to expand:* See Miralles to Luzerne, 11/25/79, in Wharton, ed. *Revolutionary Diplomatic Correspondence*, III:414.

208 *"Poor Don Juan"*: For the quote, see RM to Kitty Livingston, 5/16/80, in Huntington. For notes on Miralles and RM, see McCadden, "Juan de Miralles"; Cummins, *Spanish Observers*, pp. 173–74; Buel, *In Irons*, pp. 180–82; see also Johnson, "El Niño"; and Kline, *Gouverneur Morris*, pp. 226–28.

208 *"the most powerful merchant"*: Kline, *Gouverneur Morris*, p. 229.

209 *A barrel of flour cost $5:* Flour prices from Sumner, *Financier*, II:274.

209 *Morris no longer held a monopoly:* Cummins, *Spanish Observers*, p. 180.

209 *"our port is filled":* Liss, *Atlantic Empires*, p. 115.

209 *"When the American war commenced":* Sumner, *Financier*, II:272.

209 *"The idea that Robert Morris":* Abernethy, *Western Lands*, p. 173.

210 *"The different states must supply":* LDC: Cyrus Griffin to Benjamin Harrison, 11/23/79.

210 *"Our magazines are absolutely empty":* GW to Joseph Reed, in Reed, *Reed*, II:190.

210 *"Money they will want":* RM to Stacey Hepburn, 12/10/79, in Queens.

211 *"discovered [in me] some casual trait":* Redwood Fisher, "Reminiscences," p. 19.

211 *Congress voted to devalue its bills:* For the forty-to-one devaluation, see *JCC* XVI:262–67; Ferguson, *Power of the Purse*, pp. 48–52; and Harlow, "Revolutionary Finance."

213 *"At first there was":* Joseph Reed to George Bryan, 5/20/80, in Reed, *Reed*, II:200.

213 *"Money is our great object":* Ibid.

213 *"The affairs of finance":* RM to Silas Deane, 3/31/80, in *Deane Papers*, IV:117.

213 *"It appears to me":* Fleming, *Washington's Secret War*, p. 223.

214 *"In modern wars":* GW to Reed, 5/28/80, in Reed, *Reed*, II:204.

214 *"The country is much recovered":* Reed to GW, 6/15/80, in ibid., p. 210.

214 *"impracticable from the beginning":* Reed to Nathanael Greene, 10/79, in ibid., p. 139.

215 *"I assure you":* GW to Reed, 5/28/80, in ibid., II:204.

215 *"depressed the spirits":* "Dissertations on Government," 2/18/86, in Foner, ed., *Writings of Thomas Paine*, II:383.

215 *"men of property":* For the first meetings see Lewis, *Bank of North America*, p. 17; for first shipment to the army, see *LDC*: Philip, Schuyler to GW 6/18/80.

215 *"The ladies have caught":* Reed to GW, 6/20/80, in Reed, *Reed*, p. 260.

215 *"Of all the absurdities":* Rawle, "Laurel Hill," p. 400.

216 *"Our greatest hopes":* LDC: James Madison to Thomas Jefferson, 6/23/80.

216 *"This patriotic fire":* LDC: John Walker to Thomas Jefferson, 6/17/80.

216 *"I happened to drop":* LDC: Robert Livingston to Philip Schuyler, 6/16/80.

216 *"subscriptions" were "far more necessary":* Thomas Paine to Blair McClenaghan, 5/80, in Foner, ed., *Writings of Thomas Paine*, II:1183.

216 *"propelled him into":* Foner, *Tom Paine*, p. 182.

216 *management of the fund quickly devolved to Morris:* For notes on the founding of the Pennsylvania Bank, see Sumner, *Financier*, II:21–23; Lewis, *Bank of North America*, pp. 16–23; and Paine, "Dissertations on Government," in Foner, ed., *Writings of Thomas Paine*, II:385; see also *LDC*: Philip Schuyler to GW, 6/18/80, n. 2.

218 *"The new plan of a Bank":* Reed to GW, 6/22/80, in Reed, *Reed*, II:215.

218 *"the party opposed to you":* GW to Reed, 7/4/80, in ibid., p. 221.

218 *"This, while serviceable":* GW to Esther Reed, 8/10/80, in ibid., p. 265.

218 *While Washington maintained a friendly tone:* For Washington's reaction to

the Pennsylvania Bank, see Flexner, *Washington in the American Revolution*, pp. 397–98.

218   *"my principal enemies"*: Reed to GW, 6/5/80, in Reed, *Reed*, II:212.

220   *"Our Assembly affairs go"*: Joseph Reed to William Henry, 12/2/80, in Reed, *Reed*, II:290.

221   *sea captain named Pierre Landais:* For notes on Landais and Lee, see Morison, *John Paul Jones*, pp. 293–301.

222   *"The political salvation"*: James Lovell to Elbridge Gerry, 9/5/80, in Burnett, *Letters of Members*, V:344, n. 5.

222   *"Arthur Lee has, I believe"*: James Wilson to Silas Deane, 1/1/81, in *Deane Papers*, IV:270.

222   *"Toryism is triumphant here"*: Arthur Lee to Elbridge Gerry, 11/26/80, in Burnett, *Letters of Members*, V:439, n. 4.

222   *"that old corrupt Serpent"*: For Lee's return to America, see Potts, *Arthur Lee*, pp. 246–51; the quote is from p. 251.

222   *"I consider Mr. Deane"*: RM to BF, 3/31/80, in *Deane Papers*, IV:120.

223   *Necker made a deep impression:* For a compelling portrait of Necker, see Harris, *Necker*, passim.

223   *"our great financier"*: Deane to RM, 9/2/80, in *Deane Papers*, IV:213–18.

10. THE OFFICE OF FINANCE

PAGE

226   *"We never stood"*: Anthony Wayne to Joseph Reed, 11/7/80 and 12/16/80, in Reed, *Reed*, II:313, 316.

226   *"The public distress is"*: GM to George Clinton, 1/26/81, in Kline, *Gouverneur Morris*, p. 184.

227   *the delegates voted without dissent:* JCC XIX:180.

228   *"exercise every power"*: Burnett, *Continental Congress*, p. 484.

229   *"The different policy"*: Ibid., p. 458.

229   *"Robert Morris would have many things"*: See ibid.; for Hamilton, see Summer, *Financier*, I:261; see also Chernow, *Alexander Hamilton*, pp. 138–39.

229   *John Sullivan proposed:* LDC: John Sullivan's committee notes, 11/7/80; see also Burnett, *Continental Congress*, p. 480.

229   *drastic steps were proposed in New England:* For the New England conventions, see Carp, *To Starve the Army*, pp. 202–3.

230   *"Our Minister of the Finances"*: Adams, *Governeur Morris*, p. 129.

231   *"Our finances want a Necker"*: LDC: Joseph Jones to GW, 2/21/81.

231   *"You may render"*: Alexander Hamilton to RM, 4/30/81, in *PRM* I:32.

231   *"I have great expectations"*: Summer, *Financier*, I:262.

231   *"The derangement of our Money Affairs"*: RM to John Jay, 7/4/81, in *PRM* I:222.

231   *"Miss Fortune is fickle"*: RM to Matthew Ridley, 2/6/81, in Gallagher, "Private Interest," p. 194.

231   *"The appointment [as Financier]"*: RM Diary, 2/21/81, in *PRM* I:8.

232 *"He feels all"*: Morris to Robert Livingston, 3/14/81, in Kline, *Gouverneur Morris*, p. 189.

232 *"The business you have undertaken"*: BF to RM, 7/26/81, in *PRM* I:391.

232 *"I felt a sort of mixture"*: John Swanwick to RM, 2/20/81, in ibid., p. 5.

233 *"relaxation from business"*: RM to the President of Congress, 5/14/81, in *PRM* I:62.

233 *"uncultivated insolent rabble"*: Maier, *Old Revolutionaries*, p. 222. For Carroll and virtue, see ibid., p. 212.

234 *the motion carried: JCC* XIX:288–89.

234 *the provision was rejected: JCC* XIX:338.

234 *the Congress capitulated:* For notes on the debate in Congress over RM's terms of acceptance, see headnote, RM to Committee of Congress, 3/26/81, in *PRM* I:20; see also Ver Steeg, *Robert Morris*, pp. 60–61.

234 *"Bob Morris sets a high price"*: John Armstrong to General Armstrong, 5/10/81, in *PMHB* 5:108.

235 *"Labyrinth of confusion"*: RM to Samuel Huntington, 5/14/81, in *PRM* I:63.

235 *"the Raising of a Revenue"*: RM to John Jay, 7/4/81, in ibid., p. 223.

235 "the absolute Necessity": RM to Philip Schuyler, 5/29/81, in ibid., p. 92 (italics underlined in the original).

235 *"The very high and honorable"*: RM to Jacques Necker, 6/15/81, in ibid., p. 149.

236 *a lengthy proposal for a bank:* Alexander Hamilton to RM, 4/30/81, in ibid., p. 31.

237 *"far short of what it ought"*: RM to Alexander Hamilton, 3/26/81, in ibid., p. 79.

238 *"the public credit has received"*: To the Public, 5/28/81, in ibid., p. 83.

238 *"swelled beyond all"*: RM to John Jay, 7/4/81, in ibid., p. 222.

238 *an additional debt load later estimated at:* Ferguson, *Power of the Purse*, p. 63.

239 *"One very strong motive"*: RM to John Jay, 7/13/81, in *PRM* I:287.

239 *"I mean to render this"*: RM to BF, 7/13/81, in ibid., p. 283; see also Ver Steeg, *Robert Morris*, pp. 67–68.

239 *"I found myself"*: RM to GW, 5/29/81, in *PRM* I:94.

240 *"I must also pledge myself"*: RM to Thomas Lowrey, 5/29/81, in *PRM* I:90.

241 *a new grant of six million livres:* For Laurens in Paris, see Ferguson, *Power of the Purse*, pp. 126–27; see also Schiff, *Great Improvisation*, pp. 273–77.

241 *all government sales of French bills:* RM Diary, and note, 6/4/81, in *PRM* I:104.

242 *"all doings in paper ceased"*: Joseph Reed to James Searle, n.d., in Reed, *Reed*, II:295.

242 *"Because the value of money"*: RM's Assembly protest is printed in ibid., p. 291.

243 *"I am Financier Elect"*: RM to GW, 6/15/81, in *PRM* I:153.

243 *He opened the emergency session:* For RM's speech, see Brunhouse, *Counter-Revolution*, p. 259, n. 29.

244 *"which I think should"*: RM to GW, 7/2/81, in *PRM* I:214.

244 *"The public necessities"*: Reed to the PA Assembly, 6/20/81, in *PA* XII:765.

245 *"Congress at his mercy"*: Reed to Nathanael Greene, 11/1/81, in Reed, *Reed*, II:373.

245 *First, he drafted his clerk John Swanwick:* For the fiscal implications of Swanwick's appointment, see Ver Steeg, *Robert Morris*, p. 81.

245 *a bit of fiscal alchemy:* See RM to Treasurer of Pennsylvania, 7/16/81, in *PRM* I:307, especially n. 3.

245 *Morris outlined his scheme:* RM to Franklin, 7/21/81, in ibid., p. 363.

246 *"the most vulgar kind of bill-kiting":* Summer, *Financier,* I:283.

246 *"An operation of this kind":* RM Statement of Accounts (1785), in *PRM* IX:693.

246 *His efforts bore fruit:* RM to Governor of Maryland, 8/28/81, in *PRM* II:143.

246 *experimenting with private contracts:* For supply contracts, see Ferguson, *Power of the Purse,* p. 1323–33; see also Ver Steeg, *Robert Morris,* pp. 106–9; and Carp, *To Starve the Army,* p. 211.

246 *"binding on the United States":* JCC XX:734.

247 *"specific supplies are at once":* Sumner, *Financier,* I:246.

247 *he presented one delegate:* Oberholtzer, *Robert Morris,* p. 287.

247 *"I would gladly give you":* RM to John Jay, 7/7/81, in *PRM* I:250, cited in Ver Steeg, *Robert Morris,* p. 69.

248 *"power, consequence and grandeur":* Ferguson, *Power of the Purse,* p. 120.

248 *"the most speedy":* RM to the governors, 6/7/81, in *PRM* I:242

248 *"Your Excellency must be":* RM to the governors, 7/16/81, in ibid., p. 305

249 *"If once an opinion":* Circular to the Governors of the States, 7/25/81, in ibid., p. 380; see also Ver Steeg, *Robert Morris,* pp. 92–94.

249 *"As to the complaint":* RM to Jonathan Trumbull, 7/31/82, in *PRM* VI:133.

250 *"it is possible":* Circular to the Governors, 7/27/81, in *PRM* I:396.

252 *"the most trifling thing":* Ferguson, *Power of the Purse,* p. 119.

252 *"all business of deliberation":* Reed to Nathanael Greene, 11/1/81, in Reed, *Reed,* II:375.

252 *"The multiplicity and Variety":* RM to Silas Deane, 6/7/81, in *PRM* I:119.

11. YORKTOWN

PAGE

253 *too feeble to mount any genuine threat:* Reviewing the years 1779–1780, Washington biographer Douglas Southall Freeman asserted, "Lack of money made defensive strategy almost the sole military policy America could pursue." Freeman, *Washington,* V:92.

254 *"cheerful and hearty Welcome":* RM recorded notes on his trip to New York in his Diary, 8/21/81, in *PRM* II:73.

255 *"a superior army":* GW to RM, Richard Peters, 8/21/71, in ibid., p. 86.

255 *the only viable option:* For the message from De Grasse, see Boatner, *Encyclopedia,* p. 1235; see also Freeman, *Washington,* V:309.

255 *"We were surprised":* Richard Peters to W. H. Harrison, 1/12/1818, in Simpson, *Eminent Philadelphians,* p. 706.

256 *"He [Holker] is a selfish merchant":* Rochambeau to Luzerne, 4/14/81, in Sullivan, *Maryland and France,* p. 83.

256 *his bid to handle the sale of French bills:* For RM's conference with the French, see Diary, 8/21/81, in *PRM* II:78.

257 *Morris met with Thomas McKean:* Ibid., p. 80.

258 *"I find money matters"*: RM to GW, 8/22/81, in ibid., p. 91.

258 *Morris first laid plans*: RM Diary, 7/27/81, and notes, in *PRM* I:394.

259 *The Morris notes soon entered circulation*: For circulation of Morris notes, see RM to Ridley and Mark Pringle, 11/13/81, in *PRM* III:181.

259 *"My personal Credit"*: RM to Benjamin Harrison, 1/15/82, in *PRM* IV:45, in Ver Steeg, *Robert Morris*, p. 87.

259 *"We are on the eve"*: RM to Governors, 8/22/81, in *PRM* II:90.

259 *"to enforce in the warmest Terms"*: GW to Governors, 9/3/81, in ibid., p. 91, n. 3.

259 *"It is needless to say"*: RM to Caesar Rodney, 1/9/81, in ibid., p. 176.

260 *"like a smothering snowstorm"*: In Phelps, *Yorktown*, p. 92.

261 *"the troops . . . have upon"*: GW to RM, 8/27/81, in *PRM* II:116.

262 *"I wish the states"*: RM to GW, 9/6/81, in ibid., p. 200.

262 *"Every day discovers to me"*: GW to RM, 9/6/81, in ibid., p. 205.

262 *spilling the silver on the ground*: Oberholtzer, *Robert Morris*, p. 88.

262 *"It will be difficult"*: Benjamin Lincoln to RM, 9/8/81, in *PRM* II:220.

262 *"It seems as if every person"*: RM Diary, 9/11/81, in ibid., p. 244.

263 *"I supplied the Pay Master"*: RM to Benjamin Lincoln, 9/11/81, in ibid., p. 252.

263 *"The late Movements"*: RM to Reed, 9/20/81, in ibid., p. 309.

263 *"I need not mention"*: Thomas Paine to RM, 9/20/81, in ibid., p. 314.

264 *"contrary to my Inclinations"*: RM to the President of Congress, 9/8/81, in ibid., p. 217.

264 *"When I tell you"*: Nathanael Greene to RM, 8/18/81, in ibid., p. 69.

264 *"I by no means hold myself"*: RM to William Heath, 10/16/81, in *PRM* III:64.

264 *"I hope and trust"*: RM to Nathanael Greene, 11/10/81, in *PRM* II:228.

265 *"I am afraid I shall"*: Tench Tilghman to RM, 6/24/81, in *PRM* I:175.

266 *"your Character, Situation"*: RM to Robert Smith, 7/14/81, in ibid., p. 318.

266 *"a man full of spirit"*: Francisco Rendón to Juan Manuel de Cagigal, 7/15/81, Library of Congress.

266 *a draft letter advising John Jay*: RM to John Jay, 8/15/81, in *PRM* II:65, n. 1. For the entire Havana project, see Oberholtzer, *Robert Morris*, pp. 100–104.

266 *Young Laurens "brusqued" Vergennes*: For "brusqued," see BF to William Carmichael, 8/24/81, in Wharton, ed, *Revolutionary, Diplomatic Correspondence*, IV:660.

267 *typically detailed instructions*: RM Diary, 9/10/81, and RM to Tench Francis, 9/11/81, in *PRM* II:222, 246.

268 *just another army supply train*: For additional notes on the "treasure train," see Oberholtzer, *Robert Morris*, pp. 104–7.

268 *He laid out his policy*: RM to President of Congress, 8/28/81, in *PRM* II:124.

270 *"No Nation ever had"*: Nathanael Greene to RM, 8/18/81, in ibid., p. 69.

271 *"amount to more money"*: RM to James Lovell, 9/7/81, in ibid., p. 209; see also William Bingham to RM, 8/7/81, in ibid., p. 31.

271 *Morris reasoned that failure*: RM to the President of Congress, 11/14/82, in *PRM* VII:48.

271 *"Mr. Morris has taken"*: Affidavit of Thomas Mason, Pleasants Collection, HSP.

272 *"stripped of every thing"*: James Lovell to BF, 5/9/81, in Franklin Papers, APS; see also Nuxoll, *Munitions Merchants*, p. 476.

272 *the dispute festered for years:* See Stephen Ceronio to RM 6/23/81, and notes, in *PRM* I:171, and RM to Stephen Ceronio, RM to Bernard Lavaud, both 10/5/81, in *PRM* III:23–25; see also Nuxoll, *Munitions Merchants*, 456–65.

272 *"When I undertook the Agency"*: James, "Oliver Pollock, Financier," p. 76.

273 *"I have remarked"*: RM to Benjamin Harrison, 1/15/82, in *PRM* IV:45. For notes on Pollock, see also RM Diary, 9/10/81, n. 10, in *PRM* II:226.

273 *Johnson refused to render a verdict:* For Deane's efforts to settle his accounts, see Hilton, *Silas Deane*, pp. 94–97.

273 *"already conquered"*: Francis Dana to John Adams, 1/1/81, in *Deane Papers*, IV:273.

273 *"Poor Mr. Deane"*: Beaumarchais to Vergennes, 12/2/80, in ibid., p. 265.

274 *"I have examined"*: Silas Deane to RM, 6/10/81, in *PRM* I:128.

275 *the letters published in October:* Some historians have alleged that Deane wrote the letters of 1781 at the behest of the British ministry in return for a bribe. See Boyd, "Silas Deane," II:167–68. But this, as with much relating to Deane, remains in dispute, and like all the charges of peculation by Deane, is argued against by his unremitting poverty. See Hilton, *Silas Deane*, pp. 102–5.

275 *"Strange as it is"*: Joseph Reed to Nathanael Greene, 11/1/81, in Reed, *Reed*, p. 374.

275 *"Our former friend"*: BF to RM, 3/30/82, in *PRM* IV:486.

275 *"ex parte, erroneous"*: Senate committee report of 1841, in Hilton, *Silas Deane*, p. 121.

276 *Tilghman reported to Congress:* For Tilghman's journey and the cash award from Congress, see Fleming, *Perils of Peace*, p. 24.

276 *smash every window:* Ibid., p. 26.

277 *"a very considerable debt"*: GW to RM, 11/19/81, in *PRM* III:207.

12. EXECUTIVE ACTION

PAGE

278 *no mood for pomp and display:* Fleming, *Perils of Peace*, p. 41.

278 *Morris sat down with Washington:* For the meeting with GW and Lafayette, see RM Diary, 11/26/81, in *PRM* III:253.

279 *"the advantageous use"*: Luzerne to RM, 9/26/81, in *PRM* II:357.

279 *"have neither been accustomed"*: RM to Luzerne, 11/3/81, in *PRM* III:132.

279 *"I am now to address you"*: RM, Circular to the Governors, 10/19/81, in ibid., p. 83.

280 *"an additional proof"*: RM to Luzerne, 11/3/81, in ibid., p. 133.

280 *"After the great success"*: Luzerne to RM, 11/4/81, in ibid., p. 139.

281 *"It is impossible"*: RM to Luzerne, 11/6/81, in ibid., p. 156.

281 *"my future utility absolutely destroyed"*: RM to Luzerne, 11/22/81, in ibid., p. 233.

281 *Luzerne was unmoved:* Luzerne to RM, 11/24/81, in ibid., p. 246.

281 *"Notwithstanding my pressing instances"*: RM to BF, 11/27/81, in ibid., p. 264.

282 *"I have no hope"*: Gouverneur Morris to Nathanael Greene, 12/24/81, in ibid., p. 439.

283 *"this immense Republic"*: Ibid.

283 *"America is so extensive"*: RM to BF, 11/27/81, in ibid., p. 264.

283 *"Remember that if"*: RM to Comte de Noailles, 11/26/81, in ibid., p. 255.

284 *"perfectly disposed"*: RM Diary, 11/28/81, in ibid., p. 296.

284 *"This house will answer"*: RM Diary, 11/30/81, in ibid., p. 303.

284 *"The plot is deep"*: Arthur Lee to Thomas McKean, 8/26/81, in Potts, *Arthur Lee*, p. 252.

284 *Gouverneur's nephew Lewis Morris*: Kline, *Gouverneur Morris*, p. 215.

285 *"his great bulk and his loose jowel"*: Lincoln is described in Boatner, *Encyclopedia*, p. 636, citing Flexner.

286 *"or some daring Genius"*: Livingston to James Duane, 5/20/80, in Dangerfield, *Robert Livingston*, p. 124.

286 *"may have the pernicious tendency"*: GW to the States, 1/31/82, in Fitzpatrick, ed., *Writings of Washington*, IX:436.

286 *"The Savior of our Country"*: Jackson, "Washington in Philadelphia," p. 135.

287 *"Urge in the most pressing manner"*: RM to William Duer, 2/7/82, in *PRM* IV:181.

288 *"the cheapest, most certain"*: For notes on the Morris contracts, see Ver Steeg, *Robert Morris*, pp. 106–7 and 141–46. The quote is on p. 107.

288 *"your Excellency must be"*: RM to GW, 6/4/82, in *PRM* V:332.

288 *"If the military should disband"*: GW to RM, 6/16/82, in ibid., p. 417.

288 *"an exception from the general Rule"*: RM Diary, 12/28/81, in *PRM* III:453.

288 *"This gentleman's distress"*: For St. Clair, see Oberholtzer, *Robert Morris*, p. 176.

289 *"kindly, & at present"*: *LDC*: Samuel Osgood to John Lowell, 11/13/81.

290 *"a want of power"*: *LDC*: James Madison to Edmund Pendleton, 1/8/82.

290 *"When the bank was first opened here"*: Among the many sources on the Bank of North America, see James, "Bank of North America"; Nuxoll, "Bank of North America"; Ver Steeg, *Robert Morris*, pp. 84–87. For the Willing quote, see James, "Bank of North America," p. 63; for Osgood, see *LDC*: Samuel Osgood to John Lowell, 1/23/82.

290 *Winning acceptance for the bank notes*: On circulation of banknotes, see Rappaport, *Hostility to Banks*, p. 32; Ferguson, *Power of the Purse*, p. 138; and Ver Steeg, *Robert Morris*, p. 116.

290 *"the commonest things become intricate"*: RM to the President of Congress, 1/15/82, in *PRM* IV:25.

291 *"Let me once more entreat"*: RM, Circular to the Governors, 1/3/82, in *PRM* III:481.

291 *"Many people flatter themselves"*: RM to the Governors, 2/9/82, in ibid., *PRM* IV:191.

291 *"I am so habituated"*: RM to Daniel of St. Thomas Jennifer, 6/11/82, in *PRM* V:379.

292 *"I told them plainly"*: RM Diary, 2/8/82, in ibid., p. 188.

292 *"somewhat out of my province":* GW to the States, 1/22/82, in Fitzpatrick, ed., *Writings of Washington*, IX:433.

292 *"What, then, is to be done?":* Livingston to the States, 2/19/82, in Wharton, ed., *Revolutionary Diplomatic Correspondence*, V:181.

293 *"men whose political principles":* Paine, *American Crisis* III, in Foner, ed., *Writings of Thomas Paine*, I:73.

293 *"The people of America":* Thomas Paine to Joseph Reed, 6/4/80, in Reed, *Reed*, II:218.

294 *"There never was a man":* Sarah Franklin Bache to BF, 1/14/81, in Keane, *Tom Paine*, p. 206.

294 *"I now felt myself":* Ibid., p. 215.

294 *"that for the Service":* RM Diary, 9/18/81, in *PRM* III:290.

295 *"Robert Morris assured me":* Thomas Paine to Jonathan Williams, 11/26/81, in Conway, *Thomas Paine*, I:175.

295 *"the secret of my own situation":* Keane, *Tom Paine*, p. 216.

295 *"engaged Paine to write":* For Luzerne and Paine, see Keane, *Tom Paine*, p. 576, n. 25; for Paine's quote, see Foner, *Tom Paine*, p. 189.

296 *"Something might turn up":* RM Diary, 1/26/82, in *PRM* IV:116.

296 *"the important situation":* Agreement with R. R. Livingston and GW, 2/10/82, in ibid., 201. For the evening conference, see RM Diary, 2/19/82, in ibid., p. 262.

296 *"We wish to draw":* Memorandum on Thomas Paine, 2/82, in ibid., p. 327.

296 *"has proved me right":* Thomas Paine to RM, 2/20/82, in ibid., p. 279.

297 *"every man, almost without exception":* American Crisis X, in Foner, ed., *Writings of Thomas Paine*, p. 189.

297 *"to eat a few oysters":* Thomas Paine to RM, 3/17/82, in *PRM* IV:415.

298 *"licensed spies":* Oberholtzer, *Robert Morris*, p. 146.

298 *"Public opinion is always":* RM to William Churchill Houston, 10/29/82, in *PRM* VI:674.

298 *Morris made a personal appeal:* RM Diary, 2/13/82, in *PRM* IV:225.

299 *Nor did the new receivers share:* For notes on the Continental receivers, see Ver Steeg, *Robert Morris*, p. 101.

299 *"I cannot hope":* Hamilton to RM, 7/22/82, in *PRM* VI:7. For Hamilton's tenure as a tax receiver, see Chernow, *Alexander Hamilton*, pp. 170–71.

299 *"The habitual inattention":* For the delegations of Congress, see notes to RM to President of Congress, 5/17/82, in *PRM* V:204; for the quotes, see RM Diary, 5/24/82, in ibid., p. 247.

300 *"generally to be convinced":* For the report of the envoys, see *JCC* XXII:397; for their bills, see RM Diary, 5/27/82, in *PRM* V:269.

300 *"It is only by a Kind of Miracle":* RM to De Grasse, 5/16/82, in ibid., p. 193.

300 *"What I had afloat":* RM to Richard Butler, 7/18/82, in ibid., p. 597.

301 *Barney promptly achieved a sensational victory:* For notes on Barney and the *Hyder Ally*, see ibid., p. 147; and Russell, *Haym Salomon*, p. 200.

301 *Congress moved to sweeten the deal:* For notes on domestic loans issued by Congress, see Ferguson, *Power of the Purse*, pp. 36–37.

302   *"the general interest"*: RM Diary, 6/26/82, in *PRM* V:483.

302   *"I advised these Gentlemen"*: RM Diary, 7/9/82, in ibid., p. 548.

302   *"the Merit of being among"*: Remonstrance, published as Appendix II, *PRM* VI:695.

303   *"Interest, happiness, freedom and Glory"*: RM Diary, 6/28/82, in *PRM* V:495.

303   *"First they stimulate Industry"*: RM to the President of Congress, 7/29/82, in *PRM* VI:56.

304   *"persons possessed of knowledge"*: Carey, *Bank Debates*, p. 51.

13. FIGHTING FOR FUNDS

PAGE

307   *"Mr. Morris has become a new star"*: Benjamin Rush to Horatio Gates, 9/5/81, in *PRM* VII:xxv.

307   *"Order and economy"*: Livingston to John Jay, 2/2/82, in Sumner, *Financier*, II:33.

307   *"Your conduct, activity, and address"*: BF to RM, 8/12/82, in ibid., p. 56.

308   *"You may very truly tell"*: RM to Gouverneur Morris, 4/3/82, in *PRM* IV:510.

308   *"The greatest part of my time"*: RM Diary, 2/2/82, in *PRM* III:476.

308   *often ran past midnight:* For business before breakfast, see Diary, 5/18/82, in *PRM* V:216; for after midnight, see Diary, 3/28/82, in *PRM* IV:467.

308   *"Finding that the daily"*: RM Diary, 6/15/82, in *PRM* V:414; see also Oberholtzer, *Robert Morris*, p. 172.

309   *"he must have patience"*: For Smith, see RM to James Smith, 11/26/81, in *PRM* II:356; and RM Diary, 2/16/82, in *PRM* IV:261.

309   *"Col. Pickering applies for Money"*: RM Diary, 5/7/82, in *PRM* V:117.

309   *This was tricky business:* For notes on establishing credit for the bank, see Oberholtzer, *Robert Morris*, pp. 108–9; Lewis, *Bank of North America*, pp. 41–42. RM employed a similar scheme to support the Morris notes; see Hayfield, "Conyngham Reminiscences," p. 220.

309   *Morris intervened by persuading Luzerne:* For Luzerne's intervention in favor of the bank, see O'Donnell, *Luzerne*, p. 191.

310   *"on his Private obligation"*: RM Diary, 5/23/82, in *PRM* V:242.

310   *"How I am enabled"*: RM to Richard Butler, 7/18/82, in ibid., p. 597.

310   *The delayed payments:* For delays in payment and the problems that resulted, see Sands & Co. to RM, 9/11/82, in *PRM* VI:356.

310   *"wrongly named"*: Sands has been the subject of much historical writing; see GW to RM, 5/17/82, in *PRM* V:209; for the quote, see Fleming, *Perils of Peace*, p. 187.

310   *"Mr. Sands"*: GW to RM, 6/16/82, in *PRM* V:417.

311   *"instantly quit the execution"*: William Duer to RM, 8/2/82, in *PRM* VI:126.

311   *"I am tied here to be baited"*: RM to GW, 7/9/82, in ibid., p. 552.

311   *"It is not my wish"*: GW to RM, 10/2/82, in ibid., p. 476.

312   *"useless by the total Stagnation"*: RM to GW, 9/9/82, in ibid., p. 345.

312   *"I wish most sincerely"*: RM to Matthew Ridley, 10/6/82, in ibid., p. 509.

313 *"but do not conceal":* For notes on the views of France, see ibid., p. 463, n. 9; for the quote, see Sumner, *Financier*, II:59.

313 *a loan from Holland:* For notes on the Dutch loan, see Ferguson, *Power of the Purse*, pp. 128–29. David Howell, the primary opponent of the impost in Congress, cited the loan as evidence of America's healthy credit; see *LDC*: Howell to Nicholas Brown, 9/19/82; Howell to John Carter, 10/16/82; and Howell to Nicholas Brown, 11/30/82.

313 *Adams specifically asked:* John Adams's restrictions on the Dutch loan are noted in *PRM* VI:353, n. 3; the venture to Havana is described in ibid., p. 425, n. 1.

314 *"Strange that the Financier":* James Duane to Philip Schuyler, 6/4/82, in *PRM* V:227, n. 3.

314 *"Anarchy and Confusion":* Benjamin Harrison to RM, 12/28/81, in *PRM* III:461.

314 *"have no right":* Benjamin Harrison to RM, 2/7/82, in *PRM* IV:186.

315 *"The accumulation of Offices":* *LDC*: Arthur Lee to Samuel Adams, 8/6/82.

315 *"Our embarrassments for money":* *LDC*: Arthur Lee to Francis Dana, 6/6/82.

315 *"The prevailing temper":* James Madison to Edmund Randolph, 7/2/82, in Hutchinson, ed., *Papers of James Madison*, IV:386.

315 *"My charity I own":* James Madison to Edmund Randolph, 6/82, in Sumner, *Financier*, II:53.

316 *"expose to just censure":* James Madison to Edmund Randolph, 7/16/82, in Hutchinson, ed., *Papers of James Madison*, IV:419.

316 *"from a conviction":* RM Diary, 6/12/82, in *PRM* V:385.

316 *"All the movements":* James Madison to Edmund Randolph, 7/16/82, in Hutchinson, ed., *Papers of James Madison*, IV:419.

316 *"that Congress did not mean":* *PRM* V:386, n. 1.

316 *"every other" American diplomat:* *LDC*: Arthur Lee to Congress, 7/12/82.

317 *"his word of honor":* *LDC*: Charles Thomson's notes of debates, 7/25/82; see also *JCC* XXI:833.

317 *"Manifest injustice":* Arthur Lee to RM, 11/2/82, in *PRM* VII:6.

317 *"I cannot dispense":* RM to Arthur Lee, 11/18/82, in ibid., p. 59.

317 *Morris had already obtained:* RM to President of Congress, 11/14/82, in *PRM* VII:48.

317 *"may become necessary":* For notes on the tax committee, see *PRM* IV:318, n. 4.

317 *"large sums of money":* *LDC*: Charles Thomson's notes of debates, 7/25/82.

318 *Lee detested Wharton:* Lee described Wharton as "avowedly an agent for the enemies to our cause & our Country, an Insolvent and a profligate adventurer." Wharton was a rival to Lee in land speculations. *LDC*: Arthur Lee to Samuel Adams, 4/21/82.

318 *"the object of almost daily attack":* *PRM* V:388.

318 *Very little was produced:* For notes on Lee's inquiry into French funds, see ibid., p. 253, n. 7.

318 *"There is a misteriousness":* For Morris's thinking on Beaumarchais, see Morton and Spinelli, *Beaumarchais*, p. 284; the letters quoted can also be found in *PRM* V:244 and 281.

318 *"Congress should not pay any attention":* For Luzerne, see RM Diary, 7/9/82, in *PRM* V:547.

319 *Morris formed an alliance:* For Lee, Morris, and Beaumarchais, see Beaumarchais to Morris, 6/3/82, and notes, in ibid., p. 318.

319 *"the Impost Law will":* RM Diary, 7/2/82, in ibid., p. 513.

319 *the mercantile Brown brothers of Providence:* A fourth Brown brother, Moses Brown, had worked with John to establish the college. He broke with his brother over the question of slavery, but remained his ally in business affairs. For their saga, see Rappleye, *Sons of Providence*, passim.

320 *Howell scored a "smashing" victory:* For the debate in Rhode Island and the quotes from the newspaper debate, see the excellent treatment in Polishook, *Rhode Island and the Union*, pp. 57–73.

320 *"As you go Southward": LDC*: David Howell to Welcome Arnold, 8/3/82.

320 *"all the members of Congress": LDC*: David Howell to Gov. William Greene, 7/30/82.

321 *"by increasing temptations":* Howell recounted his testimony in ibid.

321 *"the Tax is voluntary":* RM to Gov. William Greene, 8/2/82, in *PRM* VI:123.

322 *"a long conversation":* RM Diary, 9/2/82, in ibid., p. 294.

322 *"we shall on that day":* Contractors to RM, 9/11/82, in ibid., p. 356.

322 *"consider how your army":* RM to GW, 8/29/82, in ibid., p. 282.

322 *"at present I really know not":* RM to GW, 9/9/82, in ibid., p. 345.

322 *"ruinous system":* GW to RM, 9/22/82, in ibid., p. 416.

323 *Carter was a man of mystery:* For background on John Carter, see Chernow, *Alexander Hamilton*, p. 134.

323 *"I confess to you":* RM to Comfort Sands & Co., 10/10/82, in *PRM* VI:551.

323 *"Our feelings, Sir":* Sands, Livingston & Co. to RM, 10/21/82, in ibid., p. 640.

324 *"I didn't bid for the contract":* For notes on Duer and his partners, see *PRM* VII:46, n. 3; see also Ver Steeg, *Robert Morris*, pp. 160–61. The quote is from Ver Steeg.

324 *"For upwards of two months":* The Greene quote is from Ver Steeg, *Robert Morris*, p. 151; Lincoln is quoted in ibid., p. 157.

324 *"The negligence of the several states":* RM to the President of Congress, 10/21/82, in *PRM* VI:635.

324 *"How long is a Nation":* RM to the Governors, 10/21/82, in ibid., p. 631.

325 *"It must be remembered":* RM to Rhode Island Governor William Greene, 10/24/82, in ibid., p. 655.

325 *nine states to one:* For the vote demanding an answer from Rhode Island, see *JCC* XXIII:643.

326 *"If ever there was a Cause": LDC*: David Howell to Theodore Foster, 10/12/82.

326 *"candor and prudence": LDC*: David Howell to William Greene, 10/14/82.

326 *"the most crowded":* For the Rhode Island vote, see Rappleye, *Sons of Providence*, p. 218.

326 *In Pennsylvania and Maryland:* For the actions of the public creditors in Pennsylvania and Maryland, see headnotes in *PRM* VII:81, 145.

327 *"our system of administration"*: Madison Notes of Debates, 12/4/82, in *JCC* XXIII:861.

327 *"the necessity of the impost"*: Madison's notes are in ibid., p. 81.

327 *"He left this place"*: James Madison to Edmund Randolph, 10/8/72, in Hutchinson, ed., *Paper of James Madison*, V:186, and notes.

328 *Lee managed to turn back:* Edmund Randolph to James Madison, 12/13/82, in ibid., p. 399.

328 *Harrison did not even know:* Benjamin Harrison to Virginia Delegates, 1/4/83, in ibid., p. 431, n. 3.

328 *"The fatal repeal"*: Edmund Randolph to Madison, 7/7/83, in Burnett, ed., *Letters of Members*, VII:21, n. 2.

329 *"a piece of prudence"*: *PRM* VII:82 (headnote).

329 *"casually mentioned"*: *LDC*: Samuel Osgood to John Lowell, 1/6/83.

329 *"The most intelligent members"*: Madison Notes of Debates, 12/4/82, in *JCC* XXIII:861.

330 *"Colossus, who not only"*: Joseph Reed to George Bryan, 12/25/82, in Reed, *Reed*, II:390.

14. A DESPERATE GAMBIT

331 *"We have borne"*: To the Congress Assembled, December 1782, in *JCC* XXIV:291.

332 *"I have . . . the satisfaction"*: GW to William Heath, 2/5/83, in Carp, *To Starve the Army*, p. 391.

333 *"no objection"*: For Washington's prior knowledge of the petition, and for the quotes, see *PRM* VII:249, n. 3.

333 *"The Army have Swords"*: GW to John Jay, 1/1/83, in ibid., p. 256.

334 *"it was impossible"*: Madison Notes of Debate, 1/7/83, in *JCC* XXV:847.

335 *"unwarrantable and dishonorable"*: Ibid., p. 849.

336 *"painted their sufferings"*: Ibid., p. 853.

337 *"They must have patience"*: RM Diary, 1/17/83, in *PRM* VII:315.

337 *"We are all aground"*: *LDC*: Eliphalet Dyer to William Williams, 1/10/83.

337 *"was extolled as the infallible"*: *LDC*: Jonothan Arnold to William Greene, 1/8/03.

338 *"impress the general utility"*: RM to Thomas Paine, 2/4/83, in *PRM* VII:400.

338 *"Mr. Paine has been handled"*: David Howell to Benjamin Rush, 2/8/83, in ibid., p. 85.

339 *"I had no alternative"*: RM to Nathanael Greene, 3/14/83, in ibid., p. 574.

339 *"I am heartily tired"*: RM to Horatio Gates, 1/28/83, in ibid., p. 378.

339 *"I hope my Successor"*: RM to GW 2/27/83 in ibid., p. 475.

340 *"as a source of fresh hopes"*: Madison Notes of Debate, 1/24/83, in *JCC* XXV:862.

340 *"to sink or swim"*: Ibid, p. 886 (Wilson), p. 874 (Madison), and p. 878 (Lee); see also Henderson, *Party Politics*, pp. 330–31.

341 *"During the War"*: Gouvernor Morris to Henry Knox, 2/7/83, in *PRM* VII:417.

341 *Brooks also carried:* For the funds carried by Brooks, see the notes in ibid., p. 332.

342 *"He betray'd it"*: John Armstrong, Jr., to Horatio Gates, 4/29/83, in Burnett, ed., *Letters of Members*, VII:155, n. 3.

342 *"guide the torrent"*: *LDC*: Alexander Hamilton to GW, 2/13/83.

342 *strong personal ties to McDougall:* For McDougal's ties to Gouverneur Morris and Hamilton, see Kline, *Gouverneur Morris*, pp. 257–58.

342 *a matter of speculation:* The most confident proponent of the conspiracy theory is Richard Kohn, who laid it out in his article "The Inside History of the Newburgh Conspiracy," and a later book, *Eagle and Sword*. But Kohn acknowledges that at the core his case is "circumstantial" (see "Newburgh Conspiracy," p. 193, n. 19; p. 203, n. 51). As regards Robert Morris, Kohn asserts that "The financier . . . cynically encouraged their hope for a coup," then adds in a footnote, "This is speculation" (p. 200, n. 42). For further comment on Kohn, see the notes in *PRM* VII:471. The thirdhand reference to Morris is a statement William Duer made to Rufus King in 1788. Several of the basic facts in that account, including Duer's presence in the army camp, are demonstrably false. The statement is in King, *Rufus King*, I:621.

342 *"the Financier is suspected"*: GW to Alexander Hamilton, 4/4/83, in Fitzpatrick, ed., *Writings of Washington*, XXVI:291.

342 *It was Gouverneur:* GW to Alexander Hamilton, 4/16/83, in ibid., p. 304.

342 *"Civil commotions"*: GW to Alexander Hamilton, 3/4/83, in ibid., p. 277.

343 *"your ideas"*: Henry Knox to Gouverneur Morris, 2/21/83, in *PRM* VII:448.

343 *"can only exist in one point"*: Henry Knox to Alexander McDougall, 2/21/83, in Kohn, "Newburgh Conspiracy," p. 203.

343 *"great joy"*: James Madison Notes of Debates, 2/13/82, in *JCC* XXV:898.

344 *"informed the company"*: Ibid., p. 906.

344 *"Without dissent or observation"*: James Madison quoted in headnote, *PRM* VII:463.

345 *"The speculations are various"*: Edmund Randolph to James Madison, 3/15/83, in Kaminski, ed., *Founders on the Founders*, p. 436.

345 *"Your office is neither"*: John Jay to RM, 7/20/83, in ibid., p. 439.

346 *"lengthy & warm debates"*: This quote and those that follow are from James Madison's notes, in headnote, ibid., p. 464.

346 *the first proposal for wholesale federal assumption:* Ver Steeg comments on this report in *Robert Morris*, p. 175. The report can be found in *JCC* XXIV:173.

346 "Justice requires": RM to the President of Congress, 3/8/83, in *PRM* VII:525.

347 *"timid wretch"*: John Armstrong, Jr., to Horatio Gates, 4/29/83, in Burnett, ed., *Letters of Members*, VII:155, n. 3.

348 *"We were in a state"*: GW to Alexander Hamilton, 3/12/83, in Styrett, ed., *Papers of Alexander Hamilton*, III:286.

348 *"suffering courage"*: The "Newburgh Address" is printed in *JCC* XXIV:295.

348 *Ides of March:* The portentous date is noted in Flexner, *Perils of Peace*, p. 269.

348 *"exquisitely critical"*: William Duer, in King, *Rufus King*, I:622.

348 *"anonymous production"*: This sketch of Washington's speech at Newburgh is drawn from Kohn, "Newburgh Conspiracy," pp. 209–10; Flexner, *Perils of Peace*, pp. 269–71; and the text of the speech, in *JCC* XXIV:306–10.

349 *"There is something"*: GW to Alexander Hamilton, 4/4/83, in Stylett, ed., *Papers of Alexander Hamilton*, III:291.

349 *"There are two classes"*: *LDC*: Alexander Hamilton to GW, 4/8/83.

351 *"By some designing"*: RM to GW, 5/29/83, in *PRM* VIII:130.

351 *The name Lee chose:* Lee's authorship of the "Lucius" letters was never confirmed, and the printer of the *Freeman's Journal*, where they were published, denied that Lee wrote them. But the style and substance are distinctly his, and many of his contemporaries held Lee to be the author. Even if he did not write them, he certainly approved of them, sending copies to several correspondents. One Lee biographer credits Lee with "Lucius;" a second makes no reference to the letters. See the note in *PRM* VII:502, 506.

352 *"If what you say"*: "Lucius," 3/5/83, in ibid., p. 504.

352 *" 'I Have done'"*: "Lucius," 3/12/83, in ibid., p. 559.

352 *"Writers for a News Paper"*: RM to the President of Congress, 3/17/83, in ibid., p. 595.

352 *"Will you condescend"*: "Lucius," 4/9/83, in ibid., p. 685.

353 *"What a pity"*: "Lucius," 4/9/83, in ibid., p. 689.

353 *"I confess myself"*: "Lucius," 4/23/83, in ibid., p. 744.

354 *a "virulent attack"*: RM Diary, 3/12/83, in ibid, p. 557.

355 *"There are certainly not merchants"*: Hezekiah Wetmore to John Pierce, 2/16/83, in headnote, ibid., p. 332.

355 *"a Gentleman of amiable manners"*: GW to RM, 3/12/83, in ibid., p. 562.

355 *"To be disbanded at last"*: GW to Theodoric Bland, 4/4/83, in Fitzpatrick, ed., *Writings of Washington*, XXVI:285.

356 *"but little Hope"*: RM to a Committee of Congress, 4/14/83, in *PRM* VII:701.

356 *"I wish for Nothing"*: RM Diary, 5/1/83, in ibid., p. 766.

356 *a visit by Daniel Parker:* RM Diary, 5/1/83, in ibid., p. 766.

356 *"as fast as possible"*: RM Diary, 5/3/83, in ibid., p. 789.

15. FINAL SETTLEMENTS

PAGE

358 *hostilities continued through April:* For the order of Congress to cease hostilities, see *PRM* VII:635, n. 1.

358 *"We have many reports"*: RM to Horatio Gates, 2/25/83, in ibid., p. 459.

358 *"returned to Morris' "*: Platt, "Jeremiah Wadsworth," p. 28.

358 *"We are now in the ecstasy"*: RM to unknown, 4/10/83, in *PRM* VII:693.

359 *"Acts of excess"*: Quote is from GW to the President of Congress, 4/18/83, in Fitzpatrick, ed., *Writings of Washington*, XXVI:330.

359 *a field officer read:* For Washington's handling of the news of peace, see Fleming, *Perils of Peace*, pp. 281–82.

360 *"They are more quiet"*: Jedediah Huntington to GW, 5/16/83, in GW Papers, Library of Congress, cited in *PRM* VIII:53, n. 18. For notes on the situation at camp, see ibid., pp. 47–49.

360 *"Pray do not delay"*: GW to RM, 6/3/83, in ibid., p. 158.

360 *"I am to sign them":* RM to GW, 6/5/83, in ibid., p. 172.

360 *"starved, ragged and meager":* Corporal Joseph Plumb Martin, in Fleming, *Perils of Peace*, p. 288.

360 *"without a shilling":* Pvt. Bernardus Swarthout, in *PRM* VII:53, n. 20.

361 *Events moved rapidly:* There are many accounts of the clash at Philadelphia that led to the removal of Congress. I relied primarily on two excellent articles: Kenneth Bowling, "New Light on the Philadelphia Mutiny of 1783," and Mary Gallagher, "Reinterpreting the 'Very Trifling Mutiny' at Philadelphia in June 1783." I also drew quotes and context from Fleming, *Perils of Peace*; Burnett, *Continental Congress*; Chernow, *Alexander Hamilton*; and the notes and diary entries in *PRM* VIII.

364 *Morris secretly funded a broker:* RM Diary, 4/15/83, in *PRM* VII:705.

365 *in league with the army contractors:* John Chaloner to Jeremiah Wadsworth, 6/22/83, quoted in the headnote, *PRM* VIII:225.

365 *"Mr. R. Morris has lately":* For the report and for the Rush letter, see ibid., p. 122, n. 2.

365 *"a Slanderous Report":* RM to the Governors of the States, 7/28/83, in ibid., p. 349.

366 *"I conceive great hopes":* The quotes can be found in ibid., p. 663.

366 *"The department of finance":* Summer, *Financier,* II:110.

366 *"This recommendation":* Charles Thomson to Hannah Thomson, 9/16/83, in Sheridan and Murrin, eds., *Congress at Princeton*, p. 54.

367 *"Things seem to be":* LDC: Stephen Higginson to Nathaniel Gorham, 8/5/83.

367 *"and spent the afternoon":* RM Diary, 7/4/83, in *PRM* VIII:244.

367 *"the Superintendent of Finance":* RM to Arthur Lee, 10/11/83, in ibid., p. 614; see also Ferguson, *Power of the Purse*, p. 172.

367 *"the frequent applications":* RM to the President of Congress, 9/13/83, in *PRM* VIII:511.

367 *"The superintendent has answered":* LDC: Arthur Lee to James Warren, 9/17/83.

368 *The agreement was signed:* For the terms, see Memorandum of Agreement, 3/20/83, in *PRM* VII:616.

369 *"But the real truth":* John Vaughan to RM, 6/2/83, in *PRM* VIII:145.

369 *"A very considerable treasure":* RM to Benjamin Vaughan, 11/27/83; Benjamin Vaughan to John Vaughan, both in ibid., p. 787.

370 *"Holker is full of schemes":* RM to Matthew Ridley, 10/6/82, in *PRM* VI:511.

370 *"Ye beneficent!":* John Ledyard to Isaac Ledyard, 7/83, in *PRM* VIII:865.

370 *The partners he found:* For planning stages of the China venture, see Appendix I in ibid., pp. 857–82; see also Smith, *Empress of China*, passim.

371 *Morris outlined a new program:* RM to the President of Congress, 7/30/82, in *PRM* VI:94.

372 *"Until revenues can":* RM to the President of Congress, 7/10/83, in *PRM* VIII:265.

372 *"She will sell":* RM to Thomas Russell, 8/12/83 and 8/19/83, in ibid., pp. 425, 442.

372 *"would doubtless be converted":* RM to Thomas Read, 8/19/83, in ibid., p. 442.

372 "very small": Daniel Parker to John Holker, 9/16/83, in ibid., p. 326, n. 5.

373 *"Your purchase has"*: RM to Thomas Russell, 10/9/83, in ibid., p. 596.

373 *"I find that"*: Stephen Higginson to Arthur Lee, 10/83, in Jameson, "Letters of Higginson," p. 711.

373 *"I am sending"*: RM to Jay, 11/27/83, in *PRM* VIII:785.

375 *"establish American credit"*: RM to Willinks, 5/8/83, in ibid., p. 17.

375 *"there is a Basis"*: RM to Willinks, 7/25/83, in ibid., p. 339.

375 *"Being in great distress"*: RM Diary, 7/30/83, in ibid., p. 358.

375 *Morris decided to forge ahead:* For the run-up to this decision, see headnote in ibid., p. 387.

375 *"one more rascally attempt"*: LDC: Thomas Fitzsimmons to Richard Peters, 11/6/83.

375 *Morris managed to turn:* RM Diary, 11/3/83, in *PRM* VIII:700.

376 *cargoes of tobacco to Europe:* For RM's tobacco shipments in 1782 and 1783, see Davis, "William Constable," pp. 45, 49, 50.

376 *"catastrophe to American credit"*: *PRM* VIII:391.

376 *"Money in general extremely scarce"*: BF to RM, 12/24/83, in ibid., p. 838.

377 *"With a great deal"*: John Adams to Congress, 3/4/84, in Wharton, ed., *Revolutionary Diplomatic Correspondence*, VI:785.

377 *Adams later boasted:* John Adams to Arthur Lee, 1/31/85, in Summer, *Financier*, II:116.

377 *"I wish I were"*: John Adams to RM, 5/21/83, in *PRM* VIII:108.

377 *"Creditors at home"*: John Adams to RM, 7/11/83, in ibid., p. 276.

378 *"All Property"*: BF to RM, 12/25/83, in ibid., p. 838.

379 *the "phantom" committee:* For notes on the inactivity at Congress, see headnote to Appendix I in *PRM* IX:583.

379 *"The master should know"*: From the "Statement of Accounts," printed as Appendix III in ibid., p. 691.

379 *close his accounts with a balance:* For the final tally, see Ferguson, *Power of the Purse*, p. 139, and the statement of Joseph Nourse, 3/19/1790, printed in *PRM* IX:928.

380 *"he and his immoral Assistant"*: *PRM* IX:585.

380 *"I will tell you"*: LDC: Samuel Osgood to Stephen Higginson, 2/2/84.

380 *"with five million dollars"*: Madison quoted by John Constable; the quote is in Ferguson, *Power of the Purse*, p. 139.

381 *"No treason has operated"*: Preamble to the "Statement of Accounts," in *PRM* IX, Appendix III:688; the quotes are from pp. 697–98.

16. THE GREAT BANK DEBATE

PAGE

385 *the Sons of Saint Tammany:* For the Sons of Saint Tammany, see Cabeen, "The Society of the Sons of St. Tammany"; for the march to Morris's house, see ibid., p. 222, and Jackson, "Washington in Philadelphia," p. 138.

386 *"young American adventurers"*: Woodhouse, "Voyage of the Empress of China," p. 24.

387 *an estimate, which found Holker owing:* For Holker's response to the comptroller's report, see *PRM* IX:11, n. 2.

387 *they severed all joint concerns:* For the fallout of RM and Holker, see John Holker to RM, 1/4/83, and notes, in *PRM* VII:272, and RM to John Rucker, 6/18/74, and notes, in *PRM* IX:407. For the breakup of their enterprises, see RM to John Holker, 3/25/84, in ibid., p. 205.

389 *he was a surprising character:* For background on Constable, see Murdoch, "Benedict Arnold and the Charming Nancy," passim; see also Davis, *William Constable*, quote on p. 10.

389 *He had come to America:* For background on Rucker, see RM to John Rucker, 6/18/84, in *PRM* IX:418, n. 11.

389 *"everything seems at a Stand":* For notes on the postwar recession, see Platt, "Jeremiah Wadsworth," pp. 61–67; the Colt quote is at p. 67. The RM quote is from RM to Nathanael Greene, 6/28/85, in Queens.

390 *Morris remained a principal:* For notes on Morris and the China trade, see Smith, "The Empress of Chine"; Gallagher, "Charting a New Course for the China Trade"; Woodhouse, "Voyage of the Empress of China"; and Appendix I of *PRM* VIII. For Parker's career in Europe, see Ferguson, *Power of the Purse*, p. 260.

391 *"This business I am told":* Barbara Vaughan to Peter Ridley, 11/3/84, in Ridley Papers, MA Hist. Soc.

391 *"Mr. Pettit":* Rebecca Vaughan to Kitty Livingston, 4/9/85, in ibid.

391 *The case dragged on:* For the Morris-Holker dispute, see the headnote for RM to Arbitrators, 11/4/84, in Appendix I, *PRM* IX:597; see also Brunhouse, *Counter-Revolution*, p. 167; and Kline, *Gouverneur Morris* pp. 299–300.

392 *Nicholson disputed Morris's application:* For John Nicholson's case against Morris, see the headnote for RM to John Dickinson, 11/9/82, in *PRM* VII:29; see also Brunhouse, *Counter-Revolution*, p. 167.

392 *"I have been prevented":* RM to Tilghman, 6/27/85, in RM Papers, NYPL.

393 *The sponsors were a mix:* For notes on the sponsors of the new bank, see Gouverneur Morris to Alexander Hamilton, 1/27/84, in *PRM* IX:69; and John Chaloner to Jeremiah Wadsworth, 2/14/84, in Platt, *Jeremiah Wadsworth*, p. 140.

393 *"the destruction of the Bank":* Carey, *Bank Debates*, p. 107.

393 *a hearing was set:* The challenge of the new bank and the debate over the charter are detailed in Rappaport, *Hostility to Banks*, pp. 50–68.

394 *he recognized that:* On Morris as a factor, see ibid., p. 91, and Brunhouse, *Counter-Revolution*, p. 151. For Morris's mind-set, see Ferguson, *Power of the Purse*, p. 174.

394 *"all power may be centered":* Rappaport, *Hostility to Banks*, p. 60.

394 *Thomas Willing reported:* For Willing's appearance at the Assembly, see ibid., p. 71.

395 *"The accumulation":* Assembly committee report, from ibid., p. 97.

396 *"would hurt our merchants:"* Ibid., p. 99.

396 *"Our Assembly":* Thomas Willing to William Bingham, 8/30/85, in Balch, ed., *Willing Letters*, p. 112.

396 *James Wilson spoke:* The Wilson-Sergeant debate is reprised in Rappaport, *Hostility to Banks* pp. 102–18.

398 *Deposits shrank:* Lewis, *Bank of North America,* p. 14.

398 *the urban traders and artisans:* For the sentiment of the city artisans, see the editor's headnote in Foner, ed., *Writings of Thomas Paine,* II:368.

398 *tracts defending the bank:* For samples of the articles supporting the bank, see Wilson, "Bank of North America," pp. 8–9, p. 24.

398 *a bid for president:* On RM's possible candidacy for president, see Brunhouse, *Counter-Revolution,* p. 177.

398 *To both he gave his assent:* Franklin recounts his dealings with both parties in Brands, *The First American,* p. 655.

399 *"determined to take":* Jeremiah Wadsworth to Alexander Hamilton, 11/11/85, in Syrett, ed., *Papers of Alexander Hamilton,* III:633.

399 *"To leave so considerable":* Alexander Hamilton to Jeremiah Wadsworth, 10/29/85, in ibid., p. 625.

400 *conferences with Robert Morris:* The conferences with Wadsworth and RM are recounted in Rappaport, *Hostility to Banks,* pp. 150–51. The quote is from Wadsworth to Hamilton, 1/9/86, in Syrett, ed., *Papers of Alexander Hamilton,* III:645.

400 *one hundred thousand dollars in debts:* For Wilson's debts, see Rappaport, *Hostility to Banks,* pp. 62, 151.

400 *He won an explicit resolution:* For the results of the meeting, see Wadsworth to Hamilton, 1/9/86, in Syrett, ed., *Papers of Alexander Hamilton,* III:645; and Rappaport, *Hostility to Banks,* p. 152.

401 *"It must, therefore":* Pelatiah Webster, "An Essay on Credit: In Which the Doctrine of Banks Is Considered, and Some Remarks on the Present State of the Bank of North America," 2/10/86.

402 *"I feel myself":* Thomas Paine, "Dissertations on Government; The Affairs of the Bank; and Paper Money," 2/18/86, in Foner, ed., *Writings of Thomas Paine,* II:367.

403 *"In the winter of 1778":* Thomas Paine, "To the Printers," 4/7/86, in ibid., p. 419.

403 *"exceeds its powers":* The committee report is reproduced in Carey, *Bank Debates,* pp. 14–16.

404 *"No subject of debate":* Thomas Paine, "To the Printers," 4/4/86, in Foner, ed., *Writings of Thomas Paine,* p. 417.

405 *"I rejoice that":* This and all subsequent quotes from Morris are presented in Carey, *Bank Debates.* This was a landmark piece of journalism, the first verbatim transcript of an extended legislative debate ever printed in America.

405 *"I am told":* The quote is from William Pierce, Georgia delegate to the Constitutional Convention, in Farrand, ed., *Records of the Federal Convention,* III:91.

409 *"the great change in sentiments":* Thomas Paine, "To the Printers," 4/3/86, in Foner, ed., *Writings of Thomas Paine,* II:417.

409 *Franklin weighed in as well:* For Franklin's support of the bank, see Brands, *The First American,* p. 663.

409 *"An important revolution":* Benjamin Rush to Richard Price, 10/27/86, in Kaminski, ed., *Founders on the Founders,* p. 441.

410 *"The people are fools"*: Brackenridge in Newlin, *Hugh Henry Brackenridge*, p. 78.

410 *"sold the good will"*: "A Farmer," in ibid., p. 79.

411 *There was a paradox:* George Rappaport remarks on this paradox in *Hostility to Banks*, p. 222.

17. THE CONSTITUTION

PAGE

412 *"brilliant beyond anything"*: Wharton, *Through Colonial Doorways*, p. 228.

412 *furnishings that marked their wealth:* Robert and Mary Morris Household Inventory, 1798, Thomas Fitzsimmons Papers, McAllister Collection, Library Company of Philadelphia.

413 *the space and the setting:* For notes on the Morris house, see Wagner, *Robert Morris*, p. 109; see also Lawler, "The President's House in Philadelphia."

413 *"profuse, incessant, and elegant"*: The quotes are from Breck, in Scudder, ed., *Recollections of Samuel Breck*, p. 203; for Mary Morris, see Griswold, *Republican Court*.

413 *then became his sponsor:* For the sponsorship of Pine, see Oberholtzer, *Robert Morris*, pp. 285–86. For RM's recommendation to Washington, see Jackson and Twohig, eds., *Diaries of George Washington*, IV:130.

413 *"to the great astonishment"*: For RM balloon experiment, see *PRM* IX; quote is from Francis Hopkinson to BF, 5/24/84, in BF Papers, APS.

413 *a new club:* For notes on the Society for Political Inquiries, see Vinson, "Society for Political Inquiries."

414 *"My avocations thru life"*: RM to Francis Hutchinson, 8/2/86, in Queens.

414 *"and every science"*: RM to Matthew Ridley, 10/14/81, in Mintz, "Robert Morris and John Jay on Education," p. 344.

414 *"a charming creature"*: RM to Kitty Livingston, 10/17/80, in Matthew Ridley Papers, MA Hist. Soc.

414 *"It is a very dangerous lesson"*: RM to Nicholas Jean Hugon de Basseville, 7/29/86, in Huntington.

415 *"My dearest"*: RM to Mary Morris, 7/12/89, in ibid.

415 *"our existence on this earth"*: RM to Mary Morris, 1/9/88, in ibid.

415 *"celebrated" stock of pigs:* For RM's "celebrated" pigs, see Platt, *Jeremiah Wadsworth*, p. 75.

415 *a second rural estate:* For the consideration of the Falls of the Delaware as the national capital, see Bowling, *The Creation of Washington, D.C.*, pp. 49, 65.

415 *designation of the site:* For consideration of the Falls of the Delaware as the national capital, see ibid.

415 *He called the place Morrisville:* RM's Morrisville estate is described in Chernow, "Robert Morris: Land Speculator," pp. 98–100; in Oberholtzer, *Robert Morris*, pp. 295–96; and in Sumner, *Financier*, II:175–76.

415 *The French tobacco contract:* For notes on the contract with the Farmers General, see the fascinating and lucid account of Price in *France and the Chesapeake*,

II:728–87. See also the headnote to the RM contract with Alexander & Williams in *PRM* IX:150.

417 *"It will be highly improper"*: Committee of Congress, 11/1/83, in *PRM* VIII: 520, n. 5.

422 *"Constable will draw"*: Gouverneur Morris to John Rucker, 2/6/86, in William Constable Papers, NYPL.

423 *"nothing less than"*: Lafayette to GW, 2/86, in Price, *France and the Chesapeake*, II:763.

423 *"I am unwilling"*: For the Virginia legislation, and RM's letter to Tench Tilghman, see Sumner, *Financier*, II:159–60.

423 *"Upon reflection"*: Price, *France and the Chesapeake*, II:771.

424 *"To the Farmers General?"*: RM to Tench Tilghman, 4/20/84, in *PRM* IX:275.

424 *"the most serious economic setback"*: Morris, *Forging the Union*, pp. 130–61. The nature and depth of economic problems after the Revolution have been the subject of continuing debate among historians, a curious controversy kept alive by ideological allegiances going back to the founding era. The depression was cited early and forcibly as an indictment of the Continental Congress by historian John Fiske, who dubbed the postwar years "The Critical Period." Fiske was disputed by later critics of the Constitution, especially Merrill Jensen in *The New Nation*, who decided that the years after the war were in fact a time of "extraordinary economic growth." Writing in 1987, Richard B. Morris in *Forging of the Union* cited "an overwhelming body of evidence" to restore Fiske's original thesis. See also Doerflinger, *Vigorous Spirit of Enterprise*, pp. 243–47, 261–73; Banning, "Political Economy," pp. 23–29; and Buel, *In Irons*, p. 253.

425 *"parade of bankruptcies"*: Doerflinger, *Vigorous Spirit of Enterprise*, p. 247.

425 *a duty on any imports*: For the New York domestic impost, see Sumner, *Financier*, II:196.

425 *"He has no talents"*: *PRM* IX:592. The second quote is from James Monroe to Thomas Jefferson, 4/12/85, in ibid.

425 *"Embarrassed situation of Finances"*: Quote is from Samuel Osgood and Walter Livingston to Governor Edmund Randolph, 12/26/87, in Potts, *Arthur Lee*, p. 273.

425 *farmed out to private parties*: For the foreign exchange contracts, see Advertisement for Contracts in *PRM* IX:95; see also Tailby, "Foreign Interest Remittances."

426 *"We have independence without"*: Arthur Lee to RHL, 4/19/86, in Potts, *Arthur Lee*, p. 273.

426 *"It is a melancholy truth"*: Tench Tilghman to Matthew Tilghman, 2/5/86, in Shreve, *Tench Tilghman*, p. 192.

427 *By 1787, Pennsylvania had retired*: For Pennsylvania assumption of federal debt, see Ferguson, "State Assumption of Federal Debt," pp. 416–17; and Arbuckle, *John Nicholson*, pp. 8–9.

427 *that influence was working against him*: For the politics of Pennsylvania assumption, see Brunhouse, *Counter-Revolution*, pp. 170–71.

427 *A similar measure in New Jersey*: For New York and New Jersey, see Ferguson, "State Assumption of Federal Debt," pp. 417–18.

427 *"It so happens"*: Thomas Paine, "Letter to George Washington," 7/30/96, in Foner, ed., *Writings of Thomas Paine*, II:691.

427 *all too apparent*: There are, of course, many other claimants to the paternity of the Constitution—too many to sort out here.

428 *"How ridiculous"*: Jacob Broome to Tench Coxe, 9/4/86, in Morris, *Forging of the Union*, p. 254.

428 *"important defects"*: The "Address of the Annapolis Convention," in ibid., pp. 256–57.

429 *"the only thing"*: Pierce Butler to Elbridge Gerry, 3/3/88, in ibid., p. 265.

430 *"the man who dares"*: Miller, *Samuel Adams*, p. 374.

430 *"disposition to repose"*: RHL to Edmund Randolph, 3/26/87, in McGauhy, *Richard Henry Lee*, p. 189.

430 *"smelt a rat"*: Bowen, *Miracle at Philadelphia*, p. 18.

431 *One undated anecdote*: The story of Gouverneur's bet with Hamilton is told in Farrand, ed., *Records of the Federal Convention*, III:85.

431 *"daily exercise"*: For Franklin's reference to his "daily exercise," see McMaster, "Where the Constitutional Convention Met."

433 *Gouverneur Morris headed him off*: For Gouverneur Morris's intervention and the larger question of banks in the Constitution, see Hammond, *Banks and Politics*, pp. 104–5.

433 *"General Washington is now"*: RM to his sons, 6/25/87, in Hart, "Mary White," p. 170.

434 *"one of the best cardplayers"*: Unsigned article, *American Heritage Magazine* 45, no. 5.

434 *making the rounds*: For Washington's social schedule, see diary entries printed in Baker, "Washington After the Revolution."

434 *"God bless you": LDC*: RM to Jay, 2/4/77. For Washington's correspondence, see Boller, *Washington and Religion*, pp. 76–81.

434 *"I do not believe"*: Boller, *Washington and Religion*, p. 89; for his declining communion, see p. 33.

434 *"the deplorable state of things"*: The episode is recounted by the early historian Jared Sparks in Farrand, ed., *Records of the Federal Convention*, III:497. James Madison, in ibid., p. 498, disputed Gouverneur's influence as a peacemaker, but acknowledged "the brilliancy of his genius." The first and last quotes are from Sparks; the second is from Madison.

435 *getting out of town*: For notes on this sojourn in the country see Jackson and Twohig, eds., *Diaries of George Washington*, IV:180–83.

436 *"When we had just got"*: On Rucker's failure of nerve, see Kline, *Gouverneur Morris*, pp. 312–13, and Tailby, "Chapers from the Busines Career of William Constable," pp. 194–203. I am also indebted to Elizabeth Nuxoll for her personal observations on Constable Rucker & Co. For the quote, see William Constable to John Porteous, in Tailby, "Foreign Interest Remittances," p. 170.

437 *"What a foolish"*: RM to William Constable, in ibid.

437 *"a little Mal apropos"*: Baker, "Washington After the Revolution," p. 182.

437 *"This paper has been":* RM to a Friend, 1/88, in Farrand, ed., *Records of the Federal Convention*, III:242.

18. THE FIRST FEDERAL CONGRESS

PAGE

438 *"the most daring attempt":* The writer is the "Centinel," 9/5/87, in Konkle, *George Bryan*, p. 312; Bryan is quoted in ibid., p. 308.

439 *"none but gentleman mobs":* For the Assembly deliberations on the Constitution, see Brunhouse, *Counter-Revolution*, pp. 200–201. For John Barry, see Bouton, *Taming Democracy*, p. 180. For the Bryan quote, see Konkle, *George Bryan*, p. 323. For a detailed account of the legislative proceedings, see Alberts, "Business of the Highest Magnitude," passim.

439 *fewer seats changing hands:* For electoral stability, see McMaster and Stone, eds., *Pennsylvania and the Federal Constitution*, p. 173.

440 *"You frequently are":* RM to Mary Morris, 11/15/87, in HL.

441 *next stop at Mount Vernon:* For the visit to Mount Vernon, see Fitzpatrick, ed., *Writings of Washington*, XIV:95.

441 *"We live well":* RM to Mary Morris, 12/2/87, in HL.

441 *"Poor Braxton":* RM to Gouverneur Morris, 4/13/85, in Queens.

441 *"settle accounts":* Gouverneur Morris to RM, 3/11/85, in Kline, *Gouverneur Morris*, p. 299.

442 *"I have at last":* RM to Matthew Ridley, 4/20/88, in Queens.

442 *Morris was awarded a judgment:* For the settlement, see Sumner, *Financier*, II:168.

442 *"I am exceedingly hurt":* RM to Mary Morris, 11/28/87, in HL.

443 *"As you know that":* Mary Morris to RM, 12/12/87, in ibid.

443 *"the fatal event":* Mary Morris to RM, 1/13/88, in ibid.

443 *"O my dearest":* Mary Morris to RM, 5/4/88, in ibid.

443 *"to make a great reform":* For the quotes, see RM to Mary Morris, 4/26/88, in ibid.

444 *"I cannot bear the idea":* RM to Mary Morris, 4/20/88, in ibid.

444 *"Mrs. White and you":* RM to Mary Morris, 4/23/88, in ibid.

444 *"although he purchased":* RM to John Marshall, 6/16/88, in Johnson, ed., *Papers of John Marshall*, V:102.

444 *This new and unexpected imbroglio:* For notes on the case against William Alexander, see ibid., p. 93.

445 *"I am on a sure footing":* For the first quote, RM to Samuel Smith; for the second, RM to Robert Gilmor & Co., 8/27/86, in Price, *France and the Chesapeake*, II:772–73.

445 *"You will see":* RM to Cary & Tilghman, 2/21/88, in Queens.

446 *"As it is probable":* RM to Samuel and John Smith, 8/22/86, in ibid.

446 *"I hope to be done":* RM to Alexander Donald, 3/29/89, in HL.

446 *"James [Wilson] the Caledonian":* These quotes from the "Centinel" appear in Konkle, *George Bryan*, pp. 317–18.

447 *"screen the numerous"*: Quotes are from *The Centinel*, No. 16, 2/26/88, in McMaster and Stone, eds., *Pennsylvania and the Federal Constitution*, p. 657.

447 *"afforded unrestrained scope"*: *The Centinel*, No. 17, 3/24/88, in ibid., p. 660.

447 *"bug writers"*: BF to RM, 7/26/81, in *PRM* I:391.

447 *"If I was to fight"*: RM to Mary Morris, 4/4/88, in Huntington.

447 *"considerable sums of money"*: RM "To the Printer," 3/21/88, in *PRM* IX:630.

448 *"For the honor"*: Arthur Lee Papers, VIII:164–87 (no date), in Queens.

448 *the whole business was left unresolved*: For the efforts to clear Morris's Secret Committee accounts, see Ferguson, *Power of the Purse*, pp. 198–202; when Lee reviewed the accounts, Ferguson remarks, "They baffled him."

448 *"for with much truth"*: GW to Mary Morris, 5/1/88, in Fitzpatrick, ed., *Writings of Washington*, XXIX:487.

449 *The interlude lasted*: For details of the family visit to Mount Vernon see Jackson and Twohig, eds., *Diaries of George Washington*, V:360.

450 *"rigid republican"*: See Maclay, ed., *Journal of William Maclay* (herein after Maclay, *Journal*), p. 177.

450 *"remains to be accounted for"*: *JCC* XXXIV:563.

450 *"the subject of this enquiry"*: Ibid., p. 564.

451 *"involved in impenetrable"*: Commissioner of Accounts Jonathan Burrell, in Ver Steeg, *Robert Morris*, p. 121.

451 *"What conclusion must"*: *The Centinel*, No. 23, 11/20/88, in DenBoer, ed., *First Federal Elections*, IV:352.

451 *"everything in my power"*: "Robert Morris to the Printer," 11/21/88, in ibid., p. 354.

452 *Constable was sure*: William Constable to James Phyn, 1/1/89, in Constable Papers, NYPL.

452 *He would negotiate extensions*: For the final stages of the tobacco contract and the dealings with Le Couteulx, see Price, *France and the Chesapeake*, II:784–85.

452 *bound for Paris*: Gouverneur Morris biographers Kline (pp. 336–37) and Adams (p. 167) say that Gouverneur was sent to hawk Robert's extensive holdings in western lands. But Morris's great land purchases came later; at this point the only important land project was the dormant scheme with Vaughan.

453 *"I never heard"*: Maclay, *Journal*, p. 266.

453 *"the common opinions"*: Ibid., p. 135.

453 *"gave the air"*: RM to Mary Morris, 3/9/89, in Huntington.

454 *to deny Charles Thomson*: For Thomson's political demise, see Bowling, "Good-by 'Charle,' " passim.

454 *Washington felt constrained*: For Washington refusing RM's offer, see Bickford and Bowling, *Birth of the Nation*, p. 24.

455 *"He knows everything"*: Custis, *Recollections*, p. 349.

455 *sometimes comical debate*: Maclay recounts the extended debate over titles in his *Journal*, pp. 26–29, 34–39.

455 *Morris joined in*: Ibid., p. 35.

456 *"the majesty of the people"*: Ibid., p. 38.

456   *"but Mrs. Washington ate"*: Ibid., p. 74.

456   *"Goddess whom I must adore"*: For the first quote, see RM to Mary Morris, 9/6/89; for the second, see RM to Mary Morris, 7/12/89, both in HL.

457   *"Your prudence will"*: RM to Mary Morris, 7/12/89, in ibid.

457   *"for I must avoid"*: RM to Mary Morris, 7/17/89, in ibid.

457   *Morris was . . . a force:* For Morris in the Senate, see the notes introducing *PRM* IX:xxxix; see also the biographical note in De Pauw, ed., *Documentary History of the First Federal Congress*, XIV:766.

457   *"attend with the utmost"*: Maclay, *Journal*, p. 65.

457   *"When I was in"*: RM to von Hoogendorp, 1784, in Nuxoll, "The Financier as Senator," p. 9.

458   *"When this attack"*: Maclay, *Journal*, p. 66.

459   *a rare personal visit:* Ibid., pp. 128–31.

460   *"Poor Madison got so"*: RM to Francis Hopkinson, 8/15/89, in HL.

461   *"the most delicate"*: Bowling, *Creation of Washington, D.C.*, p. 197.

461   *"burst and vanish"*: Ellis, *Founding Brothers*, p. 50.

461   *"an express national Compact"*: For the quotes, see RM to the President of Congress, 3/8/83, in *PRM* VII:525.

19. THE COMPROMISE OF 1790

PAGE

463   *"tend to concentrate power"*: David Howell, in Bowling, *Creation of Washington, D.C.*, p. 53.

463   *Franklin himself laid the groundwork:* For Franklin's motion, see McMaster & Stone, eds., *Pennsylvania and the Federal Constitution*, p. 61.

463   *"otherwise it will prove"*: Bowling, *Creation of Washington, D.C.*, p. 127.

464   *pressing Hamilton and John Jay:* For RM's connection to Hamilton and Jay, see Maclay, *Journal*, p. 145.

464   *Scott supported the Susquehanna:* For Scott's motion, see ibid.; for the maneuvers, see Bowling, *Creation of Washington, D.C.*, p. 137.

465   *"here I could give"*: For this round of talks, see Maclay, *Journal*, p. 146.

465   *"I hope you are gratified"*: For RM's visit with Maclay, see ibid., p. 148.

466   *"I had a long talk"*: RM to Mary Morris, 9/9/89, in HL.

466   *"running backward"*: Maclay, *Journal*, p. 162.

467   *John Adams broke the tie:* This round of voting is recounted in ibid., p. 165, and Bowling, *Creation of Washington, D.C.*, p. 157.

467   *"I am exceedingly plagued"*: RM to Mary Morris, 9/25/89, in HL.

467   *the Senate voted to postpone:* There is no record of the vote to postpone. For the decision, see Bowling, *Creation of Washington, D.C.*, p. 159; Maclay, *Journal* p. 169.

467   *"Each visitor on entering"*: Scudder, ed., *Recollections of Samuel Breck*, p. 202.

468   *"blaz'd upon"*: Letter of Molly Tilghman, in Brown, "Mr. and Mrs. William Bingham," p. 294.

468   *"Our Lilliputian"*: Quote is from Baumann, "John Swanwick," p. 141.

468 "*Ripe for a Change*": RM to Richard Peters, 8/9/89, in Brunhouse, *Counter-Revolution*, p. 223.

469 *the Assembly had approved a convention:* For the best account of the convention to revise the state constitution, see Harding, "Party Struggles."

469 *They turned to Robert Morris:* For the overtures to RM on running for governor, see Maclay, *Journal*, p. 188; see also RM to Gouverneur Morris, 10/31/90, in Sparks, *Gouverneur Morris*, III:17.

469 "*very much irritated*": William Grayson to James Madison, 10/7/89, in Styrett, ed., *Papers of Alexander Hamilton*, VII:431.

470 *Morris would not commit:* James Madison to GW, 11/20/89, in ibid., VII:451.

471 "*in the hour of extreme*": For the memorial and notes on the signers, see "Support of Public Credit," in De Pauw and Grant, eds., *Documentary History of the First Federal Congress*, VIII:258.

472 "*cement more closely*": Hamilton's "Report on Public Credit" can be located online at http://memory.loc.gov/cgi-bin/ampage?collId=llac&fileName=002/llac002.db&recNum=382; see also Chernow, *Alexander Hamilton*, pp. 297–300, and Schachner, *Alexander Hamilton*, pp. 242–46. The poem is quoted in Schachner, p. 246.

474 *mending fences back home:* Ferguson comments on Madison's motives in *Power of the Purse*, p. 298.

474 *purchase at a discount the American debt:* For the bid to sell American debt to France, see ibid., p. 266.

475 *he was forced to resign:* For Duer's manipulations, see Chernow, *Alexander Hamilton*, p. 293; and Schachner, *Alexander Hamilton*, p. 258. For more on Duer, see Jones, "William Duer and the Business of Government"; the offer to RM, and his decision to decline, are at p. 409.

475 *revived credit markets:* For the economic impact of the Constitution, see Brown, *Redeeming the Republic*, pp. 234–36.

475 "*I almost begin*": Ferguson, *Power of the Purse*, p. 318.

475 "*laughing heartily*": Maclay, *Journal*, p. 274.

475 "*a violent disposition*": Ibid., p. 275.

475 "*Never had a man*": Ibid., p. 299.

475 "*blazed away*": Ibid., p. 287.

476 "*on purpose to get room*": RM to Mary Morris, 4/25/90, in Huntington.

476 "*universal gloom*": For Washington's illness and public reaction, see Freeman, *George Washington*, VII:259–61.

476 "*the Old Gentleman*": RM to Mary Morris, 4/25/90, in Huntington.

476 "*as if by accident*": RM in Maclay, *Journal*, p. 292.

477 *Hamilton agreed:* Ibid.

477 *Now Thomas Jefferson entered:* For Jefferson's visit, see RM to Mary Morris, 6/19/90, in Huntington; see also Maclay, *Journal*, p. 294.

478 "*with the agency of Robert Morris*": For the dinner meeting, see Jefferson's memoir, titled "Anas," in Lipscomb, ed., *Jefferson Writings*, I:174.

478 "*Morris was often called out*": Maclay, *Journal*, p. 304.

480 "*exposed to the surmises*": RM "Memorial," 2/8/90, in *PRM* IX:633.

481 *Morris's petition had no precedent:* For the lack of precedent, see diGiacomantonio, "Petitioners and Their Grievances," p. 44.

481 *"it appears to the Committee":* Committee statement in *PRM* IX:636, Appendix I. n.5.

482 *"is a good Officer":* RM to Mary Morris, 8/1/90, in Huntington.

483 *"If these lands were":* RM to the President of Congress, 7/29/82, in *PRM* VI:36;
the quotes are from pp. 65–66 and 71.

485 *"It is strange":* Maclay, *Journal*, p. 126.

485 *"the best tract of Country":* RM to Gouverneur Morris, 8/8/90. For notes on RM's
purchase of the Phelps-Gorham tract, see Chernow, "Robert Morris: Land Speculator," pp. 35–49; the letter is quoted on pp. 48–49.

486 *"sacrifice . . . both of interest":* RM to Gouverneur Morris, 10/31/90, in Sparks,
Gouverneur Morris, III:17.

486 *he did not hesitate to make Morris his guest:* For RM's honored place at the president's levees, see Custis, *Recollections*.

487 *Morris stipulated a minimum:* For terms of the Genesee sale, see Chernow,
"Robert Morris: Land Speculator," pp. 50–51.

487 *Morris added another sheaf:* For the Northampton property, see ibid., p. 108.

487 *Benedict Van Pradelles:* For Van Pradelles, see ibid., p. 52; see also Vail, "Lure of
the Land Promoter."

487 *answerable to the government:* For notes on Hamilton's proposal for the bank,
see Hammond, *Banks and Politics*, pp. 114–17.

488 *"as an aristocratic engine":* For Maclay's thoughts on banking see his *Journal*,
p. 355; for RM's considerations, see ibid., p. 370.

488 *demand was overwhelming:* For the feverish sales of bank stock, see Schachner,
Alexander Hamilton, p. 282; for Morris and Fitzsimmons, see Nuxoll, "The Financier as Senator," p. 11.

20. RUIN

PAGE

490 *artisans in town were already occupied:* For the shortage of craftsmen, see Eberlein, "190, High Street," p. 166.

490 *"neat, elegant & convenient":* Riley, "Philadelphia," p. 367, n. 32.

490 *"put on your best":* Ibid., p. 27.

490 *"a frenzy" of parties:* Tobias Lear to David Humphreys, in Decatur, *Private
Affairs*, p. 195, in ibid., p. 18.

490 *more than thirty people:* For a breakdown of Washington's household, see
Eberlein, "190, High Street," p. 167.

491 *"second lady":* Ibid., p. 169.

491 *"expects your company":* Custis, *Recollections*, p. 328.

492 *"engage for all his connections":* Thomas Jefferson, "Anas," in Ford, ed., *Writings
of Thomas Jefferson*, I:254, n. 1.

492 *"a host who are systematically":* Thomas Jefferson to James Madison, 6/9/93, in
ibid., VI:290, cited in Flexner, *George Washington*, III:68.

493 *"notwithstanding any Law"*: Articles of sale in Chernow, "Robert Morris: Land Speculator," p. 54.

495 *"He has made"*: RM to Thomas Morris, 11/29/92, in Huntington. For the larger picture of the New York land deals, see Chernow, "Robert Morris: Land Speculator," pp. 35–88.

496 *"in such a seesaw situation"*: Thomas Levis to John Nicholson, 9/24/90, in Arbuckle, *John Nicholson*, p. 34.

496 *"perfect knowledge"*: Esekiel Forman to John Nicholson, 1/23/87, in ibid., p. 18.

496 *"I cannot write!"*: Samuel Baird to John Nicholson, 10/7/94, in ibid., p. 32.

497 *"the fault perhaps"*: The quote is from Hogan, ed., *Pennsylvania State Trials*, p. 160. While Nicholson was acquitted, his misconduct was amply demonstrated in correspondence that came to light long after. Arbuckle provides a sampling in his curiously sympathetic biography, *John Nicholson*, pp. 21–38, 76–78.

498 *shaking the financial world:* For the British banking crisis of 1793, see Wood, *History of Central Banking*, p. 43.

498 *Morris lost, by his estimate:* The figure is given in Friedenberg, *Life, Liberty and the Pursuit of Land*, p. 335.

500 *"Washington building lots":* For this passage on the founding of Washington, D.C., I have relied on Bordewich, *Washington*; Bowling, *Creation of Washington, D.C.*; Elkins and McKittrick, *The Age of Federalism*; and Arbuckle, *John Nicholson*. The quote is from Arbuckle, p. 115. For an insightful portrait of L'Enfant, see Bowling, *Peter Charles L'Enfant*, passim.

500 *"My dear general":* Custis, *Recollections*, p. 326.

501 *"It is true":* Chernow, "Robert Morris: Land Speculator," pp. 122–24. The quote is on p. 123.

501 *"Why are speculators":* GW to commissioners, 1/7/95, in ibid., p. 148.

502 *"the grandest ever":* Watson, *Annals of Pennsylvania*, I:409.

502 *"I am in want":* RM to Benjamin Harrison, in Oberholtzer, *Robert Morris*, p. 327.

503 *"very injurious effects":* Davis, "William Constable," p. 242.

504 *"a disagreeable spectacle":* GW to RM, 9/14/95, in *Records of the Columbia Historical Society* 17, p. 141.

504 *jailed for debt:* Arbuckle, *Pennsylvania Speculator and Patriot*, p. 127.

504 *"The property we now hold":* RM to Mary Morris, 9/7/96, in HL.

505 *One broker, in 1797, offered to buy:* Arbuckle, *John Nicholson*, p. 191.

505 *"Scenes of trouble":* RM to John Nicholson, 11/29/96, 12/4/96, in HL.

505 *"I want these wines":* Oberholtzer, *Robert Morris*, p. 271.

505 *Morris even continued buying land:* For these transactions, see Chernow, "Robert Morris: Land Speculator," pp. 206–7.

505 *"That family receives me":* James Marshall to Mary Marshall, 7/3/97; 7/5/97, in Johnson, ed., *Papers of John Marshall*, III:94, 102.

506 *"I think I can perceive":* RM to James Marshall, 7/4/96, in HL.

506 *"I am seriously uneasy":* RM to John Nicholson, 12/8/96, in ibid.

507 *"Another inundation":* RM to John Nicholson, 11/4/97, New York Historical Society.

507 *"By Heaven!"*: Oberholtzer, *Robert Morris*, p. 343.

507 *"They would have had me"*: Dunwoody's visit is recounted in ibid., p. 345, and Arbuckle, *John Nicholson*, p. 195. The quote is in Arbuckle.

507 *"My money is gone"*: Ibid., p. 197.

508 *"What an example"*: Harrison Gray Otis to his wife, 2/16/98, in Otis Papers, Massachusetts Historical Society.

508 *"I think he should"*: Elizabeth Hewson to Thomas Hewson, 9/5/97, in Hewson Family Papers, APS.

508 *"What a misfortune"*: Thomas Jefferson to James Madison, 3/12/01, in Ford, ed., *Writings of Thomas Jefferson*, VI:268.

509 *"a purgatory worthy"*: Mann, *Republic of Debtors*, p. 90.

509 *"Having no particular place"*: RM to John Nicholson, in ibid., p. 100.

509 *"the best in this house"*: Ibid.

509 *"Hotel with Gated doors"*: RM to John Nicholson, 5/11/98, in HL.

509 *"His person was neat"*: Chernow, "Robert Morris: Land Speculator," p. 217.

510 *"A man that cannot"*: RM to Thomas Morris, 3/13/98, in HL.

510 *"The punishment of my imprudence"*: RM to Nicholson, 2/8/98, in Arbuckle, *John Nicholson*, p. 198.

510 *"She received me"*: Ibid.

510 *"strongly affected"*: The first Gouverneur Morris quote is from Oberholtzer, *Robert Morris*, p. 352; the second is from Arbuckle, *John Nicholson*, p. 200.

511 *"I feel no kind of apprehension"*: RM to John Nicholson, 10/15/98, in Hart, "Mary White," p. 179.

511 *"bled, blistered, purged, sweated"*: Oberholtzer, *Robert Morris*, p. 270.

512 *Designed to limit fraud:* For the politics of the Bankruptcy Act of 1800, see Coleman, *Debtors and Creditors*, pp. 18–19.

512 *"I embrace the first"*: RM to Thomas Morris, 8/27/01, in Hart, "Mary White," p. 179.

512 *"I have every reason"*: Morris, "Account of Property," in Chernow, "Robert Morris: Land Speculator," p. 221, and Sumner, *Financier*, II:258.

512 *"My business was finished"*: RM to Thomas Morris, 12/5/01, in HL.

514 *"I will not be idle"*: RM to Thomas Morris, 4/2/02, in ibid.

514 *"very polite"*: RM to Thomas Morris, 1/31/02, in ibid.

514 *"lean, low spirited"*: Gouverneur Morris to James Parrish, in Oberholtzer, *Robert Morris*, p. 355.

514 *asked him to serve as president:* RM describes the bank project in a letter to Thomas Morris, 9/22/03, in HL.

514 *"left to me"*: Robert Morris Will, 6/13/1804, on file with the APS.

EPILOGUE

PAGE

518 *"did not dwell with small spirits"*: Oberholtzer, *Robert Morris*, p. 259.

518 *"deep-seated conflict"*: Beard quoted in Hutson, "Country, Court, and Constitution," p. 339.

519 *There was much quibbling:* For the controversy over *We the People*, see Jackson Turner Main, "Charles A. Beard and the Constitution."

519 *"What was once the grandest house":* Hofstadter is quoted in the Wikipedia article on Beard, at http://en.wikipedia.org/wiki/Charles_A._Beard.

520 *"fundamental divisions":* See Jensen, *The Articles of Confederation*, p. 7; "the masses": see p. 16.

521 *"The idea that Robert Morris":* Abernethy, *Western Lands*, pp. 171, 173.

521 *"resembled that of Hamilton's":* Ver Steeg, *Robert Morris*, p. 175.

521 *Ver Steeg was no apologist:* For his specific rebuttal to Abernethy, see ibid., p. 206, notes 39 and 40.

522 *"the inescapable choice":* Ferguson, *Power of the Purse*, pp. 118–19.

522 *"Morris was supremely competent":* Ibid., p. 139.

522 *"grimly determined":* Ibid., p. 152.

522 *"operated through henchmen":* Ibid., p. 174.

523 *"high-handed disposition . . .":* Ibid., p. 176.

523 *"the leader of the first conservative movement":* Ibid., p. 124.

523 *"a national alliance of conservatives":*Ibid., p. 337.

523 *"a break with the agrarian past":*Ibid., p. 121.

524 *That Clinton was a demagogue:* Ibid.

524 *"Morris and his associates:"* Ibid., p. 122.

525 *"competitive forces within society":* The quotes are from Ferguson's review of Jack Rakove's *The Beginnings of National Politics*. The review was published in 1981.

525 *"form a commentary on the ages":* F. W. Walbank, *The Decline of the Roman Empire*, p. 1.

525 *"presiding genius":* Ferguson, *Power of the Purse*, p. 109.

525 *"The myth still persists":* Ibid., p. 76.

526 *"The quality of the product improves":* Carl E. Prince, review of Vol. V of the *The Papers of Robert Morris*, in *PMHB* 105, p. 496.

526 *"In the long run":* Paul H. Smith, review of Vol. I of the *The Papers of Robert Morris*, in *PMHB* 98, p. 400.

527 *"will have a major impact":* Quote is from the jacket blurb offered by Allan Kulikoff, University of Georgia.

527 *"grab power":* Bouton, *Taming Democracy*, p. 70.

527 *"Morris envisioned gentlemen taking control of":* Ibid.

528 *Morris "viewed the common people":*Ibid., p. 72.

528 *"in private moments":* For the quotes, see ibid., p. 81 and note 48.

529 *"used government positions":* Ibid., p. 72.

529 *"Morris hoped to use his government-supplied wealth":* Ibid.

529 *"his past failures to persuade the public":* Ibid., p. 71.

BIBLIOGRAPHY

BOOKS

Abernethy, Thomas Perkins. Western Lands and the American Revolution (New York, 1937).

Adams, William Howard. Gouverneur Morris: An Independent Life (New Haven, 2003).

Alberts, Robert C. The Golden Voyage: The Life and Times of William Bingham, 1752–1804 (Boston, 1969).

Anders, W. G. The Price of Liberty: The Public Debt of the American Revolution (Charlottesville, Virginia, 1983).

Arbuckle, Robert D. Pennsylvania Speculator and Patriot: The Entrepreneurial John Nicholson, 1757–1800 (University Park, PA, 1975).

Augur, Helen. The Secret War of Independence (New York, 1955).

Bell, Whitfield J. Patriot Improvers: Biographical Sketches of Members of the American Philosophical Society, Vol. 2—1768 (Philadelphia, 1999).

Bemis, Samuel Flagg. The Diplomacy of the American Revolution (Bloomington, Indiana, 1935).

Bezanson, Anne. Prices and Inflation During the American Revolution (Philadelphia, 1951).

Bickford, Charlene Bangs, and Kenneth Bowling. Birth of a Nation: The First Federal Congress, 1789–1791 (Lanham, MD, 1989).

Billias, Geo. Athan. Elbridge Gerry: Founding Father and Republican Statesman (New York, 1976).

Boatner, Mark M. Encyclopedia of the American Revolution (New York, 1966).

Bordewich, Fergus M. Washington: The Making of the American Capital (New York, 2008).

Bouton, Terry. Taming Democracy: "The People," the Founders, and the Troubled Ending of the American Revolution (New York, 2007).

Bowen, Catherine Drinker. Miracle at Philadelphia, The Story of the Constitutional Convention, May to September, 1787 (Boston, 1966).

Bowling, Kenneth, The Creation of Washington, D.C.: The Idea and Location of the American Capital (Fairfax, VA, 1991).

————. Peter Charles L'Enfant: Vision, Honor and Male Friendship in the Early American Republic (Washington, D.C., 2002).

Brands, H. W. The First American: The Life and Times of Benjamin Franklin (New York, 2000).

Breen, T. H. Tobacco Culture: The Mentality of the Great Tidewater Planters on the Eve of Revolution (Princeton, 1985).

Bridenbaugh, Carl. Cities in Revolt: Urban Life in America, 1743–1776 (New York, 1955).

Brown, Roger H. Redeeming the Republic: Federalists, Taxation, and the Origins of the Constitution (Baltimore, 1993).

Brunhouse, Robert. The Counter-Revolution in Pennsylvania, 1776–1790 (Harrisburg, 1942).

Bryan, Wilhelmus Bogart. A History of the National Capital from Its Foundation (New York, 1914), Vol. 1.

Buel, Richard. In Irons: Britain's Naval Supremacy and the American Revolutionary Economy (New Haven, 1998).

Burnett, Edward C. The Continental Congress (New York, 1941).

Carp, E. Wayne. To Starve the Army at Pleasure: Continental Army Administration and American Political Culture, 1775–1783 (Chapel Hill, 1984).

Marquis de Chastellux. Travels in North America: In the Years 1780, 1781, and 1782 (London, 1787).

Chernow, Ron. Alexander Hamilton (New York, 2004).

Clary, David. Adopted Son: Washington, LaFayette, and the Friendship That Saved the Revolution (New York, 2007).

Coleman, Peter J. Debtors and Creditors in America: Insolvency, Imprisonment for Debt, and Bankruptcy, 1607–1900 (Madison, 1974).

Conway, Daniel Moncure. The Life of Thomas Paine (New York, 1893).

Cooke, Jacob E. Tench Coxe and the Early Republic (Chapel Hill, 1978).

Corbin, John. Two Frontiers of Freedom (New York, 1940).

Corner, George, ed. The Autobiography of Benjamin Rush (Princeton, 1948).

Cummins, Light Townsend. Spanish Observers and the American Revolution, 1775–1783 (Baton Rouge, 1991).

Custis, G. W. Parke. Recollections and Private Memoirs of Washington (New York, 1860).

Dangerfield, George. Chancellor Robert R. Livingston of New York, 1746–1823 (New York, 1960).

Daughan, George C. If by Sea: The Forging of the American Navy—From the American Revolution to the War of 1812 (New York, 2008).

Day, Sherman. Historical Collections of the State of Pennsylvania (Philadelphia, 1843).

Decatur, Stephen. Private Affairs of George Washington (Boston, 1933).

Doerflinger, Thomas. A Vigorous Spirit of Enterprise: Merchants and Economic Development in Revolutionary Philadelphia (Chapel Hill, 1986).

Dull, Jonathan. A Diplomatic History of the American Revolution (New Haven, 1985).

East, Robert. Business Enterprise in the American Revolutionary Era (New York, 1938).

Eberlein, H. D., and C. V. D. Hubbard. Diary of Independence Hall *(Philadelphia, 1948).*

Eisenhart, Luther, ed. Historic Philadelphia: From the Founding Until the Early Nineteenth Century *(Philadelphia, 1953).*

Elkins, Stanley, and Eric McKitrick. The Age of Federalism *(New York, 1993).*

Ellis, Joseph J. Founding Brothers: The Revolutionary Generation *(New York, 2000).*

Ernst, Joseph Albert. Money and Politics in America, 1755–1775: A Study in the Currency Act of 1764 and the Political Economy of Revolution *(Chapel Hill, 1973).*

E. James Ferguson. The Power of the Purse: A History of American Public Finance, 1776–1790 *(Chapel Hill, 1961).*

Ferris, Robert, and James Charleton. The Signers of the Constitution *(Flagstaff, 1986).*

Fischer, David Hackett. Albion's Seed: Four British Folkways in America *(New York, 1989).*

———. Washington's Crossing *(New York, 2004).*

Fleming, Thomas. Washington's Secret War: The Hidden History of Valley Forge *(New York, 2005).*

———. Liberty! The American Revolution *(New York, 1977).*

———. The Perils of Peace: America's Struggle for Survival After Yorktown *(New York, 2007).*

Flexner, James Thomas. George Washington in the American Revolution, 1775–1783 *(Boston, 1968).*

———. George Washington: Anguish and Farewell, 1793–1799 *(Boston, 1969).*

———. The Traitor and the Spy: Benedict Arnold and John André *(Syracuse, 1991).*

———. Washington: The Indispensable Man *(Boston, 1969).*

Foner, Eric. Tom Paine and Revolutionary America *(New York, 1976).*

Foster, A. Kristen. Moral Visions and Material Ambitions: Philadelphia Struggles to Define the Republic, 1776–1836 *(Lanham, MD, 2004).*

Freeman, Douglas Southall. George Washington: A Biography *(New York, 1952), 7 vols.*

Friedenberg, Daniel M. Life, Liberty, and the Pursuit of Land: The Plunder of Early America *(Buffalo, 1992).*

Gaines, James R. For Liberty and Glory: Washington, Lafayette and Their Revolutions *(New York, 2007).*

Griswold, Rufus W. The Republican Court; or, Society in the Days of Washington *(New York, 1856).*

Gruber, Ira. The Howe Brothers and the American Revolution *(Williamsburg, 1972).*

Hammond, Bray. Banks and Politics in America: From the Revolution to the Civil War *(New York, 1957).*

Hancock, David. Citizens of the World: London Merchants and the Integration of the British Atlantic Community, 1735–1785 *(London, 1995).*

Hanna, William. Ben Franklin and Pennsylvania Politics *(Stanford, 1964).*

Harris, Robert D. Necker: Reform Statesman of the Ancien Régime *(Berkeley, 1979).*

Harrison, Mary. Annals of the Ancestry of Charles Custis Harrison and Ellen Waln Harrison *(Philadelphia, 1932).*

Hawke, David. In the Midst of a Revolution *(Philadelphia, 1961).*

———. Paine *(New York, 1974).*

Hedges, James B. The Browns of Providence Plantations *(Cambridge, MA, 1952).*

Henderson, H. James. Party Politics in the Continental Congress *(New York, 1974).*

Higginbotham, Don. The War of American Independence: Military Attitudes, Policies and Practice, 1763–1789 *(New York, 1971).*

Hindle, Brooke. David Rittenhouse *(Princeton, 1964).*

Hilton, James Coy. Silas Deane: Patriot or Traitor? *(East Lansing, MI, 1975).*

Horle, Craig, ed. Lawmaking and Legislators in Pennsylvania: A Biographical Dictionary *(Philadelphia, 1991).*

Hughes, Rupert. George Washington *(New York, 1926), 3 vols.*

Hunt, Agnes. The Provincial Committees of Safety of the American Revolution *(Cleveland, 1904).*

Jackson, John. The Pennsylvania Navy, 1775–1781: The Defense of the Delaware *(New Brunswick, New Jersey, 1974).*

James, Coy Hilton. Silas Deane—Patriot or Traitor? *(East Lansing, 1975).*

Jennings, Francis. The Creation of America: Through Revolution to Empire *(Cambridge, MA, 2000).*

Jensen, Merrill. The Articles of Confederation *(Madison, 1948).*

———. The Founding of a Nation: A History of the American Revolution, 1763–1776 *(New York, 1968).*

———. The New Nation *(New York, 1950).*

Keane, John. Tom Paine *(New York, 1995).*

Kelley, Joseph Jr. Life and Times of Colonial Philadelphia *(Harrisburg, 1973).*

Kohn, Richard. The Eagle and Sword *(New York, 1975).*

———. George Bryan and the Constitution of Pennsylvania, 1731–1791 *(Philadelphia, 1922).*

Konkle, Burton Alva. Thomas Willing and the First American Financial System *(Philadelphia, 1957).*

Lewis, George E. The Indiana Company, 1763–1798: A Study in Eighteenth Century Frontier Land Speculation and Business Venture *(Glendale, CA, 1941).*

Lewis, Lawrence. A History of the Bank of North America *(Philadelphia, 1882).*

Lincoln, Charles. The Revolutionary Movement in Pennsylvania, 1760–1776 *(Philadelphia, 1901).*

Liss, Peggy. Atlantic Empires: The Network of Trade and Revolution, 1713–1826 *(Baltimore, 1983).*

Maier, Pauline. The Old Revolutionaries: Political Lives in the Age of Sam Adams *(New York, 1980).*

Main, Jackson Turner. The Anti-Federalists: Critics of the Constitution, 1781–1788 *(Williamsburg, 1961).*

Mann, Bruce. Republic of Debtors: Bankruptcy in the Age of American Independence *(Cambridge, MA, 2002).*

McDonald, Forrest. E Pluribus Unum: The Formation of the American Republic *(Cambridge, 1965).*

———. We the People: The Economic Origins of the Constitution *(Chicago, 1958).*

McDougall, Walter. Freedom Just Around the Corner: A New American History, 1585–1828 *(New York, 2004).*

McGauhy, J. Kent. Richard Henry Lee of Virginia: A Portrait of an American Revolutionary *(Lanham, MD, 2004)*.

McLachlan, Jas, ed. Princetonians, 1748–1768: A Biographical Dictionary *(Princeton, 1976)*.

Meng, John J. Conrad Alexander Gerard: Despatches and Instructions, 1778–1780 *(Baltimore, 1939)*.

Miller, John C. Sam Adams: Pioneer in Propaganda *(Boston, 1936)*.

Miller, Nathan. Sea of Glory: A Naval History of the American Revolution *(Annapolis, 1974)*.

Morgan, Edmund, und Helen Morgan. The Stamp Act Crisis: Prologue to Revolution *(Chapel Hill, 1953)*.

Morgan, Michael. Patriots and Pirates: Tales of the Delaware Coast *(New York, 2004)*.

Morison, Samuel Eliot. John Paul Jones: A Sailor's Biography *(Boston, 1959)*.

———, *ed.* Sources and Documents Illustrating the American Revolution, 1764–1788 *(New York, 1929)*.

Morris, Richard B. Peacemakers: The Great Powers and American Independence *(New York, 1965)*.

———. The Forging of the Union, 1781–1789 *(New York, 1987)*.

———. Government and Labor in Early America *(Boston, 1946, 1981)*.

Morton, Bryan, and Donald Spinelli. Beaumarchais and the American Revolution *(Lanham, MD, 2002)*.

Murphy, Orville T. Charles Gravier, Comte de Vergennes: French Diplomacy in the Age of Revolution, 1719–1787 *(Albany, 1982)*.

Nash, Gary B. The Unknown American Revolution: The Unruly Birth of Democracy and the Struggle to Create America *(New York, 2005)*.

Nelson, Craig. Thomas Paine: Enlightenment, Revolution, and the Birth of Modern Nations *(New York, 2006)*.

Nettles, Curtis. The Emergence of a National Economy, 1775–1815 *(New York, 1962)*.

Newlin, Claude Milton. The Life and Writings of Hugh Henry Brackenridge *(Princeton, 1932)*.

Nuxoll, Elizabeth. Congress and the Munitions Merchants: The Secret Committee of Trade During the American Revolution *(New York, 1985)*.

Oberholtzer, Ellis Paxson. Robert Morris: Patriot and Financier *(Philadelphia, 1903)*.

O'Donnell, William Emmett. The Chevalier de La Luzerne, French Minister to the United States, 1779–1784 *(Bruges, 1938)*.

Patton, Robert. Patriot Pirates: The Privateer War for Freedom and Fortune in the American Revolution *(New York, 2008)*.

Peckam, Howard. The War for Independence: A Military History *(Chicago, 1958)*.

Phelps, Henry. The Yorktown Campaign and the Surrender of Cornwalls, 1781 *(New York, 1881)*.

Polishook, Irwin. Rhode Island and the Union, 1774–1795 *(Evanston, IL, 1969)*.

Potts, Louis W. Arthur Lee: Virtuous Revolutionary *(Baton Rouge, 1981)*.

Price, Jacob. France and the Chesapeake: A History of the French Tobacco Monopoly, 1674–1791, and of Its Relationship to the British and American Tobacco Trades *(Ann Arbor, 1973), 2 vols.*

Rakove, Jack. The Beginnings of National Politics: An Interpretive History of the Continental Congress (New York, 1979).

Rappaport, George. Stability and Change in Revolutionary Pennsylvania (University Park, Pennsylvania, 1996).

Rappleye, Charles. Sons of Providence: The Brown Brothers, the Slave Trade, and the American Revolution (New York, 2006).

Repplier, Agnes. Philadelphia: The Place and the People (New York, 1909).

Ritcheson, Charles R. British Politics and the American Revolution (Norman, OK, 1954).

Roche, John F. Joseph Reed: A Moderate in the American Revolution (New York, 1957).

Rosswurm, Steven. Arms, Country and Class: The Philadelphia Militia and the "Lower Sort" During the American Revolution, 1775–1783 (New Brunswick, NJ, 1987).

Russell, Charles Edward. Haym Salomon and the Revolution (New York, 1930).

Ryerson, Richard Allen. The Revolution Is Now Begun: The Radical Committees of Philadelphia (Philadelphia, 1978).

Schachner, Nathan. Alexander Hamilton (New York, 1961).

Scharf, J. Thomas and Thompson Wescott. History of Philadelphia, 1609–1884 (Philadelphia, 1884), 3 vols.

Schiff, Stacy. A Great Improvisation: Franklin, France, and the Birth of America (New York, 2005).

Schlesinger, Arthur M. The Colonial Merchants and the American Revolution, 1763–1776 (New York, 1918).

Selby, John E. The Revolution in Virginia, 1775–1783 (Williamsburg, 1988).

Sellers, Charles Coleman. The Artist of the Revolution: The Early Life of Charles Wilson Peale (Hebron, CT, 1939).

Sheridan, Eugene, and John Murrin, eds. Congress at Princeton (Princeton, 1985).

Shreve, L. G. Tench Tilghman: The Education of a Revolutionary (Centreville, MD, 1982).

Simpson, Henry. The Lives of Eminent Philadelphians, Now Deceased (Philadelphia, 1859).

Smith, Charles Page. James Wilson, Founding Father, 1742–1798 (Chapel Hill, 1956).

Smith, Philip Chadwick Foster. The Empress of China (Philadelphia, 1984).

Stinchcombe, William. The American Revolution and the French Alliance (Syracuse, 1969).

Sullivan, Kathryn. Maryland and France, 1774–1789 (London, 1936).

Sumner, William Graham. The Financier and the Finances of the American Revolution (New York, 1891), 2 vols.

Thomson, Buchanan Parker. Spain: Forgotten Ally of the American Revolution (North Quincy, MA, 1976).

Van Doren, Carl. Mutiny in January: The Story of the Crisis in the Continental Army (New York, 1943).

———. Secret History of the American Revolution (New York, 1941).

Van Tyne, Claude H. The War of Independence (Boston, 1929).

Ver Steeg, Clarence. Robert Morris: Revolutionary Financier, with an Analysis of His Earlier Career (Philadelphia, 1954).

Wagner, Frederick. Robert Morris: Audacious Patriot *(New York, 1976).*

Walbank, F. W. The Decline of the Roman Empire in the West *(London, 1952).*

Watson, John F. Annals of Philadelphia and Pennsylvania, in the olden time *(Philadelphia, 1844),* 3 vols.

Wharton, Anne Hollingsworth. Through Colonial Doorways *(Philadelphia, 1893).*

Williams, William Appleman. The Contours of American History *(Cleveland, 1961).*

Wood, Gordon S. The Creation of the American Republic 1776–1787 *(Chapel Hill, 1969).*

Wood, John H. A History of Central Banking in Great Britain and the United States *(New York, 2005).*

PAPERS

Note: Alphabetized under subject, not editor.

Adams, Charles Francis, ed., The Works of John Adams, 2nd President of the United States, with a Life of the Author *(Boston, 1856), 10 vols.*

Diary of James Allen. PMHB 9, p. 187.

Lowrie, Walter, ed. American State Papers *(Washington, D.C., 1832–1861), 38 vols.*

Scudder, H. E., ed. Recollections of Samuel Breck *(Philadelphia, 1877).*

Diary of Dr. James Clitherall. PMHB 22.

Smith, Paul H., ed. Letters of Delegates to Congress, 1774–1789 *(Washington, D.C., 1976–2000), 26 vols.; available at http.//memory.loc.gov/ammem/amlaw/lwdg.html.*

Burnett, E. C., ed. Letters of the Members of the Continental Congress *(Washington, D.C., 1821), 8 vols.*

Ford, Worthington, ed. Journals of the Continental Congress *(Washington, D.C., 1834), 34 vols.; available at http://memory.loc.gov/ammem/amlaw/lwjclink.html.*

Ward, Graham Atkinson, ed. The Journal and Letters of Samuel Curwen *(Boston, 1864).*

Isham, Charles, ed. The Deane Papers *(Collections of the New-York Historical Society, 1878), 5 vols.*

Extracts from the Journal of Miss Sarah Eve. PMHB 5, p. 19.

De Pauw, Linda Grant, ed. The Documentary History of the First Federal Congress *(Baltimore, 1972), 17 vols.*

Farrand, Max, ed. Records of the Federal Convention of 1787 *(Washington, D.C., 1911), 3 vols.; available at http://memory.loc.gov/ammem/amlaw/lwfr.html.*

DenBoer, Gordon, ed. The Documentary History of the First Federal Elections *(Madison, 1989), Vol. 4.*

Kaminski, John P., ed. The Founders on the Founders: Word Portraits from the American Revolutionary Era *(Charlottesville, 2008).*

Graydon, Alexander. Memoirs of a Life, Chiefly Passed in Philadelphia *(Edinburgh, 1822).*

Styrett, Harold, ed. The Papers of Alexander Hamilton *(New York, 1961), 26 vols.*

Jameson, J. Franklin, ed. "The Letters of Stephen Higginson, 1783–1804." American Historical Association Annual Report, 1896.

Johnston, Henry P., ed. John Jay Correspondence and Public Papers *(New York, 1890),* 4 vols.

Morris, Richard B., ed. John Jay: The Making of a Revolutionary, *Unpublished Papers, (New York, 1975), 2 vols.*

Ford, Paul L. The Writings of Thomas Jefferson *(New York, 1892), 10 vols.*

Ballagh, James Curtis, ed. The Letters of Richard Henry Lee *(New York, 1911), 2 vols.*

Ford, Worthington, ed. Letters of William Lee, Sheriff and Alderman of London; Commercial Agent of the Continental Congress, 1766–1783 *(Brooklyn, 1891), 3 vols.*

Maclay, Edgar S. ed. The Journal of William Maclay *(Philadelphia, 1891); available at the Library of Congress, http://memory.loc.gov/ammem/amlaw/lwmj.html.*

Hutchinson, William T., ed. The Papers of James Madison *(Chicago, 1962), 17 vols.*

Johnson, Herbert, ed. The Papers of John Marshall *(Chapel Hill, 2002), 6 vols.*

Ferguson, E. J., ed., The Papers of Robert Morris, 1781–1784 *(Pittsburgh, 1973–1988),* 9 vols.

Henkels, Stanislaus. The Confidential Correspondence of Robert Morris *(Philadelphia, 1917).*

Foner, Philip, ed. The Complete Writings of Thomas Paine *(New York, 1945), 2 vols.*

Miller, Lillian B., ed. The Papers of Charles Willson Peale and His Family *(New Haven, 2000).*

McMaster, John B. and Frederick D. Stone, eds. Pennsylvania and the Federal Constitution, 1787–1788 *(Philadelphia, 1888).*

Hogan, Edward, ed. The Pennsylvania State Trials *(Philadelphia, 1795).*

Reed, William. The Life and Correspondence of Joseph Reed *(Philadelphia, 1847),* 2 vols.

Wharton, Francis, ed. Revolutionary Diplomatic Correspondence of the United States *(Washington, D.C., 1889), 6 vols.; available online at http://memory.loc.gov/cgi.*

Quincy, ed. The Journals of Major Samuel Shaw, First American Consul to Canton *(Boston, 1847).*

"Early Days of the Revolution in Philadelphia: Charles Thomson's Account of Opposition to the Boston Port Bill." PMHB 2, p. 411.

Jackson, Donald, and Dorothy Twohig, eds. The Diaries of George Washington *(Charlottesville, 1976), 6 vols.*

Fitzpatrick, John C., ed. The Writings of George Washington, 1745–1799 *(Washington, D.C., 1931), 39 vols.*

Balch, Thomas Willing, ed. Willing Letters and Papers *(Philadelphia, 1922).*

Carey, Mathew, ed. Debates and Proceedings of the General Assembly: on the charter of the bank *(Philadelphia, 1786).*

Duane, William, ed. Extracts from the Diary of Christopher Marshall, kept in Philadelphia and Lancaster, during the American Revolution, 1774–1781 *(Albany, 1877) Available online @ Google books.*

Larrabee, Leonard, ed. The Papers of Benjamin Franklin *(New Haven, 1959–2003), 37 vols., available online at http://franklinpapers.org/franklin/.*

Force, Peter, American Archives, 2 Series *(Washington, D.C., 1837–1853).*

Lipscomb, Andrew, ed. The Writings of Thomas Jefferson *(Washington, D.C., 1903–1904), 10 vols.*

King, Charles, The Life and Correspondence of Rufus King *(New York, 1894–1900), 4 vols.*

Abbot, WW., ed. The Papers of George Washington *(Charlottesville, 1983 <2010>).*

Johnston, Henry, ed. The Correspondence and Public Papers of John Jay *(New York, 1890–1893), 4 vols.*

Pennsylvania Archives, *8 Series (Harrisburg, PA, 1874–1935).*

Conyngham, David, Reminiscences, Proceedings of the Wyoming Historical and Geological Society 8.

ARTICLES

Abernethy, Thomas. *"The Commercial Activities of Silas Deane in France."* American Historical Review 29, *p. 477.*

Alberts, Robert C. *"Business of the Highest Magnitude."* American Heritage Magazine 22; *available at www.americanheritage.com/articles/magazine/ah/1971/2/1971_2_48 .shtml.*

Aldridge, Alfred Owen. *"Why Did Thomas Paine Write on the Bank?"* Proceedings of the American Philosophical Society 93, *p. 309.*

Alexander, John. *"The Fort Wilson Incident of 1779: A Study of the Revolutionary Crowd."* WMQ 31, *p. 589.*

Anderson, John LaVerne. *"The Impact of the American Revolution on the Governor's Councillors."* Pennsylvania History 34, *p. 131.*

Arbuckle, Robert. *"John Nicholson and the Attempt to Promote Pennsylvania Industry in the 1790s."* Pennsylvania History 42, *p. 98.*

Baker, W. S. *"The Camp at Schuylkill Falls."* PMHB 16, *p. 29.*

———. *"Washington After the Revolution, 1784 to 1799."* PMHB 16, *p. 170.*

Baldwin, Ernest. *"Joseph Galloway, the Loyalist Politician."* PMHB 26, *p. 161.*

———. *"James Madison and the Nationalists, 1780–1783."* WMQ 40, *p. 228.*

———. *"Political Economy and the Creation of the Federal Republic,"* in David Thomas Konig, ed., Devising Liberty: Preserving and Creating Freedom in the American Republic *(Stamford, CT, 2002).*

Banning, Lance. *"Republican Ideology and the Triumph of the Constitution, 1789 to 1793."* WMQ 31, *p. 167.*

Baumann, Roland. *"John Swanwick: Spokesman for 'Merchant-Republicanism' in Philadelphia, 1790–1798."* PMHB 97, *p. 131.*

Bemis, Samuel Flagg. *"British Secret Service and the French-American Alliance."* American Historical Review 29, *p. 474.*

Bezanson, Anne. *"Inflation and Controls, Pennsylvania, 1774–1779."* Journal of Economic History, *Supplement 8, p. 1.*

Bowen, H. V. *"The Bank of England During the Long Eighteenth Century, 1694–1820,"* in Richard Roberts and David Kynaston, eds., The Bank of England: Money, Power and Influence, 1694–1994 *(Oxford, 1995).*

———. *"The Federal Government and the Republican Court Move to Philadelphia, November 1790–March 1791,"* in Kenneth Bowling and Donald Kennon, eds., Neither Separate Nor Equal: Congress in the 1790s *(Athens, OH, 2000), p. 3.*

———. "Good-by 'Charle': The Lee-Adams Interest and the Political Demise of Charles Thomson, Secretary of Congress, 1774–1789." PMHB 100, p. 314.

Bowling, Kenneth. "New Light on the Philadelphia Mutiny of 1783: Federal-State Confrontation at the Close of the War for Independence." PMHB 99, p. 419.

———. "Joseph Galloway's Plans of Union for the British Empire, 1774–1778." PMHB 64, 492.

Boyd, Julian. "Silas Deane: Death by a Kindly Teacher of Treason?" WMQ 16, p. 165, 319, 515.

Bradbury, M. L. "Legal Privilege and the Bank of North America." PMHB 96, 139.

Branch, E. Douglas. "Plan for the Western Lands, 1783." PMHB 60, 287.

Brobeck, Stephen. "Revolutionary Change in Colonial Philadelphia: The Brief Life of the Proprietary Gentry." WMQ 33, p. 410.

Brown, Margaret. "William Bingham." PMHB 61, 54, 61; p. 286, 61, 386.

Brown, Kenneth. "Stephen Girard's Bank." PMHB 46, p. 29.

Brown, Richard. "The Founding Fathers of 1776 and 1787: A Collective View." WMQ 33, p. 465.

Bruchey, Stuart. "Alexander Hamilton and the State Banks, 1789 to 1795." WMQ 27, p. 347.

Buel, Richard. "The Committee Movement of 1779 and the Formation of Public Authority in Revolutionary America," in James Henretta and Michael Kammen, eds., The Transformation of Early American History: Society, Authority, and Ideology (New York, 1991).

Burnett, Edmund C. "Ciphers of the Revolutionary Period." American Historical Review, p. 329.

Cabeen, Francis Von A. "The Society of the Sons of Saint Tammany of Philadelphia." PMHB 4, p. 433.

Carson, Hampton L. "James Wilson and James Iredell." PMHB 45, 1.

Carter, Edward C. "The Birth of a Political Economist: Matthew Carey and the Recharter Fight of 1810–1811." Pennsylvania Magazine 33, p. 274.

Caughey, John. "Willing's Expedition Down the Mississippi, 1778," Louisiana Historical Quarterly 15, p. 5.

Clark, William Bell. "The John Ashmead Story, 1737–1818." PMHB 82, p. 3.

———. "That Mischievous Holker: The Story of a Privateer." PMHB 79, p. 27.

———. "The Sea Captains Club." PMHB 81, p. 56.

Cooke, Jacob. "The Compromise of 1790." WMQ 27, p. 523.

———. "Tench Coxe: Tory Merchant." PMHB 96, p. 48.

Cress, Lawrence Delbert. "Whither Columbia? Congressional Residence and the Politics of the New Nation, 1776–1787." WMQ 32, p. 581.

———. "Items from the Morris Family Collection." PMHB 70, p. 185.

Cummings, Hubertis. "Robert Morris and the Episode of the Polacre 'Victorious.'" PMHB 70, p. 239.

diGiacomantonio, William D. "Petitioners and Their Grievances: A View from the First Congress," in Kenneth Bowling and Donald Kennon, eds., House and Senate in the 1790s (Washington, D.C., 2002).

Doerflinger, Thomas. "Philadelphia Merchants and the Logic of Moderation, 1760–1775." WMQ 40, p. 197.

Eavenson, Howard. "Pennsylvania's Grand Plan of Post-Revolutionary Internal Development." PMHB 65, p. 439.

Eberlein, Harold Donaldson. "190, High Street (Market Street Below Sixth): The Home of Washington and Adams, 1790–1800," in Lather Eisenhart, ed., Historic Philadelphia (Philadelphia 1980), p. 161.

Echeverria, Durand. "The American Character: A Frenchman Views the New Republic from Philadelphia, 1777." WMQ 16, p. 376.

Egnal, Marc, and Jos. Ernst. "An Economic Interpretation of the American Revolution." WMQ 29, p. 3.

Einhorn, Nathan. "The Reception of the British Peace Offer of 1778." PMHB 16, p. 191.

Ferguson, E. James. "Business, Government, and Congressional Investigation in the Revolution." WMQ 16, p. 293.

———. "The Nationalists of 1781–1783 and the Economic Interpretation of the Constitution." Journal of American History 41, p. 241.

———. "Political Economy, Public Liberty, and the Formation of the Constitution." WMQ 50, p. 389.

———. Review of Jack Rakove's The Beginnings of National Politics. WMQ 38, p. 125.

———. State Assumption of the Federal Debt During the Confederation." Mississippi Valley Historical Review 38, p. 402.

Ferling, John. "Joseph Galloway: A Reassessment of the Motivations of a Pennsylvania Loyalist." Pennsylvania History 39, p. 163.

———. "Compromise of Conflict: The Rejection of the Galloway Alternative to Rebellion." Pennsylvania History 43, p. 4.

Fisher, Redwood. "Revolutionary Reminiscences Connected with the Life of Robert Morris, Esq." Graham's Magazine 44, p. 23.

Fiske, John. "The French Alliance and the Conway Cabal." Atlantic Monthly 16, p. 220.

Gallagher, Mary A. Y. "Charting a New Course for the China Trade: The Late Eighteenth Century American Model." American Neptune 57, p. 201.

———. "Private Interest and the Public Good: Settling the Score for the Morris-Holker Business Relationship, 1778–1790." Pennsylvania History 69, p. 179.

———. "Reinterpreting the 'Very Trifling Mutiny' at Philadelphia in 1783." PMHB 119, p. 3.

Gates, Paul. "The Role of the Land Speculator in Western Development." PMHB 66, p. 314.

Gibson, James. "The Pennsylvania Provincial Conference of 1776." PMHB 58, p. 312.

Goldstein, Kalman. "Silas Deane: Preparation for Rascality." The Historian, 43, p. 75.

Gough, Robert. "Can a Rich Man Favor Revolution? The Case of Philadelphia in 1776." Pennsylvania History 48, p. 235.

———. "Notes on the Pennsylvania Revolutionaries of 1776." PMHB 96, p. 89.

Grubb, Farley. "The Continental Dollar: How Much Was Really Issued." Journal of Economic History 68, no. 283.

Hanna, Kathryn Abbey. "Efforts of Spain to Maintain Sources of Information in the British Colonies Before 1779." Mississippi Valley Historical Review 15, p. 56.

Harding, Samuel. "Party Struggles over the First Pennsylvania Constitution." American Historical Association, Annual Report for 1894, p. 381.

Harlow, R. V. "Aspects of Revolutionary Finance." American Historical Review 35, p. 46.

Harris, C. M. "Washington's Gamble." WMQ 56, p. 526.

Harris, Richard D. "French Finances and the American War, 1777–1778." Journal of Modern History 48, p. 233.

Hart, Charles Henry. "Mary White—Mrs. Robert Morris." PMHB 2, p. 157.

———. "Robert Morris: A Sketch," PMHB 1, p. 3.

Henderson, Elizabeth. "The Northwestern Lands of Pennsylvania, 1790–1812." PMHB 60, p. 131.

Henderson, H. James. "Congressional Factionalism and the Attempt to Recall Benjamin Franklin." WMQ 27, p. 246.

———. "Constitutionalists and Republicans in the Continental Congress, 1778–1786." Pennsylvania History 36, p. 119.

Hutson, James H. "Country, Court, and Constitution: Antifederalism and the Historians." WMQ 38, p. 337.

———. "An Investigation of the Inarticulate: Philadelphia's White Oaks." WMQ 28, p. 4.

———. "John Dickinson at the Federal Constitutional Convention." WMQ 60, p. 256.

Ireland, Owen S. "The Crux of Politics: Religion and Party in Pennsylvania, 1778–1789." WMQ 42, p. 453.

———. "The Ethnic-Religious Dimension of Pennsylvania Politics, 1778–1779." WMQ 30, p. 423.

Jackson, John. "George Washington in Philadelphia," PMHB 56.

James, A. James. "Oliver Pollock, Financier of the American Revolution in the West." Mississippi Valley Historical Review 16, p. 67.

———. "Oliver Pollock and the Free Navigation of the Mississippi River." Mississippi Valley Historical Review 19, p. 331.

James, F. Cryil. "The Bank of North America and the Financial History of Philadelphia." PMHB 64, p. 36.

Jeffreys, C. P. B. "The Provincial and Revolutionary History of St. Peter's Church, Philadelphia, 1753–1783." PMHB 48, p. 354.

Jensen, Merrill. "The Cession of the Old Northwest." Mississippi Valley Historical Review 23, p. 26.

———. "The Creation of the National Domain, 1781–1784." Mississippi Valley Historical Review 26, p. 323.

Johnson, Sherry. "El Niño, Environmental Crisis, and the Emergence of Alternative Markets in the Hispanic Caribbean." WMQ 62, p. 365.

Johnson, Victor. "Robert Morris and the Provisioning of the American Army During the Campaign of 1781." Pennsylvania History 1, p. 7.

Jones, Robert F. "William Duer and the Business of Government in the Era of the American Revolution." WMQ 32, p. 393.

Keith, Charles. "The Founding of Christ Church, Philadelphia." PMHB 54, p. 307.

Ketcham, Ralph. "France and American Politics, 1763–1793." Political Science Quarterly, 78, p. 198.

Kite, Elizabeth. "French 'Secret Aid': Precursor to the French American Alliance, 1776–1777." French American Review 4, p. 143.

Klein, Milton M. "Failure of a Mission: The Drummond Peace Proposal of 1775." Huntington Library Quarterly 25, p. 343.

Klein, Philip Shriver. "Senator William Maclay." Pennsylvania History 10, p. 83.

Kohn, Richard. "Inside the History of the Newburgh Conspiracy: America and the Coup d'Etat." WMQ 27, p. 187. See also the two subsequent exchanges, with rebuttals, 29, 143, and 31, 273.

Lawler, Edward Jr. "The President's House in Philadelphia." Independence Hall Association; available at www.ushistory.org/presidentshouse/history/briefhistory.htm.

Lombard, Mildred. "James Searle: Radical Businessman of the Revolution." PMHB 59, p. 284.

Lynd, Stoughton. "Abraham Yates's History of the Movement for the United States Constitution." WMQ 20, p. 223.

Maier, Pauline. "Coming to Terms with Samuel Adams." American Historical Review 81, p. 12.

Main, Jackson Turner. "Charles A. Beard and the Constitution: A Critical Review of Forrest McDonald's We the People." WMQ 17, p. 86.

Maxey, David. "Samuel Hopkins, The Holder of the First U.S. Patent: A Study of Failure." PHMB 122, p. 3.

———. "The Union Farm: Henry Drinker's Experiment." PMHB 107, p. 610.

McCadden, Helen Matzke. "Juan de Miralles and the American Revolution." The Americas 29, p. 359.

McClurkin, A. J. "Summary of the Bank of North America Records." PMHB 64, p. 88.

McCusker, John J. "The Tonnage of the Continental Ship Alfred." PMHB 90, p. 227.

———. "Weights and Measures in the Colonial Sugar Trade: The Gallon and the Pound and Their International Equivalents." WMQ 30, p. 599.

McMaster, John B. "Where the Constitutional Convention Met." PMHB 11, p. 81.

Meistrich, Herbert. "Lord Drummond and Reconciliation." Proceedings of the New Jersey Historical Society 81, p. 260.

Meng, John. "A Footnote to Secret Aid in the American Revolution." American Historical Review 43, p. 795.

Mintz, Max M. "Robert Morris and John Jay on Education: Two Letters." PMHB 74, p. 340.

Mishoff, Willard. "Business in Philadelphia During the British Occupation, 1777–1778." PMHB 61, p. 165.

Morgan, Edmund S. "The Puritan Ethic and the American Revolution." WMQ 24, p. 3.

Muller, Leos. "Swedish Consular Reports as a Source of Business Information," in XIV International Economic History Congress, Helsinki 2006; available online at www.helsinki.fi/iehc2006/papers1/Muller1.pdf.

Murdoch, Richard. "Benedict Arnold and the Owners of the Charming Nancy." PMHB 74, p. 22.

Nash, Gary B. "Poverty and Poor Relief in Pre-Revolutionary Philadelphia." WMQ 33, p. 3.

———. "Slaves and Slaveowners in Colonial Philadelphia." WMQ 30, p. 223.

Nettles, Curtis. "The Place of Markets in the Old Colonial System." New England Quarterly 6, p. 491.

Nix, Robert, and Mary Schweitzer. "Pennsylvania's Contributions to the Writing and Ratification of the Constitution." PMHB 112, p. 3.

Nuxoll, Elizabeth. "Illegitimacy, Family Status, and Property in the Early Republic: The Morris-Croxall Family of New Jersey." New Jersey History 113, p. 3.

———, and E. James Ferguson. "Congressional Investigation of Government Corruption During the American Revolution." U.S. Capitol Historical Society, Congressional Studies 8, p. 13.

Nuxoll, Elizabeth. "The Financier as Senator," in Kenneth R. Bowling and Donald R. Kennon, eds., Neither Separate Nor Equal: Congress in the 1790s (Washington, D.C., 2000), p. 91.

———. "The Bank of North America and Robert Morris's Management of the Nation's First Fiscal Crisis." Business and Economic History 13, p. 159.

Oaks, Robert. "Big Wheels in Philadelphia: Du Simitiere's List of Carriage Owners." PMHB 95, p. 351.

O'Dwyer, Margaret. "A French Diplomat's View of Congress, 1790." WMQ 21, p. 408.

Onuf, Peter. "Toward Federalism: Virginia, Congress and the Western Lands." WMQ 34, p. 353.

Paine, Thomas. "Military Operations Near Philadelphia." PMHB 2, p. 284.

Patterson, Stephen. "After Newburgh: The Struggle for the Impost in Massachusetts," in James Kirby Martin, ed., The Human Dimensions of Nation Making: Essays on Colonial and Revolutionary America (Madison, 1976), p. 218.

Pavlovsky, Arnold M. " 'Between Hawk and Buzzard': Congress as Perceived by Its Members, 1775–1783." PMHB 101, p. 349.

Phelps, Glenn A. "The Republican General," in Don Higginbotham, ed., George Washington Reconsidered (Charlottesville, 2001), p. 165.

Plumer, Wilbur. "Consumer Credit in Colonial Philadelphia." PMHB 66, p. 385.

Pocock, J. G. A. "Virtue and Commerce in the 18th Century." Journal of Interdisciplinary History 3, p. 119.

Potts, Louis W. "Arthur Lee: A Life History in the American Revolution." Journal of Psychohistory 4, p. 513.

Powell, J. H. "John Dickinson and the Constitution." PMHB 60, p. 1.

———. "John Dickinson as President of Pennsylvania." Pennsylvania History 28, p. 254.

Rappaport, George. "The First Description of the Bank of North America." WMQ 33, p. 661.

Rawle, William Brooke. "Laurel Hill." PMHB 35, p. 397.

Riesman, Janet. "Money, Credit, and Federalist Political Economy," in Richard Beeman, Stephen Botein, and Edward Carter, eds. Beyond Confederation: Origins of the Constitution and American National Identity (Chapel Hill, 1987).

Riley, Edward M. *"Philadelphia, the Nation's Capital, 1790–1800."* Pennsylvania History 20, p. 357.

Risch, Erna. *"Immigrant Aid Societies Before 1820."* PMHB 60, p. 24.

Risjord, Norman K. *"The Compromise of 1790: New Evidence on the Dinner Table Bargain."* WMQ 33, p. 309.

Rolater, Fred. *"Charles Thomson, 'Prime Minister' of the United States."* PMHB 101, p. 322.

"Memoir of John Ross. Merchant of Philadelphia" PMHB 23, p. 77.

Rosswurm, Steven. *"The Philadelphia Militia, 1775–1783: Active Duty and Active Radicalism,"* in Ronald Hoffman and Peter Albert, eds., Arms and Independence: The Military Character of the American Revolution (*Charlottesville, 1984*).

Rowe, G. S. *"Thomas McKean and the Coming of the Revolution."* PMHB 96, p. 3.

Ryerson, R. A. *"Political Mobilization and the American Revolution: The Resistance Movement in Philadelphia, 1765 to 1776."* WMQ 31, p. 565.

Schlesinger, Arthur M. *"Politics, Propaganda, and the Philadelphia Press, 1767–1770."* PMHB 60, p. 309.

Schwartz, Anna Jacobson. *"The Beginning of Competitive Banking in Philadelphia, 1782–1809."* Journal of Political Economy 60, p. 417.

Scott, Kenneth. *"Price Control in New England During the Revolution."* New England Quarterly 19, p. 453.

Selsam, Paul. *"The Political Revolution in Pennsylvania in 1776."* Pennsylvania History 1, p. 147.

Shalhope, Robert. *"Toward a Republican Synthesis: The Emergence of an Understanding of Republicanism in American Historiography."* WMQ 29, p. 49.

Sheridan, Richard. *"The Crisis of Slave Subsistence in the British West Indies."* WMQ 33, p. 615.

Sioussat, St. George L. *"The Chevalier de La Luzerne and the Ratification of the Articles of Confederation by Maryland, 1780–1781, with Accompanying Documents."* PMHB 60, p. 391.

Skeen, C. Edward. *"The Newburgh Conspiracy Reconsidered."* WMQ 31, p. 273.

Slaski, Eugene R. *"Thomas Willing: A Study in Moderation, 1774–1778,"* PMHB 100, p. 491.

———. *"Thomas Willing: Loyalty Meant Commitment."* Pennsylvania History 47, p. 234.

Smith, Page. *"The Attack on Fort Wilson."* PMHB 78, p. 177.

———. *"David Ramsay and the Causes of the American Revolution."* WMQ 17, p. 51.

Jared Sparks. *"Review of Life of Arthur Lee."* North American Review 30, p. 454.

Stephenson, Orlando. *"The Supply of Gunpowder in 1776."* American Historical Review 30, p. 271.

Stille, Charles. *"Beaumarchais and the Lost Million."* PMHB 11, p. 619.

Stone, Frederick. *"Philadelphia Society One Hundred Years Ago."* PMHB 3, p. 361.

Swanson, Donald, and Andrew Trout. *"Alexander Hamilton, 'the Celebrated Mr. Neckar,' and Public Credit."* WMQ 47, p. 422.

Tailby, Donald C. *"Foreign Interest Remittances by the United States, 1785–1787: A Story of Malfeasance."* Business History Review 41, p. 161.

Thompson, Peter. "The Friendly Glass: Drink and Gentility in Colonial Philadelphia." PMHB 63, p. 556.

Vail, R W G. "The Lure of the Land Promoter: A Bibliographical Study of Certain New York Real Estate." University of Rochester Library Bulletin 24 (Winter 1969); available online at www.lib.rochester.edu/index.cfm?PAGE=1008.

———. "Rare Robert Morris Caricature." PMHB 60, p. 184.

Unsigned. "The Mount Regale Fishing Company of Philadelphia," PMHB 27, p. 88.

Unsigned. "Caesar Rodney's Ride," PMHB 39, p. 454.

Van Alstyne. "Great Britain, the War for Independence, and the 'Gathering Storm' in Europe, 1775–1777." Huntington Library Quarterly 27, p. 327.

Van Tyne, C. H. "French Aid Before the Alliance of 1778." American Historical Review 31, p. 20.

Vinson, Michael. "The Society for Political Inquiries: The Limits of Republican Discourse on the Eve of the Constitutional Convention." PHMB 113, p. 186.

Walker, Lewis Burd. "Life of Margaret Shippen, Wife of Benedict Arnold." PMHB 24, p. 423.

Walsh, James J. "The Chevalier de La Luzerne." Records of the American Catholic Historical Society 16, p. 184.

Warden, G. B. "The Proprietary Group in Pennsylvania, 1754–1764." WMQ 21, p. 367.

Whitaker, Arthur. "Reed and Forde: Merchant Adventurers of Philadelphia." PMHB 61, p. 237.

Wilkinson, Norman. "Robert Morris and the Treaty of Big Tree." Mississippi Valley Historical Review 40, p. 257.

Williams, Robert. "The Influences of Pennsylvania's 1776 Constitution on American Constitutionalism During the Founding Debate." PHMB 112, p. 25.

Wilson, Janet. "The Bank of North America and Pennsylvania Politics: 1781–1787." PMHB 46, p. 3.

Wood, Gordon. "Interests and Disinterestedness in the Making of the Constitution," in Richard Beeman, Stephen Botein, and Edward Carter, eds. Beyond Confederation: The Origins of the Constitution and American National Identity (Chapel Hill, 1987), p. 69.

Woodhouse, Samuel. "The Voyage of the Empress of China." PMHB 63, p. 24.

Wright, Robert E. "Thomas Willing (1731–1821): Philadelphia Financier and Forgotten Founding Father." Pennsylvania History 63, p. 525.

THESES, PAPERS, AND PAMPHLETS

Bigelow, John. "Beaumarchais the Merchant: Letters of Theveneau de Francey, 1777–1780." Paper read before the New-York Historical Society, New York, 1870.

Burt, Nathaniel. "On the Washington Mansion in Philadelphia" pamphlet (Philadelphia, 1875).

Chernow, Barbara Ann. "Robert Morris: Land Speculator, 1790–1801" (Columbia, 1974).

Davis, William A. "William Constable: New York Merchant and Land Speculator, 1772–1803" (Harvard, 1955).

Johnson, Sherry. " 'Where Has All the Flour Gone?' El Niño, Environmental Crisis, and Cuban Trade Restrictions, 1768–1778." Paper presented at the Library Company of Philadelphia, 2003; available online at www.librarycompany.org/Economics/2003Conference/papers/SJohnson.pdf.

Kline, Mary-Jo. "Gouverneur Morris and the New Nation, 1775–1788" (Columbia, 1970).

Nuxoll, Elizabeth. "Robert Morris and the Shaping of the Post-Revolutionary American Economy." Courtesy of the author.

Platt, J. D. R. "Jeremiah Wadsworth: Federalist Entrepreneur" (Columbia, 1955).

Rolater, Frederick. "The Continental Congress: A Study of the Origin of American Public Administration, 1774–1781" (University of Southern California, 1971).

Rappaport, George David. "The Sources and Early Development of the Hostility to Banks in Early American Thought" (New York University, 1970).

Tailby, Donald G. "Chapters from the Business Career of William Constable: A Merchant of Post-Revolutionary New York" (Rutgers, 1961).

Wood, George C. "Congressional Control of Foreign Relations During the American Revolution 1774–1789" (New York University, 1919).

Index

ILLUSTRATION CREDITS

1. Robert Morris, Senior, J. Hesselius, Courtesy the Philadelphia History Museum at the Atwater Kent, The Historical Society of Pennsylvania Collection. 2. Robert Morris by Robert Edge Pine, 1785, Courtesy the National Portrait Gallery, Smithsonian Institution. Images 3, 17, 20, 38 and 39: Library Company of Philadelphia 4. National Archives [image #208-LU-14]. 5. Thomas Willing by Charles Willson Peale, 1782, Courtesy the Metropolitan Museum of Art, Art Resource Inc. Images 6, 7, 8, 9, 10, 11, 13, 23, 30, 31, 32, 33, 36: Granger Collection 12. John Jay by Gilbert Stuart, finished by John Trumbull, Courtesy the National Portrait Gallery, Smithsonian Institution. 14. Library of Congress 15. Collections of the Comedie Francais / Photograph Patrick Lorette Images 16, 19 and 29: Independence National Historical Park 18. National Archives [image #19-N-12445]. 21. Gouverneur Morris and Robert Morris, 1783, by Charles Willson Peale; Courtesy the Pennsylvania Academy of Fine Arts, Philadelphia. Bequest of Richard Ashhurst. 22. National Archives [image #148-GW-1124]. 24. Courtesy The Princeton University Library, from the William Churchill Houston Coll. 25 and 26 from the Breck manuscripts collection courtesy the Library Company of Philadelphia. 27. Yale University Art Gallery 28. The Colonial Williamsburg Foundation. Gift of Mrs. George S. Robbins 33: New York Public Library. 34. Benjamin Franklin by Joseph Siffred Duplessis, 1785, Courtesy the National Portrait Gallery, Smithsonian Institution. 35. George Washington by Joseph Wright, c 1785, Courtesy the Philadelphia History Museum at the Atwater Kent. 36. Robert Morris by Gilbert Stuart, 1790, Courtesy the Granger Collection. 37. Mary Morris by Charles Willson Peale, Courtesy the National Portrait Gallery, Smithsonian Institution. 38. The President's House on Market Street, Courtesy the Library Company of Philadelphia. 39. Morris's Folly, Courtesy the Library Company of Philadelphia. 40. The Capitol Rotunda by Constantino Brumidi, Courtesy Architect of the Capitol

* Cartoon on page 479: View of Congress on the Road to Philadelphia, 1790, Courtesy the Historical Society of Pennsylvania.

* Cartoon on page 479: Robert Morris and Federal Hall, 1790, Courtesy the American Antiquarian Society

ABOUT THE AUTHOR

Charles Rappleye is an award-winning investigative journalist and editor. He has written extensively on media, law enforcement, and organized crime. His previous book, *Sons of Providence: The Brown Brothers, the Slave Trade, and the American Revolution,* won the George Washington Book Prize and the American Revolution Round Table Book Prize.